A *Backwoods Home* Anthology:

The Twenty-fourth Year

Published by
Backwoods Home Magazine
P.O. Box 712
Gold Beach, OR 97444

Copyright 2013, 2014 by *Backwoods Home Magazine*

ISBN: 978-1-62440-087-2

Editor: Dave Duffy

Senior Editor: John Silveira

Art Director: Don Childers

Contributors: *Donna Adams, Dorothy Ainsworth, Rowena Aldridge, Joe Alton, Amy Alton, Massad Ayoob, Richard Blunt, F.J. Bohan, Jackie Clay-Atkinson, Lucas Crouch, Kyle Doty, Dave Duffy, Ilene Duffy, David Eddings, Linda Gabris, Sylvia Gist, Steven Gregersen, Donna Insco, James Kash, Frank Knebel, Tom Kovach, David Lee, Patrice Lewis, Mike Lorenzen, Len McDougall, Kai Moessle, Amaury Murgado, Matt Purkeypile, Habeeb Salloum, Charles Sanders, George Smith, John Silveira, Susan Vetrone, John Whight, Kathryn Wingrove, Claire Wolfe, Jeff Yago, David Zaugg*

Cover Art: Don Childers

Layout Design and Proofreading: Lisa Nourse, Rhoda Denning, Jessie Denning, Ilene Duffy

Contents —

Issue Number 143

Issue Number 144

WE'RE ON KINDLE - SEE PAGE 2

Backwoods Home magazine

practical ideas for self-reliant living

Jan/Feb 2013
Issue #139
$5.95 US
$7.50 CAN

BOK BOK BOK!
(THE CHICKEN ISSUE)

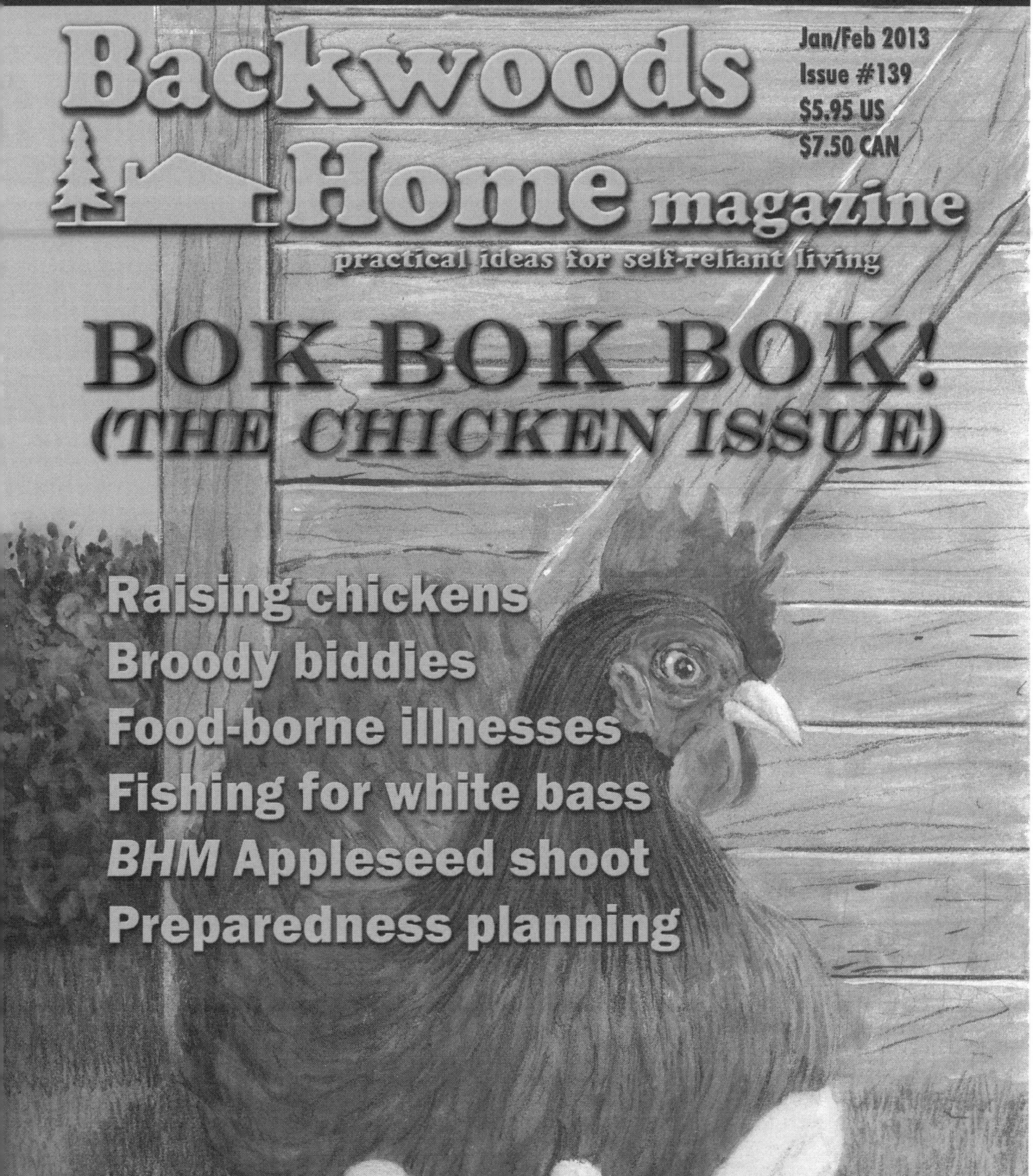

- Raising chickens
- Broody biddies
- Food-borne illnesses
- Fishing for white bass
- *BHM* Appleseed shoot
- Preparedness planning

www.backwoodshome.com

My view

Preparing for a temporary catastrophe

November's Superstorm Sandy on the Northeastern coast of the United States was our most recent grand reminder that society is fragile, most people are not ready to take care of themselves if they are temporarily displaced from their homes or if their electricity goes off for a few days, and Government is incapable of responding effectively to these sudden catastrophes.

So you have to be prepared to take care of yourself. We've said that many times in this magazine and have written many articles about it, but it still amazes me that every time a catastrophe occurs most people seem to be caught unprepared.

The true gravity of the calamity for tens of thousands of Superstorm Sandy victims, especially for those isolated on New York's Staten Island, did not make the headlines it deserved due to the Presidential election. Thousands were without adequate food, clean water, or warmth for more than two weeks as the temperatures plummeted into the 30s. Governor Cuomo has since asked the federal government for $30 billion in reconstruction aid.

Don't allow yourself to fall victim to a future storm or to any event that causes a temporary loss of electricity or compels you to leave your home for several days, and don't get caught out on the road during such an event without the ability to comfortably cope. There is no need to be inconvenienced, or worse to have your safety threatened, when it takes only a modest amount of preparation to ready yourself for most situations.

I'm going to show you how I keep myself and my family prepared as an example of what can be done. Every person's situation is somewhat unique, I think, so maybe you can borrow some ideas from me, then customize your preparedness plan to suit your own situation. My system is tailored to my personality and my family's location in the dense woods of the Pacific Northwest, next to an ocean teeming with an inexhaustible source of easy-to-catch fish. My home is also in bear country and is heavy with mountain lions so that if you're out and about, it is wise to carry a sidearm. If you live in the desert or the freezing cold Midwest, your plan will likely differ markedly from mine.

The mental plan

I have a mental preparedness plan in my head in the event of a catastrophe that calls for me to make a decision on how my family will cope with a looming disaster, and I immediately ask myself the question: Do we stay at home and weather the disaster or do we leave home?

Dave Duffy

If we can stay at home, that is the best case scenario since we are well equipped to survive a brief or long-term disaster, having an ample supply of food and supplies, gravity-fed spring water that originates a few hundred yards from the house, several heat and cooking sources that include propane and wood, several electricity sources that include a backup generator and photovoltaics, medical supplies, guns and ammo, etc. I am also relatively isolated but know all my neighbors and can count on them if survival cooperation is required.

But if we cannot stay at home for some reason (maybe my house has slid down the hill due to the earthquake, avalanches, and tsunami that is predicted to one day hit my area), then I go to my mobile plan, either in a vehicle or on foot. Hopefully, it will be in a vehicle and preferably my family will be able to transfer to our Sequoia SUV since this 4WD would make an excellent survival vehicle. This SUV is capable of being a roaming house on wheels and can traverse almost any terrrain, but, just in case, I have a well-stocked pop-up camper I can pull behind me.

In the event I must choose the mobile option, I keep three preparedness packs in the trunk of the sedan I normally drive:

- my 10-day pack, which holds the smaller items necessary for survival, such as water treatment tablets, first aid kit, fishing kit, fire starters, .45 auto, etc.
- my rifle pack, which holds my two-piece stainless steel, scoped 10/22 rifle with 10 and 30-round clips
- my golf bag

Golf bag? What's a golf bag got to do with preparedness?

I make preparedness dovetail right into other aspects of my life. Since I am semi-retired and play golf several days a week, and since I need food, water, and foul weather gear for playing golf in rainy Oregon, I share my food, water, and lightweight but very protective golf rain gear between my survival packs and golf bag. This way I am always refreshing the jerky, smoked salmon, power bars, etc., that I munch on while playing golf, and refreshing is important.

Refreshing your survival food and other supplies such as flashlight and radio batteries is vital if they are to be suitable for use in an emergency. Many people have had the sad experience of opening their survival pack to find dead batteries in their flashlight and radio, not to mention food that has become a biological experiment.

My all-important high-quality compact LED flashlight that I will rely on in my survival pack is kept in the center console of my car where I access and use it often. It has a high quality, rechargeable battery. My cell phone and iPad, both of which I consider part of my preparedness pack, are also always with me or in my car, as are the charging cords for all these devices. A cell phone and iPad are the modern day versions of the emergency shortwave radio, allowing us to keep in contact with people should we have to become mobile in an emergency. Since both my cell phone and iPad access the telephone and internet via Verizon towers (Verizon is the only service with reliable access in remote areas) and since the Internet went down for some time during Superstorm Sandy, you still need a battery-operated or wind-up emergency radio as a backup. That's in my preparedness pack.

I anticipate some of you are asking how I keep track of all this stuff, since some of it is in my preparedness pack, some in my golf bag, some in the center console of my car, and the cell phone and iPad are probably in my pocket and who knows where else.

It's a good question, and I have a sensible answer: I keep a brief laminated list in my pocket at all times. On one side is a list of things I must remember to take if I find myself in a mobile survival situation. It includes: 10-day pack, 10/22 pack, food and rain gear (from the golf bag), cell phone, iPad, camera, laptop and wand, chargers, extra water, axe, machete, Mucks, field jackets, blankets, Humless, solar panel.

On the other side of the card (you probably already guessed it) is the list of things I must remember to do to swing a golf club correctly. I refer to the golf side of the list nearly every day.

Most of the items on the list are self explanatory. A few that may not be are:

A wand is a thumb-sized Verizon device to access the Internet. It is more reliable than a satellite dish and faster. I keep it in my pocket, have used one for several years ($50 a month), and access the Internet from anywhere in the world under any conditions. If your satellite is down, or if your cable is down, chances are the wand still works just fine.

A Humless system is essentially an RV battery pack put out by Humless (humless.com) but it contains cords and adapters to charge anything, including my vehicle and whatever hooks into a USB port. It comes with a big camp light, holds a charge for a year if not used, and it can be recharged a variety of ways including using a folding solar panel that fits nicely into the trunk of my car.

Mucks are warm, comfortable, all-weather boots. Most fishermen wear them in the Pacific Northwest. Santa Claus probably wears Mucks.

10-day pack

My 10-day pack contains the following:
- water purification tablets and water purification straw
- first aid kit including prescriptions, aspirin, Advil, toothpaste and brush, floss, soap, burn ointment, antibiotic
- 2 rechargeable, powerful LED flashlights
- cold weather clothes for winter, extra rain gear
- extra socks, stocking caps, underwear
- .45 auto pistol and ammo
- high quality binoculars
- magnesium/flint fire starters, propane lighters, matches
- P38 (military can opener)
- Gerber multi-tool
- roll of strong string, plastic bags
- a few space blankets
- fishing kit (for salt and fresh)
- battery/wind-up radio
- freeze dried meals
- mess kit, canned heat
- whistle
- compass
- spare eyeglasses
- a rigid military-style knife I use mainly for prying mussels off seashore rocks
- extra cash

I also keep a small axe and machete in the trunk, along with extra water, a brick of .22 ammo, and an extra box of .45 ammo. I always carry on my person a jackknife, Spyderco knife, high-quality pocket camera, and cell phone. Why is my camera part of my preparedness pack? It just is. I'm a magazine publisher after all; I like to document stuff. You'll have quirky things as part of yours too.

My gear is not inexpensive, but it is meant to keep me and my family safe in an emergency so I invested in quality over the years. Besides, I get a lot of pleasure out of it on a fairly regular basis, as I also like to shoot my 10/22 and .45, use my Zeiss binoculars to watch whales and osprey, and like to fish occasionally.

If I am forced to leave my vehicle and go on foot, a scenario I only anticipate as the result of some extraordinary misfortune such as my car being washed away or tumbling down a hill, my 10-day pack and 10/22 pack carry easily, but I'd obviously have to leave things like the Humless system behind. The ability to stay with a vehicle is very important, as it provides shelter and protection from Nature. The best option, of course, is to stay at home, even if home has become severely damaged.

— *Dave Duffy*

Chickens

By Jackie Clay-Atkinson

Of all the livestock you can raise on a homestead, chickens should be right at the top of the list. They not only provide a family with eggs and meat, but they also provide fertilizer for the garden and consume thousands of insects that can destroy your garden. Plus, they can forage for much of their own feed.

A chicken's small size means it requires minimal housing, feed, and attention. Their non-threatening size and personality make them ideal for timid or petite new homesteaders. Children love chickens and find them fascinating. And so do I! I find myself engrossed in their daily goings-on — singing, scratching the dirt, and running after insects with their necks outstretched. They have individual personalities, like all critters. My children always had their favorite pet chickens that were exempt from butchering. These chickens loved being carried around, fed special treats, and even trained to walk on a harness and leash. Unlike dogs and cats, pet chickens will reward you with an egg a day, to boot.

If their coop is kept clean and dry, chickens are odor-free. Unless you keep a rooster, they are quiet as well. Remember that you don't *need* a rooster unless you plan on raising baby chicks from your own eggs or if you desire fertile eggs. Chickens will lay perfectly well with no rooster present.

This is a bonus for folks living in town. With no rooster to loudly proclaim his territory or greet the rising sun, your neighbors are not likely to complain about your urban homesteading endeavors. In fact, many towns and even larger cities are allowing a family to have a small number of chickens, thanks to persistent poultry owners who lobby for restrictive laws to be changed.

When deciding to include chickens on your homestead, you need to decide why you want them. Are they to be primarily pets? How about eggs? Do you want quick, tasty meat?

Or do you want all of the above? There are many breeds of chickens and if you look through poultry catalogs, such as Murray McMurray Hatchery's, you'll find many pictures and descriptions. In fact, you'll probably want to order several breeds as they are all very fascinating and beautiful. But do yourself a favor and limit the number of chickens you buy until you get the hang of poultry raising.

Pet chickens

While any chicken can be a pet if handled gently and often, some breeds lend themselves to that better

Chickens make wonderful pets. Here are our friends' daughters, Kalyssa and Kaliyan with their special hen, Lightfoot.

than others. If you are a little timid about actually having chickens, but want to try a few as pets, how about picking out some of the fancy bantams? These miniature chickens are less than half the size of standard (regular) chickens. Some are particularly friendly and lay small eggs. Among my favorites for pets are *Mille Fleur* with brown, black, and white feathers and *Cochins* which are so puffy they look like over-stuffed balls. *Ameraucanas* often have puffy beards and lay colored eggs. If you really want a larger egg, you still have many choices for an egg-laying pet. Some that come to mind are: *Standard Ameraucanas*, called "the Easter egg chickens" because they lay blue and green eggs, *Cochins* with their quiet disposition and puffy body complete with feathered feet, *Salmon Faverolles* that sport puffy beards as well as feathered legs, and *Polish*, often called the "top hat" chicken because of their puff of feathers on their head, right down over their eyes.

To make pets of these chickens, handle them from an early age by squatting down so you don't seem so large, moving slowly around them, and feeding them tidbits from your hands. Never allow small children or dogs to chase or frighten them. Soon they'll look on you as their friend and come when you call.

Egg layers

If you want to choose homestead chickens primarily for their egg-laying talents, there are many breeds to choose from. Commercial "egg factories" usually choose *White Leghorns* as they are well known for producing up to 360 eggs per year with little slow down during molting time (when chickens change feathers twice a year). These chickens are egg factories, but because of their excessive and unnatural egg production, their productive lives are short. Most use themselves up within a year's time and must be culled and replaced. In

You can save up eggs from your hens or buy hatching eggs and hatch them yourself with an inexpensive home incubator.

addition, these birds tend to be flighty and nervous.

Most homesteaders want a calm, pretty bird, even though it means sacrificing some of the bountiful egg production of the *White Leghorn*. Some alternative choices include:
- *Silver Spangled Hamburg* — a lighter-weight egg layer that has a white body liberally spangled with black feathers arranged in a pretty pattern
- *Black Minorca* — raven black with a white spot on its cheek
- *Ancona* — black with white feathers scattered about the body in an attractive pattern
- *Blue Andalusian* — a beautiful smoke-gray, erect bird

These are all white egg layers. If you prefer a bounteous egg layer that lays a brown egg, you still have many options:
- *Black Sex Link (Black Star)* — black with some degree of golden hackles (neck feathers)
- *Brown Sex Link* (Brown Star) — a shiny brown bird. They are called *Sex Links* because at hatching, the

cockerels and pullets can be differentiated by color.
- *Rhode Island Red* — a medium-sized red bird
- *Barred Rock* — striped with bars of black and white

Dual-purpose breeds

Most breeds that are noted for heavy egg production are lighter in weight, since they spend their energy making eggs instead of meat. Of course, any chicken can be butchered for meat when desired or when their egg production tapers off, but you will end up with less meat.

For this reason, many homesteaders choose a dual-purpose breed. This means that although the hen lays fewer eggs than an "egg breed," she still has good egg production. She and extra cockerels are also large enough to provide a good deal of meat when butchered.

Some of my favorite dual-purpose breeds include:
- *Dominique* — heavier with tight rose combs, black and white barred plumage, and quite a good forager,

but still lays plenty of nice brown eggs

• *White Rock* — an old standby, pure white, heavy bird (roosters weigh about 9 pounds; hens weigh 6-7 pounds) and a great layer of brown eggs

• *Buff Orpington* — about the same size as above, but looks bigger due to its puffy gold feathers. It's very gentle and is a good winter layer of big brown eggs.

There are many other dual-purpose brown egg-layers to interest homesteaders, including the *Light Brahma, New Hampshire Red, Silver Laced Wyandotte*, and the *Colombian Wyandotte.*

Some homesteaders prefer to keep two flocks of chickens (even if they live in the same coop), one for eggs and another for meat production. This can work very well, giving you a quick return on your investment with tender, juicy home-raised chicken along with plenty of eggs for the table.

Meat chickens

When one thinks of meat chickens, the popular *Cornish Rock* broiler first comes to mind. These chickens grow amazingly fast, easily reaching butchering size at 6-8 weeks of age. But although they are amazing growers, many folks (myself included!) find them unnatural and disgusting. They don't act like chickens; they don't run around in the chicken yard, scratch for bugs and seeds, or roost on poles (they huddle on the floor, instead). They eat so much that you must remove the feed in the late afternoon or they'll eat themselves to death! They do make meat fast, though, with huge breasts and a very large carcass on butchering. Don't make the mistake of trying to keep a few for eggs or to raise your own meat bird chicks. I've done that three different times, only to have the birds die of a heart attack or have their legs weaken to the point they can't use them and finally die. They aren't bred for permanence, just for a fast return.

Some breeders have addressed this and are breeding chickens that are good for meat, yet act like a chicken. They scratch, rustle for feed, and roost at night. But as they are a more natural chicken, they don't reach a butchering size quite as quickly, nor is a greater portion of their meat in breast meat, as is the Cornish Rock. Some of these meat breeds include the *Freedom Ranger* (available through JM Hatchery and Freedom Ranger Hatchery) and *Red Ranger* (available through Murray McMurray Hatchery, among others).

A very good meat chicken that requires longer to grow to butchering size of 6-7 pounds is the *Cornish*, available in several colors from white to black. We have several *White Laced Red Cornish*, which are red with each feather edged in white. The breast is very large and wide. The bird looks smaller because its feathers lay close to the body, so the weight will fool you.

We really like the *White Rock* for a meat bird. You can often buy the cockerels quite cheaply. It does take about 10 weeks to reach butchering size, but they are a natural bird, doing what chickens are supposed to do and have quite good meat-feed conversion rates. Being a pure white bird, they are easy to pluck and have a nice yellowish skin.

Starting your chicks

You can sometimes find other homesteaders who are willing to sell or barter some adult chickens, but most folks choose to buy their chickens as chicks so they can raise their own meat birds, laying hens, or pets. In the spring, you can either check out several of the poultry catalogs that offer baby chicks or go to your local feed store that carries (or special orders) baby chicks. If you choose to order from a catalog, your baby chicks will arrive at the local post office and you will receive a call to come pick them up. Baby chicks han-

Brooding chicks is easy using a heat lamp or, as with our set-up off grid, a propane heater over a small stock tank. Note the feeder and chick waterer.

dle long-distance mailing very well, so don't worry.

When we lived in the remote Montana mountains where we were snowed in until May, my late husband, Bob, had to snowmobile seven miles down to the truck so he could drive to the post office and pick up our chicks. It was so cool to hear the snowmobile whining back up the mountain, and as he got close I could hear the muffled peeps of baby chicks. He'd loosely wrapped their box in a blanket so they'd stay warm, yet not smother. We didn't lose a one, either!

Be ready when your chicks come. Baby chicks are quite tough, but they are very little babies and have specific needs. First off, they must be kept warm — warmer than just sitting in a box in the house. Most folks can easily take care of this by hanging a heat lamp a few inches off the floor of a large cardboard box or even an unused small stock tank. You do need to have something to keep your chicks "corralled" near the light, yet able to get away a little if it feels too warm. Make absolutely sure the heat lamp is wired to a fixed object, such as a screw eye, so it can't fall down to the chicks' bedding. Many fires have been started this way! The bedding should be newspaper the first day or two, then replaced with wood shavings (not sawdust as it is dusty) or ground corn cobs. The chicks will learn to eat by day two and need to know that their food is in a food tray and not to eat the bedding.

Have a thermometer in the chick brooder so you can monitor the temperature. New chicks need a temperature of 95 degrees right under the heat lamp. This temperature can be reduced by 5 degrees each week until they are feathered out. They should have room to get away from the heat if they choose. If the chicks are too cold, they will crowd together, sometimes smothering each other. Likewise, if the container has square

Chickens, when fenced out of the garden to prevent damage to plants and crops, come running for a treat of tomato.

corners, sometimes the chicks will pile together in a corner and smother each other. Keeping chicks in a container with rounded corners is a good idea, even if you round the corners by taping pieces of cardboard across them.

But what if you're off grid, like we are, and can't keep a heat lamp on? There are ways to get around this problem when you want to brood a batch of chicks. When we lived very remote up in the mountains of Montana, I built a chick brooder that used a kerosene lamp as a heat source. This worked very well and was an inexpensive way to raise a batch of chicks.

Here's a basic description of this brooder. Imagine stacked boxes, 18 inches square. The bottom box is open on the top and bottom. It's a few inches taller than the kerosene lamp you will be using (I used a lamp that had a short globe). This box has a door in one side so you can slide the lamp in and out when you need to fill it or trim the wick. There are also a couple of 1-inch holes drilled in the sides so the lamp has adequate air

supply. The box that sits over the lamp box has a bottom made out of flat tin. This tin sits over the lamp. To keep the chicks' feet from burning, I put a couple of inches of clean sand over the tin. This brooder is heated by radiant heat in the floor, via the lamp below. The top of the upper box is solid, with a hinged door to access the brooder box.

Along one side of the brooder box there is an opening a few inches high along one side. This opening faces a chick run, 18 inches wide and tall, and about 24 inches long. The bottom and sides are ¼-inch hardware cloth. It is framed with 2x2s and stands on legs long enough to line it up with the opening in the brooder box. I also added a door on top of the wire run so I could refill the feeder and waterer. Over the opening in the brooder box which faces the run, I tacked a piece of old blanket with many slots cut in it. This kept the heat in the brooder, but the chicks quickly learned to run through it when they wanted to get out and eat or drink.

Our brooder sat in our kitchen. You do need it in a reasonably warm

*Here's a beautiful little chicken coop with a fenced
and covered run to keep out predators.*

place, as the lamp won't keep chicks warm if the brooder is located outdoors or in an outbuilding with no heat. Use a thermometer to check the temperature; you may need to use two lamps at first if your house is quite cool in the spring. One additional caution: If you don't provide nighttime light, your chicks may pile and smother each other. I used a candle lamp on the table near the chick run, but you could also use a battery-operated lantern.

Another off-grid option for brooding chicks is to use a small propane heater. We've done that here in Minnesota, hanging the heater above and pointing down onto our chicks, housed in a small plastic water tank. Like the heat lamp, be *absolutely sure* that the propane heater can't fall down into the chicks' bedding. You may not only lose your chicks, but possibly your home and life!

While brooding chicks in the house is sure doable, be aware that it is not for the fastidious. Chicks create a lot of dust by the time they are large enough to go without heat. If you can't handle dust, arrange to brood your chicks in a nice, tight chicken coop.

New chicks will require water and feed as soon as they arrive. Most folks use a plastic waterer that screws onto a regular quart canning jar. You'll need one per 25 chicks. With a waterer like this, the chicks will have plenty of water, yet won't get it dirty by scratching shavings into it. Also, chicks sometimes drown in a more accessible pan. It's a good idea to use an electrolyte solution in their water for the first day or two. This helps them quickly get over the stress of being shipped to their new home. It's also a good idea to dip the beaks of each chick in the water as you release it from the shipping box. Dehydration is often a problem with new chicks that don't know where to get a drink.

Most farm stores carry chick starter feed and inexpensive metal or plastic feed troughs for chicks. These troughs have a rotating bar on top to keep chicks from getting into the feed, dirtying it with manure, and scratching it out of the pan.

While chicks can certainly be raised on plain ground feed supplemented with hardboiled eggs as Grandma used to do, most of today's homesteaders use commercial crumbled and processed chick starter to get them going.

Housing your chickens

Chickens are easy to house and their requirements are few. While some new chicken owners build beautiful and elaborate chicken cottages, it's really not necessary. Basically, there are two types of chicken housing: the chicken coop and the so-called chicken tractor. The chicken coop is a small walk-in building that contains roosts, nest boxes, and sufficient floor space for the birds in the winter. The chickens are either allowed to free range or have access to a chicken yard so they can run about, enjoy the sun, and take dust baths when they wish. Ideally, the coop should be insulated in cold climates, but as long as there are no drafts, the chickens will do fine without it. Commercial egg-layers are crammed five to an 18x18-inch wire cage where they can't even walk about, but your home flock should enjoy much more coop room. A good average is about four square feet per hen, provided that they also have an outdoor run.

A chicken coop doesn't need to be expensive. I've built two on our present homestead out of scrap lumber and material from the dump. One smaller coop we use for breeding flocks is only 6x10 feet, built as a shed addition next to our goat barn. It is built on a "foundation" of railroad ties and framed with 2x4s. It is sided with scraps of tongue and groove lumber left over from our house. The pieces ranged from two to six feet long; most folks would consider that firewood! The roof used to be two sheets of plywood, rescued from the dump and full of nails. I covered it with rolled roofing, also scrap from the dump. After it had been there for two years, I splurged and added sheet metal roofing to finish it off. The coop has two recycled windows to let in plenty of sunshine.

Our larger scrap-built coop is 8x12 feet, and houses about 25 chickens and a couple of turkeys. It's ugly, but it does the job. It is patched together with whatever plywood and OSB I could find, has two big windows, and is 2x4 framed. The roof is part left-over sheet metal and part clear corrugated fiberglass, left over from our twice-moved temporary greenhouse.

When we get our barn finished, we are going to disassemble the goat barn and two chicken coops and build one nice, pretty chicken coop with the combined materials. Until then, our chickens are perfectly happy with their homes (even though I cringe when I look at them).

Free range

Free ranging your flock is ideal because they can run any place they wish, sample seeds, insects, and greens, and have sun or shade when they want. Unfortunately, there are a couple of problems with letting your flock free range. First off, they will end up leaving chicken deposits on your porch, and scratching and eating your flowers and vegetable garden. Another issue is that those plump, gorgeous chickens are a huge temptation for predators. With totally free-range chickens, you can expect to lose some of them.

Chicken tractor

A safer alternative is to keep the chickens in a chicken tractor. This is a small coop with a nest box/roosting area on one end, and a long, wire run on the other, with wheels attached. You can easily move the whole thing every day or so. In this way, the birds can enjoy fresh ground to scratch on and eat insects and seeds, but they will be protected from predators.

They *won't* be able to dig in your flowers and eat your vegetables.

There are as many different styles of chicken tractors as there are chicken coops, but most have a basic wire run, often with handles on the end for ease of moving it, and a weathertight coop on the other. Most have a hinged door on the top of the small coop for ease of removing the eggs and a hinged door on the top of the wire run so you can easily water and feed the flock.

Even though free-range chickens and chickens in a chicken tractor will harvest plenty of pasture and insects, you still need to give them plenty of food, available at all times. (An exception is for **Cornish Rock** broilers, who overindulge if given unlimited access to feed).

Roosts and nest boxes

Chickens are naturally roosting birds when given a chance (except for sluggish, heavy **Cornish Rock** broilers). Every coop should have roosts made of rounded poles. I like my chickens' roosts screwed onto slant-ing poles so the roost poles are about a foot apart from floor to ceiling, but not one directly on top of the other (like a ladder leaning against the wall). There should be enough roosts that the chickens have "elbow" room between each other. In cold weather, they'll crowd together for warmth, and in hot weather they'll move farther apart for comfort.

When your pullets are about four months old, you should add nest boxes to the coop. There should be one available box per five pullets so they don't "argue" about who gets to use a box. The boxes can be purchased metal nest boxes or homebuilt wooden ones. I like the boxes to be about a foot wide, 18 inches deep, and a foot high, built from 1-inch lumber with a steeply slanted plywood top to prevent them from roosting on the top of the nesting boxes. There should be a pole a few inches out from the front of the boxes, so a hen can fly up, then walk down the row to choose the box she wants.

Bedding is necessary for comfort and to cushion eggs so they don't

Here's my little chicken coop, made entirely from scrap and material from the dump. It's not fancy, but it has worked for five years now.

break when they're laid or when they roll around. We use a thick layer of pine shavings or straw. The nest boxes should be about waist high to make it easier to gather the eggs and to keep the hens from soiling the boxes in their daily foraging about.

Heat is not necessary in a chicken coop. In fact, too warm an enclosed coop in the wintertime can cause an

---

Chicks and poultry supplies:

Murray McMurray Hatchery
PO Box 458
Webster City, Iowa 50595
Phone: 515-832-3280
www.mcmurrayhatchery.com

Cackle Hatchery
PO Box 529,
Lebanon, MO 65536
Phone: 417-532-4581
www.cacklehatchery.com

Meyer Hatchery
626 State Route 89
Polk, OH 44866
Phone: 888-568-9755

Welp Hatchery
PO Box 77,
Bancroft, IA 50517
Phone: 1-800-458-4473
www.welphatchery.com

Ridgway Hatchery
PO Box 306,
LaRue, Ohio 43332
Toll Free: 800-323-3825
Phone: 740-499-2163
www.ridgwayhatchery.com

Sand Hill Preservation Center
1878 230th Street
Calamus, Iowa 52729
www.sandhillpreservation.com

Nasco Farm and Ranch
PO Box 901
Fort Atkinson, WI 53538
Phone: 1-800-558-9595
www.enasco.com

---

ammonia build-up from manure and lead to respiratory diseases. In very cold climates, you can prevent chickens' combs from freezing by choosing breeds that have tight or rose combs that don't stick up, because that makes them vulnerable to freezing. If chicken combs do freeze, it looks terrible for a while, but the frozen portion will eventually fall off with no lasting ill effect.

Keeping your chickens safe from predators

What predator wouldn't relish a chicken dinner? Predators range from flying raptors such as hawks, owls, and eagles, to land critters like bears, foxes, coyotes, raccoons, possums, weasels, mink, fishers, and even pet dogs. It's hard to keep your chickens totally safe from everything that could possibly harm them, but you can do a lot to reduce the chances of them being hurt.

First of all, consider the reality of what type of predators are likely to try to get your flock. Some areas of the country have different predators than others. If you're new to chickens, ask your neighbors what kinds of predators they've had in the past.

I think the perfect chicken coop should have a cement floor. That way *nothing* can dig under it to get at your flock. If this isn't economically possible, consider a wooden floor which will significantly reduce the possibility of a predator gaining access to your chickens.

Predators, except for hawks and eagles, attack primarily at night. Be sure you always lock your chicken coop door in the evening, before dark. (I recently got lax and left the coop door open at night and lost four hens to a fox!) Even if you have your birds in a chicken tractor, be sure the coop part has a wooden floor and that you shut the access door each and every evening. If you live where there are larger predators, it's a good idea to

keep your chicken tractor closer to your house in the evening.

Be sure your coop is secure with no large cracks or knotholes. A weasel can squeeze through a knothole as big as your thumb and we just had a fox squeeze through a 3-inch crack in a box stall to kill baby turkeys. I saw it leave through the same crack!

If larger predators are common in your area, use extra heavy wire for the chicken yard and bury it along the bottom so they can't dig underneath. Use a strand of electric wire on the outside of the chicken fence to deter climbing predators like possums and raccoons. It'll also keep the stray dogs from attacking your birds. I think more chickens are killed by dogs than by all other predators combined.

Of course, large, outdoor dogs will be the best protection your chickens could have if the dogs have been trained to stay home and protect the homestead.

Egg production

At about 4-6 months of age, depending on the breed, pullets will begin to lay eggs. Their first eggs will be quite small but they'll get larger in the days to come. Hens require a minimum of 16 hours of daylight a day to maintain full egg production. In the spring and summer months, this is supplied by nature. But in the fall and winter, you need to provide extra lighting to maintain egg production. When we lived in the remote mountains, we had no power and no money to afford even a modest system of alternative power. My hens would quit laying in November and I only got a few eggs all winter long.

Now we have better light-producing capabilities, so in October, I start leaving the light on in the coop for several hours after dusk. This makes a huge difference in egg production. We get eggs all winter long.

Be aware that all chickens naturally molt twice a year, losing many of their feathers while they begin to grow new ones. At this time, most birds stop laying. This is nothing to worry about. When their new feathers grow in they'll look much prettier and will soon begin to lay again.

Food

Chickens require grit to digest food. It is stored in their crops where it functions like teeth to grind the feed they eat. When chickens are free ranged or have a large yard, they often pick up enough grit, but it's a good idea to keep a small container filled with grit available from the time chicks feather out.

In addition, a container full of crushed oyster shell is necessary so that they have adequate calcium in their diets. Calcium not only builds strong bones but also makes strong egg shells that are resistant to breakage when one hen crowds into the nest with another.

Be sure your hens have plenty of good food available at all times. In addition to what they pick up on pasture or in their yard, they should have a balanced 18% grain mix as well as oyster shell and grit. Short your hens and they'll lay less eggs. In addition to their grain, you can provide plenty of scraps from the kitchen and garden to keep them happy and laying well. We often have extra milk or whey and they enjoy having it mixed with their grain. It gives them a treat, plus it

Turkeys — the other poultry

Turkeys make a good addition to a homestead chicken flock. They eat about the same feed, require the same type of housing, and can even be housed together. There are many books and articles that repeat the old caution that chickens and turkeys cannot be housed together for fear of blackhead, mainly a turkey disease. While this is true in commercial settings, it is a very rare instance where blackhead arises on a homestead. This is primarily due to the isolation and stress-free living of a homestead flock as compared to a commercial operation. We have housed our turkeys and chickens together for half a century and have never had a bit of problem.

Our chickens and turkeys share our orchard for a yard. They get to free range, within bounds, eating bugs and fallen fruit, fertilizing the trees in the process.

Turkeys provide another form of homestead meat. We really like variety in our diet and we can get tired of chicken, chicken, chicken. So for holidays and family gatherings, we prefer turkey. Like other meats, home-raised turkey tastes way better than store-bought turkey.

Nearly all store-bought turkey comes from one commercial breed, **Broad Breasted White**. This is the Cornish Rock of turkeydom. These birds grow very quickly, are heavy breasted (as the name implies), and can weigh up to 50 pounds at maturity. While you can buy Broad Breasted White poults (baby turkeys) to raise for meat, homesteaders are usually better off with one of the heritage breeds such as **Bourbon Red**, **Narragansett, Slate,** or **Spanish Black**. The reason for this is that Broad Breasted White turkeys are so heavy that they can not usually reproduce naturally. The tom claws the back of the hens terribly when he mounts them, often causing death. Even protection such as turkey breeding saddles made of leather or canvas is often not enough to allow natural mating. Commercial flocks use artificial insemination, but that is totally impractical on the homestead.

Heritage breeds not only mate naturally, but also lay many eggs and will sit on them and raise the babies very competently. You can even save up some of the eggs before you let your hen turkey set and either set them under a broody hen or hatch them in an incubator so you raise more poults from each hen than you would normally.

We have Bourbon Reds and Narragansetts. Both of these beautiful breeds produce a large turkey at maturity and can mate normally. They do not grow as fast as commercial turkeys do, but we feel that because they grow slower the meat tastes better. Reaching 25 pounds or more at maturity, toms do need to grow for 8-10 months to be ready for the table, as opposed to six months for the commercial breeds. Take this into consideration when you are ordering poults or setting hatching eggs if you want a Thanksgiving or Christmas bird.

boosts their protein intake. I also give my chickens dampened alfalfa chaff from hay, soaked overnight in boiling water, which rehydrates the hay. It improves the yolk color in the winter and the girls love it.

Keeping excess eggs

In the spring, even a modest flock of chickens will produce a huge bounty of eggs, most laying an egg a day. We sell or barter these eggs to friends and neighbors, and there are many recipes I enjoy fixing at this time of year that require eggs, from tall meringue pies to quiches and puddings. But sometimes you end up with just too many eggs to use right away.

Freezing

Separate egg yolks from whites. To freeze the egg yolks, break clean eggs into a bowl. Stir, but do not beat. Into each cup of yolks, mix 2 Tbsp. light corn syrup (if you want to use them for baking) or 1 tsp. salt (for other uses). Package in small amounts, being sure to label what you added to the yolks so you don't make a mistake. Adding salt or corn syrup to the yolks keeps them from getting gummy. Also mark down how many yolks you have per package.

To freeze whites, separate carefully from yolks, not getting the slightest bit of yolk in the whites. Do not mix. Package as per recipe use, noting how many whites are in each package and then freeze.

Whole eggs can also be frozen. Break clean eggs into a bowl. Stir well but do not beat. To each cup of eggs, add 1 Tbsp. sugar or ½ tsp. salt, depending on how you will be using them. This prevents gumminess when you thaw them out.

Package in convenient sizes for normal use and mark whether you used sugar or salt. Thaw in refrigerator or under cold water. Don't hold in the fridge for more than 24 hours; they tend to spoil quickly after being frozen.

Frozen eggs store for about six to eight months.

Waterglassing

Waterglassing eggs is an old-time, long-term storage method. The eggs are immersed in a waterglass solution, which is sodium silicate. The waterglass solution is mixed in a sterilized, large crock and the clean, fresh, uncracked eggs are gently stacked in it with the top few inches of waterglass above the eggs at all times. The crock is stored in a cool place. You can keep eggs to use all winter this way. It works well, but I don't use this method any longer as it's extremely unpleasant to reach your bare arm into slimy cold waterglass to go after a few eggs.

Cold storage

Most folks don't realize just how long eggs will keep when stored in a cold location like a refrigerator or a cold pantry floor. Store-bought "fresh" eggs are often two or three months old before you buy them, so if you gather your own fresh eggs and carefully store them in cold conditions, they'll remain good for five or six months with no special treatment.

To tell a good egg from a bad one after long storage, float them in a bowl of water. The fresh egg will lay on the bottom. An older egg will stand on end; it's still okay to use. A bad egg will usually float completely on top. To be sure, always break older eggs individually into a cup. A bad egg will have a runny yolk, look nasty, and smell bad, to boot.

Pickling

You can pickle hardboiled eggs, then can them to use indefinitely. I like these just for snacking or for making deviled eggs when my hens are in molt and aren't laying. Here's the recipe for this quick, easy method of saving extra eggs.

```
18 whole, hardboiled, peeled eggs
1½ qts. white vinegar
2 tsp. salt
1 Tbsp. whole allspice
1 Tbsp. pickling spices
```

Mix vinegar and spices in large pot and bring to a boil. Pack whole, peeled, hardboiled eggs into a hot, sterilized jar, leaving ½-inch of headspace. Ladle boiling pickling solution over eggs, leaving ½-inch of headspace. Remove air bubbles. Make sure all eggs are covered with solution. Wipe rim of jar clean. Place hot, previously-simmered lid on jar and screw down ring firmly tight. Process for 25 minutes in a boiling water bath canner. Never let a jar of unsealed pickled eggs sit out at room temperature. You risk danger from botulism and other bacterial diseases.

You can also make mustard pickled eggs by simply adding a few things to your recipe:

```
12 whole hardboiled eggs, peeled
1 pint vinegar
1 Tbsp. mixed pickling spices
3 tsp. dry mustard
2 tsp. cornstarch
2 tsp. sugar
1 tsp. turmeric
1 tsp. salt
```

Pack eggs into hot, sterilized jars. Combine mustard and cornstarch and add enough vinegar to make a paste. Stir in more vinegar then add all of remaining ingredients, except the eggs. Stir well and heat until it boils. Ladle hot liquid over eggs, covering them and leaving ½ inch of headspace. Process for 20 minutes in a boiling water bath canner.

Health concerns

Fortunately, homestead chickens tend to be very healthy, having few common diseases and illnesses. This is because homestead chickens are generally an isolated flock that is well cared for by their owners.

Upper respiratory problems

While there a few upper respiratory diseases that are caused by viruses, just like the common cold in humans, many are caused by bacterial infection and can be treated with antibiotics given in their water. Many times upper respiratory diseases, which act like a human cold with runny eyes and nostrils, coughs, and lethargy, stem from stress. This stress includes crowding, moving a bird from one flock to another, being confined in a damp coop with poor ventilation and air circulation, or being shown in a fair or poultry show where it was exposed to many other birds' germs. Remedy the cause, such as a damp coop, then immediately begin giving the sick bird antibiotics, such as tetracycline, in its drinking water. Isolate any sick birds immediately so as not to spread the illness.

Always make sure your coop is draft-free and well bedded so that it remains dry.

Egg bound

Occasionally a hen will become egg bound. This is kind of like being constipated, but with an egg. The hen will sit in the nest box, act lethargic, and often strain as if trying to lay an egg. Use an ear syringe to insert 2 Tbsp. warmed vegetable or mineral oil into the vent around the egg. This usually results in a quick expulsion of the egg and the hen will rapidly recover. If not, and you can feel the egg, you can poke the egg with a pair of needle-nose pliers to break it, collapsing the egg, and very gently pull the pieces out so she can then pass what remains.

Mites and lice

Chickens pick up mites and chicken lice from time to time. Their feathers will look rough and broken (not to be confused with molting). The chickens will take many dust baths and pick at their feathers in an effort to remove the itching pests. These insects are very small but you can see them with the naked eye.

If your birds have an infestation, clean the coop of all old bedding, including the nest box material. Buy some pyrethrins or rotenone powder meant for poultry and dust each bird by holding it upside down by the legs and powdering the feathers, especially around the vent and under the wings. Also dust the coop when the birds are outdoors. Repeat in 10 days to ensure that any pest eggs that hatch don't cause a reinfestation.

Impacted crop

The crop is located on the lower neck, just above the breast. It holds grit and functions to grind feed so the bird can digest it. On occasion, the crop can become impacted with foreign objects or even by eating too much straw or bedding. The crop feels large and hard and the chicken becomes weak and lethargic.

You can usually remedy this problem if you catch it quick enough by dosing the bird with 2 Tbsp. vegetable oil slowly squirted into the mouth by a syringe. Don't hurry or the chicken may aspirate the oil or choke. Once the oil is all in, gently massage the oil into the mass in the crop, trying to work it apart. The bird will usually either pass the material into the digestive tract or fling the offending material out of her mouth by shaking her head violently from side to side.

Worms

Occasionally chickens will pick up internal parasites, usually roundworms. Wormy chickens are usually thin and don't lay well. Their feathers also look rough and their comb is dull. It's simple to worm your flock by adding Piperazine to the drinking water. Use as directed and repeat in 10 days to two weeks. Improvement is quick and obvious.

Bird flu

Some folks worry about their chickens giving them avian or bird flu. Yes, it is possible; however, most cases of avian flu have appeared in third world countries with minimal hygiene and chickens living in or under the hut where a family sleeps.

If bird flu happens to be found in your area, simply isolate your flock by putting wire over all openings to your coop to keep sparrows and other wild birds, which can carry the disease from one area to the other, out of your coop. If your flock has an outside run, cover it and also isolate your flock while they're outdoors. Realistically, bird flu is a minor worry to homestead flocks.

Butchering chickens

When your broilers reach butchering size or your flock has expanded too much, you face butchering time. This is not a pleasant task, to be sure, but it does not have to be traumatic either for you or your chickens.

Withhold feed from the chickens the night before and the morning of butchering. This makes the crop less full and butchering will go easier and cleaner. While you can certainly chop the heads off with a sharp axe (with the chicken's head held firmly between two spikes driven into a big stump, forming a V), using a killing cone is much better. The chicken doesn't struggle and there are no broken or bruised wings or legs from flopping around headless.

You can buy metal killing cones or make your own. (See "Build a poultry killing cone" by Allen Easterly in Issue #135, May/June 2012.) All they are is a chicken-sized funnel with a bottom opening large enough that the chicken's head and neck stick out but the wings are held firmly in place. The cone has holes drilled in the back that fit over nails or screws put in a fence post or nearby tree. To kill the chicken, hold the head with one hand, extend the neck a bit then slide a sharp knife up under the feathers of the neck and cut the throat, letting the chicken bleed out. There is little or no struggling and the chicken doesn't seem to realize what's happened.

Plucking the chicken is the next step, and it is quite easy, as long as you have a large tub of boiling hot water nearby. We butcher outdoors because it is a messy task with wet feathers and blood here and there. I keep a hose nearby to wash off our butchering table from time to time as needed.

To scald a chicken prior to plucking, hold it by the legs and dip it all the way under the surface of the boiling water for a few seconds, then remove the chicken. Pull on a wing feather and see if it pulls out easily. If not, dunk the bird again. When a chicken is correctly scalded, the feathers come out with very little effort on your part. Once the feathers slip off easily, pluck them and throw them into a nearby, lined garbage container. Once plucked, you'll eviscerate, then cool the chicken in a tub of cold water.

To clean a chicken, follow these steps:

1. Cut just below the point of breast, holding down skin. Carefully run the knife down on each side of the vent and under. Do not cut into it.

2. Gently remove the crop from the lower part of the neck, where it goes into the body, slicing it off, freeing the esophagus.

3. Reach in and pull guts out; they'll pull out in one bunch.

4. Scrape lungs loose; they're attached to the back of the ribs.

5. Cut the tail off or remove oil sac.

6. Rinse carcass inside and out and place in a bucket of fresh, cold water.

7. Pat the chicken dry and pick any pin feathers you have missed. Singe off any tiny ones by rotating the carcass over a gas burner of your kitchen stove or by twisting a newspaper into a stick, lighting it, and singeing the chicken with that.

Refrigerate your chickens overnight before cooking or canning them. Freshly-killed chickens tend to be pretty tough, regardless of age.

You can also freeze the whole chickens in a tight freezer bag (wrap this bag with white butcher wrap as well to prevent freezer burn) and, of course, you can pressure can both chicken meat and broth for use later. Canning is a good option for older birds that tend to be tougher. They become tender and make great soup, stews, and additions to many delectable recipes when canned.

Increasing your flock

While you can buy new birds, we prefer to raise our own. You can simply save a nest full of fertile eggs and let a broody hen sit on them. This is the natural way and works well with no effort on your part. (See Kash's article on page 46 in this issue for more on this.) Or you can save fertile eggs in a carton on your countertop until you have as many as you want (store for up to 7 days — if temperature is between 55° and 62° F) and then hatch them yourself in a small home incubator. Even living off grid, we've done it right in our dining room. The incubator is insulated and draws very little electricity. Incubating eggs is quite easy, provided that you follow the directions carefully. In about 21 days, you'll hear your eggs peeping and find fluffy little chicks emerging. Children are so fascinated with the process that many schools include incubating chicks as part of their science program.

The longer you have chickens, the more interested you'll become in raising them. They are such an entertaining, fun bird to have around and they earn their keep by providing fresh, tasty eggs and a pantry full of canned chicken for us to enjoy any time we want. If you don't already have a few chickens, give them a try. Δ

A Backwoods Home Anthology
The Fifth Year

Food security 101

convenience mixes make life easier

By Rowena Aldridge

Last issue we talked about some things you can do to stretch your food budget and make great use of every bit of food you buy. This article is full of convenience foods you can make yourself and keep on hand to make your life easier.

When I look at the things that are available in the stores to make cooking simpler and quicker, I see boxes and boxes of mixes filled with fat and sodium and devoid of vitamins and nutrients. When I look at the ingredient list, I see all kinds of words I can't pronounce. Then I look at the price — yikes!

So I've slowly been replacing the purchased mixes we use in our kitchen with homemade versions, and I've discovered that not only are the homemade versions tastier, they're cheaper. And because I'm in control of what exactly goes into them, I can at least control which unpronounceable ingredients I include.

Some of the ingredients called for in homemade mixes tend to make people cringe (powdered milk and bouillon granules, for instance). As an advocate of healthy eating, I sympathize, however the plain fact is that if you are struggling to put food on the table, whether due to financial strains or time constraints, these mixes will make it possible to feed everybody pretty well with minimal cost or effort at meal time. When making mixes at home, your final product will still be better for you and your family than something you could buy pre-made.

Sure, it takes time to assemble the mixes, and at first you will have to invest in some items that you haven't been keeping on hand, but in the end the total cost per individual mix will be so low that it won't be worth it to go back to the purchased mixes.

Tip: Don't try to replace everything at once. Just make note when you are running low on a mix that you normally keep, and plan to stock up on ingredients for making it yourself on your next shopping trip. This way you will only have to buy a few things at a time, and you'll only have to arrange for appropriate containment a bit at a time.

There are so many different recipes for various pantry mixes that you'll need to try a few to find which ones you like best. The following are ones I like, but you can certainly tweak them to suit your needs.

Baking mix: I use a recipe from Hillbilly Housewife (hillbillyhouse-wife.com), which can be adapted for several different kinds of flour.

For all-purpose flour:

> 9 cups flour
> 1½ Tbsp. salt
> ¼ cup baking powder
> 2 cups solid vegetable shortening

For self-rising flour (which already has salt and baking powder in it):

> 10 cups flour
> 2 cups solid vegetable shortening

Either recipe will yield the same results; just use the one that best suits your ingredients.

Mix all dry ingredients first in a large bowl. Measure the shortening by packing it down and leveling the top with your finger or a kitchen knife. Add shortening to the flour mixture, then cut or knead the shortening into the flour. Mix until the texture is like lumpy cornmeal.

Store in a tightly-sealed canister or jar. Makes 11-12 cups of baking mix that you can use anywhere Bisquick is called for.

When making a baking mix, I prefer to use vegetable shortening because it doesn't have to be refrigerated.

One of my favorite ways to use this mix is to make tortillas. Simply combine one part water with four parts

21

baking mix, knead until smooth, then tear off golf-ball sized pieces and roll them out thin on a floured surface. Toast the tortillas in a dry skillet for a few minutes until they are speckled brown. These store well in the freezer, but put pieces of waxed paper between them or they will stick together when they thaw.

Universal muffin mix: You'll find a variety of delicious muffins made with this mix at grouprecipes. com/24483/universal-muffin-mix. html. Here's the basic mix recipe.

18 cups flour
5 cups sugar
2¼ cups dry buttermilk or nonfat
   dry milk powder
6 Tbsp. baking powder
2 Tbsp. baking soda
2 Tbsp. salt
2-3 Tbsp. ground cinnamon (to
   taste)
2-3 tsp. ground nutmeg (to taste)

Combine all ingredients and store in a jar or canister in a cool, dry place.

To make 24 regular-sized muffins preheat oven to 400° F. Coat muffin tins with cooking spray. In a large bowl beat 3-4 eggs, 3 tsp. vanilla, 2 cups water, and up to 1 cup of oil or butter. Stir in 5½ cups muffin mix and any additional ingredients (2 cups of fresh fruit, shredded vegetables, nuts, or flavored chips) just until moistened. The batter should be lumpy. Fill muffin tins and bake 18-20 minutes.

This is the only sweet-bread muffin mix I use now. Husband Rudi and daughter Ella particularly like the banana muffins made from this mix and I love lemon-poppy seed.

Muffins made from this mix also freeze well. Put them on a cookie sheet and let them freeze until the outside is frosty first. That way when you put them in a storage bag they won't stick together.

Pizza dough: Okay, this isn't really a make-ahead mix, but you can make a double batch and stash the second lump of dough in the freezer.

1 Tbsp. active dry yeast
1 cup warm water (105-115° F)
1 tsp. sugar
1 tsp. salt
2 Tbsp. vegetable oil
2½ cups flour

Dissolve yeast in water. Add the rest of the ingredients and mix. Dump onto a floured surface. Knead into a smooth dough (about five minutes), then roll out and press onto a greased pizza pan. Add your toppings then bake at 450° F for 12-15 minutes until the crust looks crispy and lightly browned.

For toppings, start a bag of leftover bits of this and that. Just label the bag and stash it with the dough in the freezer. When you find cheese on sale, shred enough for a pizza and put it in the bag, too!

Cream of anything soup mix: Here's another one from Hillbilly Housewife.

4 cups powdered milk
1½ cup cornstarch
½ cup instant chicken or vegetable
   bouillon granules
4 tsp. dried onion flakes
2 tsp. dried thyme
2 tsp dried basil, crushed
1 tsp. pepper

Measure all ingredients, mix together, and pour into an airtight container.

To use this, combine 1/3 cup of the mix with 1 cup of water. Heat at medium-low heat in a small saucepan until it starts to thicken. This will make the same amount as one can of soup.

Our family loves this so much more than the stuff from the store. Using the low-sodium bouillon makes it even healthier than the canned stuff. If you prefer, you can leave out the bouillon and replace it with your own homemade broth when you make the soup. It's also great for using in things like chicken casserole or green bean casserole.

Onion soup mix:

This one is also from Hillbilly Housewife.

¾ cup instant minced onion
⅓ cup beef bouillon powder
4 tsp. onion powder
¼ tsp. crushed celery seed
¼ tsp. sugar

Combine and store in an airtight container. Five tablespoons of the mix equals one package of store-bought onion soup mix.

This is another mix in which you can leave out the bouillon and instead add broth while you're cooking. I use this mix a lot in the crock pot, and it makes a great onion dip when stirred into some sour cream or plain yogurt.

Breading mix: I live in the south. Breading things is how we roll. This mix also makes a great addition to meatloaf or salmon patties. I have been known to cheat on the seasonings and just use an equivalent amount of Old Bay seasoning because I love that stuff.

2 cups bread crumbs
¼ cup flour
3 Tbsp. paprika
2 tsp. onion powder
4 tsp. salt
2 tsp. ground oregano
½ tsp. ground red pepper
½ tsp. garlic powder

Mix all ingredients and store in a sealed container.

To cook one chicken, cut up the bird and shake the pieces with about 2/3 of a cup of the breading mix in a plastic bag. Arrange on a baking sheet and cook in 400° F oven for 50 minutes or until the juices from the chicken run clear when pierced with a knife.

You can switch up the seasonings to suit your own tastes. I like the paprika and red pepper for the color and spiciness.

Taco seasoning: Taste of Home (tasteofhome.com) has a great taco seasoning recipe that is tasty on ground beef or chicken. It also works great to season beans for burritos. You can even mix it into plain yogurt to make a tasty dip!

> 8 tsp. dried minced onion
> 2 Tbsp. chili powder
> 2 tsp. cornstarch
> 2 tsp. garlic powder
> 2 tsp. ground cumin
> 1 tsp. dried oregano
> ¼ tsp. cayenne pepper

Combine ingredients well in a small bowl. Store in an airtight container. Yields six tablespoons, so you might want to double or triple the recipe for storage.

I usually use this for making chili, too, with the addition of my double-secret chili awesome-ifying ingredients: a heaping tablespoon of cinnamon powder and just a little unsweetened cocoa.

Ranch dressing mix: The Anti-Housewife (www.antihousewife.com) has a great recipe for this. This mix works equally well for salad dressing, veggie dip, and as a delicious dressing for wrap sandwiches.

> ½ cup dried parsley
> 2 Tbsp. dried minced garlic
> 2 Tbsp. dried minced onion
> 1 Tbsp. dried dill weed
> ¼ cup onion powder
> ¼ cup garlic powder
> 1 Tbsp. salt (or less, to taste)
> 1 Tbsp. ground black pepper
> ½ tsp. red chili flakes

Pulse the parsley, garlic, and onion in a food processor. Add the other ingredients and continue processing in pulses. Store in a jar or canister.

To turn it into dressing, mix 1 tablespoon of mix with 1½ cups mayonnaise and ¾ cup cultured buttermilk. Whisk all ingredients together.

Hot cocoa mix: I always have this on hand during December, and I'm on standby to make it whenever our family watches *The Polar Express*.

> 4 cups instant nonfat dry milk
> 1½ to 2 cups powdered sugar
> 1 cup powdered non-dairy creamer
> ⅔ cup unsweetened cocoa
> 1 package of instant store-bought chocolate OR vanilla pudding mix (optional, but a tasty addition)

Whisk all ingredients together, then store in a canister or jar. Kids will like it with the full two cups of sugar. Grown-ups might like the addition of ¼ cup of instant coffee.

To turn it from mere mix into a steaming beverage to warm body and soul, place 1/3 cup of the mix in a mug, add boiling water, stir, and serve. Sometimes I dress this up by putting in a few chocolate chips or using a peppermint stick to stir it.

Russian tea mix: Ok, this is completely unhealthy and has all kinds of junk in it, but I love it. It reminds me of childhood and makes me feel like an astronaut. It also makes a great warm punch for big gatherings.

> ½ cup instant tea powder
> 2 cups Tang or other orange-flavored drink mix
> 3 oz. lemonade-flavor drink powder
> ¾ cup white sugar
> ½ tsp. ground cinnamon
> ½ tsp. ground allspice
> ¼ tsp. ground cloves

Mix all ingredients. Store in a jar or canister.

To prepare, just spoon two or three rounded teaspoons into a mug and add boiling water.

And there you have it. These are my basics. You'll know what your own basics are by looking in your pantry. There are so many mixes you can make at home that you will have plenty to keep you busy on these long winter nights.

Next issue I'll show you some of the ways I store our foods and show you why the vacuum sealer is my new best friend.

Rowena Aldridge is a former professional ballerina who now spends her days homeschooling and homemaking. She is a certified educator in a number of old-school domestic skills, but her real passion is empowering others to go out and conquer the world on their own terms.

Learn more about her classes and other projects at www.romesticity.com

(Read part one of this series in issue #138, November/December 2012.) Δ

A Backwoods Home Anthology
The Twelfth Year

* Cutting dangerous trees
* Get out of and stay out of debt
* Make your own hard cider
* Restoring a hydro unit
* The homestead greenhouse
* What do you do with all those eggs
* Build a pallet fence

* Garden seeds — a great winter pastime
* In search of the perfect cup of coffee
* This coop is for the birds
* Build your own log home in the woods
* Reading animal tracks and signs
* Spinning fiber for the homestead
* Build a split-rail fence in impossible soil

Building your chicken coop

By Jackie Clay-Atkinson

While the popular "chicken tractor" with its portable small coop and wire run is very useful for temporary housing during the nicer months of the year, in cold climates you really need a more substantial coop that won't get buried in snow or blown around in blizzards.

A chicken coop is a wonderful first building project as it's small and has minimal construction "needs." A chicken coop can be just as beautiful and fancy as the builder wants it to be. I've seen coops I'd live in: pretty and cottage-like, fanciful gnome homes, practical, no-frills simple buildings, and more than a few that are like ours — built from scrap.

No matter what your chicken coop will look like, there are several "musts." The first is a solid structure that does not leak water or wind. While good ventilation is a must, you do have to make the coop tight

Here's a coop we built from pallets and scrap lumber. The goats lived in one end and the chickens lived in the other. It was free and worked well.

enough so drafts don't blow in on your girls.

Four square feet of floor space for each adult chicken is recommended. That means your 10x12-foot coop

This is one of our current chicken coops, made entirely out of scrap. It houses a dozen hens very well.

will allow you to house 30 chickens comfortably. If you only plan on having a handful of hens, you can build a much smaller coop. You do want enough room to enter the coop to observe the birds and to clean, feed, water, and gather eggs.

My little coop is only 6x8 feet and comfortably houses a dozen hens and a rooster, but I made the door too narrow and too short. I have trouble getting in to clean out the old bedding and I've smacked my head on the sill all too many times. I should have made a wider and higher door regardless of the size of the coop.

A chicken coop can be a free-standing building or a simple sloped roof shed, built as an addition to an existing building.

Your coop's floor can simply be dirt, but be sure you build your coop on higher ground with good drainage. You don't want your coop to be damp due to standing water from rainy weather or snowmelt. Dampness leads to sick chickens in a hurry. If you choose a dirt floor, it's a good idea to bury sturdy wire down at least a foot or preferably two feet in the ground all around the sides of the coop to prevent predators from digging underneath to get at your flock. Even the neighbor's dog may attempt to kill fluttering chickens out of excitement. In this vein, make sure your coop has a solid door that is closed every single night. Most wild predators attack at night and a closed door prevents this from happening.

Chickens love sunlight, so add at least one window to your coop, preferably to the east or south. My little coop has one to the south and one to the west since the east side of the coop is built against our goat barn. Do what you can to make sure your chickens have plenty of light. The windows also let in warmth in the wintertime.

You don't have to insulate your chicken coop, but in very cold climates it is a good idea. Add insulation on the walls and also the ceiling to hold in the warmth. Cover the insulation with OSB, plywood, or paneling, as the girls love to eat up beadboard insulation and it really isn't good for them. If you do insulate your coop, it's a good idea to include some

Chickens like poles to roost on. I like to attach them to angled supports running from the floor to about shoulder height. Chickens like to "climb" from the lower poles to finally roost near the ceiling.

means for fresh air. You can install a vent in the roof or you can simply leave the small chicken access door open during the day. Even in very cold weather chickens love to go outdoors and bask in the sun and fresh air. At night when the temperature plummets, closing the small chicken door will keep the flock comfortably warm.

Include a battery of nest boxes in your coop so that there is one nest for each five hens. If you don't do this, they'll fight over who gets to lay an egg in a box and eggs will get broken or chickens will begin to lay on the floor.

Also make sure you have a ladder-like roost made of rounded poles. I like a roost that slopes from the floor to shoulder height as chickens like to "climb" up the roost and end up on the highest poles. Δ

The chicken and the egg

By Habeeb Salloum

One cannot think of our culinary world without chicken or eggs. Chicken is one of the world's most consumed meats and eggs are on the tables of the vast majority of the world population. They provide the bulk of protein to people around the globe, especially the underprivileged.

My love affair with the chicken and its egg began early in life when my parents who emigrated from Syria in the early 1920s took a homestead in southern Saskatchewan. No sooner had they ploughed the land than it turned into desert. However, this did not force them to leave the land. In their country of birth, farming had never been a life of luxury and they adapted to the new harsh life.

Chickens and their eggs helped us survive those barren years. Our chickens were not pampered. During the drought of the Depression years when our family did not have the money to buy feed, our chickens survived on the meager food they found while scratching in the barn and the surrounding fields.

Chicken meat is packed with vitamins and nutrients. It is a versatile and excellent source of protein and a healthy alternative to red meat. It has been found that the ancient way of treating a cold with chicken soup is valid even in our modern age.

Eggs are high in vitamins and minerals but low in saturated fat and calories. They are also a rich source of protein. Although eggs contain cholesterol, the nutritional benefits of these chicken offerings outweigh the slight cholesterol concerns of the diner.

These are some of my favorite chicken and egg dishes:

Chicken and almond couscous
Serves about 10

This Moroccan-type couscous is one of my favorites. The juices of the chicken, almonds, chickpeas, and raisins blend well to create a succulent dish.

2 cups couscous
2 large onions, sliced
½ cup olive oil
one chicken, about 4 pounds, cut into serving pieces
2 cups cooked chickpeas
½ cup raisins, rinsed
1 cup lightly-toasted blanched almonds
3 tsp. salt
1 tsp. pepper
1 tsp. cinnamon
1 tsp. ground coriander seeds
½ tsp. turmeric
½ tsp. nutmeg
¼ tsp. ground cloves
7 cups water
4 Tbsp. butter
½ tsp. paprika

Soak couscous in warm water for a few seconds, then quickly drain and place in the top part of the couscousiére or double boiler with a perforated top. Thoroughly break up the lumps in the couscous and set aside.

In bottom part of the couscousiére or double boiler, place onion and oil,

Chicken and almond couscous

then cook over medium heat for 10 minutes. Add remaining ingredients, except water, butter, and paprika, then stir-fry for about five minutes. Add enough water to generously cover the chicken pieces, then bring to a boil. Fit the top part with couscous to the bottom part with stew. If steam escapes between the two parts, seal the seam with a piece of flour-impregnated cloth. Cook over medium heat for one hour or until chicken is done, stirring couscous often to make sure kernels do not stick together, then stir butter into couscous and remove from heat.

Place couscous on a platter pyramid-style, then make a wide, deep well in the middle. With a slotted spoon, remove chicken pieces, chickpeas, raisins, and almonds and place in well. Sprinkle paprika over couscous then serve. Remaining stew and sauce can be served as a side dish with each person adding extra stew to taste.

Garlic chicken
Serves 6

This is a version of a Spanish recipe inherited from the Moors.

> 4 Tbsp. olive oil
> 2 pounds boned chicken breasts, cut into 1-inch-wide strips
> 1 head garlic, peeled and crushed
> 1 tsp. dried tarragon
> 1 tsp. salt
> ½ tsp. pepper
> ½ tsp. dried thyme
> ¼ tsp. cayenne pepper
> 1 cup water

Heat oil in a frying pan, then sauté chicken over medium heat for five minutes. Add garlic, then stir-fry for further two minutes. Transfer frying pan contents to a casserole.

Combine remaining ingredients, then stir into the casserole. Cover, then bake in a 350° F preheated oven for 20 minutes. Uncover, then bake for another 30 minutes or until chicken is tender. Serve hot from casserole with mashed potatoes or cooked rice.

Cantonese almond chicken

Almond, prune, and chicken stew
Serves about 8

This is my own tempting version of a Moroccan *tajine* dish.

> one chicken, about 4 pounds, cut into serving pieces
> 3 medium onions, finely chopped
> 8 cloves garlic, crushed
> ½ cup finely chopped fresh coriander leaves
> 4 Tbsp. butter
> 2 tsp. salt
> 1 tsp. pepper
> pinch of saffron
> 3 cups water
> 1 cup prunes, pitted
> 2 Tbsp. honey
> 1 tsp. cinnamon
> ½ cup blanched almonds

In a saucepan, place chicken, onions, garlic, coriander, butter, salt, pepper, saffron, and water, then bring to boil. Cover, then simmer over low heat for about 1½ hours or until the chicken is well-done, adding more water if necessary. Remove chicken pieces with a slotted spoon and place on platter. Keep warm.

Add prunes to the sauce then simmer over low heat for 10 minutes. Stir in honey and cinnamon, then continue simmering uncovered for another 10 minutes. Pour hot sauce over chicken pieces, then decorate with almonds and serve hot.

Chicken and rice
Serves about 8 to 10

In the Horn of Africa where this dish originates, it is made using a whole chicken, cut into serving pieces, and the rice is cooked with the remaining ingredients. However, I think that my version is more pleasing to the eye.

> 5 Tbsp. cooking oil
> 3 pounds chicken breast cut into 1-inch cubes
> 1½ tsp. salt
> ½ tsp. pepper
> 1 large onion, finely chopped
> 4 cloves garlic, crushed
> 2 Tbsp. coriander leaves, chopped
> 1 small hot pepper, de-seeded and finely chopped
> 1 tsp. ground cumin
> 1 tsp. ground coriander seeds
> 1 tsp. fresh ginger, grated
> ½ tsp. cinnamon
> ¼ tsp. ground cardamom seeds
> 3 Tbsp. tomato paste, diluted in ½ cup water
> 2 cups chicken broth
> 4 cups cooked rice, kept warm

27

Fried vegetables and eggs

Heat the oil in a saucepan over medium heat, then add the chicken. Sprinkle with the salt and pepper and fry, turning frequently, until the pieces begin to brown.

Stir in the onion, garlic, coriander leaves, and hot pepper, then fry over medium/low heat for about five minutes, adding a little more oil if necessary. Stir in remaining ingredients, except the rice, and bring to a boil. Cover and cook over medium/low heat for 45 minutes, adding a little more water if necessary.

Spread the rice on a serving platter then place the chicken pieces on top. Spoon the sauce over the chicken pieces and serve immediately.

Cantonese almond chicken

Serves about 6

I have dined on different versions of this dish for years, but this is my favorite.

Sauce:

1 Tbsp. cornstarch, dissolved in
   2 Tbsp. water
2 Tbsp. soy sauce
½ cup chicken broth
¼ cup white grape juice
2 tsp. sugar

Combine all the sauce ingredients in a small bowl and set aside.

1 pound chicken breast, cut into
   ½-inch cubes
4 Tbsp. thinly sliced leeks
2 cloves garlic, crushed
1 tsp. fresh ginger, grated
3 Tbsp. soy sauce
4 Tbsp. peanut or olive oil
1 cup water chestnuts, drained and
   sliced
1 cup sliced mushrooms
2 cups snow peas cut into about
   ½-inch pieces
½ cup lightly toasted whole
   almonds

Place chicken, leeks, garlic, ginger, and soy sauce in a bowl and allow to marinate for 30 minutes.

Heat oil in a wok or heavy frying pan then stir-fry chicken with the marinade over medium/high heat for four minutes. Stir in water chestnuts, mushrooms, and snow peas and continue frying for another three minutes. Add sauce then stir-fry for another three minutes. Place on a serving platter then spread almonds over top

and serve hot with cooked rice or noodles.

Cabbage and egg salad

Serves 8 to 10

This dish, a favorite of the Syrian Damascenes, makes the consumption of cabbage combined with eggs a tasty and enjoyable event.

4 cups shredded cabbage
½ cup finely chopped green onions
2 cloves garlic, crushed
4 Tbsp. olive oil
3 Tbsp. vinegar
¾ tsp. salt
½ tsp. pepper
¼ tsp. cayenne pepper
4 hard-boiled eggs, chopped
12 pitted black olives, sliced in half

Place cabbage and green onions in a mixing bowl; set aside.

Combine garlic, olive oil, vinegar, salt, pepper, and cayenne, then pour over cabbage and green onion mixture. Mix thoroughly, then place on a serving platter. Spread eggs evenly over top, then decorate with olives and serve.

Tuna omelet — *Atun tortilla*

Serves about 4

The *ajjah* (omelet), which is today prepared in the Arab East, is the twin of the Spanish tortilla (this is more like a frittata than either an American omelet or tortilla). While the Arab omelet is enjoyed at breakfast and/or at any meal, the Spanish tortilla is reserved for lunch or dinner because, in the words of my grandson's wife, our Andalusian princess, "Spaniards almost never eat eggs for breakfast."

This version is from Andalusia and is on the daily menu of many Andalusians.

4 Tbsp. olive oil plus a few drops
   extra
1 small onion, finely chopped
1 can (6.5 oz) tuna, drained and
   flaked
4 large eggs
½ tsp. salt
¼ tsp. pepper

Heat oil in a frying pan, then sauté onion over medium heat for 10 minutes. Add tuna, then sauté for a further two minutes.

In the meantime, beat eggs with salt and pepper, then stir into onion and tuna. Cook over low heat for a few minutes until bottom of omelet begins to brown, checking often with a spatula, then cover frying pan with a plate and tip over.

Add a little oil in the frying pan, then carefully return omelet to frying pan, uncooked side down. Brown for about a minute, then serve hot.

Vermicelli and eggs

Serves about 6

This dish is a unique addition to a gourmet breakfast.

> 2 cups vermicelli, broken into ½- to 1-inch pieces
> 4 Tbsp. butter
> 1 medium onion, finely chopped
> 4 Tbsp. coarsely chopped cashews
> 2 Tbsp. raisins
> 4 Tbsp. coconut flakes
> 2 Tbsp. sugar
> 4 eggs
> 1 tsp. ground cardamom
> ⅛ tsp. saffron powder

Cook vermicelli according to instructions on package, then drain and set aside.

In a frying pan, melt butter then sauté onion over medium heat for eight minutes or until lightly browned. Add cashews and raisins and stir-fry for two more minutes. Add remaining ingredients, except vermicelli, and stir-fry for another two minutes. Add vermicelli, stir-fry for one minute, then serve.

Shakshuka — Fried vegetables and eggs

Serves about 8

Made in several different ways, this North African-style dish is tasty and filling.

> 4 Tbsp. olive oil
> 1 large green pepper, seeds removed and finely chopped
> 2 medium onions, finely chopped
> 6 medium tomatoes, chopped
> 1 small hot pepper, seeds removed and finely chopped
> 4 cloves garlic, crushed
> 1½ tsp. salt
> ½ tsp. pepper
> ½ tsp. ground caraway seeds
> ½ tsp. cumin
> 6 eggs

Heat oil in a frying pan, then add remaining ingredients, except the eggs. Cover, then cook over medium/low heat for 15 minutes, stirring occasionally. Break eggs over the top, then cover again and cook over low heat for a five minutes. Serve while still hot.

Baked eggs

Serves about 4

Simple to prepare, this dish of Chinese origin is great for any meal.

> 6 eggs, beaten
> 1 cup chopped cooked shrimp
> 2 Tbsp. oyster sauce
> 2 Tbsp. water
> 2 Tbsp. sesame oil
> ¼ tsp. salt
> ¼ tsp. pepper
> 1 Tbsp. lemon juice

Thoroughly combine all ingredients then place in a greased casserole dish and bake uncovered in a 350° F preheated oven for 18 minutes. Serve hot. Δ

Baked eggs

Canning chicken — here's how I do it

By Linda Gabris

When I was kid, in the days before hydro-electricity brought the convenience of deep-freezers to rural country kitchens like ours, Mom and Grandma canned food out of necessity.

One of Mom's most prized creations was her home canned chicken. Canning chicken is a dependable, thrifty way for those who raise chickens to keep up with their surplus meat, but even those who don't grow their own chickens can still cash in on great buys at the butcher shop, supermarket, or from local farmers when chickens are being offered at prices too good to pass up.

It's also a handy way to clean up a stash of birds from the freezer that are about to expire their prime shelf life of one year. Canning them extends their shelf life. The good news is you don't have to stop at chickens — other poultry like turkey, geese, ducks, and grouse (rabbits, too) can be canned the same way.

Once you have a stash of canned chicken on the pantry shelf there are hundreds of delicious ways to put it to tasty use. One of my family's favorites is Mom's old recipe for canned chicken and dumplings. It makes a hot and hearty supper to take the chill out of winter dining and it's ready as fast as the table can be set. Try it and see if you don't agree that canned chicken can't be beat.

The pressure canner

I find that canning chicken today is much easier than it was in Mom's time because I have a pressure canner which ensures the safe canning of low-acid foods such as meats, fish, and vegetables.

In the olden days, Mom and Grandma did their canning over a crackling woodstove using what is known as a "boiling water bath" canner which involved a lot of guesswork on the canner's part. Jars of food were submerged in boiling water until it was hoped that a high enough temperature was reached inside the jar to kill bacteria or, in other words, to sterilize the food.

A boiling water bath canner is simply a large kettle. I still have Mom's big blue speckled enamel-covered pot that I use nowadays for sterilizing my canning jars, but it is not acceptable for canning low-acid foods. The boiling water bath canner can only be safely used for canning high-acid foods like jams, syrups, jellies, and other sweet things.

I must admit, even though we never got ill eating Mom's and Grandma's home-canned wares, many folks in earlier days were stricken with food poisoning from eating improperly canned foods, especially meats, fish, and vegetables. Thus, home canners today are strongly advised to only can low-acid foods using a pressure canner according to the manufacturer's directions to safeguard against botulism. A pressure canner is regulated and gauged to ensure the correct temperature for sterilizing food is reached.

Pressure canners come in various sizes to best suit your needs. If using a second-hand or older model, be sure it is in good working order. Gauges can be tested by the manufacturer or your county extension agent.

If using whole chickens, cut up the birds into uniform, serving-sized pieces.

You must use approved canning (Mason or Ball) jars that are free of nicks and have been fitted with new two-piece, self-sealing lids. Outer bands can be reused so long as they are not dented or rusty, but inner lids must never be reused. For safety's sake, steer clear of Grandma's old-style jars with glass or zinc-lined lids, rubber bands, and galvanized screw tops. They just don't cut the mustard when it comes to creating a proper seal. Lastly, do not attempt to use recycled jars that store-bought food comes in. They might not be strong enough to withstand the pressure and their lids do not have sealing compound, as real canning lids do, to ensure a proper seal.

Getting started

First, round up your canning gear: pressure canner, jars, lids, timer, jar lifter, and, of course, most importantly, the birds you wish to can. If fresh chicken is being used, ensure that they are cleaned well and all pin feathers removed. If processing previously frozen birds, thaw them overnight in the refrigerator so they will be ready to work with in the morning. I like to keep the kitchen as cool as possible while handling the birds so they land in the jar in prime shape.

Methods of packing jars

Now keep in mind there are two basic methods for canning poultry — they are known as "raw pack" and "hot pack." My favorite method for canning chicken is using the raw pack method which means that the chicken parts are packed "raw" into the prepared jars. This method not only cuts down on the work of canning chicken but also produces a delicious, tender meat without precooking it first.

One thing to keep in mind is that poultry, especially chicken, is very delicate. If not canned according to exact given timing in your pressure manual, the meat can easily fall apart in the jar. Overprocessing causes the meat to turn stringy. Under processing is not acceptable as the meat must be cooked for safe storage inside the jar. This is why one should never adjust the directions given in their manual.

Raw pack is the method I learned from Mom and the one I enjoy using most. If you are only processing a small number of birds, say about three or four whole chickens in one canning session, it works great as this amount of birds makes precisely enough to fill my canner, which accommodates up to six 1-quart sealers.

I like to tuck a sprig of fresh herb, rosemary this time, into each jar.

If you have a pressure canner with a larger capacity, you can process as many jars as your canner will hold in one session. Remember, if you have to run two or more batches through your pressure canner, keep the unprocessed jars of birds in the fridge until it is their turn for the canner. Do not leave them sitting at room temperature on the counter.

I find that one quart of canned raw-packed chicken (each jar containing one half of a breast cut into two pieces, one leg, one thigh, and one wing) makes enough meat to feed a family of four. If you need to add a couple extra pieces to each jar, you will have room in the jar to pack in another leg or thigh, or maybe two. Keep in mind the more chicken you pack into the jar, the less broth you will end up with and the less jars you will have of finished product. But you will also be able to process more birds in one batch. So take all things into consideration — how many pieces of chicken in each jar best suits your needs, how much broth you wish to have in each jar, and how many chickens you want to process to a batch.

Hot pack is the other common method of packing food into the jars. The hot pack method calls for the chicken to be precooked first. Whole or cut up chicken parts are boiled in water until tender, then cooled and deboned. Next the hot meat is packed into jars, covered with the broth in which it was cooked, then processed in the pressure canner according to directions given in the manual for hot packed poultry.

This method allows you to process two or three times as much chicken to

I can my chicken in homemade chicken broth which I make the day before.

a batch. You might find that smaller jars are more suitable for this method. Deciding on what size of jar to use revolves around how much meat you estimate your family needs per meal. Larger jars are good for company fare if you find a quart is too large for one family meal. Again, I much prefer the raw pack method mentioned above for chicken but in order to find out for yourself which method works best for you, you may wish to try them both and see.

Raw pack — here's how

So here's how I can chicken using the raw pack method. I processed three plump whole birds in this session which made six quarts of canned chicken meat in broth, excluding the necks, backs, and wing tips which I saved for making broth. You can add these pieces to the jar if you wish, but I find they are better suited for the soup pot.

On the day before canning my chickens, I always make a rich chicken stock out of about five pounds of chicken soup parts (giblets, necks, wing tips, and backs) which I buy at my butcher shop at very reasonable prices). This gives me ample broth to

have ready the next day to cover the meat in my jars for processing and yields enough leftover chicken stock for making a batch of canned chicken soup (which I usually make the day after canning chicken). This way I can also simmer the soup parts saved from my whole birds canned the day before to add to the stock pot, so nothing gets wasted.

Note: If you do not wish to cover your chicken meat with homemade chicken stock as I do, you can use store-bought stock that comes in a carton, or use bouillon powder or cubes, or even water as some home canners do. Lastly, you do not have to add any liquid at all if you do not want to, in which case you let the chicken form its own juice during processing. Of course, you might want to add salt to each jar for flavor.

The only way to decide which method you like best is to sample and see. I find that homemade stock is well worth the time and effort to make as it can be seasoned to suit your own taste. If using stock, have it ready to heat to boiling when needed. If using water, have the tea kettle ready to boil.

Begin by washing jars, then put clean jars in a large kettle of boiling water and boil five minutes to sterilize. They do not need to be sterilized as the jars and contents get sterilized during the pressure canning process, but I do it as an extra safety measure. I find it also removes any trace of other foods or odors that may be present in pre-used jars. Hold hot until ready to fill. Prepare lids as directed by manufacturer. The brand I use calls for soaking the lids in hot water to soften the sealing compound.

If using whole chickens, cut up the birds into uniform, serving-sized pieces. I use what I call the "standard" cut, removing legs, then thighs, wings, going down the back to separate back from breast, and then cutting the back into two pieces (to be put into the stock-making pile), and lastly cutting the breast in half and then into quarters. You can remove the skin if you wish but I find the chicken is much more flavorful with the skin left on. Suit yourself.

Pack cut-up raw chicken pieces into hot jars, leaving 1-inch headspace.

I like to tuck a sprig of fresh herb (this time I've used rosemary) into each jar for extra flavor and a dab of color.

Now pour boiling stock over chicken to within the required headspace. Take a spatula and push it around the chicken to remove air pockets, then add more stock as needed to ensure chicken is submerged in liquid (unless letting the chicken form its own juice, in which case no stock or water is added to the jar). I like to add a pinch of dried hot chile flakes to some of the jars for a bit of kick.

Dip a clean cloth into vinegar and wipe the rims of the filled jars to remove traces of grease which could cause an improper seal.

Put on prepared lids and lightly screw on the metal bands.

Place the filled jars in the pressure canner and process according to your own pressure canner's manual. Since pressure canners come in different sizes, makes, and models — some with a dial gauge, others with a weighted gauge — directions can vary. It is always recommended to follow your own manufacturer's directions carefully, taking the jar size you have chosen and the altitude at which you live into account. The processing times for your chicken will also vary depending on whether the meat is processed with bone-in or boneless.

After processing time is up, let pressure canner depressurize of its own accord before removing lid.

Remove jars from canner and set them on the counter to cool without disturbing. When cool, inspect each jar lid carefully to ensure it has a proper seal. Press the middle of the lid lightly with the finger. If the lid springs when touched, it is not properly sealed and the jar must be refrigerated and used as soon as possible, frozen for safekeeping, or reprocessed. The lid on a properly sealed jar should be concave — curved down slightly in the center. If the center of the lid is either flat or bulging, it should be treated as an improperly sealed jar and handled accordingly.

Safety check before eating any home canned foods

Always inspect every jar off the pantry shelf carefully before using. First, feel the jar for any signs of grease or stickiness which could indicate a leak. Look carefully for rust or discoloration around the edges of the lid. Check for bulging lid. Upon opening the jar, watch for any signs of working, bubbling, spurting, or off-odor or color. Do not eat anything that looks suspicious. Always follow the number one rule — *when in doubt, throw it out!* And, remember, if you think it is spoiled be sure to discard the contents in a safe manner where your pets or other animals will not have access to it.

Recipes

Chicken (or turkey) soup

There is no recipe, really, for homemade chicken soup. Mom's was always different from Grandma's. Mine is always different from Mom's. The bottom line is, homemade chicken soup is always good and having a few jars on the pantry shelf is super handy for any time a craving strikes.

I make mine by putting about two to three quarts of homemade chicken broth into a stock pot. As mentioned above, I make my broth out of economical soup parts. Turkey carcasses (left over from a holiday feast) also yield a huge pot of soup that can be canned for future use. You can even save bits of leftover cooked chicken and turkey and freeze it until it is time to make soup for canning and then add it to the pot.

Bring strained, skimmed broth to a boil. Add the meat which you have salvaged off the bones and any which you've saved in the freezer for the purpose. If you like meatier soup, add a few thighs when making the stock, then pick meat off the bones and chop before using. If making turkey soup from the carcass, you will find that there are lots of pickings on the bones

for the soup pot. It may be a little stringier than chicken meat but it is good nonetheless.

To the broth, add vegetables of choice (celery, carrots, cabbage, turnip, parsnips, onions) in amounts to suit taste. I love chunky vegetables in my soup so I cut them rather big. I find that chunkier pieces stand up better in the canner. I also like a good dose of barley, which does not go overly soft in home canned soups as do noodles. Some home canners add noodles, but I suggest you hold out on the noodles until the soup is opened and heated at which time the noodles can be added to the kettle. This will yield a nice firm noodle instead of one that has almost disintegrated during the canning process. Also keep in mind that starchy, flour-based ingredients do not can well and can cause cloudiness in the jar. I like to add some fresh minced or dried herbs (oregano, parsley, rosemary, and basil) to taste.

Simmer the soup for 15 minutes. Remove from heat and season with salt and pepper.

Ladle hot soup into prepared jars. I like to divide the vegetables up first

Having canned chicken and chicken soup in the pantry is handy and saves time.

Linda's canned chicken pasta supper

into the jars so each one gets an even amount, then cover with the broth.

Wipe the rims with a cloth dipped in vinegar. Put on lids and outer bands.

Set jars in pressure canner and can according to your pressure canning manual instructions given for chicken soup, making adjustments for altitude and jar size used.

Remove the jars from the depressurized canner and cool as above, checking for proper seals before storing.

Mom's canned chicken with herbed dumplings

Here's Mom's old recipe — as good today as it was years ago! It works great with canned chicken because of the quick cooking time. I like to choose recipes for canned chicken that require as little cooking time as possible.

First, make the dumpling dough:

1¼ cups flour
2 tsp. baking powder
pinch of salt and dried mixed herbs
    to taste (parsley, basil, oregano)
2 Tbsp. margarine or butter
½ cup milk (more or less)

Mix dry ingredients in bowl. Cut in margarine with fork until crumbly.

Stir in enough milk to make a soft dough.

Next, the chicken:

1 quart canned chicken with broth
¾ cup boiling water

Empty chicken from jar into saucepan. Pour one cup of boiling water into the jar to rinse out the jar and add to the chicken in the pan. Heat to boiling, drop dumpling dough by spoonfuls onto the hot chicken. Reduce heat, simmer 12 minutes without lifting the lid to peek. When time is up, test dumplings with a fork. They should be light and fluffy. If not, cross your fingers, cover the pot, and simmer a few minutes longer.

Linda's canned chicken pasta supper

My family loves this and it's so easy!

1 quart canned chicken with broth
1 cup mushrooms, thinly sliced
red peppers, finely chopped
onion, diced
garlic cloves, minced
flour and water mixture
¼ cup heavy cream
¼ cup grated Parmesan cheese
pasta, any type

Take one quart jar of canned chicken and empty it into a bowl. Gently pick out the portions of meat with a slotted spoon and place them in single layer in a buttered baking dish, reserving the gel (or broth if your chicken stock did not jell in the jar). Sprinkle the mushrooms over the top of the chicken. Scatter with red peppers, onion, and garlic. Put the reserved liquid into a saucepan and heat. Thicken with a little flour and water mixture. Remove from stove and stir in ¼ cup heavy cream and ¼ cup grated Parmesan cheese and pour over chicken. Bake uncovered in 350° F oven until bubbly, 12 to 15 minutes. In the meantime, cook pasta until tender to the tooth. Sometimes I choose spaghetti or linguine noodles, other times I'll serve it over bows or penne. Serve the chicken and sauce over the pasta with extra Parmesan on the side. Δ

Broody biddies make sense on the homestead

By James Kash

Broodiness is an avian behavior that is frowned upon in the world of agriculture. All industrial agriculturalists cull broody birds because the behavior inhibits production. But to frugal homesteaders, broodiness just makes sense. When one of the girls goes broody, this is a time to gain the many benefits, whether it's new hens for little cost or roosters for slaughter. Broody biddies come in many forms from the rather odd Muscovy duck to the small, tight-built game hen. Homestead broodies are practical, time-saving workhorses. They not only alleviate dealing with hatcheries, but they also eliminate the worry and work that comes with incubators and brooders.

Broody poultry

Turkeys and chickens are classified as "dry" poultry. They have similar nesting patterns and behav- iors. Chickens are usually the only birds to become broody in the coop on nothing but their behinds. Turkeys and chickens are the only birds that can be moved from an existing nest; they are not as protective of their nests as waterfowl. In general, it takes 21-22 days to hatch chicken eggs and 28-29 days to hatch turkey eggs. Since chickens are more popular in the industrial world, the trait has been bred out of some breeds. Chickens most noted for broody behavior are Cochins, Silkies, and game-type chickens. However, the broodier types of chickens more suitable for homestead life tend to be Buff Orpingtons, Delawares, Australorps, and New Hampshire Reds. Heritage turkey varieties usually brood no matter what; exceptions would be the broad-breasted varieties bred for commercial production which cannot successfully mate on their own. Turkeys generally only lay eggs from mid-March to late June, depending on location and weather conditions.

Broody waterfowl

Ducks and geese are classified as waterfowl because of their love and need for water. Waterfowl always locate a nesting place, lay all of their eggs, and begin pulling their down feathers for insulation toward the end of the egg-laying period. These birds cannot be moved successfully once nesting has begun. My suggestion is

J&D

that if you want them in a specific spot to incubate and brood, move them into their new home once the first egg has been laid, then lock them in there to do the job. It takes Mallard-derived breeds 28 days to hatch eggs, whereas the Muscovy takes up to 35 days to hatch eggs. I have attempted to incubate my duck eggs artificially, but allowing mama to take care of it has been more successful for me. Most Mallard-derived breeds lay year around like chickens and can set throughout the year. Muscovies, however, lay for a clutch (15 to 18 eggs) and will brood until completion. They can do this around three times a year. Muscovies are the best broody ducks, but the domestic Mallard, Ancona, and Welsh Harlequin can be good broodies as well.

It generally takes 30-33 days for mother goose to hatch her eggs. All goose breeds will generally become broody once every spring. Be careful, for they can get quite nasty if not left alone, especially the males.

Why let them set?

There are several reasons to let the girls brood eggs; one is that it is cheaper. The mother hen, duck, or goose alleviates the need to buy hatchlings or fertile eggs and incubating equipment from a hatchery. This saves you a lot of money. Broody birds save you time, too. You won't have to fool with the incubator, which means you won't have to worry about the egg turner tearing up in the middle of the incubation cycle or any other difficulty that can occur. Not to mention the care the chicks need in the brooder, which includes caring for pasty butt and hassling with the brooder lights.

Broodies are also a part of the homestead circle. They provide replacement females for your flock. Some people don't let their birds set because it interferes with egg production. My broodies create the opposite

problem, they increase production. Sure that hen is out of production for around 10 weeks, and on average you may lose around 45 to 50 eggs from that hen in this time frame. But she will start to lay eggs again. Not only will she lay, but her daughters will as well, close to six months after hatching. Say that the mother hen hatches five pullets, and if these girls lay around 4 to 5 eggs apiece each week, in the same time it took to grow out the chicks, they potentially could lay around 220 to 250 eggs, collectively. Also all the extra males can be converted into nutritious meat for table use; I consider these freebies. Mother hens, regardless of species, also teach their offspring to forage much earlier and waterfowl teach swimming earlier as well.

So, you have a broody?

The telltale signs of a broody chicken usually include squawking, irritability, and being very protective of her nest. These are the early signs. The hard-core broody chickens pull some feathers from their breast area so that they can be closer to the eggs. They assume the football pose to try and attack other birds around the feeder. My Muscovy ducks usually start peeping very quickly when I get near them, whether they are on the nest or even getting feed or water, as well as displaying the signs chickens normally show. The ducks will pull lots of fluffy down near the end of the laying cycle. Geese will also pull out down feathers, and the gander and the goose both get very protective of the nest and its area. It is recommended they be allowed to nest privately because they can get mean with children, pets, and other livestock.

Now that you have figured out you have a broody biddie, the first thing to do is make sure she is committed and then leave her be for a couple days, wherever she may start setting. Moving her too early can cause her to abandon the project altogether. Next,

you need to determine where you should put her. It is a mess waiting to happen if she wants to set where there are two dozen other hens laying in her nest. The roosters can aggravate them, as well. The same thing will happen with the ducks; the drake will sometimes irritate the duck until she abandons the nest.

Moving a broody hen

Here's how I move a broody chicken. After dusk has settled, I take a cat carrier or something of the sort to put her in, making sure the box has enough bedding (preferably hay). I also toss out the eggs under her (if she has any) because generally new eggs have been laid every day since she started and if they weren't collected it can cause the hatches to be scrambled up. I take her to the new residence in the taxi, and give her 8 to 12 fertilized eggs that were collected that day. This is a good range to have — too many and she can't cover them. After I put in the eggs, I also make sure her cage is latched. Twenty-four hours after the eggs are put in, she probably has settled and has begun to incubate the eggs. I open the door of the cage and give her access to food and water. I also write down the first 24-hour period that has been completed as day one, and then figure it down to 21 days to get an estimate on the hatch date. I usually bring broodies to our spare coop, but there are other options, such as a broody box in the main coop, a rabbit hutch, or any place that protects her from predators and the elements.

I like to do just the opposite for my duck. You may think it's crazy but it gave me a near perfect hatch. She went broody in the main coop, and since you can't move waterfowl, I moved everyone else to the spare coop. On that hatch I got 16 ducklings from 17 eggs. I did leave her in there with the others once just to see how the hatch would go, and the eggs rotted in the shell and the coop started to smell. It wasn't pleasant.

I keep my broody mamas on the same feed they're used to until a few days before the hatch date, then I switch them to a non-medicated chick starter.

Hatching time

When it is hatch time, do not interfere. You will be tempted, but restrain yourself. It usually hinders the process rather than helping it. I must say it is quite an experience to peer in at the mama hen and see her with her new babies — there is nothing like it! It's important to clean the nest out, so when mama hen leaves the nest with her brood you can sneak in and retrieve the shell scraps and any eggs that did not hatch. I usually let mama and the chicks stay in privacy for about a week. Some people do not like the rest of the flock to mingle with the babies until they are around two months old or so, but I like to get them out young. This helps the older birds get used to them while the chicks still have mom to protect them.

Mother hens are very good about getting the chicks up the ramp and into the house every night. As each week goes by and you watch them grow, they begin to stray farther from mom. Then, after about eight or so weeks, she is done raising her brood and will return to laying eggs.

Common concerns

Here are some common worries poultry owners have. Usually during incubation you notice that mother hen, duck, or goose is not eating or drinking very much, if at all. This is normal — some get up every day to eat and some wait almost a week. It differs from bird to bird and species to species. Weather also has a lot to do with it. If it's hot they usually get up more often for the eggs to breathe.

Another worry is what to do when they go broody in the winter. This doesn't bother me too much, however I am in Kentucky and winters are not as cold and bitter as Minnesota. When I had a hen go broody in the winter, I put her in the corner of my uninsulated coop with plenty of bedding beneath her and between her box and the floor. Plus I stacked a few bales of straw around her for added insulation. It worked wonderfully.

Another thing to know is that the mother bird will not defecate much; usually it comes out in large, smelly globs when she gets up to eat. This is very normal for broody birds.

Because of her limited feeding and the energy it takes to brood the eggs she will lose some size to her. This is normal, but you'll need to watch her. I have heard of it killing a hen if her eggs do not hatch and she keeps setting for a few months. This has never happened to me.

Broody birds are homestead workhorses. They are cost effective by providing new females for the flock as well as excess males for table use. They make incubating easier on you, because they do the work and you reap the benefits. The brooding behavior can vary from breed to breed and species to species, but with a little knowledge you can make the broody bird a working part of your homestead. Δ

Ayoob on Firearms

BHM hosts Appleseed marksmanship event

Long a supporter of the Appleseed concept, *Backwoods Home Magazine* hosted one in Gold Beach, Oregon, in second quarter 2012. Naturally, a good time was had by all. I had the good fortune to be in attendance. Let me tell you how it went, 'cause it's happening again next year, and ya wanna know what to expect if you come.

Prelude

I came to the event by rental car via Portland, Oregon, and it was a spectacular drive. You can see why the Gold Beach area is such a draw for those who swelter in summer heat in Portland, as they did when we went through. The run along the Pacific will find you pulling over frequently to take pictures.

At the foot of the steep cliffs, great black islands of rock rise like ragged

Yes, there was some pageantry involved.

monoliths from the Pacific. If you can, budget time to do the tourist thing in Gold Beach. The harbor area

reminded me of the Boston wharves of my youth. It was a trip down memory lane to watch boats of all sizes scooting out of the fog banks to shore as bad weather threatened.

After all these years of writing for the magazine and submitting manuscripts from three thousand miles away on the opposite coast, it was a pleasure to tour the magazine's home office and meet all the staff. Previously, I had only gotten to know Dave Duffy and John Silveira face to face. The entire *Backwoods Home* team was friendly and welcoming, not only to us but to readers and Appleseed shooters who had also arrived early.

The place is the epitome of everything a family-run small business should be. Laughter in the workplace. People who genuinely enjoy what they're doing, and care about the people they're doing it for. Go to the website and click on the video of

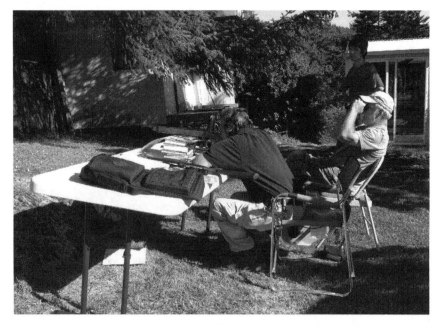

Be sighted in before you go. Here Mas and Dave Duffy do a pre-event sight-in with the Duffy family's Ruger .22s.

"Clara's Office Tour." That's pretty much the tenor of the place.

While you're there visit the Rogue Outdoor Store. It's a gun shop with old and new alike, nestled within a sporting goods and fishing/camping supply operation that makes you feel as if you've gone back to what such places must have been like in the 1940s. The owner and his well-trained crew make you welcome, and they know their stuff. A little wandering will find you at Gold Beach Books, one of the best bookstores this side of the famous Powell's in Portland. (Bring a bib, so you don't drool on all the rare collectors' editions.) Walk the waterfront amidst the gulls and the pelicans. Visit Fely's Cafe on the Brookings waterfront, a tiny, family-run diner attached to the laundromat there, where they cook your burgers to order. It takes you on a little trip back in time. Speaking of which, you want to visit the '50s diner, Happy Days Malt Shop, with the great old car collection on premises. ("What do you mean, antiques? I used to *drive* one of those...and one of *those*, dammit!") And for some gourmet drop-dead delicious seafood,

Philip Wylie, aided by Appleseed staffer using rifle stock as prop, shows the attendees the recommended prone position.

you can visit Spinner's Seafood, Steak & Chop House, run by Dave Duffy's golf-playing pal, Dewey Powers. The folks at *Backwoods Home* will be happy to show you where they all are.

The watchful instructor is there to ensure safety, and also fine-tune shooters' techniques.

Behind the scenes

Preparation had begun long before the first *Backwoods Home* Appleseed. Ted Fitzgerald had graciously donated the use of his range in Brookings, a short distance from Gold Beach. It was literally up in the clouds with a breathtaking view when there was time to take a break from one's sight picture. Only those of us who've set up shooting matches know how much work goes into them. The Duffy family now knows and appreciates that.

The whimsically self-named Revolutionary War Veterans' Association (RWVA), the group which sponsors Appleseed, had rounded up roughly a dozen volunteers to make the event run smoothly and productively. They were led by Carol Wylie, the "shoot boss," and her husband Philip, stalwart Appleseeders and gun owners' civil rights activists, who had flown all the way from their home in Illinois.

There was pasture grass to be mowed and target lines to be set up in front of the towering natural berm, or

With a stiff neck, Dave is allowed to shoot from sitting while Annie Tuttle, left, and the rest are firing from the required prone.

bullet backstop. There were tables to be set up and Porta-Potties to be placed. There were distances to be measured and parking to be arranged. It all went according to plan, with much of the *BHM* crew volunteering to do the work. For the Wylies and the Appleseed volunteers, this wasn't their first rodeo.

The range is pastureland when folks aren't shooting there. Cow pies were cleared off the firing line itself, but not entirely from the space between there and the target line, and there was the small matter of going forward to retrieve targets for scoring and replacement. No one, not even the city folks, were heard to complain without laughing about their own complaint. I figure it was part of the charm of the place. The host entity was, after all, *Backwoods Home Magazine*. I don't think anyone was expecting to go prone on Astroturf...

On the firing line. There were plenty of safety officers to keep an eye on everyone despite the rolling pastureland.

The ride to the range was sometimes dizzying. There were narrow mountain roads, a bit washed out here and there by a recent storm, with no guard rails or road shoulders. The weather was as close to perfect as could be imagined. The closest we came to rain in two days was more like mist, and it was never cold enough to need more than a sweater. Most of the time, there was a gentle breeze to blow the gunsmoke away.

It was a perfect venue for a big bunch of folks who love guns, and love their country even more, to get together and shoot.

The shoot

Appleseed is set up so attendees can shoot either day, or both; most people preferred both days. There were a few who could only make Saturday, and a very few who could only make Sunday, but some 67 shooters spent the entire weekend on the range.

There were male and female and there were old and young. The oldest shooter I personally met was 77, and there were several kids whose ages could be expressed in a single digit. There were multiple people with physical handicaps. Fortunately, Appleseed understands how that goes and makes provisions. The event can be shot from a wheelchair. If it's possible for you to get into (and out of) belly-down prone, but a neck injury keeps you from raising your head enough to aim from there, you can substitute the sitting position instead. Some shooters have been allowed to use bipods and shooting rests due to physical challenges.

The guns of Appleseed

Though the core of the apple's seed, in this case, is the military-style rifle — which is what the original Patriots brought to the battlefield, after all — Appleseed allows the .22 rimfire. This is a good thing in this time of inflation, tight money, and skyrocketing ammo costs. At other Appleseeds I've attended, there have been a sprinkling of 5.56mm rifles, and thirty-calibers. At the *Backwoods Home* Appleseed, I saw but one centerfire rifle: an HK91 or clone thereof, in 7.62mm NATO. Its user did pretty darn good with it, too.

The Appleseed uses a course of fire they call AQT, which stands for Army Qualification Test. All shooting is timed. The time constraints are not flat-out rapid combat fire in pace, but the operative term in "time constraints" is still *constraints*. All the shooters on the line but one at this particular event shot semiautomatic rifles. Their fingers never needed to leave the triggers once the shooting started, except to reload of course, or when their string of fire was done.

The exception was one young lad who caught my attention by shooting a mid-Twentieth century Mossberg bolt action .22 target rifle. The kid ran that bolt deftly, and he shot very well. Appleseed legend has it that the single highest score ever recorded on the AQT was posted by a septuagenarian who had been shooting NRA small-bore rifle matches since he was a kid. They say he accomplished the feat with an iron-sighted bolt action .22 rifle. I'm guessing the great old Winchester Model 52 target rifle, but of course, that's only a guess…

As is typical of Appleseed matches, the single most popular rifle on the line was the Ruger 10/22. There is a reason Ruger has sold millions of these rifles…yes, "millions" in the plural. They work, and they're accurate enough to get the job done. The 10/22 is the basic component of Appleseed's LTR (Liberty Training Rifle), when equipped with a precision-adjustable aperture sight system and marksman's loop sling. However, most of the shooters who make their way to the coveted Rifleman's Patch (more on that momentarily) do so with telescopic sights on their 10/22s.

Marlin autoloaders were a strong second in popularity. You want the

Annie Tuttle with one of her first runs on Appleseed's signature Redcoat targets.

ones with quick-change box magazines like those of the 10/22, which are much faster for timed reloads than tubular magazines. There was also the occasional Remington on the line, and even an old post-WWII Savage/Stevens with tube magazine.

I saw several AR15 clones in .22 Long Rifle. The single most popular was the Smith & Wesson M&P (Military & Police). I furnished one of these to my sweetie's grandson to use at the last Appleseed I attended before this one, when we were getting him a head start on USMC basic training. (The kid did great in both venues, by the way.) A Smith & Wesson M&P 15/.22 was also the choice of the top scoring rifle shooter at the *Backwoods Home* Appleseed, who posted an awesome 244 out of 250 possible points on the AQT. He

had bought the rifle a week or so before the shoot.

Setting your sights on Appleseed

A huge percentage of our nation's warfighters now have optical sights on their M4s and M16s, and the same is true of the patrol rifles now resting in the police cars that protect our communities on the home front. It should be no surprise that optical sights ruled at the *Backwoods Home* Appleseed, too.

The tie-breaking "center-V ring" on the targets 25 paces away, centered in silhouettes scaled to represent enemy soldiers at distances up to hundreds of yards away, are small marks. The "V" in the "big one" that you'll shoot from offhand (standing) is about the size of a bottlecap. The smallest, rep-

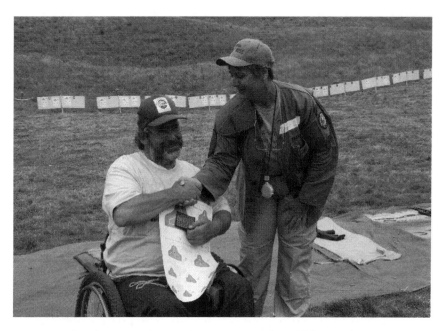

Carol congratulates a shooter on winning a Rifleman patch.

licating the longest range, is the diameter of a #2 lead pencil. You need precise aim to do your best. The magnification of a telescopic sight helps to achieve that precise aim.

In precision marksmanship — which is definitely what Appleseed is about — the magnification of a powerful scope is a huge help. If you are grouping a bit off-center, you can see it through the high-magnification telescopic sight; many people *can't* see .22 caliber bullet holes that far away with the naked eye. You'll only see it when you go forward to retrieve the target and find that your hits are "off the mark" … and that's way too late to be doing anything about it.

There is a reason so many hunters use scopes. There is a reason why, in the National Patrol Rifle Championships, so many of the winning cops have sights that magnify what they are aiming at. There is a reason the telescopic sight is the signature feature of a sniper rifle, and of course, these are all the same reasons why I would respectfully recommend that you "scope" your rifle if you want to do your best at Appleseed. The member of the Duffy family who

outshot all of his many relatives at this match knows what I'm talking about: Robby Duffy shot his high-of-the-family score and won his Rifleman's Patch shooting a .22 that had a telescopic sight on top of it.

A time to shoot, a time to talk

History lectures are a signature feature of an Appleseed event, which are scattered through the two days. The purpose is to remind the attendees of the patriotism which created this

country, and which led to the Right to Keep and Bear Arms being placed second among the freedoms guaranteed in the Bill of Rights.

What has most impressed me in the Appleseeds I've attended is how this is handled. The staff instructors lecture on the lessons learned in the American Revolution, and do so from the perspective of the individual Americans who fought in that conflict. Not just the political macrocosm, and not even just from the perspective of those who were the designated combatants under the aegis of the Continental Army. Some of the female lecturers will put on a bonnet correct to a woman of the time, when they act out the role of the Colonial housewife who captured several Redcoats at gunpoint. I watched an Appleseed veteran don the tri-cornered hat of a militiaman and act out the part of a private citizen called to battle against professional soldiers, and who — alongside his brothers — prevailed against armed oppressors from a foreign shore. At that moment, the pasture high in the Oregon hills seemed to become the hedges and fields where the Americans fought against the might of the most powerful army Europe could send forth — and won.

Another cornerstone of the Appleseed experience is reminding

The Clean Dozen: the volunteers from Appleseed who made it all work

those attending just how personal warfare is, reminding them that it's about the butcher's bill for freedom. The toll of personal heartbreak and the tax on personal courage that every international conflict entails. How individual liberty and individual sacrifice entwine for the greater good of a free society. These people get the point across better than most history teachers, because they're communicating it for the love of all it stands for.

Bottom line

The *Backwoods Home* Appleseed was, in the end, hugely successful. Some nine attendees earned the Expert-level ranking that won them the coveted Rifleman's Patch. Two of them did so from wheelchairs. Many more fought hard to do so, and whether or not they made it, it improved their marksmanship skills and kindled a fire in their bellies to win that Patch the *next* time.

The match ran smoothly. In the time of the Founders; women sewed the flags, carried ammunition, ministered to the wounded, and gathered information from behind enemy lines. In today's thankfully more enlightened times, women were "on the line" with the men, shooting. Carol Wylie, I thought, did an excellent job as "shoot boss," the exemplification of Scarlett O'Hara in *Gone With the Wind* — that is, "Steel under velvet." Well done, Carol!

The day after the match, when I drove wistfully away from Gold Beach, I was glad I had come. I had seen both of the *Backwoods Home* families in action: the staff that runs the place, and the family who created it. A bunch of the Duffys were on the line, two generations' worth, showing the same perseverance and diligence which made the magazine all that it is today.

It was a wonderful experience. It will be next time, too. I hope you can make it there! Δ

The Best of the First Two Years
Our first big anthology!
In these 12 issues you'll find:

* A little knowledge and sweat can build a home for under $10,000
* Tepee to cabin to dream house
* From the foundation up, house-building is forgiving
* A first time horse buyer's guide
* A greenhouse offers advantages for the organic gardener
* Canning meat
* Backwoods Home recipes
* In pursuit of independence
* Canning blueberries
* How we keep humming along on the homestead
* Pioneer women on the trail west
* Some tips on first aid readiness for remote areas
* Whip grafting—the key to producing fruit variety
* The basics of backyard beekeeping
* Co-planting in the vegetable garden
* How to make soap—from fat to finish
* The instant greenhouse
* The old time spring house
* Getting started in a firewood business
* For battling ants or growing earthworms, try coffee grounds
* Sawmills: a firm foundation to homesteading

Chicken can make you sick
How to prevent and treat food-borne illness

*By Joe Alton, M.D.
and Amy Alton, A.R.N.P.*

Although there might be some controversy as to which species of fowl was the first to be domesticated, there is no disagreement about which poultry meat is most consumed — it's chicken. In 2008, the average American adult ate 85 pounds of chicken over the course of the year.

Today, the chicken proverbially "crosses the road" of cultural boundaries with ease. Except in a few specific circumstances, all nations and religions allow it "to get to the other side" of their kitchens (but not much further).

There are few protein sources that can be produced in great quantities as efficiently as chicken. There are, however, significant medical issues that can occur before that broiler gets to the table. Mass production practices, inappropriate use of drugs, and contamination are some of the factors that contribute to the risk of infectious disease.

The popularity of chicken and other poultry products makes it highly likely to be a source of food-borne illness. Certain disease-causing organisms (called "pathogens") are not uncommon intestinal inhabitants of even apparently healthy chickens. *Salmonella* is one of the worst offenders when it comes to causing illness in poultry and humans alike. There are more than 2000 strains of *Salmonella*, ranging from benign to possibly life-threatening. Typhoid fever (*Salmonella typhi*) is an example.

A 2011 outbreak of *Salmonella Heidelberg* contamination in ground turkey caused one human death and

Even healthy-looking chickens can be home to disease-causing pathogens such as Salmonella.

100 hospitalizations, not to mention the disposal of 36 million pounds of meat. This resistant strain of bacteria probably developed as a result of the indiscriminate use of antibiotics that are given, often daily, to birds in mass-production facilities.

These antibiotics are not given to treat an illness; rather, it was found that poultry given antibiotics grew more quickly and got to market faster. For this reason, 80% of the antibiotics used in the United States are given to livestock, regardless of whether there is an illness to treat or not. Antibiotic resistance is becoming a major issue among both poultry and humans as a result.

Other common causes of food-borne diarrheal disease include:

• *Campylobacter jejuni* — Frequently caused by poor food preparation practices, it is one of the most common causes of diarrheal disease.

• *Clostridium perfringens* — High-temperature resistant spores become activated when food is kept warm for long periods of time, as might be seen in a hospital food service or school cafeteria.

• *Listeria monocytogenes* — Seen in poorly refrigerated poultry or poultry used well after its "sell by" date.

• *Staphylococcus aureus* — Not uncommon on human skin or respiratory passages. May easily contaminate food that requires mixing by hand.

• *Escherichia coli* (E. coli) — Intestinal bacteria commonly present in poultry. Many different strains range from normal inhabitant to virulent pathogen.

• *Vibrio cholerae* — Cholera is an epidemic disease caused by using contaminated water in food preparation.

Clean water

Water is commonly used in cleaning, preparing, and cooking chicken, and failure to ensure that water is clean or sterilized is a very easy way to allow infections to occur. Even the clearest mountain stream may be contaminated by bacteria or parasites.

Simply filtering water through gravel or sand will eliminate particulate matter, but may not eliminate pathogens. Good methods to sterilize water include:

• Boiling — Bringing water to a roiling boil will kill most pathogens.

• Chlorine — Bleach is a simple way to kill bacteria; 8-10 drops per gallon of water will be sufficient in most cases.

• Tincture of iodine — 2% iodine works well when 12 drops is added to a gallon of water.

• Ultraviolet radiation — Direct sunlight has enough UV radiation to kill most bacteria. Leave a mostly full bottle in the sun for 6-8 hours after shaking vigorously. This releases oxygen into the water, which helps the process along.

Food preparation surfaces

Properly cleaning food and food preparation surfaces (and allowing those surfaces to dry) is a key to preventing disease. Many fail to realize that their own hands are a food preparation surface. Washing hands thoroughly prior to preparing food is not just a good idea, it is the ounce of prevention that will prevent the need for a pound of cure.

Other food preparation surfaces, such as countertops, cutting boards, dishes, and utensils, should also be cleaned with hot water and soap before using them. Soap may not kill all germs, but it helps to dislodge them from surfaces. If available in good supply, use paper towels to clean surfaces. Cloth kitchen towels used and kept damp day after day are laden with bacteria. If electricity is available, place the damp towel in the microwave for three minutes on high. If not, place in boiling water.

Raw chicken is notorious for having its "juices" contaminate food. Always prepare meats separately from fruits and vegetables. Wash counter surfaces and allow them to dry before preparing a new food item; this will prevent cross-contamination of residual chicken juices to subsequent food items.

Safe ways to handle chicken

An important way to avoid getting sick from handling chicken and other poultry meats starts at the store (if that's where you're getting them). Packages of chicken should always feel cold to the touch, and like all meats, should be the last items chosen before you leave the market. Using plastic bags from the produce section, wrap the package of chicken in them. This will avoid any chicken juice from contaminating other products you buy.

Once home, don't dilly-dally. Get your chicken into the refrigerator at 40 degrees or colder or, alternatively, freeze it at 0 degrees Fahrenheit. Thaw frozen chicken in the refrigerator or in cold water, not at room temperature on the kitchen counter. This may be an overnight process for boneless breasts, or up to two days for a whole broiler. If you want to cook the chicken right away, use the microwave to thaw it. Even if thawed in the refrigerator, chicken should be cooked within 24 hours.

Some strange facts: The government doesn't require "use by" dates on poultry, but most producers put a date on anyway. Also, the term "fresh" on a chicken package means something quite specific: It hasn't ever been stored at lower than 26 degrees Fahrenheit. If it has spent any time whatsoever at 0 degrees Fahrenheit, it must be referred to as "frozen" or "previously frozen." If stored between 26 degrees and 0 degrees Fahrenheit, it is considered neither "fresh" nor "frozen."

If you're the type that prefers a very fresh (that is, alive) chicken for the pot, be certain to look for healthy, energetic birds with bright feathers. Birds that are weak, lethargic, slow to eat or drink, have discolored wattles, or have a "pasty" vent due to diarrhea are to be avoided. In many breeds, old birds can be differentiated from young birds: older chickens will have fading of the colors on the beak and comb.

Cooking the chicken

Many are surprised when I say that a very important piece of medical equipment is a meat thermometer. Yet, undercooked chicken or other

One of the greatest contamination risks is letting the chicken "juices" contaminate other food.

meats, even if previously frozen, are common causes of disease. In a remote setting without electricity, thorough cooking on both sides is sometimes problematic. Despite this, it's imperative to assure that meats reach an appropriate safe temperature and remain consistently at that temperature until cooked; this varies by the type of meat:

Beef — 145° F
Pork — 150° F
Lamb — 160° F
Poultry — 165° F
Ground Meats — 160° F
Sauces and Gravy — 165° F
Soups with Meat — 165° F
Fish — 145° F

Diarrheal disease from contaminated food

Illness caused by food contamination, especially as it relates to chicken, usually manifests as diarrhea. *Salmonella* (and various other infections) will also present as fever, vomiting, and abdominal pain within a day or two after a contaminated item is consumed, sometimes sooner. Symptoms last for four to seven days, even in self-limited disease, during which time a significant risk to health exists.

Water is the critical component in your body; 75% of the body's weight is composed of it. Fluids are lost naturally as a result of breathing, sweating, urinating, and having bowel movements. When the body's water content drops and is not replenished, it is referred to as "dehydration." Until the 20th century, most deaths in war resulted not from spears, arrows, bullets, or shrapnel, but from dehydration caused by diarrheal disease.

Although each dehydrated individual may present differently, you can expect symptoms with as little as 1% total water content loss. The sensation of thirst is triggered, which then informs the body to replace the fluids. If this does not occur, just 2% water loss will cause dry mouth, fatigue,

weakness, and muscle cramps. Work efficiency begins to suffer.

Further water loss causes an increase in body temperature, heart rate (above 100 beats per minute), and respirations (more than 20 per minute). The body makes an effort to conserve water; therefore the urine appears darker and less volume is produced. Fainting and headaches are not unusual at this stage.

Once dehydration has become severe (6% total water content loss), more serious symptoms such as loss of coordination, confusion, delirium, and even seizures may occur. The skin appears dry and withered and tends to stay elevated ("tenting") when lifted. At 10-20% body water loss, organ malfunction ensues and permanent disability or death may be the result.

The caregiver's obligation is to identify dehydration early, when simple oral rehydration will eliminate the problem. An excellent form of oral rehydration is the dilution of Gatorade with water in a 50% solution. Gatorade is essentially colored sweat and is superior to plain water due to the presence of "electrolytes," such as potassium.

Here is the World Health Organization's recipe for preparing oral rehydration fluid:

1 Tbsp. salt (sodium chloride)
6-8 Tbsp. sugar (dextrose)
½ Tbsp. salt substitute (potassium chloride)
pinch of baking soda (sodium bicarbonate)

Dilute in one liter of water (for children, make a weaker solution by diluting in two liters of water).

Once the patient is able to tolerate fluids by mouth, you can slowly advance the diet and give over-the-counter anti-diarrheals, such as Loperamide, by mouth. Certain foods are easily tolerated and decrease the loss of fluids by decreasing the frequency of bowel movements. These

comprise the B.R.A.T. diet, so named because of its usefulness in treating pediatric patients. It consists of bananas, rice, applesauce, and dry toast.

In proven cases of infectious diarrheal disease such as *Salmonella*, the use of antibiotics may be indicated. Quinolones and fluoroquinolones such as Cipro (ciprofloxacin) are considered drugs of choice when treatment is needed. In most circumstances, however, antibiotics should be used only with great caution, as the main side effect of antibiotics is … diarrhea!

For more information about poultry and your health:

http://www.fsis.usda.gov/fact_sheets/chicken_from_farm_to_table/index.asp

Joe and Amy Alton are the authors of the #1 Amazon Bestseller *The Doom and Bloom Survival Medicine Handbook.* **They have more than 250 articles regarding medical preparedness on their website at www.doomandbloom.net.** Δ

Ask Jackie

If you have a question about rural living, send it in to Jackie Clay and she'll try to answer it. Address your letter to Ask Jackie, PO Box 712, Gold Beach, OR 97444. Questions will only be answered in this column. — *Editor*

New lids

When I buy new canning jars there is a new lid and ring on the jars. The lids are usually stuck tight to the jars and there is a definite impression of the jar rim on the lid when removed. Can these lids be used for canning? I always buy new lids separately just to be sure.

Susan Holmes
Moselle, Mississippi

Yes, you can use these lids. I have to laugh — they tell us not to re-use regular metal lids, then they send them to us that way, which leaves indentations just like used lids. Just be sure to simmer the lids in water before using them and they'll be just fine. —*Jackie*

Canning legumes

I am relatively new to canning. I am using it mostly to offset the high cost of commercially canned legumes, which we use a lot of. Since there are only two of us and I primarily use them in recipes, I can mostly half pints and some pints of black-eyed peas, garbanzos, pintos, and white beans. When I use the old fashioned metal lids I can see and feel that they are sealed. I do not feel as confident with the reusable Tattler lids. I have a Presto pressure canner, the smaller one that can do 12 half pints and 10 pints. I cook them with 12 pounds of pressure for 60 or 75 minutes respectively since we live somewhere between 3,500 and 4,000 feet altitude. Here are my questions:

1. When I put water to the bottom line in the canner, where it says the water should be, it seems to be getting into the jars because they are more full when I take them out than when I put them in. Is it because the water in the canner is too high for the half pint jars or because I am not screwing on the lids tight enough?

2. How do I know for sure the Tattler lids have sealed? I am not seeing the dent in the middle I grew to know with the old metal lids.

3. Should liquid cover the beans, with absolutely no bean sticking up through the liquid?

4. Is it OK to let jars cool in the canner without tightening the lids?

Eve Garlyn
Kingman, Arizona

All legumes swell during processing, so they squash the liquid up to the top more than when you can vegetables.

The indentation on the Tattler lids may not be as pronounced as it is with the metal lids, but if you feel the top of the lid with your fingertip, you should feel the indentation in the middle. You should also be able to see it from the side of the jar.

You only need to screw the rings firmly tight, not excessively tight. With the Tattler lids, you screw the rings snug, but only fingertip snug, which is even less tight than with the metal lids. After processing, you quickly finish tightening the rings firmly tight. The term "firmly tight" means as snug as you can get them without undue force. You don't want to grit your teeth and force the rings tight because you may crack the glass rim.

Jackie Clay

You don't have to worry about having liquid covering every bean. Jars with a bean or two showing above the liquid will keep just as well as those in which all the beans are covered completely.

It is *never* a good idea to let jars cool in the canner. This often causes incomplete seals that release in storage. I know because I did just that and had 18 quarts of sweet corn ruined in my pantry. You don't tighten the rings after processing with metal two-piece lids but you *do* tighten the rings immediately after processing with the Tattler lids, just like we used to do with the old zinc lids and rubbers. If you don't tighten the rings on Tattler lids, many will not seal.

—*Jackie*

Making sauerkraut

My wife was excited to find a method of making kraut that she was hoping was the way her grandfather had done it. She remembers him making it in canning jars. So last June we cut up some cabbage and did it according to the directions. I believe it was 1 tsp. of salt, sugar, and vinegar in a quart jar packed with shredded cabbage. Filled the jars with boiling water and then gave them a hot water bath. After two months of anticipation we tried our kraut and found it BLAND. It was more like canned wilt-

ed cabbage and not the expected strong flavor of sauerkraut. Do you have a method of making kraut in canning jars, or must we find us a crock?

Jeff Pence
Greenfield, Ohio

Yes, you can make it in individual jars, but to tell you the truth, it's easier and less messy to just go ahead and use a crock. Here's the way to do it in jars, if you really want to go that route:

Shred cabbage and pack tightly into quart jars up to ½ inch from the top.

Add 1 tsp. canning salt and 1 tsp. sugar to the top of each quart.

Pour boiling water into each jar up to the top of the kraut. Use a knife gently inserted into the jar to remove any bubbles.

Put on canning lids and screw on cap loosely, not tight. Put the jars in a sink or pan so that any bubbling water won't make a mess. Let ferment for 24 hours.

Remove the caps, remove any scum if necessary, and refill with boiling water as needed. Seal as tightly as you can with your hand. Let ferment for 3 days.

Remove cap, remove any scum, refill with boiling water as needed. Wash lid then bring it to simmering and wipe rim of jar clean. Place lid on jar and screw down ring firmly tight. Process in a boiling water bath canner for 20 minutes (quarts) or 15 minutes (pints). If you live at an altitude above 1,000 feet, consult your canning book for directions on increasing your processing time to suit your altitude, if necessary.

Your cabbage was really canned cabbage, not fermented sauerkraut, so that's why it was bland. Remember, canned cabbage must be processed in a pressure canner while fermented sauerkraut can be safely water bath processed. *—Jackie*

Herb that repels bees

Back in the olden days, I remember reading about an herb that repels bees. Of course I can't remember what it was. Do you happen to know? I have several books and papers on herbs, but none mention a bee repellent.

One of the few great pleasures left to me is feeding hummingbirds but swarms of bees and wasps are making this almost impossible. Some crawl inside the feeders (don't ask me how) and drown there, in such numbers that the hummers can't feed, even before the dead bees sour the nectar. Refilling with fresh nectar every two days has become burdensome. Adding insult to injury, the larger wasps and hornets cluster on the feeder ports and won't let me or the birds near. All of my feeders have "bee guards."

Rubbing petroleum jelly around the ports did not work. I put out several wasp traps, baited with the same sugar solution, but while I catch masses of flies, the wasps prefer it in the feeders.

Phyl Hubbard
Corydon, Indiana

A mixture of lemongrass and rosemary works well for most folks. If you simmer the crushed herbs in oil of citronella, it's said to further enhance the repelling power of the two herbs. Burt's Bees has a spray made of these herbs that works great for most gardeners. Try baiting your wasp traps with soda pop. They love it and flock to it in hordes. Yellow jackets also like meat. I've had good luck putting a piece of meat inside one wasp trap and soda in others.

—Jackie

Making stock from bones

Some years ago I was reading Heloise. There was a mention in the book of making stock from bones in a pressure canner at 15 pounds pressure. Does anyone out there do this?

Where can I get more information? I did pressure can chicken bones for an hour at 15 pounds pressure but it didn't turn them to soup stock; it did soften them. I'd like to recycle my bones to soup stock.

Also what are ways to use eggshells? And what are ways to use the brown paper bags from the store?

Alice Lane
Portland, Oregon

I always make soup stock from my chicken, turkey, and beef bones. I don't bother pressure canning them but simply simmer them for a few hours on the back of our wood stove in plenty of water, flavored with seasonings we like. I add salt to enhance the flavor of the broth. You make broth from the bones and water; you don't make stock from just the bones.

Eggshells can be crushed and fed to chickens or other poultry to help strengthen bones and build thick, strong eggshells. You can also put a handful in each tomato and pepper hole when you plant them to help provide calcium, which discourages blossom end rot.

One way I use brown paper bags from the store is to cover the counter when I prepare vegetables. I open a bag flat and chop the vegetables on it, with the bag catching the waste. Then I can pick up the bag and carry the waste to the chickens or pigs. I bury the bag in the compost pile, where it composts over time. Instead of using paper bags, why not buy a canvas bag or two to take to the grocery store? Then you can reuse these bags nearly forever! *—Jackie*

Spots on pickled vegetables

Sometimes I find chalky-looking white dots on pickled vegetables, about the size of a pin tip; I often see them on store-canned/jarred capers, but I also had them recently show up on my pickled asparagus (which had just turned two years old... I know that is reaching the outer limits of "approved" keep dates, but we know that they would at least hold until we needed holiday treats this year!).

Do you know what these spots are? If so, are they anything to be concerned about?

Shawn Prenzlow
Woodinville, Washington

These spots are from the formation of a flavonoid glycoside, rutin, which is found in asparagus. It is a healthful component but it can look nasty on pickled asparagus. Two-year-old pickles are not old; I've got some that are 10 years old in my pantry. But the longer pickled asparagus remains in storage, the more possible it is to find the stems dotted with rutin spots. They won't hurt you a bit and are actually good for you! It is vitamin P1. —*Jackie*

Ghost peppers

I just heard of a hot pepper called ghost pepper. The person that told me of it said it couldn't be sold in the United States unless you signed for it. Have you ever heard of this pepper and where would you get seeds for it. I would like to try growing it next year.

Judy Hiatt
Marysville, Kansas

Yes, I've heard of Ghost peppers. They're the hottest possible pepper, reportedly. Of course the name makes them popular! It is a long-season pepper, coming from India. It is called *Bhut Jolokia* there. You can find seeds at Totally Tomatoes and Pepper Joe's. Like all very hot peppers, please wear rubber gloves when chopping or de-seeding it. —*Jackie*

Storing meat in fat

I was talking to my mom about what was done to preserve food back when … She said that her mom used to pack meat in fat in a crock and store it in the root cellar and they ate it all

winter. But other than you put rendered fat in the crock, then a layer of meat, more fat, then meat until the crock was full, that was all she could remember. Do you know how it was done? Was the meat cooked or raw? I am trying to get off the grid so I am interested in trying it. I can and dry already.

Eileen Bisson
Philomath, Oregon

My grandmother did this too. She sterilized the crock with boiling water and then air dried it. She fried the meat (she used pork) and packed it in lard in the crock, in layers, with melted lard between them. The crock, when full, was topped off with another layer of lard. She removed the meat one layer at a time, keeping the top covered with a layer of lard to seal out air. She then heated the meat thoroughly before it was eaten.

I can't really recommend this, as there are always possibilities of spoilage and botulism. Instead, I can up my meat. I pack big pieces, like pork chops, in wide-mouth jars, and ground meat and stewing meat go in regular-mouth jars. That way you never have to worry about spoilage or food safety. —*Jackie*

Canning potatoes

I got a sale on potatoes, both regular and baking size, and canned all. I tried to follow directions and boiled for two minutes, but after taking the cans out of the pressure canner, I noticed that some were mushy looking which is not a big deal since they will be mashed potatoes. Can the mashed part be prevented, maybe by boiling less time or putting the potatoes in the water after it has come to a boil?

C. N.
Wagoner, Oklahoma

This does happen with many varieties of potatoes, especially larger ones. For whole potatoes, you can raw pack them, pour boiling water over them,

and process for 45 minutes for quarts and pints, which is a longer processing time than if you pre-boiled them. For diced potatoes, you would pack raw, pour on boiling water, then process quarts or pints for 45 minutes. Both are processed at 10 pounds pressure. If you live at an altitude above 1,000 feet, consult your canning book for directions on increasing your pressure to suit your altitude. —*Jackie*

Free bummer pigs

I recently was given two small pigs, a runt and a cripple, left over from a nursery to finishing pen. One has a skin problem on his ears. The other, the smaller, has a swollen knee. Can you give me any suggestions on what to do for them. Otherwise they are eating corn screenings from our corn dryer, and produce scraps that I give them. Will that be enough to turn them into bacon and chops?

Benay Cole
Granite Falls, Minnesota

The one with the skin problem on the ears may have mange mites; it frequently shows up on the ears as thickened scales. Other indications are scrubbing its sides on the stall walls and feeder. We've had real good luck using horse paste wormer Ivermectin, inserted either in the mouth or inside a filled cake doughnut like a Twinkie. Otherwise, injectable works very well, too. Mange mites are very common in pigs.

The swollen knee may be a bigger problem. It's often an infection. Sometimes giving a course of antibiotics such as injectable tetracycline or penicillin will do the trick. If you can handle the pig, it also might help to rub a heating or cooling ointment into the swelling twice a day.

No, just feeding corn screenings won't be enough to raise those little pigs. With their tough start, I'd give them 18% pig feed wet with milk or calf milk replacer until they begin to grow nicely. Then you can quit the milk and drop their feed down to 16% pig feed until they are more than 100 pounds. At that point, you should be able to add your corn screenings. Give them all the scraps you want, anytime. They'll appreciate it. — *Jackie*

Size of coop

I am getting ready to mix my flocks of chickens. I have 10 hens from last year and 35 hens and roosters from this year's brood. I figure we will end up with maybe 20 hens from the new flock.

I have a 4x6 coop that was fine for the 10 birds but seems small for 25-30 hens. I found one reference to 4 sq ft/hen if they have access to a run.

That seems too big as it would be 10x12 or so. Any idea how big to go on the coop?

Also I heard that you should put a roost above the nesting boxes to keep the hens from staying in the nesting boxes. Is that true?

Erica Kardelis
Helper, Utah

You're right; your 4x6-foot coop is way too small for 30 hens. I'd double that size or better, if possible. You can sometimes get by with smaller quarters, but in the winter, when they are indoors most of the time, they can become stressed from crowding and end up with respiratory diseases or they'll begin picking on one another.

No, don't put the roost above the nest boxes as it'll encourage the hens to stop to roost in the lower nest boxes. To keep them from roosting on the nest boxes, fasten a steeply sloped piece of plywood over the boxes so they can't stand on top. They'll move on to roost where they should, keeping the nests much cleaner. —*Jackie*

Soaking wicks

I have been trying out oil lamps. I am confused about soaking the wick. Some say yes some say no. I eventually did it (I use KleanHeat kerosene).

It smoked so bad I blew it out. Do I have to soak the wick? My grandma never did, she just lit it.

Cheryle Aguirre
Santa Maria, California

I don't soak my wicks. I just insert them into the lamp, drape them into the filled reservoir, wait a few minutes, and light the lamp. —*Jackie*

Moving plants

I am moving from Illinois to Michigan in the next month or so. I know I will not have time to prepare a spot for everything I would like to transplant. I was wondering if I could still take some things and how to keep them happy until spring? Fridge? Bucket of sand left outside?

I would like to take some rhubarb, horseradish, strawberries and walking onions. I figured the berry bushes would be a wash.

Dawn Norcross
Orion, Illinois

Yes, you sure can take some plants with you. I'd simply dig a trench in your new yard and heel them in until spring. Make sure the soil is packed down firmly over all the roots, then mulch only the roots (so mice and voles don't get in and eat all the tops). This should work, even for your berry bushes. —*Jackie*

Storing food in a wet cellar

I have metal canning shelves in a "wet" cellar. We have a dirt (over slate slabs) floor with a creek running under the cellar and a spring in the corner (in a 50 gal. drum). I have a few light bulbs that turn on when I go down to the freezer, water softener, furnace. Should I cover the shelving with dark blankets to prevent the light from shining on the canned food? I go down about once/day. Also, can I store foods in food-grade buckets even though we have a "wet" cellar. I also have a pantry upstairs, but it's full and quite small.

Melody
Upstate New York

No, your canned goods will be fine with light bulbs shining on them. When storage recommendations say a "cool, dark place" it means no sunlight beating through lots of windows onto your jars of food. The only thing light bulbs will do is maybe make your potatoes try to sprout and they can even get green shoulders from that little bit of light.

If your wet cellar is damp with condensation, I probably wouldn't store buckets of dry food down there unless you have tight-fitting, airtight, gasketed lids; dampness will definitely damage stored dry foods. —*Jackie*

Fluid loss during canning

I am canning meat for the first time. What causes fluid loss during canning and how can I avoid it? I filled with fluid to within one inch and lost up to an inch.

Debbie Kornelli
Hillsdale, New York

Usually, loss of fluid is caused by fluctuations in pressure during canning (11 pounds, climbing to 15, then back down quickly, for example), taking jars out of the canner too soon after the pressure returns to zero after processing (let 'em sit for five minutes after a zero reading to ensure that it is truly zero), or not removing air bubbles when you pack your jars. The meat is still good and it will not affect the taste. —*Jackie*

LATE WINTER WHITEOUT: FISHING FOR WHITE BASS

By Frank Knebel

By late winter many of us are scratching our heads trying to figure out what to do. Hunting season is still about a month away and the large mouth bass are shivering and waiting for the water to warm up. So what to do, what to do?

Well, instead of moping around and driving the family nuts, load them up, hook up the boat, and tear out after one of the most voracious predators found in our freshwaters — the little ol' white bass. These small fish are as feisty and aggressive as aggravated piranhas. They travel in large compact schools with only one thing in mind — to feed! The sight of a white bass feeding frenzy is hard to miss as they drive thousands of shad to the surface and out of the water. If this happens near shore, the terrified baitfish have been known to swim right up onto the bank in an effort to escape the slaughter!

When the first cold fronts move in, the white bass, also commonly called sand bass or sandies, having spent all summer terrorizing the gizzard or threadfin populations, begin moving up the lake driven by the same urge that many species, humans included, find the cold nights of winter good for — propagation. They migrate into the rivers and creeks that feed the lakes and reservoirs and move upstream, sometimes for miles in search of just the right place. Often this is a sandbar or a rocky stretch of streambed. Here they concentrate and when all of the conditions are just right — the water temperature, current, daylight (or lack of), maybe even the moon phase and a thousand other possible things — the spawn erupts into a frenzied flurry matched only by the dedication with which they feed. Typically this all begins in December, gathers steam in January, builds pressure in February, and explodes in March. By late April it's all over.

White bass (*Morone chrysops*) are a legitimate freshwater member of the temperate bass family *Percichthyidae* (try saying that after a couple of sips of firewater). This includes the white perch, striped bass, hybrid stripers (which happen to be stripers crossed with white bass), and yellow bass. The white bass can be easily confused with its cousins, and often is.

Originally the white bass ranged from the Great Lakes, south to Arkansas, Kansas, and Missouri, and from the Mississippi to the west slope of the Alleghenies. However, this voracious little predator has been introduced throughout the rest of the South and the Southwestern states. Though it can be found in large streams and rivers, the sandies prefer the large open waters of natural and man-made lakes; the only exception is during the winter spawn when they migrate into the tributaries.

The smaller males go first, followed a week or so later by the females. When the water temperature reaches somewhere between 58-62°F, usually at night and in flowing water, the fun begins. The female releases 25,000 to one million eggs that are fertilized by the male as they exit. These then drift and sink until they lodge down in the rocks and pebbles or sunken logs and debris. If there are good currents to keep the eggs alive and viable, and the planets and moon line up just

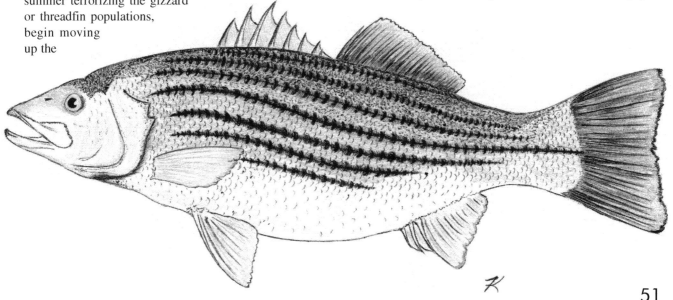

51

right, and all is well with world, the eggs will hatch in two to three days.

If running water isn't available, white bass have been known to spawn along open, wind-swept beaches and sandbars where the wind creates current. It is not unusual for there to be a failed hatch from time to time. This is the reason you often see a large difference in sizes of white bass. Nature has a way of taking care of its own and if every spawn were to be successful, the shad populations would be in real trouble.

Once a successful hatch does take place, the fry form dense schools and immediately begin their acts of terrorism on plankton and move progressively up the ladder until they are primarily devouring shad. Perch, brim, crappie, and the black basses also occasionally find themselves on the menu of these ravenous hordes until they become too large for the sandies to put in their mouths.

At a year old, the white bass typically will measure 5-8 inches and will weigh just shy of ½ pound. At three years it will have doubled up to 13-16 inches and will tip the scales at over a pound and by five years of age will be considered a monster at 15-17 inches and will weigh 2 pounds. Most don't make it though since even a four-year-old sandy is considered an ancient. I'm sure that the shad sure appreciate that fact of life.

As previously mentioned, white bass prefer the open water of lakes and reservoirs. In the early winter as they begin to set the stage for their mass migrations into the tributaries, they can be targeted out on the waters of the upper end of the lake. These pre-spawn fish can be hungry as long as the water isn't too cold. If the lake is below 50°F, stay home and organize your tackle box (unless you hear that they have already moved into the creeks). But if the lake water is warmer than that, look for feeding activity on the surface. A pair of binoculars will sure help you with this.

Identifying your catch

White bass can be differentiated from its cousins by several easily noticed features:

Stripes: White bass stripes tend to be somewhat fainter than those of its cousins. Also, with the white bass, only one, the lateral line stripe, extends all the way to the tail. Striped bass have several stripes that extend to the tail while the hybrid's stripes are broken and staggered in appearance. Yellow bass have distinct stripes and the lower ones are broken just above the anal fin. Yellow bass also tend to be — well — yellow.

Body shape: Stripers are the slender models while the whites, yellows, and hybrids are their pot-bellied kin. Stripers are only 1/3 as deep as they are long. The other tend to be deeper with their depth over 1/3 or their overall length.

Tongue "tooth" palates: White bass have a single patch of "teeth" in the mid-rear portion of their tongue whereas the stripers and hybrids have a double patch. The yellow bass has none at all.

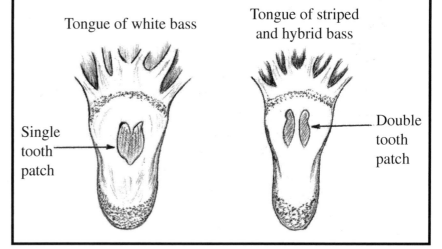

Tongue of white bass — Single tooth patch

Tongue of striped and hybrid bass — Double tooth patch

Look for frenzied feeding action and shad busting out of the water. If your lake or reservoir hosts a population or is a stopover for migrating cormorants, gulls, or pelicans during the winter months, look for working birds, especially over shallower flats and bars. When you see diving birds, get over there; you have just located a school. Even if you only locate a gull or a pelican or two sitting on the water, it's worth checking out. Oftentimes the birds know that the fish are down there and are just hanging out waiting for the frenzy to kick off. A sonar unit/fishfinder, especially one that has side-scan, is extremely helpful in locating white bass schools suspended in the lake or in the rivers and creeks.

Once you locate a school of surface feeders, don't run right into the chaos of the frenzy. Kill the engine well upwind of the slaughter so that you will drift alongside the school. If your boat is equipped with a trolling motor, make use of it to hold a position within casting distance of the school, but not so close as to spook them. If the school sounds (dives) and disappears, don't panic. Most likely they will surface again nearby.

A surface-feeding school of white bass is a great thing for the family to see. Light or ultralight action rods and spinning reels or spin-cast outfits increase the fun and make the most out of these small fighters. Small silver spoons, lipless cranks like the Rat-L-Trap, Super Spot, or Rattlin'

Rapala are all great baits in the 1½ to 2-inch lengths. In-line spinners like Rooster Tails and small spinners with white or chartreuse skirts and willow blades are also lethal to sandies. Fly fisherman can have a real blast too! Streamers are the way to go, again in white, red and white, chartreuse, or white and chartreuse. No matter your chosen weapon, expect the action to be fast and furious and more than a little chaotic.

Should the sandies not be feeding yet when you locate a school on your sonar, you can sometimes chum them into action (where legal) by tossing out ground shad or finely-chopped pieces of shad along with a few live ones embedded in a gently-pressed ball of sand and fish or those lures already mentioned. As those sand balls sink, they break up and release the shad at various levels and add action to your chum which will often drive these little predators crazy. But for some reason, should they still be tight-lipped and refuse to rise to the occasion, try a white jig or silver jigging spoon. Just maybe you'll clunk one on the head.

Once the spawn migration is under way, head up the tributaries and look for pinch points such as sand bars, log jams, or anything which halts upstream progress such as a dam or rock outcropping. Search these obstacles and structures thoroughly, especially on the downstream sections, remembering that they spawn into the current. These obstacles and pinch points concentrate several already densely-packed schools together and once you find them you'll be busy as all get out. If the waters are up from late winter rains, like they probably will be, explore the normally shallow feeder creeks, especially the clearer ones. Again, a sonar/fishfinder sure will come in handy.

A couple more tips: Should you catch one sandy in a spot, keep plugging that spot because you have just located a school. These fish will not wander around on their own. If your sonar shows that the fish are there and you're getting occasional hits, but nothing solid, slow down your retrieve and then slow it down some more. Remember, that water is on the chilly side and the fish may be moving a little slow.

Pay attention to the weather, also. Any change that drives the barometer up or down will usually kick the sandies off into a ravenous, voracious frenzy of shad-slaughtering action. This change in the barometer doesn't need to be a big one either. A simple change in wind direction or the passage of a weak front, cold or warm, will often do the trick. After a front passes, the barometer will be on the rise and the fish will be crazy active. However, once the pressure peaks and then stabilizes, the bite will most times shut down. It'll normally take a couple of days for the fish to come back around and work their appetites back into action. This time of year can have some rather fickle fishing patterns and with the changing weather and climate that we've experienced over the past couple of years, if you are able to guess the pattern consistently, you need to buy a lottery ticket or go to Vegas.

While they aren't a big, colorful beast of the depths and they don't have a multi-billion dollar industry focused solely on them or have a million strong cult-like following, white bass can hit hard and put up a fast, determined fight on light tackle. They are the perfect fish for those inexpensive box-store kid combos and offer plenty of action to hook a kid for life. On top of all that, they will get you up off of the couch and provide the makings for a fine winter fish-fry. Besides, what else have you got to do? Δ

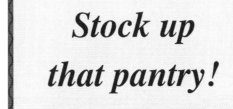

Building and using wattle fences

By Kathryn Wingrove

Wattle fences are made by weaving material in and out of posts in the ground. They were often used on the small farms of Victorian England. In fact, during those times there were craftsmen who made their living by making movable wattle fences called hurdles. This craft has gone by the wayside as more modern fencing options have come into use, but wattle fencing can still offer an inexpensive way to provide a fence wherever needed. Wattle hurdles can provide easy-to-move fencing to temporarily separate livestock or pastures. They are easy to make, require no special equipment, and can be made from many different materials. In fact, wattle fences are a great way to clear out the undergrowth in a woodlot or elsewhere around the property. It is hard to see how the knowledge has almost been lost when there are so many benefits to wattle fencing.

The first wattle fences we made around our little farm were designed to keep the ducks out of our garden beds. Since our duck pond was in the middle of the garden space, we had a terrible time with the ducks eating all of our leafy greens and tearing up whatever they wanted to taste. A wattle fence around each garden bed was a good solution because the ducks were kept out of the plants, but they were still near enough that we were able to reap their bug-hunting benefits.

To build this fence we selected some 2-inch diameter oak and bamboo for the stakes. The wood works better if it is green and fresh. We placed these stakes two feet apart all around each section of the beds, leaving a space for an entrance into each section. Next we took some long branches and small trees that needed to be cleaned out of the pasture and woodlot. These trees averaged between two to three inches in diameter. You want the trees and branches thin enough to be flexible, but long

enough to wind around several of the posts for added stability. On the first fencing section we didn't get the branches and trees long enough, so we had to do some tweaking later to improve the stability of the fence. However, for the next sections we chose trees that were 10 to 12 feet in length, which allowed them to wind in and out of several posts. This gave the rest of the fencing sections much more stability and we had very little adjusting to do afterwards. This garden fence was only two feet high, just enough to provide a visual barrier to keep the ducks out of the garden spaces while the seedlings were coming up.

The next wattle fence we built was to fence in a yard for the chickens around the chicken coop. Our flock of chickens had decided that they didn't need to go back to the coop at night. Instead they chose places like my front porch, the goat barn, and my children's play equipment to roost on at night. This was, of course, unacceptable because of the mess they left behind. It became such a hassle to catch 30 chickens roosting in various places around my house, yard, and barn that we decided to build a fenced-in chicken yard. This fence needed to be much stouter than the little garden fence we had previously built so the upright supports were approximately four inches in diameter and about five feet tall. We spiked one end of the support with a hatchet before driving them into the ground with a sledgehammer. These posts were spaced two feet apart. Again, we used tall thin trees that were at least 12 feet in length and averaged about 3 inches in diameter to weave around the supports. We started weaving at one corner on the outside of post 1, moving inside to post 2, again outside to post 3, then inside to post 4, and so on until the branch ended. If we ended on post 5 then the next branch was started on the opposite side of post 4 from the other branch already

crossing it. Continuing in this fashion, we "wove" the branches together to form a sort of basket-type weave, giving the fence more strength and no weak spots. We built this fence to a height of four feet and it was strong enough that the goats stood on the fence trying to reach tree branches and never broke through or damaged it. All of the small branch cleanings off the trees were used to stick upright into the uppermost weave, giving an additional three feet of height to the fence and creating a screen to keep chickens from flying over. This fence has worked well to contain most of our flock, but we have had two or three determined hens that have managed to work themselves over and through the upright twigs.

Wattle fencing is certainly cheap enough, using materials that otherwise have little use. It doesn't take much time. The garden fencing took about two full days to gather and cut the materials and then put them into place. The chicken fence took about a week to complete.

The best benefit yet has been the compliments that we get from visitors to the farm about how great the fences look. They certainly do have an aesthetic appeal. The only drawback we have found is that when we use smaller stuff like twigs and thin branches the fence settles and loses height. We have experienced this in the garden. However, it has been easy to fix as we smash the horizontal twigs down a bit and then add new ones to the top. We also had a couple of the upright posts in the garden rot at the ground and we simply wiggled them a bit to get the bottom to fresh dirt and pushed them back down. When they get too short to use, they won't be that difficult to replace. We certainly recommend using wattle fences around the homestead and will be implementing more of them in our future. Δ

Roast your own coffee

By Kyle Doty

I wouldn't call it a trend, but roasting your own coffee at home is definitely growing in popularity. Home roasting enterprises like Sweet Maria's (sweetmarias.com) and Seven Bridges (breworganic.com) have sprung up on the web and have enjoyed success since opening their virtual doors. Families who would like to take a more organic and frontier-like approach to their morning habit have turned to such companies in search of a better brew.

But why would anyone want to roast their own coffee? Coffee is delicate and begins to lose its robust flavor and aroma only days after roasting and it goes stale even quicker when it's ground. That means that the coffee you buy at the grocery store has already been stale for weeks — sometimes months.

We started home roasting because once we tasted the difference between fresh, home-roasted coffee and the other, stale option, we were sold. There are many ways to roast coffee at home: an expensive home roaster that does all the work for you, an old electric hot air popcorn popper, a Whirley Pop™ popcorn popper that goes right on the stove top, or even on a baking sheet in the oven.

We chose to use a Whirley Pop™ because we wanted to assure customers that we were literally hand-roasting our coffee. The Whirley Pop™ is cheap, efficient, and produces an excellent batch of coffee.

The beans

We start by ordering Organic Fair Trade green coffee beans because we want to make sure that the farmer who produced the beans is getting paid a fair wage. The green (raw) beans cost about a quarter the price of good quality roasted coffee. We buy five to ten pounds at a time. Green coffee beans won't go bad; just store them in the pantry or someplace similar. We have to keep a lot on hand because we also sell fresh-roasted coffee by the pound.

Roasting beans with a Whirley Pop™

First, heat up the popper. We put it on our electric stove with the heat turned up to high. Then pour in the desired amount of green coffee beans and turn the stove down to a high-medium heat. We set the dial for the burner just a line or two above medium. For the Whirley Pop™ it's not recommended to try to roast more than one pound of coffee at a time. We try to stick closer to half a pound at a time so we can ensure a more even roast.

It is imperative that you keep the beans stirring around by using the gear. You don't want to leave the beans sitting in the bottom of the pot or they will burn. You'll stir the beans for roughly 13-15 minutes. Every stove is different.

Turn the heat down to medium when the beans start to crack. You want to listen to the different cracking sounds the beans make. The cracking sound is moisture being expelled from the beans; it's the indicator that the beans are roasting. There are two sounds to listen for, and they're called first and second crack. The first crack is a louder sound that is spaced apart by about 30 seconds to a minute and then the second crack will start. You'll have to train your ear to hear the difference, but the second crack is lighter and more rapid sounding, like a bonfire crackling. If you are doing a dark roast, it'll get very smoky and you'll start to see oil on the beans. If you are doing more of the recommended roast for the specific region of beans, you won't go much past the second crack. This will give you more of a medium roast and you will taste the hints and notes of the coffee better.

When the beans are roasted to your desired color, transfer the freshly-roasted beans to a baking pan that you've set up beforehand. For a dark roast, the beans should have an oily look to them. For light to medium roasts they will look a little dry. Make sure that the beans have an even color to them. After transferring the beans to the baking sheet, make sure that they are evenly distributed, then turn on a small fan to help the cooling pro-

We use a stove-top Whirley Pop™ to roast small batches of Organic Fair Trade coffee. The Whirley Pop™ is cheap, easy-to-use, and efficient.

cess. It is necessary to agitate the beans using a wooden spoon to remove the chaff that is still attached to the beans. The chaff is the outer shell that peels off during roasting and it will fall off when stirred. It's messy, but there is no way around it. The beans will take about 20 minutes to cool.

Once they are cool to the touch you want to store them. We use a degassing can that we bought online for less than $10. A degassing can is a convenient way of storing your whole beans. It is also perfectly acceptable to use seal tight bags with a degassing valve to store your coffee. Degassing is important because freshly roasted coffee releases CO_2 up to 10 days after roasting. If you were to place your coffee into a seal tight bag without a degassing valve, it would expand the bag and possibly break it. Degassing is also important because as well as allowing CO_2 to escape, the can and the seal tight bags keep oxygen from getting in and making your beans go stale quicker.

You may have to play with the process a bit in order to get just the right roast. It takes time to hear the different cracks, determine how much smoke signals that the roast is almost complete, and figure out which roast is dark and which one is light to medium. We recommend a medium roast because dark roasts cook out the flavor of the coffee.

You may not be interested in selling coffee by the pound, but if you are, you can realistically earn an extra $300 to $500 per year from your kitchen stove. You will also have the satisfaction of creating a great cup of coffee with your own two hands. Whether you are going for a small enterprise or just trying to get a good cup of joe, home roasting is the best and most rewarding option. Δ

Plant a tree in the name of love

By Susan Vetrone

My Uncle Mike was not embarrassed to tell you that he talked to trees. When someone he loved passed away, he planted a tree in their honor. Occasionally, he would walk through his yard and gently pat a trunk and say, "Hello Al, beautiful morning" or "Hey Robby, think I'll go fishing."

I must be a softie, because it wasn't long after I bought my first house that I replicated Uncle Mike's tribute to those he loved. I planted a blue spruce for my grandmother — a feisty cook who spoke English flavored with a thick Italian accent. Grandma was very much alive when I planted the tree, but it gave me great pleasure to walk past the sapling and think of her. Over the 19 years that I owned the house, the tree grew tall and impressive, while my grandmother became short and soft. Grandma's tree made me feel closer to her somehow, even though she was 100 miles away.

A few weeks after her 90th birthday, Grandma left us and with her passing so went her generous spirit, tomato sauce recipe, and unconditional love.

That summer was also time for me to sell the house. I had watched Grandma's tree grow from less than a foot tall to higher than the roof line. I had whispered into that tree as I spread mulch and mowed around it. I had trimmed the tree for fragrant holiday accents and looked out the picture window at snow resting on the branches. Over time, it became a magnificently shaped gray-blue tree.

The house held happy and not-so-happy memories, and the new place had more land, a creek, and a fresh start, so the house wasn't as hard to leave as Grandma's tree.

After months of open houses, newspaper ads, and anxiety, the next-door neighbor bought the place for his frail father. After we shook hands on the deal, I asked his plans for the large tree between the houses. I feared that the now massive spruce was in the way and that the new owner had plans to remove it to shorten the walk between the two houses. I was assured that the tree would be left as-is and he even teased that I could visit my rooted friend whenever I liked.

Over the last few years I have come to love my new life in the woods.

I planted this blue spruce for my grandmother. Even though I don't live in this house anymore, I still drive by once in a while to say "hi" to Grandma.

Sadly, my property now has a tree named "Johnny" for a friend who left us too soon. There is always a concern that trees in our climate won't make it through the harsh Ohio winter or may wither from lack of sunlight in the woods, but Johnny hangs on, just like the spirit of my long-time pal.

I hope that there won't be a need for any new tree additions, though I flirt with the idea of planting another one for Grandma. If I do, the next tree will flower and be deciduous as she loved to shuffle through leaves in the fall.

My uncle was right about planting and naming trees for the people we love. Sometimes long after dark when the neighbors won't think that I am stalking them, I drive by my old house and look at that big blue spruce and say, "Hi Grandma, beautiful night."

Tree planting tips

There are many reasons to plant trees: shade, fruit or nuts, privacy, habitat for animals and birds, enhanced scenery, or the feeling of satisfaction of putting down roots or replacing what we take from the earth.

It can be fun for children to plant a tree of their own height and take birthday photos next to the tree every year and see which grows taller faster. This is an opportunity for them to learn the fundamentals of tree planting and be invested in the nature around them.

Tree planting basics will vary based on your climate and tree type, but these are a few items to consider before you get started.

• Plant in the spring or early fall in most parts of the country, for most tree types. Spring is preferred so that trees can benefit from the rainfall and become established before summer's heat and dryness.

• Select your tree type considering its appearance year round, if it will

drop any unwanted debris, if it has an acceptable amount of maintenance, and if it will work in your climate.

• Plant in an area that offers the appropriate amount of sunlight and climate requirements (rainfall, temperatures, soil conditions, etc.).

• Consider the tree size at maturity and if it will interfere with overhead wires or underground pipe lines. If you are uncertain as to the location of your cables, gas and water lines, and septic tanks, contact your utilities prior to digging.

• Dig according to the instructions for that tree type. The hole will likely need to be 2-3 times as wide as the root ball to allow for root expansion and not to restrict growth. The depth will likely be the height of the roots. The dirt along the bottom and sides of the hole should be loose.

• Mix in old compost, composted manure, peat moss, or other organic matter to make the dirt nutrient rich. If organic filler is not available, there are products that you can purchase. Good dirt is a key to success.

• Remove the string, burlap, or container holding the root structure. Using your hands, gently loosen the dirt and roots along the sides and bottom of the root ball. This is particularly important if it is pot or root bound. This will allow it to establish roots in its new location faster. Place tree in the middle of the hole.

• Add your enhanced dirt around the tree and step back and look at it. Is the most beautiful view facing your house or path? Is the trunk straight? When it is where you like it, add more soil so that the hole is filled even with the top of the roots. Do not compress.

• Add a few of inches of mulch to retain moisture, beautify, protect, and reduce weeding. Do not use plastic sheeting as it will reduce air circulation and water penetration.

• Thoroughly water after planting and at least once a week afterwards. Water should penetrate at least 12-15 inches deep. Water more frequently in the summer or in dry climates.

• Many tree types require a good deal of water the first year and a hose with a slow trickle may do the trick.

• Don't let ivy or other parasitic plants grow up the tree as they can sap some of the tree's nutrients and strangle the trunk.

• Stake the tree to help it stay straight. Don't let the stake rub against the tree trunk and only leave it in place as long as it needs to be stabilized.

Once your tree is in place, you may choose to fertilize and prune. Otherwise, there isn't much to do but enjoy your new addition over the years to come. Δ

Home air pistol range keeps shooting skills sharp

By George Smith

A home air pistol range should be simple and inexpensive. Here are a few practical tips on setting one up so you can keep hand-eye coordination, trigger control, and mental shooting skills sharp wherever you live. If weather discourages you from using your outdoor range, or you prefer a more casual and discreet shooting option, an indoor CO_2 range is for you.

A good CO_2 pistol allows for both slow and rapid, single and double action shooting. Safe targets can be made from common household materials and shooting supplies for a CO_2 pistol are inexpensive.

Targets and setup

To make a target, I took an appropriately sized cardboard box and chose a filling material appropriate to the gun's power. In this case, a plastic packing tape-coated piece of cardboard sandwiched between layers of tightly wadded-up newspaper keeps the projectiles from going through the back of the target. The crumpled paper toward the front of the target helps prevent ricochets by randomly redirecting pellets as they bounce back off the plastic-coated layer. Don't use plastic packing tape or other tough tape on the front of the target — while a fresh CO_2 cartridge will be strong enough to push the pellets through it, the last few with a waning CO_2 pressure will ricochet back at you and the room. Other possibilities inside the target include a piece of soft wood or a tough rubber material like that used for flooring in weight and multipurpose rooms.

I fixed the target at chest height on an inexpensive easel using masking tape. An old blanket protects the wall behind the target and minimizes ricochets from any stray shots, while a piece of newspaper on the floor collects any pellets that make it through or around the target.

Supplies for creating and maintaining a variety of interesting target shapes are surprisingly simple: masking tape and a red marker. I use masking tape to define spaces for targets, then draw a variety of shapes in red marker, such as bullseye, open circle, and so on. Standard paper targets can also be used. I set the easel up in front of a wall and directly underneath a light.

With both six- and ten-pellet magazines, I can work with a variety of shooting scenarios. The emphasis is on thoughtful, safe shooting. In my setup, I can shoot from standing, sitting, or stair positions at distances of 10 to 15 feet, either single or double action. By varying the lights, I can also mix in well-lit or poorly-lit conditions, and whether or not I'm using prescription glasses.

After shooting, I inspect the target and reconfigure it for the next magazine by covering hits with masking tape and redrawing the red targets as needed.

Safety

Though there is some risk with any projectile, it can be minimized with attention to strict range safety. This means keeping the range clear of people, pets, and objects that might be damaged behind or even in front of the target. I always use eye protection, whether including a prescription lens or not. And, it bears repeating, do *not* use tough plastic or other tape on the front of the target.

Proper handling of the lead is also part of a safe, responsible indoor range. Lead is toxic to the central (brain and spinal cord) and peripheral nerves (in the arms, leg, torso, and face). It is particularly harmful during the development of young brains and bodies. Take this seriously and think about what you're doing, including hand-washing after handling pellets.

One solution is to reuse the lead by melting it. Otherwise, safe and responsible collection, storage, and disposal is necessary. I keep the used lead all in one place, shaking the pellets out of the target when I replace it, along with those collected from the floor, for future reuse or recycling. This is better than repeatedly scattering them into the trash, where they may attain wide distribution and cause harm.

A local shooting range may be able to help with disposing of your lead if they responsibly handle their own spent bullets. Toxicology departments in hospitals and universities may also have appropriate facilities. Where you store your materials and whether there are children around is also important to consider.

Costs

After the initial expense of the gun, your only costs should be your shooting supplies. I get CO_2 cartridges in boxes of 40 for a bit less than a dollar each, and tins of flat — or cone — faced target pellets run \$3-5. For my modest daily shooting practice with one or two extended sessions a month, the total cost is around \$5 a month. I spend an additional \$10 each year on a few red markers and rolls of tape.

Benefits

Using this setup consistently has resulted in marked improvements in my accuracy through proper sighting, concentration, and trigger pull. Watching the groups get smaller, and watching them stay small with consistent practice is rewarding, and a valuable contribution to hand-eye coordi-nation and perhaps brain health (focus, attention, fine-motor, and any kind of real practice). It's a pleasant, brief activity that is easily available and can range from one magazine of six shots most days to more elaborate or special purpose sessions.

Mixing up precision shooting with quicker action can also help me pre-pare mentally for upcoming real-world events. For example, to get in the right frame of mind for the higher amplitude snap shooting of skeet, I'm going to run a few double-action magazines more quickly than I nor-mally shoot, and I'll do it safely and inexpensively in the basement. Of course, this does not fully replicate shooting with rimfire or centerfire pistols, but some of the skills do transfer — and it's fun.

Conclusion

As a final note, I turn the target around so that when I'm not using it, anyone using the basement is not con-fronted with targets and ballistics. I keep the air pistol in a standard zip-pered pouch unobtrusively on a shelf — easily accessible but not out in the open. Pellet tins and the box of CO_2 cartridges are close by and equally discreet. If you have children around, a different strategy will be more appropriate.

Here's hoping that you, too, may find a safely designed home CO_2 pis-tol range useful and fun. Δ

Put a rope handle on your splitting maul

By John Whight

Our house is heated by firewood cut off of our property. Heating with wood requires someone to process it. That someone is usually just me, but my wife sometimes helps. All our wood is split with a wood-handled splitting maul. (I tried a fiber-glass handle for a few years, but it seemed to be harder on the arms and shoulders.) Our wood is cut and split in the middle of the winter, and frozen wood for splitting is hard on the wooden handle of the splitting maul. Usually after a year or two of splitting, the maul would need a new handle. The wooden handle gets torn up right by the connection point of the maul head and the handle. This is where a two-foot piece of old rope comes in. The rope prevents the fro-zen wood from tearing up the handle. It also acts as a shock absorber for when the handle hits the block instead of the maul head hitting the block and usually prevents the handle from snapping off.

The orange tape you see in the picture is fiberglass rein-forced tape. I wrap it around the handle at about the 10- to 12-inch mark. This absorbs the splitting vibration and pre-vents the handle from splitting lengthwise. Two or three wraps is all that is needed. The wooden maul in the picture has really performed well. It has lasted four years and has split 24 cords of wood. With the new rope wrapping on it, I figure to get at least four more years out of the handle. Putting the rope buffer on the handle is very easy. All you need is rope (I used some of my wife's old clothesline), sil-icone sealer, and a knife.

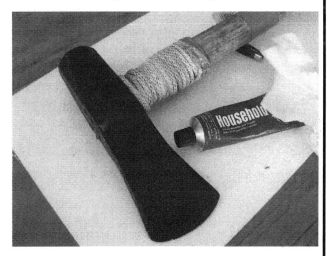

A piece of old rope wrapped around the handle of my splitting maul helps prolong the life of the handle by acting as a shock absorber and buffer against frozen wood.

Directions: Apply a ¼-inch bead of silicone around the handle where it meets the head. Press the rope into the sili-cone before it starts to harden. It really holds the rope in place. Continue wrapping the handle until you have about four inches protected, then apply a small bead of silicone on top of the handle and inter-wrap the rope on itself a cou-ple of times. Trim off the excess rope. After trimming, coat the top of the wrapped rope with the silicone to help pre-vent unraveling. Let the silicone cure for a couple of days before using. Δ

Quick, easy, and cheap tire repairs

By Steven Gregersen

I've repaired hundreds of tires by removing them from the rims and patching the holes. Patches and glue are cheap, but now that I no longer work as a mechanic, I don't have access to a tire machine to remove the tire from the rim. Since the patch must be applied to the inside of the tire, I needed to find a new way of fixing flat tires. Then I discovered tire plugs. For less than $10 I can get the tools and materials to fix five flat tires, and sometimes I don't even have to take the tire off the car. All I need is a tire plug kit sold in most hardware or auto parts stores and a way to re-inflate the tire. (We use a small, portable 12-volt air compressor.) Tire plug kits may vary slightly in appearance, but they all have a few plugs, glue, a tool for rasping out the hole, and another tool for installing the plug. Here's how to use them.

Locate the leak

Many times you can see a nail or other sharp object in the tire or hear the air escaping from the puncture, but in tougher cases you may need to submerge the tire in water and look for bubbles. If you don't have a tank large enough to submerge the tire you can slowly run water over the tread and watch for bubbles.

The tire (in photo 1) had a slow leak that took about three days to deflate the tire. The "large" bubble in the photo is about ¼ inch in diameter. This tire is off my truck and even with 70 pounds of pressure it was still difficult to find the leak. That's about twice the maximum pressure in a standard car tire but within specs for a truck tire. (Note: Never inflate a tire beyond the maximum pressure set by the manufacturer.)

The bad guy here is this tiny sliver of metal that worked its way through the tread and steel belts (photo 2). Its small size will make the next step difficult.

I purchased the kit in photo 3 from a local discount store for less than $10. From left to right you'll see the plugs (the kit came with five but I've used three already), the installation tool, the "reamer," and the cement. You can buy more plugs if you use all of those supplied in the kit. Replacement plugs usually come with another tube of rubber cement. There are different varieties of tire repair kits but the primary difference will be in the plug itself. I prefer the "rope" type plugs over the plastic ones.

Once you've found the hole and removed the nail (or whatever else punctured the tire) it's time to deflate the tire. Remove the valve stem cap and hold the center "stud" down until the tire is deflated. Next, ream out the hole (photo 4). Making the hole bigger may seem counterproductive, but it's a necessary step in repairing the leak. The rasp's rounded tip will follow the hole through to the inside of the tire. Once through, work the rasp back and forth a few times. Now remove it and coat it liberally with rubber cement and run it through a few more times. By now you should have some rubberized "dust" around the outside of the hole.

Thread a plug through the slot on the installation tool (photo 5), liberally apply rubber cement to the plug and tool, then push the plug in through the hole to the depth recommended by the kit's manufacturer (photo 6). In this case they suggest leaving about ¼ inch of the plug above the tire's outside surface. Twist the tool's handle and pull it out of the tire. The plug will remain in the hole (photo 7).

You may trim off the excess, but I usually leave it as is. Now inflate the tire to the manufacturer's recommended pressure and reinstall it on the vehicle.

One of the added benefits of using plugs is that you can repair your tires anywhere. I carry some plugs and a 12-volt air pump in my truck. There have been times when I've run nails through a tire while out cutting firewood. Fifteen minutes of work and I was back on the road again. It was a lot easier than changing a tire on a loaded truck.

Using plugs is an easy, fast, reliable, and cheap way to repair flat tires on your vehicle. The kit is widely available. The only other thing you'll need is a way to reinflate the tire. I often use a 12-volt compressor ($10 and up depending upon the model chosen) but a hand pump will work if that's all you have. There's really no good reason not to have one of these kits on hand. Δ

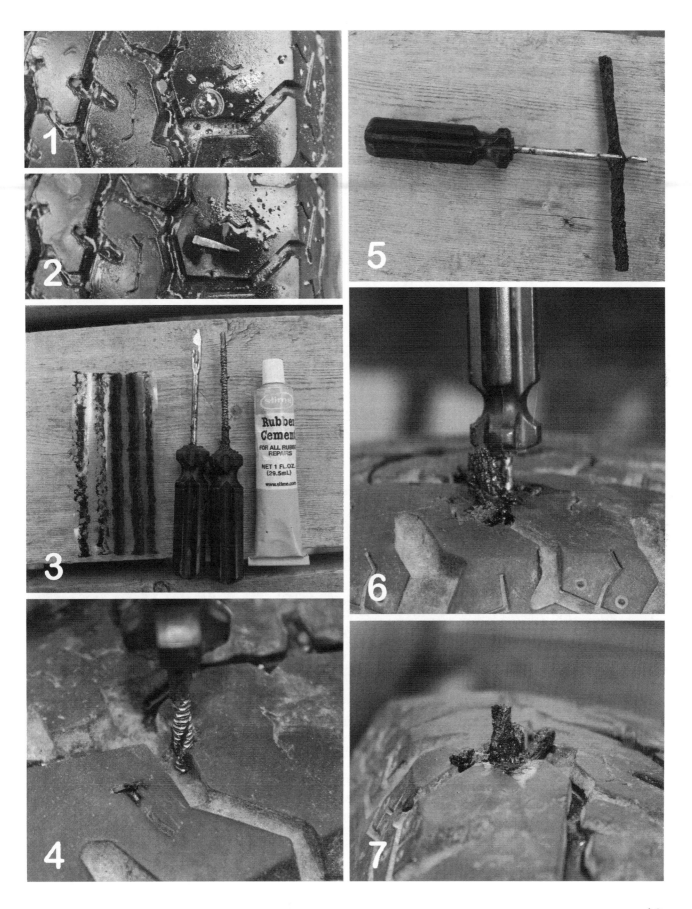

CAJETA –
A SWEET GOATS' MILK TREAT

By Donna Adams

Cajeta is very similar to the popular caramel sauce, *dulce de leche*, made from cows' milk. Cajeta, with its roots in the Mexican city of Celaya, is the goats' milk version. It's a delicious, rich, thick, and dark caramel sauce which is wonderful for making flans, drizzling over granola or ice cream, or for dipping strawberries and sliced fruit into. That's if you don't eat it all by the spoonful as soon as it's ready.

For years, I've been using my fresh goats' milk to make an array of cheeses, yogurts, and other treats, but little did I know all this time I could be making such a delicious caramel sauce with it, and with very little effort.

Cajeta

2 quarts goats' milk
2 cups granulated sugar
2-inch cinnamon stick
½ tsp. baking soda, dissolved in
   1 Tbsp. water

In a large saucepan, bring the milk, sugar, and cinnamon stick to a simmer, stirring frequently.

Remove from heat, add the baking soda, and stir to combine. When the bubbles disappear, return the pan to medium heat. Bring to a brisk simmer, stirring frequently, until the mixture begins to turn golden brown; it takes about an hour.

Continue to simmer until the mixture thickens to the consistency and color of maple syrup — about 20 minutes more.

You need to watch the cajeta very closely until it's really turned dark and has started to thicken up because

A jar of cajeta sauce

it will flash and boil over, just like maple syrup. Don't wander off to check an email, answer the phone, or feed the dogs because you'll have a huge sticky mess to clean up. Trust me, I learned the hard way.

Once thickened and dark, remove from the heat, strain through a fine mesh sieve, and set aside to cool. Store in the fridge in a sterilized glass jar for a couple of weeks.

Cajeta ice cream

After your first taste of this rich, tangy sauce, you'll be hooked and it's likely to become a new favorite treat with the entire family.

Here are a couple of recipes using cajeta:

Homemade cajeta ice cream

This is a very simple ice cream you can make quickly and with only a few ingredients — no machine required. You can mix up the flavors by adding some maple syrup or vanilla.

> 1 cup heavy whipping cream
> ½ cup cajeta
> 1 cup milk

In a small bowl with a lid, stir together the cream and cajeta. Whisk in the milk. Whisk vigorously for a couple of minutes, then seal your container and place in the freezer. After an hour, take out the ice cream and stir well. Put the container back in the freezer. In about five hours your ice cream should be firm. Serve on its own with fruit or a nice slice of pie.

Butterscotch cake with cajeta cream

This is a lovely golden cake, drizzled with sticky sweet cajeta cream. I made this cake while camping on our land in Alaska.

> 2 Tbsp. cajeta
> 2 Tbsp. heavy cream
> 1 cup of butter, softened
> 1 Tbsp. vanilla extract
> pinch of salt
> 1 cup brown sugar
> 1 Tbsp. honey
> 2 eggs
> 1 cup cake flour
> 1 cup all-purpose flour
> ½ cup milk

To make the cajeta cream:

Combine the cajeta and the heavy cream in a heavy-bottomed saucepan on low heat. Cook, stirring constantly until mixed and starting to simmer. Remove from heat. Blend to a smooth consistency if lumps have formed. Set aside.

To make the cake:

Pre-heat oven to 350° F. Grease an 8-inch round cake tin.

Cream butter with vanilla, salt, sugar, honey, and eggs. Beat until well combined.

Add flours and milk. Beat for a minute until fluffy and smooth. Scoop mixture into prepared tin. Bake for approximately 50-60 minutes until golden and a toothpick inserted into the center comes out clean.

Allow to stand for 10 minutes, then turn out cake onto a wire rack. Cool completely before drizzling with the cajeta cream. Δ

Butterscotch cake with cajeta cream

The Last Word

The coming ice age

I'm putting my apocalyptic ice age novel, *Danielle Kidnapped,* on Amazon's Kindle and also producing a paperback version on Amazon's website. (See the ad on page 65.) The next two books in the trilogy will be titled *Danielle Discovered* and *Danielle Betrayed*. They're about the crash of civilization that follows the onset of the next glacial epoch in the earth's history and a young girl's determination to keep herself, her baby sister, and ultimately the man she falls in love with, alive. In a deeper sense, the novels are about what happens to human dignity and freedom, the kinds of people who will prey on you, and the kinds who will become unlikely heroes in the face of catastrophe.

"An ice age?" you ask. (I can hear you laughing.) "It's *global warming*, John! Ask Al Gore."

But here's a piece of news Al Gore isn't going to tell you, nor are a great many liberal academics or media people: We have been in an ice age for the last 2.58 million years — and it's not over yet. The only reason we're not up to our ears in ice, right now, is because we're in an interglacial epoch—a warming period between glaciations—and unless the ice age is actually over, another glacial epoch is coming. When? No one knows. It could start this year or it could start 10,000 years from now, and when it happens it's going to come on fast, and it won't be pretty.

Is global warming real?

The global warming advocates (most of whom are unaware that we're in an ice age) are fond of saying, "The science of global warming is settled." The fact is, like the Theory of Relativity, quantum mechanics, evolution, and anything else that's meaningful in science, global warming is a *theory*. Theories are never "settled." But the trouble with the theory of global warming is that, as it currently stands, it has less scientific footing than those other theories. But that's not the way the politicians, bureaucrats, and capitalists who intend to cash in on it present it. They present it as virtual certainty which, someday, it will be, no matter what we do, but they don't really know. The fact is, there's too little data to determine if the earth's in a long-term warming trend or if any warming that *may* be being detected is just part of the regular cyclic hot-and-cold weather that's been occurring for the last 10,000 years, i.e., when the last glacial epoch ended, or if the ice age itself is ending.

So, to my way of thinking, there are only two takes on today's climate. On the one hand, if the ice age is finally ending, the earth is going to warm up *no matter what we do*. Period. The glaciers atop Greenland and Antarctica are going to melt as the planet reverts to the warmer climate that existed for tens of millions of years before the current ice age began. We could shut off all our factories, stop *all* our burning of fossil fuels, and even stop breathing and we won't — and can't — stop the warming period that's going to follow this ice age.

On the other hand, if the ice age isn't over and there's another glacial epoch coming — and there have been more than a dozen during this ice age — we'd better pray that all the CO_2 we've been pumping into the atmosphere can stop it because that may be the only thing that saves most, if not all, of humanity.

What will happen if an ice age begins?

The scientific evidence indicates that when a glacial epoch begins or ends, it will be obvious in just a few short years. At the beginning of the last glaciation, the British Isles apparently went from a climate much like today's to being buried under 100 feet of ice in two decades. Soon after, much of North America and Europe were under as much as two miles of ice. That includes almost all of Canada and much of the northern United States. Worse, in even earlier ice ages, the earth got so cold that the entire planet was one huge snowball, i.e., there were glaciers from the poles to the equator. Could that happen again? The future is *all* theory. My own guess, based on things too detailed to go into here, is that the next glaciation will not cover the entire planet. But just covering most of North America and Europe, and much of Asia, is going to bring changes you're not going to like.

The liberals are right about one thing: Climate change is coming and the earth is about to either get warmer or colder, but it's going to happen no matter what we do. It always has; it always will.

So, lay in food, guns, and medical supplies, and make sure you wear a sweater because I think the glaciers are coming, again. And read the *Danielle* trilogy. It may give you a hint of how desperate things may get.

— John Silveira

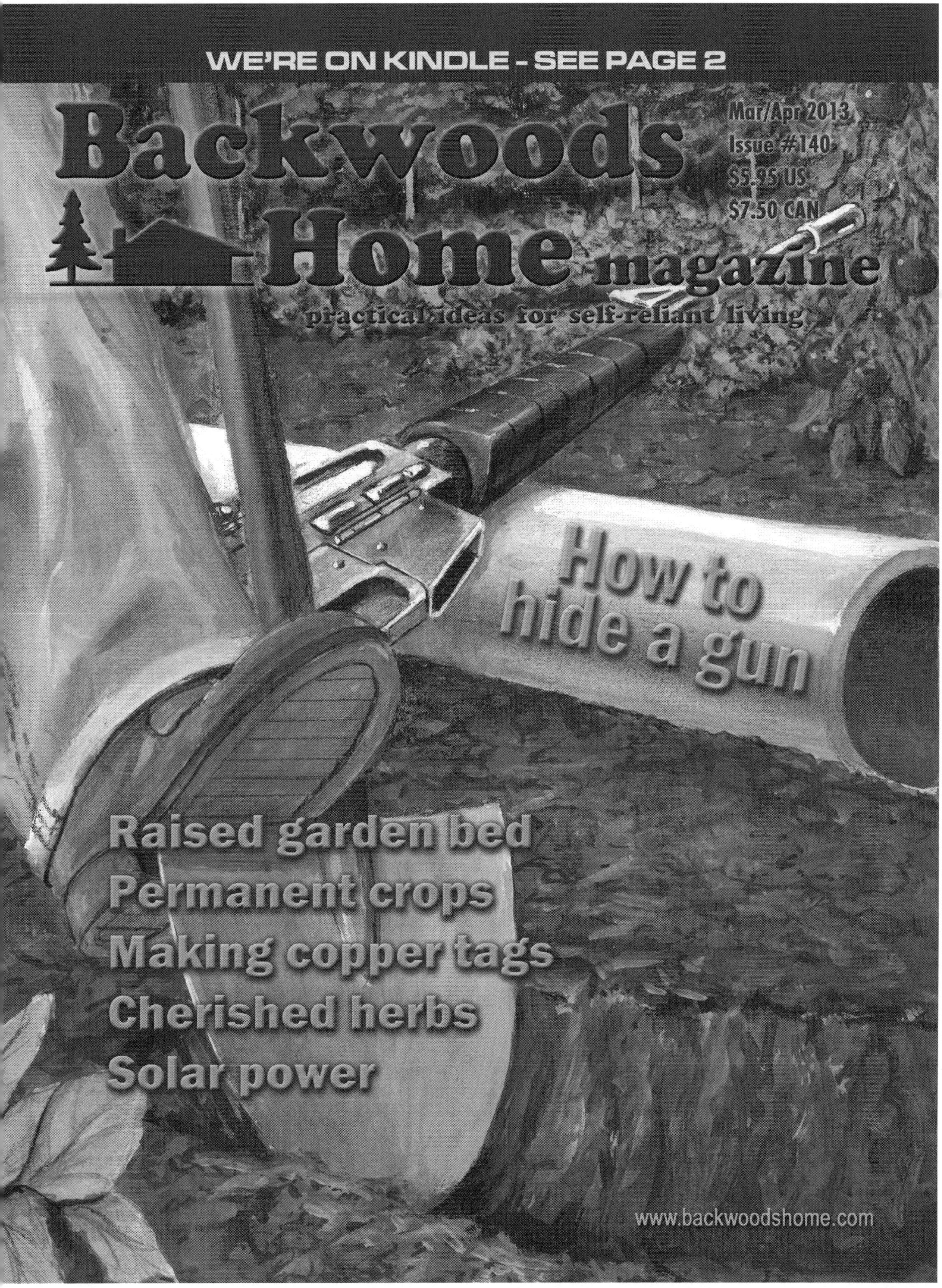
WE'RE ON KINDLE - SEE PAGE 2
Backwoods Home magazine
practical ideas for self-reliant living
Mar/Apr 2013
Issue #140
$5.95 US
$7.50 CAN
How to hide a gun
Raised garden bed
Permanent crops
Making copper tags
Cherished herbs
Solar power
www.backwoodshome.com

My view

The Newtown atrocity and "gun control"

In mid-December of 2012, a mentally disturbed twenty-year-old whose escalating aberrant behavior had gone untreated and unchecked murdered his own mother, stole her guns, and entered the Sandy Hook Elementary School in Newtown, Connecticut. When he realized police were approaching, he committed suicide … but by then, he had already murdered 20 helpless little kids and half a dozen almost equally helpless adults who had been unable to protect the children.

There had been mass murders before in America and elsewhere, some with higher death tolls, but what struck all our hearts with this one was that the killer had chosen the youngest, the most innocent, the most helpless of victims. And the national cry went up, "We've got to do *something!*"

A close cousin to the mentality of "We've got to do *something"* is the mentality of *"Someone* must be punished!" More than even they perhaps realized, a huge number of media denizens, politicians, and ordinary folks looked consciously or subconsciously for a target on which to focus their righteous rage. "Crazy people?" No, it had been politically incorrect to hate them for decades. But what did the media instantly make the symbol of the atrocity? The stolen Bushmaster AR15 .223 rifle, of course. And, from the outset, the mainstream media and certain politicians: Guns, and the people who lawfully owned them. A President who had long been anti-gun but had kept those leanings on a leash during his first term, now slipped the leash at the first opportunity after his re-election.

The result is probably the most focused attack on gun owners' civil rights in the long history of this highly polarized debate. The *Backwoods Home* editorial staff asked me to cover this topic for this issue, so given the short (deadline) notice forced by circumstances, some of what you're about to read now was taken from my series on these matters at the *Backwoods Home* blogs, beginning on December 15, 2012, at www.backwoodshome.com/blogs/massadayoob.

First line of protection

If my first reaction was that of father and grandfather, my second was that of threat manager. My life includes 38 years of carrying a badge and a gun, and more than 40 years now of teaching cops how to deal with lethal threat. The first thing I had to say on the *Backwoods Home* blog was this, from 12/15/12:

"The atrocity at the Connecticut elementary school will not be the last such horror, nor was it the first or even the worst. Go back to the year 1764, in what is now Franklin County, Pennsylvania. The first: during Pontiac's Rebellion in the wake of the French and Indian War, four "warriors" entered a schoolhouse and slaughtered the headmaster and 10 children. The worst: in 1927, a crazed monster beat his wife to death, then triggered a bombing in an elementary school in Bath, Michigan, killing 38 kids and several adults.

"I'll repeat what I said in the Wall Street Journal op-ed section and on the Today show in 1999, after the Columbine High School atrocity: if we simply prepared teachers to handle this type of crisis the way we teach them to handle fires and medical emergencies, the death toll would drop dramatically. We don't hear of mass deaths of children in school fires these days: fire drills have long since been commonplace, led by trained school staff, not to mention sprinkler systems and smoke alarms and strategically placed fire extinguishers that can nip a blaze in the bud while firefighters are en route. In the past, if someone "dropped dead," people would cry and wring their hands and wail, "When will the ambulance get here?" Today, almost every responsible adult knows CPR; most schools have easily-operated Automatic Electronic Defibrillators readily accessible; and a heart attack victim's chance of surviving until the paramedics arrive to take over is now far greater.

"The same principle works for defending against mass murders … it just doesn't work HERE because it is politically incorrect to employ it HERE. After the Ma'alot massacre in 1974, Israel instituted a policy in which volunteer school personnel, parents, and grandparents received special training from the civil guard, and were seeded throughout the schools armed with discreetly concealed 9mm semiautomatic pistols. Since that time, there has been no successful mass murder at an Israeli school, and every attempt at such has been quickly shortstopped by the good guys' gunfire, with minimal casualties among the innocent. Similar programs are in place in Peru and the Phillipines, with similarly successful results.

"Unfortunately, in this country, logic has been buried under political correctness. Those in power whose ego is invested in *brie et Chablis* values that include scorn for the peasantry they accuse of "clinging to guns and Bibles" will never see that logic. Children will continue to die in "gun-free zones" — hunting preserves for psychopathic murderers — and the cowardly murderers will continue to surrender or kill themselves as soon as armed good guys show up … far too late."

Almost a week after that appeared in the blog, Wayne LaPierre of the NRA walked into an ambush of a press conference in which he also recommended an armed presence in schools. The media went ape on him, one of the Rupert Murdoch newspapers printing an entire front page that read "Gun Nut: NRA Loon in Bizarre Rant." (Funny … years before, Bill Clinton had made the exact same recommendation of armed guards in schools … but the mainstream media chose to overlook that.)

Mental health care issues

Anyone who actually deals with the violent mentally ill can tell you that the American system for helping and sequestering them is broken, and has been for decades. It certainly became a focus for the "we've got to do *something*" mentality, but it just as quickly became apparent that both political poles were going to keep arm's length distance from doing anything meaningful in that quarter.

On the left, it was the ACLU itself that was instrumental in closing down asylums, "de-institutionalizing" potentially dangerous mental patients, and "mainstreaming" them back to the streets. The criminal justice community and the emergency medical community can tell you how many of those abandoned people who couldn't live normally found a "mainstream" that swept them into homelessness, living in the streets, and eventually ending up in prison … or dead … after committing horrible crimes that forced their imprisonment, or carrying out violent attacks which forced good people to kill them in lawful defense of selves and others.

On the right, from the tightly-knit military community to the gun owners' groups, there had already been concerns about soldiers suffering from Post Traumatic Stress Disorder being ignorantly and falsely designated as a danger to themselves and others, and stripped of such civil rights as firearms ownership. In a time when even the psychiatric community was vehemently divided as to what did and did not constitute mental illness for the forthcoming DSM-5, the fifth edition Diagnostic and Statistical Manual of Mental Disorders, who the hell was going to be able to predict the next mass killer? As obviously important as it was, this issue was too complex and volatile for lawmakers and editorialists alike to touch.

Logically enough, and in a similar vein, many analysts have pointed out the inescapable fact that a huge percentage of the perpetrators of mass murders have been on psychotropic drugs. "Psych drugs" from Ritalin to Prozac and beyond do indeed have a history of occasional bad side effects. These are often caused by the patient going off them without medical supervision or permission, which brings us back to the issue of unsupervised mental patients. The doctors tell us that something occurs called "decompensation." The epilepsy sufferer who has been controlling his seizures with Dilantin is likely to suffer the worst grand mal seizure of his medical history if he suddenly stops taking it. Similarly, if the paranoid schizophrenic who has

been stable while taking Lithium stops "cold turkey" instead of tapering off, he is likely to soon act out the worst psychotic break of his psychiatric history.

Understood … but we are back to mandated, supervised care issues here, and the huge civil rights issues that accompany them. Let me leave "big pharma" accusations out of it, just as I leave "NRA as a death merchant lobby" out of it, and simply say this: Psychiatric medication is not my field of subject matter expertise. However, there are strong arguments that for every medicated patient who snaps and does something horrible, there are a great many more who benefit from those drugs, as do their friends and families and neighbors. When the thing does more good than harm, it needs to stay. If you think about it, the fact that GUNS do far more good than harm is one of the greatest arguments for maintaining gun owners' civil rights. I see hypocrisy at the edge of the "ban psychotropic drugs" argument, another reason I for one tread lightly there.

Hardening the easy target

It is easy to see why blaming gun owners was the easy choice for political and media people seeking a target for the nation's rage. A general public which does not really understand either firearms or the dynamics of human firearms is vulnerable to the BS that is being spewed by anti-gun extremists and a strikingly sycophantic media. Much of the public apparently still believes that semiautomatic firearms and automatic firearms are the same thing. To be legally correct, "semiautomatic" firearms fire one shot for every pull of the trigger, and only one; a true automatic weapon is a machine gun that hoses a sustained rat-tat-tat-tat for so long as a single pull holds the trigger back. And what of those scary more-than-ten-round magazines which became such an issue after the Newtown atrocity? The question arises, who needs those for anything but nefarious purposes?

Semiautomatic firearms and "high capacity" magazines

There are lots of sound reasons why ordinary law-abiding people need those semiautomatic firearms with magazines that can hold more than 10 cartridges.

"For one thing, defensive firearms are meant to be "equalizers," force multipliers that can allow one good person to defend against multiple evil people. To allow one good person to defend against a single evil person so much stronger and/or bigger and/or more violent than he or she, that the attacker's potentially lethal assault can be stopped. History shows that it often takes many gunshots to stop even a single determined aggressor. Most police officers have seen the famous autopsy photo in the cops-only textbook, *Street Survival,* of the armed robber who soaked up 33 police 9mm bullets before he stopped trying to kill the

The Feinstein bill about to be presented to Congress is nothing less than Draconian in terms of gun owners' civil rights. It would ban firearms that have been responsibly owned by American citizens for more than a century, would prevent their legal transfer to one's designated heirs, and would require many of those arms to be registered as if they were machine guns.

officers. Do a Google search for Lance Thomas, the Los Angeles area watch shop owner who was in many shoot-outs with multiple gang bangers who tried to rob and murder him. He shot several of them, and discovered that it took so many hits to stop them that he placed multiple loaded handguns every few feet along his workbench. That's not possible in a home, or when lawfully carrying concealed on the street: a semiautomatic pistol with a substantial cartridge capacity makes much more sense for that defensive application.

I teach every year in southern Arizona, and each year I see more Americans along the border with AR15s and similar rifles in their ranch vehicles and even their regular cars. There have been cases where innocent ranchers and working cops alike have been jeopardized by multiple, heavily armed drug smugglers and human traffickers in desert fights far from police response and backup. A semiautomatic rifle with a substantial magazine capacity can be reassuring in such situations.

"In the last twenty years, we have seen epic mob violence in American streets. During the Rodney King riots in Los Angeles, Korean storekeepers armed with AR15s kept their stores and livelihoods — and lives — from the torches of inflamed crowds because the mob feared their force multipliers. There have been bands of roving, violent predators as lately as this year during Superstorm Sandy. And the "flash mob violence" phenomenon of recent years has left many urban dwellers picturing themselves as the lone victim of a feral human wolfpack.

"And, if you will, one more stark and simple thing: Americans have historically modeled their choices of home protection and personal defense handguns on what the cops carried. When the police carried .38 revolvers as a rule, the .38 caliber revolver was the single most popular choice among armed citizens. In the 1980s and into the 1990s, cops switched *en masse* to semiautomatic pistols. So did the gun-buying public. Today, the most popular handgun among police seems to be the 16-shot, .40 caliber Glock semiautomatic. Not surprisingly, the general public has gone to pistols bracketing that caliber in power (9mm, .40, .45) with similar enthusiasm. The American police establishment has also largely switched from the 12-gauge shot-gun which was also the traditional American home defense weapon, to the AR15 patrol rifle with 30-round magazine … and, not surprisingly, the law-abiding citizenry has followed suit there, too.

"The reasoning is strikingly clear. The cops are the experts on the current criminal trends. If they have determined that a "high capacity" semiautomatic pistol and a .223 semiautomatic rifle with 30-round magazines are the best firearms for them to use to protect people like me and my family, they are obviously the best things for us to use to protect ourselves and our families."

And, about the Second Amendment

The Feinstein bill about to be presented to Congress is nothing less than Draconian in terms of gun owners' civil rights. It would ban firearms that have been responsibly owned by American citizens for more than a century, would prevent their legal transfer to one's designated heirs, and would require many of those arms to be registered as if they were machine guns. History shows that registration of firearms precedes and facilitates their confiscation by totalitarian and genocidal entities, a pattern repeated heavily throughout the Twentieth century. For that reason alone, it is abhorrent to American values.

History and biology alike tell us the predator preys on the helpless, and that only strongly-armed good people prevail against strongly-armed evil people. It is equally true in the macrocosm of nation-states, and the microcosm of individuals protecting the innocent one (or more) at a time. Yes, there are evil things which jeopardize the innocent. But any impartial, professional evaluation that is driven by logic and history instead of by blind and uninformed emotion tells us that only the countervailing violence of the Forces of Good can defeat the violent Forces of Evil.

— *Massad Ayoob*

Read Massad Ayoob's blog at
www.backwoodshome.com/blogs/MassadAyoob

Garden injuries

By Joe Alton, M.D.

Cuts and scrapes are the most likely wounds gardeners incur (hopefully, not on that green thumb of yours). In many cases, these could have been prevented by simply using hand protection. Start off your gardening efforts by obtaining a good pair of work gloves; most injuries will occur on your hands.

You can expect to be at risk for the following mishaps in the garden:

Minor cuts (scratches): These tears in the skin only penetrate the "epidermis" (superficial skin layer) and become infected on an infrequent basis in a healthy person.

Abrasions (scrapes): A portion of the epidermis has been scraped off, exposing the dermis. You probably have experienced plenty of these as a child.

Contusions (bruises): These result from blunt trauma and do not penetrate the skin at all. However, there is bleeding into the skin from blood vessels that have been disrupted by the impact.

All of the above minor injuries can be easily treated. Wash the wound anywhere that the epidermis has been violated. The use of an antiseptic such as Betadine (Povidone-iodine solution), honey, or triple antibiotic ointment, such as Neosporin or Bactroban, will be helpful to prevent infection. Ibuprofen and acetaminophen are useful over-the-counter drugs to treat minor pain.

Minor bleeding can be stopped with a wet styptic pencil, an item normally used for shaving cuts. The wound, if it broke the skin, should have a pro-

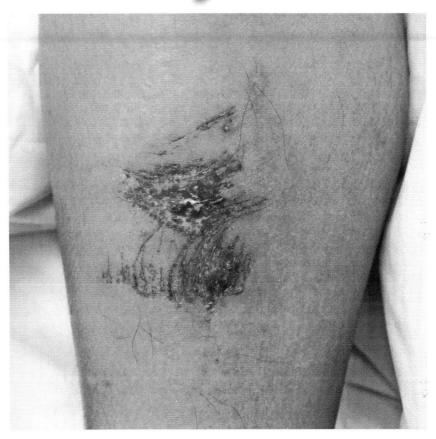

Typical abrasion

tective adhesive bandage (such as a Band-Aid) to prevent infection.

Applying pressure and ice wherever a bruise seems to be spreading will stop it from getting bigger. Bruises will change color over time from blackish-blue to brown to yellow. Bruises may be gravity-dependent and may descend slightly as time goes on.

The Liquid Skin bandage is an excellent way to cover a minor injury with some advantages over a regular bandage. Apply it once to the cut or scrape; it dries within a minute or so and seals the wound. It also stops

minor bleeding and won't peel off during baths. There are various brands (Band-Aid Liquid Bandage, New Skin, Curad, 3M Nexcare No-Sting liquid bandage) and many come as a convenient spray. These injuries will heal over the next 7-10 days, dependent on the amount of skin area affected.

If you have one of the minor injuries mentioned above, why not consider natural remedies? Here's an alternative process to deal with these issues:

1) Stop minor bleeding with herbal blood clotting agents and compress

the area with gauze. Substances that clot blood are called "hemostatic" agents. These include:

• Essential oils — geranium, helichrysum, lavender, cypress, myrrh, or hyssop.

• Medicinal herbs — yarrow tincture, or directly apply cayenne pepper powder or cinnamon powder.

2) After minor bleeding is stopped, the wound should be cleaned with an herbal antiseptic. Mix a few drops of oil with sterile water and wash out the wound thoroughly. Essential oils with antiseptic properties include:

• Lavender
• Tea tree
• Rosemary
• Eucalyptus
• Peppermint

Apply herbal antiseptic to the wound in a 50/50 mix with carrier oils such as olive or coconut oil. Other natural antiseptics include garlic, raw unprocessed honey, echinacea, witch hazel, and St. John's wort.

3) If needed, use natural pain relievers such as:

• Geranium oil
• Helichrysum oil
• Ginger oil
• Rosemary oil
• Oregano oil

Apply 2-4 drops of a 50/50 dilution around the wound's edges.

4) Dress the wound using clean gauze. Do not wrap too tightly.

5) Twice daily, change the dressing, reapply antiseptic, and observe for infection until healed.

An infected wound will appear red, swollen, and warm to the touch. In these cases, the use of antibiotics such as Amoxicillin 500 mg orally for 7-10 days is curative.

Sunburns

Another common medical problem a gardener will be at risk for is sunburn. The severity of the burn injury depends on the percentage of the total body surface that is burned, and on the degree (depth) of the burn injury.

First degree burns are very common, such as simple sunburn. The injury will appear red, warm, and dry, and will be painful to the touch. These burns frequently affect large areas of the torso; immersion in a cool bath is a good idea or, at least, running cool water over the injury.

Placing a cool moist cloth or Spenco 2nd Skin on the area will give some relief, as will common anti-inflammatory medicines such as Ibuprofen. Aloe vera or zinc oxide cream is also an effective treatment.

Usually, the discomfort improves after 24 hours or so, as only the superficial skin layer, the epidermis,

is affected. Avoid tight clothing and try to wear light fabrics, such as cotton.

Second degree burns are deeper, going partially through the skin, and will be moist and have blisters with reddened bases. The area will have a tendency to weep clear or whitish fluid. The area will appear slightly swollen, so remove rings and bracelets.

To treat second degree burns:

• Run cool water over the injury for 10-15 minutes (avoid ice).

• Apply moist skin dressings such as Spenco 2nd Skin.

• Give oral pain relief such as Ibuprofen.

• Apply anesthetic ointment such as Benzocaine.

• Use silver sulfadiazine (Silvadene) creams to help prevent infection.

• Consider antibiotic ointment if slow to heal.

• Lance only large blisters.

• Avoid removing burned skin.

I had a significant second degree burn as a child (they called it "sun poisoning" back then) and my little brother thought it was a good idea to peel off some skin. He ended up with a 10-inch x 2-inch strip of skin in his hands. Do not peel off skin from a second degree burn.

There is a deeper degree of burn known as "third degree." This is a major injury that is highly unlikely from simple exposure to the sun.

Again, an ounce of prevention is worth a pound of cure. To avoid getting burned:

• Do not sunbathe (a tan is *not* healthy).

• Avoid peak sun hours (11 a.m. to 4 p.m.).

• Wear long pants and sleeves, hats, and sunglasses.

• Spend some time in the shade.

If you cannot avoid extended exposure to sunlight, be certain to apply a sunblock. It should be applied prior to going outside and frequently throughout the day. Even water resistant/

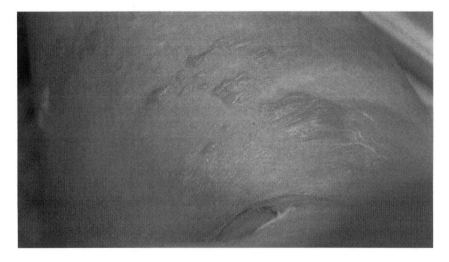

Second degree burn (Photo: CJR80)

proof sunscreens should be reapplied every 1 to 2 hours. Most people fail to put enough on their skin; be generous in your application.

A sunblock and a sunscreen are not the same thing. Sunblocks contain tiny particles that "block" and reflect UV light. A sunscreen contains substances that absorb UV light, thus preventing it from penetrating the skin. Many commercial products contain both.

The SPF (Sun Protection Factor) rating system was developed in 1962 to measure the capacity of a product to block UV radiation. It measures the length of time your skin will be protected from burning.

A SPF (sun protection factor) of at least 15 is recommended. It takes about 20 minutes without sunscreen for your skin to turn red. A product that is SPF 15 should delay burning by a factor of 15, or about 5 hours or so. Higher SPF ratings give more protection, and might be beneficial to those with fair skin.

Insect bites

There so many insects, both beneficial and harmful, in the garden that you can expect to regularly get bitten by them. Insect bites usually cause pain with local redness, itching, and swelling but are rarely life-threatening.

For most victims, the offender will be a bee, wasp, or hornet. A bee will leave its stinger in the victim, but wasps take their stingers with them and can sting again. Even though you won't get stung again by the same bee, they send out a scent that informs nearby bees that an attack is underway. As such, you should leave the area whether the culprit was a bee, wasp, or hornet.

The best way to reduce any reaction to bee venom is to remove the bee stinger as quickly as possible. Pull it out with tweezers or, if possible, your fingers. The longer bee stingers are allowed to remain in the body, the

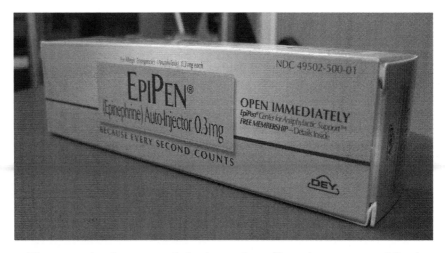

Those experiencing an anaphylactic reaction will require treatment with epinephrine. An EpiPen has a pre-measured dose cartridge for quick delivery.

higher chance there is for a severe reaction.

Most bee and wasp stings heal with little or no treatment. For those who experience only local reactions, the following actions will be sufficient:

1. Clean the area thoroughly.
2. Remove the stinger if visible.
3. Place cold packs and anesthetic ointments to relieve discomfort and local swelling.
4. Control itching and redness with oral antihistamines such as Benadryl or Claritin.
5. Give acetaminophen or ibuprofen to reduce discomfort.
6. Apply antibiotic ointments to prevent infection.

Topical essential oils may be applied (after removing the stinger) with beneficial effect. Use Lavandin, helichrysum, tea tree, or peppermint oil, applying 1 or 2 drops to the affected area, 3 times a day. A baking soda paste (baking soda mixed with a small amount of water) may be useful when applied to a sting wound.

Although most of these injuries are relatively minor, there are quite a few people who are allergic to the toxins in the stings. Some are so allergic that they will have what is called an "anaphylactic reaction." Instead of just local symptoms like rashes and itching, they will experience dizziness,

difficulty breathing, and/or faintness. Severe swelling is seen in some, which can be life-threatening if it closes the person's airways.

Those experiencing an anaphylactic reaction will require treatment with epinephrine as well as antihistamines. People who are aware that they are highly allergic to stings should carry antihistamines and epinephrine on their person whenever they go outside.

Epinephrine is available in a pre-measured dose cartridge known as the "EpiPen" (there is a pediatric version, as well). The EpiPen is a prescription medication, but few doctors would begrudge a request for one. Make sure to make them aware that you will be outside and may be exposed to possible causes of anaphylaxis. As a matter of fact, it may be wise to have several EpiPens in your possession if you have allergies.

Other medical issues for the gardener include spider bites, snake bites, mosquito-borne illness, and pathogens (disease-causing organisms) that reside in the soil. Next issue, we'll explore these subjects.

Joe and Amy Alton are the authors of the #1 Amazon Best seller *The Doom and Bloom Survival Medicine Handbook.* **They have more than 250 articles regarding medical preparedness on their website at www.doomandbloom.net.** Δ

Plant once — harvest for years

By Jackie Clay-Atkinson

Year after year we start seeds, till the ground, plant, weed, harvest, then tear it all out at the end of the season. It's a lot of work, no doubt. But there are some plants you can plant once that will produce a lifetime of food after they are established. Old-timers knew the value of these plants and added them to their new homesteads. Pioneers carefully wrapped and tended baby fruit trees, grapevines, rhubarb, and asparagus roots in their covered wagons. Maybe it's time to lighten your annual workload by adding some of these hard-working plants to your garden. If you do, you'll reap the rewards for many years.

Asparagus can be planted anywhere, in rows, in flower beds, or even in a corner of the lawn.

Asparagus

Asparagus is perhaps the easiest, most commonly grown permanent crop. A small family can easily use 25 roots, planted on the edge of a small garden, along a fence, or here and there among flower beds. More roots will give you plenty for dehydrating and canning; asparagus handles both very well. Asparagus plants are ferny, airy, and pretty. They easily blend in well in the back of flower beds, and don't crowd flowering plants at all.

When you plant asparagus from seed, it usually takes four years before you get an appreciable harvest of asparagus from your row or bed. By planting one-year-old roots, you save a year and can usually begin harvesting lightly in three years. And by planting two-year-old roots, you can

again save another year, lightly harvesting your first good spears in two years. Varieties such as the all-male Jersey Knight, Jersey Giant, and Jersey Supreme produce the most (and fattest) spears, while the cheaper old variety Mary Washington will give you quite a lot of asparagus for very little money. As asparagus is a one-time purchase, I chose Jersey Supreme and Jersey Giant for our plantings and have had great luck.

Preparing your asparagus beds for planting is quite important because your asparagus will be there for a long, long time. Till the soil well, then work in abundant rotted manure and compost. Asparagus requires a lot of nutrients to grow and produce well.

I dig a wide furrow 18 inches deep. If I'm planting a bed, I make three parallel furrows about 18 inches apart. Mound up a little rotted compost every two feet and gently spread the octopus-like roots over it. The crown should be well below the top of your furrow. Pull some more compost/soil mixture over the roots, covering the crowns by about two inches. Your trench should be only two-thirds full. Water well, but do not keep the area soggy.

As the asparagus sends out spears, gently add more soil and compost to the trench until it is even with the soil level. The spears will continue growing. *Never* pick any spears the first year or you will severely damage your plant and its ability to thrive. Be patient. If you've planted two-year-old roots, you will probably get a few fat spears the following spring. You may harvest a few of them to satisfy your impatience, but only take the very biggest ones, and lightly at that. Then let the plant go on to mature; it'll help the root system develop. To harvest spears, cut them off with a sharp knife, just below the surface of the soil. This encourages more new spears to grow and reduces the incidence of disease.

The next year you'll be able to widen your harvesting window to about 2-3 weeks, again only picking the fattest spears. After that, you can pick your spears until they begin to get small or tough. At that point, let the ferns develop and the plant store up nutrients to grow strong roots and prepare for winter.

I mulch my asparagus well every spring before it starts to grow; asparagus pokes up nicely through mulch and the mulch not only prevents weeds but keeps the roots moist during dry spells.

After the asparagus is finished and the ferns have dried in the fall, I toss several inches of rotted manure over the bed. This decomposes over the winter and nourishes the whole bed. *Never* use fresh manure on the bed, especially in the spring. It can lead to *E. coli* bacteria on your fresh spears.

Chives

Chives are one of the easiest and most useful of all small garden permanent plantings. I've seen them planted in pots on the decks of inner-city apartments, brought inside and placed in a sunny window for winter harvest. Because the bushy, onion-like tubular leaves are so attractive, they look good planted on the easily-accessible edges of flower beds. Even the lavender-colored chive flowers are edible.

In the spring, I start my chives from seed in small pots in a sunny windowsill. When the weather is settled, they

Disguised amidst this pretty flower bed are herbs, asparagus, and multiplier onions.

can easily be set out where they will stay. With a little watering and weeding, the plants soon spread out and produce tons of tasty greens. I harvest mine when they are at least four inches tall, before the flowers bud, by clipping the whole plant off with kitchen scissors. The harvested leaves can be snipped into small pieces and added to cottage cheese, soft cheeses, soups, stews, salads, and many other recipes. We like them on freshly baked potatoes and even on mashed potatoes. The chive leaves dehydrate easily and quickly, retaining both their flavor and color, to be rehydrated to use later on. I usually let some of my chives go on to flower and keep others clipped short until fall, when I let them grow so the leaves can nourish the plant over winter.

Jerusalem artichokes

Like asparagus, Jerusalem artichokes (also called sun chokes) are at home on the edge of the garden or tucked here and there around the yard. They are not from Jerusalem nor are they an artichoke, but instead are a member of the sunflower family and native to this continent. They form a large bushy plant and have pretty yellow sunflower-like blooms in the late summer. Under the soil, they form quite large, rounded tubers, almost like potatoes. These are crunchy, sweet, and great additions to stir fries, salads, or eaten chilled and raw! The first time I planted them, my youngest son, David, was two. He asked what those things were, so I cut one in half with my pocket knife, peeled it, and handed it to him. He finished it right down and then proceeded to eat half of the tubers that I had in the bag to plant! He's 20 now, and still likes them, and we have a large patch down in the corner of our garden where I can see their pretty blooms from the house.

Mushrooms, such as these Shaggy Manes, can be introduced into your yard.

Jerusalem artichokes produce many large tubers per plant, along with a bunch of smaller ones. While you dig the large ones in the fall, you never can get all of the tubers. Any that are left in the ground will go on to make new plants, each producing lots of new tubers. If you want, you can also dig smaller tubers and replant them in a different location to increase your planting.

Like asparagus, you can plant Jerusalem artichokes in the back of flower beds, along your house, or across one end of your suburban yard, as a tall privacy hedge that will give you plenty of good eating.

Jerusalem artichokes are easy to plant. Just spade up a nice spot, add some rotted compost, if you wish, then plant a small tuber (or a cut piece of a large one) about three inches deep. Water and keep weed-free. Soon, plants will emerge and begin to grow lustily. They are a tough plant, despite their pretty looks. Once planted, they will produce for years.

Horseradish

Horseradish is one of our favorite condiments; its hot, spicy flavor perks up any meat or fish dish. It is a long, tan-colored root; the leaves that grow from it are strap-like and tough.

Horseradish is so easy to grow that it can become invasive, especially in your garden. It's a good idea to plant it in an isolated area or container — not in the garden or in your flower bed.

I planted my horseradish 200 feet from our home gardens and flower beds; I figure that by the time it invades those, I'll be long gone. Plant your horseradish bed as far from domestic plantings as you practically can. Till up a spot, add rotted compost if you wish, then plant the roots on a slight angle, wide end up. If you're planting crowns, keep the growing crown up. Plant the top of the roots about two inches deep, and crowns just below the soil surface. Water and keep weed-free until growing well. The more you weed and water, the thicker your roots will be and the less work it will be to make your own horseradish sauce; the roots must be well scrubbed or peeled before grating and thicker roots yield more end product than do thinner ones.

I harvest my horseradish in the late fall after a few cold snaps, but before the ground freezes. Using a potato fork or shovel, I carefully dig the whole plant, being careful not to cut the root. Like Jerusalem artichokes, you always leave some small roots behind, and every one of them will grow and spread. Once planted, I don't think you'll ever have to plant horseradish again.

Mushrooms

Few people think of mushrooms as a "vegetable" or as a homestead crop, but they can be just that. With most of today's canned mushrooms coming from China and Indonesia, more and more people are thinking about growing their own mushrooms at home. The indoor "mushroom kits" were a start, but now there are many more economical and permanent sources of a wide variety of mushrooms available for home growers.

Such common varieties as Morels, Chicken of the Woods, Oyster, Lion's Mane, and Button can all be easily grown in small areas on the homestead. You can "plant" them in a corner of your garden, in an unused part of your lawn, or even on the edge of the woods. Some varieties, such as Shiitake and Portabella, require drilling holes in stumps or logs and placing plugs containing mushroom spawn in them. Other kinds only require mixing with compost or wood chips, sprinkling over a raked area, and watering in. There are several companies that deal extensively in mushroom growing supplies, but the one I've dealt with is Fungi Perfecti which has a very wide variety of mushrooms available, as well as a lot of information.

It often takes a while to get a mushroom bed or "patch" started, but once you do, it will last for years and years with little care. Harvests of many pounds of great mushrooms are definitely possible for even the smallest grower.

Onions

While most people think of onions as an annual crop, there are two kinds of onions that are perennial: potato onions and multiplier onions. Multiplier onions are the most common, and are available in many seed and nursery catalogs. Multiplier onions are also known as "walking onions" because they form a cluster of little onion bulbs in the summer, on a seed stalk. As fall lengthens, the stalk bends over and the already-sprouting bulbs touch the soil and root. So, after a while, your permanent onions that started out on one end of the garden, may have moved to an entirely different spot! These onions make terrific spring and early summer green onions and some of the topset bulbs are large enough to peel and pickle. Grandma had several multiplier onions in her asparagus patch, so it didn't matter much where they

Rhubarb is one of the very first plants to provide "fruit" for pies in the springtime. Two plants give plenty for baking, sauce, and canning.

walked. Mine are there, too. You can plant several in flower beds, near the back, yet in an accessible spot, as they are tall, handsome plants.

Potato onions also make top-set bulbs, but the great thing about them is that they also make a "nest" of rather large onions underground. Some are as large as smaller storage onions. They taste great and store very well over winter in your cellar. You can remove the larger underground onions to store or use, taking some of the smaller ones to pickle, as well as some of the larger topset bulbs. Then, by planting the smaller bulbs, both topsets and underground bulbs, you can keep your potato onion planting going forever. Potato onions are available from Potato Garden, 12101 2135 Rd, Austin, CO 81410. (www.potatogarden.com, phone: 877-313-7783)

Rhubarb

Rhubarb is a nearly indispensable plant for anyone wanting to have "quick fruit" for pies, desserts, and preserves. While technically a vegetable, it's called "pie plant" for good reason. Its red and green stalks are tart and succulent, making terrific

pies, jams, and preserves. And, best of all, it grows very quickly into a lusty and useful plant. By planting a couple of two-year-old or older roots, you'll be able to harvest lightly the next spring. From there on out, you'll have all you could ever want.

Rhubarb is a gorgeous plant with huge leaves. It makes a terrific background plant for a corner of a suburban yard (in place of the "fancy" Great Gunnera, highly touted in nursery catalogs). And, as rhubarb is easily divided when it gets a few years old, you can usually get a root or two from a friend for free!

Rhubarb loves plenty of rotted manure, so put an 8-inch-deep layer around it in the spring and fall, and soon your plant will be huge.

There are plenty of other plants you can use in your edible landscape, including a whole array of herbs and fruit, which I haven't even touched on, but by now I'm sure your mental wheels are turning. If you need more information on growing any of these permanent crops, my book, *Growing and Canning Your Own Food*, has a lot more information than I could squeeze into this article. Δ

HIDING A GUN: THE RULES OF THREE

By Claire Wolfe

My friend Jack pulled the car into a grassy clearing. We donned rubber boots, fetched a metal detector and digging tools from the trunk, and headed off along a game trail. Our mission: To dig up and test fire a pistol Jack had buried years ago.

The trail disappeared into a wetland, which Jack crossed with confidence. The muddy water was only about six inches deep where he walked, but I couldn't see the bottom so I waded gingerly after him. It was at this point I discovered that my borrowed waterproof boots — weren't. I squished along after Jack. By the time I emerged onto dry land, he was standing well ahead of me, next to the stump of an old cedar that had been logged a hundred years ago.

"It's buried right here," Jack told me confidently. "Between this stump and that sapling."

I was dubious. The "sapling" wasn't exactly a sapling anymore. It had grown into a mid-sized alder tree. Besides, Jack had history with not being able to relocate a buried firearm. Back in 2004, I had mocked him in one of my Backwoods Home Hardyville columns for that very thing, an SKS he couldn't relocate.

Nevertheless, he set to breaking up roots. I followed with a shovel.

"I didn't bury it very deep," he said. "We shouldn't have too much trouble."

They're at it again. The politicians in Washington, DC, and their media mouthpieces everywhere are in full cry, threatening more restrictions on our right to own guns.

My friend Jack, carrying a metal detector and digging implements, heads toward a game trail that leads to the site where he buried a pistol many years ago. The game trail is right in front of him but strangers would be unlikely to spot it because of the quick-growing blackberry bramble that's obscured it.

In response, Americans are rushing to buy firearms, particularly those that might be targets of the next ban. Without a doubt, many guns are going underground or into other hiding places. When Draconian restrictions take effect, millions more firearms will get tucked into walls, haylofts, hollow trees, and waterproof containers buried in the woods.

There are people who say, "When it's time to bury the guns, it's actually time to dig them up and use them." They have a point. But in fact, there are plenty of good reasons to hide guns, now or at any other time. And we're not talking about simply concealing a gun to have it handy in home, office, or hotel room. We're talking about hardcore, long-term hiding — stashing guns against some urgent future need.

Three reasons to hide a gun

You might want to hide a firearm just to have a spare if your others get stolen or damaged in a disaster.

You might want to hide a firearm if you are a peaceable person who is nevertheless forbidden to own a gun because of some misdeed in your past or some arbitrary state law.

And of course, you might want to hide a firearm if you fear nationwide bans and confiscations but realize that you can't stand alone against the gun banners.

Three types of guns you might want to hide

You might want to hide a spare carry pistol away from your home in case your everyday carry gun is stolen or damaged.

You might want to hide any firearm that's being banned.

Or — as in the Clinton era, the last time people rushed to hide firearms — you might want to stash any cheap, but reliable semi-automatic rifle in a common caliber. SKSs were popular stash guns then. AK-47s are good, too. You probably don't want to tuck away your best battle rifle or your most beautiful, precise, scoped bolt action hunting gun (or, as politicians will eventually call it, your "sniper rifle"). But that's up to what you can afford to sequester and what you want to have at hand if the you-know-what ever hits the rotary airfoil. Because, make no mistake, a buried battle gun is a SHTF tool.

And of course, in all cases, you're also securing ammunition for that gun and any tools you might need to make your well-hidden firearm work for you.

Whatever type of gun you choose, one of the most important steps is to prepare it well for long-term storage. You need to ensure that the firearm you eventually retrieve will be ready to use — and not a rusted hulk.

Three ways to prep your gun for hiding

My friend Jack favors the very simplest method of preparing a firearm for hiding. He leaves the gun fully assembled, wraps it in vapor-phase inhibitor paper (also known as volatile corrosion inhibitor or VCI paper), adds desiccants (see sidebar) to keep down humidity, then places gun and ammo into a tightly-sealed container. His SKS spent nearly 10 years underground in this condition and was perfectly fine — and ready to shoot — once he finally he unearthed it.

Still, such a casual approach horrifies a lot of people — and it definitely lacks failsafes. My own preference: disassemble the firearm, coat every bit with a film of high quality gun oil like Break-Free, wrap each part separately, and *then* seal everything in a waterproof container with desiccants. Some people I've known take the extra step of pulling oxygen out of the container using a vacuum or piece of dry ice. You can also get VCI corrosion-resistant gun bags (including more pricey VCI vacuum bags) from places like MidwayUSA.com or Brownells.

Some old-timers I know disassemble their guns for hiding, but instead of coating parts with Break-Free, they use Cosmoline. Cosmoline is the now nearly-generic term for a brown, gooey, Vaseline-like preservative that's been used for decades to rust-proof firearms. You may have encountered it if you ever bought a surplus military rifle. Commonly, such rifles have been literally dipped in a vat of Cosmoline at some point and will have the goop in every cranny even after being superficially cleaned. You might want to go the Cosmoline route if you expect your firearm to be hidden for a really long time — for instance, if you intend it for your yet-unborn grandchild. You can buy Cosmoline or similar pricey, corrosion-proofing preservatives online. But if you go that way, whoever resurrects the gun will need to have mineral spirits, a soaking tub, and brushes on hand.

Any time you store a gun disassembled, you need to store any tools required to clean and reassemble it. Maybe instructions, too. I know I might forget how to reassemble a gun that I hadn't touched in years.

Three types of storage containers

An appropriate storage container depends on your climate and where you plan to hide your gun.

One of the most popular and secure methods of gun hiding is burying. And the most popular container for burying a gun is ordinary Schedule-40 PVC pipe from any hardware store or plumbing supply store. You'll need a piece of pipe with sufficient diameter and length to hold your firearm, ammunition, and tools (unless you plan to store the ammo and tools separately). You'll also need end caps and sealant. Preferably you'll buy all this where you're not known, and you'll use cash, not a check or credit card. One of the caps should be permanently sealed on. The second cap may be a threaded one with a rubber gasket — but only if you are very sure of an excellent seal. My friend Jack cemented both ends when he buried his SKS. Then he also buried a saw nearby, wrapped in VCI paper, to open the storage tube.

In addition to being buried, a tightly sealed PVC tube can also be submerged in murky water or in a slurry. Painted with appropriate camouflage, it can be hoisted into a tree or into the rafters of a barn or otherwise used to hide its contents in plain sight.

If you're lucky enough to find one at a gun show or surplus store, guns and other objects can also be hidden in old plastic mortar cases, which already have threaded lids with very tight rubber-gasket seals.

A pistol can be hidden in a tightly sealed metal ammo box — again, well oiled and with desiccants added. This is how Jack hid the pistol we were searching for. Because it was going into damp ground, he placed the ammo can inside a larger ammo can, a plastic knockoff this time. He added desiccants to that, as well. Both ammo cans had their lids sealed with caulk. Then he wrapped the entire assembly in a plastic bag and duct-taped the heck out of it. As a final precaution, when he set everything into the ground, he upended a white plastic tub over the rest. This would

After two sessions of digging and detecting, this is what finally emerged from the spot where Jack and I searched. A well-sealed plastic ammo box wrapped in a trash bag and thoroughly duct-taped. Inside the plastic box is an equally well-sealed metal ammo box. Both boxes contain desiccants. Inside the metal box is a pistol wrapped in corrosion-proofing paper. Once Jack finally got all the seals opened, that pistol emerged in ready-to-fire condition.

turn out to be the one truly useless step.

Bonus: If your climate is very, very dry and you're stashing a gun above ground in a spot you're certain will never get wet, you may not need any container at all. Just place your well-oiled, VCI-wrapped firearm "naked" in its hiding place (e.g. inside a wall, under floorboards). Always include desiccants. Even in dry climates, hidey-holes can still get humid.

Three places to hide a gun

The first thing to know is where *not* to hide a gun. Do not hide it in or around your home unless you've figured out a way to make it undetectable — not only to opportunistic burglars, but also to metal detectors, ground-penetrating radar, and even gun-sniffing dogs (yes, there are dogs specially trained for this job; they're actually taught to alert to gun oils, powders, or firing residue).

Of course it's fine — and routine — to place everyday firearms in secure locations around the house. But remember, that's not what we're talking about here. We're talking about the gun or guns that you'll go get when the other guns are gone or when government agents are on a confiscation campaign. So unless you have extensive, difficult-to-search property, or some insanely clever and difficult hiding method, it's best to hide firearms *away from home.*

Three common places are: underground, above eye level, or right in plain sight, but so disguised nobody sees what you've hidden.

Undergound: Because this is one of the most popular, durable, and most secure methods — but also one of the trickiest — we'll spend the most time on it. You've prepared your firearm using one of the three methods above. You've sealed it inside a

PVC pipe, complete with desiccants, ammo, and tools. Now what?

Find a spot where you can be unobserved.

A spot where you can be confident everything is likely to stay undisturbed for years.

A spot where nobody but you is ever likely to spend time.

A spot with landmarks you can recognize — now and 10 years from now.

A spot with lots of old metal objects strewn about is a plus.

So is a spot where the soil has already been disturbed; this makes digging easier and could help foil ground-penetrating radar if anyone became serious enough about gun confiscation to try to use that against you. But disturbed ground is optional and may not be ideal for other reasons. It may be in a place with too much traffic, for instance. You can't have everything, so make your own best choices.

Your chosen caching location might be in the woods. Or an old, disused junkyard. Could be the grounds of an abandoned factory. Or a high sandy ledge in a desert canyon. Could be property belonging to a law-abiding relative (less likely to come under scrutiny than you and your own property).

Now, having found the ideal spot, dig. There are two schools of thought on this, particularly when burying a rifle: vertical and horizontal.

Inserting that precious PVC tube into the ground vertically gives your gun a much smaller — and much less gun-like — signature to metal detectors. That's good. Unfortunately, it's also much harder to dig a deep enough hole. Superman with a manual post-holer could do it. But you may need a mechanical auger.

To further compound the problem, your container should go entirely below the local frost line — which in places like Wisconsin can be as deep as four feet. And that's for the *top* of the container. Bury too shallowly and frost heave could crack your container or eventually thrust it to the surface.

Unburying a vertically buried container can also be a problem. Even after you've uncovered the first foot or so of the tube, the ground is going to cling hard. You might need a winch, a hand-cranked come-along, a rope, or at least a lot of muscle to haul your stash out of the ground. (See Charles Wood's excellent article in Issue #115 (Jan/Feb 2009) of *Backwoods Home* for more helpful details on burying and unburying firearms. He used the vertical method.)

In the Pacific Northwest, where my friend Jack buried his guns, it's less of a problem. The ground doesn't freeze more than a few inches down. Nevertheless, Jack opted for the easy method when he hid his SKS. He went horizontal. This is where having a lot of metal debris in the vicinity really helps to hide the telltale signature of a long, narrow object like a rifle.

After burying, be sure to cover the spot with the native topsoil, leaves, needles, bark, or metal garbage to disguise it.

Above eye level: It's a funny thing; people don't look up. You can hide something in a tree or in rafters. You can hide something in the clerestory of an old factory or warehouse. Or in the trim at the top of a building. Or even in a false gutter on a house. And unless they're really determinedly searching for it, people simply won't see it because they don't look up. Of course, it's still best to use camouflage techniques when hiding firearms in such places. Also, when it comes to trees or old buildings, you should consider these only as temporary hiding places — a few years, at most. Buildings get demolished. Trees are logged or fall over in storms. When you hide in such places, you need to go back frequently to

check on your stash — and that itself can compromise security.

In plain sight: Above eye level isn't the only place you can hide something in plain sight. A reader of my blog told about U.S. soldiers finding a rifle in an old heap of junk in Iraq. Its barrel had been protruding out of the garbage for months before anybody realized what it was. Then they pulled it out — and found that it fired perfectly.

Plain sight doesn't necessarily mean your firearm is "right out there," either. It can mean misdirection. For instance, you could stash a firearm far back on a deep shelf behind rusty old tools. Or in an ancient, obviously broken refrigerator. Or under a rusted truck. Gun parts could lie undetected for years at the bottoms of toolboxes or in junk drawers. (Always remembering moisture-proof containers, vapor-phase inhibitors, desiccants, and plenty of gun oil.)

Take advantage of local features, too. For instance, if you live in an area that has stone walls, you may find that some of these have loose gravel centers — perfect places to stash a gun. Lonely ponds and hollow stumps can be fine hiding places if your container is 100% waterproof. Use your imagination and your local geography.

There are thousands of possible places and ways to hide guns. As my friend Jack learned from his SKS misadventure, the real problem isn't hiding a gun. It's finding it again. Which brings us back to the gun-seeking expedition that opened this article.

As Jack and I dug (and dug) in search of the pistol he'd hidden between the cedar stump and the former sapling, both of us were recalling his last adventure in gun hiding.

Back in the Clinton era, he put his SKS underground — and thought he was being very, very careful about

---

What are desiccants?

Desiccants are essential to the safe, long-term storage of firearms. They are small objects designed to prevent humidity build-up inside sealed containers.

You're undoubtedly familiar with one type of desiccant — the little packets of silica gel crystals that come with everything from electronics to dehydrated foods. You can save those and use them when you need a dry, sealed environment. (They can help keep rust down in toolboxes, among other applications.) Heat them up a little to dry out the crystals before re-using.

You can also get silica gel crystals and make your own desiccant packs. The crystals are sold at craft stores for drying flowers. Certain types of cat litter — only those identified as "crystal litter" — are made of silica gel. Just put the crystals inside a porous container and you're ready to go. A nylon stocking will do. So will a vitamin bottle with a coffee filter replacing its lid.

In a pinch? If you're in a hurry to stash a gun and you don't have time or money to do anything else, just toss a cup of uncooked rice into a sock, tie the sock closed (leaving the rice as loose as possible for greater absorption), and drop it into your container before sealing.

---

memorizing its location. I'll let him tell about that:

"I remember well the 8-inch PVC tubing, end caps glued in place, buried 13 feet northeast of a prominent rock placed in the middle of an old, private logging road. Also marked by a blaze slashed in an alder tree.

"Fast forward 10 years or so. The road had grown up in brush and

Carl Bussjaeger photo: This isolated, metal-strewn patch of woods is an ideal location for burying a gun. The rubble can help hide the signature of a buried firearm from a metal detector. In this case, the nature of the rubble — the ruins of a horse-drawn wagon and a Prohibition-era moonshiner's still — also indicates that the spot has been undisturbed for a long time.

trees. I'll never know where that rock got off to, or the marked tree." He had nothing to point to his hiding spot.

Jack brought in a cheap metal detector. No luck. He traded that in for the best metal detector he could find and went back to work. Days later ... "The SKS and goodies were about 25 feet from where I'd been looking. All clean and dry, in pristine condition."

So now, years later, we were looking for a pistol and Jack had made absolutely sure of his landmarks. That old stump that had been there for 100 years wasn't going anywhere. Yet we dug and we dug. And we ran the metal detector in an increasingly wide circle. And we found nothing.

"I guess you're starting to question my judgment, aren't you?" he finally asked.

"Question it?" I laughed. "Oh no, Jack. I've gone way beyond merely questioning it."

We went back to digging.

Three ways to note the location of your stash

If you have chosen a really secure hiding place, even you may have trouble finding it again. Landmarks? Don't rely on them. Remember, trees fall or get cut down. Old cars get hauled away. Old houses and sheds collapse or get salvaged. Logging roads get re-cut, blocked off, or overgrown. Flash floods wash away even big boulders.

Today, of course, there are super-easy, high-tech ways to mark hiding spots. I can already hear younger readers saying, "Hey, I'll just mark the spot with the GPS in my smartphone." Easy peasy — and foolish. First of all, your cellphone is a tracking device and smartphones are the worst of all. Worse, police are increasingly able to scoop up that data without warrants or other formalities. In fact (and I wish this were just paranoia, but it's not), there's even a

growing network of "locator towers," essentially fake cellphone towers owned and operated by law enforcement whose only purpose is to spy continuously on all of us.

So no. If you value your stash and your freedom, don't even *bring* your cellphone to your hiding spot. If you do bring it, have it turned off and preferably remove its battery. Certainly do not use it to mark a location you want kept secret.

You could mark the spot with a standalone GPS unit which is not known to be owned by you and which itself is kept in a secure location. But even this is a flawed method *if used by itself*, since GPS units can get lost, stolen, broken, or simply wiped of data. A standalone GPS unit should be just one part of your site-marking strategy.

In previous sections, we've treated our "rule of threes" as an either/or. But when it comes to identifying the location of your cache and being able to find it again, one method alone is not enough. You should mark the location of your hidden weapon in three different ways. You should have a compass or a GPS unit (or both) and know how to use them.

First, identify the location visually, preferably using distant and/or virtually immovable features of the landscape. Mountain peaks, waterfalls, house-sized boulders, freeway interchanges, ancient monuments, etc. *Then* you can take note of nearby trees, rocks, and other objects as a backup. It's probably more useful to make note of the terrain than features on the terrain. Note whether the ground rises or falls around your stash, or how many paces the stash is from a nearby hillock.

Second, take compass headings to your cache location from at least three different recognizable objects. Again, you should choose objects that aren't likely to move. But if you take a heading from a power pole, a tree, and a boulder, and 10 years later the tree has fallen down, you still have other things to guide you.

In using a compass you must know the *declination* in your area — that is, how much magnetic north varies from true north. Later, when you're ready to go back to find your hidden tools, you should check the declination *again* (NOAA has a website for this: www.ngdc.noaa.gov/geomag-web/#declination). Magnetic north drifts from year to year. I was aware of this but didn't realize how much the drift could impact caching until Carl Bussjaeger, a writer and a reader of my blog, alerted me. Then I checked. Turns out, over 10 or 15 years, the change in declination in a given area could easily be enough to put you many feet away from your hidden stuff if you don't adjust for it. (It's easier than it may sound, though.)

Finally, you should mark the location with your standalone GPS unit (and remember, *never, ever* with a cellphone). Then, when you get home, transfer those coordinates to a piece of paper or an encrypted computer file (along with your compass headings), and erase them from the GPS unit.

If you write the coordinates down, disguise them in some way. One blog reader who works in security suggested making them look like a phone number and putting them in your address book. It goes without saying that you should hide or disguise your record of the coordinates very well — but not so well that you can't find it years later. But then, that's why you use three marking methods; if one fails, you still have the others.

Three bonus suggestions

In Britain, where they've lost most of their gun rights, rural folks long ago became experienced at keeping their firearms hidden. One of my blog readers from that part of the world suggests getting a roll of heavy-gauge underground cable. Dig a trench

between a house and barn or house and workshop. Lay the firearm, in its waterproof PVC pipe, at the bottom of the trench, then partially backfill. Now run the cable in the trench between the two buildings about two feet above the firearm. Gun grabbers who detect metal may dig down, find the cable, and believe there's nothing else there. "Police and soldiers hate to dig," he notes. Here in the Pacific Northwest, where my friend Jack buried his guns, loggers often leave behind enormously thick steel cable that's used to "yard" trees. It's common to stumble upon great lengths of it on old logging sites. A snaky coil of that would look natural and also disguise the signature of metal underneath.

Hide a gun that not only uses common ammunition — but uses common ammunition of a caliber that any potential enemy might use. In a pinch, you may need to do some "borrowing."

Finally, keep your mouth shut. Don't even *tell* people that you've hidden a gun, let alone *where* you've hidden it. Keep the entire act of caching on a strict need-to-know basis.

That day, we searched and searched for Jack's hidden pistol. He and I dug for an hour between the cedar stump and the now-grown sapling. It got to the point where I feared the young alder might fall on us because we'd chopped away most of its roots. We dug pit after pit around those trees, getting occasional, hopeful blips from Jack's metal detector.

Every once in a while we'd get excited, thinking we spotted a bit of the white plastic tub over the pistol box. But those were just learning experiences: alder roots are white

inside and can look a lot like plastic fragments when you've been chopping at them.

"Next time, use a hot pink container."

We dug until we were thoroughly tired, muddy, and fed up. We never did find the pistol.

Three days later, Jack went back by himself, this time carrying a long piece of sharpened rebar to probe the ground in an organized grid. He found the pistol less than a foot from our network of pits. "We were standing right on it," he laughed. And it was in one of the several spots where the metal detector had given us hopeful, but weak and inconclusive, blips. We just hadn't dug wide enough.

Oh, and just like the SKS before it, the pistol came out of its muddy hole in the ground in prime condition, ready to fire.

For more information, check out these three articles online:

Charles Wood, *BHM* Issue #115 (Jan/Feb 2009): "Bury a gun and ammo for 15 Years" www.backwoodshome.com/articles2/wood115.html

Claire Wolfe, "SKScapades" (2004 article based on Jack's experience finding his rifle): www.backwoodshome.com/columns/wolfe040815.html

U.S. Army Special Forces Unconventional Warfare Manual (see Appendix D for caching information): http://info.publicintelligence.net/USArmy-UW.pdf

Author's note: Thank you to my friend Jack for the trust, the grins, and the information. Thanks also to the Commentariat of the Backwoods Home Living Freedom blog, with a special nod to Carl Bussjaeger for going the extra mile for this article. Δ

Claire Wolfe has written about freedom-related topics for *Backwoods Home Magazine* for years. Read more of her articles at www.backwoodshome.com or read her blog at www.backwoodshome.com/blogs/ClaireWolfe.

What's the difference?

Grid-tied
Grid-connected
Off-grid

By Jeffrey R. Yago, P.E., CEM

Several weeks ago I received a call from a woman in Florida complaining that they just had a power outage lasting several days and her solar system quit working. Although I had no idea who she was and never had anything to do with the installation of her solar system, she was very distressed and I wanted to at least point her in the right direction.

After a few questions it was clear that what she had purchased was a "grid-tie" solar system, and these systems must be "tied" to a working utility grid to operate. These systems do not have any battery backup capability, so their only function is to sell solar-generated power back to the utility grid, which offsets some or all of the metered usage for a given month. Any month the solar-generated power exceeds metered usage of the homeowner, the utility will credit this excess towards a future month when the utility demand exceeds solar generation.

Some states offer tax credits or utility rebates in addition to the federal 30% income tax credits for a solar system purchase. Some states also have very high electric rates which can make a solar grid-tie system economically justifiable when combined with these tax credits and rebates. Unfortunately, if you live in a state with historically low electric rates and no rebate programs, most likely your solar system purchase will never reach a break-even point.

Getting back to our Florida homeowner, either the person selling her

Roof-mounted grid-tie array

system never made it clear to her or she didn't understand the differences in solar system design, but no solar system will supply power when the grid fails unless it includes an inverter connected to a battery bank. In fact, in order to meet various codes and testing requirements, a manufacturer must demonstrate their grid-tie inverter will shut down immediately if there is a loss of grid power. This will prevent sending power onto a non-energized utility line that could endanger utility workers repairing equipment who would not expect the line to be energized from the opposite direction. These inverters must also demonstrate they have "anti-islanding" capability in order to receive

their safety rating. Islanding involves several nearby homes on the same utility line with each having a grid-tie solar inverter.

It is theoretically possible for multiple nearby inverters on a non-energized section of power line to "see" the power feeding back into this isolated (island) power line from other nearby inverters and think the grid is still working. All grid-tie inverters must demonstrate they will not be fooled by any power back-fed from other nearby inverters and will remain off during a power outage. In other words, a "grid-tie" inverter cannot by design, and will not under any circumstances, continue to feed power back into the local utility grid or the home during a power outage.

Since grid-tie inverters do not require batteries, expensive battery wiring, or special battery room design considerations, a grid-tie system will cost less than a solar system that requires batteries. However, do not expect the lower-cost grid-tie solar system to provide emergency backup power during a power outage as it cannot and will not.

One of the newest grid-tie system designs uses micro-inverters. Unlike a typical wall-mounted inverter, a small DC to AC micro-inverter is attached to the back of each roof-mounted solar module. These are plugged into a special weatherproof 240-volt AC buss cable which ties directly into any nearby circuit breaker panel. While greatly simplifying system installation, micro-inverter systems still operate as a grid-tie system and cannot provide emergency backup power during a power outage.

At the opposite end of the solar system design spectrum is the "off-grid" solar system. This system design requires an inverter designed to operate using a large solar-charged battery bank and has absolutely no utility connection. If there are days or weeks of poor weather conditions when solar battery charging cannot keep up with the daily electrical needs of the home, a propane or diesel-fueled generator is started. Since the generator is only used to recharge the battery bank and then shut off, a major advantage of this system design is that the generator may only need to operate a few hours per week when solar output is low.

Since a truly off-grid solar system is the main, and sometimes only, source of electrical power for the home, these systems will typically include a custom-designed battery room full of very large and heavy batteries. However, with the addition of a generator, these hybrid system designs can now size the battery bank for only

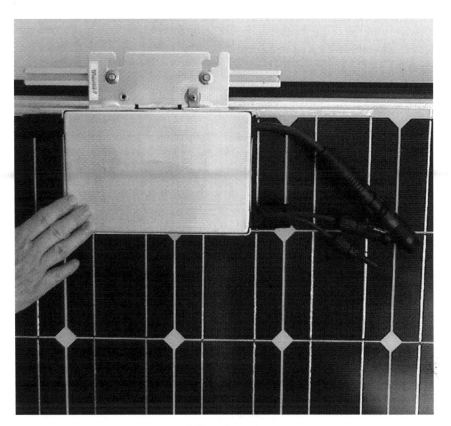

Micro-inverter

a few days of autonomy instead of five or more days typically required for non-generator systems. Although all solar systems can use the same solar modules, solar arrays intended for grid-tie applications usually have all solar modules wired in series to supply 500 or more volts DC to a grid-tie inverter. An off-grid solar array usually has the modules wired in parallel to provide somewhere in the lower 28- to 54-volt range depending on battery voltage.

Newer solar charger technology now allows using a higher solar array voltage than the battery voltage to keep wire sizes and installation cost down, but the National Electric Code still limits battery voltage in homes to 48-volt DC. This tends to keep the off-grid solar array voltage to much lower values than used for a grid-tie solar system.

Somewhere in the middle of these two extremes is the "grid-connected" solar system. Like the off-grid solar

Grid-tie inverter

Grid-connected battery inverter system and generator sub-panel

system, a grid-connected system will include a battery bank and an inverter designed to operate from battery power. However, since this system is also connected to the utility grid, most of the time the system is using the grid instead of the solar array to power the house and keep the batteries fully charged. This system will include a separate electrical sub-panel to supply backup emergency power to all critical loads, which typically include the kitchen outlets, refrigerator, most interior lighting, well pump, television, and any computer and Internet equipment. Except for homes with an extremely large solar system, this sub-panel will not supply power to any electrical heating appliances, air conditioner, electric hot water tank, electric stove, or heat pump. If these must be powered during a power outage, they will be connected to a second sub-panel supplied only by the utility grid and backup generator.

Many inverters designed for a grid-connected application can also sell power back to the utility grid just like a grid-tie system, but are typically slightly less efficient due to the additional battery charging components.

However, most of my clients considering a grid-connected system that include batteries and a generator are more concerned with having a reliable source of backup power for extended periods when a generator-only system would soon run out of fuel. For these clients, any savings on their monthly electric bill from the solar array is considered a bonus to owning this system, but utility savings was not the main reason for their solar system purchase.

Regardless of which system you may be considering, there are many options available. For example, most systems can include remote meters that indicate how well your system is performing and display system alarm or service messages. They can also display how much power the solar array is generating, and how much solar power is being sold back to the local utility. Metering equipment is also available for systems having a battery bank that display battery state-of-charge, rate of discharge, and when battery maintenance is required.

Solar buying decision

If you are looking for ways to reduce your electric bills, your first priority is to replace all lighting and appliances with those having the best energy savings ratings. Concentrate on those lights and appliances that operate the most hours per month, and don't forget that heat pumps, air conditioners, and hot water heaters over 15 years old are much less efficient than today's models, and can provide just as much savings on your electric bill as a solar system if replaced. Once you have done all you can do through improved efficiency, a solar system can provide additional savings each year for many years. If you are primarily concerned with the reliability of the utility grid or constant power outages, then a grid-connected solar system with both battery and generator backup may be just what you need.

Off-grid dual inverter system with AC and DC breaker panels

There is now a national certification for solar installers that is both difficult to obtain and requires continuing education to maintain. Be sure to ask if your solar dealer has a North American Board of Certified Energy Practitioners (NABCEP) certification which will insure the highest level of solar installation qualifications and ethical business practices. Also keep in mind the United States is currently being flooded with very low-cost solar modules and inverters made in China. When comparing proposals between different solar system installers, if one proposal is substantially lower than all others, they most likely are using imported solar hardware. While this may be less of a concern for household products expected to last two or three years, product quality and knowing that the manufacturer and installer will still be in business during the entire life of your system is a concern when most solar systems are expected to last 25 years.

Final thoughts

An easy way to compare cost proposals from multiple solar vendors is to go on the Internet to the free PVWatts website which is maintained by the National Renewable Energy Laboratory (NREL). By answering a few questions about the size and type of solar system you are considering and the proposed location, this easy-to-use website will generate an instant estimate of the month-by-month and yearly projected solar power generation and electric bill savings. Since many solar installers also use this web site to generate system payback estimates for their proposal to you, you can input your own more realistic values since some marketing proposals may have highly questionable system efficiency and utility cost data to make their proposals more attractive. In fact, while PVWatts is considered very accurate if realistic data is given, I have actually reviewed proposals from solar contractors that used system efficiency values greater than perfect, and electric rates at cost levels that may never be reached during the life of your system.

Go to: www.nrel.gov/rredc/pvwatts

Battery-based inverter systems may require a separate battery room and heavy tray batteries.

Jeff Yago is a licensed professional engineer and certified energy manager with more than 30 years of experience in the energy conservation field. He has extensive solar photovoltaic and emergency preparedness experience, and has authored numerous articles and texts. His website is www.dtisolar.com. Δ

Low-cost raised beds

By Lucas Crouch

I don't have a perfect garden, but since I started gardening seven years ago, I have worked toward that goal. Experimentation and luck have helped me develop a raised bed that is pretty close to ideal for my circumstances. It might be what you're looking for, too.

In my garden, I have tried to make sure things are inexpensive, durable, and as organic as possible. And since I live in coastal Florida at an elevation of a few feet, it must also be termite-proof and resistant to flooding.

The materials you'll need are silt fencing, schedule 40 PVC pipe, and metal fence stakes (T-posts). You could just use PVC in the corners, but the fence posts do have some advantages. If you have critter or pet problems, you can use these taller corners to hold up fencing. It also helps to keep a garden hose from getting into the beds and damaging the plants. A fence post on the end of the bed can also be used to hold a wire trellis. You could also use wooden stakes, but I prefer products that last several years

Inexpensive and durable, silt fencing makes nice raised beds. Fencing can be attached to the taller fence stakes in the corners.

and do not invite termites near my home.

Silt fencing is available at your local big hardware store. It is environmentally safe, does not degrade in the sun, and will keep dirt from washing out the sides of the bed. It comes in a 3 x 50-foot roll and costs about $20.

PVC pipe is about $2 for a ten-foot piece. I recommend schedule 40 pipe

because it will hold up better to a hammer when you drive it into the ground. Granted, PVC is not a food-grade plastic, but since it is used on the exterior of the bed, any chemicals that leach into the bed should be minimal.

Cut the roll of silt fence into three 1-foot sections. The edges might fray, but this will not cause any issues. Cut the PVC pipe into 2-foot long sections, angling one end so that it will drive into the ground easier. Leave the other end flat.

Now you are ready to lay out your garden. Start with the corners. Drive the PVC pipe about halfway into the ground. Once you have the four corners in, roll out the silt fence. To help hold it in place, I used some twine to wrap the silt fence to the corners. But overlapping a foot or so of material will also work. Once the silt fence is in place, add additional pipes on the outside of the silt fence. The bottom three inches of the silt fence should lay on the ground toward the inside of the raised bed. That will leave about nine inches for your side of the bed.

Additional PVC can be used as a trellis.

This will keep dirt from running out underneath the silt fence.

If you wish, you can add a weed liner at this point. I find it useless against dollar weed, which makes up half of my yard, but you may have better luck. You can add newspaper, shredded paper, or whatever you prefer.

Now add the dirt. The dirt will push the lining out, but the pipes will hold the lining in place. (The more pipes you use, the fewer bulges you will have.) I put down a layer of grass clippings on the bottom followed by a layer of dirt, and then topped it off with compost.

I use different-sized beds in my garden. For my pole beans and tomatoes, I prefer a 24-inch bed. For peppers, squash, beets, broccoli, and others, I use a narrower bed.

This type of raised bed has some advantages. Since I can reach my plants from either side, I never have to walk on my garden. The soil stays loose without ever using a hoe or tiller. Pulling the occasional weed also helps to aerate the soil.

Because the beds are raised with space between them, you won't be adding dirt where you don't need it. Walkways are for walking, not growing. This inexpensive style of raised bed will save you money. By giving the water plenty of places to go, flooding will also be minimized.

There are some things I wish I had done when laying out my garden. Leaving space for a lawnmower between the rows would have been helpful. If you use a weed eater between the rows, be careful that you don't cut the silt fencing. Patches are easy enough to make, but who wants the extra work?

There is no such thing as a perfect garden. But over the last seven years, I have become quite proud of mine. It puts food on my table, food in my pantry, and gives me plenty of pictures for social media. It does exactly what a garden is supposed to do. Δ

A Backwoods Home Anthology
The Fifth Year

* Odd-jobbin' can be a country goldmine
* How to keep those excess eggs
* Make better pizza at home than you can buy
* How we bought our country home
* Cooking with dried fruit
* Garden huckleberries
* Short season gardening
* The 10 most useful herbs
* Simplified concrete and masonry work
* Raising sheep
* Free supplies for your homestead
* Learning in the pickle patch
* Good-bye old friend
* Three great bread recipes
* Firewood: how and what to buy
* A bit about ducks
* Choosing superior bedding plants
* How to build the fence you need
* Improving poor garden soil
* Learn the basics of wall framing
* Build a fieldstone chimney
* Sun oven cookery
* Determined woman builds distinctive vertical log studio
* Turkeys — fun and profitable and not as dumb as you think
* Raising fish in the farm pond
* You have to learn to shovel crap before you learn to be the boss
* How to build a low-cost log lifter
* Choosing and using a wood cookstove

From waterbed to hotbed

By David Zaugg

As far as I know, I'm the only person that is using a used waterbed as a germination bed in the greenhouse. Living in Utah's colder climate, I like to take advantage of natural heat sources in the early spring. By utilizing this easy setup, I can simultaneously get an early start on my seeds *and* save a few dollars on my gas bill.

Years ago, I noticed the growth of grass and weeds in the early spring on the south side of our machine shed. To take advantage of this reflected heat I placed three 4x8-foot cold frames there to raise some bedding plants. After a couple of years, we erected a 20x36-foot lean-to hoop greenhouse using PVC pipe. The east and west ends were framed with windows and a ventilating fan. We covered the PVC pipes with a double greenhouse cover and used a green-

Here you can see the railroad ties that are the foundation of the south side of the greenhouse. We drilled holes in the ties and drove rebar lengths to anchor the ties and the lower 1-inch conduit pipe. The upper ends of the 1-inch pipes are slipped into 1¼-inch conduit pipe which forms the top of the greenhouse support and is anchored to the side of the machine shop. The bends in the lower pipe were made with a pipe bender. This cover was $100 from Growers Supply and should last six years. The north wall of the greenhouse is the machine shed with straw bales stacked against the wall in the shed for insulation, since the shed is open to the east and unheated.

Raised beds are built in the middle of the greenhouse, and water-filled drums run along the north side to absorb heat. The fan controller is by the thermometer. The wrought iron supports came from salvage and are good for interior supports since they don't shade the growing plants.

house inflation blower to blow heated air between the covers for insulation. We bought a used downdraft furnace for $30 and piped the heat to the far end of the greenhouse. The cold air return sucked the cooler air back to the furnace — setting up our greenhouse circulation. We had to bring a 1.5-inch gas line about 120 feet from the house gas meter. We made a 6x24-foot raised bed in the middle for winter crops. That first year, we put boards over the furnace pipe on the south and built a long plant stand on the north.

Under the plant stand there are fourteen 55-gallon poly drums full of water and painted black and brown to aid heat absorption. For a few years I used some homemade germination boxes with heated cable under sand to propagate my seedlings. We added a few shelves on the north wall and covered the raised beds in the middle with pallets.

We grew 225 flats of tomatoes, peppers, and other vegetables that we planted out in the field. When August came along we were busy picking, packing, and delivering produce to more than seven grocery stores. We got about four years out of that cover before the inner layer shredded due to chemical deterioration along the PVC pipe. I was told that a latex paint barrier would solve that, but it didn't. I painted the PVC but the next cover deteriorated too. Since I had overheated the greenhouse one summer, the PVC pipe was convex instead of concave, so we replaced it with lengths of metal conduit pipe and that solved the deterioration problem. I wasn't happy with the unreliable cable-heated germinators so I purchased a couple of waterbed heaters at a thrift store and used 3-foot lengths of 16-inch Nu-Flex irrigation pipe as small waterbeds.

I just elevated the ends of the pipe to keep the water in. This gave me nice even-heated germination beds and worked much better than the unreliable cable. My experience with my little waterbed germinators told me what to look for and I eventually found a king-size waterbed for $50. I built a platform for the bed using the frames that came with it, then lined it with black plastic. I placed the heat pad under the bladder and filled it with water. I had plenty of room to germinate all my seedlings with room to spare for 20 flats of bedding plants. My waterbed has worked great as a seed germinator. The thermostat turns off the heater in the morning as the sun takes over the heating of the water, and my ventilation fan keeps the air temperature in the greenhouse at about 80° F during the day. I haven't turned the gas on for the past three seasons but my bedding plants thrive with warm roots. When real

A sturdy platform is required to support the weight of the water. Mine is supported by a piece of plywood on top of 2x6s on cement blocks. I drain it each fall and refill it at the beginning of the germination season

cold weather is forecast I'll throw a light cover over the plants to keep in the heat. A commercial heating mat large enough for one flat is listed at $36.95 in the greenhouse supply catalog. They are asking $55.95 for a two-flat size and $92.95 for a four-flat size. I really haven't figured out

These sugar snap peas were planted in late January or February, and supported so they could grow to the top of the greenhouse and start back down again. Salvaged windows fill the end of the greenhouse, which is built on a foundation of cement blocks.

We started 225 flats of tomatoes, peppers, and other veggies in the greenhouse.

several batches of greens through the winter.

On the 5th of February, we harvested spinach, lettuce, and chard from the unheated greenhouse, which I'm treating as an unheated "high tunnel" for the winter. Data from USU Extension shows that we could triple our production if we placed row covers over the tender plants in the high tunnel. Yesterday I planted lettuce, spinach, radishes, sugar snap peas, and potatoes. These will be producing about the time our neighbors start to plant their gardens. We are at 4,200 feet elevation but have had a mild winter this year. About the first of March, I will unpack the waterbed and set up my germination bed for another spring season. I'll grow an early garden in the raised bed and use the table on the north to grow out any bedding plants that won't fit on the waterbed. I certainly won't be growing 225 flats this year, but I could! Δ

how much electricity my waterbed/hotbed is using but the heat pad is rated at 360 watts. Last September, I planted some winter greens in the greenhouse raised beds. We picked

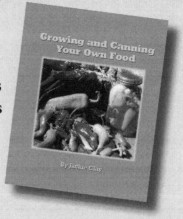

Ask Jackie

If you have a question about rural living, send it in to Jackie Clay and she'll try to answer it. Address your letter to Ask Jackie, PO Box 712, Gold Beach, OR 97444. Questions will only be answered in this column.
— Editor

Incubator

Can you tell me what the temperature control should be in a still air incubator to hatch chickens? I have the incubator but no book to go with it and I don't want to be guessing and lose the time and money that it takes to buy the eggs at the price hatcheries charge now.

Brenda Jarrell
Varnville, South Carolina

The temperature used in most still air incubators is 102° F. Incubating eggs isn't hard but is a bit fussy. I'd suggest going somewhere or calling a hatchery that sells incubators and getting a copy of an incubator instruction booklet so you don't make a mistake and lose chicks, time, and money.
— Jackie

Introducing baby chicks

I'd like to know how you go about integrating the newer clan of baby chicks to the older clan of layers. Do you just wait until the youngest are big enough to protect themselves or what?

Linda Waltman
Sweet Home, Oregon

We partition off the coop and when the chicks are well feathered out we put the newbies in one side and the older birds in the other side. That way the old birds can see them but not attack them. After a couple of weeks we take down the partition at night and let the birds mingle in the morning with supervision to make sure the older birds don't get overly aggressive. There's always some chasing that goes on but we don't let it get out of hand. We have always had good luck doing this. Make sure the chickens have plenty of room so the chicks can run away from any aggressive birds. *— Jackie*

Best homestead chickens

What breed, in your opinion, are the best foragers, are reasonably broody, are prolific large brown egg layers, cold hardy, and can be a dual-purpose chicken. Just a good all around homestead chicken, I'm not askin' for the world am I?

V. Ginger Borgeson
Johnstown, Colorado

I think the chicken breed that would best suit your needs is the old-fashioned Dominique. It's been around for hundreds of years and excels in foraging as well as being able to brood its own eggs, lay big brown eggs, and is also cold hardy, having a rose comb. It's the old "pioneer" homestead breed and should do well for you. *— Jackie*

Canning sausage

A neighbor of mine is making sausage and is wanting to can it. However he wants to can it raw in the jar (fill a PVC pipe and push it into the jar) and not in patties like you suggest. Is this safe to do or should I go advise him against it. This neighbor also built his pressure canner from an old hydraulic tank cleaned out real good. It holds around 70 quarts at a time. It works great and

Jackie Clay

reminded my mother of the old community canners when she was a kid.
Marshall Owen
Pine Bluff, Arkansas

Packing raw ground meat into a jar and processing it is no longer considered safe. It's a very dense food and it's difficult to ensure that the center of the food gets heated sufficiently hot enough for safe processing. When you lightly fry patties then put them in a jar they can move about during processing as the steam pressure in the jar wiggles them. Therefore, they can be heated sufficiently in the middle. An alternative is to break up the sausage and lightly pan fry it like ground hamburger, then pack it into the jar.

It sounds like your neighbor is highly inventive. I do hope he installed a couple of safety valves or plugs in his pressure canner so it can't over-pressure. That would make a big bang!
— Jackie

Corn mushroom

This is in regard to the article on corn. (Issue #136, July/August 2012) In a Mexican restaurant they offered corn mushroom. I ordered it. It was sauteed with garlic. The owner said this was very popular in Mexico. It is the fungus that grows on an ear of

93

corn. It was served with a corn tortilla and it was good. Do you use this fungus? It would be nice to be able to use something we always threw away.

Joe VanBiber
Blue Springs, Missouri

The "corn mushroom" is actually smut, that black, ugly corn fungus. Corn mushroom sounds nicer, doesn't it? I have cooked with it but haven't for years as smut isn't as common here in Minnesota as it was in New Mexico, where I learned to eat it. You just cut it off when it is still quite young, before it dries and the spores get dusty. Sort of like cooking with puffball mushrooms. Eating smut is sort of like eating garden weeds like purslane, pigweed, and lamb's quarter. It sure makes you feel good to be eating something you used to hate.

— *Jackie*

Old beans

My wife and I love dry beans, but lately we have had some trouble getting them to soften when we cook them. We usually do an overnight soak but they just won't soften up. What are we doing wrong? There is so much conflicting information out there, like not salting them until you are about to eat them, not adding anything acidic until they soften, adding baking soda, cooking them longer, and some people claim that the beans are too old. This last one worries me because we have a pretty large stockpile of beans in food-grade buckets with gamma lids. Is there a chance these will go bad or get too old to cook? Anyway, the internet failed me in my quest for an answer so I thought I'd ask the master!

Russ Hall
Austin, Texas

I think you have old beans. Now this isn't a terrible thing. When mine get old and don't want to soften, I just use them to can up a recipe like canned pintos, baked beans, bean soup, etc. They will soften when canned and then they'll be handy for instant use for years to come. You can cook them longer, too, should you want to only use dry beans and not can them. But they usually need to be boiled quite a bit longer even if you plan on baking them after initial cooking. (Crock pots work wonders as does sitting a Dutch oven on top of the wood stove to simmer the beans for hours.) — *Jackie*

Making cheese

I have been studying the how on making cheese. Nowhere can I find how to make cheese without a store-bought culture. Is it the same way as yogurt? In the past I know they didn't get it online. So how do you start to make a cheese without the store-bought starter culture? Also are soft cheese culture methods different than hard cheese?

William Rusch
Homestead, Florida

I seldom use purchased culture to make my cheese. I usually use cultured buttermilk instead, then I can keep the culture going in my own buttermilk, indefinitely. Some cheeses need specific other cultures that must be bought and even these can be recultured over and over again so you don't need to keep buying cultures. Some soft cheeses like lemon or vinegar cheeses don't need a culture at all. But most do and the buttermilk works fine. I'd suggest picking up a copy of Mary Jane Toth's book, *Goats Produce Too*, which is full of cultured cheese recipes which don't require purchased cultures. If you are using cow milk, the recipes are the same. I do buy my rennet in liquid form, but you use very little and it is inexpensive. Even that can be made with either vegetable sources or from a piece of a very young calf's stomach lining if you wish. — *Jackie*

Sick sheep

I found one of our sheep sluggish this morning. He did not want to get up on his feet, but slept on and off. I tried to find some illnesses that he could have, but came up only with over eating. I gave him some bicarbonate sodium (2 teaspoons in a quart of water). 3 hours later he died. The other 3 females seem to be alert as usual. They have access to a big round bale of alfalfa outside, and get a cup of oats each. Question: Could overeating actually kill him? Do I need to take precautions for the girls?

Is the meat still usable — like dog food? I presume it would not be safe for human consumption, since I don't know why he died.

Tary Flemino
Madison, Minnesota

When an animal acts "off," like your sheep, take his temperature rectally. (Make sure you know the normal temperature of your homestead animals.) Often such an animal is suffering from some type of infection such as pneumonia, which is often fast-acting and can kill quickly without immediate antibiotic therapy via inter-muscular injection. I really don't think it was overeating. I'd keep a close watch on your ewes and at the first sign of lethargy or another symptom such as snotty nose, being off feed, etc., take their temp and call your vet.

No, I wouldn't feed the meat to your dogs. — *Jackie*

Growing Brussels sprouts

We're just pulling the last of our Brussels sprouts and have a question. I have read that some people remove the leaves from the stalks when growing Brussels sprouts through the summer. Is this something you do or recommend?

Wendy Hause
Gregory, Michigan

As the first sprouts get big enough to harvest, I usually start pulling the leaves off the bottom of the plant, leaving those on the very top. As I harvest more, more leaves go. I think this helps put more strength and growth into the remaining smaller sprouts. — *Jackie*

Naked oats

I hate to ask you a question to which you have already posted an answer, but I have searched your blog to no avail on finding it. You mentioned a type of "naked" wheat for homesteaders that was easy to clean. Would you please tell me the name again and where to purchase it.

R. Berry
South Carolina

Not naked wheat; naked oats. Wheat is very easy to clean. It falls right out of the husk when you thresh it. Oats do not, so growing "naked" or hulless oats is a great idea for homesteaders. These oats are *Avena nuda* and are sold by seed companies under various names such as Nuda and Streaker. — *Jackie*

Canning milk

We recently got to meet you at the self-reliance expo in Arlington, Texas. We just bought a jersey cow and have lots of milk. I have your book, "Growing and Canning Your Own Food." You have a recipe in there on canning milk. I canned some milk using the water bath method. What is the shelf life of this milk? Also, is the cream supposed to rise to the top in the jars after canning?

Teresa Clepper
Hamilton, Texas

Like other canned foods, milk is good for years. Canned milk isn't really like fresh milk in appearance or taste — more like condensed milk. Yes, it often separates in storage. Just shake up the jar before opening it.

Have you ever made cheese? With such a good cow, you really should try some of the easy cheeses like *queso blanco* made with vinegar or soft French cheese made with only buttermilk as a culture and a small amount of rennet to set the curds. It only takes a few minutes and is very easy. Once you try soft cheeses, which you can use like cream cheese, you'll want to try some hard cheeses like Mozzarella (also very easy) and cheddar. Two good books are *Goats Produce Too* by Mary Jane Toth and *Home Cheese Making* by Ricki Carroll. Have fun! — *Jackie*

Storing onions

Each year we grow onions, 200-300, and store them (strung up) in the cellar. This year the majority are going bad, both the yellow and the white ones. What did we do wrong?

Emmy Lou Fairfield
Moyie Springs, Idaho

Did you have the drought this summer/fall? We did and even with watering our onions were stressed, making them susceptible to neck rot, a common fungal disease in onions. When it's dry, you water (of course) and when you water your garden just prior to harvesting your onions (or it rains quite a bit), the fungus attacks the onion near the base of the leaves and works its way down into the onions' scales, causing them to get spongy and soft, finally rotting the whole onion. In drier conditions at harvest, the fungus is kept in check and seldom causes any problems.

This year, be sure to have your onion rows nice and dry for the week prior to harvest and don't let the onions remain in the garden after the tops have gone brown. — *Jackie*

Pear juice

I had a lot of pears this past summer and was wondering if I could use the peelings and cores to make pear juice.

Gale Heny
Powell, Wyoming

Lucky you! My pear trees are still babies and I won't see a pear for a couple more years. Yes, you could make pear juice using peelings and cores but it would take a whole lot of them to get a pint of juice. This is why most folks cook up diced whole pears (peel, core, and all) to make pear juice. You just simmer them slowly in a large pot using a bit of water or juice (apple or pear) to prevent scorching until the pears begin to cook and produce their own juice. You'll also get a whole lot more juice if you use a steam juicer like a Mehu-Liisa (which our last seminar attendees bought us for a thank-you gift!). — *Jackie*

Sweet corn and beans

We decided to make use of some of our land that was doing nothing for us, and my husband tilled up a very large space for another garden. We have a short growing season in western Washington, with temperatures that don't get very hot, and we're wondering, what's the best type of sweet corn you would recommend? Also, I've always canned my green beans, but my husband doesn't like them because they come out kind of mushy. I follow the directions for time and pressure, so I was thinking that maybe I'm not growing the right kind of bean that would be good for canning. Do you have any favorites for canning?

Julie McCord
Port Orchard, Washington

We usually don't have hot summer temperatures either so we must grow a shorter-season, cold-tolerant variety. We've had good luck with *Quickie* (a bi-color), *Seneca Horizon*, and *Northern Extra Sweet* (both yellow).

95

Northern Extra Sweet is a super sweet corn and must be isolated from other corns growing in your garden to avoid cross-pollination and lack-of-taste corn.

Why don't you try *Provider* green beans. That's our old standby. I can always count on them coming out perfect and tasting great when canned. There *is* a great difference in the taste of different varieties of green beans! *Provider* is an old garden bean that not only provides plenty of beans to eat and can but has thick meat, no strings, and great flavor. I hope they do well for you too. — *Jackie*

Cracking nuts

I would like to purchase a nutcracker that is able to crack black walnuts. I have an abundance of the black walnuts and some of my butter nuts will be ready. I have looked in some back issues but was unable to locate the ads.

Also, do you recall a book called "Acorns & Eat 'Em"? I wish to use some of them for flour to cook with this winter.

> *Guy Hudson*
> *Red Creek, New York*

Many seed catalogs now carry great nutcrackers that make use of leverage to easily crack walnuts and other nuts leaving large pieces and smiling folks around the table. I can sure remember using the hammer and rock method and sending nutshells flying all over the room and picking out tiny, tiny pieces. I used one of the newer leverage-type nutcrackers to crack pecans at my friend Juanita's ranch in New Mexico. We did it off and on all winter while visiting around the kitchen table. They sure work fast and nice. They are a bit pricey, being around $50, but will last forever and you'll be *so* glad you bought one!

The book you mention is by Suellen Ocean and is available on Amazon.com and it gives lots of information on eating acorns. I did an article years back on using acorns as food. It was in Issue #79 (Jan/Feb 2003) and you can read it online on the *BHM* website. — *Jackie*

Canning dried beans

I really love reading your column – it's the primary reason I subscribe...

I've been canning for a long time, but one thing I have not tried and wondered if you had. Can you place dried beans in a jar, add hot water, then seal and can them in the pressure cooker without things exploding? Or do you always need to cook them first then can them? I have done it the second way but have been timid about trying to go from the dried state — though it would be handy.

> *Rose Marie Kern*
> *Albuquerque, New Mexico*

A reader says he cans dry beans regularly by placing ¾ cup rinsed dry beans in a pint jar then filling the jar, leaving 1 inch of headspace and processing for 75 minutes at 10 pounds pressure. I really haven't gotten around to trying that yet. I do my hurry-up method of canning dry beans, which I love. You rinse the beans then drain and cover with boiling water, then bring them to a boil. Boil 2 (two!) minutes then remove from heat and let stand for 2 hours. Bring to a boil then drain, reserving the liquid. Pack jars with beans, leaving 1 inch of headspace. Ladle hot liquid over them, leaving 1 inch of headspace. Remove air bubbles. Process pints for 65 minutes and quarts for 75 minutes at 10 pounds pressure. If you live at an altitude above 1,000 feet, consult your canning book for directions on increasing your pressure to suit your altitude if necessary. — *Jackie*

Enough land?

I am a single wannabe survivalist homesteader with no dependents on a very fixed income. I figure it's best to buy land for just me and sell later if I should be blessed with a husband and children. Do you agree?

If an acre garden is big enough for a family, is 1/3 of an acre big enough for me? Is that large enough to incorporate the small fruits and small orchard? If not, how much extra land should I anticipate needing? Ideally, for animals I would keep one draft horse, one goat, a small flock of chickens, and my beautiful Bassett Hound. How much acreage should I anticipate needing for food requirements and housing/exercise requirements?

How do you find time to work off the homestead? Could you please suggest some jobs compatible with survival homesteading?

> *Darlene*
> *Ontario, Canada*

Search hard for the largest place you can afford. It sure sucks to plant fruit trees, berries, fix up a house to be perfect, then because your circumstances change, sell out and move to a larger homestead. But don't overdo either the land or expense as it will cause stress especially in the financial department. Been there; done that.

Well cared for, 1/3 of an acre is plenty for one person. It is *not* enough for a draft horse. Now I have been a horse person all my life and currently have several. But they have 60 acres of pasture to roam on and we still have to feed hay. Horses are wonderful but they are expensive to own and maintain ... especially when you don't have a large enough acreage to support them at least during the summer. Horses eat ... well ... like a horse. A small homestead of an acre *is* enough to add fruit trees, small fruits, a small flock of chickens, and perhaps a milk goat or two. *And* your Bassett Hound!

I don't work off of the homestead. Being a writer, I work right at home and am happy I can do this as I can work when my homestead work is less pressing and still get everything (mostly!) done. Of course, a lot of homesteaders must work off of the homestead. You can work and homestead but things around home move at a slower pace because of it, so don't let that get you down. You will accomplish your goals, step by step, if you go slowly. A lot of homesteaders work part-time as home-care workers for the elderly and handicapped, do sewing, child care, run bed and breakfasts, write, do artwork and other crafts, yard work, and much more. Let your talents and likes guide you.

The very best of luck finding your dream homestead! I'm rooting for you. — *Jackie*

Pickling grape leaves

...Grape leaves are edible. The Greek Orthodox Church pickles grape leaves and uses them as wraps. They stuff them with a tasty filling and sell them as finger food at an annual summer bazaar.

Would you or have you published the recipe for pickling grape leaves?
Margaret Okagawa
Denver, Colorado

Here's a recipe for you to use that is pretty tasty:

30-40 grape leaves, stems removed
1 tsp. pickling salt
¼ cup lemon juice

Bring a large pot of water to a boil and add salt. Have your water bath canner hot and ready for jars. Have a large bowl of cold water standing ready.

Boil the grape leaves for 30-45 seconds, then plunge into the ice water to cool. Drain them once the leaves are all cool. Take about six grape leaves at a time and roll them up into a cigar from the side. You will need to fold over the top of the leaf end to fit into the pint jar. Pack the grape leaves into the jar, making sure you have ½ inch of headspace. Boil 1 cup of water in a small saucepan and add the lemon juice. Boil for a minute or two, then pour over the grape leaves. Remove any air bubbles. Wipe the edge of the pint jar clean, place a hot, previously simmered lid on the jar and screw down the ring firmly tight. Process for 15 minutes in a boiling water bath.

This makes only a pint of pickled leaves but don't try to double or triple it or you'll sacrifice quality of the pickled leaves. — *Jackie*

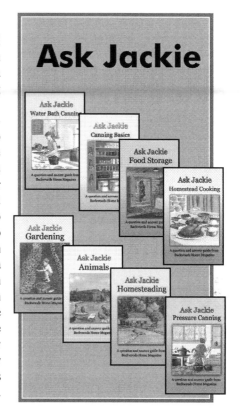

Herbs that I cherish

By Habeeb Salloum

My larder of herbs includes, among others, parsley, dill, marjoram, oregano, rosemary, sage, savory, and tarragon. However, going down my list of herbs, there are four that I cherish above all the others and I use often in my cooking. They are coriander leaves, mint, basil, and thyme. I usually plant them in my small garden and they supply my kitchen year-round, except when I need to use the fresh variety in winter.

Coriander leaves

Coriander leaves (also known as cilantro) is my herb *par excellence* — in my view the all-around tastiest herb. Fresh coriander is one of the oldest condiments known to man and today is the most widely-consumed fresh herb. However, for some it is an offensive herb. Strange as it may seem, there are some who despise its taste and abhor its smell. On the other hand, the vast majority who use it in their cuisine are addicted to its very name.

I vividly remember my first experience when I was served a stew cooked with fresh coriander leaves. A family friend who had recently arrived from the Middle East prepared the dish. That day my culinary experience was revolutionized. I went into raptures after the meal just thinking about the delicious taste of this savory herb. From that first taste more than half a century ago, I have become a fanatical advocate of this exquisite parsley-like plant.

Rich in Vitamins A and C, these aromatic leaves are employed worldwide in cooking. In Latin American and eastern cuisine they are used as a basic flavoring ingredient in a vast number of dishes. The sapid leaves of coriander are as important to the culinary artists in these lands as parsley is to the western housewife.

Numerous types of salads, sauces, curries, soups, stews, and meat loaves are made tempting by the utilization of this appetizing herb. Furthermore, in the same fashion as parsley, the strongly-scented leaves are employed to garnish the main course platters. In any event, it matters not if this historic herb is used to please the taste or please the eye, as its effect is always tremendous.

During the summer months, when coriander is plentiful, the fresh leaves and stems can be washed, then frozen in plastic bags. They will keep for a long period of time and are excellent in soups and stews. When ready to use, as much as is needed should be chopped, then the remainder returned to the freezer. The taste will only vary slightly from the leaves that are fresh.

Mint

My second most important herb is *mint* — an herb my mother used in her cooking on our farm in southern Saskatchewan. One of the most popular garden herbs that is cultivated worldwide, mint comes in some 2000 varieties. Even though most types of mint can be used interchangeably, only peppermint and spearmint are usually found in stores.

Like all other mints, spearmint is a perennial that sprouts from quick spreading roots or cuttings. It grows

Burghul and chickpea salad

easily, not from seeds, but is spread rapidly by way of wandering deep-reaching roots which, if not checked, quickly become an unwanted garden weed. Valued for its insect-repelling qualities, it matures into a green, square-stemmed plant with bright lance-shaped leaves and lilac or pink flowers. Its leaves can be picked at any time, but are at their best when young and tender before the plant flowers.

Modern research has established that most of the ancient uses of mint in the medical field have a firm base. Today, mint is utilized to give medicine a pleasant taste; and for its anti-flatulent, anti-spasmodic, carminative, and stimulant attributes. It has been found that it helps in easing nausea, relieving diarrhea, and stimulating the menstrual flow. A few drops of mint oil mixed with water help to alleviate symptoms of the common cold or flu, colic in babies, insomnia, and head or toothaches. Yet, in spite of its medical attributes, mint's main use is for culinary purposes.

In the Middle East and North Africa, mint leaves are utilized in every course of the meal, from appetizers to desserts and beverages, especially tea. In addition, mint is often used to give a tang to a wide variety of yogurt and stuffed vegetable dishes. Throughout Europe and North America, mint is employed in a sauce for roast lamb and to enhance the roast itself. Mint leaves wrapped around whole garlic cloves, then placed in incisions throughout the leg of lamb are used to heighten the flavor of the meat.

Mint goes well with beans, burghul (cooked crushed wheat), carrots, eggplants, lentils, peas, potatoes, and tomatoes. It adds much to the taste of fruit and other salads and jellies, as well as all types of sauces and soups.

The leaves are at their epitome of flavor when picked fresh. If wrapped with a damp towel and placed in a refrigerator, they will keep for about a

Fresh coriander leaves with yogurt

week. The leaves can be dried, but they lose some of their flavor and aroma. I usually cut my mint patch two to four times a year and dry them in the sun. I give my friends little portions but still have more than I can use — all from a 2x4-foot patch.

One teaspoon of dried, finely crushed mint leaves may be substituted for four tablespoons of fresh mint. Last, but not least, mint is one of the great garnishing herbs.

Basil

The third herb on my menu of herbs is *basil* — a sweet, highly aromatic herb, easily grown from seed both indoors and outdoors. Besides its pleasant scent, it gives an ornamental touch to any setting. When mature, some species reach the height of 18 inches. However, most basil plants are at their best when about 6 inches high. At this stage their perfume, taste, and re-growing ability is at its strongest.

When the tips of the branches are nipped at this height, before the plant blooms, it can be utilized the whole year. Easily grown in gardening pots indoors, or in any type of garden, a never-ending supply of fresh basil is always available in my home.

An important culinary herb, basil has a strong aroma that enhances the lure of cabbage, eggplant, onions, potatoes, spinach, zucchini, and especially tomatoes. The flavor of the leaves and stem of fresh basil, with a taste somewhat like cloves, gives a sweetish mild zest to pastas, salads, sauces, soups, stews, and vegetables. It also adds a gentle, somewhat minty taste to scrambled eggs, meat loaves, and other meat, chicken, and fish dishes.

Fresh basil, when harvested, is very perishable. The leaves bruise easily and the herb only keeps for a short period in the refrigerator. Yet, it will last for weeks in a deep freeze.

Wash, dry, then finely chop the basil leaves and place in a plastic ice cube tray. Cover leaves with water and freeze, then store the frozen cubes in a plastic bag. When it's time to use, place a cube directly into any simmering dish as soon as it is removed from the heat.

Basil, oregano, rosemary, and savory go well together in a good number of foods. However, if used by itself, basil is at its epitome of greatness when used in tomato dishes. Fresh or dried, it enriches the taste of

Chicken with thyme and fried potatoes

tomatoes, especially in salads or as a pizza topping.

To be effective, this delightful herb must not be added while the food is cooking. It should be stirred in a few seconds before the food is removed from the heat. If added too soon it will lose its delicate heady aroma.

Of course, the fragrance of the fresh herb is more superior to the dried. However, in most of North America, fresh basil, except in large urban centers, is sometimes hard to find on the shelves of vegetable markets. Only dried basil is usually available. When dried, the leaves tend to turn dark and develop a noticeably stronger taste than when fresh, but they can always be employed as a substitute. In all recipes that call for fresh basil, one teaspoon dried can be substituted for two tablespoons fresh.

Thyme

The fourth herb that I usually have in my herb garden is **thyme** — an herb with a subtle, pleasant aroma and a slightly minty flavor. It grows wild in fields, along roadsides and road banks, as well as lawns and any other place it is introduced. However,

like myself, those with gardens usually plant a small patch in the corner of their gardens and often grow enough to cover their needs and supply the neighbors — fresh in summer and dried in winter.

A woody perennial that comes in several varieties, thyme grows to between 6 and 12 inches in height. Thyme can be grown from seeds to transplants — most nurseries carry transplants in spring and summer. The soil should be sandy and open to the sun. If the climate is cold in winter the plants should be protected by mulching.

The leaves can be picked fresh and used throughout the summer, but they are at their best in flavor and aroma just before flowering. In autumn, cut the stems with the leaves and hang in small bunches to dry for winter use.

In the medicinal world, thyme is high in vitamin C, iron, and niacin. The leaves, stems, and flowers can be brewed for stimulant tea. Also, the herb helps to relieve headaches and sore throats and has antiseptic, aromatic, carminative, diuretic, diaphoretic, and antispasmodic qualities.

However, it is in the kitchen that thyme reaches its excellence. It goes well in seasoning blends for chowders, fish sauces, poultry and stuffing, as well as pizzas, soups, stews, and spaghetti. It enhances the taste of cheese dishes, custards, croquettes, eggs, lamb, tomatoes, and veal. A mixture of garlic and thyme rubbed over meat roasts gives them a special mouth-watering quality.

Recipes

Fresh coriander leaves with yogurt

Serves 6 to 8

This dish is usually served as a side dish with stuffed lamb or any other fatty meat.

4 cups plain yogurt
2 cups very finely chopped fresh coriander leaves, thoroughly washed
4 cloves garlic, crushed
1 tsp. salt

Thoroughly combine all ingredients. Chill and serve.

Coriander, meat, and pea stew

Serves about 8

4 Tbsp. butter
2 pounds beef or lamb, cut into ¾-inch cubes
1 cup finely chopped fresh coriander leaves
3 medium-sized onions, chopped
4 cloves garlic, crushed
4 medium tomatoes, finely chopped
2 cups water
2 tsp. salt
1 tsp. pepper
½ tsp. cumin
½ tsp. allspice
⅛ tsp. cayenne
3 cups fresh or frozen peas

Melt butter in a saucepan, then add meat and sauté over medium heat for 10 minutes. Add coriander leaves, onions, and garlic, then sauté for a further 5 minutes. Transfer to a casserole, stir in tomatoes, water, salt, pepper, cumin, allspice, and cayenne, then cover. Place in a 350° F preheated oven for 1½ hours, adding more water if necessary. Stir in peas, then cook for a further 30 minutes or until meat and peas are cooked, adding a little more water if necessary. Serve hot with mashed potatoes or cooked rice.

Burghul and chickpea salad
Serves 8 to 10

This salad becomes crunchier and tastier if ½ cup of dried chickpeas is substituted for 1 cup of cooked. The dried chickpeas should be soaked overnight then drained. After this, put the chickpeas, a handful at a time, in a small cloth bag then roll with a rolling pin to break them up. Remove loose skin before using.

½ cup fine burghul, soaked in warm water for 10 minutes, then water pressed out
1 large bunch parsley, finely chopped
1 cup cooked chickpeas
1 small bunch green onions, finely chopped
3 medium tomatoes, finely chopped
1 medium cucumber, about 5 inches long, finely chopped
1½ cups chopped fresh mint
3 Tbsp. olive oil
4 Tbsp. lemon juice
1 tsp. salt
½ tsp. pepper
⅛ tsp. cayenne

Place burghul and all vegetable ingredients in a salad bowl, stir and set aside. Thoroughly mix remaining ingredients, pour over vegetables and stir. Chill for about 1 hour, then toss and serve.

A medicinal mint beverage

Simple to prepare, this pleasant drink can be used to relieve a whole series of stomach ailments and headaches.

½ cup firmly-packed fresh mint leaves
1 tablespoon honey
2 cups boiling water

Place mint and honey in a teapot, then pour in the boiling water. Cover and allow to steep for 1 hour before drinking.

Sun-dried tomato chickpea dip
Serves 4 to 6

Fresh mint leaves can be used as a substitute for basil leaves when making this healthy vegetarian spread for sandwiches.

½ cup chopped, drained sun-dried tomatoes (that have been preserved in oil)
1 cup cooked chickpeas
4 Tbsp. extra virgin olive oil
¼ cup firmly packed fresh basil or mint leaves
4 cloves garlic
½ tsp. salt
½ tsp. pepper
½ tsp. dried oregano

Place all the ingredients in food processer and blend until smooth. Spread on a serving platter. Scoop up with crackers or spread on slices of bread.

Tomato basil salad
Serves from 6 to 8

5 medium-sized tomatoes, quartered, then thinly sliced
1 small onion, very finely chopped
6 Tbsp. finely chopped fresh basil or 3 tsp. crushed dried basil
2 cloves garlic, crushed
½ cup finely chopped parsley
4 Tbsp. vinegar
3 Tbsp. olive oil
¾ tsp. salt
½ tsp. pepper

Place tomatoes and onion in a salad bowl, then gently toss and set aside.

In a small bowl, just before serving, thoroughly mix remaining ingredients. Pour over tomatoes and onion then toss and serve.

Chicken with thyme
Serves 4 to 6

A couscousiére or a double boiler with a top that is perforated is a necessity when preparing this dish.

1 chicken, 3 to 4 pounds, cut into large pieces
3 tsp. salt, divided
1½ tsp. pepper, divided
1 packed cup chopped fresh thyme
1 medium onion, finely chopped
½ cup white grape juice
¼ cup vinegar
6 Tbsp. butter
½ cup finely chopped green onions

Sprinkle the chicken pieces with 2½ tsp. of the salt and 1 tsp. of the pepper, then place in top part of a couscousiére and set aside.

Fill bottom part of couscousiére with water then bring to boil. Fit the top part of couscousiére over bottom then spread thyme over chicken and cover. If there is steam escaping, seal upper and lower together with a flour-impregnated piece of cloth. Steam over medium/high heat for about 1½ hours or until chicken is done.

In the meantime, place onion, grape juice, vinegar, and remaining salt and pepper in a small saucepan, then simmer uncovered over medium heat until liquid has been reduced to less than half. Add butter and green onions, then stir-fry for 2 minutes to make sauce.

Place chicken pieces on a serving platter, then spread piping hot sauce evenly over top and serve with fried or mashed potatoes. Δ

Old-fashioned homemade cakes

By Linda Gabris

When I was a girl, Mom and Grandma made all their cakes from scratch. In fact, I had never heard of a store-bought cake mix until I went off to school in the city and saw boxed cake mixes sitting on the supermarket shelf, with some of them even claiming that all you needed to add was water!

The first commercial packaged cake mixes were introduced to the public in the 1920s. They certainly were available in Mom and Grandma's time, but were probably considered "too dear" for their budgets or too hard to come by in small country grocery stores. And besides, Old World cooks like Mom and Grandma took a lot of pride in their ability to bake a cake from scratch.

Although there's no denying that store-bought cake mixes are handy for today's busy homemakers, there really is nothing more satisfying than baking an old-fashioned cake from scratch. The good news is, it doesn't take a whole lot more time than making one from a box. You'll also find that homemade cakes are easier on the budget, not to mention tastier.

The prominent ingredient in most cakes is flour. There are two types of flour that you will see called for in the majority of cake recipes. You will notice that my recipes below simply call for all-purpose flour. It is versatile, reasonably priced, and well-suited for cakes as well as other baked goods. Today, however, many newer cake recipes call for "cake" flour, which is a flour geared especially for cake baking.

The difference between all-purpose flour and cake flour is that all-purpose flour has slightly higher protein

Aunt Mernie's raspberry jelly roll and double-chocolate cake are two old-fashioned, made-from-scratch cakes that my family loves.

content and is made from a blend of both hard and soft wheat. Cake flour is lower in protein and is made from soft wheat alone. All-purpose flour is somewhat cheaper than cake flour (at least where I shop), which is why it is the standard flour that I use for baking cakes. However, if you find a cake recipe that distinctively calls for cake flour, you can easily turn all-purpose flour into cake flour by following the simple directions in the sidebar.

I always smile to myself remembering the first thing Mom taught me about baking a cake. It was to get a "good hot fire" going in the woodstove by using kindling in order to preheat the oven to the needed temperature and then keeping the fire "built up" just right to maintain the proper heat.

Turn all-purpose flour into cake flour substitute

Measure out the called for amount of all-purpose flour that you need for a particular recipe into a bowl. For every cup of flour that you measured, take out two tablespoons of the flour and return it to the bin. Now sift the flour several times and it can now be used in place of cake flour in any recipe. However, for an even better substitute, you can replace the two tablespoons of all-purpose flour with 2 tablespoons of cornstarch. Adding the gluten-free cornstarch will give you a much lighter flour (less flour, lower protein content). Now sift the flour/cornstarch mixture through a sieve back and forth several times and you have cake flour equal to that which is specially bought — and you saved money by making your own!

Mom's old McClary woodstove had a built-in oven thermometer. To me it always seemed pretty darn tricky to maintain the exact heat long enough to bake the perfect cake, but Mom and Grandma had success every time. Today I have an electric stove that takes away the guesswork, but the bottom line is, you should bake cakes at the correct given temperature for the required time, placing the pans in the center of the oven using the center rack position, unless otherwise stated. If baking more than one cake, don't let the pans touch each other or the sides of the oven. Try to stagger them so they all get equal exposure to the heat.

A few other tricks to successful cake baking is to use the proper size of pan called for in a recipe. If the pan is too large, the batter will be spread too thin and the cake will come out flat, dry, and overcooked. If the pan is too small, the batter will rise and run over the sides of the pan and the cake may not bake all the way through to the center, causing it to be heavy and doughy instead of light and fluffy. Choose pans that will properly accommodate the batter, filled about half full, spreading and leveling the

Spread the raspberry filling on the cake while it is still warm and pliable, then roll up inside a towel and leave it until completely cool.

batter evenly. Of course, you can go ahead and use different sized pans than called for in a recipe if you take into consideration the equivalence of the pan sizes called for and those you wish to substitute.

For instance, you can use two 8-inch round pans for a two layer cake or use one 9-inch or 10-inch square pan if you just want a one-lay-er cake. I find that the batter which fills two or three 8- or 9-inch round pans makes enough for one large oblong cake (9x13x2-inch). Rather than overfilling a pan, it is better to take the excess batter and bake it as cupcakes. Since using pan sizes that are not specified in a recipe may alter baking times, it is best for beginners to stick with the required size of pan until you get a knack for adjusting the time accordingly.

When a recipe calls for greasing the pan, I use a balled up piece of waxed paper and a small knob of shortening or butter for spreading the grease evenly. If it calls for greasing and flouring the pan, I add a spoonful or two of flour to the greased pan and shake it around until the flour is spread evenly, then tap the pan over the sink to rid excess flour that has not adhered. If using non-stick pans, you will not need to grease them unless you find your pans are losing their coating. Some cakes tend to stick even when the pan is greased and floured, such as with a jelly roll, which is why the pan is greased and then lined with waxed paper and greased again. This ensures the cake

Double-chocolate cake

Mom's yellow cake with caramel sauce

can be turned out of the pan with ease.

Mom also taught me to round up all the ingredients called for in a recipe before starting. By doing so, the eggs and the fat — usually shortening, butter, or lard — will be at room temperature, which makes them easier to work with. If a cake recipes calls for oil it usually refers to vegetable oil, unless otherwise stated.

Although I typically use medium to large eggs, if I happen to only have small eggs on hand I tend to figure that three smaller eggs equal about two larger ones. A small variation in the amount of egg shouldn't make a huge difference in the outcome of most cakes — unless making an angel food cake, in which case you want to be precise with the egg measure.

Unless otherwise specified, when a cake batter calls for sugar it usually means white granulated sugar. Most cake recipes call for a pinch of salt. From what I gather, adding salt helps to draw out the other flavors in the cake but salt can easily be omitted by those like me who are trying to cut down a little on our families' salt intake or are on a salt-free diet alto-

gether. I have included the salt measures in Mom and Grandma's old recipes because they had it written down in their ingredients. Over the years, I have omitted salt from my cake recipes without noticing any difference. Suit yourself. After you have beaten the cake batter, use a spatula to scrape down the sides of the bowl so that you don't have unmixed batter around the bowl's rim. I usually scrape it down nearing the end of the beating time.

Always remember to only check cake for doneness when time is up! As Mom used to warn, "If you open the oven door too soon to peek, the draft will cause the cake to fall." Cake is done when the top springs back when lightly pressed with the fingertips or in Mom's words, "When a broom straw inserted into the center of the cake comes out clean." Of course, these days a toothpick is my choice of a testing stick.

After removing cake from the oven, let it stand about 5 to 10 minutes in the pan before turning it out. Cool on a rack before frosting. (Angel food, sponge, and chiffon types of cakes

must be cooled completely in the inverted pan).

Mom and Grandma used old-fashioned handheld egg beaters (rotary beaters) for mixing their cake batters as they didn't have an electric model such as the one I use today. I use a handheld electric mixer but there's an old saying I remember hearing as a girl, "If you have to mix a cake by hand with a spoon, it calls for 225 strokes and they must all be in the same direction." Talk about giving your arm a good workout!

So let's bake a cake. Here are some mouthwatering, economical homemade cakes that you might want to try. Some are old family recipes like Mom's yellow cake with caramel sauce that actually melts in your mouth and Grandma's gingerbread, a moist, spicy cake that everybody loves. Be sure to try my pretty holiday cherry cake, made from maraschino cherries, which is always a hit around Christmas time, and tomato soup cake, which was a recipe I saved off the label of a soup can when I was a young housewife back in the 70s — a very strange cake that is surprisingly good.

Recipes

Mom's yellow cake with caramel sauce

Serve a wedge of this moist yellow cake with the rich buttery-caramel sauce drizzled over the top and watch it disappear off the plate! You can serve the cake and the sauce warm as a cold weather "comfort" dessert or serve it cold to take the heat off hot weather dining. Makes two 8-inch round layer cakes. I like this recipe because I serve one of the cakes fresh and the other one I freeze for another day's dessert when time is running short. One cake can be cut into six servings. However, if you think you have the need for a larger cake for a particular occasion, you can bake the batter in a large 9x13x2-inch pan. This will yield nice uniform square pieces of cake, making up to 12 servings. Serve with caramel sauce, recipe below, drizzled over top.

> 2½ cups all-purpose flour
> 3 tsp. baking powder
> ¼ tsp. salt (optional)
> ¾ cup butter, margarine, or shortening
> 1¼ cups sugar
> 3 eggs
> 2 tsp. vanilla
> 1 cup milk

Grease and flour pans. Mix flour, baking powder, and salt into a bowl. In a large mixing bowl, cream fat, adding sugar gradually, beating until well blended. Add eggs, one at a time, beating well after each addition. Stir in vanilla. Add dry ingredients, alternately with the milk, mix well. Pour into prepared pans. Bake in preheated 350° F oven for 35 minutes or until done to the toothpick test.

Caramel sauce:

> 1½ cups packed brown sugar
> 1½ cups boiling water
> 2 Tbsp. cornstarch blended into ¼ cup cold water
> 1 tsp. vanilla
> 1½ Tbsp. butter

Like Mom, I use a medium-sized cast iron skillet for caramelizing (melting down) the brown sugar but any heavy-bottomed saucepan will do. Put brown sugar in skillet and heat, stirring constantly, until it melts and turns golden brown. Slowly, very slowly — otherwise it'll bubble out over the pan — add boiling water. The melted sugar will turn brittle instantly. Cook until the brittle sugar dissolves back into liquid. Slowly blend in the cornstarch/water mixture and cook, stirring constantly, until thick and glossy clear. Remove from heat. Stir in vanilla and butter. Leftover sauce saves indefinitely in the fridge in capped jar and is excellent spooned over ice cream and plain puddings that need to be dressed up with a little something special.

Grandma's gingerbread

I love gingerbread, especially when served with a dollop of fresh whipped cream on top! When I was a kid, this was Grandma's special Christmas treat. Today I make it whenever a gingerbread craving strikes. This makes a 9x13x2-inch pan and the moist, spicy cake actually improves with age, but you'll have to hide it if you want to see for yourself!

Grandma's gingerbread

> 2¾ cups all-purpose flour
> 3 tsp. baking powder
> ½ cup lard or shortening (Grandma used homemade lard in hers and it was delicious)
> 1 cup brown sugar
> 1 cup molasses
> ½ tsp. salt (optional)
> 2 tsp. ginger
> ½ tsp. each nutmeg and cinnamon
> ¼ tsp. cloves
> 1 cup boiling water
> 1 tsp. baking soda
> 2 beaten eggs

Grease and flour pan. Put flour and baking powder into a bowl. In another bowl, cream fat and brown sugar until light and fluffy. Blend in molasses, salt, and spices. Pour boiling water over baking soda in a dish and when it fizzles add to the molasses mixture. This causes a reaction that turns the batter very light and airy in the bowl! Stir the flour mixture into the molasses mixture. Add eggs and beat until blended. Pour into prepared pan, bake in preheated oven, 325° F for 45 minutes, or until done to the toothpick test.

Holiday cherry cake

This is a pretty cake that's baked loaf style. My kids love it! It is good enough to come to the table without frosting for any weeknight supper dessert, but for festive occasions, I like to use Cherry-butter frosting topped with halved red and green maraschino cherries! Makes a 9x5x3-inch loaf.

> 1½ cups all-purpose flour
> 2 tsp. baking powder
> ¼ tsp. nutmeg
> ⅓ cup butter
> ¾ cup sugar
> 2 eggs
> ¼ cup milk
> ¼ cup cherry juice from the jar in which you removed the cherries
> 1 cup sliced red and/or green maraschino cherries
> 1 to 2 Tbsp. flour

Holiday cherry cake

Grease and flour pan. Put flour, baking powder, and nutmeg into a bowl. In another bowl, cream butter while gradually adding sugar. Beat until light and fluffy. Beat in eggs, one at a time. Mix milk and cherry juice together. Add dry ingredients alternatively with milk and cherry juice, beating until smooth. Put sliced cherries into a bowl and sprinkle with 2 tablespoons flour, dredging them well. This will help distribute them evenly throughout the cake. Fold cherries into batter. Bake in preheated 350° F oven for 50 minutes or until done to the toothpick test. Turn out of pan and cool. For ease of slicing, wrap cooled loaf in waxed paper or plastic wrap and let stand a day. Serve plain or with the easy Cherry-butter frosting, below.

Cherry-butter frosting

¼ cup soft butter
3 (or more) cups icing (powdered) sugar
2 to 3 Tbsp. milk
2 to 3 Tbsp. cherry juice reserved from the maraschino jar

Beat butter until light and fluffy. Gradually beat in sugar alternately with milk and cherry juice until you have a thick, creamy pink frosting of spreading consistency, using more milk or cherry juice (for deeper color and flavor) if too thick to spread and more icing sugar if too thin to hold its shape. Leftover frosting can be saved in a capped container in the fridge indefinitely. Leftover frosting is excellent for dressing up everyday cookies or muffins so don't worry if the batch is too big for the cake as it won't go to waste.

Double-chocolate cake

Everyone loves chocolate cake. This recipe makes two 8-inch round cakes and since it uses two types of chocolate, it is super "chocolatey" and good! I like to layer the cakes and frost with rich chocolate frosting. Great for a chocolate-lover's birthday! I happened upon this recipe one time when I was halfway through mixing up a chocolate cake only to find that my cocoa can was running low and I was a couple spoonfuls short of the needed amount of cocoa powder. I improvised by melting a square of unsweetened chocolate and adding it directly to the batter and it worked great. Since then I've kept the recipe using the two chocolates!

1¾ cup all-purpose flour
¼ tsp. baking soda
1½ tsp. baking powder
¼ cup cocoa powder
½ cup shortening
1¼ cups sugar
2 eggs
1 square (1 oz.) unsweetened chocolate, melted
1 tsp. vanilla
1 cup milk

Grease and flour pans. Mix dry ingredients, including cocoa powder into a bowl. In a mixing bowl, cream shortening, adding sugar gradually and beating after each addition. Add eggs, one at a time, and beat well. Stir in melted chocolate and vanilla. Add dry ingredients alternately with milk, blending well after each addition. Beat until batter is smooth. Pour into prepared pans. Bake in preheated oven 350° F for 50 minutes or until done to the toothpick test. Cool in pans 10 minutes, then turn out and cool completely before frosting.

Cocoa butter frosting

¼ cup soft butter or margarine
3 to 4 cups icing (powdered) sugar
4 Tbsp. cocoa powder
6 to 8 Tbsp. milk
1 tsp. vanilla extract

Cream butter. Mix 3 cups sugar with cocoa powder. Gradually beat sugar mixture into butter, alternately with milk and vanilla, until of spreading consistency, adding more sugar if too thin, or more milk if too thick. You can also adjust the cocoa powder, adding more for darker, richer frosting or less for lighter flavor and color. Top frosted cake with grated chocolate and/or finely shredded coconut, if desired.

Aunt Mernie's raspberry jelly roll

My aunt made the best raspberry jelly roll ever! I can't help but wonder if it was simply because she was so generous with her huge slices. In any event, like Aunt Mernie, I always use homemade raspberry jam for this sweet roll but store-bought jam will certainly do.

> 1 cup all-purpose flour
> 2 tsp. baking powder
> ¼ tsp. salt (optional)
> 4 eggs, separated
> ¾ cup sugar
> 1 Tbsp. lemon juice plus 2 Tbsp. water
> 1 Tbsp. finely grated lemon rind
> 1 cup raspberry jam

Grease a 15x10½x¾-inch jelly roll pan and line with waxed paper, then grease paper. Mix flour, baking powder, and salt together in a bowl. In a mixing bowl, beat egg yolks until thick and yellow; gradually beat in sugar. Stir in lemon-water and rind. Gradually fold in dry ingredients. Beat egg whites until stiff, gently fold into batter. Spread batter evenly into prepared pan.

Bake in a preheated oven at 325° F for 15 minutes or until lightly browned and springs back to the touch. In the meantime, lay a clean tea-towel on the cupboard and sieve powdered sugar evenly over top. When cake is done, remove from oven and immediately turn out onto the cloth. Peel waxed paper off the cake and trim crusts from sides if uneven. Spread jelly roll with the jam, roll up lengthwise, working while the cake is still hot and pliable. Keep cake wrapped until cool. Unwrap, sprinkle with additional powdered sugar, and cut into slices. Wrap leftover jelly roll in plastic wrap to keep it fresh. This makes about 12 slices.

Variations: you can fill a jelly roll with any kind of jam or jelly, whipped cream, softened ice cream, lemon curd (from the recipe below which makes a memorable tart filling) or almost any sweet thing that can be spread and rolled.

Spicy tomato soup cake

Here is my adapted version of the old 70's tomato soup cake. Good now as it was away back then! Makes a 9x13x2-inch pan.

> 2½ cups all-purpose flour
> 1 cup sugar
> 3 tsp. baking powder
> 1 tsp. baking soda
> 1 tsp. cinnamon
> ½ tsp. nutmeg
> ¼ tsp. cloves
> 1 (10 ounce) can of tomato soup
> ½ cup shortening
> 2 eggs
> ¼ cup water
> 1 cup raisins or currants
> ½ cup chopped walnuts (or omit and add more raisins or currants)

Grease and flour pan. Mix all the dry ingredients in a bowl. In another bowl, beat soup with the shortening until blended. Add the eggs and water and beat well. Add the wet ingredients to the dry ingredients and beat about 2 or 3 minutes. Stir in the walnuts (or dried fruit if using). Pour into prepared pan and bake in preheated oven 350° F for 40 minutes or until done to the toothpick test. Cool in the pan. You can turn the cake out but I usually frost it right in the pan. Try it with maple-butter frosting, recipe below.

Maple-butter frosting

> ¼ cup butter (or margarine)
> 1 tsp. maple extract (a little more for richer maple flavor)
> 5 (or more) Tbsp. milk
> 3 cups icing (powdered) sugar

Cream butter. Add maple extract to milk. Gradually beat sugar into the butter, alternately with milk, until of spreading consistency. Add more sugar if too thin, or more milk if too thick.

Lemon curd

> ½ cup butter
> ¾ cup sugar
> juice of 4 squeezed lemons
> 3 Tbsp. very finely grated lemon zest
> 6 egg yolks (save whites for another purpose)

Melt butter in saucepan. Whisk in sugar, juice, zest, and yolks, beating until smooth. Cook over low heat, whisking constantly, until thickened, about 5 minutes. Be careful not to let it scorch! Cool and use as spread for jelly roll or whatever recipe you have that calls for lemon curd. Leftovers can be stored in capped container in fridge, keeping indefinitely. Δ

Ayoob on Firearms

Why you should try competition shooting

Massad Ayoob

Ever spent day after day hunting in miserable weather, only to finally get a shot at the winter meat supply… and blow it?

I have. My formative experience with that in my early teens taught me it was time to try a little competition. In that time and place, the 1960s in New Hampshire, the logical venue was a turkey shoot. In different parts of the United States, in different places, "turkey shoot" has meant and still means different things. Sometimes it's a round of skeet or trap, with a turkey as a prize. In the days of the pioneers, it meant a live turkey in a crate a far piece from the shooters, and whoever shot the turkey's head off won the bird. In my time and place, it was done primarily with "deer rifles" on "deer targets." One event was Standing Deer, with the target posted on a frame a hundred yards away. The other staple course of fire was Running Deer, the same target at the same distance, but rolling across the field of fire on a pulley. You fired three to five shots on the standing deer, depending on the host club's rules, and three on the briefly-exposed runner. Ten or so guys would fork over an entry fee, and whoever got the highest scoring hits on the deer's anatomy won a frozen Butterball turkey. Hence, the name "turkey shoot."

I couldn't help but notice that the guys I met at the turkey shoot were a whole lot more likely to answer yes to the standard rural greeting of November — "Got your deer yet?" — than the rank and file deer hunters of my acquaintance. Yes, I realize that correlation is not causation. However, correlation is sure a clue!

As my life and research wore on, I discovered that the deer woods weren't the only place where a correlation could be found between those who shot rifles in competition and those who used them for more serious business. America's greatest hero in World War I, Sergeant Alvin York, fed his family in part by winning turkey shoots with his old-fashioned rifle in the Tennessee hills. That same skill set worked well for him with an Army-issued bolt action .30-06 rifle (historians still debate whether it was a 1903 Springfield or a 1917 Enfield) and a Colt .45 caliber semiautomatic pistol. We do know that he littered the battlefield with enemy dead, captured a huge number of intimidated German soldiers alive, and won the Congressional Medal of Honor.

One of York's contemporaries was Herbert McBride. He may or may not have killed as many enemy soldiers as York, though he certainly killed his share, but he left much more insight in his own written words than York as a legacy for the following generations. He was a competitive rifle shooter in formal NRA-type disciplines before he shipped overseas,

Author, right, happily accepts ILEETA Cup in 2011. He says the trophy is just the icing on the cake, and the nourishment of competitive shooting comes from learning to "run the gun" under pressure.

and significantly, he titled his memoirs *A Rifleman Went to War.* Therein, McBride wrote, "Every bit of information that may be picked up on the range will prove useful in war. True, it will not always — nor often — be possible to assume the exact, orthodox positions used in competitions and there is the matter of adjusting oneself — mentally and physically — to the stress and strain of battle but, just the same, all those fundamental principles will have an important, even if sub-conscious influence, tending to increase the rifleman's effectiveness."

In World War II, one man who had the same experience was Lt. Col. John George. In his book *Shots Fired in Anger: A Rifleman's View of the War in the Pacific, 1942-1945,* George wrote that having been a competitive rifle shooter before joining up stood him in very good stead in jungle combat in the Pacific Islands.

In Vietnam, no American fighting man emerged more famous than Carlos Hathcock, the star of the Marine Scout-Sniper program, with 93 confirmed kills. Prior to being deployed, he had won the Wimbledon Cup, the championship of long-range high power rifle shooting. In Charles Henderson's excellent biography of Hathcock, *Marine Sniper: 93 Confirmed Kills,* the master rifleman explained that he dominated the battlefield the way he had learned to dominate the competitive rifle range. He put himself in a mental "bubble," focusing only on tasks and targets. The enemy learned to fear him so much they put a bounty on him.

Fast forward to the present. Lots of reports have come back from Afghanistan of soldiers and Marines who had learned fast, accurate shooting in modern American "three-gun" competition where the AR-type rifle is a staple. It turns out that their competition experiences applied remarkably well in actual combat from Iraq to Afghanistan.

Handgunning

While the rifle is primarily a battle weapon in its life-saving role, the handgun excels as a reactive weapon in self-defense, simply because it's so portable that it's more likely to be accessible in the face of a sudden, unexpected, potentially lethal assault. Here again, we tend to see some common threads among those who have survived multiple shootouts. One of those commonalities is experience in competitive shooting.

Wyatt Earp was known to shoot in the informal revolver matches in the cow-towns. It made him deadly with a gun when it counted, on what some euphemistically call "the two-way range." This, too, has remained a constant over time. In WWI, the aforementioned Sergeant York was credited with dropping about half a dozen charging enemy soldiers with as many shots from his Colt .45 pistol. Delf "Jelly" Bryce, one of the gunfighters recruited by J. Edgar Hoover into the FBI when armed accountants and lawyers didn't fare well against thugs like the Dillinger gang, was famous for his amazing skill in quick draw and point shooting. What many miss is that his career in law enforcement — and gunfighting — began when he was hired by an Oklahoma police chief who saw him effortlessly win a pistol match.

I never met Bryce, more's the pity, and I only *look* old enough to have known Wyatt Earp. I have, however, had the privilege of knowing such men as Col. Charles Askins, Jr., Jim Cirillo, and Bill Allard.

Before Col. Askins won acclaim as a gun writer, he had become famous as a Border Patrol gunfighter...and as one of the best competitive pistol shots in the country. He won the National Pistol Championship in the 1930s, and gave an excellent account of himself in ground combat in North Africa and in Europe in World War II.

Bill Allard and Jim Cirillo were frequently partners on the famed NYPD Stakeout Squad, whose job was interdicting armed robbers who already had guns in their hands. Bill led the squad in the number of "kills," followed closely by Jim. Both were avid competitors and staff firearms instructors on NYPD before they volunteered for the assignment that would put them so frequently in harm's way. Allard preferred conventional bullseye shooting, and eventually won the National Championship. Cirillo won many titles in PPC, the practical police course fired at distances from seven to fifty yards, though he was a pioneer in today's practical shooting disciplines including the International Defensive Pistol Association and particularly the International Practical Shooting Confederation.

All three of these men told me to my face that what they had learned in competition had been hugely helpful in surviving shootouts with armed and deadly opponents. Not a one of them ever stopped a bullet from one of their opponents' guns. Askins and Cirillo, sadly, are no longer with us,

In Paul Kirchner's bio, famed police gunfighter Jim Cirillo credited his match shooting for much of his success in shootouts.

109

but each left a legacy of writing. Looking up Col. Charles Askins, Jr. on amazon.com will lead you to a rich trove of his published works. Cirillo's astute observations on how competitive shooting helped him to survive shootouts can be found in his own book *Guns, Bullets and Gunfights,* and in Paul Kirchner's excellent biography of him, *Jim Cirillo's Tales of the Stakeout Squad.* Both are published by Paladin Press. Bill Allard discussed it articulately and emphatically when I interviewed him for the ProArms Podcast, which you can download at no charge from http://ht.ly/fFdIO.

With handguns as well as with rifles — with any type of firearm, really — there are two kinds of "stress shooting moments" for which competition experience can help prepare you. One, as we've seen, is the situation where you're fighting for your life and have to shoot an enraged animal that's about to kill you or yours, whether the target walks on two legs or four. The other situation that's analogous is the hunting field.

Over my lifetime, I've seen hunting with handguns evolve from a stunt or a survival necessity to a specialized

En route to winning International Defensive Pistol Association match, John Strayer slides into designated cover position from full run during one stage of fire.

branch of hunting all its own. If you're into the handgun hunting sport, you're probably familiar with these two names: J.D. Jones and John Taffin. Both have well over forty years as authoritative writers in the world of the gun. Both are famous for their handgun hunting exploits.

And, significantly, both have a history as winning competitive shooters in relevant disciplines. Before handgunning was shut down in Great Britain circa 1996, they had some splendid long-range handgun shoots at the fabled range at Bisley Camp, which drew hundreds and hundreds of the best shooters from around the world. J.D. Jones won at least one of those. Back in the day, John Taffin wasn't just a proponent of the International Metallic Handgun Shooting Association, he was one of the men to beat at the game. After you've blown enough steel critters off their pedestals from two hundred LONG steps away, you pretty much have the feel of things.

Does anyone think that John and J.D. might have been helped in their long histories of difficult one-shot kills on wild game at unpredictable ranges by honing their skills in long range competition with the same type of guns they took into the hunting fields? Well, do you think their quarry went potty in the woods?

Shotguns

The shotgun with buckshot has a long history in combat; in the Twentieth century alone it proved so effective in the trenches of World War I that the Germans complained bitterly about Americans using it...my old friend and mentor Bill Jordan used one cleaning out pillboxes in the Pacific until the paper shotshells of the time swelled so badly in the jungle humidity that they wouldn't feed

In Wisconsin, camera catches beginning of Marcus Kranz' record-setting run, 5 rounds of 00 buckshot from his Benelli shotgun hitting 7-yard target in less than 7/10 of a second. His speed record stood for years, only beaten by Tim Forshey in 2011 by a few hundredths of a second.

reliably, and he switched to a Thompson submachinegun...and my friend and colleague from the Masters of Defense knife project James "Patches" Watson used an Ithaca Model 37 12 gauge pump gun to good effect as Richard Marcinko's SEAL point man in Vietnam. Scatterguns are still used today by our military. They remain a staple in America's home defense armory, and are still well-represented in police department armories, even in the time of the patrol rifle.

From the hunting side of things, while the slug-loaded shotgun remains a popular bear defense gun in Alaska and a popular deer gun in "shotgun only" jurisdictions, the main place the scattergun holds in the hunting sports is bird and small game shooting, with birdshot. Here we're talking fast-moving targets that need to be "led" by the shooter...and the classic shotgun sports, trap and skeet on the fast-flying discs called "clay birds," are great for learning lead and follow-through.

As riflemen and pistoleros have "practical shooting" matches, shotgunners have for some time benefited from the popular modern gun game called "sporting clays." Here, you find the targets presented from unexpected spots at unexpected times, sometimes popping nearly straight up, sometimes scooting low to the ground like a running rabbit, or a flightless or low-flying bird. The majority of hunters I've talked to who shoot the clay bird games, particularly sporting clays, tell me it has helped them connect with more real targets in the hunting fields. I have no reason to disbelieve them.

What's really going on

Why does competition shooting seem to give such a strong advantage to the practitioner when he or she has to fire "when the chips are down"? It seems to be a psychological conditioning thing.

Police officer competes with his patrol rifle, a red dot sighted Ruger Mini-14, during a three-gun match in Yakima, Washington.

What the cop or soldier calls "pucker factor" and the hunter calls "buck fever" is known to the competitive shooter as "match nerves." It all comes from the same source. We humans tend to be vulnerable to a mentality of "this is *it!*" The sudden realization that performance is now very, very important tends to trip the "fight or flight" response that's hardwired into our brains and adrenal systems.

Adrenaline (epinephrine) is instantly released to course rapidly through our bodies. It brings super strength for a short period of time. It also brings tremors, which hit the hands first and soon thereafter, the legs. The heart pounds and the lungs work like bellows, to get heavily oxygenated blood pumping fast through our system, to "fuel the furnace" for the strenuous physical effort our "survival instinct" prepares us for. Vasoconstriction occurs, redirecting blood away from our extremities and into our major muscle groups and viscera. This is what makes frightened Caucasians appear to turn deathly pale, and it is what makes us stronger, but also clumsier when we are under stress. Instinct tells us to focus on the threat, not the front sight. Instinct tells us to run, not to stand and deliver

what needs to be delivered to get the immediate job done in the very narrow time frame we have within which to accomplish that mission. Only acclimation to stress allows us to overcome those instincts, use the gun most efficiently, and "get the job done."

Sighting in on "the back forty" doesn't prepare us for that. Plinking tin cans off a fence doesn't prepare us for that. Casual shooting on the gun club range doesn't prepare us for that.

Competition, on the other hand...

In competition, people are watching you. Sometimes, in major matches, huge galleries of spectators. I dunno if that gets your blood pressure up, but it sure has that effect on me. In competition your ego is riding on the outcome. The scores are going to be published, and archived somewhere to live forever. Maybe friends and family are watching. *It matters!* If it's a big match, you've spent a lot on time and travel and practice, and now it is — cue the drum roll here — *The Moment of Truth.*

In 1979, the very first Bianchi Cup match was held at the Chapman Academy range in Columbia, Missouri. In those days, you had to be at least a state champion to get an invitation to compete. I shot that match on the same squad with the aforementioned Jim Cirillo. It was the highest-dollar-prize tournament in handgun shooting history to date, and you could cut the tension with a knife. Jim and I were walking between Match II and Match III together when he mentioned that he'd never felt stress like this in any of his gunfights. I asked him why he thought that was. He replied that in the gunfights, there weren't all these people watching you and there wasn't all this time to build up to it. Talk about "teachable moments!"

What competition shooting does for you is this: it makes shooting under stress the norm. Instead of "this is it!" or "this is the moment of truth!" what goes through your mind is a laser-like focus on what needs to be done to make each necessary shot perfect. The small but critical details — the draw of the pistol, the mounting of the shotgun to the shoulder, the safety catch snapping into the "fire" position" — happen reflexively.

Whether the stakes on the table are fresh meat versus grits for supper, or the far higher stakes of life versus death, if all other things are equal the advantage goes to the person most inured to shooting under stress in a moment when *no do-over will be allowed*, and it's *now or never*. Competition shooting is simply the most readily available avenue for building that experience.

We all know that a shooting match is not a gunfight, but people tend to forget that a gunfight *is* a shooting match. The person with the most experience shooting that gun fast and straight under pressure is the person who — again, with all other things being equal — will have an advantage which is very much worth acquiring.

Final advice: Don't tell me "I don't want to shoot in competition, because I'm afraid I'll come in dead last." First, if your skills are that rusty, don't you want to know *now* in time to polish them up? But, perhaps more important, the person who's likely to come in last is the person who gave up midway through because they weren't doing well enough to please their precious ego...or the person who did something stupid and unsafe with a gun, and was disqualified. You aren't either of *those* people, are you?

And even in the unlikely event that you do come in last, always remember this: You came in ahead of a few thousand people who like to *think* they're a cool honcho of the gun, but didn't have the guts to put their skill on the line in public at a match.

The kind of guts *you* just proved you have, when you competed. Δ

The Best of the First Two Years

Our first big anthology!

In these 12 issues you'll find:

- ❋ A little knowledge and sweat can build a home for under $10,000
- ❋ Tepee to cabin to dream house
- ❋ From the foundation up, house-building is forgiving
- ❋ A first time horse buyer's guide
- ❋ Canning meat
- ❋ Backwoods Home recipes
- ❋ In pursuit of independence
- ❋ Canning blueberries
- ❋ Pioneer women on the trail west
- ❋ Some tips on first aid readiness
- ❋ Whip grafting—the key to producing fruit variety
- ❋ Sawmills: a firm foundation to homesteading
- ❋ The basics of backyard beekeeping
- ❋ How to make soap
- ❋ The instant greenhouse
- ❋ The old time spring house
- ❋ For battling ants or growing earth worms, try coffee grounds

Drinking problems

By Len McDougall

We'd been road-camping for the past week, exploring the vast public forests in Michigan's Upper Peninsula, from the geologically ancient Huron Mountains to the Driggs River. We were aware and wary of parasitic pathogens in the waters we drank, so even the most pristine rushing whitewaters were boiled or treated with iodine before being drunk or used to cook.

On the way back home, Phil began to feel ill. He developed severe gastrointestinal distress, with considerable pain, nausea, and diarrhea. The next day, those symptoms were joined by a high fever, achiness, and general malaise. A trip to the doctor and a stool sample later, and Phil had the bad news that he'd contracted a parasitic intestinal cyst.

Worse, there was no accepted medical cure to expel the creatures once they'd gotten a foothold; the prognosis was frequent bouts of flu-like illness until the cysts matured, laid their eggs, and were expelled as waste, typically two months after infestation. The worst part was that Phil made his living as a contract roofer, and the added trips up and down ladders cost him in more ways than one.

Every freshwater source on earth is home to parasitic flagellates like *Giardia lamblia,* and cysts like *Cryptosporidium parvum,* which the CDC estimates will afflict 80% of Americans in their lifetimes. In tropical climates, there are also parasitic worms that may infest victims' livers, intestines, lungs, or hearts. The USFWS also warns that tapeworms, which are not aquatic, could be contracted from hard-to-drown eggs washed into waters from infected scats.

A hit with day hikers and kayakers, squeeze-bottle filters work just by filling the bottle with untreated water, screwing on the cap and attached filter, and squeezing pure drinking water from the spout.

Boiling water (212° F) for two minutes renders harmless all living organisms within. Boiling does not lessen the concentration or toxicity of most chemicals, like the gasoline and solvents that are inevitably contained in floodwaters, or botulism spores that can only be destroyed by temperatures above 350° F in a pressure cooker. During a flood, concentrations of petrochemicals and heavy metals are usually low enough not to be immediately health-threatening, but urban floodwaters are invariably contaminated with sewage, as evidenced by the epidemic of cholera, typhoid, giardia, and other waterborne pathogens that ensued in the aftermath of Hurricane Katrina. Never drink water containing engine coolant or other toxins, because being sick and thirsty is worse than just being thirsty.

Potassium iodide tablets in the prescribed concentration (or three drops of Tincture of Iodine per quart of water) will kill bacteria, viruses, and free-swimming flagellates like Giardia. Iodine will not kill parasitic intestinal cysts, like *Cryptosporidium*

or *Cyclospora*. The same is true for Halazone (chlorine) tablets. Katadyn's MicroPur (Dichloroisocyanurate dihydrate) tablets kill everything, but even they require a four-hour wait to ensure the demise of tough cysts. MSR's MIOX micropurifier uses raw water, salt, and batteries to produce a "cocktail" of bug-killers similar to MicroPur tabs; so long as those three elements are present, the MIOX can continue to sterilize water, albeit one liter at a time, which made it a godsend after the Indian Ocean tsunami of 2004.

Portable backpacker-type water filters are a must-have for even the most urban survival kits. Failures at water treatment facilities are not uncommon, and probably most people who use municipal tapwater have received a warning to boil or filter it at some point. There are numerous makes and models, but all drinking water filter-purifiers are EPA-mandated to remove 99.98% of organisms larger than viruses, which takes some of the guesswork out of selecting one. Filters can reduce chemical and heavy-metal concentrations by as

Even in the dead of winter, parasites and other aquatic pathogens remain viable, just waiting to be awakened by the warmth of a host's internal organs.

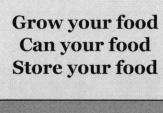
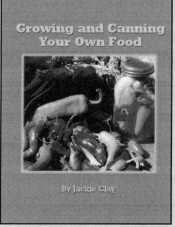

much as 80%, and most are rated to provide at least 200 gallons of drinking water. Disposable filter-cartridge models are shorter-lived than more expensive ceramic-element models but ceramic filters clog more easily and require frequent cleaning. Operational life between replacement or cleanings is dependent on how much matter is stopped by the filter, so avoid murky water.

Most backpacking water filters employ a hand-pump unit that sucks in and forces untreated water through its filter and into a drinking container. Some consist of a collapsible bag filled with untreated water and hung up so that gravity and the water's own weight forces it through a filter.

If you want go super light, there's the squeeze-bottle type, like Katadyn's new MyBottle, which has an internal replaceable filter attached to the drinking spout. This almost science-fiction filter uses hand pressure to drive untreated water through a filter, then out through a drinking spout as potable water. This filter is almost indistinguishable from an ordinary water bottle, and if you remove its filter cartridge, it can be filled with other beverages. Prices for basic filter models begin at under $50, ranging upward to more than $100 for professional-grade units.

Len McDougall is the author of more than a dozen books and has been a wilderness survival instructor for more than 25 years. His first novel, *The Mackinaw Incident*, will be published this summer. He lives in Michigan's Upper Peninsula. Δ

Sterno and the Blue Hill Stove

By Amaury Murgado

I'm going on my 26th year as a first responder in law enforcement. During that time I have learned that being prepared is a lot better than being miserable. Something else I've learned over the years is to have backups to everything important that you carry. This philosophy is exemplified in an adage found in military circles that states, "One is none and two is one." I'd like to share a simple backup to emergency preparedness that has fallen out of use — canned Sterno. There are a few tricks of the trade that may make you reconsider Sterno as a viable option.

Many people think Sterno is outdated because of the advances made in camping and backpacking stoves since its development in the late 1800s. But I don't consider it outdated or archaic. The trick to any technology is to use it in a way that plays into its strengths and match those strengths with your needs.

Sterno has many good attributes. It's almost odorless, its gel form is hard to spill, and it is designed so it can be used indoors. There are very few survival-type heat tabs or military surplus-type sources that can make the same claims. You can find Sterno (or something similar) in most grocery stores or retailers that sell cooking or camping supplies. Because it's readily available and relatively inexpensive, you are more prone to have it around and therefore have it ready for use.

I find that Sterno is a particularly realistic option when used as a backup or travel stove. It's very easy to set up and break down. Pop the cap off, and light it; put the cap back on, and put it away. There are no extra fuel bottles to worry about and no assembly required. You can store it in a go-bag or place it on a shelf in your garage or pantry.

Sterno works well in the field or at home.

Still, the can of Sterno by itself only gets you so far as it's a heat source and nothing else. You still need some type of stove attachment or other setup to place cookware over it. I have used the Sterno folding stove before and found the combination a little cumbersome. However, I found a little device that has really made me start appreciating Sterno even more. It's a small stainless steel fire ring that fits on top of the larger Sterno can. It's called the Blue Hill Stove and it turns every can of Sterno into a lightweight and portable stove. The whole kit never gets any bigger than the can itself as the ring stores underneath the can.

The Blue Hill Stove has three built-in detents that hold a cup, small pot, or other cookware. It has a sturdy design and works well under field and at-home conditions. The ring's design helps keep the cooking surface closer to the heat source and yet allows for good air flow to feed the flame.

Because of its relatively compact size, you can carry it with you almost anywhere. For example, I keep a set in my car's survival kit and one in my motorcycle saddlebags to use during emergencies. I also keep one in my patrol car as a backup to my primary backpacking stove which is located in my readiness bag.

Carrying this combo stored in your vehicles gives you options. You never know when you might have to spend hours in the middle of nowhere because of bad timing, inclement weather, or just plain bad luck. I have found that many a stressful situation has been made less stressful by simply warming up a cup of instant soup, coffee, or hot chocolate. It takes your mind off of things and gives you a few moments to regroup.

A Backwoods Home Anthology
The Ninth Year

❋ Build your own solar hot tub
❋ Make mead the easy way
❋ Plant fruit trees, pick big bucks
❋ Make "split pulley" bookends
❋ Grow unusual plants
❋ Install your own septic system
❋ Compost the quickie way
❋ Remembering the good life
❋ Build a fish pond, just for fun
❋ Build your own portable forge

❋ Try growing the popular potato
❋ Kerosene lamps — a brilliant idea
❋ Convert dead space to closet space
❋ Try this gravel road waterbreak
❋ Cash in on those windfalls
❋ Whole-grain sourdough recipes
❋ Victory gardens
❋ Long term food storage
❋ Use common herbs to treat the
   common cold

Having four or five cans of Sterno spread around for your individual needs (car, home, workshop, etc.) won't break the bank either. Since each can burns for a little more than two hours, it's really not a bad deal.

I have dealt with many citizens in my jurisdiction that were caught in some type of natural disaster or other emergency only to find out that their generator, gas grill, or propane stove had been stolen, damaged, or had empty tanks. For those concerned with Sterno's lower heat output or longer cooking times, I never said it was ideal. If we are talking slower burn versus no burn, I'll take slower over nothing every time.

You can do a few things to make it work better. For example, you can always mix some denatured alcohol into the gel. This will make it burn a bit hotter. And of course there is always what grandma taught us about adding a bit of salt to your water or cooking with a lid. These two things will also help speed up your cooking times.

Another trick is to try to keep the cans at least halfway full when using them. I recommend using two at a time. When the first drops to halfway, seal it and start using the other can. When that one drops to halfway, open the first and combine the two. That gives you a full can to use. It's not that Sterno won't work when it's below halfway, it just seems to work better when it's closer to being full.

In 2004, I worked four hurricanes and three tropical storms back to back. Towards the end we were like walking zombies. That experience really left a deep impression on me because I was surprised at just how many people, first responders included, did not prepare well. I am always looking for ways to work smarter and not harder when it comes to being prepared. Sometimes something as simple as a can of Sterno turned compact stove can make your life a lot easier during an emergency. It could make the difference between having a hot meal or eating straight out of a can. I've done both and definitely prefer the hot meal.

Amaury Murgado is the Special Operations Lieutenant with the Osceola County (Florida) Sheriff's Office and has 26 years of law enforcement experience. He is also a retired Master Sergeant with the Army Reserve. Lieutenant Murgado also writes a monthly column for *Police Magazine* titled Best Practices.

The author is not affiliated with Blue Hill Stove. Anyone interested in finding out more about the fire ring can contact Shawn Wertz directly at houseoffire72@gmail.com or call 715-764-0484. Δ

It is very hard to see Sterno when lit, so use caution.

Lenie in the kitchen

Leftover hamburger and potato casserole

By Ilene Duffy

Our oldest sons, Jacob and Robby, are big eaters. So I get a lot of pleasure when I get the chance to don my apron when they're home from college and cook up a big meal for them. Recently, on their last day home before returning to school, I wanted to fix an extra special meal for their send-off. I started the day by remembering what was already in the fridge that needed to be used up, what I had in my pantry, and how to conjure up side dishes that would pair nicely with my blossoming idea for a casserole using leftover hamburgers.

The day before, I had made a huge batch of burgers after my three guys and three of their friends came home after snowboarding. They arrived super hungry and I was ready for them with loads of hamburgers and all the fixings. I started with about five pounds of ground beef, added three eggs, about ¾ cup of oatmeal, a large squirt of ketchup, about a half cup of water, and a bit of salt and pepper. I made the patties and fried them in hot olive oil. It must have been a huge batch since I wound up with three large hamburgers left over. Here's how I used them up.

I started preparing the casserole by using up tidbits of vegetables in the fridge. I found a bit of celery, a half of a large onion, a couple of carrots, and about a half of an orange bell pepper. I chopped everything and began frying them in hot olive oil for about five minutes. I turned off the stove to zip to the garage pantry to get two cans of cream of mushroom soup. When I got back to the kitchen, I noticed that it looked like some of the veggies from the pan were missing. Then bold as brass, husband Dave joined me in the kitchen and started scooping up spoonfuls of the cooked veggies! "Stop it … they're for the casserole!" So here's a warning from me — if you've got a hungry husband like mine, cook a few extra vegetables or guard your fry pan.

Hamburger and potato casserole

½ large onion, chopped
2 stalks of celery, chopped
2 small carrots, chopped
½ orange bell pepper, chopped
5 cloves of garlic, chopped
olive oil for frying the vegetables
3 large pre-cooked hamburgers
11 small to medium potatoes, peeled and sliced thin
2 15-oz. cans cream of mushroom soup
½ cup sour cream
¾ cup milk
¾ cup cheddar cheese, grated
2 tsp. no salt seasoning blend
½ tsp. salt
½ tsp. pepper
1 Tbsp. dried parsley
olive oil for greasing casserole dish
bread crumbs (optional)

Preparation:

Heat oven to 350° F. Chop the vegetables and garlic, heat olive oil in a fry pan, and cook vegetables for about five minutes, adding the garlic last. In a large bowl, mix the cooked vegetables and all remaining ingredients except the olive oil and bread crumbs. Mix thoroughly. Add more milk if needed to make the mixture somewhat liquidy. Pour into oiled large casserole dish. Bake for about 90 minutes. Shake a spoonful or two of bread crumbs over the top and bake another 10 minutes.

Salad with mandarin tangerines

I love this colorful salad and it's so easy to prepare. I didn't have any purple onion in the house, but it's a nice addition. The hardest thing about making this salad is having enough

A nicely browned hamburger and potato casserole along with a pretty green salad dress up the dinner table.

I grew the pumpkins. I baked the pies. The boys and Dave love them.

self control so I won't gobble up a bunch of the sweet, cold tangerines after I open up the cans.

6-8 cups of salad greens
1 cucumber, peeled and sliced
½ yellow or orange bell pepper, sliced
2 cans mandarin tangerines, drained
½ small purple onion, sliced thin
½ cup walnuts, chopped (optional)
2 Tbsp. olive oil
2 Tbsp. balsamic vinegar
½ tsp. spicy brown mustard
pinch of sugar
salt and pepper to taste
Parmesan cheese, grated

Preparation:

Add salad greens, cucumber, bell pepper, tangerines, onion, and walnuts in a salad bowl. Mix gently. In a separate bowl, wisk together the olive oil, vinegar, mustard, sugar, salt, and pepper. You might need to add a bit more vinegar if the dressing looks too thick. Right before serving, add the dressing to the salad and toss gently. Serve with grated Parmesan cheese.

Orange and date platter

This is a great little side dish that's pretty and so quick to prepare. I like to add this to the dinner table when juicy oranges are in season.

Just peel three oranges and slice crosswise. Spread on a platter. Add pitted whole dates around the edge. You can add a few pecan halves for decoration, if desired.

I grew a bunch of nice pumpkins this past year and still have a couple in storage. A proper college send-off for my college boys wouldn't be complete without a couple of their favorite pies. This is Jackie Clay's recipe that is tried and true in the Duffy household.

Pumpkin pie

1 unbaked pie crust
3 eggs
1½ cups mashed pumpkin
½ cup brown sugar
½ cup sugar
½ tsp. ground cloves
½ tsp. nutmeg
1 tsp. ginger
1 tsp. cinnamon
1 cup milk
2 tsp. butter, melted
1 Tbsp. flour

Preparation:

Pre-heat oven to 400° F. Prepare a pie crust, place in a pie pan and set aside. In a large bowl, beat eggs. Add pumpkin, sugars, and spices. Mix. Stir in milk. In a separate small bowl, melt butter, add flour and mix until smooth. Add a bit more butter to make it creamy if necessary. Add to pumpkin mix and thoroughly whisk in. Pour into pie shell. Bake for 15 minutes at 400°. Turn down heat to 350° and bake for 45 minutes or until a toothpick inserted in the center comes out clean. Δ

One last outing before heading back to college is to take Damon for his first trip to the beach.

part 3

Food security 101

Why I love my vacuum sealer (and more)

By Rowena Aldridge

In parts 1 and 2 (Issues #138 and #139), we covered basics and homemade convenience foods. Now that you've become so proficient at making delicious, nutritious, and economical foods for your family, how in the world are you going to store it all? How will you keep it from losing quality and going bad?

I do this by making frequent use of my FoodSaver® vacuum sealer. It's my BFF — best friend forever — when it comes to food storage.

Better storage means *Better Food.* Better food means *Better Health.* Better health means a *Better Nation.*

We got ours years ago. Since then they've made many improvements, but the model we have does the job very well. If you can find one at a yard sale or on Craigslist, you can set yourself up to deal with every type of food storage need.

The customary way to use the vacuum sealer is to buy foods in bulk, then divide them into smaller portions for storage in the freezer. You can also vacuum seal cooked foods and pull them out later for reheating. All you need for this purpose is a roll of vacuum sealer bags and you're good to go.

What opened my eyes to the wider food storage possibilities of the vacuum sealer was learning about canning jar sealers. These little gadgets let you put food in ordinary canning jars and completely remove the air. You can create a vacuum-sealed jar right in your own home!

Warning! *Vacuum sealing jars does not take the place of proper canning methods! The vacuum sealer has a specific purpose and place in the kitchen. When used appropriately, it will make your food storage efficient, useful, and even attractive. But don't try to use it to cut corners on food preservation. "Sorry" doesn't begin to express how you'll feel if you discover that your diligence and hard-earned money have been wasted on food that went bad from not being canned properly, or from seeing friends and loved ones become sick from eating foods you thought would nourish them.*

Let me give you an example of how vacuum-sealed canning jars can work for you. My homemade convenience mixes go into various canning jars, with the ingredients list and instructions for use right on the jars. These are relatively shelf-stable and require no extra work. No vacuum sealing for them.

But here's where the jar sealer makes itself indispensable as a frugal

119

Wartime food demonstration. Explaining methods of "extending" meats now that rationing is limiting civilian meat purchases, wartime food demonstrator Alice Burtis puts finishing touches to a meat loaf before an audience in Washington, D.C. (Source: Library of Congress)

meal tool: You can prepare a week's worth of perishable salads, soups, and healthy snacks, prepare them at home in one session, place them in canning jars, then vacuum seal them for storage. Into the refrigerator they go.

For instance, I make complete salads and put everything in one jar: dressing first, then various veggies and other salad toppings (cherry tomatoes, onion slivers, bits of celery, cheese, etc.), then lettuce on top. This way the greens are separated from the dressing and remain crisp. I also vacuum seal fresh fruit and veggie crudités, so when my daughter Ella opens the fridge and sees all the pretty jars of pretty food, it's an easy choice for her to pick something healthy rather than a cookie or a bag of chips.

But there's more to this story: By using the jar sealer to store perishables, I can extend their freshness by more than double. A head of ordinary lettuce can last up to two weeks when chopped and vacuum sealed in a jar, with no loss of quality. Cheese can go months and still look, feel, and taste

new. Even cooked foods keep longer when sealed in a jar, and that lets me use them in dishes up to a week later, making it feel like we're not eating the same meal over and over.

There are some things I don't vacuum seal. Items that get opened more than a few times a week just get regular lids or go into ziplock bags. It's easier that way, because they get used up well before they would go bad anyway.

Also, some things just do better without being sealed up tight — for example, bread crumbs, which I keep in a jar that has a muffin paper liner instead of a regular lid. After all, I want my breadcrumbs to stay stale.

Tips:

When sealing things in bags for the freezer, it is sometimes better to cut a much larger bag than needed. If I know I'll only use a small portion of something, I'll usually just put it into one big bag which then gets opened and resealed as things get used up. This saves on the number of bags I store and saves money on bags too.

(Every time you open a bag, you have to cut off the part at the top where the old seal is, thus making the bag smaller. If you start with a bag that is already the right size for a serving, once you open it, it might be too small to use again for anything but scraps. But if you start with a bigger bag, you can keep closing it, losing only the little bit at the top that you cut off when you opened it.

Dehydrated foods will last nearly forever in a vacuum-sealed container. Put crushable dehydrated foods in jars, and non-crushables in bags. You don't have to freeze them, just put them on the shelf and admire your handiwork.

Oh yes — label everything! There are few things more demoralizing than the discovery that you used cream of something soup mix to make pancakes. I put the ingredient list right on the jar if it is big enough, and sometimes the instructions too.

When canning, you must use a new, unused lid for each jar, but when using the vacuum sealer with canning jars for meal storage you can use the same lid over and over. This is what I do with lids that have been removed from previously canned foods. When I get the time, energy, and materials to do it, I'm going to paint my lids with red chalkboard paint so I can use them as labels, too!

Extreme meal planning

Okay, maybe all this food drying, canning, and sealing is not for you. Maybe you just want some simple, painless, non-time-consuming ways to feed your family well and make your groceries go as far as they can. I get that, and in fact I lived that when I was still working outside the home.

But don't be fooled by finance guy Dave Ramsey's schtick about eating "beans and rice, rice and beans" to save money. Frugality doesn't mean doing without. It means using what you have well, so that what you have is enough. And you can do that right now, with very little effort.

There are several ways you can go about this. One is the planned-leftover method, which essentially means making a little more than needed for each meal and setting some of it aside for lunch the next day. I do this, and to make this more effective I load the lunch containers before serving the meal so that the needed portions are accounted for.

The next step along this continuum is what TV cook Sandra Lee calls "Round 2 Recipes." This means setting aside some of the ingredients while you are preparing your meal and using them for a different recipe the next day. I do this sometimes too. In fact, I even do this in reverse when I'm canning (setting aside some of the food I'm prepping for jars to use for that day's meal).

Using substitutes such as corn syrup and vegetable shortening, home economist Ida Lansden shows a group of Alexandria, Virginia, women how to bake the most succulent of sugarless, butterless cakes.
(Source: Library of Congress)

Left Overs: How to Transform Them into Palatable and Wholesome Dishes
(babel.hathitrust.org/cgi/pt?id=loc.ark:/13960/t6252427g) By Mrs. S. T. Rorer, 1898. This is the book that got me started down this road. Mrs. Rorer was a very practical woman with plenty of advice on the subject, and I've learned something useful in all her books, even the one on chafing dishes.
Foods That Will Win the War and How to Cook Them
(gutenberg.org/ebooks/15464) By Goodies and Goudiss, 1918. Nobody does food like people under fire.
"That's Not Trash, That's Dinner!"
(nytimes.com/2011/07/27/dining/thats-not-trash-thats-dinner.html) A *New York Times* article for those who want a few modern-day examples of using absolutely everything.

But the level I'm going to encourage you to shoot for is the one in which every morsel left in the pan at the end of a meal and every dab left at the bottom of a can and every drip at the end of a jar is assessed for its potential to become part of a new dish in a new meal. This is not as hard as it sounds; it just takes a little practice. To get you started, here are some of my favorite tips for turning what might be considered waste into nutritious, healthy, fun dishes and meals.

General ideas:

Set a jar or other container in the fridge and put in it any little bit of leftover veggies and cold meat — the last few olives in the jar, that half a boiled egg that you forgot to put in the lunch box, etc. When you have enough, chop them all up, mix with some vinaigrette and serve in a lettuce wrap (mix with a little mayo and some lemon juice and serve in a pita or mix with some salsa and serve rolled up in a tortilla).

Combine leftover rice or that one last corn muffin, some leftover chopped meat, that last bit of onion or garlic, some herbs and seasoning, then stuff them in a hollowed-out tomato, sweet pepper (or heck, even a hot pepper if you like!), squash, zucchini, or eggplant. Then stand them in water or stock in a pan and heat in the oven until browned on top.

Croquettes can be made from just about anything. If you have meat or chicken or fish, chop it finely, add herbs and seasoning, an egg, and enough breadcrumbs/leftover rice/unsweetened cereal/plain oatmeal to hold it all together. Form into small patties, heat in a pan until browned, and serve with a sauce: gravy or tomato sauce/ketchup for meat, white sauce for chicken, soy sauce for fish. Offer them on a platter with some tartar or cucumber sauce and you have a fabulous brunch entrée!

Save leftover bits of fruit together in a jar in the fridge and when you have enough, make a fruit pot pie. You might not even need to add sugar — just thicken any juices with a little cornstarch on the stove, pour the whole thing into a prepared pie crust and bake. Or if you prefer, mix some crumbled graham crackers with a little butter and press them into the bottom of a pan, pour the fruit and thickened juice on top, and chill for a delicious mixed fruit tart.

This and that:

When you finish a jar of pickles, slice up some veggies and put them in the jar with the juice overnight — instant refrigerator pickled veggies!

You can also use the pickle juice to make a delicious salad dressing. Just mix three parts oil to one part pickle juice. Add a little sugar if it's too tart for your taste.

Stale cheese — the stuff that has gotten hard around the edges — can be grated and stored in a jar. Mix it with breadcrumbs to make a tasty casserole topping or sprinkle it on crackers and pop them in the oven to make an easy snack.

Speaking of breadcrumbs — save any piece of bread that's going stale, toast it, and crumble it into a jar. You can add Italian seasoning mix to make your own seasoned breadcrumbs. Mixing different breads makes a wonderful crumb that has more depth of flavor.

Save the juice from a can of stewed tomatoes to use for flavoring soups, stews, or stocks.

The same goes for the last tablespoon of mashed potatoes, which can be used to thicken a gravy or to make the sauce in the crock pot.

Don't slice a citrus fruit if you don't need an actual slice. Just poke a hole in the side to squeeze out some juice, then plug the hole with a piece of a toothpick. Save the slicing for when you really need the fruit.

I could go on, but there are so many great resources available elsewhere that I'll put some of my favorite links in a sidebar.

Food security

Food security means different things to different people. Some think of it as having enough to eat. Some feel it's knowing their food is of a certain level of quality. Some think of it as always being able to acquire food when they need it.

For me, it's knowing that we are prepared for many different situations — loss of work, loss of electricity, zombie apocalypse, whatever. It means making sure that every penny of our food budget goes as far as it can — that I honor the hard work my husband, Rudi, does to provide for our family by protecting the resources we have and using them to their fullest. This gives me peace of mind and self-confidence that helps me not panic when things get scary.

With that in mind, here are a few more tips that work for me:

Don't put all your eggs in one basket (or your squash, or your plums, or your beef stew). Having half an acre of veggies processed and in the freezer will not do you much good if the power goes out and all your food goes bad. Nor would your food security be enhanced by discovering that you had a canning failure on 20 pounds of beef.

This is why I recommend that you take the time to buy or preserve your foods in a variety of states, if possible. Freeze some uncooked, some prepared. Can some, dehydrate some. Store some as full meals and some as separate ingredients. Yes, it's more work, but it also grants peace of mind, not to mention the convenience of having a wider array of options available when planning and preparing meals.

Meat is a specialty item. I don't dehydrate meats for food storage because they don't last as long as meats that are properly canned or frozen. It's the fat that even very lean meat has to make it go rancid over time. At most, good home dehydrated jerky will last a few weeks without freezing. However, it does make a tasty, nutritious, lightweight food to carry for camping or a road trip, so I try to plan ahead and have some on hand for short-term needs.

It doesn't have to be all or nothing. The main reason people choose to put up big lots of a given food at one time is that it's more efficient. After all, if you're chopping vegetables and filling jars, chopping and filling a little more only takes a little more time because you're already set up for it. But small-batch preserving might be right up your alley, not to mention that having a few jars of this and that is a great way to start building up a good pantry.

It doesn't have to be all at once. Maybe the idea of big-scale preserving *does* appeal to you. Don't go overboard and burn out! Choose one thing, do that, repeat. You'll get into a groove and before you know it, you'll be looking for more places to stash your treasure.

The main thing is that you *can* take steps to make your family's menus inviting, delicious, and healthy. You *can* save money doing it. And you *can* find great satisfaction in it. I do, and you will too. Just start and you might be amazed at what you achieve.

Rowena Aldridge is a former professional ballerina who now spends her days homeschooling and homemaking. She is a certified educator in a number of old-school domestic skills, but her real passion is empowering others to go out and conquer the world on their own terms.

Learn more about her classes and other projects at www.romesticity.com

(Read part one of this series in issue #138, November/December 2012 and part two in issue #139, January/February 2013.) Δ

Of sawbucks and Charlie

By F.J. Bohan

I first became aware of sawbucks many years ago when an older and wiser friend suggested that I build one after he took note that I had purchased my first chainsaw. I remember his words like it was yesterday.

"F.J., you'll be wanting to keep that bar clean and the blade sharp," Charlie said. (We'll call him Charlie, since that was his name.) "You'll need to be building a sawbuck to cut your firewood off of."

Charlie would go on and on about how it takes so long to sharpen the blade, it only makes sense that I don't run the blade through dirt or rocks in the ground, and how a sawbuck would also keep me well-balanced and perhaps even keep me from stumbling or falling while the chainsaw was revved up and running. At the time, Charlie had some interesting notions that I sometimes wroteoff as the ramblings of an old man.

Charlie was also the guy who told me that just because I had a 20-inch

Finished sawbuck

bar, it didn't mean I could tackle a 40-inch tree. Those words were still fresh in my mind a few weeks later, because one of the first trees I tackled was indeed a 40-inch diameter oak.

A carriage bolt holds the pallets together.

It was a stately tree that stood about 100 feet tall in a clearing that had allowed it to become full and well-balanced. There was enough firewood in that tree to last me three years! After cutting and wedging and more cutting, I witnessed the oak drop straight down, maintaining its perfect balance as it settled and trapped 18 inches of my 20-inch bar.

As I stood 200 feet away from the now-freed giant, I pondered how I was going to get the tree to fall over and save my chainsaw. Since Charlie wasn't around to tell me how to do it, I had to figure it out myself.

It ended up that I carefully removed my saw from the trapped bar and pulled the tree over with a long heavy rope, several lengths of 3/8-inch chain, and a large truck. By happy chance the giant cooperated by falling in the direction I had wanted, rather than the opposite direction which, without doubt, would have seen both me and the truck become a flying spectacle of sorts. Once the tree was

Position of plywood brace

down and my saw put back together, I felt a lot better.

I didn't get any firewood cut that day (having spent the entire time just trying to get the tree to fall down); however, the next day when I started cutting those 40-inch diameter logs, I did get some satisfaction in knowing how wrong Charlie was about the sawbuck. I could hardly lift a single 16-inch length of the 40-inch diameter log into the back of my pickup, let alone lift an eight-foot length to place on a sawbuck!

Years later, out west in the high desert of Arizona, I fired up the saw to do some woodcutting. At some point, when I reached down with the saw to cut a log, I lost my balance and stumbled just a bit. The blade tip touched the ground and caught a small section of a limb that had been just cut. I released the trigger as soon as I could, but it wasn't soon enough to prevent the cut limb from being thrown back at me at a very high velocity and striking me right square in the knee.

The cut limb hit me with enough force to drop me right there where I was standing. I was flat on my back,

holding my knee, and in the "assess the injury" mode when my wife called out for me. At first, when it occurred to her that I had just been involved in a chainsaw-related accident, she was hesitant to come help, fearing what she may see.

I eventually coaxed her into helping me stand up and get into the cabin through a series of heartfelt pleas and a strong promise that I wasn't bleeding. She had me sit down and fixed me a cup of coffee. I couldn't decide which hurt more: my knee, my back, or my pride. I knew that if Charlie had been around, he would have told me how a sawbuck keeps your work in front of you and is easier on your back. I continued sipping my coffee and wondered if Charlie had been right about sawbucks.

Over the years I have purchased quite a few saws, too many chains, and far too many files. I can't count how many times my blades have been run through the dirt, chipped by rocks, and re-sharpened in the driving cold wind and deep snows of winter.

Later that season I got around to actually building a sawbuck.

Regrettably, when we sold our Arizona ranch, it went along with it. This was most unfortunate since, now that we have settled back east, I once again find the need for a sawbuck.

Nonetheless, I came to the conclusion that, being in need of firewood again and getting closer to being the same age as Charlie was when he first mentioned it, it was time to build another sawbuck.

After sitting down with a cup of coffee to think about it, I realized that there are probably as many designs of sawbucks as there are men like Charlie who tout them. While they may all be somewhat different in size or design, sawbucks can make cutting firewood a bit safer and greatly reduce the opportunity for your saw blade to run through rocks and dirt, not to mention making wood cutting easier on your back.

I sketched my plans and had a material list made out, along with a general idea of the cost, and was about ready to head out to our local big box lumber store when my wife told me to sit down. She suggested I save some money by cleaning up around the shed and using some of those old pallets I had laying around.

I was hesitant in accepting her suggestion at first; after all, those pallets were going to be used one day for something really important that needed to be stacked on a pallet. Not wanting to appear too eager, I finished my coffee before telling her that this was indeed a good idea.

With two of the stoutest pallets I could find, two ½x6-inch carriage bolts, a few nails, and some scrap plywood, I put together a sawbuck in short order that would have made Charlie proud.

F.J. Bohan is the author of *Living on the Edge: A Family's Journey to Self-Sufficiency,* Paladin Press 2012. Δ

GROWING PEACH TREES

By Tom Kovach

There are two basic types of peach trees to choose from; the standard size (15 to 20 feet tall), or the genetic dwarf peach tree (4 feet to 10 feet tall). Both types produce an eye-catching canopy of delicate, pink or white flowers in the spring and juicy, sweet, fuzzy-skinned fruit when they ripen in the summer.

A standard peach tree will spread 18 to 22 feet wide; whereas the dwarf peach tree will need only 5 to 8 feet of space and can even be grown in containers.

The peaches themselves are classified as either freestone or clingstone. In clingstone peaches, the flesh sticks to the pit. In freestone peaches, the body of the fruit easily breaks free from the pit, making these varieties a better choice for canning and other cooking uses.

Buy bare root trees in spring from sources that offer at least a one-year guarantee on the plant. Avoid container-grown trees with uneven leaf growth, as they may be stressed. Do not buy bare root trees in the summer.

Peach trees can be successfully grown in growing Zones 5 through 9. They all require full sun and some shelter from the wind. On the average, a mature peach tree can yield anywhere from 2 to 3 bushels of fruit in one season. They are a great addition to any yard or garden.

Planting and aftercare

Soak roots of bare root trees in a tub of water for several hours (but not more than 24 hours). Then plant the trees as soon as possible.

Dig a hole twice as wide and one-and-a-half times as deep as the root mass. Mix soil from the hole with 1 part compost to 2 parts of soil. Prune off any twisted, broken, or dead roots. Form a cone of the soil mix in the hole. Spread the roots down around the mound. Adjust the level of the tree so that the bud union (where the stem joins the rootstock) sits one inch above ground level. Fill with soil. Firm down and water. Thin the peaches when they are about one inch in diameter. Allow about 6 to 10 inches

between each fruit on a branch. Spray the tree with dormant oil (horticultural oil) in early spring of the next year, before any buds open. This will kill any insects and eggs.

Peach trees require at least six hours of sunshine a day, so plant the trees in a sunny, sheltered location away from chilling winds. Peaches like well-drained, rich, sandy soil with plenty of organic matter, such as compost.

Harvesting

In the summer, start harvesting your peaches when they are firm, ripe, and have attained their mature color. Harvest white-fleshed peaches when they are yellowish-white on the outside. Harvest yellow-fleshed peaches when they have a red blush on the outside. Twist the fruit off the stem.

A low yield and poor-quality fruit are signs that the tree is not receiving adequate nutrients. Gently dig 1 to 11/2 pounds of all-purpose fertilizer into the soil each spring, and prune when the tree is dormant to promote new growth. Nitrogen deficiency can cause slow growth and light green or yellow leaves. Apply nitrogen-rich fertilizer in early summer. Peach leaf curl causes the leaves to develop swollen, bumpy, red areas, and can weaken the entire tree. Spray with Bordeaux or lime-sulfur mixture in late autumn, and again in spring, just before flower buds begin to swell.

After harvesting fruit, store at 60 to 70° F, for best flavor. They will be ready to eat in 24 hours. The following year, after the first harvest in early spring, prune at least one-third of the previous year's growth. If the peach tree appears vigorous, you can trim one-half of the previous year's growth.

Standard peaches

Belle Of Georgia: Has firm fruit with juicy, white flesh; large tree; late season; disease resistant. Pit type: Freestone.

Hale Haven: Oval-shaped fruit; excellent for canning and freezing; skin is bruise-resistant. Pit type: Freestone.

J.H. Hale: Deep crimson, almost fuzzless skin; needs another variety close by to grow fruit. Pit type: Freestone.

Elberta: Most popular peach tree; fruit has golden yellow flesh; very good keeper. Pit type: Freestone.

Red Haven: Yellow flesh and dark red, smooth skin; very juicy; tolerates cold well. Pit type: Semi-freestone.

Reliance: Pink flowers; fruit has juicy, yellow, very sweet flesh; tolerates cold well. Pit type: Freestone.

Dwarf peaches

Garden Sun: Fruit has yellow flesh; full flavored; good for canning and preserves. Pit Type: Freestone.

Frost Peach: Juicy, very sweet flesh; tree produces heavy yield; resistant to peach leaf curl. Pit type: Freestone.

Dwarf Golden Jubilee: Large fruit; soft, yellow skin with a red blush; tree produces heavy yield. Pit type: Freestone.

Honey Babe: Sweet, yellow flesh; mid-season; attractive red-blushed, lightly fuzzy skin. Pit type: Freestone.

Southern Flame: Small fruit has firm, yellow flesh and subtle flavor; mid-season. Pit type: Freestone.

Stark Sensation: Fruit has rich, yellow flesh; excellent for containers; tolerates cold well. Pit type: Clingstone. Δ

Make your own permanent copper tags

By Jackie Clay-Atkinson

I'm sure we've all been there: getting new fruit trees, shrubs, or perennials and planting them carefully with their paper or little wrap-around plastic name tags so we'll remember just what and where they are growing. Then a year or two later, we look and *no tag*. Was that tree a Chestnut crab? Or was it a Honeycrisp apple? Is that bush a blueberry? Or is it the Crimson Passion bush cherry?

Did one of your trees die? With no name tag, you don't know what to buy to replace it. Maybe one of your plums produces fantastic plums, but with the tag lost, you don't know what it was and you want to buy another. Darn, darn, and double darn!

Even name tags made of sturdy plastic with the name written on in permanent marker don't work. If the plastic doesn't photodegrade, the "permanent" ink disappears over a few months' time in the weather. And paper tags? Maybe after a few months you can still see a trace of the paper and some tape clinging to a branch.

Wooden tags in the ground *do* last longer, if written on with pencil. But they tend to get kicked out, run over by lawn mowers or tillers, and dug up by chickens and other ground birds.

After decades of frustration and nearly 30 new trees sitting in buckets waiting to be planted, my creative husband, Will, decided to do better — much better. We'd been looking at stamped metal name tags in one of our nursery catalogs at nearly $3 a pop. I almost ordered 10, figuring

maybe I could renew the tags on the remaining 20 trees and shrubs until I could afford another 10 … and so on.

Will had another idea. We visit the dump quite a bit … more for "shopping" than actually dumping. At the dump, Will picked up many lengths of copper water line from contractors remodeling homes.

With a small vise to hold the pipe firmly, he cut one inch wide rings (you could also cut them wider in order to add the word "Apple," "Pear," "Plum," etc. on top of the variety name) from ¾-inch copper pipe with our Sawzall (reciprocating saw) with a metal cutting blade. When he had 30 rings, he sawed down one side of each one so he could open up the ring to lie flat.

He then gently sanded all rough edges with our grinder so that they wouldn't snag our fingers later on.

We had purchased a metal stamping kit from Harbor Freight weeks ago for less than $20. Each stamp has a letter on the end and you strike the other end with a hammer to indent the letter. He laid each tag on a piece of heavy steel (he used a short piece of railroad track; you could use the top of a vise) and carefully stamped the name of each tree into the copper. As copper is a fairly soft metal, this was easily done.

Once each tag was stamped with the name, Will used a drill with a 1/8-inch bit to drill a hole in the end of it so it could be wired onto the tree or shrub. We had a bunch of short lengths of copper house wiring left over from various projects so Will stripped the insulation from several feet of wire and then cut it into 6-inch lengths, one for each tree tag.

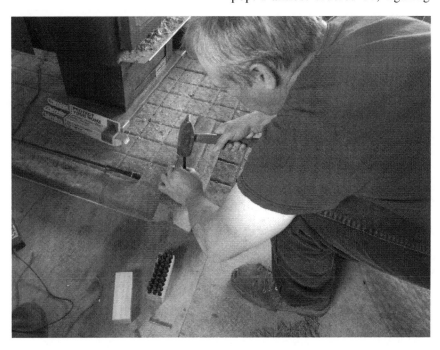

Will stamping each letter on copper tag. Notice stamping kit to his left.

Steps to making the tags: Cut rings of ¾-inch copper pipe 1 inch wide. Cut down one side. Flatten out to make blank for tag. Grind or sand edges smooth. Stamp name on tag and drill hole in end. You're done! Hang tag with copper wire looped gently around tree branch.

Then it was my turn. I got to match up each tree tag with the tree in the orchard. I fastened each tag by tying a nice big loop of wire to a sturdy uppermost branch as near to eye level as possible, with the stamped side easily visible. It's important to use a big loop so as the tree grows the loop won't become tight, cutting into the tender bark. I've also found that over the years, the tree grows taller and I need to move the tags a little so they remain easily visible.

I left the old plastic tags on the trees, and now, just three years later, only a very few trees still have the tags in place. But each and every copper tag is still on the trees and will be nearly forever — I can't imagine one ever wearing out.

Besides using these tags for fruit trees, fruiting shrubs, and other bushes around the place, you can also tack them onto a sturdy wooden post to mark grape vines, bramble, and small fruit rows. If you do that, it works best if you drill a hole on each end of the tag so you can tack or screw the tag flat onto the stake. Likewise, if you only have a few tomatoes or peppers every year in the garden, you could easily make tags on stakes to mark each variety. This also works for perennial flowers as well.

Another use we've found for our copper tags is on our goats' collars. In the spring, it's handy for those kid goats to have their own collars with not only their name but the names of their mother and father so we don't get mixed up. "Was Candy out of Trieste or Clown?" or "Was Ghost sired by Thor or Rocky?" We make a wider tag and stamp the kid's name on top and the name of the sire and dam beneath it. How easy!

The very best thing is that our wonderful copper tags cost nothing at all after you've taken into consideration the inexpensive stamping kit. And we'll be stamping out tags for years and years to come. Δ

WE'RE ON KINDLE - SEE PAGE 3

Backwoods Home magazine

practical ideas for self-reliant living

May/June 2013
Issue #141
$5.95 US
$7.50 CAN

Tomatoes
Queen of the garden

Real rye bread
Emergency lighting
Drought landscaping
"Gun Control" for dummies

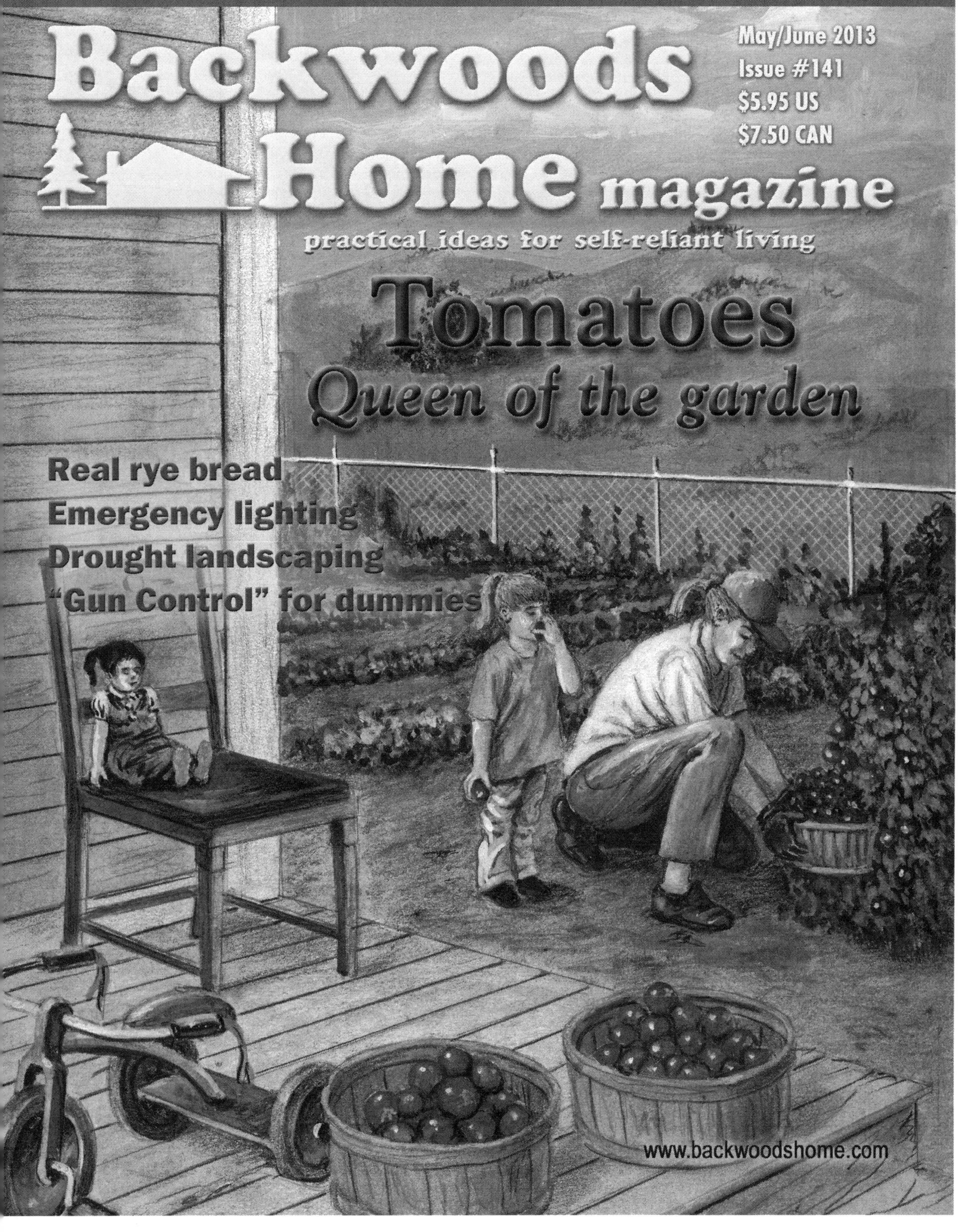

www.backwoodshome.com

My view

How a high school band triumphed over a bureaucracy and union that tried to kill it

There are few victories sweeter in life than that of young teenagers triumphing over organized mean-spirited adults in positions of seemingly absolute power. This is a story that comes out of my own home town of Gold Beach, Oregon. It pits the high school band, consisting of 15 teenagers ranging in age from 15 to 18, against the powerful local teacher's union that tried to shut the band down because their unpaid volunteer band director, who everybody agreed was doing a good job, did not possess an Oregon teaching credential.

As far as the kids were concerned, it was simply a matter of wanting to play music. They had nearly won the District Festival competition last year under the same uncredentialed band director, and they figured they had a good chance of winning it all this year.

But for the teacher's union it was a matter of revenge, not against the band or its director, but against the school superintendent who had presided over teacher layoffs forced by the economic downturn in recent years. The band itself was nearly a casualty of the bad economy, but the school superintendent, Jeff Davis, made it possible for it to survive by allowing an unpaid volunteer to teach it.

That volunteer happened to be Lenie Duffy, who is also the business manager for *Backwoods Home Magazine*. She felt she had no choice. The previous band director, another volunteer, had died suddenly of a heart attack. The last "paid" band director had taken a job in another district two years previous, in part to escape looming teacher layoffs.

Lenie had significant credentials. Before becoming *BHM's* business manager 20 years ago, she had been a "credentialed" California teacher for 9 years. And for the past 15 years, she has been an unpaid volunteer in our local schools' classrooms, spending the last 5 years as the choir's piano accompanist, and the last year plus as band director. Everybody — students, parents, teachers, even the union activists — heaped praise on her for her work with the band, and she was even nominated a couple of months ago as the town's "volunteer of the year." But she did not have an Oregon teaching credential!

The union, frustrated by the superintendent and fearing more layoffs, secretly filed a complaint with the state's Teacher Standards and Practices Commission (TSPC). They simply could not allow an unpaid volunteer, no matter how good, to fill a position that their contract said was worth about $80,000 a year in compensation. It set a bad precedent, as far as they were concerned.

Especially because the school district a few towns north of Gold Beach, in the town of Reedsport, had recently allowed the opening of a charter school, in which half the teachers could be "volunteers" or lower paid people drawn

The Gold Beach High School Band now practices in the BHM building, after being forced out of the school.

from the community. The only requirements were knowing your subject and knowing how to teach it to kids. The union had spent heavily in a vain effort to stop the charter school in Reedsport. It had been a humiliating and bitter defeat, and they did not want the idea of unpaid volunteers gaining traction in Gold Beach.

The TSPC, after lengthy deliberation, informed Davis he should cancel the class, and he did. The news hit Gold Beach like the Grinch descending on the town. "How could they!" many in the town gasped. It was the talk of the coffee shops and everyone was on the band's side.

The kids took to their social media of choice, Facebook, condemning the teacher's union with harsh, sometimes obscene, language. On the afternoon they were supposed to report to the school library instead of the band room, they staged a mass sit-in on the concrete steps that led to the band room. The local newspaper went wild with letters of complaint from parents and community members.

The union reps went on damage control. Their goal, they insisted, was not to hurt the kids. They told the local volunteer choir director, whose class they had also forced into cancellation, that they did it *"for the good of the kids,"* arguing that only credentialed teachers should be allowed to teach children.

But here's where this sad saga turns more sensible.

Backwoods Home Magazine decided to help the kids fight back against the teacher's union. I and *BHM's* Senior Editor John Silveira, Ad Manager Jeff Ferguson, and Technology Manager Al Boulley moved out of our offices and made room for a "band room." The band reformed itself into an off-campus club, just like the high school golf club *BHM* sponsors. In fact, the golf club subsequently held an emergency meeting and agreed to donate $1,000 (nearly half of its funds) to the band to show its support. The band relocated to the *BHM* building and now practices there as a club, free from any further threat from the teacher's union. They will lose the half credit they should have earned for the semester, but they will still get to put on their scheduled concerts and compete at the District Festival.

There are two important lessons that the band kids, or anyone else, can learn from this incident:

1) Don't let bullies and tyrants push you around. They can only control you if you let them.

2) There is always a solution to a problem. Pointing out the culprits is fine, but quickly find the solution and get on with what you want to do.

And there is, of course, a further lesson we as a society should understand from what has transpired in Gold Beach: Teacher's unions are meant to protect teachers, not students.

Teacher's unions, and the monopoly over education they and their local school districts have enjoyed for many years, are, in fact, destructive to our children and their education. During the recent teacher layoffs that so upset our local union, it was the newer, enthusiastic teachers who were laid off while the union protected their entrenched activists. Students, including my three sons, had complained openly that only the best teachers had been let go.

Like most unions, the teacher's union's formula for job security favors the inept, burnt-out survivors among them, while sacrificing bright new talent. It breeds well-paid mediocrity among their ranks, which leads to mediocre achievement by students.

In these difficult economic times, teacher's unions feel under siege because school districts can no longer afford the existing monopoly. Union control is being replaced by private schools and charter schools where lower priced, and often much more valuable, teaching talent can be recruited. Our local union's assertion that only "credentialed" teachers should be allowed to teach students is absurd even to the most casual observer.

In my area, teacher's unions have come begging to the taxpayers many times to help them continue their destructive monopoly over our kids' educations. But the taxpayers keep saying no because they have seen too much of what just happened in Gold Beach.

Bravo to the Gold Beach High School Band, and bravo to their unpaid volunteer teacher. Together, with just a little help from the private sector, they just defeated the bully in the schoolyard. — *Dave Duffy*

Tomatoes —
Queen of the garden

By Jackie Clay

If potatoes are the "King" of the garden, the tomato is the "Queen." There is no other crop that can be used in such a variety of foods. I put up hundreds of jars of not only whole tomatoes, crushed tomatoes, and tomato juice, but also three different tomato-based salsas, three different tomato sauces (plain, Italian seasoned, and Mexican sauce for enchiladas), three different barbecue sauces (plain, chipotle, and honey), two different types of chili (one with beans and one with beans and meat), three different spaghetti sauces (mushroom, meat, and black olive, plain with peppers and onions, and basil, garlic, onion, peppers, and meat), taco sauce, pizza sauce, stewed tomatoes, tomato preserves, and plenty of tomato-based recipes such as meatballs in tomato sauce, tomato sauce with meat and rice, and tomatoes and corn. I also dehydrate tomato slices and make tomato powder, fry sliced green tomatoes, and make faux apple pie from hard green tomatoes.

A whole lot of my pantry depends on the tomatoes that we grow each year in our garden. To top it off, tomatoes are very high in lycopene, which has been proven to reduce the incidence of many types of cancer. And they taste great, too!

Every year I grow some of my old standby tomato varieties; ones that I can count on, no matter what. Some

Tomatoes are the queen of the garden. They have so many different uses. Here, a big harvest of tomatoes from our garden waits to become canned for winter.

are hybrids, but many are old-time, open-pollinated tomato varieties from which I save seed each year. I've grown varieties such as Oregon Spring, Silvery Fir Tree, Early Beefsteak, Punta Banda, and Polish Linguisa for years on homesteads in Minnesota, New Mexico, and Montana. But each year, we try different varieties to see how they perform for us. Some do really well, so we add them to our string of favorites.

In the catalogs, each and every tomato variety sounds perfect. Living in cold Zone 3, we look at the maturity dates. Nearly every one of our tomatoes is a 75-day tomato or earlier. We rarely grow a 90-day tomato as they never make it for us.

We've decided to begin writing down each and every variety of tomato we try to grow and make a garden map so we know where they are planted. That way, when harvest comes along we can evaluate the different varieties of tomatoes as they are ripening and being used.

These are the varieties we planted last year, and how they turned out: (Determinate means a "bush" type that sets all of its ripe fruit and then basically quits. Indeterminates are a "vine" type tomato that must be caged or staked to keep them from sprawling. They set ripe fruit and keep on blooming and developing ripe fruit until fall.)

Bush Goliath (Hybrid)

Large, blemish-free red tomato, juicy and great for fresh eating, and for canned tomatoes and juice. Not terribly productive, but it made the cut for this year. Determinate.

Polfast (Hybrid)

Medium-sized, early red tomatoes, quite productive and great for fresh eating. I canned many of these. They definitely made the cut for this year. Indeterminate.

Early Girl (Hybrid)

Medium-large red tomatoes, juicy and flavorful. Not productive enough for us. Dumped for this year. Determinate.

Bush Beefsteak

Large, round, juicy red tomatoes, few blemishes and very productive. I can a lot of them every year so they made the cut for this year. Determinate.

Silvery Fir Tree

Medium-sized orange, tender, juicy tomatoes. Don't hold well on the vine and the vine quits all at once; if you don't pick the tomatoes, they quickly develop bad spots and begin rotting. *But* it's hugely productive and the first ripe tomatoes in our garden. The bush is low and open with lacy fern-like leaves; a pretty plant. Best caged or staked. Taste is okay, and canned tomatoes very good. It's prone to blight, though, so if it's a problem in your area, you might not want to grow it. We'll have it in our garden again this year. Determinate.

Brandymaster

This is a red hybrid type of Brandywine. It was earlier and more productive for us than Brandywine, having a similar taste and appearance. Not as many blemishes as Brandywine. Not hugely productive, though, nor was the taste so fantastic that we won't replace it. Good canning, but not much of it. It won't be back in our garden this year. Indeterminate.

Brandywine

This old-fashioned beefsteak tomato kind of disappointed us. We knew it was a late tomato (85-90 days) but wanted to give it a try here. It was late and not even moderately productive. The taste disappointed us, too. Maybe it tastes better somewhere else? It also had quite a few blemishes and bumps so was hard to clean up to can. Sorry, but it won't be back.

Oregon Spring

This is one of my favorites. It has never let me down and is always hugely productive. It has an orange-red, fat, juicy, medium-sized tomato with a tender skin. I use it a lot for sauces, stewed and canned tomatoes. Good flavor and hardiness. Of course it'll be back this year! Determinate, open bush type.

Super Bush (Hybrid)

This late tomato has large, red round fruit with a good flavor. The bush is super-strong with a sturdy central stem. It's moderately productive, but I love the appearance of the bush and taste of the tomatoes. It'll be back this year, although not too many as it is not very productive. Determinate.

Orange-Fleshed Purple Smudge

This medium-sized tomato is gorgeous with a bright orange background and purple shading on the top, edging down the sides. The tomato itself is meaty and tasty. But the skin is thin and once the tomatoes are ripe, you'd better use them quickly; they do not keep well on the vine or in a basket in the house. They do make great sauce. We'll grow a few this year, but not the five plants we grew last year — we got tired of rotten tomatoes! Indeterminate.

Violet Jasper

Small, round, striped tomato. Larger than a cherry tomato, smaller than most regular tomatoes. Productive and tasty, but again, does not hold well on the vine or after picking. Gorgeous color; green with violet-purple stripes. Great in salads or for fresh eating. I may plant one or two this year, but no more than that as there are better, more useful tomatoes available. Indeterminate.

Tomcat (Hybrid)

This is a medium-small red tomato that surprised us the first time we grew it. It is hugely productive and has become one of my favorites. Plan on caging it or staking it strongly or the productive vines will tip over due to their weight. Good taste and juicy, but meaty enough to make great sauces. Indeterminate.

Rocky (Hybrid)

Medium, plum-shaped meaty tomato, quite early and moderately pro-

133

Here is our final fall picking of our 2010 tomatoes of all varieties. The green ones continue ripening in the boxes and pails until nearly Thanksgiving.

ductive. It has a good, rich flavor and made plenty of great, thick sauce. We'll be planting it again this year. It produced only so-so, but we'll give it another try. I don't like to ditch a variety after only a year. Indeterminate.

Jubilee

Medium-sized bright yellow, quite meaty tomato with good flavor. Quite productive and blemish-free. I mixed Jubilees in with my other red tomatoes for sauce and the resulting sauce was bright orange and very pretty.

It'll be back this year. It's also great in colorful tomato salads! Indeterminate.

Cherokee Purple

This old heritage tomato is large with a dark purple/green/red color. It has some bumps and ridges and is prone to blemishes. But it has great flavor and is very productive. Because of the blemishes, it does tend to develop rotten spots. I'll grow a plant or two, but hold it to that. It's great

for fresh eating, but just so-so for canning. Indeterminate.

Polish Linguisa

This is one of my favorites, but it *is* a late tomato (85-90 days). It produces huge, paste-type tomatoes that resemble peppers — long, fat, and flat. They are very meaty and tasty. Unfortunately, they do not keep real well due to blemishes. Because they are so productive and meaty, I'll always grow them, but not depend on them too much. Indeterminate.

Gold Medal

An absolutely gorgeous, very large, yellow-gold tomato with red streaks and marbling. Very tasty, meaty, and sweet. Unfortunately, it is a late tomato (85-90 days) and it does develop blemishes. But because of its other attributes, I will grow it again this year. Indeterminate. Must be staked or caged as it has a huge vine with many fruit and will tip over.

Early Cascade (Hybrid—no longer available)

Early Cascade was an old Seminis Seed Company variety that I grew for decades. When Monsanto bought out Seminis, they discarded Early Cascade. I still have a few old seeds, planting half last year. And fortunately, in the past, I bred them back from hybrid, developing my own open-pollinated variety. Last year, I isolated a few plants and saved the seeds to begin the process again. This is a very early producer of firm, smallish cluster tomatoes that ripen reliably in the garden. Great taste for an early, and they produce right through to fall when I pick green tomatoes to finish ripening in the house. I use them for about every tomato product I can. Indeterminate.

Punta Banda

This is a wild red Mexican tomato that is hugely productive, making it one of our favorites. It is a sprawling vine with tons of small tomatoes, just a little larger than cherry tomatoes. Great paste tomatoes as they are very meaty and easy to prepare in a tomato squeezer. I just pull off the stem end and toss them in the squeezer. No blemishes at all. As far as I know, this is only available through Native Seeds/SEARCH in Arizona. It will always be in our garden! Indeterminate, sprawling open vine.

Siberian

Very early small to medium-sized flavorful tomato. Quite productive red fruits. I would have liked to see more production, so we'll plant a plant or two to see if it'll make the cut this year. This is one of my friend, Jeri's favorites, and is more productive for her, so we'll see. Indeterminate.

Juliet

Early, oval, red cherry-type tomato. Good flavor and production. This is a meaty tomato with no blemishes, so I canned a lot of them, both in sauces and as whole tomatoes, last year. They definitely will be with us again! Indeterminate.

Sun Sugar

This orange cherry tomato is great. We've grown it for three years now and it's so tasty and sweet that I can't save enough to dehydrate (which it's great for). Everyone who passes through the garden and house garden grazes on handfuls of these little treats. Very productive and I'll still plant more this year. Oh, yeah! Indeterminate.

Sweet Pea Currant and Red Currant

These were not productive or flavorful. The skin was very thick. A disappointment. Indeterminate.

Tigerella

Small, beautiful, hugely productive red and yellow striped tomatoes. They are round and juicy with great flavor, making them nice for mixed salads. They do tend to rot on the vine pretty quickly, so pick 'em a little early and use them up. I'll plant more, but only a couple of plants for fresh eating, although two years ago I did use a lot of them in my sauces. Quite productive little buggers. Indeterminate.

Note: If you live in a very warm summer area, consider only planting tomato varieties that do well in high-heat conditions. I found this out when we lived in New Mexico. You'd think that because we were in Zone 5 that we could grow just about any tomato! Wrong. I never had worse tomatoes in my life. I discovered that it was because some tomatoes really don't like hot summers — either they don't set fruit or the fruit doesn't ripen well. After planting more heat-tolerant varieties, we had much better luck.

Starting your own tomatoes

As you can see by our tomato trials, very few of these tomatoes are available at local garden centers in the spring. Most of them carry only a few kinds of tomatoes, and most of those are nothing to brag about. Sure you'll get some tomatoes, but they usually aren't hugely productive or especially tasty. And very few are non-hybrids if you want to save your own seeds. While hybrids *do* produce seed, the resulting plants are not going to be what the mother plant's tomatoes were like. A lot of "volunteer" tomatoes pop up in our garden each year from tomatoes that have ripened and gotten squashed or rotted before we got them picked. After being tilled under, the seeds spring up in unexpected places the next year. Some of them are from hybrid tomatoes, too. And, to tell the truth, I can't tell one from the other, once the plants are mature! I weed out volunteers growing in undesirable spots and leave the ones alone that can be left. I hate to kill anything that produces food! So I have tomatoes in my melons, potatoes, corn, onions, and even in my carrots. We think it gives a free spirit to the garden.

But to depend on a certain type of tomato each year, a gardener should plant open-pollinated tomatoes in order to save seed that is dependable. The seed will produce tomatoes just like its mother plant.

Choosing tomato varieties is largely a personal preference. We choose early varieties for most of our crop as we only have about 100 frost-free days, and of those, many are quite cool. Decide what you'll be using most of your tomatoes for. Are you just wanting some for salads? More

Tomatoes are the backbone of our pantry.
Here, jars of spaghetti sauce are in the water bath canner.

Wall O' Water plant protectors save tomatoes from late spring cold snaps like this one when temperatures dropped to 18 degrees and we got a foot of snow.

you plan on setting them out before your last frost date in the spring, they must have good protection. I've used water-filled Wall O' Water plant protectors for decades now, and can't imagine gardening without them. These little 18-inch-high tipis have individual cells that encircle the tomato plant. You hold them open with an upside down 5-gallon plastic bucket, then fill each cell with water from the hose. The bucket is removed and the top tips in, effectively protecting the young plants to way below freezing. The company says they won't freeze at 18 degrees and I agree; I've had a foot of snow and 18 degrees for several days. My tomatoes not only lived, but thrived!

You can also house your tomatoes under hoop houses or other forms of a plastic greenhouse. This won't protect them in as low of temperatures, but they will allow you to set your plants out when there is a chance of moderate frost.

As we use Wall O' Waters, I set my tomato plants out in late April, with our last frost date being about the second week in June. Sometimes the tops get nipped, but the roots are very strong and the plants quickly rebound. I start my seeds in the house in March. You don't want huge plants to set out, but nice, sturdy young tomatoes grow quickly outside into great productive plants.

You can start your seeds in just about any type of container. I've used recycled Styrofoam cups, plastic pop bottles, refrigerator containers, and even recycled trays that held sterile surgical instruments. Anything will work if it's deep and relatively strong. Be sure to poke a hole in the bottom so they don't retain too much water. Wet seed-starting medium will cause the seeds or plants to rot.

While you can certainly start your seeds in homemade seed-starting medium, made of one part well rotted compost, one part vermiculite, and one part finely ground peat moss, it is

for fresh eating? Do you plan on extensive canning? Will you be making lots of sauces and salsa? If so, you'll probably want more meaty paste varieties to make your job quicker and easier. (There'll be much less cooking down if you use paste tomatoes.)

Order your seeds early, so you have a great selection. More people are gardening today, so sometimes late selections are sold out. While most seed catalogs sell tomato seeds, some of our favorites are:
- Baker Creek Heirloom Seeds
- Totally Tomatoes
- Tomato Growers Supply
- Seed Savers Exchange
- Sand Hill Preservation Center

Starting your seeds

You should start your tomato seeds about 8-10 weeks before you plan on setting them out in the garden. Tomatoes cannot take any frost, so if necessary to "cook" this mix to kill any seeds or pathogens present in it. You can accomplish this by mixing your soil, then putting it in a roasting pan in the oven. Bake it at 250° F for an hour and your new soil will be sterile.

Or you can buy seed-starting medium. If you plan on this, talk to a nursery or greenhouse in your area and see if you can buy a bag of professional seed-starting medium. It's much better than what you will find at local stores.

I've started to use Jiffy-7 peat pellets to start my tomatoes and peppers. These are expanded in warm water and placed in my trays. By planting two seeds in each pellet, I'm generally assured of at least one strong seedling. I also put my trays inside a plastic bag. Used bread bags or shopping bags work great — just twist them shut after planting your seeds and place the tray in a warm place (70-80 degrees is best). These seeds usually germinate within a week's time; watch carefully after three days so that they don't grow leggy, searching for sunlight.

Once the plants have germinated and are poking through the soil, clip off the extra plant in a peat pellet so the remaining one can grow strong. I hate it, but it's necessary. When plants grown in containers of seed starting soil have three sets of leaves, gently transplant each one into its own pot or container. I set my peat pellet into a Styrofoam cup with a hole poked in the bottom, then fill under and around it with more soil, leaving about half an inch of room below the rim of the cup. This lets you water easily, yet the plant can still get enough light.

I grow my seedlings on a table, in our greenhouse/back room where there are plenty of south-facing windows and a four-foot shop light hung about three inches above the plants. This gives them extra light during the short days of early spring. If you notice your plants leaning toward the window, simply turn the trays every day so they grow straight.

As the plants grow stronger and stronger, nearing your planting date, begin setting the plants outdoors in a sheltered spot with some sun for at least an hour a day to begin with. Protect them from extreme sun and wind as both will kill young, tender plants. This process is called "hardening off." Increase the outdoor period by an hour a day until they remain outside all day. Be very careful that the plants do not dry out; sun and wind can quickly dry young plants in smaller pots.

Plant your baby tomatoes in the garden, protected against frost by Wall O' Waters or other frost protection if planting earlier than your last predicted frost date. If you get caught with unprotected plants and a frost is predicted, cover them with plastic two-liter pop bottles or gallon jugs with the bottoms cut out or even plastic buckets. This will *not* protect them from a freeze, but will save them from moderate frosts.

Staking and/or caging your tomato plants

Throughout my many years of gardening, I've learned the value of staking or caging my tomatoes. Without it, my plants became a tangled mass in the garden — making weeding, watering, and even harvesting a chore. Besides that, tomatoes laying on the ground as they ripen are more prone to insect and rodent damage as well as rot from ground contact.

Store-bought tomato cages, for the most part, are pretty much useless. They are so lightweight and narrow at the bottom that they easily tip over when weighted down by plants and fruit. They are usually too short for all except small determinate plants that don't grow too tall.

There are several alternative options and we've tried them all. The search for the perfect tomato cage, or at least one that is sturdy, long-lasting and reasonably priced, is ongoing. The best are the heavy-duty colored cages, coming in red, green, blue, and even

Here's Will and some of his caged tomatoes in the fall.

137

Do Will's tomato cages really work?
Here I am, in July, among our caged tomatoes!

pink and purple. (Okay, I haven't tried pink or purple!)

One of the best homesteader-friendly tomato cages we've found is built out of concrete reinforcing wire. This wire is 10 gauge and comes in 5 x 150-foot rolls at a cost of $89.95 from Lowe's. Yes, I know — *ouch*! But if you keep your eyes open, you might find some for free. We have found a lot at the dump and friends have given us some. Our friends, Warren and Betty, had quite a bit of wire lying in a trailer in their yard. It was rusty but in good shape. They wanted the trailer and the wire gone, so we helped them out. Keep your eyes open and don't be afraid to ask. Sometimes you can also find it on Craigslist or in your local shopper. If not, you'll have to bite the bullet and buy it. The good news is that a roll makes about thirty 18-inch in diameter by 60-inch high cages, which are used for indeterminate tomatoes or sixty 18-inch in diameter by 30-inch half-high cages for determinate plants. If you have a neighbor or friend who would also like some cages, you could both end up with a lot of tomato cages. Most people don't need as many cages as we do. We planted 70 tomatoes in cages last year and we just planted the extra 90 in a row. (We hate to throw away anything! I just planted too many tomato plants last year.)

The cost for these cages comes out to about $3.33 for the tall cages and $1.66 for the short ones. Not cheap, but they are much bigger and sturdier than nearly any other cages and will last for years and years. They do have two drawbacks; they come in one color only (a rust brown patina) and they don't stack for storage. Ours get thrown in a pile on the edge of the garden. And they do just fine there and are handy for next year.

To make the cages, you just need wire cutters or bolt cutters to cut the wire and a gloved hand to bend the wires so they hook the ends together to form the cylinder. Be careful, the cut wire is sharp.

Since the cages do not stick into the ground, we use wooden stakes, or lightweight 6-foot metal posts inside the cages, to anchor them firmly in place. The tomatoes love those cages and will grow rampantly upward. All you need to do is to tuck the branches of the plant through the wire squares as it grows.

Another option we've used is welded wire stock panels. By driving a metal post in at each end of the 16-foot panel and adding one in the center, then planting your tomatoes close to the fence, you have an instant trellis that is strong and can easily be reached through to harvest. And by adding another panel about a foot away from the first one, you have the plants effectively sandwiched in between the two sections of stock panel. It's easy to tuck the growing branches out both sides to hold the plants firmly in place. No wind will ever knock down these tomatoes! Because you're growing them on this trellis, you can plant them about 18 to 24 inches apart (depending on the mature size of the plant).

Of course, you can also just let your tomatoes ramble on the ground. You'll still get many tomatoes, but you'll also find them harder to tend and harvest. And you will have more incidence of rotted fruit and disease among your plants.

To prune or not to prune?

Much has been written about the need to prune your tomatoes during their growing season. Personally, I have not pruned my tomatoes in years and they have produced very well for me. Extra work around here is never enjoyed. Sometimes, though, it is a good idea to prune your tomato plants. If your plants have experienced late blight or another disease, pruning improves airflow around and through your plants. Dampness helps breed disease. To prune your tomatoes, clip off the "extra" branches and sprouts which grow between the main branches of your tomato vine and the main stem. You can even root these sprouts in a glass of water to get more tomato plants for free! It only takes a few days for the sprouts to root and in a week, they will have vigorous roots and can be planted in the garden.

Sometimes it is beneficial, when nearing fall frosts, to clip off indeterminate tomato vines so that the plant will put all its energy into developing and ripening fruit.

Watering your plants

While you can water your plants with an ordinary garden sprinkler, we've found that our tomatoes do much better when watered by drip irrigation or a soaker hose. We lay our soaker hose after we pull our Wall O' Waters, then mulch with straw on top of them. At this time, we cage our tomatoes. Be careful not to puncture your soaker hose as you drive in stakes! If tomatoes do not receive adequate water as fruits form, especially the first fruits, many often develop a black spot on the blossom end. This is called blossom end rot and is caused by infrequent watering, stress, and low calcium in the soil. While you can spray the plants with a calcium solution, it's usually easier and cheaper to just ensure that the plants get adequate water. If you've had this problem in your plants, even with adequate watering, it's a good idea to put a handful of crushed eggshells under each plant as you plant them or otherwise provide them with supplemental calcium.

If you've had a problem with late blight in your tomatoes, consider using only a soaker hose or drip irrigation. Late blight just loves damp conditions that occur after the heavy, dense plants are watered by overhead sprinklers!

Common tomato pests

While small insect pests are possible in the garden, when you grow an organic garden, you seldom are bothered by these as natural predators keep them in check. Some of these small insects include: thrips, spider mites, aphids, and flea beetles. All of these insects are very small and barely visible to the naked eye. They usually cause leaf damage first, so if you see signs of small-critter chewing spots on leaves, look very closely for the culprits. You may need to spray or powder with rotenone or pyrethrins, but if the damage is not significant, I leave them alone. Usually you'll find predatory "good" insects coming in to clean house for you soon.

Larger insects, such as the tomato hornworm, are often quite damaging to your plants and to the fruit itself. If you suddenly see an area where nearly all the leaf has been eaten off, often leaving just the ribs, look closely for dark green roundish balls of frass (hornworm poop). Tomato hornworms are very large (as large as your finger), fat, and green with a "horn" on the back end. They look fierce and "click" their jaws and thrash their horn, as if to sting you, but they do not bite or sting. Just pick them and squash them with your foot. I used to immediately pick and squash every one I found in my garden. But then I found that they are actually the larval

Grow your own food
Can your own food

stage of the hummingbird moth that we really love to watch in the flower garden! So now I only pick and squash them if they are eating the heck out of a plant, choosing to sacrifice a few tomato branches in order to observe a truly unique pollinator at work. The moths are pretty and hover around the flowers, sipping nectar just like hummingbirds.

The cutworm is a common plant pest in many areas. This grayish, fat

*Tomato cuttings can easily be rooted in a few days
to produce more plants like the mother plant.*

"worm" is seen in the shallow soil. When you dig one up, it curls up tightly as a defense. Unfortunately, it lives up to its name, chewing the base of newly-planted tomatoes, peppers, and other garden plants so badly that they are cut right off and die. An occasional cutworm is not much of a problem; I just pick them and squash them as I run across them. When they are common in your garden, the best defense is to make a collar out of light cardboard for each young plant. The collar should cover the plant stem ½-inch or so below the soil surface and extend about 2 inches above it. With this protection, the cutworm cannot "cut" and your plants soon are large enough to withstand its chewing.

Other larger tomato pests include the Colorado potato beetle, corn earworms, and army worms. When these are few, you can hand pick and destroy. When they become voracious, it's time to treat with organic controls or spray/powder with rotenone. Some organic controls include spraying with Bt (a natural bacteria only harmful to insects that consume it). Bt is often sold as Bonide or Thuricide. Other natural controls include spraying with Pyola (from Gardens Alive!) and covering your plants with floating row cover before the insects attack them.

One often unseen tomato pest is the root nematode. This causes plants to be stunted, unproductive, and sometimes die. If you pull an affected plant, it will have short, knobby roots that do not look healthy. Burn the affected plants. If this is a common problem in your garden, you might consider releasing beneficial nematodes into your garden in the spring. These are predators of the root nematode and after watering or spraying them into your soil, they will quickly multiply and overcome emerging root nematodes before they do damage to your tomatoes.

Tomato diseases

There are several common tomato diseases, which include Fusarium Wilt, Septoria Leaf Spot, early blight, and late blight. They cause the plants to lose leaves, have spotted and yellowed leaves, and they sometimes cause plants to wilt and die. There are very good disease identification photos and information online or through your local Extension Office, usually located in your courthouse. Many of these diseases are "contagious," with wind-borne late blight spores traveling many miles. Planting resistant varieties and maintaining good practices (staking and caging tomatoes, pulling infected plants, and rotating tomato growing rows with other crops, such as corn or beans) usually helps avoid these problems.

There are also decent organic sprays that do a fairly good job treating and preventing these diseases.

Planting disease and insect-resistant tomato varieties

One way you can keep from having unhappy tomato gardening experiences is to plant tomato varieties that are resistant to disease problems that are common in your area. In most seed catalogs, you'll notice a series of letters after the name of each tomato variety. These letters reveal what diseases the tomato is resistant to:

• V = resistant to Verticillium Wilt
• F = resistant to Fusarium Wilt
• N = resistant to root nematodes
• A = resistant to Alternaria
• T = resistant to Tobacco mosaic virus
• St = resistant to Stemphylium (Grey Leaf Spot).

Fortunately, very few tomato growers experience *any* of these problems, so don't let all this bother you. The only insect pests I've had were the tomato hornworm, and these were not a problem at all. We have had some early blight in our tomatoes, but by rotating our crops and destroying affected plants, we have always harvested tons of tomatoes.

Saving tomato seeds

Tomatoes are among the easiest of crops to save your own seeds from. But in order to ensure that the seeds you save will produce tomatoes like the parent plants, it's best to plant an open pollinated (non-hybrid) variety that is isolated from other tomatoes by as much distance as possible. I plant the varieties I plan on saving seeds from in beds more than 300 feet from our main garden. Plant several plants of that variety to ensure genetic diversity, which makes for healthier plants down the road.

To save the seeds of these tomatoes, just wait until several of the nicest tomatoes are very ripe. Then scoop out the seeds and "gel" and place them into a small container of water. Let them set out at room temperature for three days. During this time, a layer of fungus or mold will probably grow on the top. Don't let that worry you. Pour the cup out into a strainer and wash well under lukewarm water, gently rubbing the tomato seeds across the strainer to remove any leftover clinging gel or mold. Let drip dry well, then pour out onto a piece of waxed paper. I've used a plain pie pan or cookie sheet, but sometimes the seeds tend to stick. Once the seeds are dry, remove them from the paper and again let dry to ensure that all seed surfaces are very dry. Then pour the seeds into an airtight container. A very small jar, such as baby food jar, works well. These seeds should remain viable for several years.

I hope you'll enjoy growing lots of tomatoes this year. They are such a widely useful fruit and so good for you, too. I think I could eat them every single day, in one way or another, and never get tired of them! Δ

More self-reliance in
Emergency Preparedness
and Survival Guide

Use solar landscape lights for emergencies

By Jeffrey R. Yago, P. E., CEM

People own all kinds of household items that can be used to make life easier during an emergency, yet never realize their dual use. During a recent week-long power outage, I knew an older couple who were telling me how hard it had been for them in their all-electric house without power and no way to stay warm, cook, or wash. I knew they owned an RV camper that had battery-powered lights, battery-powered water pump, and a propane stove, furnace, and refrigerator, so I asked why they didn't stay in their RV. They told me they had never thought of it!

While this may seem like an extreme example, there are all kinds of solar-powered landscape lights that can be used during power outages to illuminate your home, yet most people never think of it. We see solar landscape lighting everywhere these days, and many are priced cheaper than light bulbs.

A quality solar landscape light is an excellent way to illuminate any room of your home during an extended power outage, and since it is being recharged each day by the sun, it is always ready to use in an emergency. By modifying the mounting post to make it easier to pull up and take inside each night during a power outage, you will no longer worry about dead flashlight batteries or a generator with an empty fuel tank next time the power goes out.

While even the lowest cost solar landscape lights I tested still worked fairly well, I found that models having a larger output work better for illuminating the rooms in your home during a power outage. The smallest single LED solar landscape light has a lighting output between 0.8 to 1.2 lumens, which averages 1.0 lumen.

Solar-powered landscape lights in dark room. Note different light patterns and brightness.

A lumen is a measurement of how much light a given source generates that can be seen by the human eye, with one lumen equal to one "foot-candle." One foot-candle is the amount of light output measured from a standard candle at a distance of one foot. Solar landscape lights are identified with an output rating as a multiplier of this basic unit. For example, a larger solar-powered landscape light may have an advertised rating of 24X. This just means it puts out 24 times more light than a one-lumen solar landscape light.

While most solar landscape lights now have LED lamps, you still want to make sure they are identified as having "LED" lamps to minimize battery drain and extend lamp life. To keep manufacturing costs low, many of the solar landscape lights I tested were furnished with a lower-capacity rechargeable battery having a typical operating life of about two years. When buying a replacement battery, try to purchase a battery having a higher capacity rating than the original to improve performance.

More expensive solar-powered landscape lights may include a manu-al switch that lets you adjust the number of hours the light stays on each night, which typically is from six to ten hours. During the winter months, with shorter daylight hours, it is not unusual to have darkness by 5 pm, which means a six-hour setting will turn off by 11 pm. This may not meet your outdoor illumination needs for walkways and driveways, but the higher 10-hour settings could exceed the battery charge if poor weather conditions in your area limit the daytime solar recharging process.

Batteries

Lower-cost, solar-powered landscape lights usually have only one battery, and there does not seem to be a standard battery type, battery voltage, or battery size across brands and models of the solar lights I tested. Just as a car battery capacity is rated in amp-hours, smaller batteries are rated in milliamp-hours (m-Ah) which is the same type of charge capacity rating, but using a scale 1,000 times smaller. For example, a 1,100 m-Ah battery would equal 1.1 amp-hours of charge using the larger scale of measurement.

Top: Small-medium-large solar-powered landscape lights showing relative size of lenses and solar cells. Middle: Solar-powered landscape light batteries come in multiple sizes and voltages.

Brand	Voltage	Type	m-Ah
Yards and Beyond	1.2 volts	NiCd-NiCad	850
Jiawei Technology	1.2 volts	NiCd-NiCad	900
Moonrays	1.2 volts	NiMh	1500
Boston Harbor	1.2 volts	NiMh	1500
Blue Generic	3.2 volts	LiFePO4	300
Portfoli	3.2 volts	LiFePO4	400
Yards and Beyond	3.2 volts	LiFePO4	850
Pathscapes	3.2 volts	LiFePO4	1000
Tenergy	3.2 volts	LiFePO4	3100

Many of the larger solar landscape lights are designed to use a single 3.2 volt 800 m-Ah Lithium Iron Phosphate (LiFePO4) battery, while the less expensive units I tested came with a single 1.2 volt 850 m-Ah nickel-cadmium (NiCad) battery. While most solar landscape lights use "AA" size batteries, many of the batteries I found in the larger solar lights were the same length as an "AA" battery, but much larger in diameter so these will not fit in the same battery compartment. Several of the solar lights I tested came with 1.2 volt Nickel-Metal-Hydride (NiMH) battery, so care must be taken when purchasing replacement batteries to buy the correct size, type, and voltage to match your fixture requirements.

I also found that you can purchase a replacement battery having the same exact physical size and voltage as the original, but with double the m-Ah rating for only 20% more in cost. I recommend replacing the lower rated batteries with higher capacity batteries to improve performance. The table on this page shows the different milliamp-hour (m-Ah) ratings of several replacement batteries I tested grouped by battery physical size. This table shows there can be a significant difference in charge capacity for the same physical size battery depending on brand and cost.

If you do decide to replace the original battery in your solar lights with a battery having a higher m-Ah charge capacity, you will need more hours of sun to fully recharge a higher-capacity battery given the same solar conditions since the solar cell size did not change.

If you decide to use your solar-powered landscape lights just for emergencies and plan to store them inside until the next power outage, be sure to remove the batteries after they have been fully recharged. This will avoid the lights trying to turn back on after being packed away.

Comparisons

It's not easy to compare solar-powered landscape light performance or know which brand and size is best for your dual-purpose emergency lighting needs, as there are so many brands and models to choose from. However, I found the smaller lights priced in the $5 to $10 range will provide enough light to illuminate a hallway, bathroom, or stairs for up to four hours per night, but will not provide enough light to adequately illuminate a kitchen or bedroom. Four hours of battery life per night is also too short for most room lighting needs during a power outage.

I was very pleased with the larger "24X" size solar landscape lights that came packaged two-per-box at a cost of $40, or $20 per light. These came standard with a larger battery and a solar cell that was almost 3-inches square. Each light contained two very bright LED bulbs and a switch allowing you to adjust the number of hours the light stays on each night. While still not equal to the illumination of a standard room ceiling light, during an extended power outage solar landscape lights having a "24X" or higher rating should provide plenty of light to let you easily move around in a living room or prepare meals in a kitchen. They also make a good bedside reading light or task light for crafts.

Make sure the top of the solar light you buy has a large solar cell — the larger the better. A large flat top will also help protect the light housing below and keep the lens clear of rain, snow, and dirt. Those solar lights shaped like a tube do not have enough top surface for a large solar cell and will have a limited light output and shorter run time. Look for lights having clear, not frosted, external lenses and interior mirror reflectors; both features help distribute the light out in all directions from the tiny LED lamps. Finally, check the battery milliamp and "X" ratings listed on the package. The higher values will provide longer run time and brighter illumination.

Landscape light supports

You want your solar landscape lights to always be ready for the next power outage, but they will normally remain outside each night illuminating your walks or driveways. During a power outage you want to make it easy to move them indoors each night and then back outside each morning. Since most solar landscape lights are supplied with some type of long tube support having a pointed end to drive into the ground, I cut an 18-inch long piece of 1-inch PVC pipe to enclose this support tube.

I drove this PVC pipe into the ground at the same location of each solar landscape light, leaving approximately 12 inches above ground. I then removed the point from the end of the support tube and inserted this tube into the PVC pipe. You may be able to use a ¾-inch size PVC pipe for smaller solar landscape lights. I then made a separate wooden base which included a 6-inch-long section of the same size PVC pipe pressed into a drilled hole sized for a very tight fit, resulting in a great lamp base. Make sure you do not drill all the way through the bottom board as you want a smooth flat bottom. The base was made from a short piece of 2x6 wood block glued to the top of a 2x10 wood block. Both boards are 15/8-inch thick, so the resulting lamp base will be 3¼-inch high with 3 inches of PVC pipe sticking out of the top and 3 inches of pipe extending down inside the base. I sanded, then painted the base with a "stone" colored spray paint. You can glue a piece of felt to the bottom to protect table tops.

During a power outage you should have one lamp base in each bedroom, bath, stairwell, kitchen, and family room, then before dark you would bring in the solar landscape lights and insert them into these wooden bases. Match solar light size with room illumination requirements if you purchased several sizes. Since these solar landscape lights are inserted in PVC pipe and not driven into the ground, their

Homemade solar-powered landscape light base made from scrap lumber.

tube posts will not be covered with dirt and will be easy to pull out. Each morning move all solar landscape lights back outside to recharge their batteries and get ready to use again if the power is still out.

Final thoughts

Be sure to locate your solar-powered landscape lights where they will receive plenty of sun each day. Avoid placing them near large shade trees or under shrubbery since any shade blocking the sun will significantly reduce their operating hours. A good indication is to check for shading from three hours before noon to three hours after noon on a sunny day. If not shaded during these hours you can expect good overall performance.

Like everything else, you get what you pay for, so if you want your solar landscape lights to also serve as emergency lighting during a power outage, be sure to purchase the larger and higher-quality lights and keep extra high-capacity rechargeable batteries on hand. Since the solar cells and LED lamps will never need replacement, the rechargeable batteries are the only spare parts you will ever need.

Jeff Yago is a licensed professional engineer and certified energy manager with more than 30 years of experience in the energy conservation field. He has extensive solar photovoltaic and emergency preparedness experience, and has authored numerous articles and texts. His website is www.dtisolar.com. Δ

Rotten luck: The skinny on composting

By Patrice Lewis

For much of human history, people have tried to prevent things from rotting. Literally every food preservation method we've come up with in the past few thousand years (freeze drying, dehydrating, salting, canning, refrigerating, freezing, etc.), up to and including keeping animals alive until the day they're consumed, is done in an effort to prevent food from going bad.

But rotting is actually a vital component to our existence. Imagine our world without the diligent munching of untold quadrillions of agreeable microbes. We would be layered with undecomposed corpses (of both plants and animals) stretching back into the mists of time. Yuck.

So we can thank microbes the world over for doing a dirty but necessary job on our behalf. And it's even possible, with a little help from science, to tailor those microbial appetites to our benefit on the homestead.

I refer, of course, to composting.

The science of composting is just that — a science. Reams have been written on the proper and methodical approach to getting things to rot. *The Rodale Guide to Composting* alone stretches to an impressive 17 chapters and 382 densely-packed pages addressing the subject from every possible angle, from small-scale to industrial applications.

Many gardening magazines and catalogs would have you believe that composting requires expensive and sophisticated tools and equipment. A

Our "helter-skelter" compost pile — newer materials on top, three-year-old compost at bottom. Happy chicken thrown in for free.

quick glance through an upscale retailer's website reveals a "back porch compost tumbler" for $249.95 and a kitchen compost bucket for $29.95. Yikes.

All this implies that composting is an intricate, slightly terrifying, and very expensive subject. What if I do it wrong? What if I don't provide enough water? What if my compost pile doesn't heat up enough? What if I can't afford the expensive equipment?

Fortunately, as the rotting bananas in your fruit bowl will attest, composting is as easy as pie. And all the components can be obtained for free.

Join me now in the not-as-stinky-as-you'd-think world of microbial activi-

ty and learn how to exploit rot to your benefit.

Black gold

I'll start by addressing the role composting plays on our own 20-acre homestead in north Idaho.

After moving here in 2003, we were dismayed to learn that our soil is heavy with clay and has a very difficult time producing anything except weeds (which grow with enthusiasm). We tilled and tilled and tilled compost (and sand) into the soil in an effort to improve it, with lackluster results. After years of increasingly frustrating attempts to get the unyielding dirt to give back something besides dog fennel and hawkweed, I gave up entirely the concept of planting a garden in the ground. Instead, I've switched to tire gardening (watch for a future article on this subject). Now all my veggies are grown in what are essentially miniature raised beds.

There have been some concerns about tires leaching dangerous chemicals into soil, but these concerns appear to stem from shredded tires (or tire dust) or from burning tires, but not from whole tires. Tires are long-lasting and almost impossible to decompose under ordinary conditions, so my concerns about any potential leaching is nonexistent. People have grown many food and ornamental plants in tires for decades with no adverse effects.

Our tires are filled, from top to bottom, with compost. I don't even bother mixing it with dirt anymore — just compost. The rotting remains of our endless barn-muckings have quite literally saved our garden.

To wax philosophical for a moment, I see homesteading as a circle. In a complete circle, all things on the farm are interconnected. The challenge is to link and connect as much of that circle as we can, without relying on outside sources. Without the compost provided by our livestock, that circle would be virtually impossible to close.

Thanks to the daily output of our 12 head of cattle, one horse, and a flock of chickens, we have compost in abundance. Piled unscientifically into an enormous heap, within three years the material has broken down into rich, black, loamy, beautiful stuff which vegetables adore.

Compost has long been called black gold among farmers and homesteaders, and they're right. On a farm, compost's value is beyond compare, especially when it comes to improving bad soil.

The science of compost

So what's the big deal about compost? Why can't plants just ... grow?

Plants, as you know, require nutrients. The most basic are NPK (Nitrogen-Phosphorus-Potassium) in various ratios. Depending on where you live, the native soil may be deficient in these nutrients in anywhere from modest to alarming quantities.

Compost helps reintroduce some of these nutrients back into the soil, benefiting whatever is planted. Additionally, depending on what went into the compost to begin with, compost can provide the trace micronutrients in which plants are often deficient — elements such as zinc, boron, molybdenum, iron, iodine, etc. These nutrients are slow-released into the soil to provide maximum benefit to the plants.

Compost offers additional benefits. It increases the friability of soil (how loose and workable it is). At either end of the friability scale, clay is too dense for plant roots to penetrate, and pure sand is too loose, poor in nutrients, and won't retain water. Compost helps at both ends; it can break up the heavy density of clay, or it can bind together and provide nutrients to sandy soil.

Compost also invites useful organisms to help with the soil-building process. Worms, those humble but glorious gardener's friends, are attracted to compost-rich environments. But other beneficial insects as well as microorganisms become inoculated into soil as well. Good compost is not dead, but is alive and teeming with life, which works symbiotically with soil to produce happy plants.

What a compost pile needs

It's the action of those unthanked microbes that are responsible for successful composting. Microbes break down larger things — banana peels, cow manure, ageing lettuce — while digesting them. This digestion process results in the release of elements in a form that plants can use. That's why rot is such a critical component of the natural cycle. Animal and vegetable materials all contain critical nutrients, but not in a form usable to plants. But if the material is decomposed and mixed with soil, then the nutrients are released into a form plants can use.

A wheelbarrow full of compost, destined for the garden.

Compost filling a tire, ready for planting.

But microbes can't work in a vacuum. They need certain conditions in order to survive and do their job. Specifically they need four things:

• **Energy** (in the form of carbon). Microbial carbon is supplied through whatever dry, bulky vegetative waste you have on hand: leaves, straw, cornstalks, even sawdust.

• **Protein** (in the form of nitrogen). Nitrogen (sometimes called an Activator) is what stimulates the microbes, and is found in grass clippings, green vegetation, and such additives as kelp meal or blood meal. (Microbes need much less nitrogen than they do carbon, so don't overdo the protein.)

• **Oxygen**. Oxygen merely means that microbes must operate in an aerobic (as opposed to an airless anaerobic) environment. Occasionally turning your compost pile provides this; alternately, the actions of worms and other soil dwellers help aerate the compost as well, though it will take longer.

• **Moisture**. Moisture is necessary for rot to happen. In fact, reducing moisture (dehydration) is an ancient form of food preservation, since microbial action requires some moisture in order to work. But too much moisture — a waterlogged compost pile — will slow down microbial action as well, since it contributes to an anaerobic environment. That's why adequate drainage is necessary for compost piles.

Activators

A special note about activators. Activators are additives that jump-start the microbial activity by providing a shot of nitrogen, which stimulates the microbes to decompose the carbons. You don't want to add a lot of activators to your compost pile; a little goes a long way. However, those small amounts of activators are handy to get things moving.

To illustrate: On our homestead, we have about two steers a year slaughtered for meat. A mobile butcher comes to our place to dispatch the steer. He guts and quarters the animal before bringing the carcass to his facility for hanging and cutting.

During this process, the animal must naturally be bled out. We provide an empty trash can or large 30-gallon tub to drain the blood. And then we take that blood and pour it over our compost pile.

Before you say "Ewww, yuck!" consider that blood is an excellent microbial activator and increases the speed of the composting. In modest quantities, blood is an excellent additive to a compost pile. Besides, what better way to get rid of it?

For those without a natural source of blood, blood meal is available for purchase from gardening centers. This is simply blood from slaughterhouses that has been collected, dried, and powdered.

There are a lot of animal-product "meals" that can be added to a compost pile as activators. Blood meal, bone meal, horn meal, hoof meal, fish meal … these are all superb additions. For those preferring concentrated activators of non-animal origin, consider alfalfa meal or cottonseed meal.

Building a compost pile

So how do you make a proper compost pile? There are two schools of thought: **the scientific approach** and the **helter-skelter method**. Frankly you'll succeed either way, but the scientific method is quicker.

Scientific approach

Ideally, a compost pile consists of a ratio of two parts vegetable matter (leaves, grass, straw) to one part animal matter (manure). The ratio of carbon to nitrogen should be about 30:1, meaning you should have 30 times more dry bulky vegetative waste than nitrogen-rich sources such as grass clippings or sea kelp.

Materials should be mixed rather than thickly layered; or at least layered thinly. If you pour several cubic yards of grass clippings onto your compost pile, for example, it's likely to compress into a stinky anaerobic sludge. However if you first dry the clippings (or take the green clippings and mix them thoroughly with leaves) before adding them to the compost pile, the materials will break down more efficiently and with less smell. Avoid grass clippings or other materials that have been heavily sprayed with pesticides or herbicides.

Leaves are particularly useful. Here in north Idaho we're surrounded by almost pure conifers; but for those lucky souls who live in deciduous areas, leaves are one of your greatest assets. Left alone, leaves compost very slowly; but decomposed leaves are one of the best possible natural composts. The richness of eastern gardens grown in "humus" illustrates this.

So rather than complain about the massive volume of leaves you have to rake each fall, instead layer those leaves into your compost pile and wait for the goodness to come forth. If possible, chop or shred the leaves first. This will reduce matting and speed up the decomposition. Mix the chopped leaves with other stuff and the leaves will decompose about four times faster than if they were simply piled and left alone.

Helter-skelter method

We aren't nearly as scientific about compost on our farm, nor are we in a hurry for everything to decompose. You might say we follow the helter-skelter method of composting. There is a certain messy exuberance associated with this kind of composting. I don't have the time or interest to get too scientific about things. When I'm cleaning the barn, I'm not thinking about whether my ratio of vegetable matter-to-animal matter is stable; I just want to dump the wheelbarrow and finish the stall.

Yet somehow it works. Peeking out from the bottom of our massive mound of barn waste is some of the most beautiful rich black gold you'll ever see. In the spring I fork it into the wheelbarrow, trundle it over to the garden, and fill a tire with it, and know that whatever I plant — corn or tomatoes or broccoli or beans — will appreciate the results. And when those plants are harvested, whatever

Fresh livestock manure can damage plants, but composting it turns it into a rich activator for crops.

is left over — cornstalks or tomato stems or broccoli leaves or bean pods — will go into the compost pile, get broken down, and ultimately be ready to grow another round of food. The homesteading circle closes a bit more.

What shouldn't be composted

Not all waste can be thrown on a compost pile. While theoretically anything organic can be composted, the reality is that some organic materials are harder to compost than others.

Some of the tough, stubborn items that take a long time to break down include corncobs, palm fronds, cotton stalks, twigs and branches, walnut or pecan shells, etc. These items *will* eventually break down, but it may take years. Make sure your "stubborn" materials are well-layered with more easily composted items, and they will compost a bit faster ... though you may still have to pluck the occasional incompletely-composted corncob from your otherwise-composted materials and toss it back in the pile for another season.

However, these stubborn organic items can be resolved simply by chopping or crushing. The smaller the piece, the quicker it rots. It might be worthwhile to rent a shredder at the end of the season and run your larger or more stubborn organic waste through it.

There are other items that you should avoid adding to a compost pile, notably meat trimmings, animal fats, and grease. It's not that these things won't decompose, but they'll do so at a much slower pace, and meanwhile they'll attract pests such as rats and flies. If you do add meat scraps to your compost pile, make sure they're in small quantities and are buried deep within the pile. Grease and fats hinder composting by literally coating the vegetative matter and providing an anaerobic environment, which drastically slows decomposition.

And no matter how precious and clean you think Fido and Fifi are, dog and cat poop can contain disease microorganisms and should *not* be added to a compost pile.

What about human waste? While it can certainly be composted effective-

147

ly, I would keep it separate from your standard compost pile. For additional details on composting human waste, see *The Humanure Handbook* (available at *BHM,* book #SS90, $25, write in your order on page 96).

Why livestock manure should be composted

If you have livestock, you must do something with their output, and the most logical thing to do is to compost it. What is manure, after all, except vegetative material that has passed through the digestive tracts of animals? The material is broken down in the animals' bodies and emerges as a concentrated activator for compost.

Fresh manure is too concentrated to be put directly on plants. And some manures — particularly those of chickens, sheep, and horses — are called "hot manures" because their intense activity can create so much heat that it will kill not only beneficial organisms (like worms) but anything growing in it (like vegetables).

So it's best to compost all animal manures. Under ideal and scientific conditions, this process will take anywhere from a couple weeks to a few months. Under helter-skelter conditions (and heavily mixed with hay), we give it about three years.

Thermophilic composting

To many people, "composting" is synonymous with "heat." If their compost pile doesn't achieve a high temperature, they consider it a failure.

Fear not, thermophilic composting isn't always necessary for successful compost.

Heat plays an excellent factor in killing weed seeds or pathogenic organisms. But if you're simply composting the remains of kitchen waste, thermophilic composting isn't necessary. Don't become so obsessed with

An interview with a worm composter

For those unable or uninterested in larger-scale composting, it's still possible to compost kitchen scraps indoors by using worm composting.

I'd heard of this in theory, but it wasn't until I saw worm composting in action that I became deeply impressed. I visited some friends (Kurt and Cindy) who have an active worm composting system for their kitchen scraps. Because it was still winter when I interviewed them, they had brought the composter indoors and placed it in a seldom-used shower stall until warmer weather permitted them to put the composter on the porch.

The first thing I noticed — or rather, *didn't* notice — about this system was its odor (or lack thereof). Despite the small enclosed bathroom location, there was no noticeable odor whatever. However, they did have a few fruit flies buzzing over the composter. And when I say "a few," I'm talking about three or four, that's it. (There are probably more fruit flies when the composter is outdoors.)

This particular composter consisted of four stackable trays with solid sides and mesh bottoms. A lid closes over the top tray, and the trays are arrayed on a four-footed solid base to elevate the composter by about 12 inches. The base collects the liquid (worm tea) which drains to the bottom and is harvested with a spigot.

Kurt told me he started with the first tray into which he placed some shredded (non-glossy) newspaper. He moistened them until the newspaper stuck to the tray. The moistened newspapers should be about an inch thick. Then he added tiny red worms he purchased online. One pound of worms (which are shipped in soil) contains about 10,000 tiny baby worms. Kurt added both the soil and the worms to the tray. On the top tray he put a week's worth of kitchen scraps (carrot peelings, potato peelings, onion skins, eggshells, coffee grounds, etc.). He didn't chop the scraps or crush the eggshells, though doing so would allow the worms to break down the organic material more quickly; he just added them to the top of the tray and spread them out evenly. Then he closed the lid and left the worms alone.

When the bottom tray gets full, Kurt adds another tray on top, repeating the process of adding shredded news-

papers and moistening them before piling kitchen scraps on top. When the worms deplete the nutrients in the first tray, they start to migrate upward through the mesh into the next tray (hungry worms always move upward). Kurt repeats the process until all four trays are stacked. By the time the worms get to the top tray, the bottom tray shouldn't have any worms at all and the compost can be used directly on plants. The bottom tray mostly consists of worm castings (an ideal plant food) and has absolutely no odor. Once Kurt empties the bottom tray, he then stacks it on top when he's ready.

Meanwhile, the worms breed. Kurt estimates that his initial one pound of worms now totals about five pounds. How fast the worms work their way up to the top tray depends on the number of worms you start with, but in Kurt's case it takes about three to four months to cycle through all four trays.

An important side bonus (besides the worm castings) is worm tea, the liquefied drainage from the compost. This "tea" is a concentrated fertilizer and is in high demand among gardeners. Kurt drains the liquid via a spigot into an old measuring cup, which he high temperatures that you become discouraged if your pile doesn't get hot.

In a nutshell, heat is beneficial if you need to kill weed seeds, destroy harmful pathogens, or decompose materials at maximum speed. But heat will also kill beneficial organisms such as worms, and it requires more frequent turning of the pile. So consider what you're composting before obsessing too much about heat.

Urban composting

Since not everyone lives on a farm, I'll address what I call Urban Composting. This is simply taking all organic waste from your home and yard (grass clippings, leaves, chipped branches, kitchen waste, etc.), and turning it into something usable.

You can use a dedicated garbage can or metal barrel. Drill holes in the sides and bottom to help in aeration, then prop the can up on bricks or cinder blocks to allow bottom ventilation. It would also be helpful to insert a perforated PVC pipe or other airy option into the center of the garbage can to permit air to penetrate the interior of the can. You can secure the lid and give the can a good rolling a couple times a week to increase aeration.

A bin made of pallets also works well. Composting yard and kitchen waste will not only provide you with usable material for container gardening or small raised beds, but it's less material that will end up in the landfill (and might even reduce your utility bills).

What about those who don't have yards? What if you live in an apartment or condo? Fear not, you can still compost on a small scale using earthworms (see Sidebar article). Worm composting is virtually odor-free, self-contained, and even potentially profitable.

then pours into empty one-gallon milk jugs. The tea is far too concentrated to be used directly and must be diluted with water at approximately a 1:20 ratio. Kurt told me it's possible to sell diluted worm tea for $4 to $5 a gallon. It takes him about two or three months to fill a gallon jug, depending on how moist the kitchen scraps are (melon rinds have more water than eggshells, for example).

Kurt said all kitchen scraps can be composted in this manner except meat scraps, milk products, and citrus (which might kill the worms). He also said not all worms are suitable for worm composting — it's best to purchase composting worms from a reputable source. A rule of thumb is to purchase twice as many pounds of worms as the amount of kitchen waste you produce each day. If you produce about half a pound of kitchen scraps a day, then start with one pound of worms.

The worm composting system is essentially maintenance free. Once it's set up, it doesn't require mixing or adding water or anything else except harvesting the finished compost and draining the worm tea. However worms must be kept in moderate temperatures. They don't

Top tray gets the fresh kitchen scraps

work as efficiently below 55° F or above 80° F. In cold climates, they would do best sheltered in a garage or even indoors; in hot climates, consider a basement or other cool location. Worms work in the dark, so make sure your composting system is not in direct sunlight or other bright light that will discourage worms from working at top efficiency.

Altogether, I found worm composting to be an elegant and efficient system of composting. I came from the interview deeply impressed and anxious to experiment with this system of composting on my own. Δ

Quicker compost

As you may have gathered, usable compost can either be made quickly or slowly depending on how precise and scientific you want to be. In his excellent book *Let it Rot!* (available at *BHM*, book #GL15, $12.95, write in your order on page 96), Stu Campbell covers (among other techniques) what he terms the University of California Method for fast thermophilic compost, which is worth mentioning.

The three principles of the U of C method are: (1) chop or shred the organic materials to increase surface area; (2) blend together the carbon and nitrogen materials, i.e. mix up the manure with the chopped leaves and grass clippings; and (3) turn the compost pile frequently, at least every three days, to increase aeration and expose all the materials to the heat from the center of the pile.

To experiment with this method, Mr. Campbell fenced a spot four by five feet in size and layered it with leaves of many kinds, some already-rotting sticks, and some seedy first-cut hay. All the material was chopped or shredded. As he layered the pile, every three or four inches he sprinkled alfalfa meal (a microbial activator) and dampened the pile with a hose. Every 18 inches or so, he added a layer of coarse unchopped hay to provide air channels into the pile.

When the pile was five feet high, he stacked hay bales around the cage (for insulation) and layered the top with flakes of compressed hay, also for insulation. He diligently turned the pile every few days.

The result? Heat activation began almost immediately. Within two weeks, the pile had begun to cool down (meaning microbial action was nearly complete) and, while not everything was perfectly broken down, it was certainly usable as gardening material.

This technique demonstrates the potential speed with which composting can happen under careful and precise conditions.

Speed factors

The three biggest factors which influence the speed at which decomposition happens are aeration, moisture, and material size.

Aeration

Aeration can be increased in a number of ways, both passive and active, depending on the nature of your compost pile and how much work you want to do.

Try vertically inserting things that will increase air flow such as perforated PVC pipes, a tightly-rolled section of chicken wire, or even bundles of cornstalks — anything to help air reach the lower levels of a pile.

If your pile is contained in a compost tumbler or a barrel or garbage can, give it a spin every few days to shake things up. If your pile is stationary and you feel you need a physical workout, turn it over with a pitchfork. Anything that introduces air into the bowels of a pile will increase the speed of decomposition.

Moisture

Ideally, the amount of moisture in a compost pile should be like the amount of moisture in a wrung-out sponge. In real life, it's not always possible to achieve this point of perfection. Fortunately, compost piles are reasonably forgiving when it comes to water. However …

Too much moisture means the compost pile goes into anaerobic condition, which drastically slows decomposition. If you live in an extremely wet climate, tarp your pile so it doesn't become waterlogged.

Too little moisture means the compost pile simply never activates. You'll have to water your pile. If you live in an arid climate where water is precious, use gray water to moisten your pile (dishwater is not recommended because the soaps and greases can coat the material in the pile, which slows decomposition).

Watering a dry compost pile with a hose can be tricky because most of the time water will only penetrate the top inch or two. It's better to dampen a pile as you turn it, or sprinkle the pile in layers as you build it. Once water is inside a pile, it won't easily evaporate; so make sure your pile is well-moistened as it grows.

Material size

While most of the time compostable materials are small in size, there will be times you'll have larger materials to decompose. This might include cornstalks, branches, large vegetable rinds or stems (broccoli stems come to mind), or other stubborn materials. Fear not, these will all break down eventually; but they'll break down a lot faster if they're chopped or shredded first. Remember the smaller the material, the larger relative surface area it has, and the faster it rots.

Chopping or shredding, besides increasing the surface area of the materials, has the added advantage of more material fitting into a smaller container. Your intact Christmas tree takes up a lot more room in a compost pile than your chipped Christmas tree.

If you're composting things that tend to mat, such as leaves or grass clippings, take whatever steps are necessary to reduce the matting potential. Leaves can be chopped. Grass clippings can be dried. Matting increases the likelihood of the material going into anaerobic condition, slowing down the decomposition process.

And above all, it's fun

While it might sound odd to get overjoyed by rot, in fact composting is a deeply satisfying factor of farm life. It's nice to be able to take what most people see as revolting garbage and make something highly useful and even valuable out of it — for free. Those who compost are modern-day Rumpelstiltskins who spin (black) gold out of straw. Δ

Making túró –
Hungarian curd cheese

By Linda Gabris

I learned how to make *túró* — accent on the *u* and *o*, (pronounced *too-ro*) — many years ago from a cherished family recipe handed down to me from my Hungarian mother-in-law who claimed the recipe was older than Hungary itself!

Even though my mother-in-law liked to embellish when telling Old World stories, she took a lot of pride in her culinary skills and was always on the serious side when it came to sharing her cherished secrets for making authentic Hungarian creations such as *túró*.

Túró, also known as "farmer's cheese," is similar to and easily mistaken for cottage cheese, but it does not contain as much liquid as cottage cheese. In North American kitchens, one might liken it to cream cheese, but *túró* has a looser texture, a lower fat content, and contains no salt.

It is often associated with Belgium's *quark*, France's *fromage frais,* and Italy's *ricotta* cheese, yet it is distinctly different. As my mother-in-law used to say in her beautiful Hungarian accent, *"túró is túró …"*

Once you've made a batch of *túró* and sampled it in some of Hungary's most famous, time-honored recipes and put it to use in some of your own unique homemade creations, you'll love it!

I find that *túró* is a very adaptable cheese to work with and makes a suitable substitute for cottage cheese and ricotta cheese in almost any recipe, especially for dishes like lasagna and other types of pasta fillings, salads,

Draining the túró, separating the curds from the whey

and in baking recipes calling for these types of fresh cheeses.

Túró can be eaten plain and simple, served with a slice of toast for breakfast, or as luncheon fare. As a child, my husband fondly remembers eating fried slices of bread rubbed with fresh garlic, spread with homemade pork lard speckled with cracklings, and crowned with a sprinkling of *túró*. He

said it was a powerful breakfast that kept a kid "full of spunk and spark all day!"

My family enjoys *túró* mixed with minced sweet peppers, cucumbers, and onions or fresh chives served with crackers as a fast and easy appetizer or as a salad dish. I find that folding in a handful of flaked smoked salmon gives the spread gourmet flair, making it a super quick and tasty appetizer for drop-in guests.

For an elegant dessert, simply drizzle *túró* with honey or scatter it with fresh fruit or berries such as blueberries or blackberries. Use a small crystal dessert bowl to hold a couple spoons of crumbled *túró* and it looks as good as it tastes!

In Hungary, *túró* is commonly used as stuffing for strudel, pancakes, dumplings, and pasta dishes. It is the secret ingredient in many of the country's famous pastries and baked goods such as *túrós rácsos, pite, toltelek,* and *pogácsa* (cheesecakes, bars, strudels, and biscuits).

And not to be forgotten is a traditional *túró leves* (soup) recipe that was popular in Hungary during the war years, especially amongst country folks who had access to fresh milk. The broth is made from whey and the noodles are made with *túró* filling. It is delightfully different and refreshingly delicious; it's hard to imagine that this soup was once considered a "poor man's" dish.

In earlier days, I made *túró* (as I was taught to make it) from a bounty of fresh whole milk supplied daily by the family cow. These days, with no cows in the barnyard anymore, I've updated the recipe to use store-bought milk which, for many folks today, is much easier to come by.

Below are step-by-step directions for making what I call "New World" *túró* as well as some authentic recipes handed down to me from my mother-in-law.

Túró

> 1 gallon (4 liters) of 3.25 percent milk
>
> 1 quart (1 liter) 3.25 percent cultured buttermilk (make sure that the buttermilk contains "active culture" printed on the carton)

In the Old World, country cooks like my mother-in-law commonly made *túró* out of fresh, whole, unpasteurized milk. Many diehards tend to argue that *túró* cannot be made otherwise. But it *can* be made when you use buttermilk with an active culture that has the power to "work" the pasteurized milk. However, I have not had luck making it out of "lesser" or "weaker" milks so use those specified above for sure results.

Pour the milk and buttermilk into a large stainless steel, oven-proof kettle that has a lid. I use my stockpot. Cover and set in a warm place. I sit my pot in the sunroom in the summer and by the hearth in colder weather. Leave the milk sitting in a warm place for about 24 hours (maybe longer if needed) until the mixture has the consistency of thick yogurt. At this point, you can take some out and use it in place of plain yogurt, if needed for a particular recipe.

After the milk has reached the consistency of thick yogurt, heat the oven to 200° F or lowest setting available. If you have a wood stove with a warming oven, the warming oven is an ideal place to set the pot. Place the pot in the oven with the lid on.

Leave the pot in the oven for six to eight hours or overnight until the curd has separated from the whey. Test it by sliding a spatula down the side of the pot and pushing the curds over so you can see if they have completely separated from the whey. It should have homogeneous (uniform-sized) curds throughout. If the curds have not formed and still resemble yogurt, the *túró* is not yet ready. Leave it in the oven an hour or two longer or until it is completely separated. You will have a mass of curds that hold their ground and stand together firmly over the top of the whey.

Take a large sieve and line it with cheesecloth. Place it over another stockpot or a large bowl. When the *túró* is ready, pour the contents into the cheesecloth-lined sieve, catching the curds and allowing the whey to drain through to the other pot. The whey will drain quite freely, but let the curds drip for a couple of hours for good measure. This will allow the *túró* to set well.

After it has dripped dry, turn the *túró* out of the cheesecloth into a bowl and it is ready to use. You should have about six cups of *túró*. It can be stored in a lidded container in the fridge for up to two weeks or it can be frozen.

Do not throw out the whey, as it contains water-soluble proteins, vitamins, and minerals that are well-worth cashing in on. You can simply put it into a capped bottle and keep it in the fridge as a healthy drink,

Linda's túró supper

claimed by my mother-in-law (who was also a well-respected herbalist in her native country) to be good for flushing impurities from the body. Add a little honey and a wedge of lemon and you'll find it a very pleasant drink.

I use whey as a soup and stock base and as liquid replacement for water in bread baking, and in other recipes to add extra nutrients as well as "raising" power. It can also be used as a fermenting agent for helping to start the working action in pickles and sauerkraut.

For those who have pigs and chickens, the whey can be used as a supplement for their diet. Whey can be added to the "swill" to help break down grains and other hog feeds. If you make your own dog food as I do, use the whey in place of water in the recipes for extra boost. And if you still have some excess whey, it makes good plant food for watering flower and vegetable gardens.

Túró soup

This soup is said to be of Turkish origin, brought into Hungary during the Turkish occupation. My mother-in-law's original recipe calls for three dried bay leaves, but I prefer dill over bay in my pot. Try them both and see which one tickles your fancy. Makes four to six servings.

4 cups whey
1 cup water
2 Tbsp. fresh minced dill (or 1 tsp. dried dill)
3 cloves mashed garlic
2 Tbsp. flour
1 cup sour cream
salt and pepper to taste

Put whey and water in soup pan. Add dill and garlic. Cover and simmer five minutes. Whisk flour into sour cream, stir into soup, whisking until blended. Heat through. Season with salt and pepper. Serve in bowls with fried *túró* noodles (recipe below) scattered over top and a pinch of fresh minced dill to garnish.

Túró and spinach-stuffed manicotti ready to bake

Fried *túró* noodles

2 cups flour
2 eggs
water
1 cup *túró*
fat for frying (I use homemade pork lard but shortening or vegetable oil can be used)

Put flour in a bowl, break in eggs, and mix well, adding enough water to form workable dough. In the war years in the old country, when eggs were hard to come by (unless you were country folks with your own chickens), this noodle dough was often made without them. It can still be made this way, producing a softer noodle. I like the harder, firmer texture which two or even three eggs produce. Knead until smooth, form into a ball, and place on a floured board. Roll into a long thin rectangle. Sprinkle with crumbled *túró*. Fold in half. Run the rolling pin over the dough until it is smooth and the *túró* is sealed inside. Using a sharp knife, cut into one-inch squares. Heat fat in castiron or heavy skillet and fry noodles on both sides until lightly golden. This recipe makes a big batch of noodles. I use half of the noodles for

the soup recipe above and the other half of the noodles for the main course dish below which I simply call Linda's *túró* supper. If not using the excess noodles on the same day as the soup, they can be frozen or stored in the fridge in a covered container for up to a week.

Linda's *túró* supper

2 Tbsp. pork lard or shortening
2 Hungarian sausages (kolbasz) sliced thinly. I use homemade kolbasz but you can use any similar store-bought sausage including smokies or wieners. When my kids were little they loved this dish made with sliced "hot-dogs" in place of spicier sausages.
3 cups shredded cabbage
1 minced onion
1 chopped pepper
1 tsp. caraway seeds
½ batch of fried *túró* noodles from previous recipe
¼ cup crumbled *túró* for garnish

Heat fat in large skillet, fry sausages about three minutes. If you are not using ready-to-eat sausages, cook the uncooked sausages until meat is done. Add the vegetables and caraway

153

seeds. Cook, stirring constantly until cabbage is tender. Add the fried *túró* noodles and heat through. Transfer to a platter and sprinkle with crumbled *túró* upon serving. Serves four.

Túró and spinach-stuffed manicotti

Here's one of my family's favorite weeknight suppers. I use wild greens such as stinging nettles or dandelions in spring, and lamb's quarters (pigweed) in summer in place of spinach. This helps take some of the demand off my garden patch of spinach, making the homegrown greens go much further on the table.

1 Tbsp. olive oil
1 small minced onion
2 Tbsp. minced sweet peppers
4 cloves minced garlic
1½ cups *túró*, crumbled
1 cup grated Mozzarella cheese
1 tsp. dried Italian mixed herbs (or pinch each of basil, oregano, parsley, and thyme)
salt and pepper to taste
1 packed cup of cooked spinach, or wild greens of choice, patted dry with paper towels, and chopped
1 egg
1 Tbsp. crushed hot chiles (or sweet paprika if you don't like the heat)
1 box manicotti
1 quart (or about 3 cups) of homemade pasta sauce (or storebought spaghetti or tomato sauce)
¾ cup grated Parmesan cheese

Heat the oil in skillet, sauté onion, pepper, and garlic until soft. Empty into a bowl and add *túró*, Mozzarella, seasonings, spinach, egg, and crushed chiles or paprika. Mix until well blended.

Cook manicotti according to package directions. Drain and stuff the tubes with the filling. Put two cups of sauce into a baking dish and lay the tubes into the sauce in a single row. Drizzle remaining sauce over top and sprinkle with the Parmesan. Cover the dish with foil. Bake in preheated 350°

F oven for 30 minutes. Uncover and let stand at room temperature about five minutes before serving. Serves four to six.

Túró scones

These tasty scones are delicious served with soup or as the bread of the day. In Hungary, they are often served with butter and jam as breakfast fare.

3 cups flour
1 envelope dry active yeast
1½ cups *túró*
1 cup margarine or butter
1 egg yolk for the dough (and another egg yolk for brushing, saving the whites for another purpose)

Combine all ingredients except the yolk for brushing, adding a little water if needed to form a ball. Knead on floured surface until smooth. Cover and let rest in fridge for an hour.

Remove dough from fridge and roll on floured surface into a large circle. Brush half the circle with beaten egg yolk. Fold over and brush half of the dough again with beaten yolk. Repeat one more time. Now roll the dough out to about ½-inch thickness. Cut

into small circles and brush tops with egg. Place on ungreased baking sheet and let rest at room temperature for about an hour. Preheat oven to 425° F and bake scones 25 minutes or until puffed and golden. Makes 18 small scones.

Túró and potato perogies

Dough:

3 cups flour
pinch salt
2 eggs
2 Tbsp. vegetable oil
½ cup or more hot water

Measure the flour into a bowl. Sprinkle with salt. Mix eggs, oil, and ½ cup of water and mix to form a soft dough, adding more water if needed. Turn out onto a floured surface and knead with floured hands until smooth and elastic. Wrap in plastic and set in fridge until chilled. In the meantime, make the filling.

Filling:

2 potatoes
1 Tbsp. lard or vegetable oil
1 minced onion
1 cup *túró*
½ cup grated cheddar cheese
salt and pepper to taste

Crepes with túró filling

Boil potatoes until tender, drain and mash. Heat fat in skillet and fry onion until golden. Mix potato, onion, *túró*, and cheddar cheese. Season with salt and pepper.

To assemble, roll dough into large thin circle on floured board. Using a perogy or cookie cutter, cut into 5-inch circles. Place a spoonful of filling on half of the circle, leaving room for the seam. Fold over and pinch to seal.

To fry: Heat fat in castiron or heavy skillet and fry perogies on both sides until golden. Pat with paper towels and place on platter. When fried in this manner, perogies can be eaten out of hand served with a tangy dipping sauce as an appetizer or as inexpensive finger food for parties.

To boil: Bring a large kettle of lightly-salted water to a boil, drop perogies into water, and cook uncovered about three minutes. Drain and serve.

Palacsinta (crepes) with *túró* filling

These thin crepes are filled with fruit or berry-flavored *túró* for a delightfully sweet breakfast treat or dessert dish.

Crepes:

3 eggs
pinch of salt
2 cups flour
1½ cups milk
oil for frying

Beat eggs and salt with a whisk. Gradually add flour alternately with milk, beating after each addition until smooth. Batter should be fairly thin so it can be poured. For best results, let batter rest an hour at room temperature before using. Heat oil in skillet, pour in batter, and tilt pan in order to make large, thin pancakes, cooking one at a time until all are made. Fill crepes with *túró* filling of choice, roll up, and sprinkle with confectioners' sugar upon serving.

Túró filling:

Mix 1½ cups *túró* with 1 Tbsp. lemon juice and three to four Tbsp.

apricot or peach preserves or jam (my mother-in-law's favorite filling). They are delicious, but be sure to try raspberry, strawberry, blueberry, or other jams of choice for endless variety.

Túró cheesecake

Here's a cheesecake to die for! My family loves it.

1¼ cups flour
¾ cup butter
2 egg yolks
1/3 cup sugar
1 tsp. baking powder
2 tsp. grated lemon zest
2 Tbsp. sour cream
2 eggs, separated
2½ cups *túró*
1 tsp. vanilla
1 whole egg

Put flour in bowl, cut in butter until crumbly. Add egg yolks, sugar, baking powder, lemon zest, and sour cream; mix with fork until crumbly. Using your hands, lightly gather up the dough and form into a ball. Place ¾ of the dough into a greased 9-inch square pan, pat down lightly and evenly. Bake in preheated 375° F oven 10 minutes or until golden. Make the filling by beating egg whites until stiff, set aside. Blend *túró* with egg yolks, sugar, and vanilla. Fold in the beaten egg whites. Spread filling over the baked dough. Roll remaining dough and cut into strips. Place in latticework fashion over filling. Beat remaining egg with one teaspoon of water. Brush over the top and bake 30 minutes. When cool, cut into squares. Serve with blueberry preserves drizzled over the top, if desired. Cut into small squares to serve, as this is a very rich dessert.

Túró custard bars

These modern-day bars call for instant pudding which makes them richly flavored, creamy smooth, and so delicious. They are sure to become a family favorite. And for variety you can use different flavored puddings such as vanilla, coconut, butterscotch, or chocolate.

Pastry:

2 cups flour
½ cup butter
½ cup sugar
3 eggs

Filling:

1½ cups *túró*
½ cup icing sugar
¼ cup heavy cream
1 tsp. grated lemon zest
1 package instant pudding mix prepared according to package directions

Grease a 9-inch square baking dish. Combine pastry ingredients until mixture can be lightly gathered into a ball. Divide in half. Pat half into the dish and bake in preheated 375° F oven 15 minutes or until golden. Turn out onto foil and cut into small squares while still warm. This will be the top. Pat remaining dough in dish and bake as above. Cool.

To make the filling, puree *túró*, icing sugar, and cream in blender until smooth. Add to the prepared pudding and whisk until completely blended. A hand-held egg-beater does a good job at blending the *túró* with the pudding.

Pour filling over pastry and cover with the top pieces of ready-cut squares, setting them back into their proper places. Δ

Make manure tea for great fertilizer

By James Kash

Springtime is coming and so is one of most homesteaders' favorite hobbies: gardening. In order to garden successfully, many resources are needed. These include: fertilizers, seeds, hand- and gas-powered tools, and a form of pest control. Many of these items can be bought once or successfully reproduced year after year. Conventional fertilizer, on the other hand, must be used each year for good harvest, and depending on your garden's size, you can use quite a bit each season. What about those of us who want to garden as close to organic as possible, and who want a fertilizer that won't break the bank? We need to make a cheap, efficient fertilizer right here at the homestead.

Manure tea is a great solution for homesteaders. Manure and compost are some of the earth's finest fertilizers and soil amendments. Many of us apply it on our gardens in the fall and use it to side dress plants in the spring. What about those of us who don't have heaping supplies of rotted manure and compost? You can make manure tea; it uses less manure, but is still just as good.

What do I need to make it?

Manure tea is easy to make and you need very little to do it. The most important ingredient is manure, of course. It will need to be fairly fresh, not overly composted. I usually make it from rabbit manure, but it can be made from cattle manure, and I am sure horse, goat, or sheep manure would work as well. I have never

Making manure tea is a great way to take advantage of a small manure supply in a large garden.

made it from poultry manure. I feel that it is probably a little too stout to use, and their diet is different from ruminant-like animals. You will need a water source, either a full bucket standing by or a water hose. Then you will also need a 5-gallon bucket to keep the tea in and a lid of some sort. You will also need a shovel to scoop up the manure and to stir the bucket up with.

How do I make it?

This is so easy to make, and takes hardly any time to do. The first thing you need to do is rinse out your bucket. The bucket does not have to be sparkly clean, just so you get out any residue of what was previously in there. You can never be too sure. Pour that water out. Next, fill 1/3 of the

bucket with good, rich manure. Sometimes my rabbit manure has a little bit of leftover hay in it, which is fine, but if there is too much hay then the resulting manure tea may not be strong enough.

Now fill up your bucket of manure with water to within a few inches of the bucket rim. If you fill the bucket too much it can slosh out, and believe me, that is not a pleasant smell on the hands or clothes. Take a shovel or other tool and stir it up, just to make sure it mixes fairly well.

Leave the full bucket where it will not be bothered for a couple weeks; I put ours in the unused chicken run, where livestock and pets won't bother it, and the smell won't be noticeable. Cover the bucket with a board or some other type of lid. This keeps out debris and rainwater, which can dilute the tea. The tea needs to "steep" for two weeks, and then it can be successfully used in the garden.

How do I use the tea?

I like to just go into a row of vegetables with a full bucket and a plastic cup (this is one instance where disposable is great), and I dip out a portion for each plant, depending on its needs. I pour it right at the base of the plant, and then continue until each one is done. By the time the two weeks has ended, most of the manure will have settled back in the bottom. I like to dump this onto the compost pile after I have gotten out all of the tea. You can continue using the tea after the two week period, as long as it stays covered.

Good crops for manure tea

Manure tea is a great alternative to high-nitrogen commercial fertilizers, and helps you make the most of the precious black gold.

The best crops for manure tea are very heavy feeders of nitrogen. These include: corn, summer squash, pumpkins, cucumbers, winter squash, and melons. These vegetables, to produce efficiently, need a lot of nitrogen and that is the best part about manure tea. You can have a very small supply of manure, and make the most of it and grow bushels and bushels of these vegetables. You also have vegetables like cabbage and broccoli that work well with manure tea too, but don't need as much nitrogen as the others. So their portions of manure tea wouldn't be as much as corn. The heavy nitrogen vegetables (listed above) usually get at least two full cups during their growing cycle, and usually, the earlier the better. This is where mulching for pumpkins, squash, cucumbers, and melons works well. Mulch helps them retain the manure tea even better because it doesn't all soak into the ground at once; with mulching very little will go to waste.

Vegetables like peppers, beans, peas, potatoes, and tomatoes that get too much nitrogen will grow enormous vines and practically no fruit. Beans and peas actually return nitrogen to the soil. This past year, I used a very little bit of manure tea on our potatoes and they did great, huge vines and huge potatoes. However, if I had given a full plastic cup (as opposed to the third of a cup), they would not have done well at all. Manure tea can work well with these veggies; you just have to have other soil amendments with it. These amendments can include wood ashes, compost, bone meal, fishmeal, etc. They are good sources of phosphorous, potassium, and other essential nutrients.

Manure tea is a great organic alternative to commercial high-nitrogen fertilizers, and is even better for self-reliant homesteaders. It is so easy to make, and you really can't beat the price. Δ

A Backwoods Home Anthology
The Sixteenth Year

Demystifying real rye bread

By Richard Blunt

R ye has been a popular bread grain in many parts of Europe for hundreds of years, second only to wheat. Popular regional rye breads can be found in Russia, Germany, Poland, the Czech Republic, Austria, Italy, and France. In spite of the large number of Americans whose ancestors emigrated here from those countries, breads made with rye are not as popular here as they are in Europe. This is unfortunate because a properly-made loaf of rye, containing a balanced combination of rye and wheat flour, or *all* rye flour, will emerge from the oven with a unique aroma that only rye can contribute.

Rye has a distinct flavor, and produces a loaf of bread with "crumb" (texture of the inner loaf) that is a little more dense than wheat. By varying the amount of rye flour in the formula, and extending fermentation, you can customize this bread to your personal preference. An excellent loaf of rye bread can be made with only 12 percent rye flour, a fermented wheat-flour starter, a pinch of commercial yeast, salt, and water. The result will be a loaf with stunning flavor, texture, and good keeping quality. As more rye flour is incorporated into the dough, the finished bread will develop more flavor and texture.

Sadly, very few bakeries in this country produce rye bread. Of the few that do, most fake it by combining a high volume of wheat flour with a small amount of white rye flour, which has very little flavor. This mass-produced bread is usually leavened with a high percentage of commercial yeast to save time. When made properly, a loaf of rye bread

Caraway rye bread

contains a certain amount of natural acidity, usually provided by some form of fermented flour starter. I will cover this in more detail later.

Commercial rye bread is usually mixed, proofed, baked, packaged, and shipped to the stores the same day. This type of hasty production results in bread with a marshmallow-like texture and very little flavor. Any flavor these loaves may have is often the by-product of incorporating excessive amounts of caraway seeds into the mix, along with concentrates of lactic and/or acetic acids to mimic the taste of natural sourdough. The overuse of these ingredients completely masks the clean, robust flavor of the rye flour and often insults the palate with an overly-sour and potent caraway flavor.

Unless you are fortunate enough to have a relative, friend, or neighbor with roots in one of the Eastern or Northern European countries, with a talent and love for baking bread, your experience with rye bread is probably limited to these fake commercial loaves. It is important to understand that properly-made rye bread has a firm but light texture, and a robust balanced flavor that can be further enhanced with the addition of toasted nuts, seeds, dried fruits, and a variety of whole herbs and spices, including caraway, in moderate amounts.

If you are one of a vast majority in this country to whom the robust flavor and bold texture of Old World rye bread may be a little out of your comfort zone, take heart. By using some simple basic techniques developed by master bakers, along with the modifications that I have added to the formulas presented here, you can take maximum advantage of the unique characteristics to rye flour and successfully bake this wonderful bread in your own kitchen, customizing the loaf to your personal taste. You do not have to live next to an artisan bakery or order an expensive frozen loaf from an online bakery to discover the joys of Old World rye bread. All you need is a good formula, a little patience, and some basic baking equipment and supplies.

I grew up in a Boston neighborhood where home-baked whole-grain breads were common in many households. My mother's favorites were the rye breads with roots in Eastern and Northern Europe. These breads were usually made with a high percentage of rye flour (70 percent or more) and were leavened with a rye sourdough starter and no commercial yeast.

My mother's fascination with these breads began when a neighbor gave her a small piece of raw bread dough wrapped in waxed paper. She told my mother that it was a piece of dough saved from a loaf of rye that she had made the day before. She taught my mother how to assemble, mix, proof, and bake a loaf of the same bread using this "old dough," as she called it. On another occasion, this neighbor gave my mother a small glass bowl with about one-half cup of what she called, "Old World rye sourdough mother culture." She advised my mother to use this old dough soon, because it contained fresh baking yeast that would only remain active for another day. The rye mother culture, she said, would be fine if she kept it in a refrigerator. She came back a few days later with a recipe for a caraway rye bread containing 40 percent rye flour. She taught my mother how to prepare this loaf using the rye mother culture. The loaf made with the old dough contained only 15 percent dark rye flour, but had plenty of rye flavor and texture, making it a great all-purpose bread for sandwiches and toast.

My mother fell in love with this bread after her first bite, and it soon became a standard in our house. On holidays and special occasions she would often increase the amount of rye flour in the recipe and add dried fruit, nuts, and spices. With these additions she transformed this basic sandwich bread into one that could be sliced and eaten with little embellishment, except for a small amount of smoked salmon or sharp cheese. This same neighbor also taught my mother how to prepare and bake with an all-rye flour sourdough starter.

Sadly, I hadn't given much thought to this wonderful bread of my youth for several years until reading a short article in the weekly food section of my local newspaper. The article outlined the differences between the mass-produced rye breads sold in supermarkets and traditional Old World rye breads of Eastern and Northern Europe. The article inspired me to once again dig into my mother's mountain of old recipes until I found her long-forgotten sourdough rye bread formula. We will be working with an updated version of this proven formula when we get to the recipe section.

After a long absence from baking breads made with rye flour, I quickly discovered that I had forgotten many of the distinct differences between it and wheat flour. As a result, the first loaves that I baked, using my mother's recipe, were dense, pasty, and lifeless. After repairing my damaged ego, I called my baker friend Mike, and asked his advice on how to proceed.

He reinforced my suspicion that rye flour has some unique characteristics that must be taken into consideration when incorporated into any bread formula. He suggested that I read selected works of a couple of master bakers with extensive knowledge and experience working with rye flour. I spent

Equipment and supplies for making rye bread: KitchenAid stand mixer, King Arthur bread flour, Bob's Red Mill Dark Rye Flour, 3 packs of instant yeast, nonstick cooling rack, silicone spatula, instant read thermometer, cast iron Dutch oven, stainless steel bowl for final proofing, pot holder, plastic and stainless bench scrapers, digital scale, straight edge razor, stainless measuring spoons, sewing scissors, parchment paper, stainless measuring cups.

Final proof in plastic bowls

six months reading articles and books written by these bakers. As a result of their genius, and my mom's old recipe, I was able to assemble and successfully bake about 60 wonderful loaves of rye using varying amounts of rye flour. The most important thing this effort taught me was to park most of my experience baking with wheat flour at the door when I enter the kitchen to bake rye bread.

There are several distinct differences between rye and wheat flour. Understanding these differences and embracing some different but simple flour-handling techniques will consistently produce rye bread with great flavor, a moist and tender crumb, and excellent keeping quality.

Before we look at some of the differences, I would like to offer you a bit of advice: Please don't let the following facts about rye flour, and how it differs from wheat flour in bread baking, discourage you from adding rye bread to your baking schedule. Successful techniques for working with rye flour have been developed and implemented by professional bakers. As you read on, you will discover that mixing, fermenting, proofing, and baking a successful loaf of rye bread does take a little more time

but far less effort than preparing a loaf of wheat bread. For example, tiresome kneading is greatly minimized, or eliminated, from bread formulas containing rye flour. If you give the dough enough time, it will do most of the work for you.

Rye bread represents an area of great potential for anyone willing to take time to understand the very special production requirements that are necessary when baking with rye flour. Excellent rye breads can contain from a minimum of 12 percent rye, combined with whole wheat or other specialty flours, and up to 100 percent rye flour, to make an endless variety of breads with interesting flavors and textures.

Adding rye flour to a bread formula changes how the dough is mixed, fermented, proofed, baked, and eaten. Like wheat, rye flour contains gluten, the protein that provides structure to bread dough. This structure is referred to as the gluten network, which makes it possible for the dough to capture carbon dioxide gas produced during yeast fermentation and which causes the bread to rise during the proofing and baking. Cutting into a loaf of artisan French bread and comparing the crumb to that of a loaf

of commercial white bread will reveal how different baking procedures can affect the texture of a loaf of bread.

Since rye flour contains considerably less gluten than wheat flour, it will not form a strong gluten structure similar to wheat's. As a result, rye bread will always have a structure that is more dense than wheat bread. Rye flour also contains more bran, fiber, and minerals than wheat and because of that it will absorb more water. This extra water will potentially produce bread with a pasty crumb unless care is taken by the baker.

The high bran content in rye flour also contributes to lower volume in the finished bread. The bran pieces act like razors, cutting the gluten network and allowing some of the volume-producing gas to escape. Rye also has a higher percentage of fermentable sugars than wheat which can cause a loaf to quickly over-ferment and collapse. A high percentage of a polysaccharide (called pentosan) also causes rye flour to absorb extra water. This complex sugar competes with the gluten in the flour for moisture. Pentosans are fragile and can break down if the dough is not gently mixed. This breakdown will result in bread with a sticky and pasty crumb.

Finally, rye flour is loaded with amylase enzymes. The main function of this enzyme is to convert starch into sugar. As the loaf bakes, and the internal temperature reaches about 125° F, the starches in the rye begin to absorb water and swell to form the crumb. At this temperature the amylases are also in an active state of converting starch to sugar. Sugar does not contribute to crumb formation. These enzymes will not be destroyed until the internal temperature of the loaf reaches about 176° F. This will result in a gummy and pasty crumb unless the baker has adopted procedures to avoid it. Professional bakers call this a "starch attack." Wheat flour doesn't have this problem for two reasons: it doesn't have as many amylase enzymes as rye, and wheat starch gelatinizes at a much higher temperature. To inhibit the decomposing effects of amylase enzymes in their rye loaves, professional bakers use an essential tool. Depending on just how it was developed, this vital ingredient goes by several names: sourdough seed culture, pre-ferment, poolish, and biga, to name a few. What all of these cultures have in common is their ability to develop lactic and acetic acids, wild yeasts, and bacteria that are beneficial to bread, especially rye bread. The lactic and acetic acids limit the decomposing activity of amylase enzymes, and produce a loaf with a more stable crumb. The wild yeasts and beneficial bacteria add more volume and flavor to the finished loaf.

A pure sourdough culture is simply a mixture of flour and water that has initially been aged at room temperature, under controlled and monitored conditions, until the development of wild yeasts, lactic and acetic acids, and beneficial bacteria become well established. The active seed culture is then stored under refrigeration and kept healthy with regular feedings of flour and water. A properly maintained sourdough seed culture will live longer than the baker who created it. Cultivating and baking with a homegrown sourdough is an effort that requires consistency in the use of time and temperature management.

I bake a variety of breads using sourdough cultures and yeasted pre-ferments. For the bread formulas we will be preparing here, we will be using the same pre-fermented, "old dough" starter that my mother used for many years to leaven her rye bread. This starter incorporates a tiny amount of commercial yeast mixed with some wheat flour, salt, and water.

After the initial mixing, the dough is covered and allowed to ferment for 12 to 16 hours. This extended fermentation increases the number of yeast

Rustic country rye bread

cells in the starter, and supports the development of lactic and acetic acids, and flavor-producing beneficial bacteria. The final dough is mixed with a little more yeast, water, and salt along with a mixture of dark rye flour and wheat bread flour. The dough is allowed to ferment, in bulk, for about 2½ to 3 hours. Finally, it is shaped and proofed for about another hour before baking. As you can see, the most important resource here is time management. When you step into the kitchen to bake any of these breads, plan on the bread coming out of the oven in about 24 hours. Using a yeasted pre-ferment is not intended to be a substitute for a mature sourdough seed culture for producing a first class loaf of rye bread.

In comparison, a pure sourdough culture adds more flavor, and extends keeping quality of the bread. But these pure cultures require ongoing maintenance to keep them fresh and active. A yeasted pre-ferment also adds flavor and extended keeping-quality to a loaf. However, there are some practical reasons for the casual baker to use a pre-ferment when baking light- and medium-textured rye breads. All of a prepared pre-ferment is incorporated into the final dough. Also, a pre-ferment takes the same

amount of time to develop as it does to refresh a pure sourdough culture. The small amount of commercial yeast used in the pre-ferment formula adds extra lift and lighter crumb to the finished loaf. If you are interested in developing a rye or wheat flour sourdough seed culture, I will be glad to cover the subject in another article.

Equipment and supplies

To bake any of the breads that I offer here, you need only five basic ingredients: rye flour, wheat bread flour, salt, water, and instant dried yeast. To this basic set of ingredients you can add dried fruits, roasted nuts, aromatic spices, and a wide variety of whole grains and seeds.

The definition for rye flour, as it is sold in this country, can be (and often is) confusing. The most visible distributers of rye flour to home bakers are: King Arthur Flour, Bob's Red Mill, Hodgson Mill, and Arrowhead Mills. The rye products of these distributors can be purchased online or in your local supermarket. I have baked bread using rye flour from all of these companies with good results. However, the flour descriptions on the bags can be misleading, depending on which brand of rye flour you buy. For example, King Arthur distributes medium rye flour that has the germ and some of the bran sifted out, and is ground fine. Bob's Red Mill distributes flour labeled Dark Rye that is also ground fine. It is very difficult for an untrained eye to determine any difference between the two flours. Both flours produced bread of similar taste and texture. Hodgson Mill distributes flour labeled Stone Ground Rye. The only difference that I could detect between this flour and Bob's Dark Rye flour is the Hodgson Mill flour is a coarser grind. The coarse grind of this flour produces a loaf that is a little denser than a loaf made with the fine-ground flour.

When I first started this project, I rotated between all of the different rye flour brands that were available to me, hoping to find the one that produced the best and most consistent loaf. Unfortunately, this made it impossible for me to determine the cause of a problem when a loaf didn't bake up as I expected. To solve this problem I decided to use only one rye flour for all of my baking. The Dark Rye flour sold by Bob's Red Mill proved to suit my needs for several reasons: it is available in all of the supermarkets in my area, it is packaged in two-pound bags, which can be used in a couple of weeks (like any

whole grain flour, rye will spoil if kept too long), and it is a fine-ground flour that yields the best results with my recipes. I paired this flour with King Arthur's standard unbleached, high-gluten bread flour to add lift and structure to the loaf. Both of these flours are sold in most supermarkets and are usually fresh. Fresh flour is essential when baking rye bread. Old or stale rye flour can produce a loaf with off, and sometimes rancid, flavors.

The flour of choice for the breads I present here is the **dark rye flour**. The milling process for this flour includes most of the outer portion of the endosperm. The additional bran gives this flour a darker color. (See sidebar for other rye flours.)

Listed below is some basic equipment that will help make your rye-baking experience more enjoyable:

1. **A sturdy electric mixer.** I have a KitchenAid stand mixer that I use for all mixing functions. Powerful mixers like this can be a little pricey but, if you like to bake bread, owning one of these mixers is a wise investment. My KitchenAid is 25 years old and is still running strong.

2. **A 10-inch cast iron Dutch oven.** I believe that every kitchen should have one of these. Dutch ovens are

almost indestructible and are available with ceramic coating for cooking everything from breads to soups and stews. To bake the breads offered here, I suggest a pre-seasoned Lodge brand Dutch oven. They are available at Amazon or Walmart for less than $30.

3. **A plastic or metal blade bench scraper.** Rye dough tends to be a little sticky. A bench scraper is a great tool for efficient cleanup.

4. At least **two silicone spatulas with 2½-inch-wide blades.** These are indispensable for scraping sticky bread dough from the mixer or other bowl. The silicone blades are also heat resistant.

5. **An instant-read food thermometer** that will record temperatures above 210° F. These thermometers are a must for determining just when a loaf of bread is ready to be removed from the oven. You can buy one from any store that sells kitchen equipment. A good one that will record temperatures from -40° F to over 300° F will cost as little as $20.

6. **A roll of silicone parchment paper.** This paper becomes non-stick when it reaches 160° F. I use it to line the bowl for the final proofing of bread dough. When I am ready to bake the loaf, this paper makes transferring the loaf to the Dutch oven painless and prevents the loaf from sticking to the pot.

7. **One or two 9-inch plastic or stainless steel bowls** to hold the dough for final proofing.

8. **A straightedge razor blade** or **pair of sharp sewing scissors** for making cuts in the dough before baking.

9. **A nonstick cooling rack.**

10. **A pair of high-quality pot holders or oven mitts.** Since you will be cooking your bread in a Dutch oven at a temperature of about 500° F, protection against burns is necessary.

11. **A digital food scale** for weighing ingredients like flour and water. Scooping flour and eyeballing the

Walnut and cranberry rye bread

correct level of water, even in a container designed for liquid measure, isn't accurate enough for a baker looking for consistency. Often even small variations in flour or water can result in loaves that lack consistency. Bread baking demands that the baker measure accurately. For the formulas that are presented here, flour and water require accurate measurement. A digital scale is a must for accurate measurement.

12. **A good set of plastic or stainless steel measuring spoons.** I own two very accurate sets of measuring spoons: a stainless steel set manufactured by Cuisipro that I bought for $12, and a set of plastic spoons manufactured by OXO Good Grips that cost only $6. Both sets measure accurately, but I prefer the stainless steel for durability.

The formulas

The breads featured in this section do not contain a lot of rye flour. However, due to the unique flavoring quality of rye, all of these breads have a very recognizable rye taste, and a firm but light crumb.

Each formula produces a high volume of pre-fermented flour starter that contains a small percentage of commercial yeast. This starter is subjected to a long fermentation that develops the mild acids, wild yeast, and beneficial bacteria that minimize problems with the rye flour and add flavor and volume to the loaf. The total amount of flour, yeast, and salt remains consistent for all three formulas. The flour proportions are adjusted as the amount of rye flour increases. In the formula with **Walnuts and cranberries** I have increased the amount of water to 11½ ounces to compensate for the increased amount of rye flour. The preparation method for the three formulas is also consistent and will only be outlined with the **Rustic country bread**. So, for the last two recipes, return to the preparation method for

this recipe because, except for the inclusion of other ingredients (such as the cranberries and walnuts in the third recipe), the baking method is the same.

At last! It is time to bake. Let's have some fun.

In each of the three recipes, I've listed *all* of the ingredients under the heading "overall formula," so you know what ingredients to assemble before you start. Some of the ingredients will go into the "pre-ferment," some into the "final dough," and some will go into both.

Rustic country bread with 12 percent rye flour

Overall formula

14 oz. wheat bread flour
2 oz. dark rye flour
11 oz. water
2½ tsp. salt
⅜ tsp. instant yeast

Pre-ferment

8 oz. wheat bread flour
⅛ tsp. instant yeast
1 tsp. salt
5 oz. water

Final dough

6 oz. wheat bread flour
2 oz. dark rye flour
¼ tsp. instant yeast
1½ tsp. salt
6 oz. water
All of the pre-ferment

Method:
Pre-ferment: Combine the bread flour, instant yeast, and salt in a small bowl and stir to combine. Add the water and mix until the dough is just smooth and all of the flour is incorporated into the dough. Cover the bowl with plastic wrap; let it stand at about 70° F for 12 to 16 hours. When the pre-ferment is ready to use it will be domed and just beginning to collapse or dent down in the center.

Mixing the final dough: Add all ingredients to the mixer except the

pre-ferment. With the dough hook attached, mix the dough for three minutes on the first speed on a KitchenAid, or low on another mixer, to blend all of the ingredients. As the dough is coming together, add the pre-ferment in chunks. If the dough seems dry, add water in very small amounts to correct the hydration.

(If this is your first effort preparing bread like this, I suggest that you resist making any changes in the formula at this time. After sampling the first slice of the finished bread you can make note of any adjustments, and incorporate them into the next loaf.)

Finish the mixing on the second speed if using a KitchenAid mixer, or medium speed for other mixers, for about 2½ minutes. Take care to maintain the mixing times that I have established. Overmixing rye flour, or mixing it too vigorously, will result in the problems, such as sticky, pasty crumb, that I outlined above.

Bulk fermentation and folding: After mixing is complete, the dough will be transferred to a suitable-size bowl that has been sprayed with a nonstick spray (like Pam), covered, and allowed to ferment for 2½ hours. During this time the dough must be folded twice. What is folding and how is it done? Due to the delicate nature of bread dough that contains rye flour, traditional kneading is not an effective way of developing a gluten structure in the dough. Depending on the amount of rye flour the dough contains, kneading it goes from difficult to impossible because rye flour makes the dough sticky. Folding is the answer to this problem, at least in these formulas. But as the amount of rye flour increases, even folding becomes impossible — and unnecessary.

How do we fold dough?

1. Flour the work surface, using enough flour to prevent the dough from sticking to the counter.

2. Turn the dough out of the bowl onto the counter.

3. Gently lift about a third of the dough from the right or left side of the bulk and bring it to the middle. Pat it down so that it holds its place. Brush off any excess flour from the fold.

4. Repeat this procedure on the opposite side of the dough.

5. Now reach over and lift a third of the dough from the far side in front of you. Once again, brush any excess flour to avoid incorporating it into the dough before patting into the bulk. Repeat this with the third of dough closest to you.

6. Folding is complete. Gently lift the dough from the counter and place it back into the bowl with the folds on the bottom.

During bulk fermentation, the dough will be folded twice at 50-minute intervals.

Final fermentation: Line a 9-inch bowl with two 17-inch pieces of silicone parchment paper. One piece will be placed from right to left and the other from front to back. When it is time to bake, the bread will be lifted into the Dutch oven, along with the parchment paper, which will prevent the bread from sticking while it bakes. Cover the bowl with plastic wrap and ferment it for 1¼ to 1½ hours at about 70° F.

Baking and cooling: When the final fermentation is complete, remove the plastic wrap from the bowl. Make a six-inch slash about ½ inch deep with a new single-edge razor blade in the center of the dough and dust the dough with a little bread flour.

If a razor doesn't produce the desired cut, a small pair of sharp sewing scissors can be substituted. Simply open the scissor blades, when you are ready to cut, then poke the lower blade about ¾ of an inch into the dough and start cutting, moving the scissors forward with each cut.

We will start baking this bread in a cold oven with the Dutch oven lid in place. The trapped steam created with this method will add volume to the finished loaf. We will finish the loaf with lid removed to promote browning.

So, lift the dough, using the parchment paper, and carefully place it into the Dutch oven and cover with the lid. Place the Dutch oven on an oven rack in the lower-middle position of the cold oven. Heat the oven to 425° F. Once that oven temperature has been reached, continue baking the bread for 30 minutes.

Carefully remove the lid and continue to bake another 15 minutes. Now, insert the thermometer into the bread and bake the bread until it reaches an internal temperature of 210° F.

Carefully remove the Dutch oven from your oven and place on the stove top. Remove the bread from the pot and place on a wire rack. Cool the bread to room temperature, about two hours.

This method is the same method you'll use in the next two recipes.

Light rye with 22 percent rye flour with caraway seed

Overall formula

12½ oz. bread flour
3½ oz. dark rye flour
11 oz. water
⅜ tsp. instant yeast
2½ tsp. salt
2 tsp. caraway seed, lightly toasted in a small skillet and set it aside to cool before adding it to the dough

Pre-ferment

8 oz. bread flour
5 oz. water
1 tsp. salt
⅛ tsp. instant yeast

Final dough

4½ oz. bread flour
3½ oz. dark rye flour
2 tsp. toasted caraway seed
1½ tsp. salt
¼ tsp. instant yeast
6 oz. water
All of the pre-ferment

Types of rye flour

If you decide that home-baked rye bread suits your tastes, we can discuss how to use the other rye products at another time. Here is a list of other rye grain products usually available in supermarkets or specialty food stores.

White rye flour. This flour is milled from the very center of the rye endosperm. Most of the bran and germ are removed during the milling process. This flour is almost white and has very little rye flavor.

Medium rye flour. This flour is the milled from the entire endosperm of the grain along with some of the bran and fiber from the outer portion of the endosperm.

Whole rye/pumpernickel flour. This flour is the whole rye berry that has been coarsely milled.

Rye flakes are the whole rye berries that are usually steamed to soften them, then rolled into flakes that resemble old-fashioned oatmeal, and can be cooked like old-fashioned oatmeal. Add some fruit and a little yogurt for an interesting and healthful breakfast.

Rye chops are whole rye berries that are chopped and resemble steel cut oats or buckwheat. This type of rye can also be cooked like steel cut oats and eaten for breakfast.

Rye berries are whole rye grain that has not been milled. Like wheat berries, rye berries must be cooked before adding them to a bread formula.

Method:

To bake, use the method from the first recipe.

Walnut and cranberry with 30 percent rye

Overall formula

11¼ oz. high-gluten bread flour
4¾ oz. dark rye flour
11½ oz. water
2½ tsp. salt
⅜ tsp. instant yeast
2 oz. dried cranberries
2 oz. walnuts, coarsely chopped
  and lightly toasted

Pre-ferment

8 oz. high-gluten bread flour
5 oz. water
1 tsp. salt
⅛ tsp. instant yeast

Final dough

3¼ oz. high-gluten bread flour
4¾ oz. dark rye flour
6½ oz. water
1½ tsp. salt
⅛ tsp. instant yeast
2 oz. dried cranberries
2 oz. walnuts, coarsely chopped
  and lightly toasted

Method:

Use the method for the first recipe except add the cranberries and walnuts to the dough in the final minute of mixing. After that, continue to use the method from the first recipe.

I hope I have given you enough meaningful insight into the often misunderstood and often ignored world of rye berry. Please give these formulas a try. You will not be disappointed. Δ

For more great recipes go to our website

www.backwoodshome.com

The Best of the First Two Years

Our first big anthology!

In these 12 issues you'll find:

* A little knowledge and sweat can build a home
    for under $10,000
* Tepee to cabin to dream house
* From the foundation up, house-building is forgiving
* A first time horse buyer's guide
* A greenhouse offers advantages for the organic gardener
* Canning meat
* Backwoods Home recipes
* In pursuit of independence
* Canning blueberries
* How we keep humming along on the homestead
* Pioneer women on the trail west
* Some tips on first aid readiness for remote areas
* Whip grafting—the key to producing fruit variety
* The basics of backyard beekeeping
* Co-planting in the vegetable garden
* How to make soap—from fat to finish
* The instant greenhouse
* The old time spring house
* Getting started in a firewood business
* For battling ants or growing earthworms,
    try coffee grounds
* Sawmills: a firm foundation to homesteading

Ayoob on Firearms

"Gun control" for dummies

Massad Ayoob

Barack Obama, outspokenly anti-gun for his entire political career, fooled an amazing number of gun owners by keeping a "hands off" attitude toward Second Amendment issues until his first term was over and his second secured. Then, when a madman slaughtered 20 helpless children and half a dozen teachers in an unprotected elementary school, he and his political cohorts pulled the trigger on an anti-gun campaign that had long stood cocked and ready.

The result was the most savage attack on the civil rights of firearms owners that I've seen in a reasonably long lifetime. In violation of the Constitution of the State of New York, Governor Andrew Cuomo rammed through the most Draconian legislation seen in the modern history of American firearms ownership, and did it literally in the dark of night without the mandatory discussion period his state's constitution demands. Gun bans. No more than seven cartridges per magazine. Ironically, they called it the SAFE Act.

Colorado followed, its legislators blatantly ignoring the overwhelming number of constituents who clearly opposed it. It was reported that Michael Bloomberg, the obsessively anti-gun mayor of New York City, told Democrats in the Colorado state house that if they opposed the gun and magazine bans, he would use his billions to fund other Democrats to unseat them in the next election. At this writing, more state-level dominoes are in line to fall in the same direction.

Throughout, the mainstream American media has for the most part cast aside pretense of impartiality and rooted for "assault weapon bans." Bill O'Reilly commented in January 2013 that CNN had turned into a 24/7 gun control telethon. It wasn't that much of an exaggeration.

From call-in talk shows I've participated in, to reader mail, to just reading clueless editorials and letters to the editors in newspapers around the country, I've seen an appalling lack of knowledge and critical thinking applied to this issue.

In the time of the Low Information Voter, you're not going to be able to educate the co-worker, the relative, the neighbor you're discussing it with in the entirety of the vast body of Second Amendment scholarship. So, let's suggest some short-and-sweet answers that bring Truth and Logic into the game.

Punish *who* for *what*?

They want to take away your property, and/or limit your ability to buy such property in the future, even though that property (semi-automatic firearms) has been perfectly legal for non-felons to own for more than a century? Because criminals use them?

We're talking about *criminals.* We call them that because they break the law and commit crimes. They are planning to commit murder, one of the most heinous crimes in the history of civilized humanity, and they're going to be deterred by a law against having the particular murder weapon they want to use? No one with three digit IQ can seriously believe that ... can they?

You'll hear the argument, "But if they're against the law for anyone to have, the bad guys won't be able to get them at all."

Things against the law are the stock in trade of criminals. Coca plants for cocaine, and opium poppies for heroin, do not thrive in North America. Yet a huge criminal drug trade continues to thrive. Both sides of this polarized debate agree that there are some 300 million firearms in the United States; no magic electromagnet from the sky is going to come down and suck them up. Firearms are the most durable of durable goods.

Moreover, they're not that hard to make. Ask the Brits who fought the IRA: anyone with a Bridgeport lathe can make a functional copy of a Sten submachine gun. Back in the 1950s, juvenile delinquents made zip guns out of radio antennas and rubber bands, and a functional sawed off shotgun using low-power shells can be fashioned out of PVC pipe. And, with new 3-D "printing" technology ...

The old saying is true: "When guns are outlawed, only outlaws will have guns." It's true on two levels. Law-abiding people, by definition, will abide by the law and turn their guns in if confiscatory laws are passed. Law-breaking people, by definition, will not. The criminals will have guns, and the good people won't.

The other side of that is, good people will now be made into criminals — even felons, the way most of this legislation is written — even though all they've done is merely possess something that has been legal for Americans to possess for more than a century. A huge percentage of the population — and in some parts of the country, perhaps actually a majority of the population — will be made criminals by a stroke of the pen.

When bad people do bad things, society should punish the bad people, not the good people who did not do bad things. Suppose the day before the Sandy Hook Elementary School atrocity someone had asked the little kids there, "If a naughty child writes graffiti on the school walls, would it be fair to take crayons away from all the rest of you?"

I would suspect those little kids would have answered, "No! *We* didn't do anything wrong. Why should we be punished? Punish the one who did the bad thing. And by the way, why didn't the teachers stop the bad boy from doing that?"

Yet before the terrible next day was over, we were hearing calls that this gun and that magazine should be banned from all good people, because of what one monster did, with a rifle he had to murder his own mother to steal. Yet realistic calls for armed security at schools met with derision.

When elected leaders and media spokespersons aren't as smart as we'd expect six- to eight-year-old children to be, it's time for someone to explain "gun control" for dummies.

Malum prohibitum, malum in se

Early in law school, future lawyers learn the difference between *malum prohibitum* and *malum in se*. "*Malum in se*" means the thing is evil in and of itself: crimes such as murder or rape, for example. "*Malum prohibitum*" means the thing is bad because we passed a law against it: carrying a gun in New York City without a permit, for example, when it's perfectly legal to do the same in Arizona or Vermont. Or owning full capacity magazines and semiautomatic pistols and rifles in which to use them. Legal since the technology existed, and now, suddenly, a felony.

Prohibition

When you tell the public, "You can no longer have something you've always been allowed to have," it's not "control," it's *prohibition*. Less than a hundred years ago — in the memory of some still living Americans — our nation's leaders turned the Volstead Act into law. We all remember how well *that* worked out. And let's not talk about how successful the "war on drugs" has been.

The history of it is, when self-righteous do-gooders say "I don't want it or like it, so therefore, you can't have it," the result never seems to turn out well. In the instant case, we have the mayors of New York and Chicago protected at public expense by huge phalanxes of bodyguards paid for with taxpayers' funds, telling the unprotected citizens that they have no right to protect themselves, their homes, and their families with the tools most suited to that task. When the well-protected tell the unprotected they don't need protection, massive nationwide non-compliance is going to be the predictable outcome.

What's being widely proposed now has nothing to do with "common sense" or "safety." When pushed to the wall, the sponsors often admit that they don't expect their proffered legislation to prevent any mass-murders. The most common default answer they give us is, "We have to do *something*."

Well, let's see. "Something" like making it illegal for you to bequeath your valuable firearms to your heirs without them paying a huge and unfair "added inheritance tax" to do it. (Some of those pushing for "Universal Background Checks" have picked up on your resistance to that and are re-writing their bills to make half-hearted exceptions … but if they had reasonably considered their legislation before offering it, they would have included such provisions beforehand. Tells you something about their thought processes …)

"Something" like making you register your long-owned Ruger Mini-14, your AR15, even the Marlin or Ruger

Some current "universal background check" schemes would make it impossible for you to lend a gun to a friend, or borrow one. Here Terri Strayer, left, coaches a friend on how to shoot a snub-nosed .38.

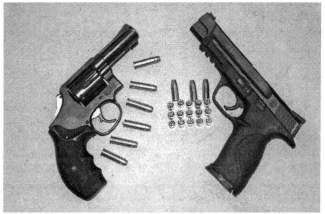

Smith & Wesson Military & Police handguns show how times change. Revolver, left, holds 6 .38 Special cartridges. Today's cop is more likely to carry autoloader, right, designed to hold 18 9mm rounds.

Gabby Giffords proudly owned a 16-shot Glock 19, identical to the one she was shot with.

.22 rifle you take to an Appleseed shoot where people learn gun safety and marksmanship, and celebrate American history. The prohibitionists ask, "Why should you worry about registering your gun? That's just to keep criminals from having them."

Uh ... excuse me, but ... *felons don't have to register their guns!* Remember one of those other Amendments, the Fifth one? Where you are not required to incriminate yourself? Long ago, in 1968, the United States Supreme Court made that ruling. Look up *Haynes v. United States*. It was an eight-to-one decision, by the way.

You are a law-abiding citizen? You are *not* a felon? Poor you: under some of the currently proposed legislation, your failure to register your weapon in a timely manner will *make* you one ... but since you weren't a felon before, don't expect protection under the Haynes precedent.

And, make no mistake: history shows that when tyrannical regimes have taken over countries and set upon a path of repression and even genocide, the first thing they do is disarm the target populace. Hitler's Nazis did it in reverse, restoring gun rights lost after WWI to "good Germans," but not to the targeted Jews. Look it up: it's part and parcel of the ugly history of genocide.

Registration is the first step to that disarmament. They have to know where the guns are before they can take them. Remember what triggered Concord and Lexington?

The right to self-defense

Lord Blackstone, the great commentator on the Common Law, said that self-protection was the highest of all human rights. We live in a nation of well over 300 million people, with fewer than one million police officers to protect them. Those officers are assigned to work 40 hours out of every 168 hour week, and we have to consider vacation, court time, sick time, training time, and all of that. Put it together, and it's no surprise that estimates of average police response time to emergencies around the country hover around eleven minutes.

A lot of bad things can happen in eleven minutes. My friends in Alaskan law enforcement tell me that in the most remote areas, response

Current "assault weapon ban" proposals would criminalize most of the .22 rifles used by shooters at an Appleseed event, like this one in Hernando, Florida.

time might take until the next day, depending on the weather.

Even in more urban areas, police from Chicago to Oakland have stopped responding to certain serious felonies because they just don't have the manpower to do it in this economically depressed society. Some of the more honest police chiefs and sheriffs are telling their citizens to arm themselves.

And, even if you're around the corner from Police Headquarters when you're attacked, *you have to survive the attack long enough to summon police assistance.* From violent home invasions to vicious "flash mob" attacks on the street, multiple assailants are involved. Gunfights are so fast-moving that no police department of any significant size has ever compiled a 100% hit ratio in officer-involved shootings. Add to that the fact that even fatal wounds do not immediately neutralize violent criminals.

Multiple attackers threatening your family ... not all of your shots will necessarily hit ... not all those that hit will strike center ... and even not all of those may instantly stop the attack. Put that all in your computer, add it up, carry the one ... nope, a New York compliant seven-shot firearm just may not add up to survival.

Don't take advice from hypocrites

Dianne Feinstein, author of the current national "prohibition" legislation, is on film and on record saying that if she'd had the clout, she'd have told "Mr. and Mrs. America, turn 'em all in" — yes, all firearms. Oddly enough, Senator Feinstein does not take her own advice. She was one of about six people (on the city Board of Supervisors) who had permits to carry a loaded gun in that city. When she jumped on the "gun control" bandwagon, she said that she was going to be the first to turn in her gun and stop the carnage.

Feinstein had a permit with two five-shot .38 caliber revolvers on it. She turned in the cheap one, kept the expensive one, and kept the permit. God knows what she has now to protect herself; to my knowledge, her permit remains active and her gun(s) remain in her possession.

New York Senator Charles Schumer, Feinstein's gun prohibitionist *doppelganger* on the East Coast, reportedly has a permit to carry a loaded gun where he lives. (Rumor has it that the gun on his permit is a Colt .38.) Interestingly, he does not seem to have ever responded to that, in any way ...

Gabrielle Giffords rode to Congress from the state of Arizona in part on a very pro-Second Amendment stance, in which she proudly and publicly stated that she carried a 16-shot Glock 19 9mm pistol. Tragically, she was shot and almost died among the corpses of others in the mass-murder by Jared Lee Loughner, who used an identical pistol. She subsequently found herself on the anti-gun bandwagon, along with her husband, Mark Kelly. In March of 2013, Kelly was observed buying an AR15 rifle — the type of gun he had said loudly and publicly no one had a right or need to own. Knowing he'd been spotted, he announced that he had made the purchase to show how easy it was, and that he intended all along to donate the gun to the Tucson Police Department. All I could think was, "Yes, your honor, I bought that heroin and cocaine, but it was just to demonstrate the scope of the drug problem ... and I was planning to turn it over to the DEA ... honest!"

Don't take advice from the clueless

In first quarter 2013, Vice President Joe Biden, a long-time gun prohibitionist, said that all anyone needed for home defense was a double barrel shotgun, and that he had advised his wife to step out on the balcony and

Joe Biden says a two-shot double barrel shotgun is all you need for home defense. In a time of multiple-perpetrator armed home invasions, the author respectfully disagrees.

empty it into the air if there was trouble. In a world where "what goes up must come down," the man a heartbeat away from command of the free world had advised the public to commit something easily construable as criminal negligence. He compounded it later by suggesting that the same double barrel shotgun just be fired through the door ... at about the same time that a South African athlete was being charged with murder for doing exactly that, according to his alibi, and accidentally killing his girlfriend.

Bottom line

The most divisive debate in our country at this time is not something which requires rocket science to decipher. It simply comes down to common sense. Explain your position clearly and succinctly. Know the issues, know the answers.

And hope that truth and logic will prevail ... though that will only happen if the truth and the logic get across to those who have been blatantly lied to and grossly misinformed. Δ

Drought tolerant landscaping

By Dorothy Ainsworth

What would a homestead look like without any trees? Mars comes to mind: barren, windswept, desolate, and uninviting. There would be nothing alive to climb on, play hide-and-seek behind, sit and read a book against, or have a picnic under. There'd be no shade, no birds, no fruit and nuts, no autumn leaves, no branches to hang a swing from, and no bark for lovers to carve their initials in and revisit when they're old. Oh, and no oxygen to breathe!

Trees are the magnificent culmination of evolutionary genius. They run on solar energy and give back oxygen, so not only do they decorate the

Dorothy on her barren land in 1981

Same spot years later

earth, but they clean the air. They help slow climate change by absorbing carbon dioxide, and they conserve topsoil. In the world of solar technology, plants of any kind are way ahead of the game of harnessing the sun's rays, and their diversity of leaf design is mind-boggling.

According to the Arbor Day Foundation, a mature leafy tree produces as much oxygen in a season as 10 people inhale in a year!

Landscaping decisions are tough and not always what we would aesthetically prefer, but each plant we choose has to fit the soil and climate conditions we have to offer. In this article I will tell what trees and bushes I chose for my property, and why.

Leyland Cypress

When I bought 10 acres back in 1981 on the hot thirsty side of Ashland, Oregon, all there was on the land was star-thistle, poison oak, buckbrush, and a couple of old live-oaks that looked half-dead. I was determined to change all that, so for starters, as soon as I drilled a well and hooked up a hose, I bought 50 one-gallon-size Leyland Cypress trees at $5 each and planted them 5 feet apart along the front of the property that runs parallel to the road.

I would have liked to buy larger trees, but with more time than money, I had no choice but to be patient. I was too engrossed in developing the property and building a house to do anything but *visualize* what those tiny trees would look like someday. That illusive "someday" is now here and the trees are 10 feet wide and 50 feet tall — in fact so tall that the power company had to trim them from their lines last year! They provide a thick barrier against traffic noise and fumes and are a gorgeous sight to behold.

Leyland Cypresses are drought resistant, insect resistant, deer resistant, and the fastest-growing evergreens there are (about 2 feet a year). They are low-maintenance, grow almost anywhere in any kind of soil, and look lush, plush, and beautiful. They form a dense privacy screen and a formidable windbreak. They even keep free-range errant cows out of my yard!

Leyland Cypresses thrive in Zones 6-10 but their kissin' cousins, Thuja Green Giants, hold up better in colder climates, Zones 5-8. They both like plenty of sun and do best in fairly well-drained soil, but then, not many species of trees like wet feet all the time.

Southern Oregon only gets 20 inches of rainfall a year, so I store well-water in a large holding tank and let gravity do its drip-irrigation all over the property via a maze of inexpensive ¾-inch poly-pipe, with an ice-

New row of Leyland Cypress behind Dorothy and "Mitzi" on mountain bike in 1983

Leyland Cypress now (view from the road)

pick hole punched wherever there's a plant. This poor-man's system works great and I've had very few casualties even during extreme drought years.

Deodar Cedar and juniper

The Deodar Cedar is another evergreen that does well under harsh conditions. I found that out "the easy way" by buying a 4-inch seedling in a 4-inch pot for $1.79 at Sprouse-Reitz 30 years ago (now extinct like Woolworth's). I poked it in the ground where I could keep an eye on it and watered it with a cup, and now that eye has to look 60 feet up to see the top. Before long I'll need binoculars! Others I've planted have taken off with the same rapid growth. Their sweeping branches hang elegantly like flared skirts with lacey edges of velvety new growth. The needles are

Barn fence with Pampas grass

soft and touchable, and the wood is fragrant. They are beautiful trees, and I highly recommend them.

Every once in a while a tree chooses me. A small juniper with its tiny roots intact jumped off a logging truck as it went by my property and I scooped it off the road and stuck it in the ground. Now it's a huge and handsome bluish-green tree with juniper berries galore on it. If I were a drinker I could make my own gin!

Poplars

I'm too busy multitasking to fuss over any *one* task (such as landscaping) so whatever I plant better be able to mostly take care of itself. Drought-tolerant hybrid poplars fit that description, so I bought 20 of them at $10 each back in the '80s, and planted them 12 feet apart along the west side of my future house site. The house is now finished and they provide shade in the summer and dazzle us with golden leaves in autumn that create a natural bed of mulch when they fall. (No, I don't rake leaves!) I planted some evergreens behind them so when the poplars are bare, Douglas Firs, Ponderosa Pines, and Blue

Spruces take over the job of wind protection.

Poplars send out runners (surface roots with new shoots sticking up) so I took cuttings with a sharp shovel and transplanted dozens of them all over the property and around a pond fed by a windmill. Those lucky trees at the pond got all the water they could drink so they've grown huge

and now provide a cool heavenly oasis where the dogs and kids hang out when it's 100 degrees in the summer.

A combination of evergreens and deciduous trees for practical as well as aesthetic reasons grace the land with plenty of seasonal color and a variety of shapes, sizes, and textures to gaze upon: globes and ovals, wide-spreading, columnar, open-headed, pyramidal, and weeping. Alternating the two types in the same row or with one row behind the other provides back-up wind protection in the winter.

Another drought resistant tree is the silver poplar. Twenty-five years ago, I took root cuttings from a friend's yard (Yes, I'm the Root Bandit) and planted a double row of what looked like scrawny little stems poking out of the ground along the road that curves around a piano studio I built. From those tiny starts grew long graceful trunks supporting high branches filled with shimmering leaves that sway in the breeze. The leaves are green on one side and white on the other and they quake in the wind like their close relative, the aspen.

Studio with silver poplars in back and tulips in front

I have since taken cuttings from those second generation trees and let nature help me create even more beautiful windbreaks in other problem areas, such as near my son Eric's house. I used a tight row of Leyland Cypresses again to deflect the strong winds coming up his hill from the southwest, and planted a row of silver poplars in front of them for color and shade in three out of the four seasons.

A local nursery had a rare sale on 10-foot Lombardy Poplars several years ago, so I bought 50 of them at $10 each, and planted them 8 feet apart along the northern boundary of my property. I ran 400 feet of irrigation poly-pipe along the fence line and those trees are now about 30 feet high. Their fall color is breathtaking!

Tree of Heaven

Another friend offered me root cuttings from what most nurseries call a "weed" but is one of my favorites: The Tree of Heaven. Talk about drought resistant! This one gets the prize. You can propagate them anywhere and they grow rapidly into big strong widely-branched shade trees similar to Black Locusts. The multi-fingered "pinnate" leaves (resembling a feather's design) are delicate-looking as they hang from slender stems, but don't be fooled; these trees are tough!

I planted 10 of them strategically around the property where I want *big* shade and they are here to stay. Everywhere I look around town I see these "survivors" growing and flourishing where no other plant would dare to tread. Some have more than one trunk and support canopies that are 60 feet high and 40 feet wide. (Originally from China, they were used in medicine and for hosting silk worms.)

They are called "invasive," but that's exactly what I want where nothing else will grow without being pampered. Their life span is only about 50 years, but they continually

This bank started off with baby St. John's Wort plants set into weed cloth. The full-grown plants prevent erosion on several steep banks on my property. As a bonus, the deer don't like it.

colonize by sending out root sprouts, and the seeds have "wings." That means free labor!

Bamboo

Bamboo is another plant that has a bad reputation for being "invasive." I say: "Bring it on!" It will only spread if it gets a surplus of water, and on my dry land it doesn't. Dense "walls" of Golden Bamboo surround one of my decks, extending the indoor/outdoor living space. The deck is totally protected from wind and sun and the segmented trunks and long skinny leaves of bamboo are simply divine. It is easily transplanted from root cuttings wherever one wants a beautiful stand of green and yellow bamboo that filters the light and offers privacy and protection.

A large stand of bamboo is so impenetrable that you could hack a narrow trail into the middle and clear a flat spot to use as a meditation "room" or a kid's "clubhouse" or whatever. Bamboo is unique, versa-

tile, and fast growing. It comes in many varieties including Timber Bamboo, which is used for construction in Asia and wood products such as flooring. In my opinion bamboo is one of the most visually appealing ornamental plants there is.

Ground cover

For large and hilly areas, I prefer *rows* of trees and *banks* of ground-cover plants, with accent bushes placed here and there for bursts of fall color. St. John's Wort is a great solution if you have a steep bank and want to prevent erosion. They are drought-resistant fast-growing "creepers" and spread their tangled roots in a formidable grid to hold soil and water. I've covered two such banks with tiny starter plants the size of a quarter (and the cost of a quarter) and now they carpet the banks with a dense layer of soft green leaves. The deer don't like it, but ladybugs and honeybees abound in great numbers when the foot-high foliage blooms

Dorothy planting a row of 50 Lombardy Poplars

with bright yellow flowers in late June.

Maples and oaks

In addition to the rows of low-maintenance trees, I've been unable to resist buying a few trees for sheer beauty and dazzling fall color. Among those gorgeous trees are the maples.

The October Glory is big and hardy and turns crimson red in the fall, and the Autumn Blaze is so brilliant it looks like it's on fire when the leaves turn a phosphorescent red-orange.

I planted a Red Oak for size and longevity, and a Sugar Maple for height. The latest addition to my family of maples is a columnar Karpick

Red Maple, which stands stately like a sentinel at the end of a long row of Red-Tipped Photinia planted along the dirt road to Eric's house. Someday it will tickle the sky 50 feet up, but will remain slim at 20 feet wide. In the fall, its bright red and gold leaves look striking against the deep blue sky.

Royal Empress and Mimosa Silk Tree

Two other trees that are an absolute must to plant on just about any piece of property are the Mimosa Silk and the Royal Empress. They are both tough and fast-growing, but their beauty belies their durability.

The Royal Empress is one of the fastest-growing deciduous trees there is (3 feet a year is common), and will reach 50 feet tall and 40 feet wide in just a few years. The large leaves hang from widely-spaced branches, forming a dense umbrella of delicious shade by summer. Oddly enough, the "Empress" is late to come to the ball in the spring but stays long after the party is over before letting her hair down at midnight (late fall).

In winter, the smooth branches are covered with furry little buds that burst into fragrant pinkish-purple blossoms in the spring, like something you'd see in Hawaii. Its fragrance is a cross between jasmine and gardenia. It grows almost anywhere and has no significant pest or disease problems. It tolerates drought and most soils, and is a hardwood that lives to an old age. All this in a tree you don't have to baby! It's incredibly beautiful but almost indestructible. Even Oprah got in the act and recommended it.

When I bought mine, it looked like a tiny squash plant with a pliable green stem (trunk?) in a 6-inch container, but it cost $25! I remember thinking: *This* is a *tree?* I really had my doubts — but not for long. It has been in the ground only 4 years, is 12 feet tall, and already spreading its arms far and wide and waving gracefully like a royal empress should. I did it a favor by planting it on the lee side of Eric's house so its huge leaves would be buffered from the wind, and indeed, it is flourishing flawlessly.

The Mimosa Silk — another remarkable beauty — is unsurpassed as a hummingbird "magnet." It is easy to grow, drought-tolerant, adapts to almost any soil type, and can be planted in full sun or partial shade. Its fragrant hot-pink tropical-looking blossoms grow in clusters and face up like shimmering "cups" offering nectar to be sipped. Its smooth greenish-gray trunk supports a fluttering umbrella of fern-like leaves that is wider than the tree is tall and lends wonderful shade on a hot summer day. I like to sit and watch the "show" — where at least 20 hummingbirds at any given time flit around from flower to flower, drinking, fighting, flirting, mating, and singing. I could go down to the local bar and see the same thing, but, no thanks, I'll stay home where it's much more entertaining — under the silk tree.

Note: The Mimosa Silk is another late bloomer. Just when you think it must have died in the winter, it finally shows signs of life in late spring, but is still going strong in late fall long after all the other trees are skeletons of their former selves.

Flowering Hawthorn and Golden Chain Tree

Two more ornamental trees that offer unusual visual treats in the spring are the Flowering Hawthorn and the Golden Chain. Both do well up here on the arid savanna. I planted them in close proximity to each other 20 years ago, unaware that they would bloom at the same time and complement each other as beautifully as a multi-cultural beauty pageant. The Flowering Hawthorn's tangled "hair" reminds me of a Jamaican's dreadlocks adorned with an extravagance of dark pink rosettes, and the Golden Chain's bright yellow pendulous blossoms hang like Goldilocks' ringlets. Side by side, the contrast is stunning!

Fruit and nuts

Being a big advocate of edible landscaping, I planted a small orchard years ago and another one recently. I've found that cherry trees require the least maintenance. Apples and almonds are next, then plums and pears. Apricot and peach trees are prone to leaf curl and other diseases and need to be sprayed and pruned regularly. Apricot trees are the first to bloom in the spring and their blossoms have to be protected against frost bite. Nothing seems to bother cherry trees. I prefer standard Bings because they grow impressively huge and I'm perfectly willing to share the crop on the very top with the birds. I planted one bare-root Bing for my grandson Zane the year he was born and they are growing up together — both 12 this year!

His mother Cynthia bought a Spanish Fir as a live Christmas tree for Zane's first Christmas and they too are growing up together. The Spanish Fir has proven to be a perfectly-suited species for this hot dry land. It is very unusual and exceptionally handsome — just like Zane!

The Hall's Hardy Almond and the Hardy English Walnut trees I planted are extremely low-maintenance and very productive. Nuts are excellent survival food when all else fails. They store well and are loaded with protein and healthful Omega-3 fatty acids.

Shrubs

Ceanothus (buckbrush) is native to this land so I leave it alone to do its thing. It is also known as wild lilac and literally buzzes with bees in the spring, which also help pollinate the fruit trees. It is practically drought proof and fast-growing but stickery so I prune it back on trails or if it gets too close to a structure (fire danger) and that's it. An eye-catching variety called Blue Ceanothus is available at nurseries. The blue is so intense it appears fluorescent.

Pampas grass is one of my all-time favorite grassy shrubs. It makes an attractive impermeable hedge (the

Leyland Cypress and silver poplars set off Staghorn Sumac.

175

sharp-edged leaves can cut like a knife) but has a whimsical flair and gorgeous spires that burst into feathery bloom in the fall. It is native to southern South America so it's drought friendly and self-pruning (old spires die and make way for new ones). Because I prefer tall and wide hedges, I always buy the large standard size, but the dwarf variety would look pretty in a smaller yard as well as in containers.

I've had excellent luck with lavender, lilac, Scotch Broom, Oregon Grape, Burning Bush, and Staghorn Sumac. Red-Tipped Photinia is a given; it grows anywhere (even along a freeway), and can be trimmed into a hedge or allowed to turn into a tree (8 feet tall and 6 feet wide). The rich red tips (new growth) that come out in the spring are like eye candy wherever you look.

Forsythia is a large shrub that is the first to bloom in early spring with bright yellow tentacles of blossoms reaching out wildly in every direction and announcing that spring is here even though the calendar says it isn't.

Wild roses volunteer all over the place and provide rose hips (a good source of vitamin C). Boysenberry and blackberry vines are thickly draped over an old 100-foot long barbed-wire fence and continue to spread unchecked as long as they get water. Wild strawberries carpet the ground here and there, but I also plant regular strawberries. They propagate themselves by sending out runners so there's never a shortage. I mulch their beds with straw to withstand the winter.

Flowers

I've chosen flowers that do well in full sun: Sunflowers, climbing roses, old-fashioned hollyhocks (think grandma), morning glories, and my all-time favorite: foxglove (adorable speckled hanging bells). I've planted hundreds of bulbs: daffodils, narcissi, poppies, and irises. Every year we get surprised anew when those harbingers of spring poke their pretty little heads out of the snow. Bulbs are one of nature's most ingenious inventions!

I adore flowers but I don't clip their heads off and put them in a vase. I like everything to be free, including me.

Using the land as an artist's palette, nature herself paints the sloping hills knee-deep in purple vetch and blue lupine every spring. The sight is spectacular! Then when it all dries up it adds nitrogen to the soil. Beautiful and useful — a perfect balance.

The plan

My landscaping style is pretty "loose," and I'm certainly not an expert horticulturist. I do some google research, then just up and plant whatever catches my eye and is recommended for my area (zone). My general philosophy is "let nature take its course" and "survival of the fittest."

There has been no master plan or grand scheme, but I know what I like: Beauty, Balance, and Practicality. I do a lot of artistic visualization as I go along so the overall landscape will end up looking natural and pleasing to the eye. Sometimes I've bought shrubs and trees on impulse (on sale) and figured out where to put them after I got home. Nurseries thrive on plant lovers like me who let "green emotions" run away with their purse! (Warning: It's an easy addiction to acquire.)

My homestead is a work in progress. I water everything enough, fertilize occasionally, and mulch with hay and/or straw for winter. I should spray my fruit trees (organic oil spray) and prune them regularly but I seldom get around to it. Heck, I don't even prune my own hair very often!

Smoke tree

I'm finally winding down on planting because we're on a well and I'm forced to conserve water — and I also maintain a vegetable garden. But there's a special tree I've always wanted and it doesn't drink much — but it "smokes!" Smoke trees are like giant shrubs with unusually eye-catching clouds of gossamer pink,

North entrance to studio beautified with trees, bushes, and bamboo

white, or purple haze hovering over the inner branches which are camouflaged by the billowing "smoke." Artists have portrayed them in western desert paintings because they are so unique and enchanting to gaze upon. Once you see one, you'll never forget it.

Closing thoughts

It feels good to look about the land and know that I planted everything on it by digging each hole with a pick and a shovel. It was mildly back-breaking but not bank-breaking. It was tremendous exercise and I still have the muscles to show for it. That's the benefit-in-disguise of being economically-challenged: you have to do all your own work, and nature pays you back with strength, endurance, and a feeling of satisfaction you can't put a price on. About half my landscaping has been free for the digging. I never turn down a green gift from somebody's yard, even if I have to turn red to get it.

By plugging away over the years, I've inadvertently created a diversified ecosystem that is alive with birds (60 species documented so far), and a multitude of other critters running around night and day. When I first bought the property, only lizards, scorpions, and rattlesnakes were scurrying and slithering around. Now there's an environment that invites and nurtures all kinds of wildlife, and we're all sharing the land and enjoying the heck out of it.

My biggest trees have provided not only shade and fruit, but priceless memories (and photographs) of dogs, cats, and kids who have had great fun playing on, under, and around them. Laughter still echoes from the treehouse whenever Zane comes to visit. What could be better than that!

My advice to new property owners is to plant *now* and do everything else later. Dig a hole, add water, and nature will do the rest. The labor is short-lived but the beauty and useful-

Golden chain tree, foxglove, and California poppies

ness are forever. Grab your shovel … time is not a renewable resource!

Author's note: I've planted many more species of trees and bushes than I wrote about in this article, but there wasn't room to list them all so I described only the main ones. Δ

To read more about Dorothy's incredible projects go to:
www.backwoodshome.com

Ask Jackie

Jackie Clay

If you have a question about rural living, send it in to Jackie Clay and she'll try to answer it. Address your letter to Ask Jackie, PO Box 712, Gold Beach, OR 97444. Questions will only be answered in this column. — *Editor*

Storing potatoes

For the past four years we've been developing our gardens. In 2011 we planted potatoes for the first time, reds and Yukon Golds. At the end of the season we dug up the remaining potatoes, cleaned them all, packed them in cardboard boxes, covered them with newspaper and placed them in the crawl space under the bedroom area of our house. I have a large thermometer hanging in the crawl space and over the past years the temperature remains between 40 and 45 degrees from fall until spring. In the spring of 2012 we were still using our potatoes even though a few were sprouting.

I checked with another reference and a neighbor and it was indicated I should not clean the potatoes before storing them.

We planted again in 2012, harvested them, and stored them without cleaning them prior to storage. In early December I retrieved some and found there were small sprouts starting. By early January all of them had sprouts from 8 to 12 inches long and the potatoes were very soft. I ended up throwing them all away.

I would appreciate your guidance.

Harry Kent
Corvallis, Montana

I have rinsed and dried potatoes before storing them and also (usually) stored them without cleaning the dirt off. Really, I could see no difference in the storage ability of the potatoes.

The main thing is to let the rinsed-off potatoes dry thoroughly in the shade before storing. If they are stored wet, they will mold and quickly rot. The storage of potatoes varies from year to year unless you have monitored storage facilities (as do the big potato warehouses) where humidity and temperature are both closely controlled. Potatoes store best with quite high humidity and temperatures around 40 degrees. Any light at all and they will begin to sprout. Add warmer temperatures of only about 5-10 degrees and they'll quickly soften after that. It's also necessary to harvest your storage potatoes just before hard frosts. Harvesting early potatoes earlier in the fall results in longer storage times and often, failures in storage ability. And make sure the variety of potatoes you are growing are good storage potatoes. (Some reds don't store too long.)

We store our potatoes in big plastic totes in our basement pantry. There is no light and the humidity in the boxes is quite high. When the bottom of the lid shows condensation, I crack it open for a day or two until the humidity lessens. We have potatoes to use until we harvest our new crop the following fall. Our pantry stays at 40-45 all winter and warms up to about 55 in the summer.

Good luck this year. — *Jackie*

Excess produce and eggs

In 2012 I picked up 300 pounds of apples all colors and dehydrated all of them. Four months later apples that were dried are now soft with bugs crawling through the apples. The containers had all air removed and container was dipped in wax. Bugs still got in. What did I do wrong?

This year so far I've been given 70 pounds of green beans. How can I can them safely?

Around 2-3 days after Christmas I picked up seven 22-pound boxes of tomatoes, which I have canned to use later.

At what temperature do I can kiwi, papaya, green and orange melon, and pineapple and for how long?

How do you can eggs?

Kent McRee
Sonoma, California

How did you dehydrate your apples? Did you just air dry them or did you use a dehydrator with heat? If you just air dried them, it is possible that insect eggs present were not killed and went on to hatch in storage. Be sure that your dehydrated foods are very dry when you store them as this helps prevent insect infestation. Apples should be tough-leathery, not soft like store-bought dehydrated apple slices. I store my dehydrated fruits in gallon glass jars with screw down lids and have never had any sort of insect problem even after years and years of storage.

It's very easy to can up green beans. Just remove the stem and blossom end and cut into pieces about 1 inch long. Pack the beans into a clean canning jar, leaving 1 inch of headspace.

Add ½ tsp. salt to pints and 1 tsp. to quarts. Pour boiling water over beans, leaving 1 inch of headspace. Remove air bubbles by running a wooden spoon handle down to release any air bubbles you can see. Place a hot, previously simmered new lid on the jar and screw down the ring firmly tight. Process in a pressure canner only at 10 pounds pressure for 20 minutes (pints) or 25 minutes (quarts). You can also make dilly beans or other pickled foods from your green beans.

Good for you on canning up your bounty of tomatoes! I'm sure you'll enjoy them later and be very happy you got them.

You would water bath process your fruits for 20 minutes. Muskmelons are the exception and are best canned as "pickled muskmelon balls." This is a spiced, sweet pickle and makes canning them both tastier and safer than canning them fresh.

Eggs are only canned as pickled eggs. This is very easy to do and they'll last for years on your pantry shelves. To pickle eggs, you'll want 18 peeled, whole hardboiled eggs, 1½ quarts white vinegar, 2 tsp. salt, 1 Tbsp. whole allspice and 1 Tbsp. mixed pickling spices.

Mix vinegar and spices in a large pot and bring to a boil. Pack whole, peeled hardboiled eggs into hot, sterilized wide mouthed jar, leaving at least ½ inch of headspace. Ladle boiling pickling liquid over eggs, leaving ½ inch of headspace. Cover all eggs. Remove air bubbles. Wipe rim of jar clean, place hot, previously-simmered lid on jar and screw down ring firmly tight. Process for 25 minutes in a boiling water bath canner. Never leave unsealed pickled eggs out at room temperature. You risk danger from botulism and other bacterial diseases.

Just a hint: For all of your growing and canning questions, pick up a copy of my recent book *Growing and Canning Your Own Food*, available right here at *BHM*. It is filled with hundreds of recipes for canning a huge variety of foods for your pantry.
— *Jackie*

Zucchini blooms and stunted plants

Some of my zucchini have blooms that are on long stems; these usually end up on the ground and don't make fruits. Are these male? Only the blooms that have those little fat bumps behind them make fruits. My winter squash is the same way. Is that why some of them just fall off? Some of the long-stemmed ones are probably the ones to pick to eat, right?

My plants seemingly grow smaller. I had three that did it; a tomato, squash, and a strawberry. They all started out ok and grew up to a point and started going in reverse. I pulled them up and got rid of them. The rest of the garden is fine.

J. Wallick
Bushnell, Illinois

Yes, these are the male flowers. The flowers with the little bumps are the female flowers and have been pollinated by the male flowers which then drop off. I pick mostly the male flowers to eat but do sometimes harvest some female flowers of some very bountiful producing vines/bushes. They're great battered and fried!

Stunted garden plants often signal stress of some sort and it's up to us gardeners to find out what that is. Sometimes it's an insect pest such as whiteflies or aphids that are causing the plant to go into survival mode instead of growing. Check your plants very carefully. If that's not the problem, do a soil test. Stunting is often a result of a lack of calcium and phosphorous and can happen in just isolated spots in the garden. But sometimes the plants are just slow starters and will eventually catch up, given the chance. If you notice that again, I'd mulch the plant well with rotted compost, make sure it is watered adequately, and just wait to see what happens. Hopefully the plant will respond and begin shooting up normally. — *Jackie*

Seed descriptions

I have steadily enjoyed and been educated by you since day one! In looking through seed catalogs over the years two items have consistently been a mystery.

One item is: Describing a seed/seedling/plant as determinate or indeterminate. Exactly what does that mean?

Item two is: Very often the various seed descriptions mention 53-, 75-80-, 97- days. What do these days represent, when do you start counting days, and what happens to the edible crop after the "last" date?

One of your usual clarifying explanations would surely be a huge help.

B. Galioto
East Elmhurst, New York

Tomatoes are classified mainly into two groups, determinate and indeterminate. The determinate tomatoes are usually "bush" type and have a stout, main stem and grow to a much shorter height than do indeterminate plants. They also only produce one main-crop. The indeterminates are "vining" type tomatoes and grow very tall. They produce more and more fruit all summer and fall until the frosts do them in at last. Determinates are great for smaller gardens and often container growing. The indeterminates should be staked and caged to allow them to bear their heavy loads of fruit and not slump and sprawl all over the garden. The tomatoes stay cleaner, are easier to pick, and resist rotting much better than lying on the dirt.

The maturity dates indicate about when you can expect to begin harvesting edible food from a plant. Some plants such as peppers and tomatoes are started indoors then transplanted outside when the weather permits as they will be killed if

179

exposed to frost. So the dates to maturity of these plant seeds are referring to "from transplanting." Therefore if a tomato variety is an "80-day" tomato, it takes about 80 days for the plant to begin producing tomatoes to eat following transplanting into your garden.

This maturity date can be misleading as it depends a lot on where you live. For instance, since we are in northern Minnesota and have only about 90 frost-free days, you'd think we could only grow short-season tomatoes. But because our summer days are very long, we have more growing time than only the 90 days. Therefore we regularly harvest 90-day tomatoes and 110-day squash and pumpkins. (Pumpkins and squash seed descriptions of maturity dates are usually from direct seeding into the garden, not starting plants indoors.)

As the date refers to the approximate time the plant begins to bear, you will continue to harvest food from many plants far beyond that. Exceptions, of course, would be one-harvest crops such as cabbage, carrots, rutabagas, turnips, potatoes, etc.

I hope this clears thing up for you.

— *Jackie*

Making butter

I have access to a large amount of whipping cream. Can I make butter out of it and then can the butter? I have heard that butter made out of whipping cream cannot be canned. Maybe I need to know how to make the butter properly.

Sheryl Roberts
Houston, Alaska

Yes, you *can* make butter out of whipping cream and you are able to can it, just like butter made from fresh cream. To make good butter, just let your whipping cream set out at room temperature until it's warmed up some, then churn it. A lot of folks use a mixer or even a blender to bring it

to the stage when butter grains are forming, then dump it into a churn to finish up. It cuts down the time factor. All butter is soft when just finished. Just rinse several times in cold water and then drain and work out the remaining buttermilk with a wood paddle. Add salt to taste then pack in a container to cool. If you wish, then proceed to canning it, following directions. Good luck! — *Jackie*

Feeding meat scraps to pets

When I give meat scraps to cats, dogs, or pigs, is it better to cook it first or give it raw?

Gail Erman
Palisade, Colorado

I'm not sure there's a "better" to this question; we give both raw and cooked scraps to our animals. If there's a question of possible parasites in the meat, such as venison scraps, it's better to cook them first. Otherwise, animals were "built" to digest raw meat. Cooking is not natural. In fact, many pet breeders are now advocating feeding only raw meats to pets for better digestibility. I think it's up to each owner and each situation. I sure don't have a problem feeding a few cooked table scraps (without bones!) to our animals. And they seem to appreciate them. — *Jackie*

Canning chicken liver pâté

Can precooked chicken liver pâté be pressure canned without adding liquid? If so how long for half pints?

Paul and Pat Stine
Windber, Pennsylvania

Because chicken liver pâté is such a dense product, I wouldn't recommend canning it. This holds true of many other products such as meat loaf and puréed pumpkin pie filling. The reason for this is when canning such a dense food, the centers of the jars may not heat up sufficiently or long enough for safe canning. Better to can

the chicken livers whole, then make pâté out of them after opening each jar. — *Jackie*

Epsom salts for plants

I read an article where you mix 2 Tbsp. Epsom salts with 1 gal water and spray on lawns for a greener lawn from the magnesium. Would this be something that would help the garden too?

Mary Carman
Mount Carmel, Pennsylvania

Yes you can do this if you wish. We don't bother but we know a few people who routinely use the Epsom salts when planting their tomatoes. I pretty much rely on rotted compost.

— *Jackie*

Fruit cocktail trees

Have you ever had any experience with "fruit cocktail" trees? Could you recommend a good source of some?

Jack Kavanaugh
Groton, Connecticut

The so-called "fruit cocktail" trees are simply trees which have several different fruits grafted onto a compatible rootstock. For instance, you can buy a tree with peaches, plums, apricots, and nectarines growing on the same tree. Unlike the pictures though, the fruits will not all ripen at the same time. Some are earlier-ripening and some are later. I have not, personally, grown these due to our Zone 3 garden. It's too cold for these Zone 5-8 trees to survive. But I have grafted different apples onto the same tree. It works well and makes good use of space while adding variety to a yard. Many nurseries offer these trees, including Burgess Seed and Plant Co.

— *Jackie*

Garden injuries, part 2

By Joe Alton, M.D.

In the last issue of *Backwoods Home*, we discussed some of the hazards encountered by the homesteading gardener. Burns, cuts, abrasions, allergic reactions, and certain insect stings are, however, just some of the issues that the serious horticulturist can expect to deal with. In this issue, we will further discuss various insects and related ne'er-do-wells that can complicate your efforts to establish a successful garden.

Spiders

Although large spiders, such as tarantulas, cause painful bites, most spider bites don't even break the skin. In temperate climates, two spiders are to be especially feared: the black widow and the brown recluse.

The black widow spider is about ½ inch long and is active mostly at night. Southern black widows have a red hourglass pattern on their backs, but other sub-species don't. Although its bite has very potent venom damaging to the nervous system, the effects on each individual are quite variable. Severe pain at the site is usually the first symptom soon after the bite. Following this, you might see:

• Muscle cramps
• Abdominal pain
• Weakness
• Shakiness
• Nausea and vomiting
• Fainting
• Chest pain
• Difficulty breathing
• Disorientation

Each person will present with a variable degree of the above symptoms. The very young and the elderly are more seriously affected than most. In your exam, you can expect rises in both heart rate and blood pressure.

As its name implies, the brown recluse spider is brown and has legs

Most spider bites cause nothing more than pain, but the Black widow and brown recluse inject a potent venom which can cause serious symptoms and death.

about an inch long. Unlike most spiders, it only has six eyes instead of eight, but they are so small it is difficult to identify them from this characteristic.

Victims of brown recluse bites report them to be painless at first, but then may experience these symptoms:

• Itching
• Pain, sometimes severe, after several hours
• Fever
• Nausea and vomiting
• Blisters

The venom of the brown recluse is thought to be more potent than a rattlesnake's, although much less is injected in its bite. Substances in the venom disrupt soft tissue, which leads to local breakdown of blood vessels, skin, and fat. This process, seen in severe cases, leads to "necrosis," or death of tissues immediately surrounding the bite. Areas affected may be extensive.

As a result, the human body activates its immune response and can go haywire, destroying red blood cells, kidneys, and the ability of blood to clot appropriately. These effects can lead to coma and eventually death. Almost all deaths from brown recluse bites are recorded in children.

The treatment for spider bites includes:

• Washing the area of the bite thoroughly
• Ice to painful and swollen areas
• Pain medications such as acetaminophen/Tylenol
• Enforcing bed rest
• Warm baths for those with muscle cramps (black widow bites only; stay away from applying heat to the area with brown recluse bites)
• Antibiotics to prevent secondary bacterial infection

Suction devices are generally ineffective in removing venom from wounds. Tourniquets are also not recommended and may be dangerous.

Although antidotes known as "anti-venins" (discussed in the section on snakebite) exist and may be life-saving for venomous spider and scorpion stings, these may be scarce in remote settings or austere environments.

Most cases that are not severe will subside over the course of a few days, but the sickest patients will be nearly untreatable without the antivenin.

Ticks

Although ticks are commonly thought of as insects, they are actually arachnids like scorpions and spiders. The American dog tick carries pathogens for Rocky Mountain spotted fever, and the blacklegged tick, also known as the deer tick, carries the microscopic parasite that's responsible for Lyme disease. Some tick-borne illness is similar to influenza with regards to symptoms; it is often missed by the physician. Lyme disease sometimes has a tell-tale rash, but other tick-related diseases may not.

Most Lyme disease is caused by the larval or juvenile stages of the deer tick. These are sometimes tough to spot because they're not much bigger than a pinhead. Each larval stage feeds only once and very slowly, usually over several days. This gives the tick parasites plenty of time to get into your bloodstream. The larval ticks are most active in summer. Although most common in the Northeast, they seem to be making their way further West every year.

Ticks don't jump like fleas do; they don't fly like, well, flies, and they don't drop from trees like spiders. The larvae like to live in leaf litter, and they latch onto your lower leg as you pass by. Adults live in shrubs along game trails (hence the name Deer Tick) and seem to transmit disease less often. In inhabited areas, you might find them in woodpiles near gardens (especially in shade).

Many people don't think to protect themselves outdoors from exposure to ticks and other things like poison ivy, and many wind up being sorry they didn't. If you're going to spend the day puttering in the garden, you should be taking some precautions:

• Don't leave skin exposed below the knee.
• Wear thick socks (tuck your pants into them).
• Wear high-top boots
• Use insect repellent

Good bug repellent is going to improve your chances of avoiding bites. Citronella can be found naturally in some areas and is related to plants like lemon grass; just rub the leaves on your skin. Soybean oil and oil of eucalyptus will also work. Consider including these in your medicinal garden if your climate allows it.

It is important to know that your risk of Lyme disease or other tick-spread illness increases the longer it feeds on you. The good news is that there is generally no transmission of disease in the first 24 hours. After 48 hours, though, you have the highest chance of infection, so it pays to remove the tick as soon as possible. Ticks sometimes don't latch onto your skin for a few hours, so showering or bathing after a gardening session may simply wash them off. This is where good hygiene pays off.

If you find a tick feeding on you, remove it as soon as possible. To remove a tick, take the finest set of tweezers you have and try to grab the tick as close to your skin as you can. Pull the tick straight up; this will give you the best chance of removing it intact. If removed at an angle, the mouthparts sometimes remain in the skin, which might cause an inflammation at the site of the bite. Fortunately, it won't increase your chances of getting Lyme disease.

Afterwards, disinfect the area with Betadine (povidone-iodine solution) or apply triple antibiotic ointment. I'm sure you've heard about other methods of tick removal, such as smothering it with petroleum jelly or lighting it on fire. No method, however, is more effective than pulling it out with tweezers.

Luckily, only about 20% of deer ticks carry the Lyme disease or other parasite. A rash that appears like a bulls-eye occurs in about half of patients. If you get a rash along with flu-like symptoms that are resistant to medicines, you'll need further treatment.

Oral antibiotics will be useful to treat early stages. Amoxicillin (500 mg 3x/day for 14 days) or Doxycycline (100mg 2x/day for 14 days) should work to treat the illness. These can be obtained without a prescription in certain veterinary medications (a topic of a future article).

Scorpions

Most scorpions are harmless; in the United States, only the bark scorpion of the Southwest desert has toxins that can cause severe symptoms. In other areas of the world, however, a scorpion sting may be lethal.

Some scorpions may reach several inches long; they have eight legs and a set of pincers, and inject venom through their "tail." The nervous system is most often affected. Children are most at risk.

Symptoms you may see in victims of scorpion stings may be:
• Pain, numbness, and/or tingling in the area of the sting
• Sweating
• Weakness
• Increased saliva output
• Restlessness or twitching
• Irritability
• Difficulty swallowing
• Rapid breathing and heart rate

When you have diagnosed a scorpion sting, do the following:
• Wash the area with soap and water.
• Remove jewelry from the affected limb (swelling may occur).
• Apply cold compresses to decrease pain.

• Give an antihistamine, such as diphenhydramine (Benadryl).

• If done quickly, this may slow the venom's spread.

• Keep your patient calm.

• Limit food intake if throat is swollen.

• Give pain relievers such as Ibuprofen or Acetaminophen, but avoid narcotics, as they may suppress breathing.

• Don't cut into the wound or use suction to attempt to remove venom.

Mosquitoes

Unlike the stings of bees or wasps, mosquito bites are common vectors of various diseases. One of the most notorious diseases caused by mosquito vectors is malaria. Worldwide, one to three million deaths a year are attributed to complication from this illness.

Malaria is caused by a microscopic organism called a protozoan. When mosquitoes get a meal by biting you, they inject these microbes into your system. Once in the body, they colonize your liver. From there, they go to your blood cells and other organs. By the way, only female mosquitoes bite humans. Anaphylactic allergic reactions, not uncommonly seen with bee stings, are rarely an issue with mosquitoes.

Symptoms of malaria appear flu-like, and classically present as periodic chills, fever, and sweats. The patient becomes anemic as more blood cells are damaged by the protozoa. With times, periods between episodes become shorter and permanent organ damage may occur.

Diagnosis of malaria cannot be confirmed without a microscope, but anyone experiencing relapsing fevers with severe chills and sweating should be considered candidates for treatment. The medications, among others, used for malaria are Chloroquine, Quinine, and Quinidine. Sometimes, an antibiotic such as Doxycycline or Clindamycin is used in combination with the above.

Other mosquito-borne diseases include Yellow Fever, Dengue Fever, and West Nile Virus. The fewer mosquitoes near your retreat, the less likely you will fall victim to one of these diseases. You can decrease the population of mosquitoes in your area and improve the likelihood of preventing illness by:

• Looking for areas of standing water that could serve as mosquito breeding grounds. Drain all water that you do not depend on for survival.

• Monitoring the screens on your retreat windows and doors and repairing any holes or defects.

• Being careful to avoid outside activities at dusk or dawn. This is the time that mosquitoes are most active.

• Wear long pants and shirts whenever you venture outside.

• Having a good stockpile of insect repellents.

If you are reluctant to use chemical repellents, you may consider natural remedies. Plants that contain Citronella may be rubbed on your skin to discourage bites. Lemon balm, despite having a fragrance similar to citronella, does not have the same bug-repelling properties. Despite its name, lemon balm is actually a member of the mint family.

When you use natural substances to repel insects, re-apply frequently and feel free to combine them as needed. Besides Citronella oil, you could use:

• Lemon Eucalyptus oil
• Cinnamon oil
• Peppermint oil
• Geranium oil
• Clove oil
• Rosemary oil

The above are medical risks to anyone that is responsible for the family garden. Always be mindful of protecting your hands by wearing a good pair of gloves while cultivating your plants. As well, consider adding some of the herbs discussed in this article to your medicinal garden. In this manner, you can have a renewable source of natural remedies that may be helpful in dealing with these issues.

Joe and Amy Alton are the authors of the #1 Amazon Bestseller *The Doom and Bloom Survival Medicine Handbook*. Visit their website at www.doomandbloom.net Δ

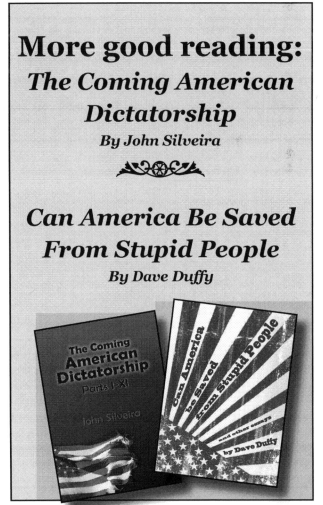

Delicious bison

By Habeeb Salloum

In North America there is a long list from which to choose when thinking of big game animals. From among these are the caribou, elk, deer, moose, and above all, the bison. Of course some of these are rare or on the endangered list.

For those who venture into the world of cooking wild game, the first thing one must know is that all game meat, with the exception of bison, has a gamey taste and the meat is lean, thus drier when overcooked. To lessen the gamey taste, all fat and silvery skin on the meat should be removed. As for alleviating dryness, a sauce can be made to go with the meat. The gamey taste that some claim they like has never been my cup of tea and therefore the only game meat that I enjoy is bison meat.

This wild animal, after being almost obliterated from the face of the earth, has made a comeback, both in the wild and on ranches. Today, its meat is found in many supermarkets in North America.

The bison occupied a place of honor in the lives of the Northern Plains Peoples — their means of survival. It was a gift of love from the Great Spirit — their essence of life; their general store, offering food, clothing, and shelter. There was no part of the animal that they did not use. They knew that bison was a healthy meat and they consumed it in various ways: pit-roasted, prepared into sausage, or dried and combined with berries, herbs, and nuts and made into pemmican.

What the Indigenous Peoples had known for hundreds of years is again being discovered today. Bison meat is one of the healthiest meats known. Modern research has established that bison meat is healthier than all the other commonly eaten red meats. Also, bison meat is lower in cholesterol, contains less fat, and has fewer calories per serving than beef, skinless chicken, lamb, pork, veal, venison, and sockeye salmon. In addition, bison meat has 40% more protein than beef and is high in iron, selenium, and Vitamin B-12.

Bison, if eaten in place of other red meats, can be beneficial to one's health and, hence, one can enjoy a juicy tender bison steak without feeling guilty. In preparing bison meat, it should be cooked on a low fire — a lower temperature than you would other types of meats. Of all the bison steaks, filet mignon, cut from the centre of the tenderloin, exemplifies the prime cut, it being the tastiest, juiciest, and most flavorful. The best meat comes from animals between the ages of 18 months and 2½ years.

Bison meat is usually prepared like beef but due to its low fat content it is easy to overcook and, thus, one must check on it sooner than other meats. To keep burgers, roasts, and steaks juicy and not allow them to dry up, they should be cooked to medium rare for the perfect balance of juice and flavor — never well-done.

The Arabs love their meat, and bison will only add to the richness of the variety of meat in their larder. These few recipes prepared in the eastern Arab style of cooking will give you an idea of how bison meat can well become a world gourmet delicacy.

Bison meat soup
Serves 6

½ pound bison shoulder meat, cut into very small pieces
4 cloves garlic, crushed
7 cups water
4 Tbsp. butter
4 Tbsp. flour
2 cups milk
¼ tsp. cayenne
1½ tsp. salt
1 tsp. pepper

Place meat, garlic, and water in a saucepan then bring to boil. Cover and cook over medium/low heat for 2 hours or until meat is well cooked.

Melt butter in another deep saucepan then stir-fry flour in the butter until flour begins to brown. Pour in meat with its juice from the other saucepan then stir in remaining ingredients. Stirring constantly, bring to boil then cook over low heat for 10 minutes. Serve piping hot.

Bison meat pie
Serves 6

As soon as this dish is cooked it should be immediately removed from the oven. If left in the oven, the tomato slices will become dry.

1 pound ground bison meat
1 cup pulverized walnuts
2 medium onions, chopped
2 cloves garlic, crushed
4 Tbsp. finely chopped fresh coriander leaves
1 tsp. crushed dried mint leaves
1 tsp. salt
½ tsp. allspice
½ tsp. pepper
2 medium tomatoes, sliced
2 Tbsp. olive oil

Place all ingredients, except tomatoes and olive oil, in a mixing bowl then thoroughly combine. Spread evenly in a greased casserole then place tomato slices evenly over top. Sprinkle with olive oil then cover and bake in a 350° F preheated oven for 1 hour or until meat is cooked. Immediately remove from oven and serve.

Bison-egg rollups
Serves 6

These egg rollups make an excellent entrée when served with fried potatoes and a tomato salad.

1 pound ground bison meat
1 medium onion, chopped
1 cup chopped parsley
1 tsp. salt
1 tsp. cumin
½ tsp. pepper
¼ tsp. allspice
⅛ tsp. cayenne
4 hard-boiled eggs
1 cup tomato sauce
½ cup water

Place all ingredients, except eggs, tomato sauce, and water, in a food processor and process into a thick paste. Divide into 4 balls then flatten out into 4 rounds. Place an egg in middle of each round, then form into a ball with meat covering the entire egg. Place in a casserole, then pour in tomato sauce and water. Cover and bake in a 350° F preheated oven for 1½ hours or until meat is cooked.

Remove from oven and allow to cool for 15 minutes, then slice balls into ¼-inch-thick slices. Place on serving platter, then spread casserole sauce over top and serve warm.

Bison and chickpea stew
Serves about 6

For stews, chickpeas can equal or outdo beans or peas as a complementary ingredient. Their taste and texture seem to blend well with all types of meat.

1 pound ground bison meat
½ cup fine bread crumbs
4 medium onions, chopped
2 cloves garlic, crushed
1 tsp. salt
½ tsp. cumin
½ tsp. allspice
½ tsp. pepper
4 Tbsp. olive oil
2 Tbsp. maple syrup or similar syrup
2 Tbsp. lemon juice
2½ cups water
1 can (19 oz.) chickpeas, undrained

Place meat, bread crumbs, half the onions, garlic, salt, cumin, allspice, and pepper in a food processor; then process into a paste. Form into small balls the size of small walnuts then set aside.

Heat oil in a frying pan, then fry meatballs until they begin to brown. Remove with slotted spoon and place in a saucepan.

In same oil, adding more if necessary, sauté remainder of onions. Place frying pan contents along with remaining ingredients over the meatballs in the saucepan, adding a little additional salt and pepper, if desired. Bring to boil and cover; then cook covered over medium/low heat for 1½ hours, adding more water if needed. Serve hot with cooked rice or mashed potatoes.

Bison burghul patties
Serves about 6

These patties are excellent when served with a tahini salad.

½ cup burghul, soaked for 10 minutes in warm water, then water squeezed out through sieve
1 pound ground bison meat
1 large onion, chopped
1 large sweet pepper, chopped
1 cup mashed potatoes
2 cloves garlic, crushed
¼ cup fine bread crumbs
½ cup finely chopped parsley
4 Tbsp. finely chopped coriander leaves
2½ tsp. salt
1 tsp. pepper
1 tsp. cumin
1 tsp. ground oregano
⅛ tsp. cayenne

Burghul and bison meatball stew

Peas with bison meat

Place all ingredients in a food processor, then process into a bread dough consistency, adding more bread crumbs if necessary. Roll dough into walnut-size balls and flatten into patties, then place in a greased baking pan, uncovered. Bake in a 350° F preheated oven for 1¼ hours or until done.

Burghul and bison meatball stew
Serves 6 to 8

A little different than the stews one is used to in the West, this dish is tasty and wholesome and one never forgets tasting it for the first time.

> 1 cup fine burghul, soaked for 10 minutes in warm water, then water squeezed out through sieve
> 1 pound ground bison meat
> 1 large onion, very finely chopped
> ½ tsp. allspice
> 2 tsp. salt, divided
> 1 tsp. paprika
> ½ tsp. pepper, divided
> ½ tsp. cumin, divided
> ¼ tsp. cayenne, divided
> 3 Tbsp. butter
> 2 large tomatoes, finely chopped
> 4 cups water

Combine burghul, meat, onion, allspice, 1½ teaspoons of salt, ½ teaspoon of paprika, ¼ teaspoon each of pepper and cumin, and ⅛ teaspoon of cayenne. Shape into balls a little smaller than walnuts and set aside.

Melt butter in a saucepan then add tomatoes and the remaining salt, paprika, pepper, cumin and cayenne. Fry over medium/low heat for 8 minutes, then add water and bring to boil. Add balls, then cover and cook over medium/low heat for 1 hour or until balls are well done. Serve with cooked rice or mashed potatoes.

Spinach with bison meat
Serves about 6

Dining on this dish makes one realize that the meat of the king of beasts on the western prairies of North America has no gamey taste — a fact that has made me a fan of its meat.

> 6 Tbsp. cooking oil
> 1 pound bison round steak, cut into ½-inch cubes
> 1 large onion, finely chopped
> 4 cloves garlic, crushed
> ½ cup finely chopped fresh coriander
> 2 cups stewed tomatoes
> 1½ tsp. salt
> 1 tsp. pepper
> 1 tsp. ground cumin
> ⅛ tsp. cayenne
> 2 cups water
> 1 pound spinach, thoroughly washed and chopped
> 2 Tbsp. lemon juice

Heat oil in a saucepan then fry meat over medium/low heat for 10 minutes. Stir in onion, garlic, and coriander then fry over medium/low heat for another 10 minutes, stirring often. Stir in tomatoes, salt, pepper, cumin, cayenne, and water. Cover then cook over medium/low heat for another 50 minutes, stirring occasionally and adding a little water if necessary. Add spinach then cook over medium/low heat for 10 minutes, stirring often and adding a little water if necessary. Stir in lemon juice and serve hot.

Peas with bison meat
Serves about 6

> 4 Tbsp. olive oil
> 1 pound bison sirloin steak, cut into ½-inch cubes
> 1 large onion, finely chopped
> 4 cloves garlic, crushed
> ½ small hot pepper seeds removed, finely chopped
> 4 cups water
> 2 cups cooked tomatoes
> 1 pound shelled fresh peas (frozen peas may be substituted)
> 1½ tsp. salt
> 1 tsp. dried and crushed oregano
> ½ tsp. pepper
> ½ tsp. cumin

Heat oil in a saucepan, then add the meat and sauté over medium/low heat for 5 minutes. Stir in onion, garlic,

and hot pepper then sauté for another 10 minutes, stirring a number of times. Add water, then cover and bring to boil. Simmer over medium/low heat for 1½ hours, stirring occasionally and adding more water if necessary. Stir in remaining ingredients then cook over medium/low heat for 20 minutes, adding more water if necessary. Serve hot with cooked rice or mashed potatoes. Δ

Reviving heat-stressed plants

By Tom Kovach

Special care is needed when dry weather conditions deprive plants of the essential moisture they need to survive. Plants showing stress from heat need immediate attention. Heat stress is a condition in which plant functions begin to shut down due to a lack of moisture available in the soil, usually as a result of hot weather and long dry spells. When plants are heat-stressed there is leaf wilt, stem wilt, and without quick action, plant death. Shallow-rooted perennials, annuals, and container plants are the most susceptible. However, even mature shrubs, trees, lawns, and plants growing in sandy soil or windy sites may also be affected.

In detecting heat stress, the first sign is usually leaf wilt. Leaves may droop or close up. This is followed by stem wilt, and entire stems may bend to the ground. Leaf edges may curl or brown and actually turn crisp. Lawns that begin to suffer heat stress usually have a silvery cast.

Water will correct the problem. Immediately water heat-stressed plants. Use a hose to get water to the roots of the plants. Apply a thorough, gentle stream of water at a rate the soil can absorb, but avoid runoff. If the plant is out of direct sun, douse leaves with a gentle spray as well, wetting all surfaces. For smaller plants put up a temporary shade, which lowers temperatures immediately to halt the damage. Also, add a thick layer of mulch around the base of the plant to cool the soil and conserve moisture. Continue watching and watering for the next few days, especially if hot, dry weather continues. Avoid any further damage by watching plants closely and watering as needed. But don't overdo the watering if the soil is moist. Too much water can also hurt plants.

Always plan ahead by mixing moisture-absorbing, organic materials such as manure or compost into the soil at planting time. Give moisture-loving plants an area that is protected from the wind. Wind, especially in dry weather, adds to the heat stress problem. Plan ahead for summer heat and hot sites such as south-facing walls by installing a drip system for young plants, annuals, perennial beds, and vegetables. Then, if a heat wave hits, you can water easily and effectively. If you live in an area with hot, dry summers, plant a garden of drought resistant plants. Watch for signs of wilt as the temperature rises. Some plants wilt on hot afternoons but are fine by morning, a warning that they need additional water or shading. Place container plantings in afternoon shade. During hot weather, be sure to water efficiently. Early morning applications provide moisture critical to survive the hottest part of the day, and little is lost to evaporation. In very hot weather, follow this with an evening watering, which adds valuable humidity in very dry climates.

Although gardeners are usually advised to avoid watering plants during the heat of the day, stressed plants are an exception. They need moisture immediately, even in hot sun. Apply water at the base to keep foliage dry and to help reduce evaporation.

Besides watering and moving some plants to more shaded areas, polymers can also be used. Polymers are water-holding crystals which absorb water and release it slowly. They help keep soil evenly moist around annuals or plants in containers.

If heat-stressed plants are discovered in time and cared for properly, the chance of recovery is very good. Check an hour or so after initial watering to see if the plant is perking up. Repeat watering and rinsing if the plant still looks stressed. It will take some time for plants to recover fully. Avoid applying fertilizer or pesticides for several days afterward so that the plants do not burn. Allowing the foliage to return to normal and feeder roots to refreshen is important in sustaining overall health after heat stress. Observe the plants carefully. After a week or two, if the plant is showing renewed vigor, you can resume normal fertilizer applications.

Heat-stressed plants can recover. But the best thing to do is to plan ahead and keep all plants properly watered so that heat stress doesn't occur. Δ

The Last Word

A reason for the Second Amendment

Right after the shooting of 20 children and 6 teachers at the Sandy Hook Elementary School in Newtown, Connecticut, I was asked by several people, "Does anyone really need assault weapons with high-capacity clips?"

My short answer was, and still is, "Yes."

When that elicits surprise, I add, "Why do cops need them?"

The usual response is, "To protect us." What I then explain is, "Cops have no obligation to protect you. Even if they promise to protect you, they don't have to, and they can't be held accountable if they don't. No police organization in this country includes in its charter the obligation to protect you. Their sole purpose is to serve the government. No citizen has ever won a case in court when they've sued because a police organization failed to protect them. Cops don't even have to stop a crime if they're witnessing one, and this has happened with undercover cops and cops on stakeouts who have witnessed heinous crimes and done nothing because they didn't want to blow their cover. In 2005, the Supreme Court ruled that the job of police is not to protect us, but to enforce the law."

If I've been allowed to get this far, I also like to add, "If the cops need the kinds of guns you would like to see outlawed, then I want them too because cops almost never show up to stop a crime, but only to take a report."

As for more stringent laws, more gun laws aren't going to prevent mass shootings. We have more than 20,000 gun laws on the books at local, state, and federal levels and they couldn't stop the Sandy Hook shooting.

However, if we really want a solution to shootings in schools, there is a solution that has worked: Israel had a problem with terrorists attacking schools, and a major part of the solution was to allow teachers, who became proficient with guns, to arm themselves. With the Israeli model, the goons just don't know which teachers may be armed and when. It worked and Israeli schools became safer overnight.

The Israeli model for protecting children in schools goes hand in hand with the argument and statistics presented by John Lott in his book, *More Guns, Less Crime*. His statistics show that for concealed carry weapons to be effective deterrents against crime, it is not necessary for everyone to be armed. In counties in the U.S. where it is legal to carry concealed firearms, crime dropped dramatically.

Still, there are those who believe we would be better off with no private ownership of guns, so let's examine the real reasons for gun ownership.

We own guns for self-defense.

We own them because they're fun, just as Corvettes, Lamborghinis, and even my Honda Accord is fun.

But the greatest reason for Americans to be armed, especially with military-style weapons with high-capacity magazines, and the real reason for the Second Amendment, is that they are our last line of defense against tyranny. The Founders included the Second Amendment as a reminder that an armed populace can resist tyranny.

Is there an American dictatorship on the horizon? I don't know. But no one could have predicted, at the close of WWI, that a country as cultured and civilized as Germany would have devolved into a nation with a government that would prey on its own people and citizens in neighboring countries, killing at least 12 million civilians because they were Jews, Gypsies, Poles, homosexuals, those with birth defects, etc.

Hundreds of studies based on an original experiment posed and conducted by Stanley Milgram, a renowned Yale University professor of social psychology, have been carried out in the almost seven decades since WWII ended to explain how a country like Germany could have turned so barbaric. What has been concluded, again and again, across many cultures including our own, is that people, no matter what their nationality, will "follow orders" and torture their fellow citizens. The studies found that roughly one third of any large population would willingly do what the German people did.

Now, imagine the difficulties Hitler and his gang would have had if the people he persecuted been armed to the teeth as the American people are today. Remember the Warsaw Ghetto where Jews made a heroic last stand on the same level as the Texans at the Alamo or the Greeks at Thermopylae? Imagine if the Jews and the others murdered had not surrendered their personal firearms when the new Nazi regime first imposed gun control? How much attention would the Nazis have had to give to a guerrilla war at home, fought by people they couldn't so easily murder because they fought back? The irony is that, had the Jews, Poles, Gypsies, etc., been armed, not only would more of them have lived, but more Allied soldiers would have lived, also.

And Germany was not an aberration. In the 20th century in the Soviet Union, 20 to 60 million died under Stalin. In China, at least 50 million were murdered, and some estimates run as high as 120 million. In Cambodia, at least 1.7 million died, as did millions in Turkey and millions in other countries — and all of these countries became "gun free" zones before the atrocities began.

How successful would these government pogroms have been had their genocidal victims been armed and able to resist? On the other hand, I don't believe any government-sponsored massacres have ever happened where the populace was armed.

So, are Americans in any danger?

Maybe! Our own government has been at war with We the People ever since the early days of the Republic, at least as far back as the Alien and Sedition Acts of 1798, which were designed to prevent criticism of government. And before oppression of blacks in the postbellum South was possible, blacks were "lawfully" disarmed so they couldn't resist. When Indians were committed to those uniquely American concentration camps we call reservations, they too were legally and lawfully denied access to weapons, as were the Japanese-Americans interned during World War II.

Are guns dangerous? Yes, they kill! They'd be useless if they didn't. But just as we trade more than 30,000 traffic deaths a year for the benefits of cars, trucks, and motorcycles, there are benefits from widespread gun ownership, including ownership of those high-capacity magazines that help make us the equal of an armed government should it turn against the people.

We shouldn't assume tyranny is impossible here. As I've pointed out in past columns, it seems we're putting in place more laws each year that would make a dictatorship possible. Laws prohibiting modern personal weapons would be the last brick in the wall. And as horrible as the shooting at the Sandy Hook Elementary School was, we cannot let it become an excuse to disarm an entire nation.

— John Silveira

A Backwoods Home Anthology
The Tenth Year

* What if the electricity goes off?
* With commonsense planning, you can survive hard times
* 7 mistakes of food storage
* Emergency gear for your vehicle
* Roll your own newspaper logs
* Build an old-fashioned smokehouse
* Plant a Y2K garden
* Compare the nutrition in wild meats to supermarket meats
* Ayoob on firearms: Home on the range with a .357
* Catch more fish with this simple feeder
* Salvaging cement blocks the easy way
* Raising your own beef for your family
* The water system
* Cost-saving baby tips
* Start your food storage on $10 a week
* Seven common medicinal plants
* A salvaged oak floor for $5
* Medical kits for self-reliant families
* Harvesting and freezing apples
* A house for an outdoor dog
* Ambidextrous chainsaw filing
* Millennium vehicles
* Raise tobacco for trade or barter in hard times
* Roughing it with plastic trash bags
* Ayoob on firearms: Defending your lifestyle
* Practical livestock for the homestead
* Try this simple slow cooker
* Keeping your food cold — Solutions to refrigeration

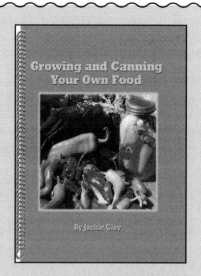

Grow your food
Can your food
Store your food

- *Gardening basics*
- *Canning supplies*
- *Growing fruit*
- *Growing and canning tomatoes*
- *Stocking up your pantry*
- *Basic staples for a pantry*
- *Great recipes*
- *Basic pantry mixes*

A Backwoods Home Anthology
The Fifth Year

❋ Odd-jobbin' can be a country goldmine
❋ How to keep those excess eggs
❋ Make better pizza at home than you can buy
❋ How we bought our country home
❋ Cooking with dried fruit
❋ Garden huckleberries
❋ Short season gardening
❋ The 10 most useful herbs
❋ Simplified concrete and masonry work
❋ Raising sheep
❋ Free supplies for your homestead
❋ Learning in the pickle patch
❋ Good-bye old friend
❋ Choosing and using a wood cookstove

❋ Three great bread recipes
❋ Build a fieldstone chimney
❋ Sun oven cookery
❋ Firewood: how and what to buy
❋ Choosing superior bedding plants
❋ A bit about ducks
❋ How to build the fence you need
❋ Improving poor garden soil
❋ Learn the basics of wall framing
❋ Determined woman builds distinctive vertical log studio
❋ Make better pizza than you can buy
❋ Good-bye old friend
❋ Turkeys — fun and profitable and not as dumb as you think
❋ Raising fish in the farm pond
❋ You have to learn to shovel crap before you learn to be the boss

Backwoods Home magazine

July/Aug 2013
Issue #142
$5.95 US
$7.50 CAN

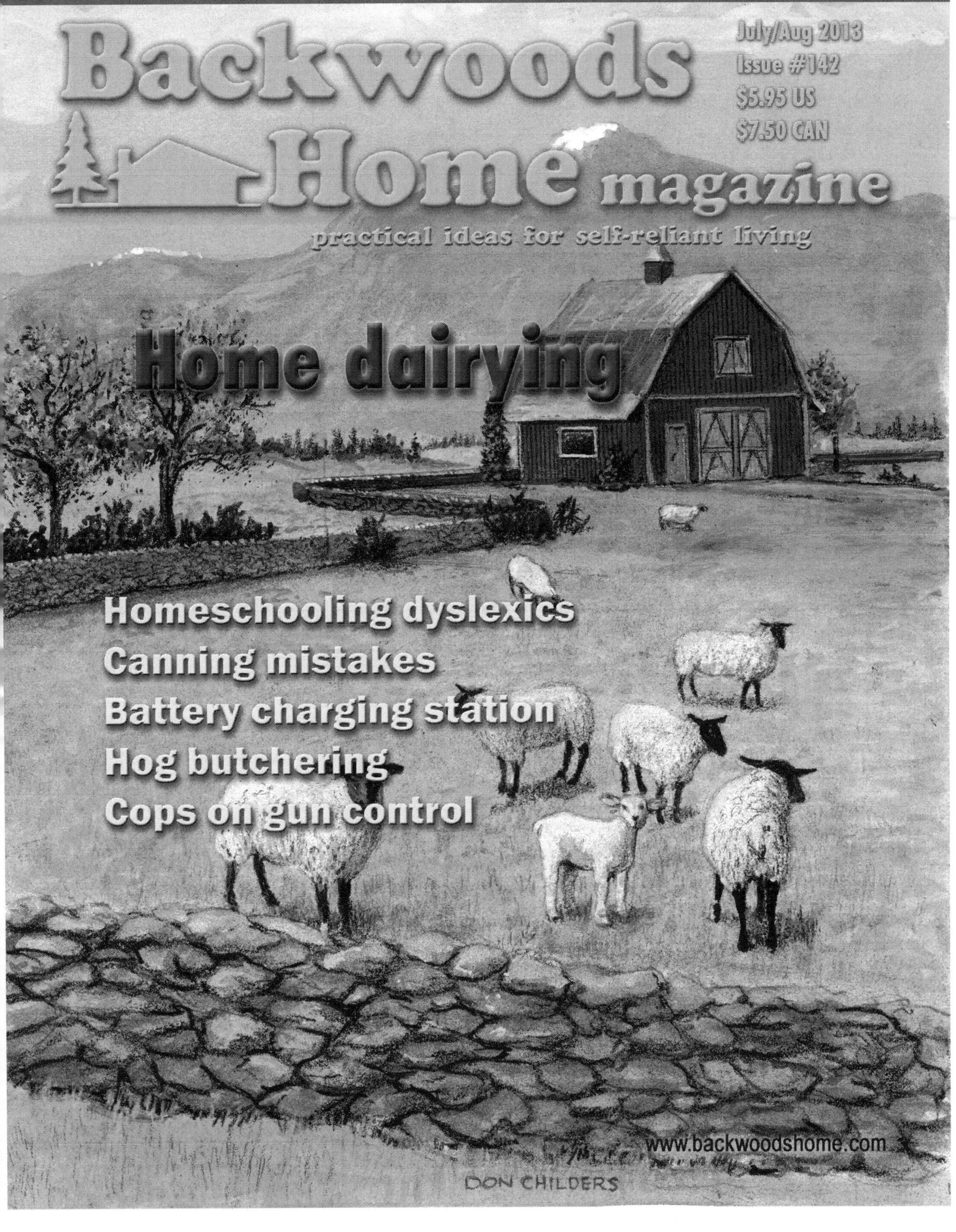

practical ideas for self-reliant living

Home dairying

Homeschooling dyslexics
Canning mistakes
Battery charging station
Hog butchering
Cops on gun control

DON CHILDERS

www.backwoodshome.com

My view

The Government intimidation factor and its effect on the health of society

How do you take the temperature of a society, that is, how do you tell if a society is healthy or sick?

Several years after the Soviet Union dissolved in 1991 under the accumulated weight of 70 plus years of oppression and debt, various public opinion survey groups complained that they couldn't rely on the answers of the former Soviet peoples because their answers reflected what they thought you wanted to hear, not what was on their mind. Pundits of the day said it was because the former Soviet societies were sick, having been controlled and mentally intimidated by their Communist masters for seven decades. They had been conditioned to give answers that would not get them in trouble with "The State."

So let's fast-forward to American society. How do you tell if we are healthy or sick? Are we as afraid of Government Authorities (The State) as the Soviet peoples were? Of course not, but there certainly is a "Government intimidation factor" at play in American society, enough to give it a temperature that indicates our society is not experiencing optimum health. Ask just about anyone for their personal stories about confronting Government.

Since my wife and I own a business (this magazine) we confront Government on a regular basis — through government forms we must fill out to comply with Government regulations, all of which come with the threat of legal action, fines, or imprisonment. My wife, Ilene, does most of this. Here's her opinion: "The bottom of the bottom of things I have to do is sending states their various sales tax forms with a check after we attend an Expo or Fair. Here we are, willing guests in their state, freely spending money on planes, hotels, and restaurants, helping their economy by taking part in an Expo that provides jobs and knowledge for their residents, then the State comes after us for their cut."

Texas is the worst, she says. Every fiscal quarter she must file a tax form with the state of Texas to let them know we have not had a physical presence in Texas to conduct business there so don't owe them any sales tax. If we fail to send them that form, they automatically fine us $50 for the quarter. Noncompliance would also mean Texas would ban us from attending the annual Self Reliance Expo near Dallas, which is not that bad an alternative since the Expo is a net financial loss for us.

Now the federal Government wants to make it even easier for states to collect sales taxes, especially those generated on the internet, so it is on the verge of passing the Marketplace Fairness Act, so named because the

I saved copies of the LA Times for about a three-week period in 1991 as the Soviet Union dissolved under the accumulated weight of 70 years of oppression and debt.

Government did not want to call it a new tax. This new tax is not a new tax at all, according to politicians who support it, but merely an attempt to collect taxes due the states. The Senate has already passed the tax with broad bipartisan support, and the House, after a few more weeks of Doublespeak to confuse their constituents, is expected to do the same.

This new Government effort to impose yet another tax on the American people comes while the news is full of admissions by the IRS that for years it has been targeting and auditing people who talk about freedom issues, especially if they criticize Government or use words like "Patriot" or "tea party." The IRS has apologized for what it termed its "absolutely inappropriate action," an interim IRS commissioner has resigned, and President Obama vowed that those responsible would be held "fully accountable."

But most of us know nothing will change. IRS intimidation has been a tool of both political parties for many years, and chances are some Government official is watching both you and me right now because we are talking openly about Government intimidation. Next year the IRS will become even more powerful as it assumes the lead role in collecting personal health insurance information to ensure we comply with new Obamacare mandates.

But our Government's heavy-handed attempt to collect taxes is only the tip of the iceberg. The last time I attended the big Midwest Renewable Energy Fair in Wisconsin, it was the Government goons at the Central Wisconsin Airport in Wausau that caused me and my daughter, Annie, the managing editor of *BHM*, stress. We were subjected to a random drug search of our luggage. When I tried to take a photo of what was going on, a Government agent curtly told me to put my camera away. I was intimidated into doing so, even though the Supreme Court has ruled again and again that it is legal to photograph police in the performance of their duties. It is surprisingly easy to be intimidated when you are suddenly confronted with a threatening situation.

Our Government's ubiquitous presence in its ongoing War on Drugs has touched many families. Many of us know someone — usually a young person pressing the limits of youthful exploration — who has been in jail due to a minor drug offense. The War on Drugs has mainly given America the highest prison incarceration rate of any country in history, dwarfing the old Soviet Union's dreaded Gulags. It is enforced by the same bureaucracy that once enforced Prohibition, that former 1920-33 full-employment scheme for Government bureaucrats, and it is gradually expanding into a War Against Prescription Drugs as our Drug Army seeks even more work for it to do. How many of you know the legal intricacies of traveling with your prescription medications? In a car? On a plane? Across state lines? I'll bet quite a few of you accidentally violate the law on a regular basis. And woe be to you if you run into a TSA bureaucrat or cop looking to score points with his supervisor by arresting you for a law you didn't even know existed.

Sometimes I think the Government's overall strategy is to have so many laws and regulations, with so many varying degrees of punishment ranging from a slap on the wrist to imprisonment, that many citizens are in a mild but fairly constant state of anxiety that they might be doing something illegal. If an IRS auditor interrogated you about your latest tax return, would you tell him what was really on your mind about their tyrannical tactics, or would you tell him what you thought you needed to say to keep out of trouble?

American society is certainly not experiencing the state of intimidation that the old Soviet peoples were prior to 1991, but we definitely have a temperature. That's why we have to keep speaking out and fighting for freedom — to keep that temperature from rising into a dangerous fever.

— *Dave Duffy*

A Backwoods Home Anthology
The Eighth Year

* Considering life in rural Arkansas
* Where I live: Nine-patch, baby, and log cabin quilts
* Here's the best way to split gnarly firewood
* Here's an easier (and cheaper) way to make wooden beams
* Rid your garden of snails and slugs — organically
* Try these 13 metal cleaning tips to keep your house shining
* I remember the day the lynx attacked
* Raise your own feed crops for your livestock
* Lay vinyl flooring the foolproof way
* These double-steep half stairs save space
* Think of it this way...Science and truth — are they related?
* Commonsense preparedness just makes sense
* Grandma will love this personal "Helping Hands" wall hanging
* Try these pasta desserts for unusual holiday fare
* Protect your small buildings from wind damage
* Winterize your animals without going broke
* Enjoy snap beans — fresh from the garden
* Set 100 steel fence posts a day with a home-made driver
* Plant your Irish potatoes this fall or winter
* From apple crisp to French tarts, tasty apple treats are just right for fall
* Here are four sure catfish baits
* Save time and energy with the fenced chicken coop/garden
* Rough day? You need to sip some yeller wine

The home dairy

By Patrice Lewis

When my husband and I decided to travel the road to greater self-sufficiency many years ago, one of the first things we discussed was the purchase of a dairy animal.

Milk is one of the most fundamental aspects of the American diet. From milk comes many superb and healthy food products: yogurt, cream, cheeses of all kinds, butter, buttermilk, sour cream, cottage cheese, ice cream, and of course just plain milk. In short, without the ability to obtain fresh milk from our own animals, our self-sufficient diet would be very different.

But we were total and complete novices when it came to livestock. Frankly I was scared spitless at the thought of getting an animal. I knew nothing about cows or goats; I knew nothing about milking or making cheese; I knew nothing at all.

But if there's one thing I've learned in life, it's that sometimes the best thing to do is just dive in. And that's what we did.

Cows vs. goats vs. sheep

Over the course of history and in many cultures, many different types of animals have been milked: cows, goats, sheep, horses, llamas, yaks, camels, water buffalo, etc. In America, the two primary dairy animals are cows and goats.

When we first decided to get a dairy animal nearly 15 years ago, we had to resolve the great cow-versus-goat debate. We learned (ahem) that people have extremely passionate opinions on the merits of both species.

There are enterprising individuals who milk other animals besides cows or goats. I had the good fortune to find a sheep dairyist nearby, one of only two licensed facilities in the state of Idaho. I will discuss the uses of sheep's milk separately; however,

for the moment let's stick to the cow vs. goat debate.

In the beginning...

Before getting a dairy animal, there are a few things to consider. What is your climate and terrain? (Some animals may be better adapted to your region than others.) What kind of infrastructure (barns and fences) do you have? What is your work schedule — how long are you away from home every day? Do you have any physical limitations? How much acreage do you have? All these factors will play a part in influencing what kind of dairy animal you get.

Cows and goats have their strengths and weaknesses. Here are some advantages of dairy cows:

• They give abundant milk with cream that separates easily.

• While not universal, in general they have few birthing problems.

• They have a longer productive breeding and milking life, often stretching 15 years.

Here are some disadvantages of dairy cows:

• The quantity of milk they give can be overwhelming.

• They are large and can be intimidating to handle.

• They are more expensive when obtaining your initial animals.

Here are some advantages of dairy goats:

• They are smaller in size and less intimidating to handle.

• They give smaller quantities of milk.

• They can graze on marginal land and control weeds.

• They eat less.

• They are less expensive to obtain your first animals.

• They usually have multiple kids, making herd expansion quicker.

Here are some disadvantages of dairy goats:

• The bucks can smell terrible and often must be kept in separate (and distant) facilities.

• They are clever at escaping fences due to their penchant for climbing.

• Some people think the milk tastes funny.

• Because they usually have multiple births, some birthing assistance may be needed if the kids are tangled in the womb.

• Their milk is naturally homogenized, which makes cream separation more difficult.

• Their milk develops a strong taste and goes "off" more quickly than cow milk.

At first glance, it would appear that the benefits of goats outweigh the benefits of cows. However in our situation, one single factor tipped the balance in favor of cows; namely, we don't like goat milk.

Of course nothing says you can't have both cows and goats. That's the beauty of choice. Get whatever dairy animal catches your fancy.

Remember, both goats and cows are *herd animals*. A solitary animal suffers from loneliness just as much as a solitary person does. Therefore try to obtain at least two animals at first. They don't necessarily have to both be milking animals; you might get a cow and calf pair, a doe with her kids, a doe and whether (castrated male), or some such combination. But giving your dairy animal company will help ensure that she remains happy.

Breeds

Over the last couple of centuries, cows and goats have been bred to perform specialized functions, usually milk vs. meat (some people keep animals for draft purposes as well). You'll get more meat from a meat breed, and you'll get more milk from a milk breed. Nothing says you can't milk a meat breed or eat a milk breed; but the specialization means you'll get more bang for your buck for whatever the breed's intended purpose is.

Some breeds are dual-purpose, meaning they give adequate amounts of both milk and meat. "Adequate" means they do not produce either product to the maximum amount preferred by *commercial* enterprises; however dual-purpose breeds are often superb choices for homesteaders. For example, we started with Dexter cattle, a small Irish dual-purpose breed. They give less milk than a Jersey and produce less meat than an Angus, but for our family, this was fine. We've since branched into Jersey and Dexter-Jersey crosses for greater milk production and maintain purebred Dexters for meat.

Among the heaviest milk-producing cow breeds are Jersey, Guernsey, Brown Swiss, and Holstein. There are many other fine breeds of cows, but these four top the list in terms of volume. However a high-volume cow may be too much milk for the average family, so keep this in mind when selecting a breed.

Dual-purpose cattle breeds are often "heritage" breeds which thrive on marginal pasturage (versus a high-grain diet) and were bred to handle local climate and terrain. For northern areas, consider a Scottish Highland or Galloway; for temperate climates, consider a Devon or Red Poll; for hot climates, consider an American Criollo, Senepol, or Ankole-Watusi. For a smaller dual-purpose breed, consider a Dexter, Welsh Black, Normande, or Dutch Belted. Be wary of certain "miniature" cattle breeds — not because the animals are bad, but because their specialty nature means the prices are usually astonishingly high.

Among the best milk-producing goat breeds are Alpine, Swiss, Toggenburg, Nubian, La Mancha, Oberhasli, and Saanen. Of the many wonderful goat breeds, these seven are best known for their milk.

Volume

A note about milking capacity: homestead animals, even high-volume breeds, seldom produce the quantities of milk a commercial dairy does. Commercial dairies must, of necessity, maximize an animal's output. They select for heavy milkers, they separate the calf or kid immediately after birth, they feed a specialized diet, and they cull older animals or animals which are poor performers.

On a homestead, maximum milk production isn't necessary or even desired. Not many people are capable of handling 10 or 15 gallons of milk a day.

There are many factors which strongly affect how much milk a cow gives: whether she has a calf on her; how much grass vs. grain she eats; even how much affection you give her. Don't be afraid to get a high-volume milk producer if you fall in love with a particular animal.

A personal example: when we decided to branch away from our history of raising pure Dexters, we bought a six-year-old Jersey cow from a commercial dairy. We immediately plunged into an udder nightmare of mastitis, scabs, and other issues.

But oh my goodness, I absolutely fell in love with our Matilda. Through all the treatments we gave her, she rewarded us with kisses and affection. Her huge beautiful brown eyes were gentle and kind. And when her udder issues cleared up (and since she didn't have a calf on her), her production dropped from a maximum of 10 gallons a day (when she was at the commercial dairy) down to five; and when she birthed her first calf on our farm, I began milking her once a day and got about two or three gallons — a manageable amount.

The important thing to remember is to choose a breed of cow or goat (and even a specific animal) that you love. The health and condition of an animal is clearly important, but so is fondness. Livestock thrive on affection, and a warm relationship with your dairy animal makes for a happy homestead. On a commercial enterprise, it isn't always possible to bond emotionally with an animal. There's no reason you can't form a loving bond on a homestead.

Infrastructure

I'm a big believer in having infrastructure in place *before* getting your animals. This means have adequate fencing and shelter before bringing home Bossy.

Fencing

Fencing is obviously necessary to keep your animals on your property and out of your (or your neighbor's) garden. Unfortunately with the price of T-posts, fencing can be pricey; but advertising for used fencing materials is one way we've obtained equipment on a budget.

Make your fences stronger than you think they should be. Livestock animals are hard on fences. They have a tendency to exert pressure either at top or bottom that will loosen the posts. Goats have a tendency to push their cleats on the lower rungs of wire fencing in order to raise themselves up. Cows have a tendency to reach over the top of fences to reach the grass on the other side (which everyone knows is *always* greener). Once an animal knows he can escape by whatever means (jumping, pushing, barreling, whatever), it's harder to keep that animal in.

Three- or four-strand wire fencing (either barbed or unbarbed wire) can be greatly strengthened by wiring sticks to the strands. This is cheaper than the twisty "fence stays" that can cost upwards of $1 apiece.

Don't skimp when it comes to building tough, sturdy perimeters. Take it from someone who has dealt with marginal fencing for decades. It is far better to do the job right the first time, than to do a half-assed job and spend the next 10 years fixing your mistakes. Additionally, have the means on hand to make repairs, both short-term emergency repairs and long-term permanent repairs.

Electric fencing

Many people put a touching but misplaced faith in those little zaps of

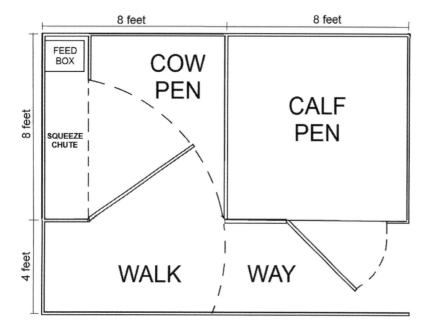

This setup works well for once-a-day milking by keeping the cow and calf separated at night. After morning milking, the cow and calf are turned out into the pasture together until evening when they're separated again.

electricity that come from electric fences, but here's the harsh truth: those little zaps won't mean diddly to an animal determined to get through.

One time we strung two hot wires across our driveway and let some cattle loose to eat down some grass. We watched, literally watched our bull mosey his way between the two hot-wire strands to get to the tender grass on the other side. We watched his skin ripple with each zap but it didn't phase him in the slightest. So don't make the mistake of thinking electric fencing *by itself* will work to keep livestock in. It won't.

Where electric fences comes in very handy is to *supplement* existing fences. When we built our bull pen, for example, we built a sturdy four-board fence and then strung hotwire at three levels around the perimeter. This keeps our bull from leaning on the fences or otherwise trying to batter through to get to a cow in heat.

Goats are more sensitive to hotwires. Since goats like to elevate themselves by putting their cleats on the bottom rungs of fences, this can be prevented by stringing a hotwire at about knee level.

A word of warning about stringing hotwire: It can come down and then entangle livestock. A few years ago in an effort to keep our cows (and horse) from leaning over and pushing down the top of our pasture fences (we have field fencing, sometimes called woven wire), we strung a hotwire on top of the fence line around the entire perimeter of the pasture. It worked fine until the next morning. An investigation revealed that a jumping deer had taken out a section. So we fixed it. The next morning, the wire was down again. Deer simply cannot see a thin wire in the dark, and over and over they got tangled in it as they jumped, until we concluded the entire experiment was useless and turned off the power.

Foolishly we never unstrung the wire, and over the next few months it

The author's younger daughter with Matilda, a purebred jersey cow

came down in numerous places as the deer caught it while jumping. And once wire is on the ground, it can catch livestock. One of our calves got tangled in a wire and led us on a merry chase until we caught her and snipped the wire off her leg. Wire can severely damage livestock. If they tangle in it, it will eventually tighten and cut off circulation.

A better alternative is electric tape, which is colored, wide, more visible, and less likely to damage livestock.

Picketing

Picketing is an option for those whose land is without adequate fencing. However picketing has its own problems. A picketed animal cannot flee a threat (predator or other frightening condition) and may hurt herself in her efforts to escape. It is also very easy for a picketed animal to become tangled in the rope. I know of one sad case where a picketed animal reared up and was impaled on the T-post to which the rope was attached. Pickets should be very low in the ground and with a ring that permits free movement of the rope.

Needless to say, picketed animals should be moved frequently in order to allow access to fresh food, and water should always be within reach.

Shelter

Some people don't believe livestock need shelter. Perhaps there are some fortunate climates where shelter isn't necessary, but personally I'm not aware of any. Your dairy animal is giving you milk; the least you can do is protect her from torrential downpours, baking heat, bitter cold, or other climatic extremes. Some of the saddest sights I've seen are animals suffering through blizzard conditions with no means of escape. Wildlife has the option to travel to a more sheltered location and bed down in hollows or behind trees; but livestock are trapped in whatever fenced place you provide and cannot go anywhere. Do them the kindness of providing a haven.

While shelter may simply mean an open-sided loafing shed, you may want to pull together something a bit more comprehensive for your animals since you'll be milking them. Milking in an open field during a downpour isn't much fun.

Cows or goats whose babies have free access to their mama's milk all day long will not have much leftover milk for you. Therefore if you want to milk your animal, you will have to separate the baby. If you want your dairy animal's full and undivided milk output, the separation should be permanent. If you want the mother to raise her baby (and, not incidentally, make your milking schedule easier), you only need to separate the baby at night and milk just in the morning (see *BHM* article *Once a day milking*, Issue #99, May/June 2006).

This means you will need two adjacent stalls, one for the mother and one for the baby. For multiple animals, you might just leave the mamas free and put the babies in a pen for the night. Above all, the mothers must be able to see and sniff their offspring while they're separated; "out of sight and out of mind" does NOT work for a cow or goat. The mothers will go crazy trying to find their babies if you hide them, and a stressed animal gives very little milk.

Additionally, a milking arrangement is necessary for comfort during your daily milking routine. While sometimes an animal can be milked simply by squatting next to her with a bucket, more often a stanchion, stall, squeeze chute, or other restraining location is necessary, especially while training a cow or doe to milk. A crate or stool can also increase your comfort (I'm at the age where my knees can't take squatting next to an animal for the amount of time it takes to milk her).

How roomy should your barn be? This depends on whether you're housing cows or goats, as well as how many animals.

Cows are comfortable in a 8x8 foot space (though a 10x10 is better), but don't try to lock more than one cow per stall or they'll argue (and, if they have horns, possibly hurt each other).

However multiple calves can be penned together without issue.

Goats can be comfortable in a space as little as 6x6 feet (though 8x8 is better). Multiple kids can be penned together at night. Kidding pens can be as small as 4x4 feet.

Coupled with a spot for milking, your barn space can be very modest indeed. For years I made do with a small cobbled-together shelter my husband built that consisted of two side-by-side stalls and one narrow walkway. For milking, my husband made a dual-purpose gate: latched, it was simply a gate to the stall; but during milking, it folded inward and made a sort of squeeze chute for the cow to hold her still while I milked. The calf pen was right next to us. The entire footprint of the shelter was about 11x16 feet.

There are endless variations on the theme of housing your animals. Your best bet is to do some pencil sketches and get an idea of what you need. Don't go too crazy — you can always add on later — but make sure you have at least moderate shelter for your cow or goat, a pen for the calf or kids, and a spot for milking.

Choosing your animal

The whole purpose of having a dairy animal, of course, is to milk her. I'm continually astounded by the number of people who keep cows or goats as "pets" but don't take advantage of the rich milk they could be harvesting.

What factors should you look for when buying a dairy animal?

Disposition

A dairy animal must be handled. A wild cow or goat who is terrified of you and has never been confined in any manner is going to be hard to milk. I know some people who had a bad-tempered, half-wild cow who kicked viciously and even bit (she didn't have horns, otherwise those would have been lethal). My friends

had to employ more and more elaborate techniques just to confine and milk the cow. They eventually butchered her and got a cow with a sweeter disposition and were stunned at the contrast in personalities. They fell in love with their new cow.

This doesn't mean an untamed animal can't be tamed, but it will take time and patience. However some animals are just plain ornery. Especially for novice milkers, ornery animals will want to make you give up milking in frustration. Better to have a sweet animal who can be handled.

Conformation

In county fairs all around the country, judges rate livestock on conformation — how close an animal gets to the ideal "breed standards."

While I do not slavishly adhere to superb conformation, over the years I've learned that extreme departures from the breed's standards can cause problems with a homestead animal, particularly when it comes to udders.

When choosing your first dairy animal, pay attention to her general health. She should have bright eyes, a glossy coat, neat hooves, no sores, and otherwise look healthy and alert.

And look at her udder attachment. While a young unbred doe or heifer may not have had her udder tested, take a look and see how well "attached" the udder is through side and back ligaments. (If possible, take a look at a young animal's mother and note the udder attachment.) On an older animal, a poor udder attachment is immediately apparent, since the udder will look stretched, pendulous, or dangly. A tight attachment means the udder (even if enlarged with milk) is carried tight and close to the body, and will continue to stay close through their productive years. With a poor udder attachment, the udder will stretch and become more and more pendulous with each successive birthing.

Ideally the udder "floor" should be level, meaning the teats point down and are the same length. In real life, a level floor is rather hard to find, and in practical terms it doesn't much affect the quality of milk obtained from the animal.

Livestock purists dislike the idea of breeding an animal with a poor udder, but the reality is most of us can't afford blue-ribbon-quality animals, and so we must make do with what we get. It is my *personal opinion* (nothing more) that for a homestead animal, the most important characteristics to look for is a sweet disposition, overall good health, and a tight udder attachment. Perfect conformation to the breed standard isn't necessary to have a successful dairy animal on a homestead.

Feeding

In some climates, dairy animals can graze year-round. Unfortunately not everyone has that option, in which case you'll have to supplement your animal's grazing with feed.

Commercial dairies supplement their animals' diet with heavy amounts of grain. Grain is high-protein and dairy animals love it; but let's face facts, it's not what they were bred to eat. Kids love cookies, but they aren't "bred" to live on cookies to the exclusion of healthier foods. Similarly, cows love grain but were bred to live on grass.

So reserve grain as a treat, a training aid, and a nutritional boost for your lactating animal; but don't get caught up in the notion that livestock *must* have grain. We've raised cows for years with nary a grain in sight.

Homestead animals are healthiest if they can obtain most of their food through grazing, during the times of year when grazing is available. Here in north Idaho, there is graze available from about early May through November, peaking in June. We rotate our animals through three different fields during these times. During the rest of the year, we either supplement with hay, or feed entirely with hay.

Keep an eye on your pasturage. Small and/or poor-quality pastures can get eaten down very rapidly, in which case you'll have to supplement with hay. Some neglectful livestock owners have the extraordinary notion that because their animals are in a field, they are getting enough to eat. But if the field is eaten down to bare dirt, the animals could be starving. Be vigilant and attentive to the needs of your animals. Besides the cruelty factor, hungry cows or goats won't give much milk.

For winter feeding, a rough rule of thumb is about 3% of body weight per day in hay. For a thousand-pound cow, this translates to 30 lbs. of hay per day, usually split between two feedings. Some people free-feed, which is fine; but you'll go through a lot more hay that way.

"Hay" is a generic term referring to dried plant material, either grasses, legumes, or a combination. Depending on your climate, terrain, rainfall, and other factors, you may have to supplement year-round.

Not all hay is created equal. Alfalfa is a high-protein high-quality feed, but it's also very expensive and a pure alfalfa diet may be too rich. Cheatgrass is a low-quality low-nutritional forage that, at least in our case, our cows loathe.

If you own enough pasture land which receives adequate rainfall, you may be able to mow and bale your own hay; otherwise you'll have to buy it. Hay prices vary from year to year, from region to region, and also vary according to what kind of hay you purchase.

Grass hay such as a timothy/brome mix, or oat hay, are excellent general choices for livestock. These are usually among the more affordable feeds as well. Because these hays are less rich in protein, a small grain supplement might be necessary.

Your livestock should also have access to minerals, either with a mineral block or with loose mineral salts.

And needless to say, water! Your animals must *always* have fresh water available.

Training to milk

Now that you've obtained your cow or goat, she must be trained to milk. Because a dairy animal isn't likely to take kindly to the indignity of having you mess with her udder, especially if she's never been milked, it's best to construct *sturdy* facilities. Cows, especially, cannot be confined in flimsy surroundings (trust me on this).

If possible, begin training your animal *before* she gives birth. Trying to introduce her to a strange new setup shortly after giving birth (when she's hormonally deranged) will be difficult. Ideally you want to introduce her to the stall, chute, or stanchion in the last months of her pregnancy so she won't be freaked when you start milking.

The number one rule of milking is *gentleness*. No matter how ornery an animal is, it won't help her disposition to yell, hit, or otherwise express your frustration with her behavior. This not only stresses you, it stresses her.

Take any and all opportunities to handle your milk animal through brushings, lead training, and other hands-on situations. The more you handle your animal, the more she'll trust you.

Never underestimate the power of a bribe when it comes to getting your cow or goat into a stall or stanchion. Put a handful of sweet feed or other treat in a feed box and gently lure the animal in. Whatever you do, do *not* close her in — let her move freely in and out until she learns it's not a terrifying situation. Keep this up for about a week.

Once she's used to the physical structure, give her some grain and confine her. She will probably strug-

This homemade goat milking stand is elevated for easier milking. It has a feed box on the other side of the headpiece.

gle, which is why construction must be sturdy. If using a squeeze chute, *it must be narrow enough that she cannot turn around.* Usually an animal will struggle for only a few minutes, after which she'll settle down and eat

her grain. Be generous with the grain at this stage — give more if necessary as a reward for settling.

This situation should continue until the animal gives birth. Gently massage her udder and run your hand

The headpiece is an area where goats can be locked in by the neck so they don't move around during milking.

around her belly and backside. If she's inclined to kick, you can either tie her near back leg, or you can run an iron rod through the stall at about the level of the hock joint to keep her from kicking.

When your cow or goat gives birth, you have two options.

• **Permanent separation.** If you remove the kids or calf from the mother right away, this ensures all the milk belongs to you. It's best to remove the baby as soon as possible, certainly within a few hours. The cow or goat will mourn for a few days as she laments the loss of her baby. You will also be responsible for feeding the baby from birth, including milking the cow or goat and bottle-feeding the colostrum-rich milk the baby so desperately needs. Permanently removing the baby also means you *must* adhere to a twice-a-day milking schedule, no exception.

• **Separation at night.** A better option for homesteaders is to just separate the calf or kids at night, and milk only in the morning. This is far less work for you, as well as healthier for both mother and baby. The animal gets to raise her baby herself; you don't have to worry about bottle feeding; and your milking schedule is easier since you only have to milk once day and can even skip a milking if you leave them together for the night.

Your first milking attempt

Okay, the day (or night) has come when it's time to put the calf or kid in a separate pen. I recommend starting when the baby is seven to fourteen days old.

The easiest way to get the calf in the pen is to lure the cow or goat inside with some grain, and the baby will follow. Have another person restrain the baby while you shove the mother back out, and lock the gate.

When you build your calf pen and milking stall, put them side by side. This will be calming for both cow and calf. The calf pen should allow the calves to be visible and "smellable" to the cow, but not "nursable." The animals should be able to touch noses but the baby should not be able to reach the mother's udder.

Don't be misled by the idea that if the baby is "out of sight, out of mind," then the mother will settle down quicker. Trust me, it doesn't work that way. The mother will go crazy looking for her baby if you've built the calf pen any distance away. If you put the calf or kid pen where the mother can sniff her baby, she'll be annoyed at the separation but not frantic.

Get ready for incredible noise the first night the baby is separated from its mother. The baby will bleat and cry. The mother will bellow or bleat like crazy. Any other animals in the vicinity will bellow in sympathy. It will sound like Jurassic Park in the barn.

The next morning, with trembling heart, you will go to the barn to milk your cow. Remember, *this will not go smoothly.* Indeed, it may be so frustrating that you're tempted to give up. Don't.

The mother, having bellowed all night, will be in a bad mood. She will also be uncomfortable because her udder is full (plus she hates being separated from her baby). So when you first put her in the milking stall and stanchion and actually have the audacity to touch her udder, she'll kick and swipe and thunder around. Don't be intimidated by the mother's restlessness and attempts to escape. Just let her thrash it out — and *don't,* under any circumstances, let her out before *you're* ready. Otherwise the cow or goat will learn that if she acts obnoxious, you'll get frustrated and let her loose. Bad lesson for a dairy animal to learn. You'll be lucky to get three ounces of milk this first day. Don't worry, things will get better.

And — no matter how much your animal thrashes and kicks — never, *ever* hit her. Believe me, the tempta-

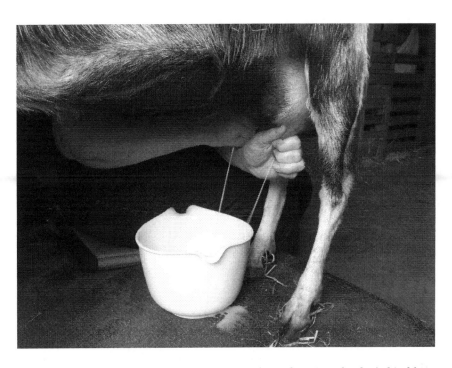

Susan milks from the side, with her left wrist braced against the doe's hind leg to keep her from kicking. Couldn't do that with a cow!

tion to punch your cow or goat when she's misbehaving can be overwhelming. Resist. You never want your dairy animal to associate anything negative while she's in the milking stall.

When you're ready to release her, immediately reward the mother by letting her baby out of the pen.

Within a week, this arrangement will start to become habit. The calves or kids will learn to file into their pen in the evening. The cow or goat will start to voluntarily go into the stanchion or milking stall in the morning. Fortunately since livestock are creatures of habit, once you establish a milking routine, the animals will fall into it as part of their daily schedule. Peace will reign once again.

Lactation

It may seem self-evident, but a cow (or goat) can't lactate until she's had a baby. And a cow can't have a calf without the cooperation of a male (or male-replacement; that is, artificial insemination).

If you have the room and the inclination to keep a bull or a buck, it's best to keep them confined separately within fences from which they can't escape. I know from experience that a bull who is determined to reach a cow in heat will barrel through gates, fences, and any other obstacle to reach his lady-love. Therefore make your fence construction as sturdy and escape-proof as possible.

Most beginners find it easier to employ the services of an obliging bull or buck belonging to someone else. Sometimes you can leave your animal at the breeder's farm and pay room and board as well as a service fee; other times the owner of a bull or buck can bring the animal to your farm and leave it there for a number of weeks. It's common to leave the cow or doe exposed to the male for two heat cycles. Cows and goats cycle about every three weeks; therefore a four-week exposure to a male usually ensures pregnancy.

Alternately, the use of artificial insemination (AI) is common. This allows you to choose the specific qualities of the male to introduce improvements to your herd. The diffi-

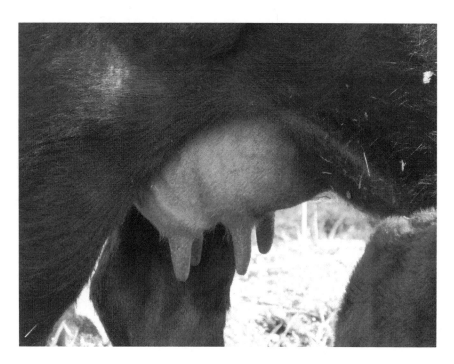

Jersey/Dexter cross, three years old, second calving, recently freshened. Note the even floor (all four teats same length) and tight udder attachment.

How to milk

Before and after every milking, the udder should be washed. While there are special "udder washes" on the market, a basin of warm water may be all that's necessary. Udders can become very dirty with caked on mud and manure, so washing is essential. It also minimizes undesirable material from falling into the milk.

Washing also stimulates the animal to "let down" her milk. Some people recommend waiting about a minute after the udder is washed to give the milk a chance to let down.

Before you start milking, give each teat a good squeeze or two into a dedicated cup. Besides eliminating the fore-milk (which may have some bacteria from being so close to the teat opening), examining the first couple of squirts for signs of mastitis is a good idea (more on mastitis later).

To milk, don't *pull* on a teat. *Squeeze.* Squeeze from the top down. I clamp the top of the teat between my thumb and first finger, then apply pressure in a downward cycle through the rest of my fingers until the milk trapped in the teat is squeezed out. Don't be afraid to squeeze hard, but be careful of *pulling.* Depending on your strength, yanking and pulling on a teat can damage tissues.

You want to squeeze in a downward motion rather than compressing all your fingers at once, which might force the milk *upward* back into the udder.

The old joke says that some of the teats give chocolate milk, others give vanilla. This actually isn't too far from the truth: the first milk coming out of the udder is skim milk; the hind milk, coming out as the udder is going dry, is pure cream. So milk the udder as dry as you can, and your milk will be richer. Obviously this won't happen the first day, when you're still learning.

Milking techniques can never be adequately described; you literally

cult thing is timing the arrival of the technician to perform the AI. Some animals have obvious heat cycles; some animals are more subtle; and it's not always easy to tell when an animal is ready to be bred. You also need to have an AI technician on call and within close driving distance to AI the cow or goat at the optimal time. We've had spotty success with AI, though other people are luckier. Until you're more experienced in watching for signs of heat in your dairy animal, it might be easier to have your animal exposed to a male.

After giving birth, a mammal produces a special milk for the baby called colostrum, which contains many critical nutrients and antibodies, and offers immunizing benefits for the calf or kid. If possible, the baby should be allowed to nurse freely for at least four days, as that is the window of nutritional opportunity to give it the best start in life.

After the first four days or so, the cow's or doe's lactation begins to stabilize in response to the baby's needs.

At this point it's fine to start milking your animal. She will gradually increase her output to accommodate not only the needs of her baby, but the needs of *you* as well.

Keep in mind that dairy animals have a lactation cycle. They do not flawlessly and uniformly produce the same quantity of milk, day after day, week after week. Rather, their milk production adjusts to demand — the needs of their baby as well as whatever you take. The amount of milk also varies from day to day depending on the amount and quality of feed, the health of the animal, and whether or not they're in their heat cycles.

The lactation cycle runs as a bell curve, peaking when the baby is about a month old and gradually decreasing until such time as the calf is weaned. Many farmers like to breed back their animals so they calve or kid about once a year, at about the same time.

A cow's gestation is about nine months and ten days. A goat's gestation is about five months (150 days).

need to learn it on the job. Everyone milks just a bit differently, so learn as you go with whatever works for you and for your dairy animal. Your milking technique will vary according to the size of the animal's teats, your hand size, and your hand strength.

After milking, it is often helpful to apply a thin coating of Bag Balm or Udder Butter or other brand of lotion in order to minimize the chances of chapping or discomfort for the cow or goat. Just remember the baby will be coming in behind you and drinking his breakfast, so don't put on such a thick coat that he gets a mouthful of lotion instead of a mouthful of milk.

As soon as you've finished milking your cow or goat, release her from the milking area and reward her by letting her rejoin her baby.

Depending on the schedule you adopt, you can usually skip an evening milking and just keep the baby on the mother all day; then separate the baby at night and milk only in the morning. Alternately you can milk in the evening as well, but expect less milk since you've been sharing it all day with the baby.

There's a rumor that animals must be milked at 4 am or some such nonsense. This is true on a commercial dairy where there are dozens or hundreds of animals to milk. But on a homestead, you can set your own schedule. If you milk twice a day, choose times that are roughly twelve hours apart. If you're an early riser, milk at 6 or 7 am and then again in the evening. If you're a night owl, milk at 10 am and 10 pm. Your choice.

Alternately, if you milk just once a day, pick your time. The only stipulation is to keep that time approximately the same each day. Livestock thrive on routine, so it's best to keep up a schedule.

One additional note: cows and goats have a strict hierarchy within a herd. Milk the dominant animal first.

Milking options

Obviously on most homesteads, milking will be done by hand. You will develop an impressively strong grip as a result. I've learned to "back down" my handshake lest I crush the other person's hand.

Hand-milking offers a number of advantages. You are up close and personal with your cow or goat, and can more easily become more aware of any problems; hand-milking is gentle on the udder; and there is something warm and elemental about hand-milking that makes you feel very connected with your animal.

But unquestionably it takes time, and if you have a hard milker it can take a toll on your hands and forearms. My first Jersey cow came to me off a commercial dairy with scabs and mastitis, as well as a three-times-a-day milking schedule. Milking her was so rough that I developed carpel tunnel syndrome and had to wear braces on my forearms for a few months. Fortunately as her udder healed, so did my arms.

For those who can afford it, milking machines are an option. These are available in single units that balance on the animal's back, strap around her belly, and the units plug onto the teats. The advantage is that the animal is milked in mere minutes. But the disadvantages are enormous: cost, noise (they are *very* noisy!), and cleaning. In fact, you lose absolutely every advantage in terms if time-savings by the amount of time it takes to properly clean a milking machine. Therefore milking machines are usually only recommended for those who have many animals to milk.

An excellent compromise for those who have physical difficulties (such as arthritis or carpel tunnel syndrome) is an EZ Milker (www.udderlyez.com) which is a hand-held trigger-operated vacuum pump which operates on the same principle as a milking machine but without the noise. Once the cup is fitted over the teat, the user gives a few pumps of the handle (which looks like the apparatus on a spray bottle) and the suction forms. This draws the milk out into either an attached pint or quart bottle. An EZ Milker has a secondary benefit in that it keeps the milk very clean when compared to an open bucket.

Purebred Jersey cow, approximately 10 years old. Note the pendulous udder with stretched ligaments and poor attachment.

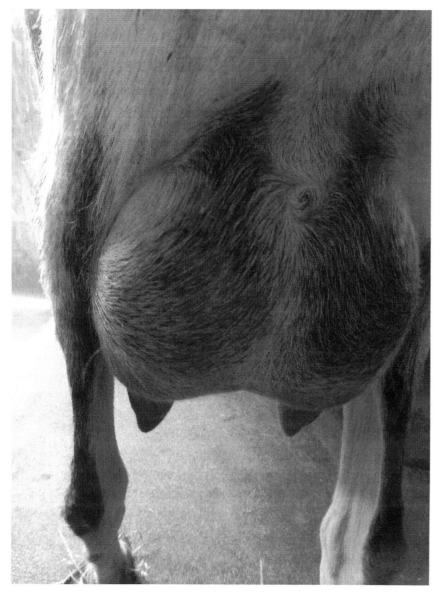

Look at this beautiful goat udder! Two teats, not four (like a cow).

Keep it clean!

Speaking of clean, your home dairy must be as clean and sterile as possible. This means a clean animal, clean milking conditions, clean equipment, and clean processing. Clean clean clean!

Livestock and barns are dirty under even the best conditions, so to the best of your ability you'll have to form your own little bubble of cleanliness. The biggest issue is keeping the milk itself clean. When it comes out of the udder, it's sterile; after that, it's up to you how clean it stays.

Stainless steel buckets and other equipment is easiest to sanitize and will last practically forever (though the initial cost is high). Seamless buckets are recommended because otherwise milk can get caught in the seams and breed bacteria.

Processing the milk

So what do you do with your bucketful of milk? Unless you're using a milking machine or milking directly into a bottle with an EZ Milker, your next step is to strain it. Straining removes any large impurities such as bits of hay or dirt.

There are commercial strainers available, which are simply disposable paper filters that fit into a funnel-shaped strainer. Or you can cobble together your own system using a colander lined with cheesecloth or muslin (wash the cloth after every use, and rinse in boiling water).

The whole idea of straining is simply to remove the impurities that fell into the milk. The milk should then be chilled.

Cow's milk separates quite easily into skim milk and cream. If you leave it in the refrigerator for any length of time, you'll notice the cream start to rise. Give it at least 12 undisturbed hours and you'll have most of the cream at the top. This can be skimmed off using a ladle or even a turkey baster. Cows without calves on them give more cream. Cows with nursing calves give less cream.

Goat's milk is naturally homogenized and won't separate easily. If you want goat cream, you'll need a cream separator (which also works for cow or any other kind of milk) which separates the heavy cream from the lighter milk through centripetal force. Cream separators come in either hand-cranked or electric varieties and are fairly expensive (several hundred dollars) but a worthwhile investment if you're serious about obtaining goat cream. I've seen many old-fashioned cream separators in antique stores sold as ornamental decorations, but be wary of buying these for farm use since certain critical internal parts may be missing.

The milk you get from your dairy animal has endless uses. From our cow's milk, I've made cheese (cream cheese, cheddar, and mozzarella are my specialties), butter, yogurt, whipped cream, ice cream, and of course plain drinking milk. Extra milk can also be used to raise other farm animals, including pigs.

Should you pasteurize your milk? Most people already have pre-determined opinions on this subject (see *BHM* article *Pasteurizing milk*, Issue #123, May/June, 2010), so I'll leave that decision up to you. In a nutshell, you may wish to pasteurize if someone in your family has a compromised immune system, you lack the means to adequately refrigerate your milk, or if you're not confident that your milk-handling equipment or facilities are the cleanest they could be. Otherwise unpasteurized milk should be fine.

If you decide to pasteurize, there are two methods of pasteurization: fast (flash) and slow. Both require the use of a double boiler (a two-gallon pot nested inside a three-gallon pot works fine) with a lid to put over the upper pot.

In the flash method, heat the milk to 161° F and hold that temperature for 15 to 20 seconds, then cool. Don't go above 161° F or the milk will taste cooked.

In the slow method, milk is heated between 140 and 150° F and held for 30 minutes.

In both methods, rapid cooling is essential. Set the pot in ice water (replacing the ice when necessary) and stir the milk constantly until the temperature reaches 60° F, then stir occasionally until the temp reaches 50° F. A sterile stainless steel spoon is recommended.

You can purchase milk pasteurizers for your home dairy. Prices range from $300 to $500. The advantage of a commercially-manufactured pasteurizer is obvious (consistent results). So is the disadvantage (price).

Remember the ultimate rule of thumb when it comes to handling and processing your milk: clean *clean CLEAN*. Sloppy milk handling can result in unpleasant taste or even dangerous contamination. Be safe, be clean.

Animal health

There are a certain number of diseases to which cows and goats are prone and for which there are a number of recommended steps.

While most of the health issues dairy animals face are a result of overcrowded conditions on commercial dairies, this doesn't excuse the home dairyist from taking care of his animals. Healthy animals mean healthy milk. Sick animals not only means the milk is questionable, but sick animals can spread illness through your herd.

I recommend a discussion with your local farm vet about a recommended vaccination course. Most dairyists want to vaccinate at least for Bang's disease (also called Brucellosis) and tuberculosis (in cows) and coccidiosis and clostridium (in goats). Others want the full course of vaccinations (often multiple vaccinations are combined into a single injection) which include IBR, PI3, BVD, BRSV virus, clostridial vaccine, Brucellosis vaccine, and leptospirosis.

Guidelines vary according to species (cows vs. goats), the age of your animal, and from state to state. Vaccinations are usually required to transport an animal over state lines.

Johne's disease, sometimes called paratuberculosis, is a fatal gastrointestinal disease which typically infects young ruminants and may not manifest itself for many months or even years. Symptoms start to occur when an animal becomes emaciated and often has diarrhea. In an infected animal, Johne's disease interferes with nutritional absorption — in effect the animal starves despite having a good appetite and eating well. Because of the prevalence of diarrhea, Johne's disease is highly contagious in a herd environment.

Since Johne's disease resists a cure (adult animals with Johne's disease must often be slaughtered), the best way to prevent an outbreak is *not* to introduce an infected animal into your herd (have the animal tested first). Additionally, newborn animals should be kept in as clean an environment as possible.

Johne's disease may be a widespread, if hushed-up, problem in commercial dairies where control is difficult. For the home dairyist, it's best to be vigilant about the conditions and circumstances under which Johne's disease can be introduced.

Worming your dairy animal is also recommended once a year. As animals graze, it's not uncommon for them to ingest parasites. A yearly worming helps keep them healthy. Worming can be done with a dewormer that can be added to grain, or a pour-on variety that is applied to the backs of the animals and absorbed through the skin.

In some areas, fly control is recommended. This can be accomplished by pouring fly control powder into cheesecloth and tying it up as a bag, then dangling the bag where the animals will brush against it.

For healthy babies, the very best thing you can do is ensure they get colostrum milk. You can do this by either keeping the baby on the mother for at least four days; or, if you remove the baby immediately, then collect the cow's or goat's colostrum milk immediately for the first four days of lactation, and feed this to the calf or kids.

Keep an eye on your animals' hooves. Elongated hooves are painful and ugly. If you're not able to trim the hooves yourselves, there are hoof trimmers who can come to your farm and do the job.

Most people recommend dehorning dairy animals when they're babies. We use dehorning paste under very careful conditions (see *BHM* article *Dehorning with dehorning paste*, Issue #128, March/April 2011); others burn the horn buds while very young. Dehorned animals are less likely to hurt you or each other.

For a peaceful farm, it is highly recommended that you castrate baby males who will not be used for breeding. This is accomplished very easily with banding. You can band a young calf or kid within a week of birth (once the testicles have descended).

A special note on mastitis

Mastitis is a bacterial infection of the udder tissue, detectible through the milk. Early stages of mastitis can be detected on special sensitive cards, something like pH paper (a drop of milk will turn the card one color if the milk is clean, another color if mastitis is detected). In the medium-early stages, the milk has little white gelatinous squiggles or ropes in it. If you're hand-milking, you can feel the squiggles coming out of the teat as well.

Mastitis is a condition that *must* be addressed immediately. Untreated and in its worst stages, mastitis can cause systematic blood poisoning and bring a cow or goat near death. Even with aggressive treatment, an animal's milking productivity can drop to nothing. A bad case of mastitis killed a quarter of the udder on one of my Jerseys.

Whatever you do, *do not drink milk with mastitis.* The milk should be discarded in a place where other animals won't be exposed to it (in other words, don't just pour it on the barn floor). Better to pour it down a sink drain. *Wash your hands thoroughly* before handling another animal, or even another teat on an infected animal, so the infection doesn't spread. You may also want to keep the infected animal quarantined from other livestock.

For early stages of mastitis, one of the best things you can do is keep the baby on the mother. The constant nursing flushes the system and may be all that's needed to clear it up.

But you need to keep checking your animal to monitor the situation, especially if there is no nursing baby. If the milk begins to turn dark, the infection is spreading. Consult with a vet and be prepared to give intramammary injections of antibiotics (this means inserting a narrow syringe into the mammary teat and injecting an antibiotic treatment).

In more advanced cases, intramuscular antibiotic treatments are required. In even more advanced cases, the teat will die. Been there, done that.

To go back to the beginning — if you notice white gelatinous squiggles or ropes in your animal's milk, cease drinking the milk and milk the animal out into a bucket dedicated to her. Mastitis usually affects one quarter at a time, and your job is to keep it from spreading to the other quarters. (Milk from unaffected quarters is safe to drink.)

Mastitis is most prevalent in animals that don't have nursing babies, because constant nursing is what keeps the udder healthy and flushed. The worst case of mastitis I've ever dealt with came from a cow we bought off a commercial dairy who had no calf on her. A year later, when this cow had a new calf, mild mastitis appeared briefly and was gone almost immediately thanks to the calf's healthy nursing.

For an infected animal that doesn't have a nursing baby on her, you'll need to milk her many times during the day — three, four, five times. The most important thing is to keep her system flushed.

Your home dairy

If you're interested in getting a dairy animal, the very best thing you can do is just grit your teeth and take the plunge. An enormous amount of knowledge of dairy animals comes from on-the-job training, and the best way to get that training is, well, on the job.

I do recommend having your infrastructure (particularly fencing) in place first; but after that, follow the Nike slogan and Just Do It. In very short order, you'll find yourself madly in love with your dairy animals and wondering why you were ever nervous about delving into home dairying in the first place.

Milking a dairy animal is one of the most elemental homestead chores there is, a process that truly brings you close to your food source. It offers greater independence from the commercial food industry and teaches self-sufficiency and an appreciation for early farmers.

So go ahead. Milk a goat or a cow. You'll be glad you did.

Patrice Lewis and her husband homestead 20 acres in north Idaho. Visit her blog at www.rural-revolution.com

The author wishes to thank Susan Sotin of St. Maries, Idaho for generously sharing her knowledge of dairy goats. Δ

Harvesting the Wild

Harvesting the Wild
gathering & using food from nature

A self-reliance guide from Backwoods Home Magazine

- *Clover*
- *Greens*
- *Asparagus*
- *Flower buds*
- *Raspberries*
- *Blueberries*
- *Wild garlic*
- *Plantain*
- *Cactus*
- *Birch syrup*
- *Acorns*
- *Hazelnuts*
- *Mushrooms*
- *Wilderness wine*

Preparing for an Appleseed event

By Massad Ayoob

Getting ready for an Appleseed event? It won't hurt to brush up on the positions you'll be exposed to there. These include prone, kneeling, sitting, and, of course, standing. In rifle shooting, the standing position is known as "off-hand."

Not getting ready for an Appleseed? It still won't hurt to brush up on classic techniques of riflery.

The basics

If you have traditional "iron sights," you align them. With an open notch rear sight, that means the front sight's post is centered in the rear notch, both level on top, with an equal amount of light on either side. If you have aperture sights, also known as "peep sights," you look through the rear aperture which you will thereafter ignore, and center the front sight therein. *Voila* — you now have *sight alignment.* Simply superimpose that alignment over the exact place you want the bullet to go, and you will have *sight picture.* From here on, keep a hard primary visual focus on the *front sight* as you press the trigger.

If you use a red dot optic or a telescopic sight (and frankly, most do their best at Appleseed with the latter), it's even easier. You'll see the aiming dot or scope reticle in the same focal plane as the target through the front sight, and you just keep that aiming indicator on the spot you want to hit as you bring the trigger to the rear.

Now comes the hard part — the trigger. Sixty years of shooting have left me convinced that trigger control is the heart of the beast, the single most important factor in delivering an accurate shot. When the decision to fire has been made, the trigger must be brought straight back. I know some people suggest doing that in stages, but the top shots I've worked with and studied under do it in a sin-

Massad Ayoob

gle-stage movement. For the time frames you'll have for Appleseed shooting, you'll be able to do it relatively slowly. Bring it back smoothly, without interruption. Smoothness is the key. Fight the urge to break the shot when the wobbly sights are crossing dead center, *now!* It's almost sure to jerk the shot far from where you wanted it to land. Instead, let it wobble in the middle, and if the trigger "breaks" by surprise, the shot will hit in the middle, and you will be less displeased with its placement. You know how folks say "perfect is the enemy of good?" That's classically true here.

If the pull on your particular rifle is light and crisp, you may get your best results by placing the tip or the pad of your trigger finger at the center of the trigger. (The "pad" of the finger generally means the whorl of your fingerprint.) However, when I'm working with a service rifle that has a heavier trigger pull — most of my AR15s, any of my M1A rifles, my department issue Ruger Mini-14 .223 or M14 .308 — I place my index finger with the crease of the distal joint centered

The conventional wisdom is to operate the trigger with the pad of the index finger, but if your gun has a heavy trigger pull, contacting at the distal joint of your trigger finger, as shown, will give you more leverage for a smooth, straight-back pull.

on the trigger. Old-time revolver shooters called this placement the "power crease" because it's where the human index finger has the most leverage to exert the most strength. Leverage is power, power is control, and control is what you need for a precision shot. No one technique delivers the best results for every shooter with every firearm.

Position shooting

As the name implies, this discipline involves shooting from various positions. Center of balance comes into it, and that varies a bit from person to person. The "gal" with her higher pelvis and shorter torso than her "guy" twin brother may not shoot from exactly the same stance as he does, even if they're the same height. Body flexibility, individual range of movement, and existing injuries or medical conditions are among the elements which must be taken into account here. I know some shooters who can manage a good kneeling position but have back issues which make the sitting position excruciatingly painful. On the flip side, I can introduce you to shooters with knee problems who find the kneeling position to be pure agony, but are perfectly comfortable firing from the sitting position.

A look up and down the firing line at an Appleseed event — or at the National Championships in Camp Perry, Ohio, or an informal match at your local gun club — will often show that no two shooters interpret a given stance exactly the same. The point is, it's not about being a clone of the club champion, it's about finding the interpretation of a given stance that works best for *you*. (I bet your club champion will be happy to help you find that right-for-you position, though!)

Let's look at some of the positions you'll be expected to shoot from if you attend an Appleseed. Most of them will be of some use to you, somewhere, whether you are competing, harvesting game, or performing pest control as part of your ranch or farm duties.

Offhand (standing)

Offhand is generally recognized to be the most difficult of positions because you're "standing on your hind legs." Your center of gravity is the highest and the wobbliest it's ever going to be, unless you ever have to take a shot from atop a stepladder.

Let's start from the bottom up. The soles and heels of both feet need to be flat on the ground. Going up on the ball of one foot will be wobbly, and will result in muscle tension and tremor. You need a good foundation, so the feet should be at least shoulder-width apart. With a particularly heavy rifle, you might want them a little wider apart than that to compensate for the outboard weight of the firearm.

Author in "precision shooting" offhand position. Shoulders are back. Note near straight line from forward heel, up leg, to support hand under floorplate of magazine of this Springfield Armory M1A SOCOM 7.62mm rifle.

Before we go any further, we need to distinguish between an "action shooting" stance and a "precision shooting" stance. "Action shooting" takes many forms: the rabid dog charging at you, the moving target, or multiple targets which must be engaged rapidly. This means high-speed shooting, which in turn demands very rapid recoil recovery and getting the sights back on target as soon as possible. To achieve this efficiently, the body has to be aggressively forward. I would want my forward knee sharply bent, my rear knee slightly bent as my rear foot digs into the ground to drive my total body weight hard in the direction of the gun and the target.

One tailors the tool to the task, and remember that in shooting, *the stance is one of your tools*. If I'm preparing for an Appleseed, I'll set those action shooting positions aside and concentrate on "precision shooting" techniques. The coiled muscles of the action shooting stances that I'd use in a three-gun speed match, a police patrol rifle qualification, or actual combat are good for rapidly engaging targets the size of a broadside deer's shoulder or the middle of a man's chest, but they aren't steady enough to guarantee hitting a bottlecap at 25 paces.

In the offhand stage of an Appleseed, that's exactly the target. The tie-breaking, maximum point "V-ring" is about the size of the cap off a bottle of soda. To nail it reliably, you want a dead-steady "precision shooting" stance. Appleseed will give you enough time that you don't need the aggressive "action shooting" posture designed for extreme rapid fire.

In the precision shooting offhand stance, it's the skeletal support structure that's doing the work, not the musculature of your body. So, moving up from the feet, the legs won't be consciously flexed, nor will they be exerting any conscious muscular "drive" in any direction. That said,

This is the version of kneeling that currently works best for Mas. Elbow is ahead of knee, not directly on it. Seen from front, there would be a straight line of skeletal support from forward heel up through leg and arm to rifle. Curled down firing thumb and trigger finger at distal joint, give maximum leverage against service rifle trigger pull weight with this AR15.

though, you don't want to consciously, rigidly lock them because that could induce muscle tremor. The easiest way I've found to do it is to conjure the advice of my late mother (and probably your mom, too): "Stand up straight." Seriously, that's all you need.

For precision rifle shooting, marksmen learned back in the distant mists of time to do something they'd never do in rapid fire: lean back *away* from the gun a little bit. If there's any likelihood at all that you'll need a very fast follow-up shot, this isn't a great idea, because it causes an exaggerated rise of the muzzle and takes longer for you to get back on target to fire again. However, if you have plenty of time, and precise accuracy is of the utmost importance — both of which are true at Appleseed — it will get you the best hits.

The reason is that skeletal support factor. You're holding a rifle out in front of you that weighs somewhere between six and ten (or more) pounds. It pulls the body forward.

Cantilevering the shooter's shoulders back invokes a magic thing in shooting: *balance*! Now, the recoil is going to rock you slightly out of balance in that position, which is why recoil recovery is so poor from that stance. But, from when the crosshairs or the front sight settle on the center of the target to when your shot breaks, that slight rearward lean of the shoulders can help you balance to a near-perfect steadiness.

The support arm's position is critical here. Most hunters will grasp the fore-end of their rifle about midway out. Most casual target shooters, or "plinkers," will do the same. Your action shooter may grasp the upper part of the magazine of his AR15, or may extend his arm *way* out there on the fore-end like a pointed finger, to "drive" the gun rapidly between multiple horizontally-arrayed targets that are wide apart from one another.

You won't be doing that kind of shooting at Appleseed. You'll be doing your best to fire one steady, perfect shot after another, with suffi-

Sitting position is fungible based on multiple interfacing aspects between specific rifle and specific shooter. Here, Mas has feet wide apart, heels dug into ground...

...and here, feet are crossed under shooter, which allows upper body to come more forward into the EoTech-sighted AR15. Use what works for YOU, says Mas.

cient time allotted to allow for recoil recovery. And to keep everything steady, you want to bring your upper arm against your body, your humerus (upper arm bone) perpendicular to the ground and parallel to your rib cage. My own felt index is triceps against outer edge of pectoral muscle.

The ideal is to get the forearm straight up and down too, and in line with that forward leg your upper body is leaning back away from. This puts a straight line from the foot, up the

long bones of the leg, through the hips, and into that support arm and the torso to which it is attached. Riflemen figured out a long time ago that with nothing else like a tree or a fence to brace the rifle on, this would give you the most solid skeleton-muscular support that the human body can deliver in a standing position.

Forward hand placement depends on the shooter and on the configuration of the rifle. If the magazine extends from the bottom of the gun to

a suitable length, the palm of the support hand can become a rest for the floorplate of the magazine, and it's dead stable. Back in my early twenties, when I shot in NRA High Power Rifle competitions with .30 caliber National Match semiautomatics furnished by the New Hampshire State Rifle and Pistol Association, I practically groveled in gratitude when I had a chance to swap my issue M1 Garand for an M14. The latter's 20-round magazine allowed me to use that hold, and it made it much easier for me in the offhand position.

If you don't have a protruding magazine, you have other options. I've seen some fine scores fired by shooters who rested the rifles on the extended fingertips of the support hand. I've seen them rest on the palm with fingers pointed toward the muzzle, and with the hand bent back so the fingers of the shooter's left hand were to the left of the rifle in front of the trigger guard. It's a classic case of "different strokes for different folks."

I learned early the classic posture of the firing hand's elbow being extended out, shoulder-high or higher, to create a "shoulder pocket" for the rifle butt between the pectoralis and the deltoid muscles. This is important with harder kicking guns, and it's the way I shoot a .30-06 Garand or a .308 M14 or M1A to this day. The well-defined shoulder pocket keeps the butt from skidding off the deltoid muscle and into that tender plexus between the deltoid and the bicep, which not only hurts but destroys shot-to-shot consistency, requiring you to almost "re-shoulder" the rifle between shots. With a light-kicking gun — a .223 caliber AR15 or the .22 rimfire that's so popular at Appleseed — the high elbow creating the shoulder pocket is less important. (When you try the high elbow/shoulder pocket, you'll notice that the gun butt is right at the collarbone. The high elbow pulls the pectoral muscle up over the bone to shield it. For some people, however, it doesn't shield it enough to take discomfort away. That's something to find out for yourself, in slow fire, with a moderately-powered rifle.)

Kneeling and sitting

The military and the NRA have traditionally taught kneeling and sitting as totally separate techniques. Appleseed gives you the choice of the two. Either is more stable by far than offhand, because they not only lower your center of gravity, but they also take you off those stilt-like standing legs and settle you into a tripodal base.

In the kneeling position, the three points of the tripod are forward foot (whose knee is up), rear leg knee, which is on the ground, and rear foot. If you are flexible enough to sit on your rear foot, you'll be that much more stable.

The key thing is how you're going to use the forward leg to brace the forward arm. Intuition will tell you to put your elbow on your kneecap, but your intuition is lying to you. Round knobby joint on round knobby joint equals wobble. Your top rifle shooters get the back edge of their upper arm just above the elbow a tad ahead of that flexed patella, and things are less likely to slip. Picture your kneeling position from a target's eye view: is the heel in line with the tibia and fibula of the lower leg and the knee? *Good.* Is the forward support arm's forearm in line with all of those? *Good.* You have a straight line of solid skeletal support.

It would be ideal if all of these bones could be straight up and down, perpendicular to the ground, but that's not always possible. We have to adjust for sloping ground between shooter and target, how high the targets might be, and how low the shooter's center of gravity can get. The leg may have to come a little back here, the forearm a little forward there.

Prone position. Note forearms vertical as much as possible, gun-side knee pulled up to help stabilize rest of body in position. Note that pistol on belt is pointed backward here on the practice range, which is why it's not allowed at Appleseed.

In the sitting position, the three points of tripodal contact are your buttocks and each of your feet. This is a *highly* interpretive position. In my younger days, I crossed my ankles because it gave me maximum support and allowed me to lean into the gun, which I always liked. Now, deep into my sixties, I'm not flexible enough to comfortably do that anymore; I have better luck these days putting my feet wide apart. Elbows ahead of knees worked for me as a young rifleman with ankles crossed; today, the best stability my aging body can give me is feet apart with the elbows on the inner thigh side of my knees. Try every variation you can think of.

Author's preferred prone position, using bottom of magazine as "unipod" stabilized on ground, is NOT allowed in Appleseed events.

You'll find what works for *you*, and that's what's most important.

Prone

Ain't no more solid hand-held shootin' position than flat on your belly. If you have neck issues, though, it can be nigh unto impossible to get your head up to the sights. My friend, Dave Duffy, elected to use the sitting position instead of prone at Appleseed for this reason. (The tenor of the rules is, you're allowed to do something harder than the other competitors, but not something easier, and sitting is universally recognized as more difficult than prone.)

Try to find a position that rests your head on the stock as much as possible; it will alleviate at least some of the neck strain. If you're firing from your right shoulder, draw your right knee up tight and flexed (vice-versa for southpaws): it'll help with natural body support and reduce muscle strain. Both elbows should be in contact with the ground, of course, but a hint here: the more vertical instead of angled your forearms can be, the more stable a platform you'll generally have.

I'm a big advocate of the unipod or monopod technique, in which the bottom of a rifle's extended magazine touches the ground. It gives tremendous added stability and won't compromise the function of a good rifle with good magazines. Unfortunately, as I discovered after my first Rifleman score was disqualified at my first Appleseed, it's not allowed in that discipline. Only the physically handicapped will get a dispensation to shoot with artificial support such as this (a bipod, for example, or shooting sticks).

A few pointers

Bring double ear protection, a billed hat, and good eye protection. In the photos, I'm hatless because I'm demonstrating on my own range and don't have anyone else's ejected hot brass to worry about. You'll see powerful .30 caliber rifles on the range at Appleseed, and you don't want their burning hot brass landing between your necessary safety glasses and your eyeballs. Hence, the billed cap. The hot brass generally comes from the other guy's rifle, not yours. Wear plugs *and* muffs if you're anywhere near someone with a high-power rifle, and not just on the .22 side of the firing line. A significant amount of the sound waves that cause the high range nerve deafness we colloquially call "shooter's ear" come through the mastoid bone; plugs don't protect against that, but muffs do. At the same time, the stems of those necessary protective glasses can break the seal of the muffs at a critical juncture; plugs give good backup.

In the photos, taken on my own range for illustration purposes, I'm wearing a pistol. *Don't* do that at Appleseed; it's not allowed. As the photos here show, prone position leaves the holstered gun pointed at the audience behind you, and is therefore forbidden by the safety rules.

Listen to the instruction. Listen to the safety commands. Take it all seriously. Those dedicated Appleseed instructors are unpaid volunteers who came to teach you what they know for their love of the art and their sense of patriotism. They deserve your attention.

I hope the above pointers will be of help. They helped me to win my own Rifleman Patch my first time at an Appleseed, and they should work for you, too. Δ

A Backwoods Home Anthology
The Fourth Year

Build your own battery charging station

By Jeffrey Yago, P.E. CEM

Let me guess — the reason many of you do not use rechargeable batteries is that every time you need to recharge an electronic device you have to wait all day for it to recharge. Normally you replace batteries when you try to operate your remote control, digital camera, or flashlight and discover the batteries are dead. You need your device to work *now*, and that means throwing out the old batteries and putting in new ones so you can use the device immediately.

The solution is to always have rechargeable batteries ready to use that are fully charged and easy to locate, as it's just as easy to switch out dead batteries with new batteries as it is to replace rechargeable batteries that are out of power with another set that are fully recharged. New rechargeable battery technology allows recharging more than 1000 times — which means you may never have to purchase regular batteries again.

In addition, since the new types of rechargeable batteries can hold their charge for a year or more, you can now recharge spare batteries then store these for future use without worrying that they will have lost their charge by the time you actually need them.

Discarded button batteries containing mercury-oxide contribute to almost 90% of the mercury going into today's landfills, while dry cell batteries contribute to half of all cadmium and nickel found in our landfills. It is estimated the United States discards more than 3 billion dry cell batteries

Completed charging station after sanding and painting

each year, which is more than 35 AA, AAA, C, D, and 9-volt size batteries per family. While this may be a reasonable national average, I think for many homes with teenagers this number will actually be far higher.

To extend the life of disposable batteries, many manufacturers are switching to heavy metals in their battery construction such as nickel, cadmium, lead, mercury, and acid. If discarded in landfills, these potentially toxic materials can leach into our lakes or groundwater, or if incinerated can become harmful airborne ash.

Two years ago I decided that maybe it really was not a good idea to discard old batteries in the trash, and

decided to save up for proper disposal since they could contain unsafe materials that should not go into a landfill. I had a large pretzel jar available and wrote "Discarded Batteries" on the side. I placed this container next to the door of our office and after two years it was completely full.

I consider my list of battery-powered devices to be similar to most readers of this magazine, yet I never imagined I could have actually gone through so many batteries so quickly. I do have a flashlight in every vehicle, several AM/FM portable radios, and can't forget all those TV and appliance remote controls, digital cameras, and battery-powered games and tools.

213

I must admit my impression of rechargeable batteries was formed years ago when they would not hold a charge for long and did not provide the same run-time as regular batteries. I also did not like having to keep up with different battery chargers for each battery size, and did not like having to wait an entire day to recharge the batteries in a device I needed to operate *now*.

After seeing this jar full of discarded AAA, AA, C, D, and 9-volt size batteries, I decided there must be a better way. I discovered that today's rechargeable batteries are much more reliable than the earlier technology I remember, and there are now more types to pick from.

The secret of switching over to only rechargeable batteries is to have a central location in your home, garage, or business specifically for storing recently recharged batteries of various sizes, and having a single charger capable of charging multiple sizes of batteries at the same time. I also found that it is much easier to make the switch to rechargeable batteries cold turkey. In other words, switch all of your flashlights, portable radios, and remote controls from non-rechargeable to rechargeable batteries

This jar full of discarded batteries is typical for many households.

at the same time. This reduces the chance of accidently discarding an expensive rechargeable battery and replacing with a low-cost non-rechargeable battery because they do look alike.

This article includes very detailed instructions for building your own charging station using basic hand tools. I suggest first taking inventory of your battery-powered devices and identifying the most common battery sizes you use. Since rechargeable batteries are not cheap, this may be a good time to start buying replacement rechargeable batteries so you will be ready to use the battery charging station as soon as it's finished. In order to always have a fresh set of rechargeable batteries, you will need extras for each size you are using. For example, if you have two remote controls that each require two "AA" size batteries, you should purchase a minimum of eight AA rechargeable batteries (2 remote controls x 2 batteries x 2 sets = 8).

It is fairly easy to find stores that sell rechargeable AA and AAA batteries; these sizes are popular for digital cameras which are known to eat batteries due to their high energy demand. Other rechargeable battery sizes are harder to find, especially for the mid-sized C cell and rectangular 9-volt battery. I ended up ordering these hard-to-find rechargeable batteries over the Internet and found some great discounts for quantity orders, so I ordered eight each of the most common sizes I needed.

Since cell phones and tablet computers have built-in rechargeable batteries, they usually require their own special battery charger. However, in an effort to centralize all battery charging, I moved my cell phone chargers to the same charging location so there is no longer a scavenger hunt each day trying to find the correct charger that matches the device I am trying to recharge.

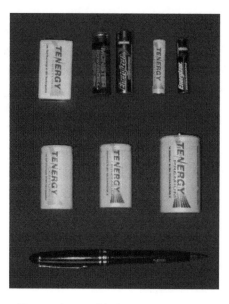

New rechargeable battery technology

Rechargeable battery technology

As mentioned in the introduction, today's rechargeable batteries are higher quality and have a much longer life than earlier designs. The most popular rechargeable batteries sold today are nickel-metal hydride (NiMH). The nickel-cadmium (NiCd) rechargeable battery is an older technology and is being replaced by the newer NiMH batteries. The NiMH battery technology will store two to three times more energy than the older NiCd technology and can be recharged more than 1000 times. There is also an updated version of the NiMH battery technology which has an extremely long self-discharge called LSD NiMH. These can hold 90% of their charge for up to a year and 75% of their charge for up to two years. Even without the LSD design feature, most rechargeable batteries will hold their full charge for at least six months.

The lithium-ion (Li-Ion) batteries typically found in today's cell phones, laptop computers, and portable power tools provide even more charge capacity while weighing less. However, most of these are either built into the device or are supplied with their own special charger that matches their unique shape and charging cycle requirements.

Battery charge capacity

When I started my conversion to all rechargeable batteries, I found a wide difference in charging capacity from one battery manufacturer to another. For example, the highest quality D cell rechargeable batteries from Sanyo have a 11,000 milliamp-hour (mAh) rating, while some cheaper rechargeable batteries were found to be in the low 8,000 mAh range. While less expensive, this 28% lower charge capacity would translate into a similar drop in device operating hours.

Since flashlight and digital camera-size batteries have a much smaller charge capacity than the amp-hour ratings used for comparing car batteries, a smaller scale milliamp-hour (mAh) rating is used, which is just amp-hours divided by 1000. A flashlight battery (D cell) with a 10,000 mAh rating will have twice the stored power of a similar-sized battery having a 5,000 mAh rating. Unfortunately, these ratings are not always easy to identify without reading the small print, so when you are shopping for rechargeable batteries, remember that the brand that costs half as much may also have half the recharge capacity.

There are some rechargeable battery brands and models that consistently out-perform all others. Professional photographers needing reliable flash performance, first responders needing life-saving portable 2-way radio communications, and field technicians needing reliable battery-powered test equipment soon learn which rechargeable batteries give the best service. Based on their recommendations and my experience, I have compiled my list of rechargeable batteries that are consistently rated highest for charge capacity and reliability. I am sure there are other brands equal or

Multi-size battery chargers

better than my list, so you can check their mAh rating against my Table ratings to see how they compare before making a purchase.

The following table compares some of the best rechargeable batteries I have found along with their corresponding capacity ratings. When shopping for rechargeable batteries, use these ratings as a benchmark.

One reason many people are getting away from the older NiCd battery technology is its "memory effect." If you try to recharge a NiCd battery when it still has some charge remaining, it will return to the discharge level you started from and will no longer provide power below this starting charge level. If you plan on using rechargeable NiCd batteries to save cost, you need

Table 1 - Rechargeable Battery Comparison		
Brand	**Size**	**Capacity**
AccuPower Evolution	D	12,000 (mAh)
Sanyo Eneloop	D	11,000
Maha Powerex	D	11,000
Tenergy Centura	D	8,000
Sanyo Eneloop	C	6,000
AccuPower Evolution	C	6,000
Maha Imedion	C	5,000
Tenergy Centura	C	5,000
Maha Powerex	C	5,000
AccuPower Mignon	AA	2,900
Sanyo Eneloop	AA	2,700
Maha Powerex	AA	2,700
AccuPower Evolution	AA	2,600
Tenergy Centura	AA	2,000
AccuPower Evolution	AAA	1,200
Maha Imedion	AAA	950
Tenergy Centura	AAA	800
Sanyo Eneloop	AAA	750
AccuPower Evolution	9 Volt	300
Sanyo Eneloop	9 Volt	300
Maha Imedion	9 Volt	200
Tenergy Centura	9 Volt	200

to make sure the battery charger has "smart charging" technology which can correct this problem.

High quality chargers can automatically tell which type of battery has been inserted and will first remove any remaining charge in an NiCd battery before starting a full charge cycle. The newer NiMH battery technology does not have this "memory effect" so your charger will fully recharge these batteries starting from any level of discharge. If you are testing batteries with a volt-meter or battery tester, keep in mind all nominal 1½ volt NiMH batteries will actually measure 1.2 volts, not 1.5 volts, when fully charged, and all nominal 9-volt NiMH batteries will actually measure 9.6 volts when at full charge.

If your budget allows, I strongly recommend using only nickel-metal hydride (NiMH) rechargeable batteries which can be recharged more than 1,000 times and do not have the memory effect problem of nickel-cadmium (NiCd) batteries.

You will also want to purchase a multipurpose battery charger that will automatically recognize which type of battery is inserted, determine its starting point charge level, and then stop charging when fully recharged. You also want a battery charger that can recharge any combination of AAA, AA, C, D, and 9-volt size batteries at the same time. The most common models will recharge four batteries at a time, while more expensive chargers are able to charge 8 to 16 batteries at a time.

I found several good quality battery chargers that were reasonably priced and had all the features I have described. The "AccuManager 20 Charger" by AccuPower costs $48 and has four charging slots plus two 9-volt battery spaces. The "Ansmann Deluxe Energy 8 Charger" has eight charging slots plus a really nice digital display that indicates the charge level of each battery individually, which I found online for $56. The

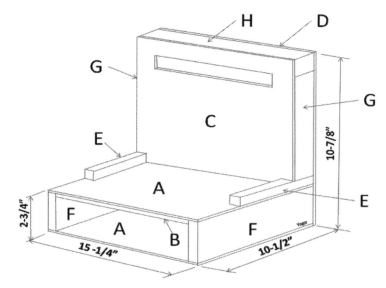

A	Drawer top and bottom	10½" x 15¼" x ⅛"
B	Drawer top brace	½" x 2" x 14¼"
C	Rear wall	15¼" x 7⅞" x ⅛"
D	Back	15¼" x 10⅞" x ⅛"
E	Deck brace (2)	1" x 1" x 7"
F	Drawer sides (2)	½" x 3" x 10½"
G	Rear wall side spacer (2)	1" x 1" x 6"
H	Rear wall top spacer	1" x 1" x 15¼"
I	Rear wall bottom spacer	1" x 1" x 13¼"

Maha Ultimate Professional Charger also has a nice digital display and space for 8 batteries. It has a slightly higher charging rate than the other lower-cost chargers and I found it online for $83.

The chargers for your cell phones, iPods, and pagers usually come with their own chargers so you will only need to relocate these chargers to your charging station.

Battery charger station

There are many advantages to doing all battery charging at a central location. For example, since all chargers will be together, you will no longer have to hunt all over for your cell phone or iPod charger. Since most battery chargers consume some electrical power even when not charging, by plugging all chargers into the same electrical strip outlet, it's easy to turn

all chargers off with one switch when not needed. Having a central battery charging station provides a good place to store extra rechargeable batteries that have been fully recharged and ready for immediate use.

Charging station construction

My goal was to make a charging station that was small and light enough to be portable when needed. All the materials including the plastic drawer were purchased at a local building supply for less than $30, not including the paint or stain you may select for a finish.

I purchased the thinner 1/8-inch cabinet plywood to make the wall sides, top, and bottom. I purchased a 4 foot length of ½ x 2-inch poplar for stiffeners, a three-foot length of 1 x 1-inch square poplar for the top

1. Organize materials needed.

2. Build bottom drawer assembly first.

3. Next, add side and rear bracing.

4. Attach rear wall bracing.

5. Frame in electrical strip.

and side spacers, and a 2-foot length of ½ x 3-inch poplar to frame in the drawer. The drawer is actually a 14-inch Plano ProLatch Stowaway Organizer with the top removed, which cost $4.97 and was also available where I purchased the wood materials. The electric strip outlet has six plugs, surge arrestor, and illuminated on/off switch and cost $13.97.

All materials were assembled with construction glue and a pneumatic finish nailer, although you could use small screws or finish nails. I installed the strip outlet before gluing on the back plate to give it a built-in look, and sanded all corners and joints before painting. Refer to the exploded drawing detail.

Closing comments

I made the entire charger station portable and purchased 12-volt car adapters for each charging device. Now if we have a power outage lasting days, I can relocate the charging station next to the generator or in whatever vehicle that is still operating. This allows me to recharge all my battery-powered devices during an extended power outage.

Finally I added a 12-watt fold-out solar module which provides a great way to power each charger during an extended power outage when fuel may not be available to operate a generator or vehicle. With a charging station that can be powered by the utility, a generator, a car 12-volt outlet, or solar module, you will no longer have to worry about power outages shutting down your cell phone or iPad, and will be able to keep your portable radio and several LED flashlights operating indefinitely.

Jeff Yago is a licensed professional engineer and certified energy manager with more than 30 years of experience in the energy conservation field. He has extensive solar photovoltaic and emergency preparedness experience, and has authored numerous articles and texts. His website is www.pvforyou.com. Δ

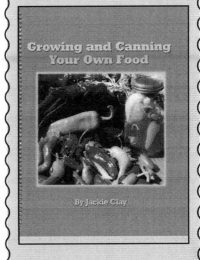

Consider sheep dairying

By Patrice Lewis

When you think of dairy animals, you usually think about cows and goats. But what about sheep?

Sheep have been milked for centuries, mostly in countries near the Mediterranean. France alone has nearly a million ewes in production. But in America, where sheep milk is far less common, there are fewer than 100 domestic sheep dairies. Yet we import millions of pounds of cheese made from sheep milk each year, which equals tens or hundreds of millions of dollars.

With the scarcity of dairy sheep facilities in America, I was delighted to learn of a sheep dairy in my immediate region. Homestead Farm (www.homesteadsheep.com) is run by John Cady, along with his business partner Shari Pratt and her husband Dale

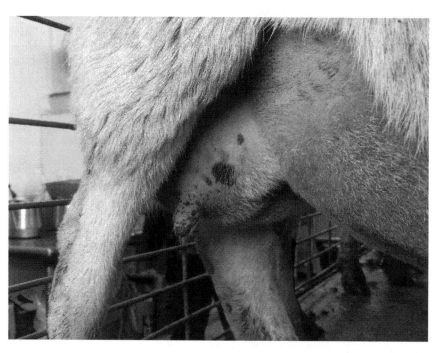

A sheep's udder is decent-sized relative to the size of the animal, but the teats are so small! How can you grab and milk a teat that size?

Like goats, sheep are most comfortable to milk on an elevated stand. (Pictured with sheep is John Cady.)

Pratt, who is a certified Master Cheesemaker. Homestead Farm is a family owned and operated artisan farm just outside of Worley, Idaho, and has perhaps the largest flock of milking Katahdin sheep in the Pacific Northwest.

Katahdin sheep is a breed that doesn't need shearing because they shed. In other words, they have fur (hair) instead of wool. This breed, in the words of Mr. Cady, "are disease resistant, parasite resistant, have fewer hoof problems, don't require shearing, and they have a brain."

A sheep's udder is decent-sized relative to the size of the animal, but because Katahdins are a meat breed, the teats are small. Homestead Farm is breeding for improved milking traits in Katahdins, including longer teats and greater milk production, to make them a true dual-purpose breed.

But in the meantime most of the ewes have small teats, and because Shari Pratt suffers from carpel tunnel syndrome, they use EZ Milkers to milk the ewes. The EZ Milkers also help keep the milk sterile. It also gives a precise measurement of how much milk each ewe gives, which helps in determining which animals to breed for future improvements to the flock.

Now here's the interesting thing about milking sheep: Unlike cows, where milk is measured in gallons; or goats, where milk is measured in quarts, sheep milk is measured in ounces. Which begs the question, why milk sheep?

The answer? Cheese!

While sheep milk is used in many products, the prince among them is cheese. Sheep milk cheese is considered a gourmet item and sells for anywhere from $35 to $90/lb. Now raising dairy sheep begins to make economic sense.

One gallon of milk makes about 1.4 pounds of cheese. One hundred pounds of milk makes approximately eight 2.5 pound wheels of cheese. On John Cady's farm, it takes about a week to get 100 pounds of milk.

The milk is frozen in food-grade plastic containers until they have enough to produce cheese. Freezing does not affect the milk's quality because the milk has such small fat molecules.

Using Dale Pratt's cheesemaking expertise, Homestead Farm produces Gouda, smoked Gouda (for which they harvest their own wood), Roquefort (blue cheese), ricotta, feta, etc. These cheeses sell for $35/lb. and up. They also make specialty custom cheese to order, such as habañeras, cumin, garlic/herb, horseradish, jalapeño, etc. These custom cheeses cost $65/pound and up. Soft cheeses such as ricotta have a limited shelf life and are therefore less costly; but hard cheeses like Gouda, which improve with age, are more expensive due to a limited supply.

Sheep's milk has small fat molecules which won't separate the cream from the milk, so making butter isn't possible without a culture. However sheep milk makes superb ice cream, yogurt, and of course fluid milk for fresh drinking. Milk can also be used for soap and skin-care products.

It takes half as much sheep milk to make cheese as it does cow or goat

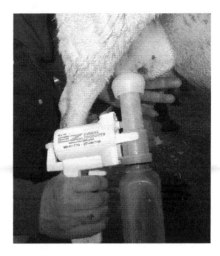

An EZ Milker is a handheld suction device that is pumped to create a vacuum to start the milk flowing. After a few pumps the milk runs out on its own.

milk. Sheep milk contains twice the calcium as cow milk. Domestic sheep average about 125 pounds of milk per lactation period (about 95 days). Unlike other kinds of milk, sheep milk can be frozen and retain its nutritional value. Many people who are allergic to other kinds of milk are more tolerant to sheep milk.

Homestead Farm also sells USDA cuts of meat. The meat from Katahdin sheep is much less "gamey" than Suffolk (the usual meat breed in the U.S.), so demand is high.

The most common dairy sheep breed is the East Friesian. This breed gives more milk but it has less fat. Katahdins give less milk but it's richer. "East Fresians are like Holsteins, Katahdins are like Jerseys," notes John Cady. "It depends on what you're looking for — quantity or richness."

As Homestead Farm demonstrates, dairy sheep have a valuable niche market for gourmet cheese, with a side benefit of filling the demand for meat. For those with the property and the interest in raising sheep, dairy sheep may be a valuable addition to a homestead. Δ

Sheep-milk cheese is considered a gourmet item and is sold in Costco for upwards of $40/pound.

Avoiding common canning mistakes

By Jackie Clay-Atkinson

Canning has been an important part of my life since I was a young girl helping my mother and grandmother can in our Detroit basement. I loved the smell of fresh peaches simmering in syrup and the pungent spices used for making pickles. I loved going out in the garden and picking fresh fruit, cucumbers, and tomatoes. I also loved our family weekend outings in the country, picking up boxes and baskets of foods to can from roadside markets and farmers' trucks.

In growing up with relatives who experienced the Depression, I soon realized what a wonderful thing it was to have a pantry chock-full of all sorts of foods to "see us by." Once properly canned and stored in the pantry, any food not eaten during the winter will remain good for years, without losing any of its gourmet taste or nutrition.

Ever since then, I've made home canning an important part of my quest for a self-reliant lifestyle. And, boy-oh-boy, have I canned a wide variety of foods! From pickles, jams, jellies, and preserves to venison, pork, beef, chicken, meals-in-a-jar, stews, soups, and nutmeats — I've canned them all.

I love teaching others about canning. For more information, check out my book, *Growing and Canning Your Own Food*, my "Ask Jackie" column in *BHM*, and my blog. I even host seminars here at our homestead.

Truthfully, I think everyone who is able should learn how to can. It is an easy, enjoyable, and frugal thing to do.

Throughout the years, I've found that there are certain common mistakes that folks (me included) have made. Over and over, I've heard "I did this and this, and then my food turned out bad." I really hate for this to happen because some people just chuck out the whole idea of canning right then and there. So, here are a few mistakes that home canners make and some advice on how to fix these mistakes.

The pressure canner blew up!

There's always a story floating around that someone's mother, aunt, or neighbor had a pressure canner that blew up in the kitchen, blowing food and glass everywhere. All I can say is, "Yeah, right…" I hear this all the time. It's the most frequently-given reason why folks don't want to try pressure canning.

Let me say here and now that it is nearly impossible for a modern pressure canner to blow up. Modern pressure canners (those built within the last 40 years or so) are equipped with

Always use a rack to prevent the jars from coming in contact with excessive heat from the burner. If you don't, the bottom of the jar may break out!

at least one fool-proof safety device — a petcock. The petcock releases steam and pressure when it gets over 15 pounds and has a hard rubber plug that pops out if the pressure gets too high. In addition, many canners, such as the All American, come with both a dial and weight. If the pressure gets too high, the weight jiggles and releases steam and pressure. No blowing up.

You do need to monitor your pressure canner while it is building pressure and during processing. Like a deep fryer, you don't just fill it and go in the other room or outside while it is doing its thing. (A long time ago, my oldest daughters decided to make French fries, so they put the potatoes in the deep fryer and went outside to sunbathe. Needless to say, they ended up having to call the fire department.) You need to monitor your canner's pressure — stay in the same room! If you want to ready another batch of food to can, that's perfectly fine. But check often to make sure the pressure isn't climbing past the pressure you are processing your food with.

As an added safety precaution, be sure to always check your petcock and steam vents before you can. Run a needle through them to make sure a bit of food hasn't blown out of a jar and gotten wedged in the vent. In the past, this is usually what blew up the old canners without safety features. The plugged vent let the steam pressure build up until the lid blew off. Again, with modern canners, this is *nearly* impossible.

The bottoms broke out of my jars

This commonly happens during water bath canning. The reason is simple: hot jars put into a cool canner or cool jars put into a boiling canner make the bottoms of the jars crack and break during processing. Always make sure your jars are hot and the canner a little below boiling before you put them together. You can hold

Be sure to put your hot, processed jars onto a folded, dry towel away from cool breezes. Setting hot jars onto a wet towel, on a bare countertop, or next to an open window can cause broken jars.

your jars in another canner full of boiling water or even hold them in a sink full of hot water so they stay reliably hot. Then pack them quickly and put them into a very warm canner. Even when pressure canning, I always take the time to heat my canner a bit so I'm not putting hot jars of food into a cold canner. By doing this simple step, I have no jar bottoms break during processing.

Another cause of broken jars is setting your jars of hot, processed food directly on a kitchen counter or table to cool. Setting them near an open window with a cool breeze blowing on them will also cause breakage. So will canning outdoors and putting the hot jars, right out of the canner, on a table in a windy area. Make sure there is no wind or breeze, and always set your hot jars on a clean, dry towel and they will cool safely … in one piece!

Tunking jars together while very hot can result in broken jars. The jars should also have enough space between them to create a good airflow. A good airflow results in a good seal.

Liquid blowing out of jars

Liquid blowing out of jars during canning can happen for a couple of reasons. The first and most common

reason is letting the pressure vary during processing. Let's say you are canning at 12 pounds pressure but it slips up to 15 pounds before you notice it. If you quickly turn off the heat and let it go to 12 pounds, then turn the heat back on a couple of times, this can cause liquid to blow out of the jars. It is better to slowly bring it back to the right pressure.

Opening the canner too soon after processing or bumping the weight a couple times to "hurry" things up will also cause liquid to blow out of the jars. Once the pressure goes back to zero after your batch of jars has processed fully, wait five minutes or so. Then release any steam and remove the lid of the canner. Don't try to save jars by over-packing food. Filling the jars past the recommended headspace will also cause liquid to blow out.

Although unsightly, the food in jars with a low liquid level is perfectly good to eat. A low liquid level does not affect the shelf life or the taste of the food.

My jars didn't seal

Having a couple of jars that don't seal in a big batch of canning is nothing to be concerned about. Reprocessing it is easy. Just reheat the food, check the jar rim for nicks or food particles, use a new, previously-

Cracks and nicks in the jar rim are a common cause of seal failures. Here, I'm checking each jar rim carefully with my finger. Be careful; sometimes nicks in the glass are sharp!

simmered lid, and re-process within 24 hours. Or, you can just refrigerate it and eat it.

However, if more than one or two jars fail to seal, there is a definite reason. And the most common reason is *not reading directions*. Canning is definitely not rocket science, but you do need to follow tested recipes and the directions for *every* food, *every* time you can it. Never rely on memory. Even with all my experience, I always open my canning book and read the directions before I can that particular food. It's a good habit to get into. And you'll have fewer failures along the way if you do.

One other thing we thought of that quite a few folks have done wrong, including my oldest son, Bill, is to begin counting the processing time in a water bath canner from the time they put the jars into the canner. This is *wrong* and can result in failed seals, mold, or fermenting foods. The time should always begin when the canner full of jars comes to a full rolling boil.

Examine every jar *before* you fill them to check for nicks or cracks in the rim of the jar. Always be sure to wipe the rim of your filled jars with a damp, clean cloth to remove any food bits or grease before putting on your lids. When they are done processing, do not wipe the jars and lids before they are cooled. If you have minerals in your water, your jars may have a whitish film on them after they come out of the canner. This film is nothing to worry about, but some folks take a towel and wipe it off before the jars have cooled. The lids will not seal properly if you do this. Wait until the jars have cooled completely, then you can take off the rings and wash the jars thoroughly under warm, soapy water with no ill effect.

When your batch of jars are through with their processing time, let the gauge return to zero or let the canner cool so there is no remaining steam if using a weight only. But do not leave the lid on the canner overnight and assume that the jars will seal just fine. Sometimes they appear to seal, but in storage, the seal releases and the food spoils. Again, *read the directions* and follow them. When the book says "let

the gauge return to zero or allow the canner to cool naturally then remove the lid and remove the jars," do just that. It does not say to leave them for several hours in the cooled canner!

My grandmother water bathed green beans

Years ago, home pressure canners weren't readily available, so people did process foods such as vegetables and even meats by holding them in a boiling water bath canner for three hours. That *usually* caused the jars to seal, although the food was terribly overcooked. But, no matter how long you hold jars of food in a water bath canner, the temperature of the food in the jars never reaches above boiling.

Boiling temperatures kill molds and yeast, along with some forms of bacteria. But it does not kill the bacteria that cause botulism (food poisoning) or their toxins. So you could boil your green beans for three hours in a water bath canner and still have toxic food in your pantry, even though the jars had sealed. To kill these bacteria, food in your jars must reach 240 degrees — a temperature which is only reached inside a steam pressure canner.

No, botulism is not common in this country, but it does occur. Do you really want to gamble your family's safety by continuing an unsafe canning practice? Again, always read the directions (from a modern canning book) for each and every food you can. All low-acid foods, including vegetables, meats, poultry, and fish (and recipes including them) must be processed in a pressure canner.

Can I reduce the processing time if I boil foods first?

Any time you can up a batch of food, you have to treat it as if you had just mixed it up fresh. This goes for your own recipes of chili, soup, and stew, as well as when you re-can large #10 cans (institutional size) from the store. It's always possible for bacteria to float into that food between cooking and canning. So to be safe, you must process that food as though it were made up fresh and follow the processing directions exactly in your canning book. If you don't, you'll have incompletely processed food that may go bad during storage or expose your family to the danger of food poisoning.

My sweet corn turned brown during canning

There are a couple of reasons why corn turns an unappetizing brown after processing. The most common is that the corn is one of the newer super-sweet varieties. Plant or buy a variety of corn that is not "extra sweet" or "unbelievably sweet." One popular variety sold is Kandy Korn, a super-sweet best seller. It is very good, eaten fresh. But it is a poor choice to can. I've done it with mixed results; some batches are fine, others turn brown.

Another possibility is that the corn was processed at too high a temperature. This often happens when a person fails to monitor the pressure gauge while the corn is processing. If you should be processing at 10 pounds pressure, don't assume that 15 will make it "better."

Make sure that water covers the corn well and that you use the correct headspace recommendations.

If you do end up with unappetizing brown corn, it is fine to eat. Most folks won't want to eat it as a side dish because of its appearance, so just use it in your recipes.

My jelly didn't set up

This just happens sometimes, even with the most experienced jam and jelly preservers, me included. Personally, I don't worry about it and just use the unset spread as syrup over pancakes or ice cream. It's sweet, fruity, and thick enough not to be runny.

I think the most common reason it doesn't set is from tweaking the recipe in your canning book. Don't add extra fruit juice to your recipe, thinking that you can get away with adding a little more sugar. It never works out and you'll be disappointed with unset spreads.

Whether you use a recipe with pectin or not, don't hurry the boiling of your spread. If your recipe calls for added pectin, add the full amount. Never double a recipe. It often does not turn out well; either it doesn't set up or it scorches.

If you've done everything right and the preserve *still* doesn't jell, you can save it and remake it again to get a firmer product. Before re-canning, just remember, some fruit preserves and jellies take up to two weeks to set up. And some fruits, such as chokecherries, are a bugger to set. Whenever I start to cook down my chokecherries, I use apple juice as a liquid, not water. The apple juice is high in natural pectin and helps the chokecherry jam or jelly to set. I also add powdered pectin.

If you want to remake your jam, jelly, or preserves that have not set up after two weeks, here's how:

Spreads made with powdered pectin, such as Sure-Jel:

To remake failed jelly or jam, only do 8 pints at one time. For each cup of spread, measure 1½ tsp. powdered pectin, 1 Tbsp. water, and 2 Tbsp. sugar. Set sugar aside in a separate bowl. Combine pectin and water in a large saucepan and bring to a boil, stirring constantly to prevent scorching. Bring the pectin and water to a boil over medium heat, stirring frequently to prevent scorching. Add unset preserves (or jam or jelly) and sugar, stirring constantly to prevent scorching and to mix thoroughly with pectin mixture. Bring to a hard boil for 30 seconds. Quickly ladle into hot jars, leaving ¼ inch of headspace. Place a hot, new, previously-simmered lid on jar and screw down the

ring firmly tight. Process in a water bath canner for the time shown in the original recipe.

Spreads made with liquid pectin, such as Certo:

To remake failed jelly or jam which has been made with liquid pectin, only do 8 pints at one time. For each cup of unset jelly, measure out 1½ tsp. liquid pectin, 3 Tbsp. sugar, and 1½ tsp. lemon juice. Place failed preserves (or jam or jelly) in a large saucepan and bring to a boil, stirring constantly to prevent scorching. Quickly stir in sugar, lemon juice, and liquid pectin. Return to rolling boil, stirring constantly. Boil hard for one minute, stirring constantly. Remove from heat. Ladle hot jam/jelly into hot jars, leaving ¼ inch of headspace. Place a new, hot, previously-simmered lid on the jar and screw down the ring firmly tight. Process in a boiling water bath canner for the time required in the original recipe.

Without added pectin (boiled down jam, jelly, or preserves):

Usually when these don't set, it means you haven't read or followed the directions correctly. Read them again and recheck your method. If it still seems right, heat the unset product in a large pot until the temperature in the recipe is reached or the jelling point is reached. Be sure the preserves slide off a clean spoon in a sheet instead of dripping off in drips. Then quickly ladle the spread into hot jars, leaving ¼ inch of headspace. Place a hot, new, previously-simmered lid on the jar and screw down the ring firmly tight. Process in a water bath canner for the time required in the original recipe.

My jars have come unsealed during storage

This happens once in a while, but it should not happen very often. If more than one jar in a large batch comes unsealed, or this starts happening frequently, you have a problem.

The most common cause is that food bits have been trapped under the lid during processing. Be sure to wipe both the rim of the jar and the threads to remove any clinging food particles before putting the lid on the jar. Another cause of food getting trapped under the lid is varying pressure during canning which often blows liquid and small food particles out of the jar during processing. These particles sometimes lodge under the lid and around the rim of the jar, causing seal failure either right away or later on.

Another common cause is, again, not following directions. If the food has not been processed for the correct time, it won't stay sealed. Never take shortcuts, thinking that 30 minutes is as good as 40 minutes in a pressure canner. Or thinking that because a soup was put into the jars boiling hot, it doesn't need to be processed as long as if it were not previously boiled.

Another common cause of seal failure in storage is packing food too tightly into a jar, not using the recommended headspace. The food swells during processing and touches the underside of the lid, sometimes causing seal failure in storage.

Not removing air trapped in the liquid when you pack your jars will also cause seals to fail in storage. Take the time to slide a plastic or wooden spatula or chopstick down inside the jars to release any air bubbles.

Finally, when the processing time is finished, don't leave the jars in the pressure canner with the lid on. I did that once because I was exhausted from a 36-hour canning session. I left a big batch in the canner, turned off the heat, and went to bed. The next day, every one of those jars of sweet corn seemed sealed, so I put them into the basement. Two weeks later, I started to smell a stink in the basement. The seals had all failed — I threw out 9 quarts and 14 pints of spoiled corn. I've never done that again!

Incorrectly exhausting steam before shutting your pressure canner can also lead to food spoilage. Most canners require 10 minutes of steady steam escaping from the vent before you begin processing by flipping down your petcock or putting your weight in place. The steam should not come out in spurts; it should be steady and vigorous. If you shut your canner too soon, the food often will not heat for long enough during processing and can spoil in storage even if the lid appears sealed.

My fruit or tomatoes are floating in liquid in the jars

This is nothing to worry about, although many beginning home canners are distressed to find this happening. The fruit crowds near the top of the jar with lots of syrup or juice below it. Raw packing the fruit is generally what causes this. If you simply heat your fruit (or tomatoes) in their syrup or juice, they won't float in the jars. Be sure to pack your fruit well without smashing it into your jars. The fruit will slightly shrink in processing.

My pickles are shriveled

This most often happens when you can whole pickles, usually sweet gherkin type pickles. There are two common causes of shriveled pickles. The first cause is that too much sugar was added to the cucumbers at one time. Follow your recipe to the letter and add the sugar over the period of time indicated. The second cause is not pricking the cucumbers with a fork before soaking them in the brine. Pricking lets the brine penetrate each cucumber, plumping it up during brining.

This condition is unappealing, but the pickles are still edible and usually quite tasty.

My pickles are soft and limp

There are several reasons that pickles get soft after processing. I believe the most common is boiling them too long. Refrigerated cukes are nice and crisp, but those left on the counter at room temperature are limp and wrinkled. Pick a recipe that requires little to no boiling before packing and a very short time in a boiling water bath canner. Grandma's best pickle recipes

Even when I've canned for more than 45 years, I always get out a canning book. It's too easy to forget a step or process at an incorrect time.

required no water bath processing and the pickles were always sealed and crisp. They were packed cold in the jars then the boiling brine was poured quickly over them and the lids and rings were fastened in place. Every jar sealed and remained sealed. Today, to keep us absolutely safe from any possible food-borne illness, experts now recommend processing all pickles in a boiling water bath — some for as little as 5 minutes and most for 10 or even 15 minutes. The longer you boil pickles, the softer they tend to get. Some folks add grape leaves or powdered alum (pickle-crisp) to the pickles to help them stay crisp, with varying results.

Another cause of limp pickles is not removing the blossom end (as opposed to the stem end) of each cucumber as it is prepared. Be sure to trim it off completely to remove any bacteria or mold-causing organisms present.

Using weak vinegar or a brine that is too weak (often made so by adding water) also causes limp pickles. Be sure to cover all of your pickles in the jar with brine. Those that stick up out of the brine will become soft and soggy. Only use 5% acidity vinegar in the brine. If you use homemade vinegar, test it to make sure it is strong enough to use in pickling. Also, use pickling salt, not common table salt. Table salt contains iodine, a necessary supplement to diets, but it can cause pickles to get soft or discolored.

Using other-than-fresh cucumbers is another very common reason for pickles going limp. Always pick your cucumbers just before pickling and be sure to wash them thoroughly. I store mine before processing in a large bowl full of cold water.

The food in my jars is getting discolored and pale

This is common when home-canned food is stored in conditions with too much heat and/or light present. An attic is very warm in the summer months and if you have windows in the attic, the light, coupled with heat, will discolor your food. Canned foods should be stored in a dark, cool location, such as a dry basement that is not subject to freezing temperatures. The discolored food looks unappetizing and may soften (especially fruit), but as long as the jars remain sealed, the food should be okay to use.

My rings and lids are getting rusty

Condensation in a damp basement can and does cause canning jar rings and lids to rust. I had this problem in the farmhouse basement we used, years ago. By simply adding a dehumidifier to our storage area, then using a small wood stove down in the basement in the winter months, my problem was solved completely.

But there can be another common cause of jar lids and rings rusting. Did you know that jars store much better if the rings are taken off of the jars before storage? Most folks just take the cooled jars to their pantry after processing. Instead, you can do what I do (what you're *supposed to do*) and remove the rings and wash the jars off with warm soapy water when they are cool. During processing, food juices often blow out of the jar and lodge between the ring and the jar threads. If you don't remove the ring and wash the jar, this remains during storage and attracts moisture, which rusts the rings and the lids. These lids eventually rust through and spoil the food. When washed, the lids last years longer.

I do sometimes store my jars with the rings on to save storage space for the rings, but I always remove the ring, wash and dry the jar, then put the ring back on.

Some people fear that if they remove the ring, the jar will come unsealed and the food ruined. This is not true. If the jar is properly sealed, removing the ring never lets the seal come undone.

My Tattler reusable jar lids don't seal reliably

Some people try the Tattler reusable canning lids and don't read the directions on the box. Or they have older jars with difficult-to-understand directions on the box. They use the lids just like they do regular lids, and that doesn't work with Tattler lids. With regular two-piece metal lids, you pack your food, wipe the rim of the jar clean, place a hot, previously-simmered lid on the jar, and screw down the ring firmly tight. Then it goes into the canner.

Tattler lids are different in the way they seal and you need to be aware of this. I use them myself; they work wonderfully for years and years *if* you follow the directions on the box. You pack your food, wipe the rim of the jar clean, place a hot, previously-simmered lid and rubber on the jar, and screw the lid only fingertip tight. Now that's *barely* snug, it's just enough to hold the lid on the jar during processing! Most folks mistakenly tighten the ring as with metal two-piece lids.

When you take the jars out of the canner, *immediately* tighten the rings all the way and set the jars on a dry folded towel to cool. This is like the old zinc lids with rubbers where the instructions say "complete the seal." If you follow these instructions, they'll seal correctly and you can reuse them over and over for decades!

Conclusion

Canning is simply a learned life skill. Like all homestead arts, the more you do, the better you'll get — and the more confident you'll get, too! I've had to deal with a lot of these common problems over the years in my own canning and with the canning my friends and *BHM* family have done. I'm hoping that by reading this article, you'll be able to solve some of your own mistakes and avoid making others. Happy canning! Δ

Keep your vittles cool with a modern spring box

By Kai Moessle

Keeping food cool without electricity isn't a huge challenge anymore. These days, propane and kerosene-powered refrigerators and freezers are readily available. However, if you're not willing (or able) to spend the rather large amount of money they cost, it seems you are doomed to an ice trip to the nearest convenience store every few days, which will cost you more over time than the refrigerator itself. That was the situation I found myself in when I started to plan for more than just the three-day-weekend stays on my property. I had planned on getting a kerosene fridge (I don't like propane), but I would need something to keep milk, butter, cheese, etc. cool until then.

Fortunately, my property has a good spring that feeds a little pond with really cold water about 10x15 feet and one foot deep. Bottles are easily kept cold by putting them right in the water along the edge, but a Tupperware with cold cuts or a ziplock bag with bread tends to float away and end up right in the middle of the pond. Starting your day trying to prod breakfast to shore with a stick or wading into 35 degree water to get it tends to put a damper on the best of moods; although your doctor will probably tell you that the latter is excellent for improving circulation in your legs.

So, after a few weeks of thinking and planning, I decided to upgrade the old spring box design to a "water jacket cooler." I figured that by finding two plastic boxes that fit inside each other with about a one-inch gap in between, I could let the spring water flow through this gap and cool the air in the inner box where I could keep my vittles.

The whole cooler would have to be located far enough below the spring pond to let gravity do the work of pumping the water. To make sure the water circulates all around, it needed to have the intake on the bottom and the outlet near the top of the outer box.

All the parts and tools needed are readily available at any hardware store or home improvement center. The dimensions of the wooden shell are based on the outer plastic box, so I would recommend buying this first and then figuring out the size and lumber necessary for the shell.

Tools used:
25-foot tape measure
hammer
24-inch hand saw
2-inch wood chisel
wooden mallet (homemade)
framing square
utility knife

Container parts:
14-gallon storage tote (inner box)
16.5-gallon storage tote (outer box)
(2) ¾-inch galvanized couplings
¾-inch galvanized close nipple
1 foot (or longer) of 1-inch PVC pipe
1-inch slip to 1-inch threaded PVC bushing
1 inch-threaded PVC coupling
5 pounds of 8d nails

Lumber list
Platform:
2 pieces 4x4x8 feet
1 piece 2x4x8 feet
4 pieces 1x6x8 feet
Wooden shell:
1 piece 2x4x8 feet
6 pieces 1x6x8 feet

Platform frame pieces

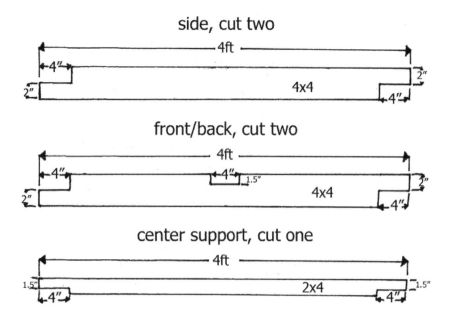

side, cut two

front/back, cut two

center support, cut one

Altogether, I didn't quite spend $100.

First on the "to-do" list is the inlet and outlet on the outer box. The inlet goes on the bottom on one side; the outlet near the top on the opposite side. To be able to use a regular garden hose as the supply pipe, I decided to use a hose bib in the intake; it's also easy to disconnect the line without any tools that way. Thread on ¾-inch coupling onto the rear end of the hose bib and the ¾-inch close nipple into the coupling (use Teflon tape on both joints for a tight seal). Next, cut a hole into the outer box along the bottom edge of one sidewall just big enough for the close nipple to fit through. Also cut the same size hole in a 2x4-inch piece of 3/8-inch-thick wood. This piece of wood reinforces the box wall somewhat on the outside and acts as a backer for the coupling to insure a watertight seal. To finish the intake, thread the wood piece on the nipple, push the nipple through the box wall, add an O-ring (or homemade rubber gasket from a piece of inner tube) and screw on the second coupling. Make it good and tight, but don't overdo it or the box wall might crack.

For the outlet, take the piece of 1-inch PVC pipe and glue on the slip-

Frame parts for the platform with tools used

to-threaded bushing. Cut a hole into the box wall on the opposite side of the intake and near the top just big enough for the threaded part of the bushing to fit through. I didn't use a backer piece here because it doesn't have to be watertight (the water flows out here anyway). Push the bushing through, screw on the 1-inch threaded coupling and — *presto!* — the outer box is done.

To set up the whole affair, you need to find a spot along your stream where you can build a small platform. The spot also needs to be low enough to keep the water outlet below the start of the intake pipe (the far end of my garden hose). If there are a lot of leaves or other debris that could get sucked

into the hose in your stream, it might be necessary to add an intake filter or tie a piece of screen across the opening.

I was lucky, since my little pond is dammed up and the stream has enough drop, I only had to go about 50 feet down from the dam. To keep the platform off the ground I used four old concrete blocks I had lying around, but some flat rocks will work too. The frame of the platform consists of four 4x4 pieces, 48 inches long with a half lap joint on each end and one 2x4 piece, 48 inches long with a half lap joint at each end. The 2x4 helps to keep the 1x6 boards from sagging when you step on the platform. Nail the frame together, set it on the blocks (or rocks), and level it in all directions. Next, cut the 1x6 to length (48 inches again) and nail on for the decking.

The wooden shell for the two boxes will vary in size, depending on the dimensions of the outer box. My shell is 26 inches wide, 21 inches deep, and 19 inches high. It's nothing more than a box without a bottom, fastened

Platform frame assembled and leveled on concrete blocks

Outer box (front) and inner box (back) on the finished platform. Note the water outlets on the outer box.

Wooden shell completed with both boxes inside. Note the two 1x3s that keep inner box from floating.

After a few hours, the inner box started to bulge inward from the water pressure, so I built a brace out of some 1x6 and 2x4 scraps.

to the platform. This not only makes it look pretty but keeps the inner box from floating up by way of two 1x3 crosspieces that slide into slits cut in the front and back walls of the shell. Of course, the inlet and outlet need openings cut as well. A lid to cover everything and to keep critters out completes the cooler shell, again built from 1x6 with 2x4 crosspieces. I also added a piece of metal roofing on top of the lid to keep rain out — you could just throw a tarp over it.

The last piece I had to build was a brace for the inner box, which had

started to bulge inward after a couple hours. It only took some of the 1x6 and 2x4 cutoffs. I also cut some left-over two-inch foam insulation to size and laid it on top of the inner box (it fits perfectly under the lid) to keep more cold air in. All that's left to do now is to hook up the intake line (garden hose) to the bib, fill it with water to start the flow, drop the other end into the water upstream, and wait a while for the inner box to cool off.

And just how cold does it get? Well, it doesn't work as well as your kitchen refrigerator, but on a 75 degree day

the inner box stays between 45 and 50 degrees, cold enough to keep my butter and cheese from melting. It might be possible to get it even colder by putting insulation between the outer box and the shell, but I haven't tried that yet. One minor problem seems to be some condensation on the inside, which is probably due to the lid not sealing airtight like on a regular fridge. As long as all the food is in plastic bags or lidded bowls, it's not that big of a deal.

Finally, as long as your water supply doesn't freeze up, you don't have to drain the cooler for winter. The lowest temperature this past winter was -24° F and the water ran steadily without even so much as a ring of ice around the outside. Δ

Some leftover 2-inch insulating foam from another project under the lid keeps the temperature down a little more.

Homeschooling your dyslexic kid

By John Silveira

I write and edit for a living. I'm the senior editor for *Backwoods Home Magazine* for which I've written numerous columns during the last 24 years. Before that I did technical writing for defense contractors. Recently I published two novels, *Danielle Kidnapped* and *The Devil You Know*, and I'll have two more completed before the end of the year, *Fossil* and *Danielle Discovered*. The trouble is, although I write, I can't read.

Okay, that isn't quite accurate. I can read some, but it's not easy. I'm dyslexic.

If you've never heard the term before, the *Merriam-Webster* definition of dyslexia is:

A variable, often familial, learning disability involving difficulties in acquiring and processing language that is typically manifested by a lack of proficiency in reading, spelling, and writing. Melinda Beck, writing in *The Wall Street Journal*, cites a Yale University report that says dyslexia is a problem with "…associating letters with spoken sounds and blending them together fluidly to make words."

They are both accurate. If you're dyslexic, you were born that way and there's no "cure" for this learning disability. You have to simply deal with it, as I've learned to deal with mine after a fairly lengthy struggle. If an adult had gotten a handle on my "disability" when I was a kid, my life would have been much easier. Too many kids, unable to read well and thinking they were stupid, gave up and fell through the cracks, even though many of them were otherwise very bright.

As many as one in five people have some degree of dyslexia, although only 12 percent of kids are diagnosed with it. Don't let your own dyslexic kid fall by the wayside. This article is an attempt to help you homeschool your dyslexic child by showing you how I learned to cope with my dyslexia.

Dyslexia is not a type of retardation. When I was diagnosed, I thought it was. But a list of famous dyslexics reads like a *Who's Who* of history and includes such notables as Albert Einstein, Thomas Edison, George Washington, Ludwig van Beethoven, Steven Spielberg, Leonardo da Vinci, and General George Patton. Dave Duffy, the publisher of this magazine, is also dyslexic.

My story

Until the ninth grade I was functionally illiterate. I was well-spoken but read fewer than 50 words per minute. I'd never read an entire novel, but could "fake" book reports. School was like a prison for me, one without parole. That's when I was diagnosed as dyslexic. I'd never heard the word before — not surprising, given my limited vocabulary at the time. I knew it had something to do with my brain and I was afraid it meant I had a form of retardation. The news made me sick. I kept it to myself for years.

However, it was also in the ninth grade that my reading began to improve. It wasn't because of the school system, but because of a kid who was to become a lifelong friend, Fred Brennion.

Fred read voraciously. Most of it seemed to be either science fiction or stories about warfare, especially fighter pilots. He told me about the books he read and they sounded fascinating. I wanted to read them, too. And since Fred had joined the Science Fiction Book Club, I joined too. He perused book titles in the racks at various bookstores and markets, so I did.

But when I attempted to read the books I bought, it was like self-inflicted torture. I read paragraphs, then reread them because I didn't know what they said. I'd often read them several times and I'd suddenly realize I'd somehow gotten the words out of order or, more often, I'd mistake one word for another and do it repeatedly. Once I understood the paragraph, I moved onto the next one, which I might get through unscathed, or I might stumble again and have to read and reread this one until it made sense. Finishing a page was an accomplishment, never mind finishing a whole book. Most of the books I started soon got put aside, and never finished, unless they were so compelling that I was willing to endure misery and frustration.

But there were a few I read from start to finish. One was a book on science and math by the Russian-born physicist, George Gamow, titled *One, Two, Three...Infinity*. It was fascinating because I was into science and I was learning stuff I was interested in. So I hung in. I started reading it in the ninth grade and finished it in the tenth. I think Fred read it in two or three days. Another took me an entire summer to read: *Kon Tiki* by Thor Heyerdahl. I stayed with it because it was an adventure that fascinated me.

Practice made ... well, not perfect, but my reading did improve as I read more and I got so I could finish a standard-size novel in maybe two months, *if it was so good that I*

titles because I can't read the subtitles fast enough. It's either watch the movie and not know what anyone's saying, or read the subtitles and not know what's going on in the movie. (Even if I limited myself to just reading the subtitles, I usually can't finish reading one before the next one flashes up on the screen.)

In the meantime, I was doing poorly in school. Between ninth grade and high school graduation, I flunked seven subjects and should have flunked eight, except that Mr. Cangiano, the ninth grade science teacher, promised an "A" to anyone who got a 95th percentile or better on the end-of-the-year standardized science test. I got a 99. At the time, no one could figure out how I got that score. Fred, by the way, got a 93, but he asked Mr. Cangiano if I was getting the "A." I didn't dare ask. Mr. Cangiano, who couldn't figure out how I got

didn't know. What he did was retest me and this time I got a 98, and then he gave me the A. The school system didn't know what to do with me because they suspected I had a very high IQ, which I did, but I was at the bottom of the class, actually finishing dead last in grades.

Order from chaos

Today, it comes as no surprise to me that I did so well on that standardized science test. In the ninth grade I'd discovered the scientific method, the step-by-step method on which modern science rests, and to a 13-year-old boy who felt he was already failing at life, it was like an extraterrestrial had landed and was revealing the secrets of the universe. It opened up a new way of looking at the world and that was why I found Gamow's book gripping and I hung in, reading it, for almost a year.

Getting good at science also saved my ego. I understood things many others did not. When I reached the 10th grade I could give a layman's explanation of Einstein's *Theory of Relativity* along with his theory of gravity, but I flunked 10th grade biology because I couldn't read the textbook used in class.

If your kid has a logical mind, encourage it. This was one of my first discoveries about dealing with dyslexia: Things are easier to learn or memorize if I can see the logic behind them.

Vocabulary

There was yet another nightmare: *Vocabulary*. My vocabulary was very limited, and when I did encounter words I didn't recognize or had forgotten the meaning of, "looking them up" was torture because that, too, involved reading and even if I found the definition, I often had to read it several times to understand it. Eventually, I gave up on the dictionary — but not for long.

Enter, again, Fred. One day he said to me, "I can spell almost any word, even if I've never heard it before — and I can probably guess its meaning."

This sounded like a joke. I cautiously asked, "How?"

"I just look at the root and then the prefix and suffix, or both."

I didn't have a clue as to what he was talking about because I didn't even know what those words meant. I was pretty sure that, if he wasn't kidding me, this was going to be something I'd never catch on to. I asked him for an example, hoping I wasn't about to become the butt of a joke.

He told me what the root of a word was. "In the word transport, the root, 'port,' means to carry. It's in other words like 'portable — able to be carried,' 'teleportation —carried over a distance,' 'import — to carry in,' 'export — to carry out' …

"The 'trans' part is the prefix and means the other side or across or beyond. So, when I hear 'transport' I know it means something like 'to carry across.' Transcontinental means across the continent. Transgalactic describes light that travels across a galaxy."

As if to show me more of this wizardry he said, "Prehistoric: the 'historic' part means history, the 'pre' means 'before.' So it's 'before written history' and it's pretty easy to get a handle on spelling it and guessing its meaning."

"Or 'archaeology.' The root word is 'archaeo,' which means old stuff and lore while the suffix, 'logy,' means something like a theory or science. So, it's the study or science of old stuff." He explained the word "biology," and related its suffix to more words like "geology," "anthropology," "cosmology…" He explained how the "phil" in "philosophy," meant "love of" and associated it with words like "philatelist," "philharmonic" and others.

I'm not saying the teachers hadn't tried to impart this stuff to me, but long before I'd ever gotten out of the first grade, I'd pretty much given up on school and had stopped listening in class so every test was a surprise and every report card was a badge of shame. I was a failure at school. But here I was, standing on a street corner in Medford, Massachusetts, and a kid my age was enlightening me, opening up the world, the way no teacher ever had.

I nodded like I'd known it all along. But I was astounded and my head was swimming. *Words actually made sense.* There was order in how most of them were formed, where previously I had perceived only chaos. Order, rules of thumb, and patterns, this was where I shined. Beginning on that day, my vocabulary started to grow just because I looked at words differently. I even (grudgingly) began to use the dictionary again because I wanted to see how words I didn't know were put together. Fred's ten-minute lesson is probably the best way to start to expand any kid's vocabulary, but it's especially important to a dyslexic such as me because his explanation was dripping with logic, and logical things I could learn.

At this time I did not know Dave Duffy. He was in downtown Boston at Cathedral High School learning Latin from the nuns as part of the regular Catholic school curriculum. Like me, he was also struggling with reading, but Latin was the ancient language from which came many of the roots, prefixes, and suffixes that Fred was teaching me. Latin would be to Dave what Fred was to me.

Reading

So I was learning to read. My vocabulary was expanding. Still, I read slowly, and I was to discover not all writing styles are "equal." Certain styles drove me crazy. I could read Hemingway, but not Faulkner. Later

on, I could read Charles Bukowski's or Richard Brautigan's poetry, but not T.S. Elliot's or Shakespeare's. Turgid and complex writing styles are so much more difficult for dyslexics that I began to avoid them then, and I even avoid them now.

So, lean toward giving your dyslexic kid clearly written prose. Give him Hemingway, Twain, Robert Louis Stevenson, etc. Although their styles are clean and simple, their stories can be enjoyably complex and we dyslexics aren't afraid of complex ideas.

If you must get complex prose, like Faulkner, David Foster Wallace, Thomas Pynchon (three writers I can't read), get them audio books. Your local library should have plenty of them. There's also text-to-speech software you can get for your computer. Even Kindle readers have text-to-speech enabled options for thousands of titles.

Writing

Even today, I don't like reading instructions or manuals. Almost invariably they're not written so a person who's as poor a reader as I can readily understand them. So, if I have to assemble something I bought, or learn a new piece of software, and it's not intuitive or there's no one around to "show me," I usually don't do it. Dave's the same way.

On the other hand, if either Dave or I have to *write* instructions for someone else, as we did when we were writing for the defense contractors, we write crystal-clear instructions because we write them so that even people who read as poorly as we do can easily read them. Though we both attribute our poor reading skills to dyslexia, we attribute our good writing skills to the same thing. We have a sizeable readership for our columns largely because we can take complex ideas and write them in such accessible prose that even a dyslexic can understand them.

Memory

I had already done lousy in grade school and was doing almost as bad when I got to college. I took seven and a half years, in and out of several colleges, before I got a degree in math. Learning was only a little easier because I read somewhat better. Not well, but better. (The last college, Suffolk University, threatened not to graduate me unless I took a remedial reading course. I refused because I already knew my problem with reading couldn't be remedied. The threat proved hollow; they gave me my degree anyway.)

But I learned something in college that I hadn't realized before: I could remember almost anything I heard. And if a class was interesting, as were the ones I took from one of my professors, Dr. Reiche, I was better off *not* to take notes, but to attend every class, and just listen to him lecture. I got nothing but "As" from him, even on the finals, for which I had not written notes from which to study. They were a breeze.

Notice how your kid learns and remembers. Does he remember what he hears better than what he sees? Or is it the other way around? Also, does he remember stuff that unfolds logically before him? To help him succeed, play to his strengths.

Spelling

I'm a pretty good speller, *now*. I'm no threat to any spelling bee champs, but I wouldn't have struggled to be good at it except that I wanted to write. To get this way, I've forced myself to memorize but mostly I've associated words the way Fred taught me to, by understanding their roots, prefixes, and suffixes. But the funny thing is, I can't spell many words off the top of my head. I can't "picture" them properly. However, the same words I can't spell off the top of my head I can spell if I'm writing them down. It's a different kind of memory and lots of people are like me. I don't

know if they're all dyslexics. So, don't be surprised if your kid can't spell a word if you ask him to spell it out loud, but he can if he's writing it down. If so, make all of his spelling tests *written*.

Delegating

If he asks you the meaning of a word, or how to spell it, or the capital of Albania (Tirana), or how to boil an egg, don't be too quick to say, "Look it up." I once spent most of an afternoon looking up the word "bureau" to see how it was spelled. To a dyslexic, the spelling of that word, and many others, makes no sense. The frustration of looking up words almost made me *never* want to look up a word, a capital, or any other fact, again. The fact that I was constantly told to "look things up" myself made me stop asking for help.

Don't be too quick to judge your student as lazy. "Looking it up" can be incredibly difficult for many dyslexics and "giving them the answer" will do something I don't think most people have thought of: it teaches them something I never learned — to "delegate," and to be able to depend on others. In a *New York Times* article, Brent Bower writes, "It has long been known that dyslexics are drawn to running their own businesses, where they can get around their weaknesses ... and play to their strengths." Gabrielle Coppola, in *Bloomberg Businessweek* cites Julie Logan, a professor of entrepreneurship at Cass Business School in London: "Being a slow reader forces you to extract only vital information, so that you're constantly getting right to the point. Dyslexics are also forced to trust and rely on others to get things done — an essential skill for anyone working to build a business. People really struggle to delegate, and these people (dyslexics) have learned to do that already ... If you're bogged down in the details, you're not out there looking at where your business needs to go."

Dave Duffy was encouraged to depend on others. He had older brothers, Bill and Hugh, who he could depend on, who would give him answers and explanations. What they were doing, whether they realized it or not, was helping Dave learn how to delegate. On the other hand, my family thought they were doing me a favor by insisting, "Look it up yourself."

Today, Dave feels confident in the people he hires. He has developed a "good built-in crap detector," he says, and hires only good people, to whom he delegates important jobs and writing assignments, and the result is that he publishes a successful magazine. I never learned to delegate or how to depend on others, so I gravitated toward things where it was me against the world; I became a good chess player, a successful poker player, a nonfiction writer, and now a novelist. While Dave became a publisher who hires and directs others, including me, I became a one-man show.

So, here's the homeschooling strategy for a dyslexic child:

Don't discourage him. Answer his questions.

Help him learn how to depend on others and delegate.

Don't try to turn him into a straight-A student. Chances are he's never going to make the honor roll.

Encourage him to focus on what he's good at — and what he enjoys. Writing, chess, math, and science saved my ego when I seemed to be failing at everything else. Mark my words, intelligent kids with learning disabilities *need* things they can be good at.

Play to your dyslexic kid's strengths, whether you're homeschooling him or if he's in a public school. And, keep in mind, if he's in a public school the teacher has 30 or more other students to attend to, so your "problem child" is likely to fall through the cracks unless *you* help him. Δ

Ask Jackie

If you have a question about rural living, send it in to Jackie Clay and she'll try to answer it. Address your letter to Ask Jackie, PO Box 712, Gold Beach, OR 97444. Questions will only be answered in this column. — *Editor*

Dual-purpose chickens

I've been reading a lot lately about Wyandotte and Australorp chickens. Both are dual-purpose, good layers (although they say the Australorp is a little better), and both are good meat birds.

Which do you prefer personally and think is better for a small ranch? Also, do you think there's a great difference in the color of the Wyandotte with regard to performance?

Barry Tietler
Cave Creek, Arizona

Personally, I like Wyandotte chickens a little better, maybe because my Grandma used to have them. But for a plain old good homestead chicken I like White Rocks unless you have a predator problem. White chickens are easier to pluck because of the pale coloring of the pin feather "dye" that is sometimes left after plucking. Predators *do* tend to pick off white birds, however! Choosing a breed of chickens is a personal decision. Choose one that appeals to you the most. All of the older breeds are still around because they have desirable traits, sort of like heritage vegetables.

No, I don't think the Wyandotte coloration has anything to do with performance. — *Jackie*

Processing deer meat

I have a question about processing deer meat. First, when we get a deer, we put it into big insulated coolers on ice and water that is really cold for 3 days, then cut it up. Sometimes it turns out good tasting, sometimes it doesn't. However, in Growing and Canning Your Own Food, under Canning Wild Game you say "Do not soak meat in water." Are we doing something wrong that could be affecting the taste? Also, is it possible to make wild game such as deer, taste like beef? I'm afraid I'm spoiled, but I just can't stand a "game" taste.

Kylee Mink
Potts Camp, Mississippi

Don't soak your meat in water. That definitely can give it an off taste and does nothing to the texture of the meat. We quickly skin and eviscerate our deer, rinse off the inside with ice-cold water, and let it drip dry. Then we insert a stick to hold the carcass open and either pack it with ice or hang it, depending on the temperature. *Never* hang meat when the temperatures are much above 35° F. And don't leave it hanging for days at a time or with the hide on. Both result in bad flavors. I always hang my skinned carcass wrapped in a clean sheet to keep dust and critters off the meat. If it is too warm to hang, I cut it up into quarters and backstrap/tenderloin chunks and pack into ice chests with the meat positioned so melting ice doesn't cause the meat to sit in the water.

A lot of "gamey" venison is simply partially spoiled or incorrectly handled meat. Handle your venison like you would a big roast from the store. Keep it clean, cold, and away from dust/critters.

When canning, add a heaping teaspoonful of powdered beef soup base instead of salt to each pint jar (2 tsp. per quart), in addition to the broth made from pre-browning the meat. This will make the venison taste more like beef. It's amazing how many

Jackie Clay

folks who "don't like venison" try this tip and now rave about it!
— *Jackie*

Sun drying fruit

We currently have two food dehydrators, used both for jerky and fruit. The end product tastes great; however, they are limited in size and require large amounts of electricity. Do you have an idea or method of drying fruit outside using the sun as the energy source? I'm unable to design an effective outdoor dehydrator able to dry fruit while escaping the threats of birds and/or insects.

Ryan Fisher
San Juan Bautista, California

One of the easiest ways to dehydrate fruits and vegetables is to simply lay your trays or nylon window screens out in your car in a sunny spot. We used to have a Suburban (when gas was cheaper!) and every day in the summer I filled the whole back with screens full of fruits and vegetables. Usually one day of this treatment would dry them. Cheap, easy, and power-free! And it protects your food from dust, birds, and insects. Watch the kids though; they soon learn to snack out the back! If you have trouble with foods getting pale from being in the sun, just drive the car to a less sunny location. Works like a charm. — *Jackie*

233

Growing stevia

Can a person grow stevia and use it in canning? If you can, how much compared to sugar?

Scott Cooper
La Grange, Kentucky

Stevia is very easy to grow. A large pot can be brought indoors during the winter so you can use it year-around, snipping off leaves to use and even dehydrate and powder. But not enough has been tried yet to use homegrown stevia in canning such as with jams, jellies, and fruits. I'll be sure to keep you and others posted as we go along. We're really excited about stevia and all of its possibilities! — *Jackie*

Cooking old beans

In response to the letter from Russell Hall in the spring issue of BHM (#140) regarding cooking old beans, I think you hit on the best solution when you mentioned canning them because they soften under pressure. I have been cooking beans in a simple pressure cooker (without a gauge) for years. I have some old beans that have been around for 12 years or more. I soak them overnight (10-12 hours), drain off the soak water (which contains the sprout prohibiting factors that interfere with digestion, produce gas, etc.), put them in the pressure cooker and cover them with fresh water. Then I add a 2 or 3 x 5-inch piece of Kombu (also called kelp) which acts as a tenderizer, and about ½ tsp. oil to prevent foaming.

Most old beans take 30-35 minutes after the pressure is up. Some like Limas or green peas take 20-25 minutes. Soy beans take the longest — 40-45 minutes. Fresh beans take even less time.

After the pressure is up, turn the burner down enough to maintain the pressure during the cooking time. When time is up, turn off the burner and allow the pressure to normalize. Then the beans are ready to season

up and use for whatever recipe you have in mind.

Patti Claire
Washburn, Tennessee

Thanks for your tips, Patti. Too many times, folks throw away old beans because they try to cook up a mess and they are "hard" no matter how long they are boiled or baked. The pressure canning/cooking makes all the difference in the world. What I like about canning those beans is that in a few hours, I can put up pints and pints of beans to use at my leisure anytime I feel like it, at the drop of a hat. Talk about convenience! — *Jackie*

Keeping seed corn

We are growing open pollinated corn and want to save some seeds for planting. We roast our corn for making corn meal because it will get buggy if we don't. Of course we can't roast our seed for planting. Seed companies put pesticides/fungicides on their seed corn. We don't want to treat our seed with chemicals. Do you know of ways to keep seed corn without it getting bugs in it? Will putting the seed in the freezer work?

Mark and Deb Wehr
Mifflinburg, Pennsylvania

Yes, you've hit on the very best way to keep your seed corn so it doesn't get buggy. Just put the corn you wish to save into airtight freezer containers (a half-pint canning jar will work well) and freeze until you are getting ready to plant. Your seeds will remain safe and viable until they go into the ground. You can also freeze your corn you plan on grinding for a few weeks. When stored in an airtight container, you should experience no further problems with insects without roasting or heating the corn. — *Jackie*

Canning ham

I have a question about canning ham. I want to can some ham for use in my dry beans. I'll be using pint jars

and using boneless, smoked ham (fully cooked). If you could give me some pointers I'd be forever grateful!

Charley Gates
Alton, Missouri

Canning ham is easy and you can use it so many different ways. I always buy up a couple 99-cent hams whenever they're on sale even though we raise our own pigs. It's cheap meat at that price. What I do is cut up smaller cubes from slices and pack into pint and half-pint jars, leaving 1 inch of headspace. Then I cut up larger cubes and pack those into pint jars. After most of the good meat is in jars, I toss the scraps into a stock pot, add water and boil for about an hour. I remove the scraps and skim off any excess fat. While it's boiling hot, I ladle into canning jars, leaving 1 inch of headspace, and remove any air bubbles. I'm careful to wipe the rim of the jars clean with a clean, hot, moist cloth. I place hot, previously simmered new lids on jars and screw down the ring firmly tight. I process pints and half pints for 75 minutes at 10 pounds pressure. If you live at an altitude above 1,000 feet consult your canning book for directions on increasing your pressure to suit your altitude.

Once these are processing, I usually return the scraps to the pot and add more water, salt, spices, and pepper if desired. Then I rinse 2-3 pounds of split peas which I add to the ham broth after it has been boiled another hour. I pick off any good remaining meat as soon as I can handle the scraps and mix with the peas. I dip out about 1/3 jar of split peas, then ladle broth over them to within 1 inch of the top of the jar. I process these in pints at 10 pounds pressure for 75 minutes. You can also do this with beans you've rinsed, brought to a boil for five minutes, and let sit for two hours. Pack the beans and ham broth/ meat scraps and process for 75 minutes (pints). It's amazing how many jars of good food you can get from one ham! — *Jackie*

Lemon or lime jelly

You've been so kind to give me recipes for a lot of other things but I would love to get a couple more.

One for lemon jelly or jam. The other for lime jelly or jam.

Should I just follow the directions for orange or is there something else that I need to do?

Tess Graves
Thomaston, Georgia

I had a hard time, but I did find a recipe for lemon jelly. But first, here's a good one for canned lemon or lime curd which is like a clear, custardy jelly. I use it like jelly and it's real good alone or in many different recipes like using it as a cake filling or cookie enhancer. Here's the lemon curd recipe. To make lime curd, substitute lime zest/juice for the lemon.

2½ cups superfine sugar
½ cup lemon zest (finely grated yellow lemon rind)
1 cup bottled lemon juice
¾ cup butter
7 large egg yolks
4 large whole eggs

Zest lemon and mix with sugar. Set aside in bowl. Juice lemon; remove seeds. Break butter into small pieces and chill in refrigerator. Measure lemon juice and set aside.

Put water into bottom of double boiler and set top in place. Heat to boiling.

Water should not be touching bottom of top pan. Remove top pan and add ingredients to pan and whisk briskly until well mixed. Sit top pan back on bottom of double boiler and heat. Stir continuously until mixture reaches 170° F. Remove top pan and continue stirring for about 5 minutes until mixture thickens. Strain through sieve to remove zest. Discard zest. Fill hot, sterilized jars to within ½ inch of the top with hot lemon curd.

Wipe rim of the jar clean and place hot, previously simmered new lid on jar and screw down ring firmly tight. Process jars for 15 minutes in a boiling water bath canner.

Caution: Do not heat the water in the canner to more than 180° F before jars are added. If the water in the canner is too hot when jars are added, the process time will not be long enough. The time it takes for the canner to reach boiling after the jars are added is expected to be 25 to 30 minutes for this product. Process time starts after the water in the canner comes to a full boil over the tops of the jars.

This will remain good for about 4 months, canned, but will eventually discolor and possibly separate so do use relatively soon after canning.

And finally, here's the lemon jelly recipe! It's very simple:

---

6 thin-skinned lemons, rinsed well
5 cups water
6 cups superfine sugar

Cut the ends off the lemons, then slice them thinly. Remove all seeds and then quarter the slices. Put them in a large, heavy-bottomed saucepan and add 5 cups water. Bring to a boil, then decrease the heat and simmer, uncovered, for 45 minutes to 1 hour, or until the lemons are soft. Make sure you cook on low heat. Watch it carefully toward the end and stir often. Add the sugar and simmer, uncovered, for another 45 minutes to 1 hour (you can add more water if it seems necessary). To test if the jam is ready, spoon a little onto a plate and tilt it. It should slide down with resistance and not just run down. If necessary, cook until it jells nicely.

To make lime jelly, substitute large limes for the lemons. Process both in a boiling water bath canner for 15 minutes. — *Jackie*

Cheese from frozen milk

I have had to dry my milk cow up. I have been freezing the milk for the past month or so to have milk until I

start milking again. Can I use the frozen milk (after I thaw it) to make cheese? If so, are there any variations on the temps or amount of rennet that I use?

Teresa Clepper
Hamilton, Texas

Yes, you can make cheese from frozen, thawed milk. The curd texture isn't as good with some cheeses. There are no differences in the temps or recipes. Just thaw and stir the milk, bringing it up to the temp first required in the recipe, and you'll do fine. — *Jackie*

Milking goats

When I separate my dairy does from their kids at night, for morning milking or separate them completely and bottle feed, the does are very easy and laid back for milking. They also milk all the way out better. When I leave the does with their kids 24/7, as I am doing now (due to not needing much milk) the does are wicked to milk. Why is that?

Mary Hartsock
Lancaster, Kentucky

They are getting in the habit of *not* being milked by you and resent you "stealing" their kids' milk! When you milk at least once a day, they are quite accepting. Usually I pick a doe or two for milking and let the kids take the milk from my other does and I don't milk them unless they are producing more (usually soon after freshening) than the kids can drink. Once the kids get vigorous, they'll snack all day, consuming much more milk than if you bottle fed them. (A gallon vs. a couple of pints!) Don't let them drink so much milk that they get diarrhea, though. I milk my better does and let the ones that are first fresheners and lesser milkers raise their kids.

— *Jackie*

More self-reliance in
Emergency Preparedness
and Survival Guide

Organic pest control

*By Amy Alton, R.N. and
Joe Alton, M.D.*

You may not realize this, but when you eat non-organic foods, you are also ingesting of number of different pesticides that have been used to produce them. Sadly, pesticides are a common occurence in our world today. Gardeners use them when their plants are threatened by harmful insects, farmers use them to lower the risk of losing their crop to infestations, and even the produce at your local supermarket has been sprayed with pesticides. Chemical pesticides sprayed on plants can make their way into your water source by a process known as leaching. If pesticides are lethal to insects, it is possible that they could have other deleterious effects to our health and environment.

With this in mind, it is wise for the home gardener to avoid these chemicals if at all possible. Organic gardening simply means that your methods are derived from living organisms and not based on the use of chemicals. Organic, effective methods of pest control do exist. Prudent planning will aid you in producing the healthiest fruits and vegetables for your family.

The best way to prevent the failure of a garden is to start with the sturdiest plants available. Healthy plants are better able to survive pest invasions. Other factors that will lead to a successful organic garden include appropriate watering, provision of nutrients, and most importantly: pest control.

*Planting healthy, well-watered plants in nutrient-rich soil
is the first step in controlling pests organically.*

Many a garden has failed due to inappropriate watering. You know that you should water your plants regularly, but a particular crop may need less water than others. Be aware of the water requirements of each fruit or vegetable you grow.

Adding nutrients to the soil or plants can help increase productivity. Instead of standard fertilizers, an organic gardener can use liquid seaweed extract to provide these nutrients. Mostly obtained from kelp, this product provides trace elements such as calcium, magnesium, sulfur, iron, zinc, and barium, which promote strong plant health. Fish emulsions are also useful.

Compost is another natural way to improve the quality of your soil. Compost is easy to produce from various leftovers in your home, such as coffee grounds, vegetable peels, and other refuse from the kitchen. Worked into the soil before planting, it improves the health of your soil and increases earthworm activity. Some people even add commercially-bought worms to their compost to benefit from their excrement (worm castings).

Manure from animals that feed on plants (such as cows, chickens, or rabbits) make healthy fertilizers. Manure needs to be mixed with hay or straw and allowed to compost before using. Before application, you should wait six to nine months or some plants may be "burned" by the high level of methane in it.

Protection from pests

Various pests will invade your garden. Even in a greenhouse, you may still experience snails, slugs, aphids, whiteflies, nematodes, and gnats.

To prevent fungus gnats, don't over-water your garden or containers. A simple trick to eliminate gnats is to place Mason jars with holes punched into the lids and filled with vinegar around the base of the plants. Fungus gnats will fly into the jar and die. You may also try placing a shallow dish, filled with baking soda and apple cider vinegar (or even a sweet soda), around your garden.

A spray of *Bacillus thuringiensis* (BT) is a microbial disease of many pests. Depending on the strain, it will kill pests ranging from fungus gnats, cabbage worms, tomato hornworms, and corn earworms. BT comes in a powder form which is mixed with water and sprayed onto the leaves or surrounding soil, depending on what pest it targets. BT should not kill any beneficial insect predators.

To eliminate slugs and snails, make a trap using a plastic soda bottle with a square opening cut into the middle. Bury it so that the opening is even with the soil. Fill the bottle with beer or a mixture of yeast and honey; slugs and snails cannot resist taking a swig. Unfortunately for them, they also drown. Commercial iron preparations such as "Sluggo" and "Escar-go!" stop snail metabolism, causing them to die in three to six days. Copper is another element that is helpful against slugs. They will not pass a barrier composed of it. Look for snails and slugs, especially at night. I find them hiding just inside the edge of containers, under a tiny bit of soil.

Whiteflies can be difficult, at best, to eliminate and may cause the organic gardener serious frustration. Rigorous sanitation and disinfection of gardening tools, gloves, and your hands are a must. Early infestations may be decreased with a strong jet of water to wash them off the leaves, but be careful not to damage the plant. There are special plant vacuums to suck them off your plants. This is

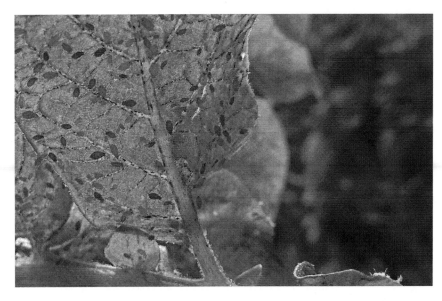

Aphid infestations, as pictured here, are easily treatable with a product called Diatomaceous Earth.

time-consuming, but it works. Make sure to prune away severely-infested leaves and dispose of them in airtight bags. Sticky traps can be used to eliminate whiteflies and other pests; however, you might kill some beneficial insects as well.

Aphids are major issues for many gardeners. Sprinkling food grade Diatomaceous Earth (DE) is an organic way to control aphids and some other pests. DE is the fossilized remains of tiny creatures called diatoms. DE works by causing fatal dehydration. To help decrease an aphid population, sprinkle DE on the top and bottom of leaves and plant parts. For slug control, place a ½-inch pile of DE around your plants as a barrier.

Nematodes are another issue that can negatively impact your garden. Nematodes are microscopic organisms that attack the root system and cause reduced growth and productivity. However, there are beneficial nematodes that can control harmful nematode populations. These can be purchased online or from a local garden supply store. The eggs are microscopic and are mixed with water and applied to the soil. Adding compost to

your soil will also reduce nematode populations.

Like nematodes, most pests have a predator. Ladybugs, for example, enjoy aphids as part of their diet. Other garden helpers include praying mantises, spiders, assassin bugs, hover-flies, lacewings, and all wasps. Many of these can also be purchased and released in your garden.

Certain flowers and herbs have evolved bug-repellent properties and should be additions to your garden. Plant flowers around the garden that repel pests. Aphids, for example, will be repelled by garlic, chives, corian-

Marigolds repel whiteflies, tomato hornworms, and nematodes.

der, anise, nasturtium, petunia, and catmint. Slugs don't like rosemary and wormwood. Cucumber beetles are repelled by tansy and radish. Whiteflies, tomato hornworms, and nematodes hate marigolds.

Mulching can be helpful. Spread mulch over freshly-planted seeds or around transplants. Many weeds are pest habitats; mulch will decrease the number of places they have to live. Besides pest control, mulch has many other benefits:

• Adds nutrients (depending on what type of mulch is used)
• Conserves moisture around the root system
• Moderates soil temperature fluctuations (keeps the soil warm in cold weather and cooler in hot weather)
• Reduces soil erosion
• Provides a barrier between fruit and soil, thus reducing rotting
• Repels slugs
• Decreases fungal diseases

To produce mulch, just use fallen leaves, straw, grass clippings, or compost.

Collars can be made around the base of plants to protect them from cutworms. These can be made from a bottomless plastic cup. They should extend a few inches above and at least

A solution of water, Neem oil, soap, and essential oil creates an effective, organic pesticide.

an inch below the surface of the ground. A barrier paper using the waxed cardboard from old milk cartons is effective against cabbage moth larva by hindering egg laying. Use a 3-inch square of the cardboard; cut two slits crosswise in the middle of the cardboard, and slip it over the newly-emerging seedling stems. This is especially helpful for broccoli, cabbage, Brussels sprouts, kale, or cauliflower.

Row covers are another method that act as a physical barrier. There are "lightweight" versions that allow good sunlight to come through but prevent pests from eating your plants. They also allow rain and fresh air to reach your plants. Heavier row covers are best used only short-term for cold protection. Remember to remove them when it is time for pollination.

Crop rotation is well-known for helping the soil, but it also helps with pest control. If you are changing the local environment of a pest with a different type of plant each planting season, they may move on.

Sometimes, a successful garden will attract critters that don't have six legs or a trail of slime. Unharvested fruit and vegetables rot, thus attracting rats, squirrels, and other rodents. Make sure to eliminate rotting fruits and vegetables, if possible, from your garden to decrease their food supply. Rodents and rabbits seem to dislike peppermint. Soak cotton balls with its essential oil and spread them around the garden. You'll have to replace these every few days or after a hard rain.

For those gardeners who have trespassers with antlers, there is always fencing. But even that isn't always enough to keep determined deer from munching on your precious plants. Deer are easily spooked, so try hanging foil, tin cans, or plates inside and around the borders of the garden for a little noise and distraction. Some say that a fragrant bar of soap is a repellent, as it confuses the deer, making

them want to move on. A homemade spray that is distasteful to many interlopers (and withstands a light rain) is made by mixing:

2 gallons water
1 cup milk
2 whole eggs
2 Tbsp. cooking oil
1 Tbsp. liquid detergent
1 oz. hot sauce

Of course, there are many organic gardening insecticidal mixtures that you can obtain. Every longtime gardener has used a number of these and has their favorite concoction. Here is one of my personal favorites:

4 cups water
½ Tbsp. Neem oil
½ Tbsp. Dr. Bronner's Tea Tree or Lavender castile soap
A few drops of tea tree essential oil

Spray lightly, covering the entire plant and the surrounding soil. Repeat every five to seven days and reapply after a hard rain. This effectively treats plant diseases as well.

Finally, don't underestimate the effectiveness of simple inspection and removal. Frequently scout the garden in the mornings and at night. Evaluate each plant from the bud to the soil, including both the upper and lower leaf surfaces. When you find a pest, squash it! There's nothing more organic than that. Also, some insects (for example, aphids) release a hormone when squashed that signals others of their species that the area is not safe.

Keeping your garden pest-free doesn't have to involve a ton of chemicals. Follow the organic methods that work for you, pay careful attention to your plants, and you'll go a long way toward having a successful growing season.

Amy and Joe Alton are members of the Master Gardener Program for their state and are experts in medicinal herb, aquaponic, raised bed, and container gardening. Δ

Hog butchering
— using everything but the squeal

By Charles Sanders

Hogs are raised throughout our neighboring Amish community for many of the same reasons old American homesteads raised them. First, hogs don't take up much space. Second, they have a very good feed to meat conversion ratio.

A healthy hog will usually eat about eight pounds of food per day. If you feed straight grain ration, that can amount to quite a bit of money being spent on feed. Fortunately, hogs are thrifty. They don't need fancy feed — they thrive on our scraps. The homestead hog can fare very well on kitchen scraps, a bit of ground feed, leftover garden produce, extra milk from goats or cows, orchard windfalls, and cornfield gleanings. Any of these supplemental feed sources help in offsetting the total cost of purchased feed, and are valuable, nutrition-wise.

Generally speaking, hogs will convert about 2 to 6 pounds of feed to one pound of gain on the animal. In comparison, cattle average about 5½ to 6½ pounds of feed per pound of gain. These statistics are for animals that are on full feed; they don't take into account the supplemental food sources we've mentioned above.

Similar to cattle, a hog will average about 57% edible meat from a live hog. So, you can estimate that a 250-pound hog (a good butchering weight) will yield about 142 pounds of edible meat.

Every winter I help friends and neighbors butcher their hogs and put

A 450-pound hog will provide a lot of delicious meat.

them up in the form of canned meat, sausages, lard, and bacon. *Levavausht* (pronounced sort of like "level-vash") or Amish head cheese is often made as well. The word is an Amish dialectic pronunciation of the Dutch word *leverworst* meaning "liver sausage."

Depending on where you live, butcherings usually occur in late winter or early spring when the temperatures are cold, but not bitterly so. Often, there are three to five animals worked up at one time. That takes a lot of time, effort, and manpower. This time, however, my friends were working up only one animal, and things went well during the process. Even with just the one animal, the 450-pounder produced a lot of meat.

Getting started

To begin with, the pig needs to be killed. This can be done quickly and humanely with a well-placed shot from an ordinary .22 caliber rifle. Pour a bit of feed out for the pig to concentrate on, then, from close range, take careful aim and kill the pig with a shot just above the eyes and just off-center on the skull. That way, the shot won't glance off the animal's skull and wound it instead of killing it.

Having killed the hog, the next step is to "bleed" it. We did this by slitting the hog's neck across the jugular veins and allowing the blood to run out. To get a good idea of where to cut the hog's neck, just feel your own jugulars and figure about the same

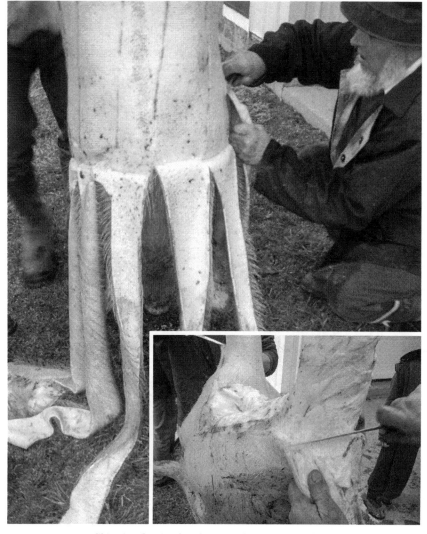

Skinning begins by skinning down the rear leg.
The strips of hide will be removed and discarded.

spot on the hog. Bleeding the hog will make a mess, so it's best to do this away from the actual butchering site. If you are planning to make blood sausage, you will need to have a vessel in which to catch the blood.

When butchering a hog, it can be either scalded or skinned. Skinning is quicker, but scalding is the preferred method if you plan to make head cheese or *levavausht*.

Scalding

Scalding takes more equipment than skinning, but the procedure goes roughly as follows:

1. Heat the water. The water in the tank should be about 160° F. Don't let it get too hot or it will cause the hair to "set" and it will be very difficult to remove.

2. Kill and stick the pig. Cut one of the jugulars so the animal will bleed out. Catch the blood if you want to make blood sausage.

3. Move it to the scalding tank. Use a tractor with a 3-point boom or a front-end loader.

4. Dip the animal and allow it to soak for a few minutes. Raise it out and scrape as much of the hair off as you can, using a hog scraper.

5. Repeat step four until the hair is removed from the animal.

We used overlapping ropes (you could use a chain) to roll the pig into the scalding water. Then we pulled back and forth, rolling the animal to and fro, making sure that it got thoroughly scalded.

Many folks use 55-gallon drums filled with hot water as their scalding tanks. Others use a big trough made for the purpose. It resembles a feed bunk but will allow the user to fill it with hot water. An old bathtub will also work.

My friends added a coffee can full of wood ashes (hickory is good) when we scalded their pigs. The lye contained in the wood ashes supposedly helps to cause the hair to slip from the hide.

Once you can easily scrape the hair from the animal, remove it and complete the scraping of the entire carcass.

Skinning

I've helped with butcherings where the animals were scalded and others where they were skinned. It's simply a matter of preference, but skinning tends to be quicker and doesn't take as much time or labor.

On this occasion, my friend chose to skin the animal. As is often the case when preparing for a Saturday butchering, we killed the hog on a Friday evening.

We began skinning by cutting around the legs just above the feet. Then, we made cuts from the back of each rear leg up towards the anus. Each rear leg was skinned down and the hide was worked down off the rump. The hide itself, especially on the sides and back, was skinned down towards the head in strips about three to four inches wide. That was to help in pulling the hide off the critter.

Once the carcass was skinned down to the neck, we cut the head off and saved it to use later. We cut open the carcass and carefully removed the anal vent and guts. All the entrails were removed. In this case, we were not going to use them for sausage casings, so we discarded them. If they were going to be used to stuff with sausage, they would have been emptied, washed, and scraped.

We used a meat saw to remove the feet and split the carcass. To split the carcass, we sawed from the tail to the neck down each side of the spine. That left three pieces consisting of two meat halves and the backbone. We hung the halves to allow them to cool overnight. This firms the meat and aids in cutting it up and processing it later.

While skinning the animal, we used the knife deftly to leave as much of the fat on the carcass as possible.

Processing

Very early the next morning, family and friends began to gather for the actual processing. The halves of the carcass were brought in to our processing area and cut into various large cuts (hams, shoulders, side meat, loins, ribs, and so on) using the meat saw and sharp knives. All of the meat except the ribs was de-boned and prepared for packing into quart jars or for grinding into sausage. The side meat was left for slicing into bacon that will be eaten fresh or taken to a local processor for curing. The ribs were cut into convenient slabs and packaged for cooking shortly after butchering or for freezing.

Since my friend and his family don't have a freezer in their home, most of the meat was packed into quart jars and pressure canned. The ladies in the group took charge of this part of the operation and it went smoothly.

One of the next chores was to set up the kettles for cooking the meat and rendering the lard. The heavy cast iron kettles were suspended from a heavy pipe frame. There are usually two or three kettles hanging over a

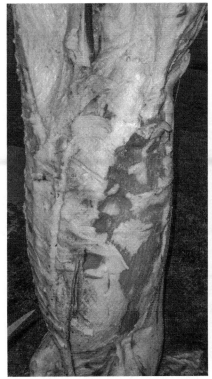

The skinned carcass, ready to open. Notice the large amount of fat present on the animal. It will be used in making lard.

long fire. In our case, only two kettles were needed.

Once all the fat was cut into small cubes, we placed it in one of the empty kettles. As the fat chunks heated, they began to liquefy. Then, we had to constantly stir the kettle to prevent the chunks from sticking and burning.

Once the lard was cooked out, we poured it into the lard press. There, all the liquid fat ran through the press and into a bucket. As soon as most of the liquid had run through, the remaining lard was "squoze" out and into the bucket.

After cranking the press and squeezing out the remainder of the liquid lard, the remaining cooked bits — the cracklings — were salted and snacked on as the work day progressed. I also took home a bag of them!

Making the sausage

Next, it was time to make the fresh pork sausage. To do that, we gathered

Getting the kettles heated up. Notice the handy adjustable hanger for the butchering kettle.

241

the meat and trimmings that had been set aside for the purpose. Good sausage requires a bit of fat in it and that had been considered in trimming the meat.

To grind the meat, we used an old Universal model 632 that has seen years of service. It was connected by a V-belt to a gasoline engine. The flywheels are of such sizes that the grinder runs at a good, slow speed.

We ground the meat and fat into sausage, then seasoned and mixed it by hand. Some of the folks seasoned with just salt and pepper; others preferred a bit more seasoning.

Once we mixed the sausage, we put it into the stuffer.

We stuffed the sausage into commercial store-bought casings. As I mentioned earlier, the hog intestines can be used, but they must be emptied, washed, and scraped beforehand, which is a time-consuming process.

In this case, we soaked the commercial casings in water to make them pliable. After soaking them for an hour or two, we fed them onto the

Pint jars of fresh pork are stacked into pressure canners. The ladies kept the two canners going for quite a while.

Left: Fresh pork loins and ribs. Right: A slab of fresh bacon.

The sausage is ground and stuffed into long ropes of sausage, then the ladies twist it into links.

spout of the sausage press, several feet at a time.

Once the press was filled with sausage, we slowly turned the crank, filling the long casing with meat. The women took the filled casings inside, to twist them into links. The women separated the links by cutting each from the others with a sharp knife.

They then boiled the individual links in a kettle of hot water. It's best to bring the temperature of the hot sausages up to cooking temperature gradually so that they don't burst.

These links are called "water sausages" since they are cooked in boiling water. Other times, we've cooked them in hot, liquid fat.

I enjoyed cooking the sausage, as it required frequent sampling to be sure the meat was done! I made sure that my sampling was accompanied by slabs of bread and mustard.

As soon as the link sausages were sufficiently cooked, the women took them inside and packed them into quart jars. They poured some hot liquid in the jars, then pressure canned them on the propane stove. After the jars were done processing and cooling, they were ready to be stored on the shelves for later use.

If the sausages had been cooked in fat, they would also have been packed into jars with the liquid fat and processed. After they cool, those sausages are encased in a white chunk of lard. Obviously, the jar must be warmed before the sausages can be fished out. The fat is poured off for later use and the sausages heated or used in recipes.

Head cheese or *Levavausht*

The making of head cheese is just a part of using all the pig that you can in butchering. To make *Levavausht*, begin by cooking all the bones remaining after trimming off the meat. Add the liver and kidneys to the kettle and allow them to cook as well. Add some strips of skin to the kettle, but keep in mind that you will only want to add hog skin that has been scalded. The skin will have been scraped clean of hair and will cook up

A kettle of cooked sausage is quickly packed into jars for canning.

to add a gelatinous quality to the finished sausage. Add jowl meat and fat, then any other meat and fat that remains.

Boil until the meat is easily removed from the bones. Lift the kettle from the fire and dip the meat onto a table where it can be picked clean from the bones.

This is a good time to have a container of salt handy as you'll probably want to nibble on pieces of kidney or liver as you work. After picking the meat from the bones, run the whole lot — meat, organs, cooked skin, and all — through the sausage grinder. Mix it with a bit of seasoning, then either stuff it into casings or containers.

My friends decided to keep some of the meat and sausage fresh and put it in freezer bags. They planned on taking the fresh meat to a small locker facility where families rent freezer space. Dozens of families in the neighborhood take advantage of the facility.

For my efforts, I brought home a bag of cracklings and a big bag of bulk sausage (I divided that into smaller packages and froze it.)

The whole operation of butchering and putting up a hog takes several people and a lot of work. It makes for a couple of long, busy days. It is a good and worthwhile time, though. Besides producing a lot of food, I got to spend time with good friends and make some new ones as well. It was, indeed, time well-spent. Δ

The lard is squeezed out through a press into a waiting bucket. The kids enjoy this part of the operation, especially eating the hot, fresh hog cracklings afterwards!

Ayoob on Firearms

The current "Gun control" push: A cop's eye view

Massad Ayoob

First, a word of explanation. The reason "gun control" is in quotes in the title and in this sentence is because, for a very long time, the prohibitionists have made it more about control of the general public than about controlling criminal misuse of lethal weapons. Of late, the prohibitionists have played their word-spin again, changing the name of their product to "firearms safety" and "firearms responsibility."

Um ... sorry. You'll have to look long and hard to find, among the ranks of the prohibitionists, anyone who has actually taught a firearms safety class. Since 1871, the leading firearms safety training entity in the United States and probably the world has been the National Rifle Association, an organization which has been venomously demonized by those who would now usurp all they've done to further the disarming of American citizens.

But, enough of partisan semantics. I've been asked by the editorial staff to write this particular article because, even though I'm the Firearms Editor and not the Justice System Editor, I became by default the "resident cop" at *Backwoods Home*. I recently passed the 39 year mark of carrying a badge and a gun for the protection of the public. (I did it part time, which is why I didn't burn out from it and lasted this long.) Nineteen of those years were spent as chair of the Firearms and Deadly Force Training Committee for ASLET, the American Society of Law Enforcement Trainers, and a partially overlapping 10 years as a member of the Advisory Board of ILEETA, the International Law Enforcement Educators and Trainers Association. I've also taught for IALEFI, the International Association of Law Enforcement Firearms Instructors, both stateside and abroad. It's safe to say that the decades have given me a pretty good handle on what cops think about guns ... and about "gun control."

The view from the street

In mid-April of 2013, roughly four months after the atrocity at the Sandy Hook Elementary School in Newtown, Connecticut that triggered the strongest politico-media push for "gun control" in our nation's history, I was at the annual conference of the above-mentioned ILEETA, attended by more than 700 police trainers from around the nation and the world. I was one of many attending a panel discussion on Active Shooter Response when something interesting happened.

Since the Columbine High School atrocity in 1999, mass murders by gunfire have become known as "active shooter" events. It was pointed out by some of the panelists that this is an unfortunate term; what was really under discussion was immediate response to mass murder. "Active shooter," historically, has meant someone lawfully using firearms, from a hunter sighting in for deer season to a target shooter at a match to a member of a police department pistol team.

Partway through the discussion, a panel member looked down at a text message on his smartphone, and raised his hand to interrupt. He announced that he had just received a message that the Universal Background Check bill had failed to pass in the United States Senate.

And, spontaneously, the packed classroom of police instructors burst into applause.

While I was at ILEETA, I couldn't help but notice that NRA had not one but two booths at the concurrent Law Enforcement Vendors Expo. One represented NRA's Law Enforcement Division, which teaches dozens of police firearms instructors' schools around the country each year. The other showcased NRA's firearms safety programs for the public. (One class at ILEETA revolved around a police department that teaches CCW (Concealed Carry Weapon) courses for private citizens, the tuition fees supplementing the agency's training budget.) By contrast, the anti-gun groups were notable by their absence. No surprise; they had nothing to offer real, working cops, and probably knew that streetwise police officers would see through them, anyway.

Street reality

The media and the prohibitionists had told the public that America's police had wanted banning of semiautomatic rifles, and of magazines that held more than 10 cartridges; that had already failed in the Senate. Even

245

*More than 700 police instructors attended the
International Law Enforcement Educators and Trainers conference.*

background checks for transfer of firearms ownership had now failed? Shouldn't the cops have responded with an anguished chorus of "Boo"?

No.

Because these were the *real* cops, the trainers of the next generation of *real* street cops, and they knew the *reality*.

They knew that the sick monster who had slain 20 children and 6 adults in Newtown had murdered his own mother to steal the guns she had lawfully purchased in Connecticut, one of the nation's toughest "gun control" states, and that no background check could have stopped his evil depredation.

Many of the cops in that audience, myself included, had been the first responding officer to situations where innocent victims had saved themselves from deadly danger with defensive firearms ... the only reason they were still alive to talk to us when we got there. Every cop in that audience worked hard to be proactive, to prevent crime. But each also understood that in a nation of more than 300 million people, with only about 800,000 cops, law enforcement is

really more reactive than proactive. Cops can't be everywhere. They can't predict where the most evil and violent criminals will strike. They can only respond as fast as they can when they "get the call."

At the time that announcement was made at ILEETA, the panelists had already discussed the timelines police

have to deal with. The call has to come in to 9-1-1. The message has to be relayed from the dispatchers to the officers in the field. Those officers have to GET THERE, and none of them can suspend the time/space continuum and freeze the situation until they arrive. Average police response time to emergency calls in this country seems to run around eleven minutes, from the call coming in to the first responding officer arriving at the danger scene.

The horror of Sandy Hook was in the minds of the ILEETA audience more profoundly than it was in the minds of most of the prohibitionists. Every cop in the ILEETA audience had pictured themselves as the first responding officer, or the trainer of that officer, or the supervisor responsible for that officer.

Every cop in that large classroom empathized the horror those first officers faced when they got there, to discover that the killer had already killed himself and that there was absolutely nothing they could do to bring 20 innocent little children and their 6 helplessly slain protectors back to life. And each of them knew something else: it would have been far bet-

*NRA had a booth promoting their "civilian" firearms training programs at
ILEETA, separate from the NRA Law Enforcement Division booth.*

ter to have been the first to find a school resource officer, a private security guard, or even a schoolteacher with a smoking gun in her hand standing over the corpse of a dead would-be murderer, the only casualty of the day.

ILEETA vis-à-vis NRA

Not long after the ILEETA conference in the Chicago suburb of Wheeling, Illinois, I attended the annual members' meeting of the NRA in Houston, Texas. A record 86,000-plus NRA members attended. Among the throngs inside the convention center were many law enforcement officers, some in uniform. They chatted pleasantly with the armed citizens and firearms industry people in the aisles. Across the street were anti-gun protest groups whose numbers ranged from half a dozen to a reported 50 at one point. Police were assigned there. They kept a respectful distance, showing no indication of wishing to interact with the protesters while their brother officers were fraternizing with the gun folks inside. (Of course, the press gave the tiny clutch of protesters as much coverage as the vast crowd of pro-gun people, but that's another story.)

Understanding a misunderstanding

The media and anti-gun politicians constantly tell the public that cops want more "gun control" and even gun bans. You'll hear the same from high profile police chiefs who, despite the usual rule that police officers can't take political positions while speaking as members of the law enforcement agency, will flank the President or some other politician who makes an anti-gun speech. Why does that happen?

In the great majority of communities, municipal police chiefs are appointed by the mayor, the city manager, or the city council. If those political entities are anti-gun, you

NRA's Law Enforcement Division booth at the ILEETA seminar.

may be sure that they will either appoint an anti-gun candidate, or make it clear to the appointee that he will speak the lines he is given or he will no longer be Chief. As a general rule, police rank is only protected by Civil Service up to Captain level. Higher than that, and the high ranking cop "serves at the pleasure" of the appointing authority. If he doesn't toe their line, he can be busted back down to Captain and replaced by someone who responds more obediently to the puppet strings.

Sheriffs are a different matter. The high sheriff of the county is an *elected* official, and "serves at the pleasure" of … the voters. This is probably why you see relatively more sheriffs than police chiefs or commissioners standing up for gun owners' civil rights and refusing to be sock puppets for anti-gun politicians.

Pro-gun lawmen

In May of 2013, attorney David Kopel — a legendary champion of gun owners' civil rights — filed a suit against Colorado Governor John Hickenlooper. The governor had signed into law Draconian legislation that severely hampered firearms

transfers between law-abiding citizens and criminalized, among other things, any magazine that could be made to hold more than 15 cartridges — which, mechanically speaking, is almost every pistol or rifle magazine in existence. Joining as plaintiffs in that suit were (at this writing) 55 of the 64 high sheriffs in the state of Colorado. Does that, perhaps, tell us something?

If the Colorado law was one major victory for the gun prohibitionists, certainly the ironically-named SAFE Act in New York State was another. Among other things this sloppily-cobbled law limited magazines to no more than seven cartridges, and criminalized the mere possession of a magazine even capable of holding more than ten. Violating the New York State Constitution, which requires a certain period of time for reflection, analysis, and debate before it can be passed, this classic example of feel-good legislation was ramrodded through literally in the dark of night. It was so poorly crafted that it initially neglected to exempt law enforcement, an error that would later be repaired. By May of 2013, the first arrest had been made, a motorist who had nine cartridges in the magazine of his otherwise legal pistol, instead of the maximum seven.

The Police Benevolent Association representing New York State Police Troopers took public exception to the law. On April 16, 2013, reporter Teri Weaver wrote:

"Syracuse, N.Y. — The union representing New York State Police say they believe the state's stricter gun laws could put law enforcement officers at risk.

"In an email release on Monday, the New York State Troopers PBA said its 6,000-member group "holds widely shared concerns" about the NY Safe Act. Nonetheless, the union takes exception to some state lawmakers accusing the troopers of failing to enforce the law.

"'The individual members of this union did not write the terms of the bill nor vote on its passage,' the release said. 'We urge the citizens of New York state to remember that troopers are simply tasked with the lawful mandate to enforce the laws of

An NRA member pats a mounted police officer's horse outside the Convention Center at the NRA annual meeting.

the state, regardless of their personal opinion of such laws.'

"The Safe Act bans certain semi-automatic guns now labeled as assault weapons. Monday was the first day gun owners had to register these assault weapons with the state; a ban on magazines larger than 10 rounds also went into effect Monday.

"The troopers are not the first law enforcement group to criticize the Safe Act. The New York State Sheriffs' Association has expressed concern about the likelihood that deputies can enforce certain provisions of the law, including background checks on private gun sales. The sheriffs group also believes many provisions of the law will only increase requirements among those who abide by the law and do little to ward against violent crimes or mass shootings.

"Here's the message, in full: 'The NY SAFE Act has been a controversial and emotional topic since its passage in January of 2013. The NYS Troopers PBA, representing more than 6,000 active and retired members, has reserved public comment as we worked within the legislative process of NYS government with the hope of affecting changes to the law. Our membership holds widely shared concerns of this new law. Additionally, we believe that actual enforcement of these new regulations will significantly increase the hazards of an already dangerous job.

Convention center was filled with a record 86,000+ NRA members in Houston this year.

"'Polls have shown that increased firearm regulations are not popular in the more rural and upstate regions of our state, which is where the majority of our members live and patrol. Additionally, some in mainstream media have already irresponsibly increased the anti-police rhetoric, which fosters additional resentment of law enforcement. Even some of our elected officials, like Senator Ranzenhofer and Assemblyman Gabryszak, are calling for a probe of our members and their efforts to meet the standards of this new law.

"'It is the responsibility of this union to defend the reputation and safety of our members. Potential legislative changes as well as pending court decisions may further alter the terms of the SAFE Act. The individual members of this union did not write the terms of the bill nor vote on its passage. We urge the citizens of New York State to remember that Troopers are simply tasked with the lawful mandate to enforce the laws of the State, regardless of their personal opinion of such laws.'"

Thank you, Ms. Weaver!

These laws adversely impact cops

A lot of the general public has missed the fact that many of these laws impact police. Let's say that a given state bans AR15s on the theory that they are "evil assault rifles." A great many law enforcement agencies (Florida Highway Patrol comes to mind) can't afford to buy AR15s for every officer, so they authorize their armed personnel to buy their own and take them on duty after appropriate training and qualification. An "assault weapon ban" written to allow these guns to be purchased only by law enforcement *agencies* takes that option off the table, and police in that situation won't have access to patrol rifles with which to protect the public and themselves. If the law is written to exempt currently sworn individual

---

The PoliceOne.Com Poll

A huge police-only Internet site, PoliceOne.Com, polled its members on "gun control" recently. It is important to note that to be on the site and part of the poll, those participating had to reveal their identities and PROVE that they were cops. Some of the results of the survey:

95.7%: ... did NOT think a federal ban on manufacture and sale of ammunition magazines that hold more than 10 rounds would reduce violent crime.

71%: ... thought a federal ban on manufacture and sale of semiautomatic firearms would have no effect on reducing violent crime.

20.5%: ... thought banning such firearms would actually have a negative effect on reducing violent crime.

81.3%: ... supported the concept of trained, armed school personnel.

---

police officers, that means that as soon as the officer retires and gives up his sworn authority, he's either a criminal if he keeps it, or has to give his personal property over to the police department.

In 2004, then-President George W. Bush signed into law HR 218, the Law Enforcement Officer Safety Act. As LEOSA stands now, any sworn (or honorably retired and currently handgun-qualified) police officer can carry a personal handgun nationwide when "on their own time." However, they are required to conform to the laws that would govern a private citizen licensed to carry in the given jurisdiction. This means that if Coloradans can't have more than a 15-round magazine ... if Californians can't have more than 10-rounders ... and if New Yorkers with permits are allowed no more than seven cartridges in a magazine ... then that applies to visiting out-of-state cops as well.

The bottom line is, when you hear someone say "The police want to ban these guns/magazines/transfers between law-abiding private citizens" ... don't believe it. Anyone who actually works with the cops on the street knows that the great majority of them want to enforce existing laws on genuine criminals, not criminalize the law-abiding citizens they've sworn an oath to protect and serve. Δ

The Last Word

The false argument about defending our freedoms

I'm tired of hearing how we should honor our veterans because they're defending our freedoms. They're not. No one in any of the Islamic countries is trying to take away our freedoms. No one in Russia, China, or North Korea gives a damn about them, either.

In reality, the only people taking away our freedoms are in Washington, DC, our statehouses, and our city halls. It is our own politicians, our own bureaucrats, and special interest groups from the Sierra Club to Monsanto, all of which are made up almost exclusively of fellow Americans and who are pressing to have laws, rules, and regulations passed that restrict our speech, our opinions, and our travel; they want to grab our guns, snatch our property, and determine what we can and cannot do with our own bodies.

It is The PATRIOT Act, the RICO Act, and a myriad of other laws and regulations that are stealing our freedoms, and not a one of them was enacted or passed by a foreign government or terrorist group. It's not al-Qaeda that's creating "free speech" zones in this country or removing people wearing political T-shirts from parade routes the President might take. It's not the Taliban that's going after the records of reporters at AP. The North Koreans aren't behind the IRS's targeting of conservative political groups.

And here's some irony for you: You know these freedoms our military is supposed to be protecting for us? Well, those of us who steadfastly demand to be able to practice those freedoms and who demand government at all levels adhere to the Constitution, are now labeled as potential domestic terrorists. Demand your freedoms and rights and you're lumped with al-Qaeda!

If our military wants to protect us from the real thieves of our rights, they're going to have to protect us from our own government.

In the meantime, I'm not denigrating those who serve in our military services. They're men and women who are willing to give their all. They go overseas and many come home in body bags or they come home maimed and crippled. But don't tell me they're doing it for our freedoms because, as I said, the Islamic terrorists, the Syrians, the North Koreans, and any of these other countries or groups don't give a damn about them. What they do care about is that we're meddling in what they consider their business whether it's supporting Israel, propping up the Saudi royal family, protecting Monsanto's overseas interests … the list goes on. And I'm not saying we should or shouldn't be

doing those things. But the real reasons for our military adventures should be part of the public debate so informed Americans can make voting decisions at the polls. We shouldn't be using phony patriotic arguments to send our kids off to die.

John Silveira

And that brings me to my second point: The people who should be protecting our freedoms are not uniformed soldiers, it's We the People. It won't matter how many of our sons and daughters die in Iraq or Afghanistan if we won't protect our rights here at home. And the sad thing is, to get rid of those who are really stealing our freedoms we don't need the Marines. All we need is a ballot. But we go to the polls year in and year out and we keep reelecting the thieves who are gutting our Constitution, while they're sending our kids off to die in wars that have nothing to do with our freedoms.

We're not losing our freedoms in lands afar, we're losing them here at home.

— John Silveira

FREE ANTHOLOGY AND BOOK SPECIAL - SEE PAGE 97

Backwoods Home magazine

Sept/Oct 2013
Issue #143
$5.95 US
$7.50 CAN

practical ideas for self-reliant living

Apple Trees

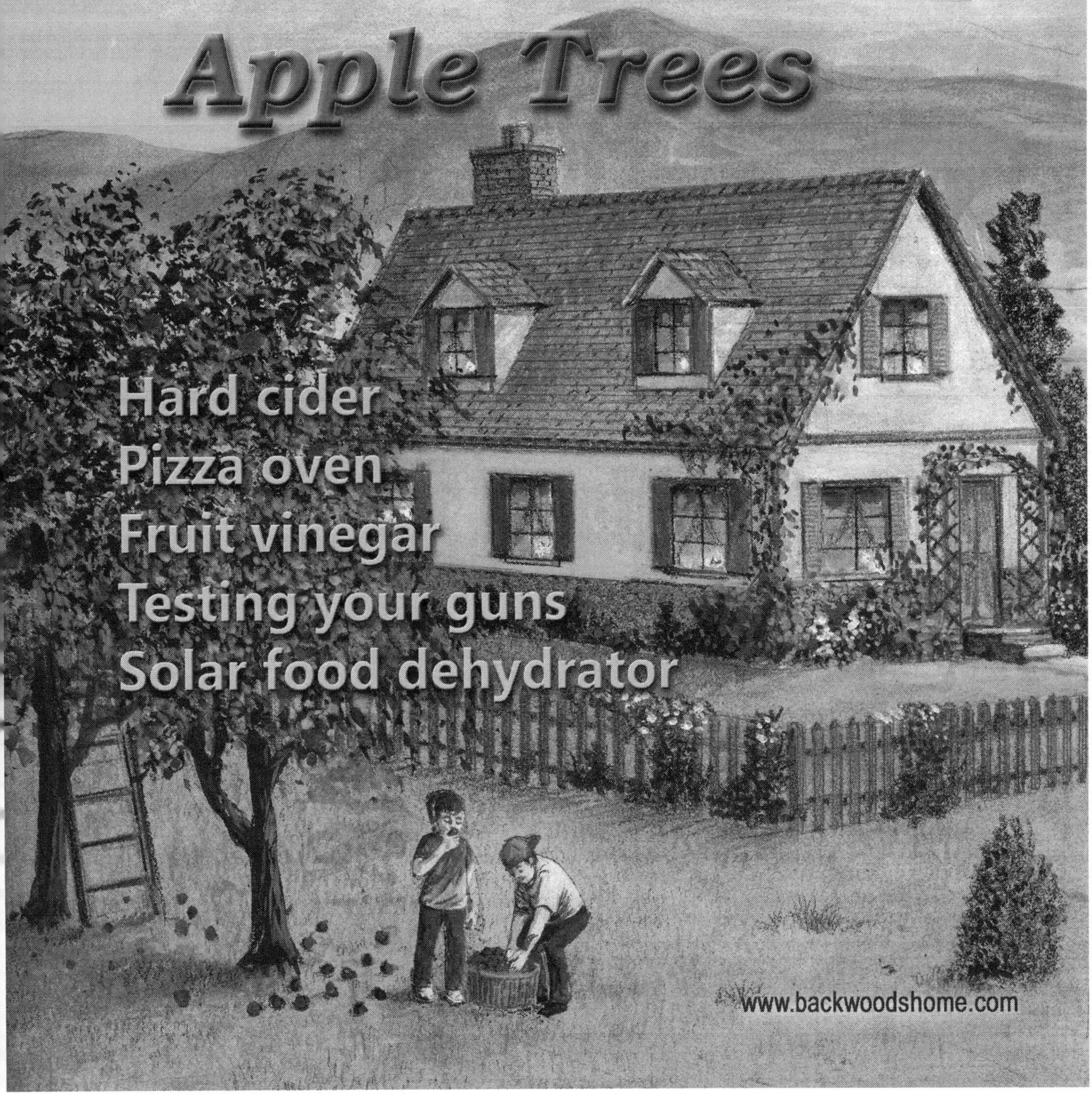

Hard cider
Pizza oven
Fruit vinegar
Testing your guns
Solar food dehydrator

www.backwoodshome.com

Apples
on your homestead

By Jackie Clay-Atkinson

Apple trees deserve a special place on every homestead, no matter how large or small. I've never met a person who didn't love a crisp apple fresh from the tree. For that matter, I've never met a person who would refuse an apple from root cellar storage during the cold of mid-winter. When I think of apples, I picture eating a sweet, crisp, juicy apple, but I can also picture all the ways I can use them in baking: apple pie, baked apples, apple bread, apple cake, apple upside-down cake, applesauce, fried apple pies, apple jelly, dehydrated apples, and even apple pectin to help set my other jams and jellies.

Luckily, apples grow in most sections of the country from frigid Zone 2 to balmy Zone 9. While they do have chilling needs to produce fruit, some varieties have quite short chilling requirements, so growing them down south is definitely possible. And while there are only a few extra-hardy varieties that will take the Arctic blasts of Zone 2, there *are* at least some. If you live somewhere in between these zones, you have the world by the tail. Even here in northern Minnesota (Zone 3) where we have some winter temperatures of

A three-year-old apple tree, bearing its second crop. Notice the six-foot-high fence surrounding our orchard to keep out deer and other pests.

252

-45° F, we are able to grow many different varieties of apples.

In fact, we have more than 20 different varieties of apples growing happily in our little orchard. The most mature are only four years old right now. Some are starting to bear and every tree looks very healthy. We can hardly wait until they are all in production!

A short apple history

Archeologists say that people have been eating apples since 6,500 B.C. The only wild apples native to North America are crab apples. Some of these are fairly large, but most are not. Some are good to eat while others are bitter and unpalatable.

Apples originated from an area around the Caspian Sea and were eventually brought to England by traders. The apple first came to the United States in the Massachusetts Bay Colony, planted by the Pilgrims and brought to the New World from England. George Washington and Thomas Jefferson both had apple orchards.

Today, there are 2,500 varieties of apples grown in the U.S. and more than 7,500 varieties grown worldwide. Of the 2,500 varieties grown in the U.S., there are more than 100 varieties grown commercially. Today, apples are grown in all 50 states, with most commercial apple orchards found in Washington, New York, Pennsylvania, California, and Virginia.

Cold climate varieties

While it is definitely possible to grow apples in colder, less hospitable climates, you do need to make some adjustments to what trees you buy and where you get them. I've made plenty of mistakes along the way (and had dead trees to show for it), so I'm hoping you'll learn from my mistakes and save yourself some discouragement.

When you live in Zone 4 or even some Zone 5 areas, you'd think that you could plant any variety of tree listed for that zone. Well, that depends. If your Zone 5 is in a very windy area with some cold temperatures during the winter, your listed Zone 5 trees may not survive. We lived in Zone 5, on the high plains of northern New Mexico. It seemed warm enough to me, so I planted several semi-dwarf Zone 5 trees. Few survived.

Since then, I've learned that when you live in an inhospitable climate with cold, stiff winds, semi-dwarf and dwarf trees often do not survive. Their rootstock is just not hardy enough to withstand the combination of cold and wind.

The same goes for folks living in Zone 2 or Zone 3. I've had better luck with trees surviving by planting only standard apples. They not only live but thrive, with little to no winter kill. Winter kill is when branches die from exposure to the cold. In severe cases, the whole tree dies to the ground.

Some folks have asked me why I'd plant standard trees when I'm more than 65 years old. Their reasoning is that those trees will get 35 feet tall and I won't be able to climb ladders to pick the fruit. My answer? That's what pruning shears are for. With selective pruning, you can easily shape a tree so it grows *out* instead of *up*. In fact, many commercial orchards routinely top their trees for that very reason. You can keep standard trees quite small, if you wish (or must), due to space constraints.

Although standard trees *can* take several years to begin to bear, if you take good care of them, most will start to bear in about three years. Those years seem to fly by on the homestead. On the other hand, if you wasted your time planting semi-dwarf trees in Zone 3 or Zone 4, those trees will most likely winter kill and have to be replanted, taking several years before they begin to produce.

Types of apple trees

Apple trees come in standard, semi-dwarf, or dwarf size. The semi-dwarfs and dwarfs are smaller trees than the standards. The semi-dwarfs usually mature to about 20 feet tall, unless you keep them pruned shorter. Dwarfs often reach only 10 feet, even without pruning. And some dwarfs are only 5-6 feet tall, making them easy to pick from.

Both semi-dwarf and dwarf trees produce full-sized fruit. In fact, they are often so covered with fruit that you must prop up the branches so the weight of the fruit doesn't split branches from the tree.

You can expect to harvest up to 20 bushels from a mature standard tree, 10 bushels from a mature semi-dwarf, and 2 bushels from a mature dwarf tree. And because semi-dwarfs and dwarfs are smaller, earlier-maturing trees than standards, they will begin bearing at a young age, often two to three years after planting.

The added benefit of planting semi-dwarf and dwarf apples is that you can plant them in a much smaller space. Even folks living in a city can usually find room for a couple of apple trees in their yard. Instead of planting ornamental trees, why not think of planting a couple of trees that are food-producing? Apple trees all have gorgeous pinkish-white blooms in the spring. You can even plant these smaller apple trees in your front yard, but expect some to be snatched, as ripe apples are tempting to passers-by.

There are also *extremely* dwarf apple trees that are suited for containers. Even if you live in an apartment, there is no reason you can't grow a few of these apple trees. And if you move, just take them with you.

Choosing apples for your own homestead

Before you go out and buy apple trees, decide what you want to use those apples for. Do you want an

Good sources for apple trees:

Specializing in northern and challenging climate trees (many Zone 4-8 trees too):

Fedco Trees
P.O. Box 520
Waterville, Maine 04903-0520
www.fedcoseeds.com/trees.htm
207-426-9900

St. Lawrence Nurseries
325 State Hwy 345
Potsdam, New York 13676
www.sln.potsdam.ny.us
315-265-6739

Main Zone fruit trees (ones that will grow almost everywhere):

Raintree Nursery
391 Butts Rd.
Morton, Washington 98356
www.raintreenursery.com
800-391-8892

Trees of Antiquity
20 Wellsona Road
Paso Robles, California 93446
www.treesofantiquity.com
805-967-9909

and try many different apples. Don't go by what you've tasted in the store! This is not a viable method as many of those apples were picked on the green side and never ripened to full flavor. I've eaten homegrown *Honeycrisp* apples that were ambrosia from the gods, and I've eaten $3.19/lb. store-bought *Honeycrisps* that were sour and tasteless.

Some types of apples are best suited for dessert, such as *Northern Spy*, *Golden Delicious,* and *Honeycrisp. Baldwin, Gravenstein, Wealthy, Harrison,* and Will's very favorite, *Pink Lady* (also called *Cripps Pink*) are apples that work well for pies. Some of these are good to eat fresh as well as being great for sauce or pie. Read the descriptions in the catalogs carefully.

On our homestead, we enjoy learning about apples and raise many old heritage varieties as well as more modern ones. As a result, we have more apple trees than the average homesteader does.

Folks ask what we will *do* with all of those bushels and bushels of apples when the trees mature. Of course, we'll eat plenty fresh. But we'll also make and can sauce and jelly, dehydrate apples, and store many for use during the winter. We plan on bartering or selling some of the excess and feeding the rest to our livestock to help out on the feed bill. All our goats, cattle, pigs, chickens, and even turkeys love apples. And apples are nutritious, too.

Buying your apple trees

Choose your apple varieties, then shop around for where you will be buying as it makes a huge difference in the end result. Simply taking the easy route and picking up a few apple trees at the local Wal-Mart or other big box store isn't such a great idea. Many times, these trees have come from far away and will either not grow in your zone or will be too leafed out to do well, once planted.

You want to plant trees that are completely dormant for best results. Although it is tempting to buy potted trees that are fully leafed out and have blooms or fruit on them, the little "sticks" (dormant smaller trees) quickly catch up to the potted trees in size and surpass them in livability and production.

You can buy your trees from a mail-order nursery and have them shipped directly to your door. Again, choose your nursery carefully, especially if you live in an inhospitable zone. Many nurseries that brag that their trees are "hardy" grow them on rootstock that is only dependably hardy in Zones 4-8. Nearly all apple trees grown and sold today are grafted trees. This means that small branches (scion wood) from the desired apple varieties are grafted onto hardy rootstock (likely a very hardy apple or crabapple). As the graft takes and grows, it becomes the top part of the tree — the fruiting part. But it needs that sturdy, hardy rootstock to survive cold and otherwise inhospitable climates.

For that reason, we only buy from St. Lawrence Nurseries and Fedco Trees. If you live in a happier zone, you have a huge selection of nursery catalogs from which to choose your trees. I'd advise one that grows their trees in a climate similar to your own for best results. If you live in a very warm climate, you want to choose a company in a warm climate that specializes in trees with low chill requirements. All apples require some period of chilling temperatures to set fruit. Fortunately, there are some newer varieties with very low chilling requirements that *will* dependably produce fruit in the warmest of zones in the U.S.

One additional tip: Don't pick a nursery that "prunes" the roots and tops of their trees like so many of the big-box nurseries are doing today. This type of pruning is detrimental to the tree and is only done to fit the tree

early summer apple for fresh eating, applesauce, and dehydrated apples? There are plenty of summer apples such as *Yellow Transparent, Duchess of Oldenburg, McIntosh,* and *Zestar.* They are great eaten fresh, used for sauce, or in a pie. But they don't keep. Their harvest window is only a few weeks — after that, they begin to soften and rot. So don't buy multiple summer apple trees unless you think you need that many.

If you want an apple that will keep well over winter in your root cellar, choose a variety such as *Honeycrisp, Baldwin, Frostbite, Winesap,* or *Sweet Sixteen.* And even winter and fall apples have a huge variety of flavors. If possible, go to an apple orchard into a package that is cheaper for the company to send in the mail. I cringe at pictures of those trees. They look butchered!

Choose your trees early after studying several catalogs and then place your order. Some of the best companies have a very early cut-off date for shipments and some of the best varieties do sell out. Although we still have snows in April when our trees typically arrive, with care they will hold well until we can plant. So don't worry about ordering too early, just tell the company where you live and they'll usually do well in sending at the proper planting time.

Planting your new trees

Your trees usually arrive via the post office or UPS. As soon as they show up, unwrap them, check for damage, and see how dry the roots are. Most roots come wrapped in shredded newspaper or sphagnum moss that is damp, then wrapped in plastic to hold in the moisture. If the roots are not wrapped this way, dampen them, add sphagnum moss or paper, and wrap loosely in plastic to keep the roots damp. They'll store fine in an unheated basement, a garage where the temperature doesn't freeze, or a root cellar. If unfrozen soil is available in your garden, you can dig a trench and lay the tree roots in it with the tops laying on the ground, then cover the roots with soil. This is called "heeling in" and it will effectively hold the trees safe until you can plant them in their permanent location.

Most of us plant our apple trees in the early spring, as it gives them all summer and fall to become strong before winter. But those folks who live in milder climates like the Northwest coast often plant their trees in the fall to take advantage of the fall and winter rains. The roots will have a chance to become established before next spring rolls around, giving your apple trees a head start.

Prepare a $100 hole for a $25 tree.
You want plenty of room for the roots in loose, amended soil.

Here, I'm pruning off sprouts from below the graft prior to planting the tree.

Planting distances

Standard trees should be planted with at least 25 feet between trees and rows. Semi-dwarf trees can be planted closer — about 15 feet apart. Dwarf trees can be closer still — about 8 feet with rows about 15 feet apart to allow for the tops to grow and room to maneuver between them to harvest. These distances also pertain to the distance away from other trees such as shade trees. If your shade tree is not grown to maturity, remember to allow for it to get bigger. Planting trees too close together results in lower apple production.

255

Prune off only dead or damaged branches from your new tree.

Here's our orchard of young trees, protected against rabbit and vole damage by aluminum window screen. You can also use plastic trunk protectors.

Planting trees for pollination

While some fruits, such as peaches, are self-pollinating, apples require another apple as a pollinator in order to produce well. So unless your nearby neighbor has an apple tree or even a crab apple, you need to plant at least two different apples for pollination. And when planting these two trees, try to keep them within 50 feet of each other for best fruiting. Also, remember to pick apples that bloom at about the same time — if they aren't blooming together, they can't pollinate each other. Generally, this means choosing pairs of trees that are either summer, fall, or winter apples.

Readying your planting holes

One of the most important things you can do to ensure that your new tree thrives is to plant it well. Many people are so busy when the trees come that they just dig a hole, barely big enough to hold the roots, put the tree in the hole, and shovel the dirt back in to cover the roots. Does it live? Maybe. Does it do well? Not usually.

It's been said that you should dig a $100 hole for a $25 tree. Dig the hole broad and deep, even if you have clay or rocky soil. Use a crowbar or pickax to remove large rocks and to help loosen the soil. Do you think the hole is deep enough? Dig it twice as deep! Then mix in some rotted compost with the native soil and add a few inches of that to the bottom of the hole. Soak your tree in a pail of water for an hour or two before planting. Situate the tree so the graft is several inches above the ground level then gently begin to sift in the mixed soil. As you fill, soak the soil with water to eliminate any air pockets. Add more soil until the tree is planted to the depth it was in the nursery row. Make a shallow, wide bowl with a berm around it to hold water. Water the tree and replace any soil that has settled.

Watering and staking

Keep the tree well-watered all through the year, giving it 1 to 2 inches weekly unless you are having very heavy rains.

If you live on sandy or gravelly soil, water your trees throughout the fall until the ground freezes. One year, we didn't water our young orchard enough, watering only until the trees' leaves had turned color and dropped. We had a lot of winter kill. Since then, we've always watered until the ground freezes and have had only minimal winter kill on a few of the new-growth branch tips.

Dwarf and semi-dwarf trees need to be staked when planted because their root system is not as strong and extensive as the roots of standard trees. Your stake should be 10 feet long (above ground) and driven in close to the tree but not so it damages the roots. Keep the tree tied loosely to the stake as it grows. Then, prune off all growth below 24 inches, maintaining the central leader to grow straight.

Pruning new trees

Newly-planted apple trees require very little, if any, pruning. Prune off only dead or broken branches. Never prune roots unless they are broken or rotten. Don't over-prune young trees as they grow because it delays production. Leave the central leader to grow, cutting off only extra trunks, suckers from the roots, and branches that cross and rub against each other. Each spring, cut off any branches or tips that have died, but other than that, leave the tree alone until it begins to bear.

Mulching

It's a good idea to keep your young trees mulched. You can use well-rotted compost, wood chips, or straw in a layer about six inches thick in a 4 to 6-foot circle around the trunk. This not only keeps down weeds and grass but it also holds moisture around the tree roots. We spread a wheelbarrow-load of rotted manure around each tree in the spring to fertilize the tree, but never in the fall. This often causes late fall growth which winter kills in the cold.

Keep the mulch and manure a few inches away from the trunk of the tree to discourage voles and mice from tunneling under the mulch and eating the bark of the tender tree trunks.

Thinning the fruit

As the trees start to bear, you'll often have smaller apples at the beginning. To get some size on the apples and to help the tree grow, it's a good idea to thin some of the apples each year. Just pluck a few immature apples from each bunch. Choose the smaller or misshapen ones. I know it's hard, after you've waited so long for fruit. As the tree gets older, you can still do this to get more large apples instead of a ton of small ones. Commercial orchards use a spray to make the tree self-thin.

Every spring, we mulch around each tree with rotted manure for fertilizer and to retain moisture around the roots. It also prevents weeds and grass from crowding the young tree.

Protecting your apple trees from pesky critters

As hard as you've worked to establish your trees, you don't want them to be killed by deer, rabbits, or mice. It's hard to imagine that something as small as a field mouse could kill a six-foot-tall tree. But they can, and do, all too often! During the winter, they'll tunnel under the snow and snack on the bark, making a white ring around the whole trunk. By the time you discover the damage, there is little chance of saving the tree. You can try a bridge graft but that is rarely a fix.

Every fall, before snowfall, wrap the lower part of the tree (as high as you can so rabbits can't eat the bark) with either plastic trunk wrap (the white tubes or spirals) or old window screen. Using ¼-inch hardware cloth is also a good option. Be sure to push the trunk guard down all the way to the ground.

In the spring, it's a good idea to remove the protection as apple borers like to use the guard as a hideout.

And don't forget deer! Oh dear, they love to snack on apple trees. They eat all the tender branches, preventing the tree from flowering in the spring. They can even eat so many branches that the tree will die. Watch out for bucks — they will thrash the young trees with their antlers when they are in rut.

I've tried all kinds of scent repellents, noise repellents, and vision repellents and they've all failed. I've scattered bags of human hair in and around our trees, turned on a small radio, let our dog roam in the orchard, and nothing worked — the deer kept coming back and damaging the trees. Finally, I'd had enough. Over the winter, I chased away the deer and saved up my money. Once spring came, I bought 8-foot steel T-posts and 6-foot 2x4-inch welded wire and totally fenced the orchard. No more deer. I know they're supposed to be

Here I am with some of our very first Norland apples last year.

the lower trunk of each tree with indoor white latex paint. After that, watch your trunk for any sign of frass. If you notice some, poke a wire into the hole and kill the borer.

One way to prevent severe insect infestation in your orchard is to keep any dropped fruit picked up. While it is normal for a young tree to drop healthy fruit in order to avoid stress and to allow for the growth of the tree itself, many dropped fruits are damaged by insects. If they are not picked up, the insect completes its cycle, ending up with more "bugs" in your orchard and more worms in your apples. We avoid this problem by having our chickens use the orchard as a chicken yard. Any fruit that drops is almost immediately eaten. If you choose to pick up dropped fruit, don't compost it, just bury or burn it so the worms and eggs are destroyed.

Apple diseases and what to do about them

Apple scab is a common apple disease caused by a fungus, evidenced by raised, tannish bumps on either the fruit or leaves. If minimal, it usually causes no harm, but if extensive, it can weaken the tree or make the crop unusable. This fungus overwinters in affected leaves and dropped fruit so you can often lessen or eliminate scab on a homestead by simply raking up the leaves and dropped fruit in the fall and burning them.

Powdery mildew can sometimes affect apple trees, causing the leaves to have a powdery gray coloration. It is a fungus that can cause the tree's leaves to die and the fruit not to form because of infected buds.

Both apple scab and powdery mildew can be prevented/treated by spraying with elemental sulfur. Folks have had good luck using Neem oil, as well.

Fire blight is a bacterial disease that often gains access to a tree during damp periods, through buds and wounds. It causes young branches to

able to jump eight feet, ten feet, and the moon. But after four years with this fence, we've never had a deer in the orchard.

If you only have a couple of trees in your yard, you can fence each one individually to save money. Wrap the fence around the tree far enough out so the small branch tips do not stick out of the wire. And use 2x4-inch wire, not wire with bigger openings as deer noses can reach in and nibble. Also, run the fence right to the ground or the deer will get on their knees and reach under. I've seen them do it!

Insect pests

Apples have a few common insect pests that can vary from area to area. It's a good idea to go to your County Extension Office, usually located in your courthouse, for information on what you may expect. Some areas, like ours, have few apple growers and few insect pests. Others have plenty of apple trees to attract bad bugs.

Two of the most common insects that make "worm holes" in apples are the codling moth (whose larvae bur-

row down into the center of the apple, leaving trails and premature apple drop) and the apple maggot (whose larvae hatch and burrow all through out the apple). Apples are also affected by aphids, which cause the leaves to roll up, weakening the tree in severe cases. Apple borers are another pest to watch out for. They tunnel into the trunk of the tree, leaving frass (sawdust and poop) outside the holes. Borers weaken the trunk until it can break right off in a wind.

Even those of us who abhor using chemicals can still keep these bugs from damaging our trees and apples. There are many organic treatments available through such companies as Gardens Alive! and ARBICO Organics. Spraying your trees periodically with Surround, a kaolin clay spray that leaves a whitish film on both leaves and fruit can be a very successful treatment. As with chemical treatments, you must get your timing right for each application and reapply following rainstorms.

You can help prevent apple borer infestation by removing any trunk protection in the spring and painting blacken, droop, and die. It is a serious disease and can quickly kill affected trees if not treated in time.

To treat fire blight, prune any blackened twigs or branches back to healthy wood and treat the pruning wound with a mixture of one part vinegar to three parts water, disinfecting your pruners between cuts to prevent spreading the disease. Then spray the tree as recommended with Bonide Liquid Copper. This product is approved for organic use and can be used during the tree's dormant period or even when there are blooms or fruit present.

Harvesting the fruit

If your tree is mature and fruiting, you can best tell when the fruit is ready for harvest by simply picking a seemingly-ripe apple and eating it. Boy, there's a task I love! If the apple tastes good, it is mature. If it tastes sour or green, it needs to stay on the tree a few days (or weeks) longer. Some varieties of trees hold their ripe fruit for several weeks where others ripen the fruit and then drop it from the tree. So don't wait too long and risk having dropped, bruised apples.

The lower apples are easy to pick; you just stand on the ground and reach up to grasp each apple, giving it a slight twist as you pull it from the tree. Higher fruits require either a stepladder or a basket picker to reach. I really like the basket picker. It is a gallon-sized wire basket with several stiff raking teeth on the top. It is mounted on a pole and you can stand on the ground and reach apples in the tops of most trees. I much prefer this to a ladder; it's safer. You can pick several apples before you lower the picker to put the apples in a basket.

Harvest fall and winter apples before the temperatures drop below 30° F. Many varieties soften and begin to rot after having been frozen.

As you harvest, separate out any insect-damaged, cut, or bruised fruit. It will not keep and will likely cause the other apples next to it to rot. The old saying is true: "One rotten apple spoils the bunch."

Storing the apples

Varieties of apples differ greatly as to the length they may be stored. Summer apples will only remain good for a few weeks at most before softening and beginning to spoil. Some fall and winter apples, such as the common *Red Delicious*, will store for 2-5 months in optimum storage conditions. Others will store longer, from over winter into spring, so first find out the storage capabilities of your apples before attempting to store them.

A refrigerator is a good storage unit for small harvests. Some folks keep a second older refrigerator in a garage or other outbuilding that does not freeze in the winter to keep the harvest from their backyard apple trees.

When you have more apples than that, storing them in an unheated root cellar that does not freeze is a good option. Apples need high humidity in storage (up to 90%) yet they need air circulation as well. Storing apples in wooden, slatted crates, in a single layer, on the floor of a root cellar works well. Some folks pack their apples gently in polyethylene bags with vent holes in them, with the opening of the bag just folded over. This holds in the humidity yet allows air circulation so the apples do not rot.

Some people say to never store apples and potatoes in the same area. The flavors can transfer and the ethylene gas given off by potatoes causes apples to go soft prematurely. We store boxes of both apples and potatoes on the floor of our unheated pantry and have had no problems, but I'd recommend *not* storing them right next to each other or in the same container.

We eat our large apples fresh and use our smallest apples for applesauce and cider. The medium-sized ones are what I use to dehydrate and can as apple slices because they're easy to peel where the smaller apples

Will enjoys a fresh apple while Domino, our mule, waits for the core. Animals like apples too!

259

are harder and require no peeling for smooth applesauce or cider. To process them for smooth (as opposed to chunky) applesauce, I just sort them to make sure there are no wormy or bruised apples, put them in a large turkey roasting pan, and put them in the oven at 300° F until they are soft. Then I just run them through my Victorio tomato strainer. The smooth sauce comes out the side, and the peels, seeds, and stems out the front.

We also hold our medium winter apples for fresh eating and fresh dessert apples all winter long.

Dehydrating apples slices

I dehydrate a lot of apple slices each year. It's extremely easy and the dried apples will last for years and remain good to eat. When I need apples, I just rehydrate and use as if they were fresh in pies, desserts, and baked goods. We find we use the dry apples as a tasty, healthy, out-of-hand snack any time during the year.

To dehydrate apples, first peel them. You can use an apple peeler, but it only works on very firm apples. Once they begin to soften, you'll have to use a paring knife. You can dehydrate slices, with the core removed or slice the apples as for pie. Then you won't have to do a thing when you want to use them, rehydrated, in a recipe later on. Make your slices about ¼- to ½-inch thick.

To prevent the apples from darkening, hold them in a bowl of water with either Fruit Fresh, salt (about 1 Tbsp. per gallon), or lemon juice (½ cup per half gallon water). Most apples will darken somewhat as they dehydrate but the taste will remain unaffected.

Remove the apples from the bowl of water with a slotted spoon and lay them on a clean towel to absorb any clinging water, then transfer them to a dehydrator tray. Place them in a single layer, filling one tray after another until all apples are used or all trays are full.

Dry at 130-135° F until leathery. If you don't have an electric dehydrator, you can dehydrate apple slices on a clean fabric screen in a warm place such as an enclosed porch or even the back of an SUV during warm, sunny weather. Once completely dry, store in an airtight container in a cool, dark location. I use gallon and half-gallon jars for this and the apples store well for years.

Canning apple products

Applesauce

As I've said, I make smooth applesauce with my Victorio strainer with apples cooked in the oven. This sauce can easily be canned up to use any time you want. You can put it up with or without sugar. If you do want to add sugar, start by adding about ¼ cup of sugar per quart of puree (or less if you prefer; go by taste). Heat mixture in a pot, stirring frequently to prevent scorching. Bring to a boil, then quickly fill jars, leaving ½-inch of headspace. Remove any air bubbles and wipe the rim of the jar clean. Place a new, previously-simmered lid on the jar and screw down the ring firmly tight. Process in a boiling water bath canner for 20 minutes for both pints and quarts. You can even do half-pints to use for baby food.

Be sure when you process in a boiling water bath canner to begin your timing when the canner reaches a full rolling boil *after* the jars have been put into the simmering water.

Also, if you live at an altitude above 1,000 feet, consult your canning book for directions on increasing your processing time to suit your altitude.

For chunky applesauce, you can either mix smooth sauce with cooked apple dices or make your entire sauce from cooked dices, as you wish. You can add sugar to taste. Process chunky sauce for the same time as smooth sauce.

You can also add ground spices, usually cinnamon and/or allspice, to the sauce near the end of cooking. It

tastes great, but be aware that canned sauce with spices is darker in color.

Canned apple slices

3-4 pounds firm apples per quart jar
sugar
water

Peel, core, and slice apples. Treat to prevent darkening, if desired. Make a light or medium syrup by mixing 2¼ cups to 31/3 cups of sugar with 5 cups water. Remove apples from liquid and gently boil in syrup for 5 minutes. Pack hot apples into hot jars leaving ½-inch of headspace. Wipe rim of jar clean and place hot, previously simmered lid on jar. Screw ring down firmly tight. Process pints or quarts in a boiling water bath canner for 20 minutes.

Apple rings in cinnamon red hot syrup

8-10 pounds apples
1½ cups sugar
½ cup red hot cinnamon candies
2 sticks cinnamon
2 tsp. whole cloves
2 cups water
1½ cups vinegar
⅔ cup light corn syrup
red food coloring if desired

Peel, core, and slice apples into rings about ½-inch thick. Treat to prevent darkening. Combine remaining ingredients in a large kettle and bring to a boil. Lift apple rings out of anti-darkening bath. Add apple rings to syrup, cover, and simmer 5 minutes. Pack rings in hot jars, leaving ½ inch of headspace. Ladle hot syrup over rings, leaving ½ inch of headspace. Remove air bubbles. Wipe rim of jar clean and place hot, previously simmered lid on jar. Screw lid down firmly tight. Process pints and quarts in a boiling water bath canner for 15 minutes.

Apple juice

24 pounds apples
2 quarts water

Remove stem and blossom ends. Chop apples and place in a large stockpot. Add water and cook until tender, stirring to prevent scorching. Strain through a damp jelly bag. Do not squeeze the bag or the juice will be cloudy. Heat juice 5 minutes at 190° F — do not boil. Ladle hot juice into hot jars, leaving ¼-inch of headspace. Wipe rim of jar clean and place hot, previously-simmered lid on jar. Screw down ring firmly tight. Process pints and quarts for 10 minutes in a boiling water bath canner.

Apple jelly

4 cups apple juice
3 cups sugar

Put apple juice in large pot, add sugar and stir. Bring to a boil over high heat, stirring constantly to prevent scorching. Boil to jelling point (until jelly slides off a clean spoon in a sheet). Remove from heat. Ladle hot jelly into hot jars, leaving ¼-inch of headspace. Wipe rim of jar clean; place hot, previously-simmered lid on jar and screw down ring firmly tight. Process 10 minutes in a boiling water bath canner.

Crab apple jelly

about 5 lbs. crab apples, making 5 cups juice
1 pkg. powdered pectin
7 cups sugar

Remove blossom end and stems of crab apples and quarter. Add a small amount of water with the crab apples in a large pot and slowly simmer until fruit is soft and juice is running. Drain in a damp jelly bag overnight or for several hours. Measure juice.

To 5 cups juice, mix pectin and stir well as you bring to a rolling boil. Add full measure of sugar all at once, stirring constantly so it does not scorch. Ladle hot jelly into hot jars, leaving ¼ inch of headspace. Wipe rim of jar clean; place hot, previously simmered lid on jar and screw down the ring firmly tight. Process for 10 minutes in a boiling water bath canner.

Canned apple pie filling

6 quarts sweet, firm apples (peeled and sliced)
5 cups apple juice (or water)
5 cups sugar
1 Tbsp. cinnamon
2½ cups water
1½ cups ClearJel
¾ cup lemon juice

Blanch sliced apples in a large pot in a gallon of water for one minute after the water begins to boil. Drain and keep slices covered and hot.

Combine apple juice (or water), sugar, cinnamon, and water in a large pot and bring to a boil, stirring frequently. Mix ClearJel with lemon juice and add to pot of syrup. Boil 1 minute, stirring constantly. Don't let it get very thick. Add apples and ladle quickly into hot quart jars to within ½-inch of the top. Wipe rim clean, place hot, previously-simmered lid on jar and screw down ring firmly tight. Process quarts for 25 minutes in a boiling water bath.

Of course, there are many more recipes for canning apples and crab apples. Most of these recipes are from my own book, *Growing and Canning Your Own Food*.

Besides recipes to can, there are also hundreds of things you can bake and cook using apples, from breads to pies, tarts, cakes, and much more.

Here are just a couple to whet your appetite. You can find a bunch more in *Jackie Clay's Pantry Cookbook*.

Apple pie
Crust:

2 cups sifted flour
1 tsp. salt
¾ cup lard or shortening
4-5 Tbsp. ice water

Filling:

5 large tart or semi-tart apples (Will's favorite variety for pies is Cripps Pink)
1 cup sugar
2 Tbsp. flour
1 tsp. cinnamon or more to taste
butter or margarine
cinnamon

Crust: Sift flour and salt into medium mixing bowl. With pastry blender or fork, cut in shortening until mixture resembles coarse cornmeal. Sprinkle with ice water, tossing light-

One of our favorite uses for apples is crisp apple pie!

ly until dough holds together in a ball that can be handled without breaking apart, yet is not sticky. Divide in halves, with one half a little larger for the bottom crust. Flatten each ball somewhat with your hands. Cover and refrigerate if you have the time. Remove from refrigerator and take out larger ball and place on a lightly-floured surface. Sprinkle flour on your rolling pin and lightly begin rolling out the dough from center to outside edges, working in alternate directions to keep a rounded shape. You can lay the pie tin upside down on your crust-in-progress to check the size you need. Remember to allow for the depth of the pan and the edges when making your decision. When the crust is the right size, gently roll it up on your rolling pin and unroll it over your pan. Trim crust at edge of pan with a knife and fill.

Filling: Peel and core apples. Quarter, then slice about ½-inch thick. Use enough apples to fill a pie pan, heaping full; they settle during baking.

Mix sugar, flour, and cinnamon in a bowl, then add to the apple slices and mix well. Place on bottom crust of pie shell. Dot the top of the apples with about five pats of butter. Dampen edges of bottom crust, trimmed to fit pie tin. Lay out top crust and cut a few slices in it for vents. (I always do

back-to-back wheat stems as a design, complete with heads of wheat on each stem, by using the blade of the knife to cut through the crust for the stems and the end of the handle to make indentations, not through the crust, for the wheat kernels, then a few light strokes with the knife tip, also not through the crust, for the beards. It makes a pretty pie!) Roll the top crust up lightly on your rolling pin and gently unroll on top of the filled pie. Trim the edges of the top crust to fit the pie tin. Use the handle of a table knife to push the two crust edges toward the center of the pie between your thumb and first finger. Repeat all around the pie and you'll have a nice fluted edge that seals in the juice and looks pretty. Rub softened butter on the top crust, then sprinkle liberally with brown sugar and sprinkle with cinnamon.

Bake on a cookie sheet at 350° F until the crust is nicely browned. (The cookie sheet makes removing the pie from the hot oven easier and safer and the sheet will contain any juice leaks so you don't have to clean your oven.)

Apple snow

2 egg whites, yolks reserved
1 cup sugar
2 tart apples, peeled and finely grated

Beat the egg whites until they are very stiff. Gradually add sugar and grated tart apples. Cover and chill.

Sauce:

2 egg yolks
1⅓ cups milk
2 Tbsp. sugar
2 Tbsp. cornstarch
1 tsp. vanilla

Beat the egg yolks, milk, sugar, and cornstarch together. Cook over medium heat, stirring constantly until thickened. Add vanilla and mix. Cover and chill.

To serve, put a spoonful of the apple mixture in each serving bowl and cover with the sauce.

Apple pancakes

2 cups flour
2 Tbsp. sugar
4 tsp. baking powder
1 tsp. salt
2 egg yolks, well-beaten (reserve the whites)
2 cups milk
2 Tbsp. butter, melted
1 cup apples, finely chopped
2 egg whites, stiffly beaten

Sift dry ingredients together. Mix egg yolks and milk. Pour into dry ingredients; mix well. Stir in butter and apple. Fold in egg whites gently. Let mixture stand for a few minutes to rise. Bake on hot, lightly-greased griddle. You may sprinkle with cinnamon sugar or confectioners' sugar and serve with whipped cream if you want.

As I've said, there are many more great ways to serve apples in your meals, from main dishes to desserts. And, of course, your family will always relish a crisp cold apple right from the tree in your yard or the cellar! I know we do. Even our Labrador, Spencer, loves apples. He begs for the cores every time I cut one open. Smart dog! Δ

Making hard cider

By Matt Purkeypile

Hard cider is an American tradition dating back to before the Revolution. In the early days of America, it was as prevalent as beer. Unlike what we teach school children, Johnny Appleseed did not wander the American frontier planting apple trees to give everyone apples to eat as they settled — he was planting orchards so that the settlers would have mature apple trees to make hard cider. This turned out to be a very profitable venture for Johnny Appleseed. Even though hard cider is as American as apple pie, it seems to have fallen out of favor.

Hard cider is simply apple juice that has been fermented to create an alcoholic beverage. It is surprisingly easy to make.

The first step in making hard cider is to get five gallons of apple juice. If you have an orchard, you can take your apples and crush them in a press to make the juice. Although some people don't find it visually appealing, having chunks of apple in the juice won't hurt anything. If you don't have a large supply of fresh apples, a good alternative is to use apple juice or cider from a grocery store. Going this route also eliminates a lot of the mess and hassle that goes into making fresh apple juice.

Once you have your five gallons of apple juice, you can add any additional flavorings you like. I find a pound of brown sugar is a good addition. To add the sugar, I usually heat a half gallon or so of the juice — enough to absorb the brown sugar, but not to the point of boiling.

My Purkeypile Hard Cider on tap at a local pub

Once you have your juice ready, it is time to turn it into hard cider. For this you'll need a container that you can seal off with an airlock. Five- or six-gallon glass carboys are ideal, although you can also use a food-grade bucket with a lid and hole for an airlock. For an airlock you'll use a rubber stopper with a hole that the airlock fits into. The airlock is essentially a device that will let gas out, but not into the container.

Before you add the juice to the container, you'll need to sanitize it; simply washing it with dish soap won't suffice. You can fill it with water and a little bit of bleach and let it sit for a few minutes to sanitize it, although make sure you rinse it several times. Another alternative I prefer is an iodine solution such as Star San. With this, you simply fill the container up with a cap or two of the solution, let it sit for a minute, then empty it. No need to rinse it, and you don't have to worry about it ruining your batch of hard cider.

Once you've sanitized the carboy or bucket, fill it with your apple juice. A funnel is essential if you're using a carboy. Once you've added all your juice, add cider yeast and put the airlock on. The yeast is what makes the magic. The yeast will multiply, using the sugar in the apple juice as its source of food. As it eats the sugar, it'll expel carbon dioxide and alcohol as by-products. This is the same process as wine and beer — all alcohol is essentially yeast "poop."

Now comes the hard part: waiting. It will take about six weeks for the yeast to finish working. It can be done as early as four weeks if you're impatient, but I've also let it sit for nearly four months without a problem.

After about a week you can rack it. Racking is when you take the cider from one carboy or bucket and siphon it into a second, leaving the accumulated yeast on the bottom. This results in cider that looks and tastes cleaner. Make sure that the tubing and second container are sterilized when you rack. If things are not sterilized, wild yeast and bacteria will compete with your alcohol yeast and contribute to foul flavors at best, and will make your batch undrinkable at worst. (This is why you sanitize everything and use an airlock.)

No need to worry if you end up with a bad batch, though. The alcohol will kill anything that will hurt you, so while it may taste terrible, you won't get sick. Sunlight will also contribute to off flavors, so if you're using a glass carboy you'll want to cover it with a dark shirt or towel. You'll know your cider is fermenting when you see the airlock bubbling after 12 to 24 hours. This subsides after a few days as the amount of sugar for the yeast decreases.

Once you've waited six weeks, it is time to bottle your cider. When bottling, first rack the cider into a bucket, following the sterilizing procedures I've mentioned before. Add a dextrose (corn sugar) solution into the bucket. Take about a pint of water and four ounces of corn sugar and boil it for five minutes to sterilize it. This additional sugar gives the remaining yeast enough to eat to naturally carbonate your cider in the bottle.

You'll also need to sterilize your racking device, bottles, and caps. The bottles and racking device can be done in a bleach or iodine solution. You'll want to boil the bottle caps in water for about five minutes. I usually keep my bottles upside down until I fill them to help prevent airborne contaminates from getting in. You'll need 48 12-ounce bottles or about 26 22-ounce bottles. These bottles don't have to be new; you can recycle commercial ones. If you use recycled bottles, make sure they don't have twist off caps — those might prevent a good seal and ruin some of your bottles of cider.

Fill all of your bottles, leaving about ½ to one inch unfilled so there is room for some air to create the carbonation. Cap each bottle with a bottle capper as soon as you fill them to minimize the chance of contamination. After you've bottled everything, let the bottles sit for 10 days or two weeks so they naturally carbonate. You'll want to reduce their exposure to sunlight, so keep them in a box or dark place. After 10 days or so, stick some bottles in the fridge overnight, then crack them open and enjoy an American tradition!

It is also possible to put your cider in kegs instead of bottles. The advantage to this is that there is less work at this stage — filling a keg is essentially like doing one big bottle instead of many small ones. There's also the appeal of having a fresh pint of cider straight from the tap. For kegging cider, use five-gallon Cornelius (soda) kegs. Any book that discusses kegging homemade beer is a good reference — the equipment and setup is

You can use a half-gallon growler from a brew pub to experiment with various recipes.

the same for cider as beer and you can even mix the two on a single system.

There is one more thing you can do with your hard cider if you want — make applejack. Applejack is essentially the hard alcohol version of cider. To do this you'll carry out a process known as freeze distilling. Fill up a pitcher of hard cider and place it in the freezer. As slush starts forming, fish this out. Continue doing this until the mixture doesn't freeze at all. Since water freezes at a much higher temperature than alcohol, what you're doing is removing the water from the mixture and leaving the alcohol and flavoring behind. In the old days people would leave barrels of cider on their porches and fish the ice off every night, leaving applejack.

A great source to get the equipment and yeast you need is a home brewing store. If you don't have a local homebrew store, an excellent online source is www.morebeer.com. They have great prices and will ship your order for free if you make a modest-sized order.

I've often said that making hard cider is so easy an elementary school student could (but probably shouldn't!) do it. I'm sure you'll find it to be the same. It is a great hobby and an economical way to make your own booze. I hope you enjoy it as much as I have. Δ

Home cider-making equipment. From left to right: a five-gallon Cornelius keg, a bottle capper, and a 6.5-gallon carboy with a sticker thermometer.

Soups from the garden

Freshly gathered vegetables make soup nutritious

By Sylvia Gist

The beauty of soup is that it can be made from practically anything — and it can be made in one pot! Some of my favorite soups are made up of totally or mostly vegetables, beginning with the first greens in the spring and going strong into the winter using stored vegetables.

I start the year by seeding some greens in the cold house (Eliot Coleman's term for a greenhouse with no heat) in February. By April or May (depending on the weather here in northern Montana), we are eating greens. We start eating salads and dishes with stir fried vegetables, but eventually I think, "I've got to do something different with all this green stuff." The soup I call "Green soup" can be made using a variety of greens, but my favorites are spinach, bok choy, mild mustards, or a mix. I find chard gives it a bitter taste, but the baby stuff might work.

Green soup

1 Tbsp. oil
3 green onions, chopped
3 cloves garlic, peeled and crushed
2 slices of fresh ginger, ¼-inch thick
1 lb. bok choy, spinach, mustard greens, or other greens
8 oz. potato, peeled and diced
3 cups water
¾ tsp. salt

Prepare bok choy by slicing it into ½-inch sections (the stalks can produce weird strings if you don't). Other greens should be chopped into one-inch pieces.

Heat oil in medium pot over medium heat. Add green onions, garlic, and ginger. Cook about 3 minutes until fragrant. Add greens, potato, water, and salt. Bring to boil, cover, reduce heat to low, and simmer for about 20 minutes until all ingredients are tender.

Transfer the solids to a food processor or blender and pulse until puréed. Add a little of the broth if necessary. Return everything to the pot, stir, and reheat, if necessary. You can add a teaspoon of sour cream on the top of each serving, if desired.

Summer soups

As summer progresses, I can hardly wait for the yellow crookneck squash to produce. Then after I've cooked up several batches with onions and bacon, I'm ready for a change. When production is in overdrive, it's time to make some into soup. Here's a recipe that I enjoy. I particularly like the mild zip that the curry powder gives. Make extra and freeze some, or freeze some chopped squash and make the recipe any time.

Yellow crookneck squash soup (6 servings)

2½ lbs. squash, chopped
1 cup onion, peeled and chopped
1 clove garlic, peeled and chopped
2 Tbsp. vegetable oil
5 cups water
¼ cup white rice, uncooked
1-1½ tsp. curry powder
salt and pepper to taste

Sauté the first three ingredients in oil until tender. Add water and bring to boil. Add rice and curry. Lower heat and simmer until vegetables are soft.

Purée in blender, in batches if necessary. Return to the pot and season with salt and pepper to taste. Add water if soup is too thick. Heat thoroughly and serve.

Versatile tomatoes

We eat tomatoes straight from the garden in salads and on sandwiches, but they also make a great base or ingredient for soup. Since I can my own stewed tomatoes, I sometimes start with them and add frozen greens, a grain such as quinoa or barley, and some spicy sausage for a quick soup in the winter.

After frost has sweetened the kale, we like to use it in soup. In both of the following recipes, fresh ripe tomatoes can be substituted for the canned ones. Both recipes have some of the same ingredients, but the results are somewhat different. If you don't have leeks, substitute onions, but use less onion, since leeks are milder. I generally add a little meat of some kind since my husband prefers it that way. The slightly spicy sausages seem to go well in these soups.

Tomato leek soup

2 large leeks
1 clove garlic, chopped
¼ cup olive oil
3 cups chicken stock
2 cups tomatoes
1 cup kale, ribs removed
1 Tbsp. quinoa, rinsed (optional)
1 tsp. thyme
1 bay leaf
1 tsp. salt
1 tsp. tamari or soy sauce
½ cup pepperoni pieces (optional)

Prepare leeks by removing top and root and cutting them in half lengthwise. Rinse, if necessary. Slice narrowly; 1/8 inch is good.

Cook garlic and leeks in oil over medium heat until they are fragrant and limp. Then add chicken stock, tomatoes, kale, quinoa, and seasonings.

Add pepperoni after tomatoes, kale, and quinoa are cooked. Heat thoroughly. (If you boil the pepperoni with the rest of the ingredients, it loses its flavor.)

Tomato kale soup (4 servings)

1 quart canned tomatoes
2 leeks
4 cups kale (measured after ribs have been removed and leaves coarsely chopped)
2 cups water
salt
8 oz. hot sausage (optional)

If using fresh tomatoes, peel and chop. Remove the root and green tops from the leeks. Wash and split lengthwise before slicing narrowly.

Put tomatoes, leeks, kale, water, and salt into large pot and cook on medium heat until tomatoes and kale are done. If you are adding sausage, precook it before adding it to the soup.

Tomato soup base

As I mentioned before, tomatoes make an excellent soup base. Here is a recipe that a friend gave me for canning a lot of end-of-the-season produce into one soup base. This recipe makes a large quantity,

Tomato leek soup

Biscuits go great with chunky tomato kale soup.

depending on the size of the cabbages, onions, and additions, so you would need a really big kettle. You could halve it and still probably have a canner full of seven quarts.

We grab a jar of this off the shelf and add a pint of canned meat and some fresh potatoes from storage to make a quick soup. Since this is almost a concentrate, I usually add a cup or two of water as I rinse out the jar. It is also possible to add pasta or a favorite grain. It's a recipe you can tailor to your liking, changing the size of the vegetables or even your choice of vegetables. Sometimes I include a bit of zucchini when it is available.

Canned tomato soup base

¼ bushel tomatoes
2 heads cabbage, chopped
2 quarts carrots, sliced
3 green peppers, seeded and
    chopped
6-8 large onions, chopped
3 stalks celery
3 quarts water
¾ cup salt
1 Tbsp. pepper

Put all in a very large pot and cook 1 hour (timing after it gets hot). Put in sterilized jars, leaving 1 inch head-space, top with sterilized lids, and process at 10 lbs. pressure for 35 minutes. Adjust for your altitude, if necessary.

Crockpot vegetable soup

In August I came up with a crockpot soup I call Italian garden vegetable soup. It is chunkier than all of the other soups and makes use of what I had from the garden along with a good dose of Italian seasoning and mild Italian sausage. Don't overdo the green beans, as they tend to overwhelm the other veggies. This one can handle whatever vegetables you have that you want to add.

Italian garden vegetable soup with sausage

green beans, cut into 1-inch lengths
summer squash, cut into ½-inch
    chunks
carrots, peeled and cut into ½-inch
    chunks
potatoes, left unpeeled and cut into
    1-inch chunks
onions, cut into 1-inch chunks
Italian seasoning, a couple of table-
    spoons for a 3 quart crockpot
1 lb. Italian sausage, cut into ½- to
    1-inch pieces and cooked sepa-
    rately

Put all except the sausage in the crockpot and cook on high for a couple of hours and then turn to low for several more. In the hour before serving, cook the sausage separately and add to the crockpot. Serve with slabs of homemade bread.

Late summer soup

Another soup that could be made when the vegetables are fresh from the garden in late summer is corn

Sweet potato squash soup

Corn chowder ready to serve

chowder. I am usually so busy eating corn on the cob and canning that I end up making this soup in the winter, using frozen corn. Canned corn could also be used — just make the liquid add up to the total.

Corn chowder (4 to 6 servings)

3 slices of bacon, cut in ½-inch pieces
¼ cup chopped onion
¼ cup chopped celery
2 cups cooked potatoes, ¼-inch cubes
1 cup water
1 tsp. salt
pinch of thyme
1 lb. frozen corn, thawed
3 cups milk (cream and lowfat mixed)

Fry the bacon in a separate frying pan until it is almost crisp. Add the onions and celery and cook until tender, then drain off the grease.

Move bacon mixture into a large saucepan with potatoes, water, salt, and thyme. Heat and simmer about 10 minutes, making sure it doesn't boil dry. Add corn and milk and heat thoroughly, but do not boil.

Fall soups

Even when the garden is in decline, frost having put the brakes on, it keeps on giving — right into fall and winter.

Another soup that can be made in the fall is sweet potato squash soup. Any of your favorite squash can be used. The blend of the two makes a mild-tasting, but sweet soup.

Sweet potato squash soup

2 cups cubed squash
2 cups cubed sweet potato
1½ cups water
½ tsp. salt
½ cup chicken stock
½ tsp. curry powder

Boil first four ingredients until tender, then blend in a blender or food processor. Add chicken stock and curry powder. Reheat. Makes 4 cups or 2 large servings.

Another squash soup that I like is one made with canned coconut milk. The squash can be previously cooked, puréed and frozen, so this soup can be made any time.

Curried squash soup with coconut milk

1 Tbsp. oil
½ cup chopped onion
1 cup mashed cooked squash
¼ cup water
½ cup canned coconut milk
1 tsp. curry powder

Sauté onion in oil until translucent. Add squash and water. Heat and purée in the blender or food processor. Return to the stove, add the coconut milk and curry powder, and heat till bubbly. Serve. Makes 1 serving.

Another "anytime" soup is potato soup; it's one of my favorites. You can add ham or bacon to this soup and serve with hearty bread for a filling lunch or dinner.

Potato soup (4 servings)

¼ cup butter
1 cup chopped onion
2 stalks celery with leaves, chopped fine
¼ cup flour
3 cups water
2½-3 cups potatoes, cubed to ½-inch
1 tsp. salt
½ cup condensed milk or cream
shredded Swiss or Parmesan cheese (optional)

Melt butter and cook onion and celery on low heat in covered pot about 15 minutes, stirring occasionally. Stir in flour until blended.

Add water, potatoes, and salt while stirring. Bring to a boil; lower heat and cook covered about 30 minutes until potatoes are done. Stir occasionally because it tends to want to stick.

Add milk and heat thoroughly. Sprinkle cheese onto each serving.

Soup can make a hearty or a light meal, depending on what you make it from. With a little planning and imagination, the garden can supply ingredients for soup year-round. Δ

In Backwoods Home Cooking you'll find: Breads, Casseroles, Cookies, Desserts, Jams & jellies, Main dishes, Pasta, Salads, Seafood, Soups, and Vegetables

Homestead security for women

By Donna Insco

In these tough economic times, many women are finding themselves alone for long hours on the homestead. As local jobs disappear, the major breadwinner may take a job with a long commute, leaving the wife and kids to run the farm. I know several farm women whose husbands are long distance truckers, and another has a husband in the military. Some women have found their place in the country and are starting out alone; others have lost their husbands due to death or divorce. In these instances, the women must provide security for the homestead.

If you find yourself in this position, have a stern talk with yourself. Are you up to the challenge? Most women depend on a man to keep them safe,

and our society encourages this by viewing women alone as prey. We expect a boyfriend or a husband to make sure that the wolf stays far from the door. I tell my own sons that it is part of a man's job to protect the women in his life.

It is easy to forget that this nation was built by the strength of women as well as men. The following thoughts and advice may help a woman who discovers that she has been promoted to head of security.

Make your place an unattractive target

Make it harder or more time consuming for someone to break in. The priority should be to slow a burglar down so much that he looks elsewhere for an easier target.

First, fence around your home and buildings, especially between your home and the road. Keep passersby as far from your house as possible, both to cut down on dealing with strangers and to keep people from casually observing what you own. In our area, a common tactic for strangers to gain access is to be "lost" and ask for directions. In the fall, armed men roam the back roads and sometimes show up at isolated farms claiming to have permission to hunt. Some truly are hunters hopelessly turned around. Others are thieves looking for easy pickings and programming locations into their GPS for future reference. Keep these sorts off of your place by fencing them out and installing a sturdy gate locked with a hardened chain and heavy padlock.

Another idea to help deter people from driving close to your buildings is to park junk equipment along your fence line. Instead of selling that broken baler for scrap, why not park it along your fence line to prevent people from simply cutting your fence and driving through? The bigger and rustier the junk the better. What? Some thieves tried to drive around your gate and ran over a mower blade unseen in the tall grass and punctured all four tires? Darn the bad luck. A couple of small signs attached to your fence warning about copperheads and rattlesnakes wouldn't hurt, either. Just make sure your junk really is junk or someone might steal it, too.

If you can afford to do so, install security cameras. They may not stop a thief, but they may take a good enough photo to identify and track the perpetrator down. If the homestead has a long driveway, a driveway alarm that sets off a chime in the house when a vehicle passes by will alert the household that someone is coming. There are many such products on the market, limited only by your pocketbook. If you have the money and like gadgets, some of them may be good investments.

Installing motion detector lights is money well spent. They can be adjusted so that the family pets don't set them off. I love ours when coming home after dark and the porch light flips on automatically, illuminating the entire front yard and eliminating dark corners. Another benefit is that I don't worry nearly so much about getting a snake bite on the way to the door.

Install good locks and deadbolts on all exterior doors of your home, and use them. It is a good idea to lock the house if you are outside, but not within sight of the house. You don't want to return from berry picking to find that someone has made themselves at home. Also, lock the doors if noisy equipment like the vacuum is being used. An elephant could come through the door while the average woman is vacuuming and she wouldn't know it until it tapped her on the shoulder with its trunk, so lock those doors. Before bed at night conduct a perimeter check of all ground floor doors and windows to ensure that all are closed and locked.

Don't forget about safeguarding equipment. It is often a mistake to leave valuable equipment such as tractors or trailers within sight of a road. We found this out the hard way after losing a nice 16-foot trailer. An acquaintance lost a tractor even though he had removed the battery. The thieves brought their own battery and drove the tractor out of the hay field and onto a waiting trailer. Don't leave the keys in any equipment, no matter how far back in the woods you are. That's an invitation criminals will be happy to accept. Lock up — or chain up — small equipment such as lawn mowers, chain saws, and especially ATVs.

Some people will steal anything. In our area, it has become common for thieves to steal air conditioning units for the copper, and even tear the plumbing out of walls in unattended homes. In a bad economy these types of crimes worsen. I once worked with a man who lived in a crime-ridden part of town who said that he knew men who would do anything for $10 — a sobering thought.

Will deadbolts, window locks, and strong gates keep a determined criminal out? No. But they will cause the bad guys to make noise and slow them down, perhaps long enough for the householder to call reinforcement and go for the guns. Look at it this

A dog is an early warning device, a deterrent to intruders, and a loyal friend.

way — if someone has just opened a gate with bolt cutters, or bypassed the gate by mowing down two fences, he isn't coming to buy farm fresh eggs. His intentions are quite clear, aren't they?

Keep dogs

In my opinion, a woman in the country absolutely must have a dog, preferably a big one. Two big dogs are even better than one because a dog is braver if he has a buddy. When we had only one dog, the coyotes and bobcats would come right up to the yard fence at night. Our dog would bark, but seemed unwilling to charge into a pack of coyotes. This changed after a suitable canine companion was acquired. Working as a team, both of our dogs are quite comfortable rushing headlong into a pack of their wild cousins. If we lived in bear or mountain lion territory, we might keep really big dogs with a hunting or guarding ancestry. We might also keep three or four of them to up the odds that one might still be standing after trying to drive a really big kitty away from the goat barn.

The homestead dog performs three jobs in a defensive situation. First and foremost, he is an early warning device. A dog's sense of smell and hearing are extraordinary, and he can see in the dark better than a human. If anything or anyone is within their sphere of influence, the dogs will know about it far sooner than we will. A good dog will be ready to do something about it immediately. Our dogs can be lying in the driveway looking like roadkill, and then suddenly leap to their feet and race to the gate, barking and snarling. Sure enough, several minutes later, a vehicle that no one heard approaching will arrive.

The second defensive job a dog performs is confronting intruders. A dog that knows what's his and is willing to defend it is far superior to a dog that simply barks. This is why I'm in favor of large dogs for the country

woman. Experts say that the size of the dog is unimportant, that even a small dog can be deterrent. That's true in the city. I once knew of a nine-pound Miniature Schnauzer that saved his owner's backside by hanging from a home invader's pant leg. The little dog was kicked like a soccer ball several times across the apartment, but pressed the attack long enough for his owner to escape and call 911 from an apartment down the hall. However, in rural areas the response time of law enforcement can be measured in hours, if they choose to respond at all.

Ladies, in the country, size does matter. A dog weighing seventy pounds or more can be a deterrent, and he is capable of doing a lot of damage in a short amount of time. It seems to be a sad truth that many bad guys are more afraid of a dog than they are of a woman with a gun in her hand. A criminal may be thinking that a woman doesn't know how to shoot a gun, or that she won't shoot, or even that she can't hit anything if she tried. But a couple of large dogs at your side strenuously voicing objections, circling around, and coming in behind the threat can be disturbing enough to give even determined men second thoughts about wrongdoing. The proper homestead dog will be saying very clearly through his aggressive actions, "Not on my watch."

What if the folks in your driveway are harmless, like the Ladies' Quilting Society out recruiting new members? Then apologize profusely and say something offhand like, "Oh, I am sorry. My dogs are extremely protective and really dislike strangers. Good thing I was here to drag them off." That statement could even be a big fat lie, but they won't know that. Word will get around that the family at the end of the road has a pack of barely controllable hounds from Hades.

Lastly, a dog willing and able to engage a threat can buy his family valuable time to escape or deploy

weapons. Pay attention to your dogs; if they sound the alarm, investigate. If the dogs bark ferociously at night and then suddenly stop, assume one of three things has happened. The intruder has left. It's not an intruder but someone you know and your dogs are now happily greeting them. Or, it is an intruder who has done great bodily harm to Fido and Spot. Hope for the first two scenarios, but be prepared for possibility number three.

Take care of your dogs. Train them to come when called and to sit and stay. Teach them to walk quietly on a leash and to ride in a vehicle. Make sure they get vaccinated with rabies and distemper vaccine every year. If your dog bites someone, law enforcement may arrive and demand to see proof of vaccination, as well as require the animal to be quarantined.

My comments on dogs are meant for women living on isolated homesteads where big aggressive dogs are unlikely to run into trouble with traffic, repairmen, delivery people, or stray children. If your dog bites someone, even while defending you, you can be sued and perhaps be financially devastated. Your faithful canine can be declared "dangerous" — especially if he has defended you in an effective manner, leaving you on shaky legal ground and your dog's future uncertain. People are innocent until proven guilty, but Fido has no such entitlement. The worst violent offenders can be cleaned up and look innocent in court. By contrast, your loyal hound with a bloody muzzle and some dude's tattered pants in his mouth is clearly guilty. Don't expect any sympathy from responding officers or the court. The response you are more likely to receive is, "For crying out loud, lady. What the heck were you doing out there all by yourself, anyway?" The homestead invader may be four-legged instead of two. Your dogs may try to drive away something bigger and more ferocious and die in the attempt. Keep firmly in mind that if your dog defends you with his teeth, he may pay for it with his life. Bury him with honor.

Stay out of feuds

If you are in the middle of a feud between locals, or if you started one, get out of it immediately. You can't afford to be drawn into unpleasantness, so don't make yourself a target by engaging in angry aggressive behavior with anyone. Sometimes odd things set people off and minor difficulties turn into long-standing hostilities. I once lived in an urban area where arguments over a parking space nearly turned four intelligent, well-educated people into homicidal idiots. In suburbia, the average stay in a house is about five years, so people think that they don't have to get along with their neighbors. In rural areas, people often stay on a place for decades, even generations. So it is of utmost importance to remain on good terms with neighbors.

If a property line is in dispute, ask the neighbor to pay half on a survey and have the problem fixed. Is livestock getting out, yours or theirs? Fix your fences to keep your animals where they belong and keep other people's livestock off of your place. If someone complains that your kids are trespassing, accept full responsibility and teach your children to stay on your own farm. My family has permission to be on several adjoining farms, and I renew this permission annually by speaking to the owners directly. Even so, we absolutely stay off of other farms during deer season unless we are after a downed deer. This also applies to friends and relatives who have permission to hunt our farm. We make sure our guests know where our property lines are and that they stay within them.

What does this have to do with homestead security? Neighbors often know more about you than you realize: your schedule, who lives in your house, even what you own. Neighbors

Encourage your kids to get off the couch, enjoy the fresh air, and practice a useful skill while they're at it.

can become crucial allies when treated fairly and respectfully. One of the easiest ways to get along is to mind your own business and let other people mind theirs. Don't pass along gossip unless you are positive it is true (and maybe not even then). You want to be known as the family that does things for themselves, so work hard and don't ask for help very often. Be willing to help others when you can. It is comforting to know that in an emergency, neighbors will arrive to help because they like you, not because they are obligated.

Be armed

If your state allows citizens to carry a concealed firearm, get a permit to do so. Maybe you are thinking that you're not very interested in firearms, plus, you don't want to go to the expense of owning and operating them, so you will just trust in the overall goodness and decency of humankind. Of course, that is your choice, but I don't share that sort of optimism. A woman living in an isolated area is foolish if she isn't armed. As previously mentioned, the response time for law enforcement in rural areas is horrendously slow due to long distances, poorly paved secondary highways, gravel roads, and weather. I can't stress this enough: if you run into trouble in a remote area, you must solve the problem yourself. Whether the predator is four-legged or two-legged, the act of physically defending yourself, your children, your livestock, and your home rests with you.

Once you acquire a carry permit, I suggest that you keep your firearm concealed even if you aren't legally required to do so. The element of surprise is intimidating. The first time a bad guy realizes a woman is armed should be when he is looking down the business end of her barrel. Seeing an obviously armed woman also scares people and sometimes causes unnecessary rumors. While your neighbors may agree in principle with your right to be armed, they may be offended that you are armed in their presence. They might speculate endlessly about what you are so afraid of. Whether a woman is armed or not is no one's business but hers, so keep that weapon concealed. Handguns and spare ammo weigh quite a bit, and it may require rethinking your wardrobe. But a firearm won't help you if it's locked in a safe and you need it right this second.

When you have decided to make a firearm part of your everyday life, you must gain the skills to use one proficiently. It takes thousands of rounds to become adept with a handgun, so buy a gun that you can afford to shoot, and then shoot almost every day. Acquire skills with long guns, also. Every homestead woman should own a .22 rifle for varmint control, small game hunting, and dispatching livestock. I also feel that she should have a shotgun, either a 20 gauge or a 12 gauge, and be skilled in its use.

Teach your children to shoot. The best way to ensure that kids are safe around firearms is to teach them safe firearm handling procedures. Enroll them in a 4-H firearm program. 4-H firearm instructors are extremely conscientious about gun safety, and the youngsters are held to a high standard. The NRA and many state conservation departments hold firearm training programs for kids, and they are usually free. Take advantage of them. An afternoon spent on the firing range with your kids can be a rewarding family activity. It teaches discipline, a lifelong skill, *and* it is fun. Don't let your kids sit on a couch playing video games when they can be out developing a useful skill.

Firearm safety begins at home, and you as a parent are responsible for enforcing it. Hold your children to rigid safety standards. I take firearms safety very seriously and I try to instill those standards in my children. I do not allow any horseplay where guns are present. Of special concern are friends or relatives who have sloppy gun handling habits. Allowing children unsupervised access to people who disregard safety can quickly lead to kids imitating them and a tragedy ensuing. I make an effort to privately point out to my kids the safe gun handling techniques (or lack thereof) of other shooters.

Talk to your kids

Have honest discussions with your children about your current circumstances. Edit your speech to avoid scaring the younger ones, but older children often want and deserve to know the true nature of events. Kids do better when they have some facts and a plan; it's why schools have fire, earthquake, and tornado drills. Gently tell them what kinds of emergencies they might face, and tell them exactly what you expect them to do during those events. If a fire breaks out, should they operate a hose, or should they just stay out of the way? If predators threaten, regardless of how many legs they walk on, how do you want your kids to respond? Have these talks with your children now, before unpleasantness occurs. In the middle of chaos they may be too frightened or intimidated to act if they don't already have a plan that you have given them.

Caution your children to say as little as possible about your situation to other people. Some kids are constantly running their mouths. In casual conversation, teenagers have told me where every valuable that their family owns is hidden, as well as their parents' entire schedules. Smaller children are even worse, as they will tell you all kinds of things that they shouldn't. Remind your own children that small bits of information can be used by criminals to hurt your family. Kids are trusting and can't be expected to decide who might be a threat; the best policy to adopt is one where your kids simply refer all questions to you.

About men

If you are truly on your own due to death or divorce, don't be in too much of a hurry to fill that empty chair at the dinner table. Ask yourself first, "Why is this man interested in me?" Remember, your land, home, livestock, and garden are valuable assets. If you think he is interested in a self-reliant lifestyle, put him to the test. Making hay or cutting wood quickly separates the men from the slackers.

Be careful who you bring home, because casual observation can reveal much about your life. Sometimes the breach in security is seemingly unintentional. Some people just can't stop talking. A woman who carries a gun should especially beware of a man who tells other people that she carries. If he can't keep his mouth shut about your weapon, what else is he blabbing about? He may be rattling on about the location of equipment keys, or where the valuables are kept, or that pile of food in your cellar. Remember the old saying about former friends making the worst of enemies? Multiply that equation by 50 if it is a disgruntled ex-boyfriend. Once you have given your seal of approval to someone, your own dogs may just stand in the driveway and watch while a former boyfriend turns into a thief.

Be sure that your prospective beau shares your views on home security. All of your steps to ensure your family's safety can be undone if a man refuses to lock doors or gates, leaves valuables laying around, or invites home unsavory friends from his past. Does he respect your concerns, or does he belittle them? In a worst-case scenario, will he stand at your side, or will he run screaming like a 10-year-old girl? Better yet is a man who will say, "I'll take care of this, honey. You get the kids to safety."

Final thoughts

I hope that you never need to defend yourself or your home from anything more concerning than an "opossum in the henhouse." But it's better to prepare now while the sun is shining, than to scramble for cover while the storm is breaking. Don't depend on anyone to do it for you. Have a plan, have the necessary skills, see to your own defense, and keep yourself safe. Δ

More self-reliance in
*Emergency Preparedness
and Survival Guide*

Build a pizza oven

By Mike Lorenzen

About a year ago, my wife and I traveled around Italy by car. We had lots of wood-fired pizza. Italians make their pizza very thin with some sauce, cheese, and very little topping. If you order pepperoni pizza, you don't get meat — just green and red peppers.

Now, I'm a man who builds what his wife wants. After our trip to Italy, it was a pizza oven. I am not a professional pizza-oven builder, but I am a homebuilder with lots of hands-on construction experience.

I decided to build an igloo-type oven. It takes a little more time than just a simple half-pipe style, but I think the igloo looks cooler and is more efficient than other types of outdoor ovens. The walls of the oven are solid red bricks, and it is built on a base of concrete blocks with a poured concrete slab foundation and top. The steel door that I made seems to help hold the heat but is not necessary. (You should not make the door self-latching for child safety reasons.)

The total cost of this project was just about $300. If you don't mind loud, obnoxious music, you can see unlimited designs of pizza-ovens being built on YouTube (with no verbal instructions).

First, decide where to build the pizza oven in your yard.

I poured the slab to fit standard 7-inch-wide CMU (concrete masonry units) without cutting or staggering blocks. (My base is 44 x 48 inches — the back wall is two blocks wide, plus the blocks that form the sides; the side walls are three blocks long.)

The slab could be a little larger than the footprint of the blocks. I made mine about 5 inches thick with 3/8-inch rebar around the sides and a cross grid of 12 inches. The forms don't have to touch the ground; you can mix the mud thick enough so that it won't run under the forms. I jabbed vertical rebar into place before the concrete got hard — one rebar for every block cell.

Once the slab is dry, lay the blocks for the base. I didn't lay my blocks with mud as I needed the block cells

The finished pizza oven, with fire lit. After heating the oven, the burned-down coals are shoveled to the back, then the pizza slipped in to bake.

275

The size of the base doesn't really matter; it just needs to be big enough to support the oven.

This styrofoam will be your guide while laying out the rest of the bricks.

reused the edge forms from the foundation slab to form the edges of the top. To hold the upper forms in place, I propped them up with some 2-inch boards around the outside of the base. Then I cut a plywood floor for the bottom form and supported it with about six vertical posts. The floor form should be cut about a half inch smaller so that it will come out after the concrete is poured. Pour the concrete into the form, then let it dry before you remove the forms.

I used thin 1¼-inch-thick fire bricks to create the floor of the oven. You could use the standard size if you want more of a heat sink. I laid out the fire bricks on top of the upper slab, then traced a circle that was about 8 inches smaller in diameter than the base was wide. This way there is room for the red oven bricks to sit around the edge of the fire bricks. To draw the circle, I measured to the center and drilled a small hole to set a nail for a pivot point, then hooked a tape measure and held a pencil to the right size and drew my circle. You can save some bricks if you mark half the circle, cut those bricks, and use the pieces for the second half.

Before laying the red oven bricks, you should know a little about mortar. I used a Type S brick mortar. The consistency should be so that when buttered on the brick in the right shape, you should be able to lay the brick in place with just a little nudge and maybe a tap with your trowel. It will probably surprise you how thin a mix you will end up making to do this. The buttering part is important in this process and needs to be shaped for the space to be filled. In this case, it needs to be thinner on the inside and thicker on the outside. If you mess up, just scrape the mortar off into the batch and try it again. Another thing that you will notice is how well the bricks will stick unsupported, especially on the wide face.

filled with concrete anyway. So I dry stacked them, using small wood wedges to tilt the stack to be plumb and straight when I filled the cells. This trick worked very well and I was now ready to form the top.

I made the top slab 6 inches thick, mostly to act as a heat sink. The vertical rebars which were sticking out of the blocks were bent to horizontal so that they laid in the top slab, then I tied in another 12-inch rebar grid. I

Pizza in the oven, ready to bake. You can see the red coals still in the oven.

The completed pizza oven is now protected by a covered patio and makes a perfect gathering spot in our yard.

or nail to hold bricks in the right place.

Bricks can be sawn with a diamond blade saw. They can be broken into a shape also, but it's not too pretty. I would recommend a wet tile saw or brick saw; the brick dust is pretty bad otherwise. They can be cut with a small side grinder with a diamond blade, but it's not as safe. Abrasive masonry blades are not very good as they wear out fast and will end up costing more.

The first course is the easiest to lay because you won't need to cut any bricks. They can be set vertically as in soldier coursing. The next course was laid vertically, but cut on the bottom and outside. For the next several courses you will need to use half bricks laid flat — because of the radius the long bricks won't work.

The closer you get to the top, the more cutting you will need to do. The bricks will need to be shaped something like a dove-tail tapered two ways. The front of the igloo is almost like a separate structure and the best way to describe joining the two sections is to say it is faked together. When I worked up to near that area, I laid up the front then joined the round part. After a few days the forms can be sawed out.

Some people cover their oven with insulation and plaster. I didn't need it to stay hot that long and I liked the look of the brick. The bricks absorb water in the rainy season, so it takes longer for them to dry out. To remedy this, I built a cute little roof over mine.

It's a good idea to start planning a patio or at least a gravel area in front of the oven, as the grass will get trampled. After a few months of frequently using our pizza oven, I decided to build a covered patio structure over it. Δ

More building projects

in all 18 anthologies

You will need a form or guide to shape the dome of the oven. I used Styrofoam sheet material cut into the round shape of the dome, then cut more pieces to cross at the middle, and more yet to divide it into eight. The inside height on my oven is 18 inches, so that's how high I cut the forms. I used nails to hold the pieces in place. You won't need the forms to keep the bricks from falling until you get near the top of the dome. I didn't always stay right on the forms until near the top when I needed a wedge

277

Ayoob on Firearms

Testing your guns

In the past, this column has touched on how to buy guns and make sure you're getting a good value. This time around, we'll talk about testing the ones you've already acquired.

It's amazing how many people have guns they haven't truly tested, sometimes haven't even fired. News alert, sports fans: they don't all come out of the box sighted in … and they don't all come out of the box *working*.

Looking back over 40-plus years of gun-writing and gun-testing for the firearms press, I recall a name-brand revolver that came in new, with its cylinder so "out of time" (its chambers not in line with the barrel in front, nor the firing pin in the rear) that it often failed to fire because the firing pin was so far off-center of the primer. I recall a .45 pistol from another famous maker (now defunct) that did the same thing.

If your gun has seen a lot of use — in your hands, or the hands of one or more previous owners — wear and tear may have taken its course. Even if your rifle has been well cared for, if it has a wooden stock, moisture may have gotten into it between seasons and warped it, causing wood to press unevenly against the barrel. This can throw the point of impact (of the bullet) away from a previously established point of aim (on what used to be a sighted-in firearm). This is one reason why wise hunters always take their hunting rifle to the range to confirm sight-in before going afield with it when hunting season rolls around.

For starters

When you get a new gun, you want to learn how to field strip and clean it. Do that before you do anything else. Do it with safety glasses on, because springs and parts sometimes go flying. (And fellas, your wife is right: *read the owner's manual first!*) If you don't have a manual, check online; most manufacturers, if still in business, will have owners' manuals online for each model, if only to cover themselves on civil liability. If your gun is "out of print," the best and most complete source I've found is Steve's Pages. Google search will get you there. It's an awesome resource for gun owners.

Check safety devices to make sure they're working. Triple check the gun, point the business end in a safe direction, and engage the safety. With the safety still "on," pull the trigger firmly. Now, removing the trigger finger and keeping the muzzle in a safe direction, release the safety to the "fire" position. If you experience the "click" of the hammer falling or the firing pin snapping forward, that would have been a shot if the gun had been loaded, and you have discovered an unsafe gun the easy way. I've known this to happen with new rifles out of the box, and have experienced it with used 1911 pistols that had been abused.

I've seen brand new guns come out of the shipping box bone-dry. Autoloaders in particular need to be lubricated to allow the long bearing surfaces within their mechanisms to work properly. Make sure there are no obstructions in the bore. You don't see as many military surplus firearms on the market today as you would have in my youth, but a lot of those came out of armories where they had been stored for a very long time, with grease and Cosmoline all over their insides and outsides, including the bore. Thick, congealed grease inside the bore (the inside of the barrel) can become an obstruction. Enough of it can raise internal pressures to the point where a "catastrophic event" occurs, that being the industry euphemism for the gun blowing up.

In the firing mechanism, accumulated crud in an old gun can literally jam up the works. A few years ago, I got a primo deal on a Colt Detective Special which had been manufactured in the year of my birth. (No mention

Mas sets up Caldwell Stable Table, which he has found ideal for accuracy testing and sighting in with rifles, on his 100-yard firing line.

of antiques here, please.) It had an incredibly low "as is" price tag on it because, the pawn shop owner said apologetically, "the action doesn't work right." I tried it, realized what had happened, and pulled out my checkbook. As soon as I got home, I turned it over to a gunsmith I trusted to work on the Colt's relatively complicated internal geometry, and he removed about 60 years' worth of hardened sludge that had accrued since its original owner filled the insides with 3-In-One Oil. I now own a very sweet, tight-grouping classic revolver made in my birth year (we gunnies like that) ... and did I mention that it was a helluva deal?

Next step

I start my test shooting at seven yards, the old "FBI combat distance," with a handgun, and at 25 yards with a rifle. That gives me an idea where the thing is hitting. "The object of shooting is to hit (your target)," said the late, great gun expert Jeff Cooper, and no one can gainsay him on this. Many years ago, a prosecutor's office in New Jersey flew me in to train their investigators and other armed personnel, and to save hassles with that state's draconian gun laws, they issued me a revolver like the ones they issued their detectives. My first priority was to test it on the range. From the 25 yard line, with all shots aimed at center chest, there were no hits there. All the shots were in a tight cluster in the right hip area of the silhouette. Closer examination of the gun showed that it had left the factory with the barrel off-center from the frame. It went back to its manufacturer that week, and I was issued another that was quickly confirmed to "shoot where it looked."

I learned over the years not to trust a gun until I had fired it 200 times, with the same ammunition and magazines I was going to have in it when I needed it. I still stand by that, though some think I'm a piker. Tactical

Testing shows whether the gun hits where aimed. Firearms expert Steve Denney uses a sight-pushing tool to adjust fixed Novak sights on Colt .45 pistol.

expert and shooting champ Ken Hackathorn and master 1911 pistol builder Hilton Yam both recommend a thousand rounds through the gun before you trust it. And those are all jam-free rounds, if it's going to pass the test: one malfunction, and unless you know it was caused by human error or one bad magazine or one identifiably defective cartridge, you go back to square one.

Particularly now — I'm writing this during the worst "ammo drought" in my relatively long lifetime as a shoot-er, and ammunition prices have gone insane — I know that's a lot to ask. But, balance the cost/risk ratio. If you've been hunting all week for that moose that's going to be winter meat in the larder, you want your gun to work. And if it's a gun you keep or carry for personal defense, the price of malfunction can literally be death.

Testing for accuracy

No human being can hold a firearm perfectly steady; that's what makes marksmanship such a challenging

CSM Ray Millican, Special Forces (ret.), uses Caldwell Matrix Shooting Rest on concrete bench at author's 25-yard firing bay to sight in S&W Military & Police CORE pistol with red dot optical sight from InSight.

endeavor. To find out what the given gun/cartridge combination can do, it has to be braced. Think sandbags. Think benchrest.

When I test firearms for accuracy, a company called Caldwell is my friend. I have full sets of their specially-shaped sandbags. I have their Stable Table installed permanently on my 100-yard range: it has adjustable bracing brackets for both the fore-end and the buttstock, and an adjustable seat to allow the shooter to be in the most solid possible firing position. There's also the shoulder-saving Lead Sled, which allows you to shoot from the bench with the machine soaking up the recoil instead of your shoulder. I wish that had existed back in the late 1980s, when I had to sight in the old-fashioned way for African hunting safaris with .458 Magnum and .375 Magnum "elephant guns."

For handguns, the gold standard is the machine rest, a specially-designed "gun vise" that holds the gun on target while you press a lever to activate the trigger, carefully re-setting the device between shots. It's complicat-

Patterning a shotgun, in this case a 20-gauge shell of #3 buckshot at "home defense distance"

ed to set up, and needs some shots to be pretty much wasted to "settle in" the machine. The Ransom brand is the platinum standard for this gold standard of robotic gun holding, though the HAMMR rest I have at my range comes very close. All that said, though, I prefer to test handguns

hand-held in a two-handed grasp with a Caldwell Matrix Rest set upon a concrete table. I discovered over the decades that if I fired a five-shot group this way, and measured not only all five hits but the best three therein, the latter measurement was always amazingly close to what the same gun and ammo would do for all five shots from a Ransom Rest.

More than a decade ago, when Cameron Hopkins was editor of *American Handgunner* magazine and I was the law enforcement editor, he challenged me to prove that and put me up against Charlie Petty, who was the handloading editor. Charlie and I tested three different handguns, me off the bench hand-held and Charlie running the same gun/ammo combinations with his Ransom Rest. We found that the "best three" of mine with "all five" of Charlie's correlated slightly more closely than did the variance between multiple groups all done on the machine rest.

How many shots for group testing? Over the years, with both rifle and pistol, five-shot groups became pretty much the standard. There is room for argument there, though. A lot of hunt-

Try the gun in simulated real world use. Here Mas wins Enhanced Service Pistol division at an IDPA match, March 2012, with Springfield XD(m) 5.25 9mm he was testing for On Target magazine. Camera has caught slide in mid-cycle, arrows point to freshly ejected casings. Photo courtesy On Target magazine.

ers felt that since even in the most difficult field stalking situation, no more than three shots would be fired at one animal, the three-shot group made the most sense. I personally can't argue with that. For a target rifle (or for that matter, target pistol) shooter, many competitors felt that a ten-shot group made more sense.

For that purpose, I can buy that too. Back when I shot the NRA High Power Rifle Competition, we fired 10-shot strings. If that was the standard we had to attain, it was obviously the standard to which we had to test the guns. You see the same today in 10-shot strings in the Project Appleseed competition. As a rifle's barrel heats up — particularly a high-powered rifle, firing high-pressured cartridges — its shot group will sometimes open up, too. (In my experience, that was most commonly manifested in a vertical stringing of the hits.) When I was preparing for my first Appleseed in 2010, I shot all 10-shot groups for sighting in. That helped me to win the coveted Rifleman's Patch at my first such event. With hotter loads in particular, the first three, and even first five shots will tend to cluster closer than all 10. That's important in 10-shot strings. Not so much when you won't need more than three shots for the moose you hope to put in the freezer to feed your family, a moose you'll hopefully bag with only one clean, humane shot.

When I hunted in South Africa, I discovered that the locals didn't sight in with three- *or* five- shot groups. They shot "pairs": two shots. That was partly because they figured you'd have one shot at the critter, and one more to fix anything you did wrong with the first before your quarry disappeared ... and partly because, having been embargoed by the west in the time of apartheid, ammunition was ridiculously expensive and extremely hard to find ... about like now in the United States.

So, how many shots do you need to fire per "group" to see how accurate your rifle or handgun is? About as many as you think you'll need to fire at The Moment of Truth.

Shotguns? They aren't grouped *per se*, unless you're shooting single-projectile rifled slugs. They're called "shotguns" because they generally discharge a cloud of spherical shot pellets: relatively large third-of-an-inch diameter, double-ought buckshot for close range deer or anti-personnel needs, or tinier pellets for birds and small game and such. Therefore, instead of being "grouped," shotguns are "patterned." The long-time standard is large sheets of white butcher paper, set on a target frame. Fire at the various distances, and see how densely the pellets hold their pattern together at each distance. This will let you know the optimum distance at which that particular load is likely to dispatch the given target you expect to be facing.

Field-testing

Once you know the gun works, and it hits center, you want to test it in the "human factor" elements when it's applied to the purposes for which you acquired it. Is it a target gun? Set up the course of fire you'll be faced with at the match, and "run the course." It's a deer rifle? If the deer move fast between the trees in the woods where you hunt and there's never time to go sitting or prone and rarely even time to go kneeling, then stand up on your hind legs and shoot from "offhand."

You'll find that the 10-pound "beanfield rifle" is awkward as hell to hold and swing on a moving target, and the fact that it puts every shot into half an inch from a bench rest at a hundred yards is suddenly absolutely meaningless to its intended purpose. You may find that the six and a half pound Winchester .30-30 carbine introduced in the year 1894 stays on target better and still hits the substantial area of a buck's lung cavity; that may be more

likely to bring home the venison in the real world scenario you're preparing yourself for. Last I knew, our most popular *Backwoods Home* writer, Jackie Clay, was bringing home deer every year with one of those Winchester '94s. If you have been using a sniper rifle in the deer thickets instead of a deer rifle, and have been making reservations for dinner instead of making venison for dinner like Jackie does, you may be looking at a classic case of not testing for the predicted firearms task.

When I test a concealed carry pistol, one thing I do is — duh! — carry it concealed for at least a full day. That lets me know whether it has sharp edges that will uncomfortably dig into the body during routine wear, for example, or become so excruciatingly uncomfortable to carry that no matter how sweet it is on the range, I'd rather be unarmed and helpless than be wearing the equivalent of a hair shirt.

Did you ever notice that when gun editors for *Field & Stream*, *Sports Afield*, or *Outdoor Life* test a hunting rifle, they actually try to go hunting with it? They want to know — and want their readers to know — how it "carries" during a long day in the field. They want to know how it comes to the shoulder when wearing the kind of clothing they'll be wearing in hunting season, not how it feels when they're sitting at a shooting bench in perfect weather with unlimited time to "get behind the gun for the shot."

In the same vein, when I'm testing a defensive handgun, I like to shoot a "combat pistol match" with it if the schedule allows. My favorite for that is the International Defensive Pistol Association (www.idpa.com). Most stages start with having to draw from concealment. You have to shoot while moving, strong hand only or weak hand only sometimes ... you have to shoot from behind cover in awkward positions ... and the shot may be at belly-to-belly distance, or 25 yards away. All of that is a great test-bed for the situations you're likely to face in the real world of self-defense handgunning.

The most often missed part of the test

The guns of a backwoods home tend to be family guns. One thing I've seen again and again in decades as a firearms instructor is the syndrome of the Alpha Male, usually the largest and strongest member of the household, burning thousands of rounds through dozens of guns to find out what works best for him (so far, so good) — but then, declaring to his petite wife, his smaller offspring, and the arthritic grandparents who live with them that "I've found the perfect gun for all of us."

If you've ever read my gun tests in magazines like *Guns, American Handgunner, On Target*, etc., you've noticed that I put those guns through multiple hands. I want to know how they'll work for big people and small people. Males and females. Big hands and small hands, long arms and short ones.

A weaker wrist may jam a semiautomatic pistol that works fine for someone with strong wrists. Conversely, a pistol that never malfunctions in a small hand, or injures that hand, may tear up the web of a large hand with its sharp-edged slide as it cycles, or cause a big thumb to accidentally hit the magazine release button of a small pistol and literally "unload the gun while trying to fire it" even though it functions perfectly

in the smaller hand. I've found that large people can adapt to a short rifle or shotgun stock much more easily than small people can adapt to long rifle or shotgun stocks. If it's going to be a "pool weapon," which any member of the household might have to employ, selecting it with a view toward the smallest, least physically capable user makes more sense than vice-versa. But *everyone* who's going to use it has to be part of the test, or the test isn't valid for the identified firearms need.

The bottom line? You test-drive the car before you buy it, you test it the way you plan to drive it, and if you're wise, everyone who's going to drive it participates in the test.

Testing guns, when you think about it, ain't a damn bit different. Δ

A Backwoods Home Anthology
The Sixth Year

❋ Here's a simple device to improve rough roads

❋ Backwoods firearms

❋ Make your own tool handles

❋ Home brew your own beer

❋ Make a heated seed germination flat

❋ Elderberries—the undiscovered fruit

❋ Wild turkey, goose, and venison for the holidays

❋ Tractor maintenance saves you more than money

❋ How to buy your first sheep

❋ Try a cement block garden

❋ Greens—delicious, nutritious, and easy to grow

❋ Raising goats can be profitable

❋ Making teas from wild plants and herbs

❋ Need a privy? Here's the right way to build one

❋ Enjoy zucchini all year

❋ Lunchbox cookies

❋ Start a home-based herb business

❋ Try these fresh ideas in your dairy

❋ Install rafters alone—the easy way

❋ Want to save fuel and firewood? Try square-split firewood

❋ This is one way to make applejack

❋ Build a homestead forge and fabricate your own hardware

❋ Soups for winter

❋ Moving to the wilderness—turning the dream to reality

❋ If you'd like to get started with chickens, here are the basics

Vegetarian chili

By Richard Blunt

Ask a room full of cooking enthusiasts to describe a hollandaise sauce and the answer will usually be something like this: "An emulsified sauce consisting of unsalted butter, egg yolks, and lemon juice combined with a little water, salt, and cayenne pepper." If you make any changes in the production procedure or ingredients, this classic sauce becomes something else. Now, if you ask the same group to describe chili, the resulting descriptions will go on for hours. Eventually this mild-mannered conversation will morph into a heated debate.

Why is this? Well, outside of a broad list of possible ingredients that define color, texture, piquancy, and very loose preparation guidelines, a universal definition for chili does not exist. For example, ask yourself if chili is a soup, a stew, or a casserole, then ask a few friends the same question, and compare answers. The issue becomes more confusing and controversial when the subject is vegetarian chili.

Many recipes for vegetarian chili rely on canned beans and chunky vegetables for substance. Some of these recipes also suggest using one of the many lackluster commercial chili powders for flavor. For a chili to be edible, it must be cooked for an extended time on low heat. Most vegetables and all canned beans turn into mush when cooked this way. In an attempt to reduce production costs, manufacturers of commercial chili powder often grind the stems and seeds of the chili pepper along with the pulp. The seeds and stems do not break down completely, even with prolonged cooking. For this reason, I

stopped using these commercial powders in all of my chili recipes.

How then, does a cook prepare a vegetarian chili that is savory, robust, and has real chili texture, using basic and easily available ingredients? I think I found the answer to this question. I believe a great chili can be made by anyone, regardless of culinary experience. However, there are some basic but simple rules that must be followed when making chili of any kind.

My intention here is to focus on chili without meat as a major component. Until recently, meatless chili has been the last chili that most cooks consider making. After correcting some of the problems that I have encountered while preparing meatless chilies, I believe I now have a vegetarian chili even meat lovers would

consider making. To create this chili, I have modified the way beans are prepared and cooked, the vegetable selection, the flavoring components, and method for achieving real chili texture.

The beans

Let's start with the beans. Canned beans are often used in a chili recipe because they are convenient and easy to use. Dried beans are sometimes regarded as a production problem because many cooks consider their preparation time consuming and their texture, after cooking, unpredictable. Old methods for preparing beans call for soaking them in cold water without added salt for 12 to 24 hours, rinsing the soaked beans in cold water, and simmering them in fresh

Dish on lower left (from top clockwise): dried Pacific kombu, fresh garlic, shiitake mushrooms. Dish on the right (from top clockwise): fresh serrano chili peppers, dried ancho chili peppers, pecan halves, dried pasilla chili, and dried pinto beans. Small bowl on the left: French lentils. Small bowl on the right: medium-grind dried bulgur. Top: bowl of chili

water for about one hour or until tender.

Often this meticulous and busy process produces beans that have not ruptured during cooking or you wind up with beans that have failed to cook completely. The solution for this problem is simple. After sorting the beans to remove unwanted material, rinse the beans in cold water and combine them with a measured amount of fresh water and salt. Bring the water to a boil, cover, and remove the pot from the heat. Soak the beans for one hour in the covered pot. After draining and rinsing the beans, they are ready to use in the formula. They will cook to perfection with the chili.

Vegetables

Most vegetables contain a high percentage of water. When vegetables are subjected to a long cooking time, they break down and leach water into the chili, causing it to become thin and soupy. In this formula I use vegetables that contain very little water, or have most of the water removed before being added to the chili. The details for this are outlined in the assembly procedure.

Chili flavor

Good chili is only possible when every ingredient in the pot serves to complement the others in quality, taste, and texture. My definition of a well-made chili is: a homogeneous mixture of ground or diced meat or vegetables, and grains or beans, nestled in a thick spicy sauce. Meat, especially, gives chili a distinctive flavor and texture. When meat is absent from the formula, the cook must compensate with alternative ingredients to achieve these results.

In my previous chili article, I introduced a flavoring method that knowledgeable professional and home cooks have been using for many years to enhance the flavor of the food they prepare. This concept, called umami (or fifth taste) combines foods that react with taste receptors on the tongue to greatly amplify the natural flavors in compound foods like chili. Umami was discovered by a Japanese physical chemistry professor in 1909 when he extracted a white compound from giant sea kelp and used it to give simple Japanese vegetable broths a savory and meaty flavor. What he had discovered was the amino acid glutamate.

In the year 2000, molecular biologists discovered a taste receptor on the tongue that reacts with glutamate to create the meaty and savory taste sensation, especially in foods that do not contain meat. Glutamates alone, however, produce a fairly weak umami taste. When combined with biological modules called nucleotides that occur naturally in many foods, the umami taste is substantially amplified.

To take advantage of this amplified umami taste, I have included ingredients in this chili that contain glutamate, along with things like kombu, tomatoes, garlic, onions, and dried shiitake mushrooms that are rich in nucleotides.

Texture

Most of the vegetarian chilies I sampled while doing research for this recipe lacked one very important chili characteristic — textural dimension. When meat is cooked for an extended period, as it is in chili, fibrous proteins in the connective tissue break down into a gel-like substance called collagen. Collagen thickens and adds texture to the chili. Since this recipe contains no meat, a substitute for collagen is necessary.

While doing research, I found a recipe that used medium-grind bulgur wheat to add texture to the finished dish. Bulgur is wheat that is partially cooked, dried, and ground. After rehydrating it in cold water for an hour, it is often used cold in salads like tabbouleh or in a pilaf, like rice. After testing it for use in this formula, I discovered it did not break down and become mushy when cooked in a liquid for more than three hours. A third of a cup of this grain also added a subtle nutty flavor to this chili, as well as all of the texture that I was looking for.

Dashi stock

The magic ingredient in this stock is a sea algae called kombu, which is cultivated and harvested in the cold waters of the North Pacific Ocean. It is high in glutamate and is one of the three components used to make this simple and tasty vegetable stock. The remaining two are shiitake mushrooms and soy sauce. The soy sauce is also high in glutamate and the mushrooms are high in nucleotides. This combination makes this stock a super umami cocktail that amplifies all of the bold and subtle flavors in this dish. This formula yields about 5½ cups of stock. This is more than enough for the main chili recipe. The remainder can be used to cook the lentils if you decide to use them.

7 cups water
2 four-inch pieces of dried kombu
   sea kelp
6 dried shiitake mushrooms
1 Tbsp. low-sodium soy sauce

Method:

1. Gently rinse the dried kombu and shiitake mushrooms under cold running water. Be careful not to rub the white minerals from the surface of the kombu leaf. Measure the seven cups of water in a suitable size pot and soak the kombu and mushrooms in this water for 15 minutes.

2. Remove the mushrooms from the water, remove the stems, cut each mushroom into quarters, and return them to the pot.

3. Bring the water to a slow simmer and cook the mixture for 15 minutes.

4. Remove and discard the mushrooms and kombu. Add the soy sauce and set the broth aside.

Vegetarian chili

8 oz. dried pinto beans, picked over
  and rinsed
2 qts. cold water
1 Tbsp. salt
1 dried ancho chile pepper
1 dried pasilla chile pepper
2 tsp. dried oregano
¼ cup pecans, lightly toasted
1 can (14-oz.) diced tomatoes,
  drained and the juice reserved to
  add later
2 Tbsp. tomato paste
1 to 2 fresh serrano chile peppers,
  stemmed and chopped (do not
  remove the seeds)
5 cloves fresh garlic, minced
3 Tbsp. vegetable oil
12 oz. yellow onions, diced
½ tsp. salt
¼ cup dry sherry
2 tsp. ground cumin
1 tsp. ground coriander
3½ cups dashi stock
⅓ cup medium-grind bulgur wheat
3 Tbsp. fresh cilantro, chopped

Method:

1. Combine the dried beans, cold water, and salt in a suitable size pot. Set the pot on a stove and bring the water to a boil over high heat. Remove the pot from the heat, cover, and let it stand for one hour.

2. Preheat the oven to 300° F.

3. Remove the stems and seeds from the dried ancho and pasilla chile peppers and cut the peppers into one-inch pieces. Place the pieces on a small cookie sheet or pie plate and toast until fragrant, about seven or eight minutes. Remove them from the oven, and set them aside to cool.

4. Grind the toasted peppers and oregano in a spice mill or electric coffee grinder until finely ground.

5. Process the pecans in a food processor until finely ground, and transfer them to a small bowl.

6. Process the drained tomatoes, tomato paste, fresh serrano chiles, and fresh garlic in a food processor until the vegetables are finely chopped, and add the mixture to the processed pecans.

7. Heat the oil in a heavy-bottom four-quart Dutch oven or sauce pot with a heat-proof lid and handle over medium-high heat until it shimmers. Add the onions and salt. Cook the onions, stirring occasionally until they begin to brown.

8. Add the sherry and continue cooking until the pan is almost dry. Reduce the heat to medium-low, then add the processed chile pepper and oregano mixture along with the ground cumin and coriander. Continue cooking while stirring the mixture for about 30 seconds.

9. Add the drained beans and dashi stock to the pot and bring to a boil over medium-high heat.

10. Remove the pot from the heat and stir in the processed tomato mixture, bulgur wheat, and reserved tomato juice.

11. Cover the pot and place it in the oven for 1½ to 2 hours or until the beans are tender.

12. When you remove the pot from the oven, the oil will have risen to the top of the chili. Do not remove this oil because it is an essential flavor and binding component that will further enhance the flavor and stability of the sauce. Stir the chili well with a wooden spoon and let it stand uncovered for 15 minutes. Stirring will release some of the starch from the beans and bulgur to create a thickened sauce that will not separate when reheated.

13. Stir in the cilantro and serve.

Optional ingredient:

Lentils make a nice addition to this chili as they add complexity to the texture. If you'd like to add some,

My definition of a well-made chili is: a homogeneous mixture of ground or diced meat or vegetables, and grains or beans, nestled in a thick spicy sauce.

while the chili is cooking, soak ¼ cup of French lentils for about one hour in warm water (about 110° F). Drain and combine them in a small casserole dish with one cup of the remaining dashi stock, cover, and place them in the oven to bake until tender, about one hour. Remove the lentils from the oven, drain, and set them aside. This variety of lentil has a rich and complex flavor and holds its shape when cooked. The reason they should be soaked and cooked separately is because the acidity of the tomatoes in the chili will prevent them from cooking properly. Add the cooked lentils when you stir in the cilantro.

How successful was my chili? My son, Michael, has been a vegetarian for the last four years. When he tried this chili, he eyed me suspiciously and said, "Dad, there's meat in this chili."

Success! I had concocted a great tasting chili I can serve to everyone. Δ

More great recipes are in
Backwoods Home Cooking

Reel in a sucker: Fishing for carp

By Frank Knebel

As I fished along the rocky shoreline of Texas' Lake Georgetown, I came to a shallow cove and immediately found a treasure trove of the small-but-feisty Guadalupe bass. One after another, they smashed my little Rebel crawdad crankbait until the bites stopped. I had been catching and releasing those little bass, but now I was seriously beginning to consider the repercussions of such a practice — I was sure that the little big-mouths that I'd been letting go had been swimming around down there and snitching on me, resulting in my sudden catch deficit. As I was pondering all of this, I continued to cast and retrieve, varying the speed in a vain attempt to get a bite. Suddenly, my lure snagged up on something. I gave the line plenty of slack and waited for the lure to float to the surface, like it normally did after hanging up on a rock. When that didn't happen, I gave the line a good jerk, hoping to either pop it loose or bend

the little hook. Well, the rock I thought I snagged turned out to be very much alive and for the next 20 minutes I fought a battle that would have made Hemingway weep.

Line peeled off of the reel and the drag sang while the light action 6½-foot rod bowed and vibrated. I had no idea what was on the other end of that line, but I guessed it was just a big gaspergou (freshwater drum). But once the battle was over, I was amazed to be looking at the bronze and pink-tinted behemoth that lay on the rocks. I had just caught a 12-pound carp on a crankbait. I later learned that one of the local old-timers kept that cove baited with corn and that he considered my 12-pounder to be "just a puppy." I also found out that while carp hitting lures isn't a real common occurrence, it's not exactly a rare one and that these suckers can weigh as

much as 80 pounds and measure five feet long!

Why carp?

Now, why in the world would anyone intentionally go out after carp? Well, for one thing, although it's bony, this fish is actually pretty tasty and is one of the most propagated fish in the world. It has been cultured in Asia and Europe for ages. In fact, though indigenous to Asia, it had been spread all across the European continent and was so common that Aristotle mentioned it repeatedly as far back as 350 B.C. (I asked my mother-in-law if she remembers hearing about them back then and she says they used to eat them all the time!)

In 1876, the United States Fish Commission imported the carp from Germany. Since then, they have spread from east to west, coast to coast. In the rest of the world they are found on every continent with the exception of Antarctica. The propagation of common carp is encouraged and often subsidized and promoted by the United

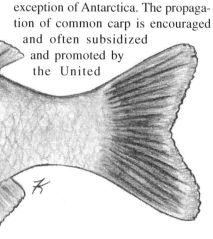

Nations in underdeveloped nations. These are not to be confused with that other Asian importation, the Asian or Silver carp, that is wreaking havoc on the upper Mississippi.

Another reason to fish for carp is that the common carp can also become a nuisance like its pesky Asian cousin. The carp mostly feed along the bottom and their rooting around muddies the water and destroys water clarity. Often placed in ponds or lakes to help keep them clean, much like putting goldfish in the horse trough, they will occasionally overpopulate and the increased rooting activity destroys the very environment they were supposed to maintain. Water quality decreases and the darker, muddy water draws more heat than clear and thereby raises the water temperature. As vegetation is consumed or uprooted, oxygen content decreases and other fish lose vital cover or elements vital to spawning, such as vegetation for eggs to cling to and cover for the fry. The stirred mud silts over the nest, smothering the eggs. The entire ecosystem is affected negatively by misguided good intentions. So it's just as important to manage carp populations as it is to manage forage and predatory fish popula-

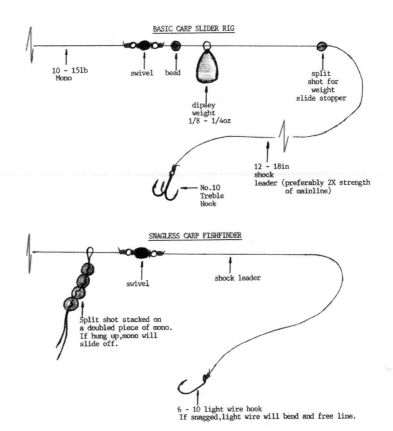

tions, especially in smaller isolated waters.

If you're a trapper, it only makes sense to target carp as they are an excellent bait for coons and mink on your water sets and even bobcat and coyote while trapping bottomlands and swamps. Once winter sets in, fish is a powerful draw to a set since by then all of the "easy" foodstuffs are long-gone. With their abundance, large size, and easy availability, it will only take a little effort (and a whole lot of fun) to lay in an entire season's supply of trap bait. Carp also make an excellent bait, chum, or base ingredient for catfish baits. Seriously, there are 1,001 uses for this "trash" fish.

Carp facts

Before we move on to the "how to catch 'em" part, let's look at the fish itself.

The common carp (*Cyprinus carpio*) belongs to the Cyprinidae family which includes the minnow. Coloration will vary depending on water clarity and ranges from a brass-green or bronze to a bright copper-gold. Often, the darker fins will appear pink, as will the belly. Both the anal and dorsal fins possess a toothed spine that can destroy nets. The common carp has a deep, humped body covered with large

---

Homemade carp doughbaits

One of the most popular is made by mixing 100% bran flakes with Big Red soda water. Mix and mash it to a thick consistency that will remain on the hook. When ready to use, ball a little up on the hook. Just remember that carp have small mouths. Doughballs should never be larger than a grape.

A bread/cheese dough is also effective. Break a few slices of stale bread up into a cotton handkerchief or bandana, cup, towel or whatever, and wet thoroughly with tap water. Squeeze all the water out of the bread through the cloth, then open and add grated sharp cheddar or blue cheese (a good ratio is 1/3 cheese to 2/3 bread) and knead. If the dough is still soggy, add cornmeal a little at a time until it makes a sticky, yet firm, dough. Be careful with the cornmeal — too much will make it brittle.

Wheaties mixed with water and mashed into a dough is a simple, effective bait. Much like us, carp can differentiate between salty, sweet, bitter, and acidic flavors. By adding a dollop of sugar, corn syrup, or anise oil to any of the above recipes, you can only improve them.

scales, and a barbel (whisker) on each side of its upper jaw that distinguishes it from others in the sucker family. It also has a small mouth for its size. The average carp weight is two to eight pounds, but 20 pounders are not uncommon.

Carp spawn in shallow water, often less than a foot deep, in the spring when the water reaches somewhere around 65° F. The spawn resembles a wild frat-party with all the thrashin' and splashin' that takes place as hundreds to thousands of these fish come together for the event. A 10-15 pound female can carry up to two million eggs. These hatch without parental care in five to ten days. Where there is an adequate food source, these fish can grow fast — a year-old carp will weigh a pound or more. Carp are also long-lived, reaching 25 years of age on average. (One made it in captivity to the ripe old age of 47!)

Carp can survive and thrive nearly everywhere and are found in all major river systems. They can tolerate the cold of the north and the heat of the south. This sucker prefers off-colored, shallow lakes where it can find plenty of organic goodies to munch on. In many bodies of water, this omnivorous fish is the dominant species. They root along the bottom and inhale both vegetable and animal matter. During algae blooms or some insect hatches, the carp can be found feeding on the surface as well. It has been accused of seeking out and gorging on gamefish eggs, but it probably doesn't do this any more than several of the sunfish species, and in all probability, less so. Plants, algae, insect larvae, worms, snails, small crustaceans, and mussels make up part of their vast diet.

There are two other varieties of the common carp: the mirror carp and the leather carp. These are rarer subspecies/variants that are cultured on farms and less likely to be encountered in the wild, especially since breeding back with common carp eliminates their unique characteristics of slick skin and few scales.

Catching carp

Like many other species of fish, the best time to catch carp is during the spring spawn while they are in shallow water. But carp are active all year, just not as concentrated. When the other fish tend to shut down and lay up during the summer heat, the carp can still be readily caught.

Patience is the key to catching carp on a rod and reel. Lacking the aggressiveness of predatory fish, they will just graze along until they come across your bait. Think of them as aquatic hogs. The best way to ensure success with these rooters is to bait a hole. Toss in a bunch of range cubes, cottonseed cake, feed corn, or milo into the area you intend to fish. If you can do this for several days in advance, so much the better.

As far as baits go, carp seems to have as many options as catfish. Dough, cheese, potatoes, carrots, corn, canned pork, canned cat food, and even marshmallows are just some of the proven producers. There is also an entire arsenal of prepared, commercially-available baits out there. But the most common baits that I have used have been corn, cheese, and doughbaits.

Fishing corn is a no-brainer, just thread several kernels of canned whole-kernel sweet corn onto a size 6-10 long-shanked hook or a No. 10 treble hook. The same goes for fishing cheese, just cut a small cube (¼ to ½-inch) of sharp cheddar or blue

---

Carp for the trapper

There are two ways to put carp up for use later in the season. The first and simplest is to just freeze it. You can freeze them whole to be cut up later or go ahead and do it now and then freeze. The easiest method is to freeze them and then cut up into chunks with a saw. One of those cheap, imported bandsaws works great for this, but be sure to clean it well after use or the wife will be wondering what went and died in the garage.

The other method to put up carp is to salt the fish. Cut into correctly-sized chunks for your sets. A chunk the size of your fist should work. Pack the cut chunks into a five-gallon bucket a layer at a time and salt each layer with pickling salt, rock salt, or even plain old table salt. You can make two-inch layers of fish with a ½-inch layer of salt on each one. Repeat until the layers are within two inches of the lip of the bucket. Then fill all the way to the top with water and press the lid on slowly so that all of the air can escape. Put up this way, it will last for years with no odor.

When ready to use, remove it from the bucket and rinse well. Then place it in a clean bucket and soak in water overnight. This helps rehydrate the fish and revitalizes its fishy aroma. The fish is still salty though, so don't use it as a prebait. Cut and frozen or salted carp can be improved even further by mixing a little fish oil, vegetable oil, anise, or asafoetida with it.

I peg the baits in pocket and cubby sets with bent welding rods that I have knocked the flux off of. This keeps the critters working the sets longer and keeps them from getting a taste. Generally it's too salty and if you miss the coon or mink on the first shot, he may not work for it again. In my experience on the Texas coast, bobcats are just looking for a trap to step into and coyotes don't seem to mind the salt too much. In fact, during the 2007-2008 season, I caught almost as many coyotes as coons on my bottom land sets using this bait. We even have a video off a game camera that shows a 'yote that had managed to miss the trap licking that salty bait like a piece of candy.

cheese and thread on the hook. However, if you're using a treble hook, push the shank of the hook through the cheese and then tie onto your line. Doughbaits are just balled up around the hook. There are several different effective recipes.

Tackle is pretty simple too. Long "cane poles" work great. Spinning outfits, especially lighter action rods, seem to be the most popular here in the U.S. for carp. Over on the other side of the Atlantic, they all use special 12-foot or longer rods specifically made for carp. A 7-foot light to medium-light rod with any reel spooled with 10-15 pound mono or one of the smaller diameter superlines will do just fine. If you are targeting bigger carp, then gun up. Get as many lines in the water as possible to increase your chances and be patient.

Rigging up is also a simple matter. All you need are the small hooks already mentioned, split-shot or some light, sliding sinkers of some sort, and small swivels. With these, you can fish on the bottom where the carp are rooting around. Using a stand-up float can help detect subtle bites. Leaders made out of the super-clear fluorocarbons of 15 pound test or so do as well but aren't necessary. You can just make a leader with your regular mono, though one made from line that is twice the breaking strength of that on your reel will serve you best

Carp for catfish

Carp are hardy and make exceptionally good big catfish baits when using trotlines, limblines, or jugs. A hand-sized carp hooked in the back above the spine will live for days or until a monster cat makes a meal out of him. Fresh-cut carp are also good when you don't have any shad — this is the go-to bait for monster gar. These can be caught in a perch trap baited with cotton seed cake. (Four to six carp are perfect.)

as a shock leader. Some basic rigs are shown in the illustration and are pretty self-explanatory.

There are two things you need to remember: keep any weight well back from the bait so that little to no resistance is felt once the carp picks up the bait, and set the hook as soon as you feel a twitch or see your float wiggle. The carp will pick up and mouth the bait for just a second before it decides if it wants to eat it or not. Don't give it the chance!

Eating carp

Carp should have all of the skin and dark meat trimmed away since it has a strong flavor. Fillets or whole fish can be steamed or baked and the white meat flaked away from the larger bones. Be sure to pick out the smaller, finer bones. The meat can then be eaten as is, in salads, or mixed into soups and gumbos. Carp can also be canned by cutting steaks or chunks and pressure cooking. This not only cooks the meat, but softens the bones. When prepping for cooking after it's been canned, just pick out the larger bones. You'll never notice the smaller ones. Carp croquettes are every bit as good as mackerel or salmon ones. Smoked carp is also something that shouldn't be overlooked. There are literally thousands of carp recipes out there on the Internet. American, Asian, and European cuisines all have a carp dish. I'm sure you can find something to satisfy even the most skeptical palate.

Conclusion

Carp fishing is a true relaxation sport. Throw out something to draw them in and cast out several rigs. Then just kick back and wait. When nothing else is biting, what have you got to lose? Take a moment, take a breath, and relax. Besides, it'll keep you out of your old lady's hair for a while. Δ

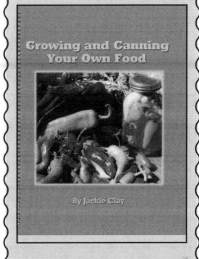

Build a passive-solar food dehydrator

By Jeffrey R. Yago, P. E., CEM

Humans have been drying fruits, herbs, nuts, vegetables, meats, and fish using just the sun for thousands of years. Early Egyptians used wooden racks to sun-dry thinly-sliced strips of meat and fish. As early as the 1700s, people were improving the dehydration process by constructing drying enclosures built over slow-burning fires. By the early 1900s, commercial dehydrators became available that included powered fans and small electric heaters similar to the designs in use today.

This article describes how you can build your own solar-powered food dehydrator, but I will not be going into detail on how to actually prepare and season foods for dehydration. There are numerous reference materials, recipes, and detailed instructions on the dehydration process, which are easy to find in other *BHM* articles and on the Internet.

Dehydrators come in every size and design imaginable. Residential units usually are about the size of a large microwave oven and use a bottom heating element to improve the drying process. Simple homemade units have been built using everything from cardboard boxes with a small light bulb in the bottom for heat, to larger homemade dehydrators made from discarded refrigerators, wooden shipping crates, and metal shelving.

The main design feature for all dehydrators is multiple porous racks that will support small slices of fruits,

The finished passive-solar dehydrator maintained a fairly constant temperature of 150° F throughout most of the day without any repositioning, which shows that this design can easily provide the temperatures required by any dehydrator recipe.

meats, or garden herbs spaced closely together while still allowing good airflow around and through these racks. Good airflow is mandatory; the goal is to slowly remove the moisture from the food, not cook it.

Most dehydrators have ventilation near the bottom, so that the air passes up through the drying racks before exiting near the top. Since heated air rises, some dehydrator designs do not require electricity and rely on natural air convection to provide the airflow.

More expensive dehydrators will include adjustable air dampers and exhaust fans to draw air through the racks and out the top. This dehydrator project includes air intake vents located on each side near the bottom, and a larger outlet vent on the back near the top.

The second design issue is the size of the enclosure, and this will be driven by the size of the racks. Since you want metal racks that are easy to clean and offer good support, while still having minimum air restriction, the racks will normally be a manufactured product. However, you can use the metal racks from a discarded refrigerator, old stove, or even commercial screening material. Once you have found or purchased the racks you want to use, this will determine the width and depth of the enclosure. The enclosure itself can be made from metal, wood, or heavy cardboard, depending on your budget and available scrap materials.

Since the fruits or meats to be dehydrated will be sliced very thin to improve moisture removal and reduce drying time, the individual shelves can be much closer together than you would normally see in a standard refrigerator or oven. In fact, shelf spacing of two to three inches is typical in both homemade and commercial dehydrators, so the number of shelves and their spacing will determine the height of your homemade solar dehydrator.

Finally, by covering the interior with reflective aluminum foil and adding a clear glass or Plexiglas® front cover, you can forget electric heating and use the sun to drive the dehydration process. Remember, this is not intended to be a high-temperature solar oven and you are not trying to cook the fruits, herbs, or meats. Almost all foods will be properly dehydrated by keeping the inside temperature between 120 and 140° F, but I recommend following the pre-seasoning, drying temperature, and drying time recommendations found in your dehydration recipes.

This dehydrator is very easy to build. Two of my grandchildren, eleven-year-old Christopher and nine-year-old Stephen, did all of the cutting and drilling to fabricate the wood components shown.

While some fruits such as thinly-sliced, peeled apples may be fully dehydrated in six hours, moist fruits such as bananas and strawberries may require 12 to 16 hours before they are fully dehydrated. Thinly-sliced meats may require slightly higher temperatures and up to 16 hours to fully transform into jerky.

Construction

I wanted to design a solar-powered dehydrator that would utilize low-cost materials and be very easy for anyone to build using basic hand tools. While you can modify my basic design to accommodate your choice of metal racks, I found some very inexpensive racks at Lowe's that are designed to fit barbeque grills. These racks are made from 12x18-inch perforated aluminum sheets and sold in packages of two for less than $5. Eight racks will cost $20 and since they were designed to cook foods on a grill, they are perfect for our needs. Eight of these racks will easily fit in a dehydrator that is 24 inches high, including extra space at the bottom and top.

To save construction time, I chose 16-inch-wide finished shelving lumber to make the sides, top, and bottom, and ¼-inch plywood to make the back. I also found a 18x24-inch stock size of pre-cut Plexiglas® and pre-formed metal rails to support the thin Plexiglas®. While I spent about $90 for all materials, if you have discard-

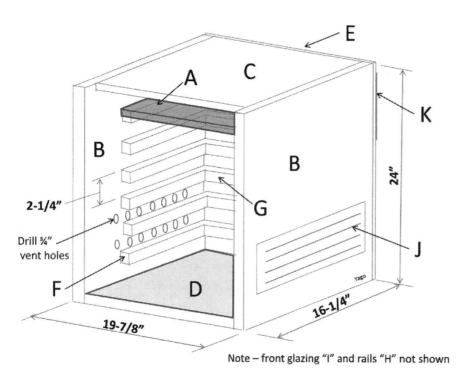

2-1/4"

Drill ¾" vent holes

19-7/8"

24"

16-1/4"

Note – front glazing "I" and rails "H" not shown

final assembly using construction adhesive in a caulking gun and a pneumatic nailer, both easy to operate with one arm. While not intentionally trying to prove this project is child's play, it does show that this solar dehydrator is fairly easy to build. And keep in mind, if you find a good deal on racks of a different size, you can modify this design as needed.

By adding a small solar-powered fan on the top, you can significantly improve the performance of this dehydrator. I have also tried to utilize a design that eliminates the possibility of insects getting inside since some types of fruits or meats have dehydrating times that exceed the typical six to eight hours of sun available per day. This could require having to leave the fruits or meats outside in the dehydrator for multiple days to fully dehydrate, depending on the weather, so insect screening is mandatory.

I have covered all exterior ventilation openings with low-cost metal louvers that include internal insect screening, and all joints are nail and glue construction for a tight fit. Once the Plexiglas® front panel is slid into position, you are ready to start dehydrating. I added a kitchen thermometer with a long probe inserted through a drilled hole near the top to monitor the inside temperature. You will want a thermometer with a range of 90 to 200° F if possible. Candy thermometers register up to 400° F, which is too high for our purposes. By periodically checking this thermometer, the drying temperature specified in the recipe can easily be maintained by orienting the dehydrator toward or away from the direct sun.

During my initial testing, this homemade solar dehydrator stayed a fairly constant 150° F throughout most of the day without any repositioning. While you may want to orient the dehydrator slightly away from the direct sun to lower this temperature,

ed appliances or scrap building materials you many not need to buy anything.

Since I recently had major shoulder surgery, my current workshop projects are seriously limited for the next few months, so I enlisted the help of two of my six grandchildren. Eleven-year-old Christopher and nine-year-old Stephen did all of the cutting and drilling to fabricate the wood components shown, so I only had to do the

Bill of materials		
Reference	**Quantity**	**Description**
A	4	Master Forge 12"x18" grill topper racks (two-pack)
B	2	3/4"x16"x24" pine shelving
C	1	3/4"x14-3/4"x18-3/8" pine shelving
D	1	3/4"x16"x18-3/8" pine shelving
E	1	1/4" pine plywood, 19-7/8"x24"
F	16	1"x2"x11-1/2" long white pine
G	8	1"x2"x18-3/8" long white pine
H	1	5/16"x22" metal screen frame rail
I	1	18"x24" acrylic clear sheet
J	2	4"x16" screened louver vent
K	1	8"x16" screened louver vent
	1	Tube construction adhesive
	1	Roll heavy oven aluminum foil
	1	Dial thermometer with probe

this does show that this design can easily provide the temperatures required by any recipe.

Step-by-step construction

1. Cut all parts as shown. Note the top is set back 1¼ inches from the front edge to clear the sliding front so it can be pulled up and out.

2. Add the rack supports to both left and right-side boards, then drill the air vents as shown between the lower two racks.

3. After cutting out the three openings in the back to fit the top louver, glue down a layer of heavy aluminum foil before adding the rear rack supports.

4. Cover the underside of the top board, and top side of the bottom board with a layer of heavy aluminum foil before final assembly.

5. Assemble the sides, back, top, and bottom using construction glue and finish nails or screws. Sand all rough surfaces and corners.

6. Finally, install the metal rails to support the removable sliding Plexiglas® front. This front Plexiglas® could also slide in grooves cut into the sides and bottom, which would eliminate the metal rails.

Since this solar dehydrator will be outside when in use, I added two coats of a semi-gloss exterior paint to all outside surfaces. However, I left all exposed interior wood surfaces unpainted to avoid paint fumes affecting the taste of the dehydrated foods. Although the bottom of this dehydrator is covered with heavy aluminum foil, you may still want to add a small pan to catch drippings if you will be dehydrating meats.

The 12x18-inch aluminum racks are fairly flexible, and since they will only be supported along the left and right edge and the back, I bent down a ½-inch lip across the front edge which significantly strengthened the racks. Since these racks are thin, it was fairly easy to bend by hand to

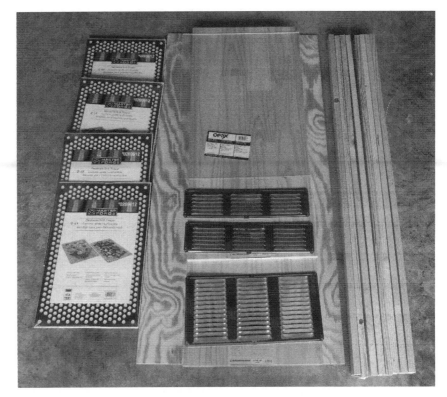

Here are all the materials needed to build a solar food dehydrator.

Completed back

Attach rack supports to each side.

form the lip with the bend passing through the first row of holes.

Conclusion

While you are free to copy my design and material selection shown, I encourage you to utilize your own discarded materials to reduce costs which may require adjusting the dimensions and construction to fit. Δ

Jeff Yago is a licensed professional engineer and certified energy manager with more than 30 years of experience in the energy conservation field. He has extensive solar and emergency preparedness experience, and has authored numerous articles and texts. His website is: www.pvforyou.com

Assemble both sides to the back.

The Last Word

Concealed carry laws reduce crime

This year, Illinois became the 50th state to allow the carrying of concealed weapons by law-abiding citizens. That's a milestone that heralds a lot of good news for crime statistics. More guns in the hands of law-abiding citizens has drastically reduced violent crime in the last quarter-century.

Back in 1986 there was only one state — Vermont — that allowed "unrestricted" concealed carry, as guaranteed by the *Second* and *Fourteenth Amendments* of the *Constitution of the United States*. That is, you didn't need a license or permit to carry a concealed weapon in Vermont. Eight others were "shall-issue" states, meaning a citizen needed a permit of some sort to carry a concealed weapon, but the state had to issue such a permit to *any* law-abiding citizen unless there was cause not to. Another 25 states had "may-issue" laws, meaning a law-abiding citizen could apply for a permit, but the state didn't have to issue it if the applicant didn't have what amounted to a "good reason." The remaining 16 were "no-issue" states, meaning just what it sounds like — the average citizen was not allowed to carry a concealed weapon under *any* circumstances.

Right now, all 50 states allow some kind of concealed carry. Five are unrestricted, 37 are shall-issue states, and only 8 are may-issue states. Had I been asked 27 years ago, I'd have said we'd never see this day. But it was difficult to get to this point because when the widespread movement to allow concealed carry began in the 1980s, the antigun people warned that more guns would lead to carnage in the streets. Every time a state considered allowing concealed carry, the antigunners foretold of fender benders and traffic disputes being settled by gunfire, and barroom arguments over who was a better center fielder, Mickey Mantle or Willie Mays, being resolved by firefights. Of course, as each successive state made concealed carry an option for its citizens, none of the antigunners' predictions came true. But this didn't stop them, because whenever another state considered allowing concealed carry, the same tired arguments were freshened up and paraded out again.

So, if we didn't get carnage, what did happen?

The May13-May19, 2013 issue of *Bloomberg Businessweek* (formerly *BusinessWeek*), a magazine wholly owned by Bloomberg, L.P., which, in turn, is 88% owned by New York City's antigun mayor, Michael Bloomberg, carried an article titled *Good News on Guns, Bad News for Gun Control*. According to the article's author, Paul M. Barrett:

• The Bureau of Justice Statistics, a federal government agency belonging to the U.S. Department of Justice, says that from 1993 to 2011, gun homicides in the United States have dropped by 39% and, according to the Pew Research Center, an American think tank organization based in Washington, D.C., the drop may be closer to 49%.

• Nonfatal gun crimes have dropped 69%.

• The average annual number of homicides in schools has dropped from 29 in the 1990s to 20 in the 2000s.

What makes this ironic is that Mayor Bloomberg is enacting some of the most stringent antigun laws in the country. So much for taking care of the people he "serves."

Barrett doesn't speculate on the reasons for the drop in gun crime, but gun proponents have, for years, said that widespread gun ownership and concealed carry licensing (exactly what has been happening since 1986) would lead to lower crime rates.

John Lott, an economist famous for authoring books such as *More Guns, Less Crime*, has done a statistical analysis of the proliferation of concealed carry laws. His research indicates that almost everywhere concealed carry has been allowed, violent-crime rates have fallen. Academics have attacked Lott on personal grounds, while disputing his studies on narrow and often esoteric grounds. Supporters, however, have repeatedly demonstrated the efficacy of his statistics.

The National Academy of Sciences has claimed there is no correlation between concealed carry and crime rates, one way or the other. What is true, however, is that no reputable study has ever backed up the antigunners' claims that laws allowing concealed carry by law-abiding citizens lead to crime increases. On the other hand, in jailhouse interviews, felons have said what they fear most is not the police, but *armed* citizens. Draw your own conclusions.

What I hope the future brings:

• More states will allow unrestricted carry.

• Better yet, the universal recognition of concealed carry permits among the states, i.e., if you've got a license from one state, the other states must honor it, just as they do drivers' licenses.

• Best would be for the states and federal government to finally honor the guarantee of the *Second Amendment*, which says, "…the right of the people to keep and *bear* Arms shall not be infringed," and forget this foolishness about licensing because the truth is that America is now safer than it has been in decades, and one of the factors in this decrease of violent crime is that there are more law-abiding citizens than ever who are "packing heat" in their homes and on the streets.

I'm one of them. — *John Silveira*

Build a balcony deck

By Dorothy Ainsworth

A balcony deck is a pleasant and inviting place to get a breath of fresh air, lounge and sip, pet the cat, read the paper, listen to the birds, and enjoy the view. From your elevated perch, you can watch the sunrise, gaze at the stars, or howl at the moon.

The charm and appeal of a deck is that it lets you go outside without leaving the house. It provides a seamless transition from indoors to outdoors without putting a foot in the dirt, and that makes it feel as good as it looks.

In my opinion, there's not a second story room in any house that wouldn't be enhanced by adding a deck to it. Why not step out onto the balcony deck of your bedroom, stretch, yawn, and greet the day ... barefoot and in your bathrobe if you like?

Decks extend our living space without costing very much. In 30 years of developing my property, I've added at least one deck onto every livable structure and onto every storage building — totaling 13 in all.

My last big project (building my son Eric's house) took six years of paying as we went and doing the labor ourselves.

To get to the finish line a little sooner, we decided to postpone building the balcony deck off the kitchen until later — or never. The deck was in the original plans and we paid the permit fee for it, but enough was enough. Fortunately, we had planned ahead and left the electrical wiring out of the place in the wall where the door might be someday, and stubbed out two sets of wires for an outlet and a porch light.

After we received the final inspection and occupancy certificate in April 2012, I hung up my carpenter's belt and considered myself retired from construction work. That silly concept was short-lived. Exactly one year later, I took the belt off its rusty nail, rescued a cute little spider from the nail pouch, and started in on the project.

Planning the deck

Eric's house is nestled into the side of a slope, with the basement buried on the west side but completely exposed on the east side. His kitchen is eight feet off the ground, sitting atop the basement. The entire east wall was tall, bare, and boring. There was nothing on it but the kitchen window twelve feet up and the basement door at ground level far over to one side. The house just didn't look balanced without a balcony deck on that side; it cried out to be built.

I figured the deck would not only be an attractive and useful addition to that side of the house, but it would also create a protected area underneath it for garden tools. It would accentuate the good features of the east side: a spectacular view, sunrises and moonrises, delicious shade in the afternoon, rainbows galore in the spring, and (being on the lee side) very little wind.

We decided on a long narrow deck that would be small, affordable ($10/sq.ft.), and would only take a couple of months to build. I had a 24-foot wall to play with, so I decided to make the deck 18 feet long and 5 feet wide. That way I could use standard lumber with very little waste and still have room to squeeze in a fire-escape stairway off the end without it extending beyond the wall and intruding onto the walkway around the house. The 90 sq.ft. deck itself would be plenty of room for a little table, some chairs, and a portable BBQ.

It was a cool April, so getting it done before the scorching summer was imperative. I sketched out some detailed plans, made a materials list, and drove the old truck to Home Depot, where I used my 12-month interest-free charge card, and got loaded up — or down — depending on whether you are looking at the height of the load, or the flatness of the tires.

Deck construction

The great thing about retrofitting a deck is that you can do all your hammering and sawing outside without disturbing anybody inside — well, until you cut the door opening in the wall. But that's just one day of inconvenience and mild torture — a small price to pay for years of future enjoyment.

Deck construction is simple and straightforward. There's nothing complicated about footings and piers, bolting or lag-screwing a ledger board

Posts set in piers, plumbed, and braced; ledger board already installed

Deck framed, piers set in concrete, now ready for deck boards

297

Notched gothic posts ready to receive fence-railing

Setting the ledger board

The next step was snapping a long horizontal level chalk line on the outside wall *three inches lower* than the finished floor on the inside. That three inches provides a 1.5-inch step-down from the house to the deck, and also allows for the 1.5-inch thick 2x6 deck boards that will be fastened on top of the ledger board later. The 1.5-inch step-down is very important so rain doesn't creep into your house.

I installed all the joist hangers on the 2x6 18-foot ledger board and its corresponding rim joist at 24 inches on center while they were still down on the saw horses. Then I lag-screwed the ledger board to the house, making sure it was lined up and squared with the piers and perfectly level from end to end.

Setting the posts

I temporarily plumbed and braced each 4x4 in place in its bracket on top of each pier. Then, working from a ladder, I was able to run a 6-foot level from the ledger board to the post and

to the house, attaching the joists, then laying down the deck boards.

Setting the piers

My first step was measuring and re-measuring, then hammering stakes in the ground and running level strings every which way — with horizontal string-levels hanging from them — to lay out the deck on the ground first so I would know where to dig the pier holes. After outlining the squares with fluorescent spray paint, I dug five large and fairly deep holes (44 inches apart) so I could wrestle the piers into them and have room to adjust their exact positions and level them before pouring concrete around them. I used piers with a hole in the top to hold adjustable brackets so I could fine-tune the deck leveling process later if I needed to.

Note: When you build a deck, the most important tools are **levels**: string-levels, a long level, a medium level, and a short (torpedo) level. The old saw: "*Plumb, level, and square*" should be muttered under your breath like a prayer as you work so you

won't end up muttering something else when you discover you just built a sloping parallelogram instead of a level rectangle.

Dorothy making rise-and-run cuts on the stair horses

make a mark to cut the post off level with the ledger board.

After taking the 4x4 posts down and cutting them off, I put them back up, re-braced them, and fastened them permanently to the post brackets with screws. I connected the posts all around with *two* sets of rim joists on all three sides to accommodate fastening long rail posts later.

Then I mixed ready-mix concrete in a wheelbarrow and poured it around each pier. I did this step at the end in case I had to make any last-minute pier adjustments.

Installing deck boards

I put L-flashing along the house side and installed the ten 5-ft. 2x6 joists. Then I screwed down all the 18-ft. 2x6 Douglas Fir kiln-dried deck boards with 3-inch deck screws and put a coat of natural sealer/stain on them. It was now time to build the deck railing.

Deck railing

To make this back deck match the front door deck/ landing/stairs, I bought the same style decorative gothic posts and picket fencing (Home Depot) and installed it as before — by notching the gothic posts and screwing them onto the rim joists surrounding the deck, then fastening the fencing to those posts.

Fire-escape stairway completed

My slot-cut trick to avoid buying expensive adjustable-angle hangers

Stairs and handrails

I built a little gate on the stair-end of the deck and then tackled the stairs. To fit the rise and run of the space, they had to be moderately steep, but still within the safety code. They are there mainly to be used as a fire escape, so the handrails are only 27 inches apart, enabling a person to safely and securely hang on with both arms while going up or down. I also put traction strips on the steps — cut from inexpensive composition roofing and screwed down with flat lath screws.

I cut the stair horses from Douglas Fir 2x12s and attached them at the top with metal hangers and at the bottom to a landing. I made handrails out of smoothly sanded 2x4s forming an upside-down "T" (screwed together) for the outside rail. I fastened it flat-side-down to the angled-cut top of

Secure landing at bottom of staircase

299

Dorothy chiseling mortises (recesses) for door hinges

4x4 posts set in concrete, and used wall brackets for the inside rail. The handrails are strong, supportive, and very inexpensive to make.

Installing the deck door

Now that the deck itself was done, it was time to cut the door opening to fit a quaint little one-of-a-kind 2-foot-wide door I bought for $50 at a builders' discount outlet. It was built from beautiful straight-grain Douglas Fir, and had a window in it to let more light into the kitchen, which made it ideal.

Eric cut the opening with a circular saw through the siding on the outside and a sheetrock saw and Sawzall on the inside. The hardest part was removing one wall stud from the mid-dle of the opening, and adding an additional stud on each side.

I then framed it all around with straight-grain kiln-dried Douglas Fir 2x10s. The three layers of siding, sheathing, and inner wall sheetrock, plus the 2x6 framing, added up to 8.25 inches, so I had to rip (cut lengthwise) one inch off of each 2x10, because a 2x10 is actually 9.25 inches. I measured and shimmed very carefully during the door jamb framing process so the door would fit the jamb with only 1/8 to 3/16-inch clearance all the way around, leaving just enough room at the bottom for the threshold.

Note: Shims are mandatory for squaring and plumbing a jamb, and for hanging a door.

I installed the door's hardware and hung it without incident. Everything fit perfectly, including the sweep on the bottom of the door as it brushed over the threshold. I used finish nails to attach molding (stops) all around the door jamb, and framed the outside of the door with siding to match the window frames.

I splashed more sealer/stain on everything and backed down the steps as I sashayed back and forth with the paint brush — and the job was done.

Closing thoughts

Building the deck had another bene-fit: I was now able to finally (and eas-ily) put rain gutters on that tall side of the house without using scaffolding. I may get ambitious and put an awning over the deck before the rainy season begins, but for now, it's BBQ time!

When (pianist) Eric wears his "Go For Baroque" T-shirt, everybody mis-reads it as "Go for Barbeque." Now he's in style either way. Δ

Picking your pressure canner: All American or Presto?

By James Kash

The garden is in full swing and you have baskets of vegetables piling up; what do you do? You can them, of course. Your mother's old granite-ware canner only works for high-acid foods like tomatoes, jams, jellies, fruits, or pickled vegetables. You *cannot* safely water bath can low-acid vegetables (this includes sweet corn, potatoes, green beans, peas, carrots, squash, greens, etc.) or any meats using the water bath canner. You will need a pressure canner for that.

Pressure canners come in many forms, brands, and sizes. Some operate using a gauge and some operate using a weight. Pressure canners are the only safe way to can low-acid vegetables, meat, and fish or any combination of those foods. I, personally, do not understand why anyone *wouldn't* want to can with a pressure canner, especially since you can get botulism from canning meats, fish, and low-acid vegetables with a water bath canner. Pressure canners use a substantially less amount of water and fuel, which I am sure all frugal home-steaders appreciate. It requires a shorter amount of time to process compared to the hugely outdated (and dangerous) instructions for canning meat, fish, and low-acid vegetables with a water bath.

Having grown up with the stories about exploding pressure canners, some readers are probably wondering why I would want that ticking time bomb in my kitchen. Here is a little secret: If you properly use your pressure canner and understand how it works, it is nearly *impossible* to blow it up. It takes just a little knowledge to properly operate one.

Essential considerations

Regardless of what brand you are buying, there are many things to consider. Costs can vary — it's worth spending a little more to get the one you want because odds are it will probably last several decades before being discarded, while paying for itself time and time again. But you want something that fits your needs and your resources.

If you are buying a pressure canner for the first time, your first instinct may be to buy a smaller one. This is understandable — the bigger canners can be quite intimidating. However, you will end up spending all night canning if you don't get a good-sized one the first time. For the sake of your time and money, do not get one under the capacity of at least nine pints and seven quarts. I consider that a small canner, but to a newbie it might seem like a large one.

Imagine this scenario — it is mid-summer, your electricity is off and won't be back on for at least a week, you just bought a whole bunch of meat on sale at the grocery, and it is in your now-hot garage in your now-dead freezer. You are working on a time frame to get it canned and if you don't, the money you spent will go down the drain. This where a good-sized canner (like the All American #921) comes in handy; you will be able to can all that meat quickly and save most, if not all, of your food.

Make sure you get a canner, not a cooker. I have seen several retailers feature pressure cookers right next to

The All American is a heavy-duty, weighted gauge pressure canner; most models are designed for large jar capacity.

With good care, pressure canners can last a very long time.

canning jars, funnels, canning lids, and water bath canners. It is very misleading. It is not safe to can in a pressure cooker.

You also need to consider your stove type because, believe it or not, all canners do not work on the same types of stoves. Some have to work on gas ranges and will damage electric ranges or not work properly if used on an electric stove. An easy compromise is a propane camp stove. If you have a gas range canner and the electricity goes out, you will still be able to use it.

Another consideration is size; if you don't have a lot of upper body strength, the largest All American (Model #941) is probably not best suited for you.

Presto versus All American

Before I begin my comparison of these two brands, I want you to know that I own both brands and like both of them very well, but for some folks they may not work as well. Presto pressure canners are some of the most common (and popular) canners in America. They are widely available online and in retail. All American canners seem to be more popular with survivalists and preppers. There are pros and cons to each brand.

All American pros

These are not your stereotypical pressure canners and they work differently than the nostalgic canner with a rubber seal. All American pressure canners are made by the Wisconsin Aluminum Foundry and have a huge diversity of sizes. This is very handy if you normally can in large batches. The smallest version, Model #910, holds four quart jars and seven pint jars. I wouldn't suggest this version, as it is too small for homestead life. In contrast, their largest canner (Model #941) holds 19 quart jars and 32 pint jars. I consider this too big and too expensive (listed at a little more than $600). However, they have models, like the Model #921, that are better suited to homestead life. It holds 7 quarts and 19 pints. This is the version I have and I enjoy it very much. It holds quite a few jars, but it isn't too heavy. It is not as pricey as the others (about $217) but will last quite a while and is extremely reliable. These canners are very sturdy and with proper care, they will probably last for generations.

Regardless of the size of your canner, All American canners must be used on a gas range. If you try to use them on an electric range, they will scratch the stove. They also have a domed bottom which, according to manufacturers, can damage the stove. If you are an off-grid homesteader and cook with propane gas, these canners work best on those stoves.

I find the best thing about this canner is its incorporation of a dial gauge and a weighted gauge. All American canners are weighted gauge canners (they regulate pressure by a special weight on the valve instead of by manual heat adjustment). With this system you are able to successfully leave your canner on a lower heat setting and it will regulate the pressure for you. With the dial, you are able to know when the inside of the canner has successfully returned to zero pounds pressure; that way there is no question when it is ready to open. With the dial you also get to watch the pressure build up. All American canners also have an emergency release valve in case the pressure reaches dangerous levels, thus exhausting the steam. Another plus with this canner is that it has a metal-to-metal seal, and will never have to be replaced — making the purchase of a yearly rubber seal obsolete.

Presto pros

Presto pressure canners are made by National Presto Industries, and come in two sizes: a 16-quart liquid capacity model (holds 7 quarts and 9 pints) and a 23-quart liquid capacity model (holds 7 quarts and 20 pints). Both models are lightweight and are well-suited for large canning jobs. The prices are also very reasonable; the 23-quart liquid capacity model costs about $120 (depending on where you buy it). Presto canners are very sturdy and will last quite a long time with good care.

One of the more favorable qualities of the Presto pressure canner is that it works on electric ranges as well as gas ranges. This canner is strictly dial gauge, meaning that in order to maintain the appropriate pressure for your elevation you must reduce and maintain the heat. This is a big plus for those in high altitudes; you will be able to successfully can at your appropriate pressure. It does have a weight on it (which will let steam exhaust after it reaches 15 pounds pressure) as well as an emergency release valve. The newer models also have a button on them that lets you know when pressure has successfully been released from the canner; the button will drop down when you can safely remove the lid. Presto pressure canners are also the most common. They are not very hard to find and are available at stores such as Walmart for very reasonable prices.

All American cons

One of the biggest advantages for the All American pressure canner is also one of its biggest disadvantages. The weighted gauge cannot be used at 11, 12, 13, or 14 pounds pressure. For example, if you live at an altitude where you have to can at 12 pounds pressure, you must use the 15-pound setting on the regulator in order to cook the food at a high enough temperature. This can overcook foods at that altitude (between 2,000 and 3,000 feet above sea level) so this would definitely be an important consideration when selecting a canner.

All American canners are not very easy to find in retail markets, so you will likely have to order it online or from a mail order catalog.

Be advised: With this canner, you must be able to lift it onto the stove (something to remember with the Model #941) and be able to securely bolt the lid down. We learned this the hard way, even with the lighter #921 model. There are multiple canners in my house. As a 16-year-old boy, I can lift the canner and bolt it down, but my 78-year-old grandmother can't do it alone with the #921 model, let alone with the larger #941.

Presto cons

One of the biggest disadvantages of the Presto pressure canner is that every year you must replace the rubber ring on the inside of the lid. These rings are not very expensive, but they are an additional expense you will have as long as you can with it. These rings are essential to make sure the canner seals to hold in steam and pressure.

Another trait some may not like is that the largest version holds no more than seven quarts, which can slow down big canning jobs.

Where can I get one?

These are the most popular brands of canners and are not very hard to locate. They can be bought new from retail stores, online, mail order, or the manufacturer.

Walmart supplies Presto pressure canners in most outlets and online, as well as the All American canners online.

Amazon has a wide range of models and sizes pooled from different stores. You can find good prices on this site.

For those of us who do not have Internet access or just prefer mail order, you can order canners from the following retailers' catalogs:

Lehman's Supply
1-888-438-5346
PO Box 270
Kidron, OH 44636
www.lehmans.com

Emergency Essentials
1-800-999-1863
653 North 1500 West
Orem, UT 84057
www.beprepared.com

Kitchen Krafts
1-800-298-5389
PO Box 442
Waukon, IA 52172
www.kitchenkrafts.com

You may also get lucky and find a gently-used canner at a thrift store or even a yard sale.

Buying a pressure canner is a big investment for homesteaders, and an important one at that. It is essential for your pantry. It is very important to buy what you need now instead of later. Being an owner of both of these great pressure canners, I must say they can be polar opposites in some

These are just some of the foods that should be canned with a pressure canner.

areas. Therefore, it is important to properly investigate and search before settling on a model that is right for you. Δ

Homemade fruit vinegar

By Patrice Lewis

For many people, late summer and early fall is fruit-canning season. Peaches, peas, apples, plums ... the possibilities for preserving the summer's bounty are unparalleled.

Preserving all this fruit also means a lot of scraps for the compost pile. Or does it?

Last year I canned up pears, apples, and peaches. But rather than simply discarding the piles of fruit peelings, I decided to do something different: make fruit vinegar.

A long history

When did mankind discover vinegar? Probably just after they discovered that fermented fruits produced a pleasing alcoholic beverage. Since it's a short hop from alcohol to vinegar, doubtless the two resources developed almost simultaneously.

While perhaps not welcomed with as much enthusiasm as wine or other fermented brew, the versatility of vinegar has been exploited for untold millennia, maybe as long as 10,000 years. Vinegars have been used as cleaning agents, beverages, medicines, preservatives, condiments, deodorizers, bathing agents, and even construction aids (splitting boulders for road construction).

A short chemistry lesson

Chemically, vinegar is simply the production of acetic acid through the fermentation of ethanol by acetic acid bacteria. The process is aerobic (requiring oxygen) rather than anaerobic. The bacterial culture is referred to (rather insultingly) as "mother," and vinegar can be formed either slowly through the natural development of the mother, or rapidly through the deliberate addition of mother.

Fermentation takes place in two stages. In the first stage, alcohol is formed. The fermenting material creates carbon dioxide bubbles, evidence that the microbes are at work. In the second stage, the alcohol turns to acid, aided by the mother. The grayish scum that forms on the surface indicates the mother is at work.

Playing with garbage

On a hot September day, I canned up 40 pints of apple bits. At the end of the day, I had an impressive amount of peels and cores. Shortly after this, I canned 125 pounds of pears, with a veritable mountain of scraps.

I put the apple and pear scraps into separate plastic food-grade bakery buckets (the pear scraps took two buckets because I had so many) with each bucket 2/3 full. Relative to the amount of apple and pear scraps, the peach peels I saved were such a small amount that I could use a one-gallon glass jar for the scraps.

I then mixed sugar into water at a ratio of 1 quart water: ¼ cup sugar (or one gallon water: 1 cup sugar), then filled the buckets with enough sugar water to cover the fruit scraps by a couple of inches.

I placed a large square of old sheeting over the mouth of each container, secured it with a rubber band, and left them alone for about two weeks.

I dated each container so I knew when I had started the fruit scraps fermenting. There's no hard and fast rule for how long fruit scraps need to ferment. In cooler weather, the process can take as long as two months; in warmer weather, as short as two weeks.

Step one: bubble, bubble, toil and trouble

It didn't take long for bubbles to start forming in the fermenting scraps — a couple days or so. If the house was quiet, I could hear the tiny bubbles popping from across the room. At this stage, vinegar is very much alive. The bubbles indicated that the bacteria and wild yeasts were eating the sugars and producing carbon dioxide as a by-product.

The cloth over the buckets not only allowed the fermenting sludge to breathe, it also kept out fruit flies and other insects which were attracted to the smell. Incidentally, the smell was very pleasant — rich and syrupy and just a wee bit sour.

After two weeks, I decided the fruit scraps were mostly done fermenting because the bubbling had slowed significantly. I later learned that a longer fermentation time is preferred. The reason for this is because the higher alcohol content of the fermented fruit will discourage all but the proper acetic acid-forming bacteria.

Nonetheless, after only two weeks, I removed the cloth cover and prepared to strain out the scraps. I was a little dismayed to see that the pear scraps had swelled to the point where there wasn't any liquidy juice that could be easily strained out. The scraps were very damp and moist with lots of liquid amongst the peelings, but everything had mushed together so much that I couldn't simply pour the scraps into a strainer and catch the juice.

I split the wet scraps into two old pillowcases and suspended them to drain overnight over large pots to catch the juice. I keep old clean pillowcases on hand for a number of draining projects. Whatever you do, do *not* use your good pillowcases

Fruit scraps can be made into fragrant fruit vinegar.

To speed up fermentation, add sugar water to the fruit scraps.

because they'll be stained forever. Some people prefer to drain in cheesecloth, which is fine. In this case, I used pillowcases because they hold higher volumes.

The only reason I had trouble with the pear scraps is because (1) I had so much of them, and (2) I didn't add enough sugar water to the pear scraps in the first place. I should have filled the buckets to the top with sugar

water, or put in fewer scraps per bucket.

One of the things I *didn't* do, but should have, was to stir the buckets once in a while (as often as once a day). If I had stirred the scraps, I would have noticed that the pear scraps didn't have quite enough liquid during the fermenting process, and I could have added more.

I had no trouble draining the apple scraps or the peach scraps because

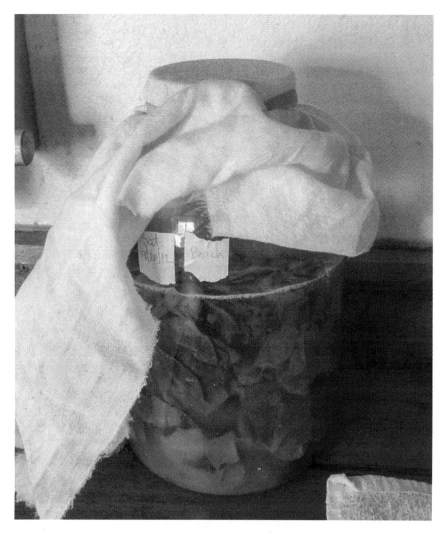

Fruit peels need to ferment for at least two weeks.
Cover with a thin cloth to keep out fruit flies.

After the fruit scraps ferment, drain and keep the liquid.

both of these fruits had enough water added. However, draining takes a *lot* of patience. Don't hesitate to let the scraps drain through a cloth-lined colander (or a suspended pillowcase) overnight.

Step two: making acid

Having drained all the fruit scraps, I poured the sharp fermented liquid into clean glass jars for the acidifying stage. I ended up with three 1-gallon jars, two ½-gallon jars, and one quart jar of proto-vinegar. I lined the jars up on my kitchen cabinet and covered them with squares of clean sheeting secured with rubber bands.

For this stage, I let the jars of liquid sit for three weeks. During this time, the proto-vinegar will develop a revolting-looking scum on top. This is the acetic acid bacteria (the mother) at work and should be left alone. I also noticed a thin layer of sediment that gradually settled to the bottom of the jars.

As with the fermentation stage, there's no hard-and-fast rule for how long the juice should acidify. However, the longer you let the proto-vinegar sit, the more acidic it becomes. It will also acidify quicker in warm temperatures. I learned, after the fact, that I probably should have let the vinegar acidify longer than three weeks. Eight weeks would have been acceptable. In fact, some sources suggest the proto-vinegar should acidify for as long as six months, so don't hurry this process. Taste the proto-vinegar periodically to determine its strength and suitability.

Storing vinegar

At the end of the acidifying process, I was faced with storing 4.25 gallons of vinegar. What to do with it all?

I could pour the vinegar into *sterile* bottles and use corks or plastic lids (never metal!) to seal them. The advantage of this is that I would be able to use the vinegar to "seed" future vinegar projects because it would still contain living mother bacteria. The disadvantage is the vinegar will look cloudy because of the presence of the mother.

I could pour the vinegar through several layers of damp cheesecloth into clean jars and then pasteurize them. This is done by putting the jars (either corked, with a plastic lid, or even uncovered) into a pot of *cold* water and gradually heating it to 145° F. This temperature needs to be held for 30 minutes, then you can remove the jars and let them cool. The advantage of this method is that the vinegar stays clear. The disadvantage is that the "mother" is killed off and the vinegar cannot be used to seed future vinegar projects.

Or, I could simply can the vinegar in a water-bath.

I chose to can the vinegar because frankly I didn't know what else to do with it, and I wanted the vinegar in long-term storage. However, **take note**: the only reason I could can the vinegar was because I used plastic Tattler reusable canning lids, *not* metal disposable lids. Vinegar cannot be stored with metal lids because the acid will gradually corrode the metal.

To can homemade vinegar, I strained the vinegar through cloth into sterile quart jars. After scalding the Tattler lids, I capped the jars and put them in a water bath for 15 minutes. Why 15 minutes? Well, I couldn't find any directions for canning homemade fruit vinegar, so I followed the directions for canning lemon juice and added five more minutes just to be safe.

The results

I now have several gallons of vinegar from something that would normally have gone into the compost pile. The vinegar is fragrant and beautiful. The different fruits produced slightly different-colored vinegar — peachy-pink for the peach vinegar, amber for the apple vinegar, and golden for the pear vinegar.

The liquid should be strained through a cloth before acidifying.

While fruit vinegar would be fine for cleaning projects, I prefer to use it in cooking. It's a wonderful addition to soups and stews, and I even splash it in spaghetti sauce. Fruit vinegars also make an excellent base for a vinaigrette salad dressing. Some people like fruit vinegar for hair rinses as well.

As you can see, making fruit vinegar is a rather lengthy process, but it's not very labor-intensive. Most of the work is passive and simply requires patience.

And best of all, it takes material that would otherwise go to waste and makes a beautiful, fragrant, useful product.

In summary

Here's the step-by-step directions for making fruit vinegar:

- Take fruit scraps (peels, cores, bruised unusable fruit, etc.) and put in a glass jar, food-grade plastic container, or ceramic crock. Chop up the larger pieces for faster results.
- Cover the fruit scraps generously with sugar water. The sugar water should be in a ratio of 1 quart water: ¼ cup sugar. Over time, the scraps may swell, so be generous in the amount of sugar water.
- Cover with cheesecloth or other thin cloth and secure with a rubber band or cord.
- Allow to ferment for at least two weeks or until the bubbles stop forming.
- Strain out the fruit scraps and preserve the juice in a new clean container (glass jars work well).

*The acidifying liquid will form a scum,
called "mother," which converts the alcohol to acid.*

- Cover with cheesecloth or other thin cloth and secure with a rubber band or cord.
- Allow this fermented juice to acidify for several weeks or even months.
- Strain through several layers of damp cloth into clean sterile jars, and use either a cork or a plastic lid to close the jar.
- If desired, pasteurize or even water bath can the vinegar.

A few last considerations

If your fruit is not organic, it would be best to scrub or wash the fruit before peeling so the peels won't have pesticide residue during the fermentation process. The oxidized (browned) scraps seem to make a better vinegar than fresh scraps. This isn't hard to arrange, as presumably the scraps are sitting by and quietly oxidizing while you're busy processing the whole fruit.

The smaller the fruit waste, the faster the fermentation. While the scraps don't have to be pulverized, you might want to chop up the really big stuff.

The wider the mouth of the container, the more wild bacteria will be cap- tured, and the faster the fermentation process will go. Do not use metal containers while fermenting the fruit or acidifying the juice. Some people say you should avoid plastic, but I used plastic food-grade bakery buckets during the fermenting stage and had no problems. If you use plastic, it should be food-grade. Glass jars or ceramic crocks are also wonderful.

If you have chlorinated city tap water, you might want to purchase distilled water to use for vinegar since the chemicals in urban water can kill or contaminate the mother. When you see a scum forming on top, don't disturb it; this is the mother. Eventually, the mother will sink toward the bottom and continue its work. However if you see *mold* forming on top, by all means skim that off. Mother isn't moldy; it's scummy.

If you want to speed up the fermentation process, you can add about a cup of Bragg's Vinegar (or other natural unfiltered vinegar, often found in health food stores) to "seed" the fermenting fruit with mother. You can also purchase "Mother of Vinegar" from such places as Lehman's.

Homemade vinegar should NOT be used for canning pickles or other fermented food. Vinegar for canning needs to be at 5% acidity level, and homemade vinegar varies wildly in its acid content. Even pH test strips cannot accurately gauge proper acidity levels in homemade vinegar.

Making fruit vinegar allows you to utilize the fruits of summer — from beginning to end. Enjoy! Δ

Fourteen quarts of fruit vinegar, ready for long-term storage.

Backwoods Home magazine

Nov/Dec 2013
Issue #144
$5.95 US
$7.50 CAN

practical ideas for self-reliant living

Growing older on the homestead

Cherry trees

Water systems

Controlling rodents

Job site solar power

Survival/utility vest

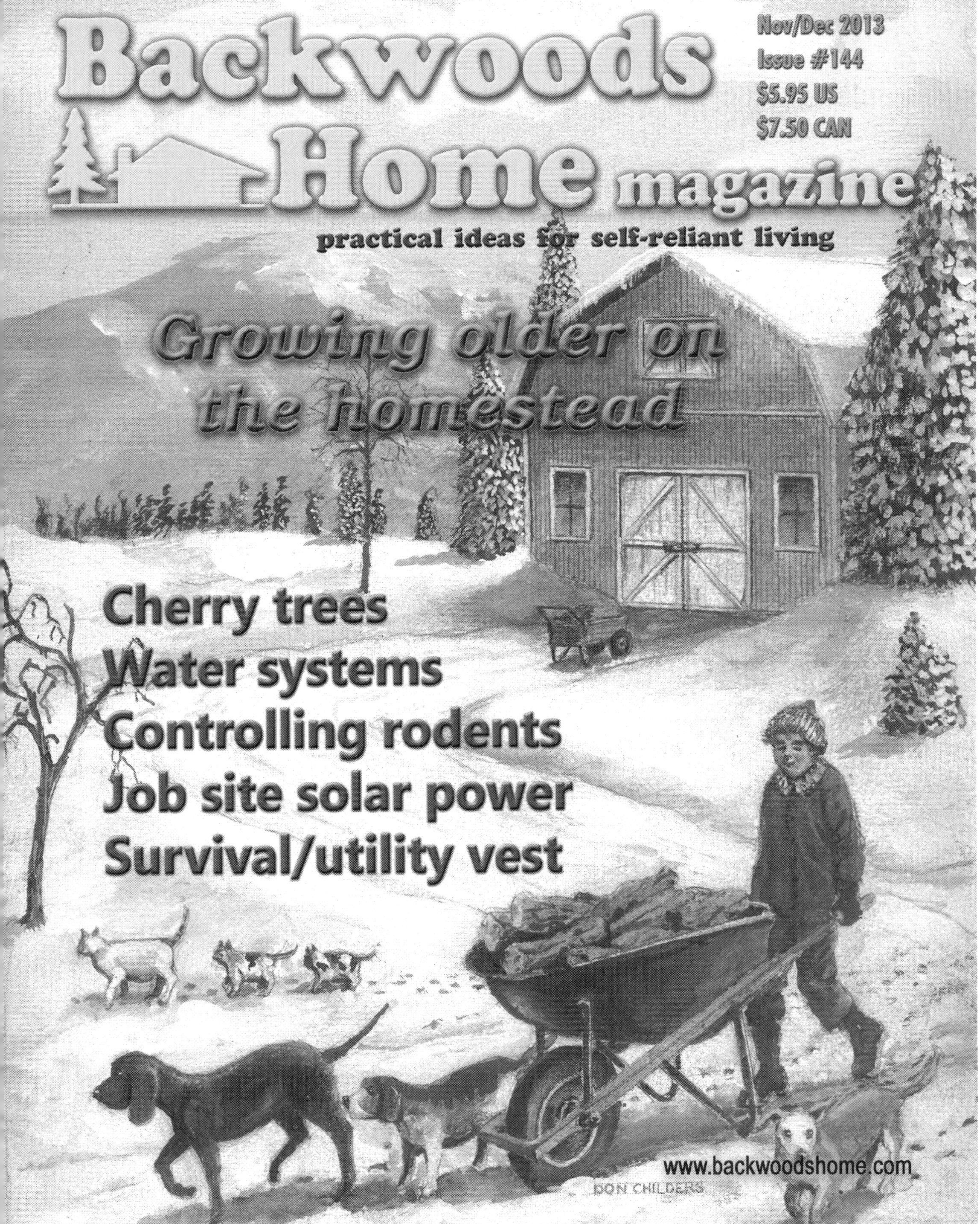

www.backwoodshome.com

DON CHILDERS

My view

How to fix your aching back using the McKenzie Method

It's hard to get anything done around the homestead if you've got an ailing back. I've had an ailing back for about 40 years, but between issues, after another debilitating encounter when my back went "out," I discovered a solution to put it back "in" that is far more permanent than my previous 40 years worth of attempts. Not only that, it is the model of self-reliance and it is free once you learn the technique.

It's called the McKenzie Method, and it's been around for almost as long as my back has been ailing, especially in New Zealand where Robin McKenzie practiced physiotherapy, specializing in spinal disorders and musculoskeletal problems. In 1980 he first published the book *Treat Your Own Back*, which is a self-help guide to relieving back pain caused by various spinal misalignments and over-stretched ligaments.

Why I never encountered this treatment method until now is a mystery to me, but better late than never I suppose. If you've got chronic back pain and are tired of dumping money into chiropractic adjustments that typically give only temporary relief, or are contemplating surgery that your doctor is not sure will cure your problem, you're going to love the McKenzie Method. It teaches you how to help yourself through proper posture and specific "extension" exercises that nudge your spinal column back into proper alignment so your back can heal. Continuing the good posture and the extension exercises after you are healed will help keep your back from going out again.

"Extension" is the key word here. Throughout my history of back pain, I've used "flexion," that is, stretching my back forward to relieve back pain. Extension is the opposite of what I and most other back pain sufferers have done for years. This article will tell you why extension exercises are more effective for the majority of ailing backs, and it will show you how to do the exercises that helped my back.

As always with medical advice, before using these exercises it's best to get evaluated by a competent physical therapist familiar with the McKenzie Method. These therapists are getting easier to find, as the McKenzie Method is gaining in popularity among physical therapists in the U.S. You can also find good information and therapists at www. mckenziemdt.org.

My discovery of the McKenzie Method came after a trip to the emergency room at Samaritan Hospital in Corvallis, Oregon, where I had been working on this issue with my daughter, Managing Editor Annie Tuttle. My back had gone "out" on the left side the previous week and my pain had gotten progressively worse, finally going into my left hip and left groin area. I had gone to the chiropractor, as usual, but his manipulations gave only temporary relief, lasting about an hour after each visit. I also got an hour-long professional massage, and that offered more temporary relief.

The pain became so severe on a Sunday morning that I thought my body was trying to pass a kidney stone, which I've had the misfortune of doing three times previously in my life. So off to the ER I went, begging for

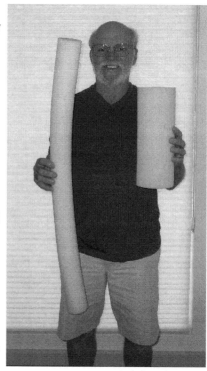

Foam lumbar rolls help maintain the back's lordosis. The small one is for sitting, the long one for sleeping.

relief. But after a welcome dose of intravenous pain medication, a CT scan pointed to a bulging disc as the culprit. I was referred to physical therapy at Samaritan Hospital Rehabilitation Services, where their enlightened physical therapists had already adopted the McKenzie Method as their primary tool to treat back pain.

My main physical therapist at Samaritan was Nathan Smith, one of only two certified McKenzie Method therapists in Corvallis. The other is his wife. I ended up at the right place with the right person at the right time.

Within a half hour of my first session at Samaritan, I began to feel relief. But what surprised me was the relief came from the "extension" exercises, which I had never encountered before.

Nathan explained that flexion (bending forward) would indeed reduce my pain because it will stretch the back muscles away from the offending nerves, but it would only be temporary relief and it would not solve the underlying mechanical problem, which he said was overstretched ligaments and a bulging disc causing pressure on nerves. In my case, the sciatic nerves were involved, causing pain in my left back, hip, and groin, and shooting it down my left leg.

The idea, Nathan said, is to encourage the bulge in the disc to migrate back between the vertebrae by opening up the front of the vertebrae through extension, then allowing the ligaments and torn tissues to heal. He cautioned me not to do any forward bending during the expected two or three weeks it would take for my back ligaments to heal. Later, after healing, I could do both extension and flexion exercises to increase my range of motion and strengthen my back muscles overall.

During my healing process, Nathan said I should read McKenzie's book, *Treat Your Own Back*. Much of this article is based on that excellent book, and if you are a chronic back sufferer like me I encourage you to go on Amazon.com and buy it for a few dollars. It will save you thousands of dollars in unnecessary chiropractic adjustments, doctors visits, and avoidable pain.

Before I get into the exercises to help heal the back, let's look at some of the reasons a back gets injured in the first place.

Most back pain occurs in the lower back. Sometimes it is the result of an injury involving a sudden overstretching of the ligaments, but most back pain is caused by improper posture that overstretches and weakens the ligaments over time. In teenagers, back pain is usually easy to remedy by teaching them how to walk and sit properly. My son, Sam, often slouches when he sits, with his butt at the front of the chair and a big space between it and the back of the chair, so he often complains of back pain. After watching my latest bout with severe back pain, he's begun to sit more upright and has experienced less back pain.

As we get older, we've often weakened our lower back ligaments by habitually overstretching them through improper bending or poor posture, and we've created a back that is more prone to injury. So we suffer from chronic bouts of back pain, as I have for many years. Sometimes, as in my most recent episode, the ligaments are so stretched that a disc between the vertebrae moves, bulging to one side or the other, causing severe pain.

Maintaining the lordosis

A key to this whole process of recurring lower back pain is whether or not we consistently maintain the lordosis, which is that hollow in the lower part of the back that is normally present if we are standing and walking with correct posture. This natural lumbar curve acts like a shock absorber for the spine. If it is too often lost, for example, from frequently bending forward or sitting for too long in a slouched position, the ligaments become too stretched, sometimes to the point of damaging surrounding soft tissues. Once the soft tissue is damaged, pain will be present until the tissue heals.

Much of the healing process for a painful back involves purposefully maintaining the lordosis, in other words, by practicing correct posture while standing, walking, sitting, and even sleeping. We supplement correct posture with extension exercises designed to allow the tissues to heal and the ligaments to stop overstretching.

Proper standing and walking posture is similar to how military personnel are taught to stand and walk: stand tall, chest out, abdomen and butt in. Keep a mild (not an exaggerated) lordosis in your lower back.

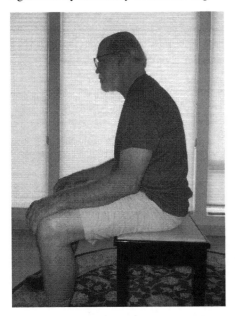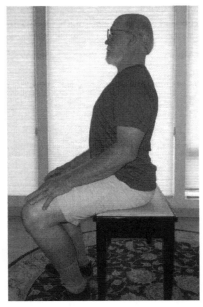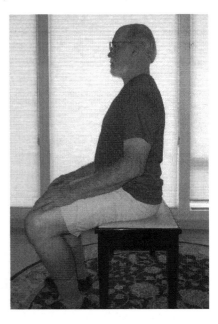

Practice correct sitting posture by sitting on a stool (or sideways on a chair with a back)
and go through these steps: 1) slouch 2) slowly raise to an extreme of good posture, accentuating the lordosis,
and hold for two or three seconds. 3) lessen the strain to achieve the correct sitting posture.
Do this 15 times, 3 times a day until you can sit correctly with relative ease.

Proper sitting posture is achieved with the aid of a lumbar roll behind you to help maintain a lordosis in the lower back. Sit tall, no slouching. Sitting is typically hard on the lower back, so it is advisable to get up often and do a couple of "standing extension" exercises (shown on facing page), plus walk around a bit. Long car rides are especially hard on backs so you should stop every hour or so and do standing extensions and walk a little.

It is recommended you sleep on your back, with a lumbar roll under your lower back to maintain the lordosis even while you sleep. Do not sleep curled up in a fetal position during the healing phase of a lower back problem because it works against what the extension exercises are trying to do. Once healed, sleeping on your side is okay so long as you have a lumbar roll tied around your waist. (These are more comfortable than you think.)

Extension exercises

Once the back is injured, doing the following extension exercises will help it heal. I'll illustrate only the extension exercises I used to heal my back. They will apply to most people, but McKenzie's book has others that may benefit you. The exercises are working if your pain moves first to the center of the back, then lessens gradually each time you do them. Do the exercises slowly and smoothly, as the back does not like jerky movements. If these exercises cause you pain, stop doing them and consult a McKenzie therapist to see which exercises you should do.

Myths about back pain

There are several myths associated with back ailments and treatment, according to McKenzie. They include:

1) Frequent manipulation via chiropractors is necessary to maintain back health. In most cases this is false. Not only that, it creates dependence and sometimes can be counterproductive. Spinal manipulation by a chiropractor or osteopath is necessary in only a handful of severe cases.

2) Ultrasound treatment and electrical muscle stimulation is beneficial to back pain. This widely used treatment option has no supporting scientific evidence.

The lower back muscles need to relax, so stay in this position for a couple of minutes. Assume this position whenever you need a break from the other exercises.

This is a preparation for the half push-up, shown next. Do several of these, staying on your elbows. Stay a minute or two each time until you feel confident in going to the half push-up. Then lie down for a few moments before commencing the half push-ups. I get a lot web surfing done during this exercise.

3) Back pain is caused by inflammation. This is generally false, although inflammation does occur in certain situations. Back pain is almost always caused by a mechanical misalignment, such as a disc displacement or sprained ligaments around the lower back vertebrae.

4) Back pain is caused by arthritis. I thought this was the cause of my pain. Turns out it is generally not the cause, and it was not the cause of my pain, although I do have arthritis on some of my upper back vertebrae.

The half push-up. It's as simple as it looks. Keep the pelvis in contact with the floor if you can. If you cannot, allow it to relax so it sinks as low as possible. Do the half push-up slowly and hold at the top for two seconds. To drop the pelvis even lower, breathe out at the top. Start with 10-15, four to six times a day. Now that my back is healed, I do 20, twice a day, to remain healed. A side benefit is I lost two inches off my waist.

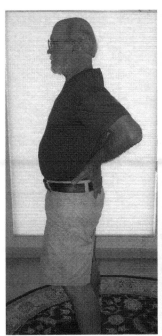 

Do these "standing extensions" throughout the day — whenever you rise from sitting, whenever your back feels a bit tight. I do them before I swing a golf club and often while walking the course.

Sitting is hard on the back. You can help maintain your lordosis with the aid of a lumbar roll. These are a must for driving if you have a back that is prone to lumbar pain.

5) Avoid sports if you have back pain. This is also false. You may have to go easy for a day or two, but the quicker you get back to your jogging, vigorous walking, swimming, golf, tennis, etc., the better.

My back healed in 10 days

In 10 days, with five physical therapy sessions and me faithfully doing the "extension" exercises four to six times a day at home, I achieved total relief from my severe back pain. From the very first day, the McKenzie therapist told me I should continue playing golf because walking was good for the back, but he told me to do the standing extensions between swings. I played golf after every therapy session. But keep in mind that if your pain has been present for many months, it will likely take longer to gain relief. Give yourself a couple of weeks of faithfully doing the exercises.

As long as I continue doing the extension exercises, along with maintaining correct posture, I expect I'll continue to have a pain-free back. I now do the extension exercises described above twice a day as part of my normal routine, plus I've added several flexion exercises, that is, exercises that have me bending my spine forward. Doing the flexion exercises once you are healed is necessary because the healed tissues and any scar tissue formed during the healing process must be made pliable again so it is not subject to overstretching and re-injury. Flexion exercises

include the several bending forward movements (toe-touching, etc.) traditionally recommended to stretch the back muscles. Go slowly when resuming the flexion exercises.

It is important to remember that every session of flexion exercises must be followed by a few extension exercises. Simple standing extensions will suffice.

I do both flexion and extension exercises now, but I do far more extension exercises. Almost every time I rise from a sitting position, I do a couple of standing extensions. And while playing golf, I perform standing extensions before I swing the club and at any time my back feels a bit tight. Good posture, of course, has become part of my life.

— *Dave Duffy*

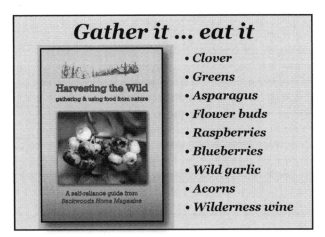

Gather it ... eat it

Harvesting the Wild
gathering & using food from nature

A self-reliance guide from
Backwoods Home Magazine

- *Clover*
- *Greens*
- *Asparagus*
- *Flower buds*
- *Raspberries*
- *Blueberries*
- *Wild garlic*
- *Acorns*
- *Wilderness wine*

Cherries
on your homestead

By Jackie Clay-Atkinson

I can remember it like it was yesterday; my playmate Kenny and me climbing up on the roof of his family's garage in Detroit so we could spend the afternoon snacking on sun-warmed *Bing* cherries from the big tree that grew in their yard. His mother picked buckets of them from a ladder, but only we adventurers thought about climbing up onto the garage roof to get at the biggest, ripest, sun-sweet cherries. And boy, did we! Lying on our backs on the hot asphalt shingles, we ate cherries until we were so full we could hardly climb back down. And so began my love affair with cherries.

Today, cherries come in all sizes from bush cherries growing only to about six feet with an eight-foot spread, to tall trees such as the old-fashioned *Bing*. And the colors also vary from the deep black wild choke-cherry and *Hansen's* bush cherry to light yellow with pinkish blush as seen in *Royal Anne* and *Rainier*.

Although there were wild cherries in the United States and Canada for centuries before the European settlers arrived, it was the colonists who first brought domestic cherries to the "New World." Cherries originally came from Europe and western Asia, becoming domesticated and popular there. From these areas, the cherry quickly gained popularity, and was

These are North Star pie cherries that grew on our homestead near Wolf Creek, Montana. The naturally semi-dwarf tree is quite hardy (to Zone 4) and has tasty cherries.

raised by ancient Greeks and Romans. The colonists brought cherries with them early in the 1600s, where they earned a place in settlers' orchards.

There are two distinct species of domestic cherry tree: the sweet cherry (*Prunus avium*), which is the most planted, and the tart or sour cherry (*Prunus cerasus*). The two types will not cross-pollinate. Most *P. cerasus* cherries are self-pollinating, whereas most *P. avium* cherries need a nearby sweet cherry tree to pollinate to ensure fruit set.

There are other common species of domestic bush, small-treed, and wild cherries, and it gets complicated when some nursery catalogs give them differing common names. For instance, the Hansen's Bush cherry is *Prunus besseyi,* but is listed by differing names in a lot of catalogs, ranging from its common name, to Western Sand cherry or Dwarf Flowering cherry. Always look for the scientific name when trying to buy one of these bush cherries.

Wild cherries in your neighborhood

Pin cherries (*Prunus pensylvanica*)

This tasty wild cherry is very abundant in most of Canada, down to the northern Midwest and Northeast coastal areas of the U.S., and south through the Appalachian Mountains.

The pin cherry is a small, graceful tree bearing bright red, tart cherries that look like miniature pie cherries. The leaves are a narrow oval in shape with a point and toothed edges. Brilliant, abundant white flowers appear in flattish clusters of about four to five flowers on stems in the spring. The bark of the pin cherry is typical "cherry," being reddish brown with lighter horizontal markings, or lenticels.

When the cherry ripens, it is bright red and hangs from long stems, often in groups of two to three. It differs from the chokecherry by having single long stems and a red color instead of dark, nearly black. (The chokecherry fruit hangs in bunches with short stems on each fruit.)

Pin cherries taste like tart cherries, only a bit more tart. They have pits, but they do make very good juice and jelly, having a pretty clear red color.

Chokecherry (*Prunus virginiana*)

The chokecherry is a very common wild cherry growing throughout much of the U.S. and Canada. Its range covers all of the northern half of the U.S, and nearly all of the Appalachians and south to Georgia as well as in the Southwest, usually in the mountains through Arizona and New Mexico. Chokecherries are also found in most of the wooded portions of Canada, from Newfoundland to western British Columbia. In drier climates, they are usually found near rivers and streams.

You wouldn't think a fruit with a name like "chokecherry" would be good to eat. It sounds poisonous! In fact, historically it's been one of the most-harvested fruits of all time. Native peoples all through the U.S.

and Canada have picked and used chokecherries for hundreds of years. Following their lead, settlers soon learned to harvest chokecherries using them primarily for jams, jellies, and preserves.

But raw chokecherries *do* have an astringent taste, especially when not quite ripe. Totally ripe chokecherries are very dark, nearly black, and soft to the touch. However, even those astringent, puckery chokecherries make excellent preserves with no trace of this yucky taste.

It is quite easy to identify chokecherries. They usually grow in a clump of small trees or large shrubs, seldom more than eight feet high. In the spring, their white flowers shine like miniature lilacs, hanging in beautiful clumps like grapes. The leaves are pointed ovals about two inches in length, with small, downward-facing teeth. The tree has no thorns. During the late summer, the cherries are red and about ¼ inch in diameter. They are unripe at this time. Later, towards fall, they ripen, hanging like bunches

Here are some of the wild pin cherries on our homestead. Notice the leaves' long, toothed edges and the cherries hanging as individuals or small bunches with longer stems. They make fantastic jelly!

Wild chokecherries often provide plenty of jelly and jam free for the picking.

of blackish grapes, often bending the flexible branches of the tree down with their heavy harvest.

We frequently pick five quart pails full of these wonderful wild cherries to make one of our favorite jellies.

Wild black cherry (*Prunus serotina*)

This common, very large cherry tree (up to 80 feet!) grows in most of the U.S. east of the Mississippi River from New Brunswick and Nova Scotia in Canada to the Gulf of Mexico. It has very long (up to six inches) oval leaves with serrated edges like the typical cherry. And like most cherries, the bark is reddish, smooth, and marked with horizontal lighter markings. In the spring you will notice large stalks of white flowers, similar to a chokecherry. Later in the fall, they will be very dark, smallish cherries (about 1/3 inch) with a pit. The flavor is sweet with sometimes a small amount of bitterness. This cherry is often a little harder to harvest due to the height of the tree, but it is well worth the effort as it makes excellent jam, jelly, and juice. As with all wild harvesting, it is important to learn to harvest these wild cherries with an experienced person.

Cherries for Zones 2-4

While some fruits, like peaches, seem like only a dream to homesteaders who live in climate-challenged areas such as high mountain elevations and extreme northern climates (Zones 2-3), we *can* grow cherries!

Okay, maybe not those huge, super sweet *Bing* and *Queen Annes*, but cherries, nevertheless. Unfortunately, so far there isn't a single variety of sweet cherry that will grow in less than Zone 4 and only a few pie cherries which are more tart than sweet cherries. One newer variety of a Zone 4 hardy sweet cherry is *Kristin*.

But when you live where winter is cold and long, *any* cherry tastes like heaven on earth!

Tree cherries

Believe it or not, you can grow some "real" tree cherries where it is cold. One of the very best is *Evans Bali*. This Canadian-bred cherry is not only hardy, but also tasty. The *Evans* is a smaller tree and the fruit is delicious and abundant. We've planted four or five here in northern Minnesota that are doing well. And I've seen videos shot in Saskatchewan of five-gallon buckets filled with *Evans Bali* cherries after harvest!

These cherries are darkish red and can actually be pitted for pies (some so-called pie cherries have more pit than meat). And although called tart cherries, they are actually quite sweet.

Another "real" pie cherry is the *Garfield Plantation*, offered by Fedco Trees. We have two of them. You can either prune them to grow as a smaller tree or let them sucker and they'll form a grove. Ours have been very hardy but are not fruiting yet. (But boy, are we waiting!)

We have also had very good luck with a Fedco and St. Lawrence *Meteor* cherry. It has grown very well and survived three winters with absolutely no winter kill and is now starting to fruit. If Will would quit eating them, I could actually bake a pie!

If you live in a more moderate cold climate, *North Star* is a good bet. I had a beautiful tree in the mountains of Montana and another in Michigan, years ago. But they just aren't hardy enough for us here.

All pie cherries are naturally semi-dwarf, self-pollinating, and can be planted in quite small yards. With their attractive shape and brilliant white flowers in the spring, they make a beautiful addition to any homestead.

Bush cherries for the north (and other places)

Luckily, there are several great bush cherries that do well here in the cold north and other climate-challenged places, such as high elevations. These bush cherries range from the old standbys like *Nanking* and *Hansen* to newcomers from Canada like the so-called "Romance" series from the University of Saskatchewan, which include *Crimson Passion*, *Juliet*, *Valentine*, *Romeo*, and *Cupid*, as well as *Carmine Jewel*. So far, I've only been able to buy *Crimson Passion* and *Carmine Jewel* to try in our garden and after two years in the ground, I'm happy enough with both of them to order more.

These are much sweeter than tart cherries and have the flavor of true sweet cherries. A big plus is the productivity. There are reports of up to 75 pounds from one bush! Unfortunately, there are few nurseries in the U.S. who carry this great line of University of Saskatchewan bush cherries. One of the best is HoneyberryUSA, which not only has great little trees, but good prices, too.

In addition to these newer bush cherries, there are a couple of other hardy bush cherries (*Prunus japonica* and *Prunus jacquemontii*) that have been developed. These are *Jan*, *Joel*, and *Joy*, producing small pie-type cherries on a four-foot bush. While not quite as hardy as the University of Saskatchewan bush cherries, these are quite nice.

Our old standby bush cherries are *Nanking* and *Hansen*. Both are hugely productive, lining the branches heavily with dark half-inch cherries. Although they are both said to be "pie cherries," I'd hate to be the one pitting them, as the pit-to-flesh ratio has more pit than meat. *But* the cherries do make excellent jam and jelly. *Hansen* is our very favorite so far, with its jam tasting like the best blackberry in the world.

Nanking is pretty tart, but when *Hansen's* bush cherries are really ripe and soft, they are great for snacking on in the orchard. We feel that *Hansen's* is one of *the* most valuable additions to our cherry "factory."

While these bush cherries are invaluable to us climate-challenged homesteaders, don't think for a minute that they are only for us. Those of you in nicer climates can enjoy them, too. They make excellent fruiting hedges and are very beautiful when in bloom, covered with white, abundant flowers from the top to bottom of each branch.

Bush cherries also make a pretty edible-landscape shrub, either free-standing in the yard or in a corner. The flowers draw butterflies and other pollinators.

Cherries for Zones 5-9

There are many varieties of wonderful sweet cherries available to Zone 5-9 homesteaders, including many which come in semi-dwarf or even dwarf sizes to fit any yard. Maybe you don't have the room for a potentially 80-foot-tall standard *Bing* cherry, but I'll bet you have room for a semi-dwarf that only reaches 8 to 10 feet. Let's take a look at some different varieties.

Bing is the "old standard" sweet cherry, which was most commonly planted in commercial orchards as well as farm and homestead plantings. The *Bing* produces large, very dark red cherries with a pleasing sweet taste.

Some other newer *Bing*-type sweet cherries include *Black Tartarian* and *Chelan*. All are great sweet cherries that make my mouth water. But take note that they do require another compatible sweet cherry nearby for a pollinator, as they are not self-fertile.

We harvested the first ripe cherry from our Meteor pie cherry tree in July 2011.

One of our two-year-old Hansen bush cherries, loaded with big, black, sweet cherries

If you have the room for two sweet cherries, by all means try a couple different varieties. If not, don't despair — there are several excellent *Bing*-type self-fertile sweet cherries. Among these are *BlackGold*, *Lapins*, *Sweetheart*, and *Benton*.

Not all sweet cherries are dark mahogany red, however, and if you'd like a pretty yellow cherry with a blush of red that is definitely more bird-resistant, you might like to try *Rainier*, *WhiteGold*, or *Stardust*.

As I've said, most sweet cherry varieties can be bought in both standard and semi-dwarf trees. Even dwarf trees are available in some varieties. But keep in mind that dwarf trees aren't as long-lasting as semi-dwarf and standards and they require staking so they won't blow over in strong winds.

Bush cherries can make a pretty landscape shrub as well as being a valuable addition to climate-challenged homesteads.

Planting your cherry tree

Cherry trees are very easy to plant, but to get the best results take the time to plant them correctly. When you get your tree, if it is bare rooted, be sure to keep the roots moist but not wet. Don't put it in a pail of water unless you plan on planting it within a few hours. Too long in the bucket results in a weak start. If you can't plant within a few days' time, you can "heel" the tree in. This means that you take the wrapping off and dig a trench or large, shallow hole in your garden and lay the tree down, covering the roots up with soil so they aren't exposed to any air. Heeled in, it'll be fine for weeks if necessary. Be sure to water well after heeling to destroy any air pockets.

Cherry trees do best when they receive sunlight during most of the day. Standard pie cherry trees can be planted about 20 feet apart in all directions. Semi-dwarf trees can be even closer and dwarf trees as close as 10 feet apart. Standard-sized sweet cherries (larger varieties) should be spaced about 30 feet apart. Semi-dwarf and dwarf varieties can be much closer.

Your new tree holes should be about twice as big as you think necessary by looking at the roots. *Never* prune your tree's roots so it will fit in a hole. This often kills the tree. By digging a very deep, wide hole, you loosen the soil nicely and can add quite a bit of rotted compost. Mix the compost with the native soil, leaving the hole deep enough so when the tree is set in the hole, the graft is a couple of inches above the bottom of a shallow dish of soil around the trunk. Place the tree in the hole, spreading the roots comfortably, then begin filling in the hole with loose soil-compost mixture. As you fill, water the tree with a hose or bucket so all air pockets are eliminated. Add more dirt until the tree is planted. Gently step on the soil all around the tree to pack it in place, then again water the tree. By leaving a gently sloped basin around the tree, water will collect in it, supplying the tree's roots with water not only when you water it, but each time it rains, as well. In arid places, I've made this basin much larger — about four feet in diameter — to collect even more rainwater.

Never plant cherry trees where it is soggy and wet. They don't like "wet feet" and will often die. If your homestead is on lower ground, consider building up a long, wide berm (sort of a raised bed) for your fruit trees. This works well, keeping the roots from getting too much moisture.

Also don't fertilize newly-planted cherry trees. Let them get adjusted to their spot. They'll get a little fertilizer from the rotted compost, enabling them to grow nicely.

Where apple trees require little pruning at planting time other than to remove any damaged branches, cherries should be pruned right after planting. This helps them get over transplanting shock quickly, sending more energy to the roots. And it also helps develop the tree's tendency to branch instead of growing only upright. (The more branches, the more cherries, and the more spread out the tree becomes, the less ladder work you'll do in the years to come.)

Make sure that you water your newly planted tree every day after planting it. The tree should receive at least a five-gallon bucket equivalent daily unless it rains heavily. After two months, you can reduce the water to twice a week provided it has not become extremely hot and dry.

Stake your dwarf and semi-dwarf trees with wooden stakes driven in on three or four sides of the tree with ropes run around the trunk to prevent wind damage. Be sure the loops around the tree are padded with soft material such as burlap and that they are not tight around the trunk. The bark of young cherry trees is easily damaged, which can result in insect attack or fungal infections.

Cherry trees that are well cared for will begin fruiting in two to four years. Hedge or bush cherries also will begin fruiting in two to four years, given good care.

Cherry varmints

Voles and rabbits

The most common pests of the cherry orchard are rabbits and voles (field mice). Both of these love to chew the bark from the trunks of young trees. And when they snack, they eat all the bark around the whole trunk, killing the tree. Voles eat under the snow so you often see no evidence of their work until the snow melts away from the trees in the spring. Then you see stark, white bands around your precious tree's trunk. Usually there is no way to save the tree. Rabbits chew on bark and tender branches while sitting on top of the snow, often early in the spring after the sap has begun to run.

Fortunately, protection from damage by these creatures is quite simple.

Every time we plant new fruit trees, we are careful to wrap the trunk up three feet or as high as we can wrap before running into many branches with aluminum window screen or hardware cloth. We usually use the hardware cloth to make corrals for our bush cherries as there is no central trunk. I tie the screen with twine, leaving it in place all summer and winter. In the spring, I remove the screen so I can prune any sprouts, if necessary. But in the fall, the screens go back on. I once had dozens of young trees killed because I failed to do this and it was a lesson I only needed to learn once!

Birds

You wouldn't think a pretty songbird would be a cherry pest. But once you've seen your beautiful little tree covered with ripening cherries full of robins or cedar waxwings — each with a fat cherry in their mouth — you'll soon see what I mean. I've picked cherries from the ground while waxwings cussed at me as they picked cherries above my head. (They pick faster than I do, too!)

Sometimes birds aren't so much a bother, especially when your cherries are bush cherries or one of the yellow blushed varieties. But those nice bright red ones sure call the birds from far and wide.

Commercial orchards often resort to gas-powered booming "cannons" which fire periodically to frighten birds away. But I much prefer to net my trees. It's quieter. Once the cherries begin to show red color, it's time to get the nets on. Net the tree top to bottom or birds will get under it and then get trapped trying to escape. With smaller trees, some folks make PVC frames and net over those. They are lightweight and easy to move.

Fortunately, most homestead cherry trees/bushes are not plagued by disease or insects. If you begin to find either, contact your local extension office for information.

Harvesting your cherries

Harvest your cherries as soon as they are fully ripe. Only pick what you will be canning or freezing each day, as they hold on the tree better than they do in the refrigerator. Cherries will not continue to ripen once picked, as some other fruits do.

Once harvested, most folks pit their cherries before canning or freezing. You can buy a nice cherry pitter which pits cherries easily or you can use a variety of methods with what you have at home. I've done a whole lot of cherries by cutting them in half with a sharp knife and flicking the pit out. Then there's the straw or chopstick method. Just hold the cherry between two fingers and poke the pit right through with either one. Or you can use a paper clip or hairpin. Hold the cherry, poke the clip in, and scoop out the pit. It only makes one hole! Same with Will's method. He uses a hemostat, just reaching in the stem end and pulling out the pit. How easy is that?

I find that sitting out on the porch swing on a nice summer day while visiting with a friend makes pitting pounds of cherries pleasant work and the time just flies by.

Preserving your harvest

While you can and should eat cherries fresh (both pie and sweet), there are plenty of ways to preserve your harvest so you can enjoy cherries year-round. If you have freezer space, one of the easiest ways to preserve moderate amounts of fresh cherries is to pit and freeze them.

One of the best ways to freeze either pie or sweet cherries is to make a syrup pack, mixing half sugar and half water together, then pouring over a freezer container of pitted cherries, covering them all and leaving ½-inch headspace. Seal, label, and freeze. These are tasty and the processing is quick.

But to prevent this precious harvest from freezer burn eventually, in case they don't get used up within about a year's time, I prefer to can most of our cherries. Once canned, they are good almost indefinitely.

Canning processing note: All times are given for altitudes of 1,000 feet or less. If you live at an altitude above 1,000, consult your canning book for directions on increasing your processing time to suit your altitude.

Canned cherries (tart or sweet)

To can cherries, stem and pit. You may pack them either raw or hot. To pack them raw, pit the cherries, then make a light or medium syrup, as you wish. Pack the cherries gently into a canning jar and shake gently to settle them in place. Ladle hot syrup over the cherries, leaving ½-inch headspace. Remove air bubbles. Wipe the rim of the jar clean; place hot, previously simmered lid on jar and screw the ring firmly tight. Process pints and quarts in a boiling water bath canner for 25 minutes.

To hot pack your cherries, pit them and measure. Put cherries in a large pot. For each quart of cherries add ½ to ¾ cup of sugar, to taste. Slowly heat while stirring to mix in sugar and prevent scorching. When sugar is dissolved and cherries are thoroughly hot, pack into hot jars. Ladle juice to cover cherries, leaving ½-inch headspace. If there is not enough juice, add boiling water to cover, leaving ½ inch of headspace. Process pints for 15 minutes and quarts for 20 minutes in a boiling water bath canner.

Fortunately, there are a lot of different recipes to can using cherries, from pie filling to conserves, jam, jelly, and preserves. Here are a few of my favorites:

Cherry jam

2 pints pitted, chopped tart pie
   cherries or *Hansen* (or other
   bush) cherries
2 Tbsp. lemon juice
1 pkg. powdered pectin
5 cups sugar

Mix pitted, chopped cherries, lemon juice, and pectin in a large pot and slowly bring to a full rolling boil that cannot be stirred down over high heat, stirring constantly to prevent scorching. Add full measure of sugar at once, stirring. Return to a full rolling boil and boil hard for one minute, stirring constantly. Remove from heat. Ladle hot jam into hot jars, leaving ¼-inch headspace. Wipe rim of jar clean; place hot, previously simmered lid on jar and screw down the ring firmly tight. Process for 15 minutes in a boiling water bath canner.

Cherry jalapeño jelly

3½ cups tart pie cherry juice or pin
   cherry juice
4 jalapeño peppers, chopped (or
   less if you want less hot jelly)
1 pkg. powdered fruit pectin
5 cups sugar
1 tsp. almond flavoring

In a small amount of water, slowly simmer cherries and chopped jalapeño until soft. Hang in a dampened jelly bag or several layers of cheesecloth overnight. Measure juice into large pot and add powdered pectin. Bring to a boil over high heat, stirring frequently. When at a full rolling boil that cannot be stirred down, add full measure of sugar, stirring well. Stir constantly to prevent scorching and return to a full boil. Boil hard for one minute. Quickly add almond flavoring. Stir. Remove from heat. Ladle hot jelly into hot jars to within ¼ inch of top. Wipe rim clean, place hot, previously-simmered lid on jar and screw down ring firmly tight. Process for 10 minutes in a boiling water bath canner.

Sweet cherry marmalade

2 quarts pitted, chopped sweet
   cherries
1½ cups chopped orange with seeds
   removed
7 cups sugar
½ cup lemon juice
2 tsp. almond extract

Combine cherries, orange, sugar, and lemon juice in a large pot. Bring to a boil over high heat, stirring con-

Here's part of a day's picking of chokecherries, ready to juice up for jelly.

stantly. Boil hard almost to jelling point, then remove from heat. Quickly add almond extract and stir. Ladle hot marmalade into hot jars, leaving ¼-inch headspace. Process 15 minutes in a boiling water bath canner.

Chokecherry jelly

apple juice
3½ cups chokecherry juice
1 pkg. powdered pectin
4½ cups sugar

Rinse cherries and remove stems. Add a small amount of apple juice to a large pot and add chokecherries. Bring to a boil, stirring frequently to prevent scorching while extracting the juice. Mix juice and pectin in a large pot and stir well while bringing up to a full rolling boil. Add full measure of sugar at once and return to a full rolling boil that cannot be stirred down, stirring constantly to prevent scorching. Boil hard for 1 minute, stirring constantly. Remove from heat. Ladle hot jelly into hot jars, leaving ¼-inch headspace. Process for 10 minutes in a boiling water bath canner.

Cherry pie filling

6 qts. pitted pie cherries
7 cups sugar
1¾ cups Clear Jel
9⅓ cups cherry juice or water
2 tsp. almond extract
¼ tsp. red food coloring (optional)
½ cup lemon juice

Heat 7 cups of cherries in a gallon of water until boiling; heat for 1 minute, then drain. Save the water to re-use; continue until all cherries have been blanched and drained; reserve juice to use unless you have real cherry juice.

Mix Clear-Jel and cherry juice or water left from boiling cherries as per recipe ingredient list. Add almond extract and food coloring if desired. Heat until this bubbles and begins to thicken; don't overcook. Add lemon juice. Fold in hot cherries. Fill hot pint jars with cherries, leaving one

With your own pie cherries, you can make plenty of scrumptious homemade cherry pies like this one that is a family favorite.

inch headspace. Remove any air bubbles. Wipe rim of jar clean, place hot, previously simmered lid on jar and screw down ring firmly tight. Process for 30 minutes in a boiling water bath canner.

Since there is abundant research showing that tart cherries are very good for you, especially the juice, why not can up some when you have a wonderful crop? Tart cherries have some of the highest levels of antioxidants of any fruit and they also have been shown to help in arthritis. It's quick and easy to can juice for you and your family right at home. Using a steam juicer such as a Mehu Liisa makes juicing very quick and easy.

Tart cherry juice

Take your hot cherry juice after extracting and pour into sterilized, hot pint canning jars, leaving ½-inch headspace. Process for 15 minutes in a boiling water bath canner.

Drink as is or add sweetener as desired since it is quite tart.

Dehydrating cherries

Dehydrating cherries is very easy and, like canning, once your cherries are dried and stored in an airtight container, they are good for decades. Not only can you use these dried cherries in many recipes, but they

make great snacks and additions to trail mix.

You may dehydrate both pie and sweet cherries and they are equally good. All you have to do is sort, rinse, stem, and pit your cherries, then lay them out on your dehydrator trays in a single layer. Dehydrate at about 165° F until leathery (like raisins). Store in an airtight container. You can use in baked goods, dry, or rehydrate to use in any cherry recipe.

Dessert recipes

As cherries are so tasty, you can eat your sweet cherries right from the freezer or canning jar or use your tart cherries in dozens of scrumptious recipes. Here are a few of my favorites:

Cherry pie
Crust:

2 cups sifted flour
1 tsp. salt
¾ lard or shortening
4-5 Tbsp. ice water

Sift flour and salt into medium mixing bowl. With pastry blender or fork, cut in shortening until mixture resembles coarse cornmeal. Sprinkle with ice water, tossing lightly until dough holds together in a ball that can be handled without breaking apart, yet is not sticky. (Add a tiny bit of extra water if necessary to reach this consistency.) Divide in halves, with one half a little larger for the bottom crust. Flatten each ball somewhat with your hands. Cover and chill if you have the time. Place larger ball on lightly floured surface. Sprinkle flour on your rolling pin and begin lightly rolling out dough from center to outside edges, working in alternate directions to keep a rounded shape. You can lay the pie tin upside down on your crust-in-progress to check the size you need. Remember to allow for the depth of the pan and the edges when making your decision. When the crust is the right size, gently roll it up on your rolling pin and unroll it over your pie pan. Press down to fit pan and trim edges with a knife. Roll out top crust.

Filling:

You can use two pints of canned cherry pie filling or you can make this filling from canned tart cherries:

> 1 quart drained pie cherries, juice reserved
> 1½ cups sugar
> ⅓ cup flour
> ⅛ tsp. salt
> 2 Tbsp. butter or margarine
> ¼ tsp. almond extract (optional but nice)
> 1 egg yolk, beaten slightly

Drain cherries, reserving 1 cup juice. Mix dry ingredients. Gently mix juice into dry ingredients, stirring well. Bring to a boil, stirring as it thickens. Stir in butter, almond extract, and cherries, then remove from heat. Pour into bottom crust. Add top crust (be sure to have vents cut in top to let out steam or cut top crust into strips and arrange a lattice top over the pie, sealing edges and fluting them to keep juice in the pie as it bakes). Paint with egg yolk to make a shiny crust; you may sprinkle on sugar, too. Bake at 400° F on a cookie sheet until top is nicely browned. (Tip: line cookie sheet with aluminum foil to make clean-up a snap.)

Cherry cobbler

> 1 quart drained sour cherries
> 2 cups sugar
> 2 Tbsp. butter
> 1 egg, beaten
> 3 cups flour
> ½ tsp. salt
> milk (enough to make a medium batter)

Mix sugar, butter, and egg together until well mixed. Add flour and salt. Mix in enough milk to make a medium batter. Pour batter into greased 13x9x2-inch cake pan. Pour drained cherries evenly over top. Bake at 375° F until top is golden and cake-like. This cobbler may also be baked in a greased Dutch oven.

You can also substitute a yellow cake mix, made up into a batter, poured into a pan with the cherries sprinkled over the top. They will sink into the batter as it rises and bakes, making a great cobbler very quickly. Tip: you may want to also sprinkle some sugar over the cherries as it may be too tart for your taste.

Cherry bars

> 1 cup butter or margarine, softened
> 2 cups sugar
> 4 eggs
> 1 tsp. vanilla
> ¼ tsp. almond extract
> 3 cups flour
> 1 tsp. salt
> 3 pints home-canned cherry pie filling

> Glaze:
> 1 cup powdered sugar
> ½ tsp. vanilla extract
> ½ tsp. almond extract
> 2-3 Tbsp. milk

> Topping:
> slivered, toasted almonds (optional but nice)

Cream butter and sugar until light and fluffy. Add eggs, beating well after each egg is added. Mix in the extracts. Mix flour and salt in small mixing bowl. Add to creamed mixture and mix well.

Spread 3 cups batter onto a greased 13x9x2-inch cake pan. Spread with pie filling evenly. Drop the remaining batter by spoonfuls over the filling. Bake at 350° F for 30-35 minutes or until a toothpick inserted in the middle comes out clean. Cool on a wire rack, in pan.

Combine the glaze ingredients and drizzle over the bars. While glaze is still moist, sprinkle on slivered toasted almonds. Cut into squares and serve.

Another easy favorite of ours is to make a chocolate cake, baked in two round pans, then between the layers, spread a pint of home canned cherry pie filling. Top it with the filling then add whipped cream on top or ice with your favorite cream cheese icing. Pretty darned good in a hurry!

As you can easily see, having a few cherries in your yard or on your homestead can be quite beneficial. Whether you choose sweet cherries or tart cherries, bush cherries or wild cherries, I don't think you'll ever be sorry. We love 'em all and can't wait for cherry season each year. Δ

Jackie Clay's Pantry Cookbook

- main courses
- side dishes
- breads
- eggs
- snacks
- desserts

- pantry mixes
- soups
- stews
- vegetables
- quick breads
- salad dressings

Rats!

Controlling rodent infestation and rodent-caused diseases

By Joe Alton, M.D.

"You dirty rat!"

True or false? From a medical standpoint, this famous line from classic gangster movies isn't too far from the truth. Rats, mice, and other rodents are well-known causes of "zoonotic" infections. A zoonotic disease is one that can be transmitted from animals to humans. The rodent you see may be asymptomatic but may serve as a "vector," and carry the disease to humans.

Rats and mice belong to the order Rodentia, from the Latin word *rodere* ("to gnaw"). This order contains various families, including beavers, porcupines, squirrels, and gophers. As you are unlikely to have an infestation of beavers in your home, we'll concentrate on rats and mice in this article. A pair of rats can have 1,500 offspring in only one year if they all survive and reproduce. Most species that cause issues for humans are known as "Old World" rats and mice. These include:

- Brown rats (*rattus norvegicus*) are also called Norway rats although they didn't originate

there. Norway, it seems, has no more rat issues than other countries. Brown rats may reach 16 inches (including the tail) and are good swimmers; the term "sewer rat" was coined for them.

- Black rats (*rattus rattus*) are thought to have introduced the

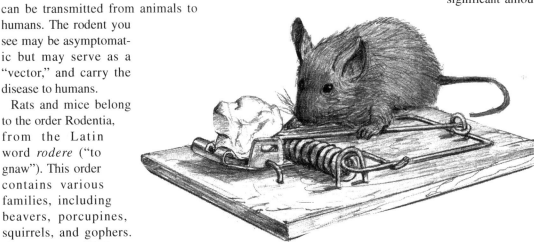

Plague to Europe through their fleas. The black rat, also called the "roof rat," is slightly smaller than its brown cousin and is an excellent climber.

- House mice (*Mus musculus*) are used to living in close quarters with humans. Mice are "nibblers" and can contaminate an entire pantry by taking a few

bites out of multiple items. Mice don't need a water source to survive; they get their fluids from food sources.

All of the above originated in Asia, reaching the Middle East in Roman times, and Europe in the Middle Ages. When these animals are introduced into new areas, they cause a significant amount of environmental and economic damage. Indeed, they are some of the world's most invasive species. Every year, a percentage of the world's food supply is contaminated by their droppings, urine, and hair. These inanimate items, known as "fomites," may contain disease-carrying organisms and render a foodstuff unfit for human consumption. It should be noted that rodents can chew through electrical wiring, and are, therefore, also a fire hazard.

Diseases

Before I go further, let me tell our readers who have rats and mice as pets that they are generally clean, intelligent creatures. I have had the privilege of working with them in university laboratories as a student. Despite this, it is indisputable that the diseases they may carry are cause for significant concern.

From a medical perspective, what diseases might one contract from a rodent or its droppings?

Plague: The Plague is caused by a bacterium known as *Yersinia pestis*. It is carried by fleas. The black rat's arrival in Europe in the Middle Ages (and with it, their fleas) caused pandemics of the disease that wiped out a third of the population. Even today, Plague exists in developing countries and there have been hundreds of cases in the United States over the past three decades.

Hantavirus: Hantavirus is transmitted by mice through urine, droppings, or saliva. These contaminants can causes a serious lung disease that may become fatal without the availability of intensive care.

Leptospirosis: Leptospirosis is caused by consuming food contaminated by rat urine. It causes a flu-like syndrome that will progress to kidney and liver failure if untreated. This disease can also be carried by certain livestock.

Lymphocytic Choriomeningitis Virus (LCMV): LCMV may be contracted from mice urine or droppings or from pets in contact with mice, such as hamsters. It causes a flu-like syndrome that occasionally causes complications in the nervous system, especially in people with weakened immune systems or pregnant women. LCMV may cause miscarriage or birth defects.

Salmonella: Salmonella may occur as a result of handling pet rats or mice, especially if they have had diarrhea. It causes severe diarrheal disease in humans, and is one good reason for owners of rats and mice to wash their hands after handling.

Rat Bite Fever: Infection with the bacterium *Streptobacillus* occurs from rat bites and scratches or from ingesting food or water contaminated with rat droppings. Abrupt onset of fevers, rashes, vomiting, and headaches are noted at first, with general deterioration afterwards. If untreated, there is a 10% death rate.

Rodent-proofing your home

Given the above, it makes sense to take measures to prevent rodent infestation in the home and to eliminate those already there. Much more effort is required to dislodge your unwanted guests once an infestation has occurred. Rodent-proof homes have been carefully evaluated for points of entry from the level of the foundation to the roofline. This includes sewer lines, bathroom vents, pipes and gutters, doors and windows, and vegetation near concrete slabs.

Techniques for rodent-proofing indoors:
- Install vent guards in bathroom or washer/dryer vents.
- Place barriers to prevent climbing rodents from going up pipes or gutters.
- Never leave food or water out overnight. Keep your countertops clean and disinfected.
- Breadboxes may seem old-fashioned, but they are there for a reason: to keep the bread away from rats and mice.
- Clean under kitchen appliances. Even a few crumbs will make a meal for a mouse or rat.
- Keep garbage disposals and sinks clean with a cup of bleach once a month.
- Never flush grease down the sink drain.
- Keep toilet lids down until needed.
- Store dry foods, even pet foods, in sealed containers at least 18 inches off the floor.
- Deny access to water by fixing leaky faucets.

Techniques for rodent-proofing outdoors:
- Trim trees so that branches don't come close to the roof.
- Contact the utility company for strategies to prevent rats from traveling along power lines to your house.
- Prevent rodents, especially rats, from tunneling under the foundation by placing flat concrete pavers or gravel extending at least 3 feet from the base of the house.
- Never leave pet food outside. Clean all bowls daily, whether they are used inside or out. Rodents love to eat dog and cat food.
- Store firewood away from your home at least 18 inches off the ground.
- Trim all vegetation that abuts the house so the ground is easily inspected.
- Eliminate tree branches that make eaves and gutters accessible.
- Remove ivy or other climbing plants from exterior walls that may hide points of entry.
- Construct barriers around birdhouses and bird feeders to prevent seed from being accessible to rodents.
- Remove any fruits or vegetables from your garden that you won't use.
- Keep garbage can lids tightly closed.
- Keep side and back yards free of debris that might serve as shelters.
- Avoid putting animal products in your compost bin.
- Seal cracks in building foundations, walls, siding, and roof joints with mesh hardware cloth, concrete patching, or other materials. Rodents only need ¼ inch of opening to gnaw their way into your home. Metal mesh scouring pads or galvanized window screening (not steel wool, which quickly deteri-

orates) may be stuffed into crevices as a temporary solution.

Identifying an infestation

If you're not sure that your home is currently rodent-free, you might consider:

- Looking for any partially eaten food, gnawed containers, or nesting material.
- Inspecting your home's interior at night with a flashlight; look closely at the bases of walls, as rats and mice prefer to travel along them. Seldom-used areas of the home should be especially targeted.
- Looking for rodent droppings. Mice and rats defecate 50 times a day; if they are in your home, you should be able to find their feces along floorboards, in attic crawl spaces, and in basements.
- Setting out a thin layer of flour or talcum powder by areas through which rats and mice might enter your home. Place additional flour or powder along floorboards; rodents prefer to travel along walls. The rodents will leave tracks which will prove their presence.
- Having cats and dogs as "mousers." They may or may not be efficient, but they usually will alert you when a rodent is near.
- Listening for squeaking and scrabbling noises inside walls at night.
- Checking for unusual smells. If there are a lot of rats in your home, you may notice an odor from their urine.

Dealing with an infestation

Once you have made the determination that you have rats or mice in your home, it's time to reduce the population. It should be noted that long-term control will be difficult if you haven't followed my earlier suggestions for indoor and outdoor sanitation.

When cleaning out a building populated with rats or mice, specific safety precautions should be followed to avoid infection. First and foremost: Remember that you should never handle a wild rodent, alive or dead, without disposable gloves. Masks, coveralls, and shoe covers should be worn when cleaning any significant infestation.

- Open windows and doors before cleaning to allow it to air out, then leave for an hour.
- Avoid raising dust if at all possible.
- Steam-clean all carpeting and upholstery.
- Clean all surfaces with a diluted bleach solution or other household disinfectant; soak areas that held dead animals, nests, or droppings.
- Wash all bedding linens, pillows, etc. with hot water and use the high heat setting on your dryer.
- Eliminate any insulation material contaminated by rodent urine, feces, or nesting material.
- Place contaminated items that cannot be thrown away (such as important documents) outside in the sun for several hours. If this isn't possible, "quarantine" the items for a week in a rodent-free area. This should give enough time for viruses to be inactivated.
- Dispose of any contaminated items or dead rodents in a plastic bag (double-bagging is better), and then place them in an exterior garbage can.
- Thoroughly wash hands after cleaning. Consider showering with soap and hot water.

There are a myriad mouse and rat-traps on the market and several poisons available to kill rodent invaders. It makes more sense to use traps, as poisons may leave you with a bunch of dead, rotting animals inside your walls. The stench may last a month or more. A deodorizer inserted through a hole drilled in the wall is sometimes required to eliminate the lingering odor.

Don't use poisons in your yard, as they may be ingested by neighborhood pets or even children. Consider trapping boxes instead. These can be snap traps, electronic "zappers," glue traps, or even catch-and-release versions. Both rats and mice will readily go for a small amount of fresh peanut butter as bait. Advice to the softhearted: Brown rats, black rats, and house mice are not native wildlife; besides other damage, some will cause casualties among endangered songbird eggs and young birds if released.

Glue traps are popular but controversial. They are better weapons against mice than rats. Unfortunately, they sometimes leave you with a live animal to kill. Throw the trap and animal into a bucket of water or strike it with a stick several times just behind the head. Another disadvantage of the glue trap is that it loses effectiveness in dusty areas or at extreme temperatures.

Snap traps should always be placed in perpendicular fashion with the bait side against the wall. Never use just one trap; place a number of them several feet apart in the rodent's usual path. Traps can be fastened to pipes with wire or thick rubber bands.

Conclusion

We share our world with many other creatures. Some of these creatures invade our homes and can damage our possessions and, more importantly, our health. With careful attention to sanitation and the occasional surgical strike, we can eliminate unwanted guests and make our homes safe environments for our families.

Joe and Amy Alton are the authors of the #1 Amazon Bestseller *The Doom and Bloom Survival Medicine Handbook.* **They have more than 250 articles regarding medical preparedness on their website at www. doomandbloom.net.** Δ

Job site solar power

Jeffrey R. Yago, P. E., CEM

If you are planning to live off-grid or are building something in a remote area without grid power, I am sure you are planning to use a generator. While I have also owned generators, I find them temperamental, noisy, and I hate to drag fuel up some mountain trail when I need to power construction tools. To wean myself off the traditional construction site generator, I found an amazing selection of high-quality power tools that operate on battery packs. In addition, if you standardize on the same brand and voltage, the same battery packs will be interchangeable with a wide array of power saws, drills, portable lights, and even radios. Keeping a spare battery pack on charge also allows a quick battery change and continued tool operation without having to wait.

When I first started buying battery-powered tools I decided to standardize on DeWALT, but there are several other good brands of battery tools that offer the same interchangeability of battery packs in multiple tools. It is amazing what you can build with just a few battery-powered tools, and a complete set is indispensable if you live off-grid or are building a remote retreat.

Most manufacturers of commercial-grade battery-powered tools with Nickel-Cadmium (NiCad) battery packs have increased their voltage from 12 volts up to 18 volts to increase tool power and extend operating time. Some battery-powered tool manufactures are switching to Lithium-ion (Li-ion) batteries which allow making smaller and lighter portable tools due to the higher energy density of this new battery technology. Although the DeWALT charger I used for this article can charge both NiCad, NiMH, and the newer Li-ion battery technology, you still should standardize on one type to make sure all of your battery packs can use the same charger.

For large solar power projects, I am a firm believer in using high-quality DC to AC inverters which allow using standard 120-volt AC appliances and power tools. Inverters are becoming much more reliable and less expensive, which allows using your existing house wiring instead of having to rewire everything for DC. However, powering 120-volt AC power tools requires a 1,500 to 3,000-watt inverter and very heavy battery bank. Some small inverters costing less than $50 are now available to power your laptop computers and video devices while in your car or truck.

Unfortunately, many of these lower cost inverters do not generate the same waveform as the utility grid, which can cause problems with the more sensitive electronic devices you want to power. It is also true that many battery chargers for recharging power tools will have very poor charging performance when connected to a low-cost modified-wave 120-volt AC inverter. Most of these low-cost inverters also have a low power conversion efficiency, and can quickly drain your car or truck battery if the engine is off while powering any 120-volt AC device.

While finding 12-volt DC appliances is more difficult than standard 120-volt AC appliances, there are many advantages to using portable 12-volt power without the need for an AC inverter. Not only will this make all wiring easier and safer than dealing with 120 volts AC, but powering 12-volt DC devices directly from a 12-volt battery is much more efficient. This is especially true if the battery supplying the power is being charged by a solar module. By fitting everything into a standard battery case, the system I am describing can

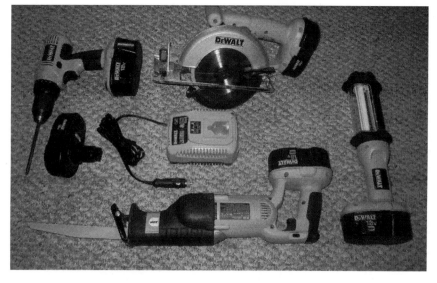

Regardless of your favorite brand, standardize all battery-powered tools to use the same battery pack.

be made totally portable. In addition to recharging power tools, this basic system can also be used to power DC appliances at a remote cabin or weekend retreat.

Electrical loads

I have mentioned in prior articles that there is an amazing selection of low-energy LED light fixtures, refrigerators, and kitchen appliances available from any boating or RV store that are designed to operate from 12 volts DC and require very little power.

I was also pleasantly surprised to find that most manufacturers of battery-powered construction tools now offer a version of their power tool battery chargers in a 12-volt DC portable model, typically called a "vehicle charger." Although harder to find and a little pricey at $65 to $95, these DC to DC chargers provide the ability to recharge your 12 to 24-volt battery-powered tools from a 12-volt battery without needing a heavy inverter or noisy generator.

This can be a real advantage if your construction project or weekend retreat is located in an area where hauling generator fuel and equipment up a mountain trail is a major effort. Although this project was intended primarily for powering tools at a remote job site, you can also use this portable solar-power system during a power outage or when camping to recharge your cell phone or power a laptop computer, since most of these devices include charging adapters to fit a 12-volt DC vehicle auxiliary outlet.

Project construction

I designed this project to require a minimum number of parts and very few wiring connections. I selected a standard Group 31 RV/Marine battery which is designed for multiple deep charge/discharge cycles while still being reasonably priced. I also found an inexpensive battery box, 10 amp

in-line DC fuse, and female cigarette lighter receptacle at a local recreational boating store. I decided to use this type of power receptacle for this project since so many portable tools and electronic devices have charging adapters that fit this type of 12-volt DC receptacle. As shown in the photo, I mounted the cigarette lighter receptacle in the box cover and wired it through the fuse to the battery using #10 standard copper wire and crimp on ring terminals. The center post of the cigarette lighter receptacle is always connected the battery positive (+) and the outer shell is always connected to the battery negative (-).

The Solar-Tech 85-watt solar module I selected for this project includes a full-size conduit box mounted on the back. To reduce costs, many solar modules are now supplied with "pigtail" wire connectors and no longer

include this conduit box. Make sure the brand and model of solar module you purchase *does* include this conduit box feature.

Also make sure the solar module is advertised for a nominal 12 volt charging voltage (17 volts peak), as manufacturers are increasing the physical size and wattage of their modules so fewer modules and wiring connections are needed for the same array total wattage. However, this increased module size also requires increasing the nominal voltage to 24 volts (35 volts peak) to keep current and wire size as small as possible, and this is too high for directly charging a 12-volt battery. While solar charge controllers are available to allow a mismatch between the solar array voltage and battery voltage so you could use a higher voltage solar module, these solar controllers tend to have a much higher cost and are too large to use in this very basic portable solar charging system.

I purchased a Morningstar SunKeeper-12 charge controller which is designed to mount into the standard ½-inch knockout opening in the solar module's conduit box and is suitable for mounting out in the weather. By locating the solar charge

Completed solar-powered portable tool charger

327

*Back view of 85-watt solar
module showing conduit
box and solar charger*

controller on the conduit box attached to the back of the solar module, you can use a 10-foot-long, 2-conductor cable with ring terminal ends for quick connect and disconnect to the battery terminals using wing nuts.

Solar sizing

Each tool charging cycle consumes an average of 7 amp-hours of battery capacity (7 amp charge rate for 1 hour). The Group 31 RV/Marine battery used for this project has 100 to 115 amp-hours of charge capacity, depending on price and brand. To avoid discharging this battery below 50% (which will help increase battery life), we will have approximately 50 amp-hours of useful charge capacity. This equals seven battery tool recharges (50 amp-hour/7 amp-hour) before the RV/Marine battery will need to be recharged. Of course, the actual number of tool recharges will depend on ambient temperature, battery age, and depth-of-discharge of the tool battery.

We estimated this Group 31 solar battery will require 50 amp-hours of solar charging to replace what the battery tool charging took away. Assuming we have an average of five hours of full sun per day, this will require a solar module capable of providing 5 amps of output to fully recharge this size battery in two days. (50 amp-hours/5 amps = 10 hours).

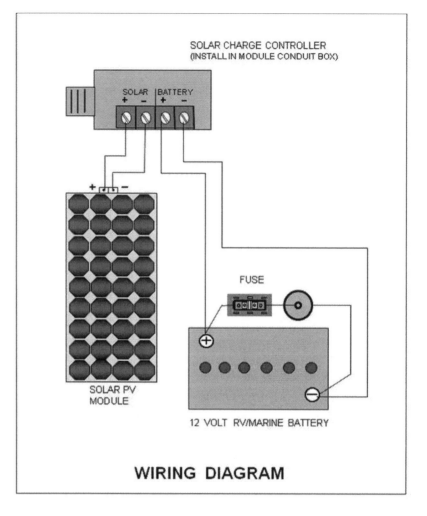

SOLAR CHARGE CONTROLLER
(INSTALL IN MODULE CONDUIT BOX)

SOLAR | BATTERY
+ − | + −

SOLAR PV MODULE

FUSE

12 VOLT RV/MARINE BATTERY

WIRING DIAGRAM

*Close-up view of battery box cigarette receptacle and
12-volt DC-powered battery pack charger*

A typical 85-watt solar module designed to charge 12-volt batteries will typically have a peak output of 5.1 amps, so I selected an 85-watt module. This smaller wattage module is also fairly easy for one person to carry, while still large enough to provide a reasonable amount of solar power. Your solar module can be larger or smaller than my 85-watt module selection, which will reduce or increase the number of days it takes to fully recharge the RV/Marine battery.

I have also omitted solar and charging efficiency considerations to simplify our example calculation. I have also assumed a clear blue sky all day, no module shading, and proper module solar orientation. When these factors are taken into consideration, you will most likely only convert approximately 70% of any solar module's nameplate output rating into useful battery charging. Do not be surprised if it actually takes a little longer to fully recharge the battery you select.

A Backwoods Home Anthology
The Fifteenth Year

* Canning basics
* Benefits of mulching
* Water and winter tree injury
* Birch tree syrup
* Selecting a breed of chicken
* Grow your own dishrags
* Solar & propane powered super home
* How to shoot a handgun accurately
* Make a poor man's safe
* Hogs belong on the homestead
* Fighting tomato blight
* Water is the key to gardening
* Herb boxes from fence boards
* Controlling aphids
* Dairy goats are for you!
* The poor man's ceramic knife sharpener
* Protect your house from lightning
* Double wall adobe construction
* Living with kerosene
* Save money when you buy your next vehicle
* Tree planting tips
* Sweet big fat squash that keep all winter
* Removing pine sap
* Split shake siding the modern way
* Beekeeping basics

Sources

While most major manufacturers of battery-powered hand tools offer an "in-vehicle" charger, these are not easy to find in your local retail store. If you cannot find them locally, there are several Internet sites that sell in-vehicle chargers. Order the charger that matches your brand of battery-powered tools, and be sure the charger matches the voltage and chemistry of your battery packs.

* DeWalt #DC9319 7.2-volt to 18-volt vehicle charger: www.factoryauthorizedoutlet.com

* Makita #DC18SE 18-volt/Lithium-ion vehicle charger: www.tylertool.com

* Bosch #BC006 7.2-volt to 24-volt vehicle charger: www.toolup.com

* Milwaukee #M12 12-volt Lithium-ion wall and vehicle charger: www.milwaukeetool.com

* Milwaukee #M18 18-volt Lithium-ion wall and vehicle charger: www.milwaukeetool.com

* Ryobi One+ 18-volt dual chemistry in-vehicle charger: www.homedepot.com

Conclusions

It feels really rewarding to build something off-grid in a remote area with the convenience of labor-saving power tools without having to deal with a noisy generator. It's also nice to have a portable solar-charging system instead of having to keep your truck running while using a DC to AC inverter to power your tools and tool chargers. When not needed to recharge power tools at a job site, this portable solar-charging system can be used for camping or during emergency power outages. This solar module with built-in solar charge controller can even be used to recharge your RV camper batteries when dry camping.

Jeff Yago is a licensed professional engineer and certified energy manager with more than 30 years of experience in the energy conservation field. With his extensive solar and emergency preparedness experience, he has authored numerous articles and texts. His website is www.pvforyou.com Δ

Homestead water

By Patrice Lewis

It is the most necessary of homestead requirements: water. It is literally a make-or-break resource.

There are some parts of our country blessed with an abundant and never-ending supply of water. These areas receive plentiful rainfall and/or have springs or other groundwater sources that never fail. To those homesteaders fortunate enough to live in such places, congratulations.

But for many other locations, water is a constant source of concern because it's either undependable, less than pure, and/or hard to find (or reach). Most of these places, it seems, are where population is low and therefore particularly attractive to homesteaders who yearn to settle far away from the city lights. To these folks I say, *be careful.* A cavalier attitude toward water can spell disaster for your homesteading plans.

I confess I never gave much thought to the issue of water before moving rural, 23 years ago. In the city, water is just *there.* When you turn on your faucet, it issues forth, clean and potable, without fail. Growing up in California, we paid attention to governmental pleas to conserve water whenever there was a drought (which was most of the time), but by and large I never doubted that I could fill my glass whenever I wanted.

But gradually, as my husband and I embarked on our newly-married life in the city, we began asking a series of "What if?" questions. Such as, "What if city water *wasn't* available? How would we survive?" In this day of increased awareness about disruptions in city services caused by anything from natural disasters to terror-

Count yourself lucky if you have a river on your homestead. This is one of two rivers that runs through managing editor Annie Tuttle's property.

ism, it doesn't take a rocket scientist to deduce that urban water sources are vulnerable to interruptions.

These kinds of concerns ultimately led us to leaving the city and embarking on our first rural adventure in 1993. Thus began our education on the need and availability of this critical resource.

This article cannot be entirely comprehensive in addressing everyone's water issues. Your situation will depend on your rainfall, climate, soil and groundwater conditions, and finances. Hopefully, this article will allow you to better assess your situation and determine what action you need to take in order to secure a regular source of water.

Variable criteria

The trouble with discussing the issue of water is the vast number of variables involved. Is your property bare or developed? Is your home off-grid or on conventional power? What is your annual rainfall? Is your rainfall seasonal or year-round? What is your water source — well, pond, creek, spring, runoff, hauled in? What is your anticipated water usage — household use only, small garden, large garden, livestock, irrigation? What are your storage options — jugs in the basement, cistern, storage tank, pond, elevated gravity-fed tank? What are the practical alternatives to address water issues? And can you afford them?

Your budget will help determine solutions to your water challenges. By "budget" I mean everything from where and how much property you purchase, to what kind of backup water systems you're able to afford.

Our story

Our first rural home was in southwest Oregon. The region had cool rainy winters and hot dry summers. The property had an 11 gallons per minute (gpm) well 80 feet deep. Urban novices though we were, we knew enough to have the well capacity as well as water quality tested before we made an offer on the house. We lived in that house for ten years and never (well, rarely) gave the well another thought. The water was delicious, dependable, and abundant.

Ten years ago we moved to rural north Idaho (with cold snowy winters and warm dry summers) and suddenly the issue of water played a much larger part in our lives.

This time we were a little less diligent about researching the well. We knew the well flowed at a decidedly modest 4 gpm and was a dazzling 590 feet deep, but we made the mistake of taking the seller's word about dependability. Our biggest concern was whether or not the well could go dry, but the sellers assured us that had never happened during their ownership. Still, we could get by on 4 gpm, and the house and property was otherwise suited to our needs. So we made an offer, clinched the deal, and a short time later moved in.

Two weeks later, the well went dry.

It went dry literally in the middle of a shower. Grumpily I toweled the sticky soap from my skin and my husband and I wondered what the heck to do.

In talking with neighbors, we basically learned the sellers had lied to us. It turns out the well often went dry. In fact, it went dry so frequently that there was a well-sharing clause with the neighbor's house, with the piping already in place. Our new neighbors kindly allowed us to renew the well-sharing and we paid them a monthly fee. This arrangement lasted for an entire year while we scraped together the money for a new well.

We had two drilling options for the well. Option One: We could drill an entirely new well at a cost of approximately $15,000. Option Two: We could re-drill the existing well and deepen it further, at an approximate cost of $7,000. While Option Two sounds like the logical choice, the trouble was there was no guarantee of hitting water, in which case we would have to fall back to Option One and pay for *both* scenarios.

We decided to take Option Two. The reason behind this calculated risk was because my husband (an engineering geologist by education) pulled the well logs for all the neighboring six properties and found that there was a fairly consistent and abundant water table at approximately 600 feet deep. Our existing well was 590 feet deep.

Could it be the original drillers had come up a mere ten feet short of punching through into the aquifer? It was certainly possible, since our well was the first one drilled in our neighborhood, 15 years before. The original owner had no way of knowing that more water was available just a bit deeper.

The well drillers arrived, they drilled out the old PVC pipe, and then continued to drill downward. Sure enough, at almost exactly 600 feet in depth — ten feet deeper than the original well — they punched through into a beautiful aquifer. Our well suddenly gushed at 30 gallons per minute. Eureka!

To be safe, the drillers went down another ten feet for a total depth of 610 feet. They re-inserted the original well pump (which, ironically, only pumps 5 gallons per minute) and we haven't had a stitch of trouble with our well ever since.

But the depth and vulnerability of our deep well has never left the backs of our minds. When the power goes out, we lose water because we lose the well pump. We're high on the prairie, ground water is very deep, and we have no springs or streams. Hand pumps aren't possible at that depth. For years we investigated wind and solar alternatives. There are some arrays that could service a well that deep; but we didn't have the money to pay for them. So our search for an alternative water source continued.

A few years ago we sprang for a 1500-gallon above-ground water tank,

Our well hasn't given us any trouble since drilling it deeper, but when the power goes out, we lose water because we lose the well pump.

331

An above-ground water tank can be used to store rain runoff from the roof.

with the idea that we would hook it up to roof runoff. This will provide us with drinking and wash water but won't be sufficient to water a garden or our livestock.

Our final solution (to date) was to dig a stock pond, which was actually more economical than we anticipated (more on this later).

So, after 10 years and a lot of thought, we now have three backup water sources (we call this the Rule of Three — backups to the backups to the backups) on our homestead. First backup: Stored water (about 40 gallons) for immediate use. Second backup: 1,500-gallon water tank for household and limited stock water. Third backup: a stock pond along with a pump and filter system for household use, stock water, and garden water.

Water sources

There are three primary sources for water: rainfall, groundwater, and surface water.

Rainfall. The advantages of rainfall are obvious. It's free, it's available, and it blankets everything. Depending on climate and location, even arid places often receive enough rainfall to harvest for homestead use, such as capturing roof runoff into cisterns, rain barrels, or other catchments. Sadly, there are some places where local governments place restrictions on such practices, so check your local rulings before harvesting rainwater.

The most obvious catchment system for rainwater is roofing. A roof is a large and relatively clean flat surface with (hopefully) a non-leaking and water-shedding composition. Catchment systems are fairly easy to set up, merely gutters leading to a holding tank, cistern, or pond. If your rainfall is seasonal, your catchment system can be designed with enough capacity to get you through the dry season with normal usage. Keep in mind the needs of your garden and/or livestock.

Groundwater. Groundwater can only be accessed with a well. In pioneering days, a well was hand-dug and of necessity fairly shallow. It was usually about three feet wide and accessed with a bucket and windlass; or later, with a hand pump. Our old house in Oregon had such a hand-dug well, a beautiful stone-lined antiquity located under the front porch. If you're lucky enough to have such a well, I suggest keeping it available for emergency use, and to keep a stout cover over the top to keep out animals, pets, children, and contaminants.

Today most wells are drilled and are about four to six inches in diameter, typically cased with PVC pipe. An electric well pump, located either adjacent to the well-head or at the bottom of the well, will deliver the water to your home. Wells have three measurements to consider: depth, flow rate, and static water level. The depth is just that — how far down the drillers needed to go in order to reach the aquifer. Flow rate is how many gallons per minute seep into the well hole. Static water level is how far up the well hole the water is pushed after whatever confining layers above the water table have been breached. In our case, our well is 610 feet deep with a flow rate of 30 gpm and a static water level of about 450 feet.

Static water level is important to know because if you need to hand-harvest your well water using a well bucket, sometimes called a well cylinder, you'll need to know what kind of distance you'll be pulling upward. Sometimes the static water level is too deep to efficiently use a well bucket, other times it's not.

If your static water level is not too deep, a hand pump can be a lifesaving device for times when you're without power (or live off-grid). However, hand pumps, which move water mechanically, are limited in effectiveness by static water level depth. If the static water level is greater than 200 feet, the water column (the amount of water in the pipe) is too "heavy" to lift; and the force required to lift water from that depth will be too great for practical use.

Aside from a standard AC electrical pump, for deeper wells (such as ours) there are really only two other practical options for bringing water to the surface. One is a solar array to power a specially-designed electric well pump; and the other is a windmill to pump the water to the surface mechanically

Windmills are highly effective and relatively simple (meaning, less maintenance) devices for pumping water from deep sources. The downside for us was price. We investigated a windmill for our needs and were quoted a price of $18,000, which I believe was reasonable. The trouble is we don't have $18,000 lying around, so we were unable to take advantage of that option.

It also goes without saying that a windmill will do you very little good if you live in a place that gets no wind.

Alternately, a solar rig can be set up to power just the well pump (as opposed to powering an entire household). This consists of a solar panel hooked to a submersible well pump. Prices are more affordable than a windmill, though its more complex nature may mean greater maintenance. And for a consistent flow when the sun isn't shining, a bank of batteries is necessary.

In both these cases (windmill or solar power), it would be best to talk to a knowledgeable sales rep from a specialized retailer about your specific needs. Both options have a long and well-established history of providing water in remote or difficult locations (think Texas hill country or Australian Outback) and are well worth the price. As a reminder, though, if the wind isn't blowing or the sun isn't shining, eventually the well is useless.

Surface water. If available, surface water is a tremendous blessing. A pond, spring, or stream can be used for either emergency household use (filter as necessary) or for everyday livestock and garden use. Once again, there may or may not be governmen-

tal restrictions on the use of surface water, so you need to research with due diligence whatever local restrictions may be in place.

How much water do you need?

If you're like us, your daily indoor water usage can be very modest, far below the national average of 80 to 400 gallons per day (depending on which sources you consult). Perhaps you reduce your water usage through such water-saving devices as low-flow shower heads, composting toilets, and efficient washing machines.

However be careful of judging your homestead water needs by your indoor use. If you have livestock and/or a garden, your water usage will increase, often dramatically. I have a quarter-acre garden which must be

watered daily during the dry summer months, a process that takes two hours. If we estimate three gallons per minute during the watering process, this comes to about 360 gallons per day just to water the garden. We are looking to make the garden more efficient in both time and water usage by installing a drip irrigation system. Mulching also greatly assists in reducing evaporation and reserving water. Nonetheless, a garden requires water. So do livestock. Can't escape that.

These considerations must be factored in when calculating the amount of daily water you have available from a well, spring, roof runoff, or especially if you're trucking in water.

So let's do a modest exercise. I will try to estimate how much water our family of four uses on a typical hot

Dorothy Ainsworth's water system includes a tank that she built herself and a water pumping windmill. Note the flag that is on a float in the tank. Dorothy can tell at a glance what the water level is in the tank.

You may have to haul water to your homestead as Jackie Clay did at one time.

summer day, both indoor and outdoor use.

Washing dishes: 10 gallons.
Washing a load of laundry: 25 gallons.
Four showers: 40 gallons (low-flow shower head)
Toilet flushing: 25 gallons
Drinking: 2 gallons.
Livestock: 100 gallons
Quarter-acre garden: approximately 350 gallons
TOTAL: 552

Now let's multiply that amount through three dry months (90 days):

49,680 gallons. This is the amount of water, in theory, our homestead would need over the course of a typically dry summer. Fortunately, it's rare in our region to have 90 straight days without rain; but that's extremely typical for such places as southern Oregon or central California.

This is why it's useful to employ catchment systems such as a house or barn roof. If we were to utilize our barn roof and catch rainwater, how much water could we expect?

Our barn is 36x48 feet. Each roof side is approximately 912 square feet in size. During a medium-sized rain-storm in which a quarter-inch of rain falls, this means 38 cubic feet or about 290 gallons can run off the roof and into a cistern or pond. Multiply this through additional rainstorms, and we have a decent amount of water available before the dry months hit.

That's why catchment systems are so useful in drier climates. A large cistern or (better) a stock pond can greatly alleviate water woes and allow ample opportunity to keep your livestock and garden happy.

Look before you leap

Those who already have their homesteads have doubtless given a great deal of thought to water. But what about those who are trying to get into the homesteading lifestyle? What should you consider before purchasing a piece of property to fulfill your homesteading dreams?

The fact of the matter is, water is too critical a component of any homestead to skimp on proper research and forethought. Before buying a piece of bare land, for example, get a serious and reputable quote for how much it will cost and/or what it will take to develop a dependable source of water. Far too many city folks buy their piece of rural property for a song, and then are dismayed to learn it will cost thousands or tens of thousands of dollars to sink a well, buy and install a pump, and install a pressure-tank controller... as well as the necessary plumbing.

But as our story demonstrates, even developed property can have water problems. Springs, wells, and creeks can all go dry. The old "Rule of Three" applies just as much to water sources as to anything else.

If you're just beginning your homesteading journey and are looking for suitable land, water availability should be your primary consideration. In some dry places, I know of people who haul in water from a distant location once or twice a week, but I find that option a little scary. What happens if your vehicle breaks down or you can't get gasoline to power your vehicle or the distant water source is no longer available?

We also know some people who have taken the windmill and solar route for providing water from their deep well. Additionally, they've taken the precaution of digging a stock pond. In short, they are capable of obtaining water, whether on or off-grid.

I truly believe it's vital that every homestead have a non-electric water source. If you have a spring or year-round stream or pond or other surface water, make sure you have the means to filter it for safe drinking. Alternately, look into harvesting roof runoff (again, with the means to filter it). If your well is not too deep, get a hand pump for those times when there is no power available for the electric pump to function.

Remember that cities are thirsty, thirsty entities, and are famous for usurping water rights from rural areas in order to fill swimming pools and provide green golf courses. In some classic examples, farmers were liter-

---

Moving water uphill

Some people may be fortunate enough to have a rapidly-moving creek or stream downhill from where they need water. What happens if you want to pump water uphill to water your garden or supply your household?

A centuries-old technique is to use a ram pump, which is powered by the kinetic energy of the flowing water itself. Commercially-made ram pumps are available for around $600. For do-it-yourselfers, there are online plans and instructions that allow you to build a ram pump with materials commonly available in hardware stores for around $100 or less.

---

ally left with dust in their fields while their water rights were diverted to the nearest big city. Keep this in mind before purchasing property with no natural water source.

It is *essential* that you investigate the water rights for a piece of property prior to purchasing — and make sure those water rights stay in your name for the lifetime of your property ownership.

Well contaminants

Before purchasing property with a well, it is important to get the water tested for contaminants. Private wells are not covered by the EPA regulations that protect public drinking water systems. It is the buyer's responsibility to test well water.

Well water can become contaminated either through naturally-occurring chemicals and minerals, or through man-made issues (herbicides, pesticides, animal feed operations, malfunctioning wastewater treatment facilities, etc.). While shallower wells are more subject to surface contamination, deep wells are affected by anything impacting the water table or aquifer.

Some of the common contaminants tested on private wells include coliform bacteria, nitrates, and volatile organic compounds.

Well buckets

If your water source is a well and the depth is too great to allow for a hand pump, a common emergency backup to get water from the well is a well bucket, sometimes called a bullet or torpedo bucket.

Modern wells usually have casings ranging from four to six inches in diameter, which makes for very narrow conditions for alternate water capture. You can't just drop a bucket on a rope down the well and hoist water aloft.

Well, actually you can... but it takes a specialized bucket to fit within modern wells. A well bucket is a

metal or PVC tube narrower than the interior diameter of the well casing. At the bottom is a flap valve which opens and allows water to enter the tube, and then seals shut by the weight of the water as the tube is lifted out of the well.

The amount of water lifted with a well bucket depends on the diameter and length of the tube. For example, a well bucket 52 inches in length and 3.5 inches in diameter will hold 1.9 gallons. Commercially-made well buckets are sold in many places online, but they are also easy to make from readily-available parts at any hardware store.

Depending on the depth of your well, a well bucket may require a windlass in order to more efficiently bring up water. Our well is 610 feet deep with a static water level of 450 feet, and a windlass will make the task of using a well bucket infinitely easier. Make sure you have adequate lengths of paracord or other sturdy nylon cordage on hand to lower the bucket to the depth of the static water level.

However, using a well bucket is not a simple matter of dropping a bucket into a hole. You must first remove the existing electric well pump and piping in order to have room for the well bucket. For this reason, a well bucket would only be practical during a long-term power outage and not during a blackout of short duration. Keep stored water on hand for temporary power outages.

By the way, if your well is less than 200 feet deep, consider getting a hand pump for alternate water access. While expensive, they are reliable and efficient.

Consider a stock pond

If water is not abundant in your area, you may have to create your own abundance. In north Idaho where we can easily go three months (during the summer) utterly without rain, we

We solved our long-term water needs by digging a stock pond.

solved our long-term water needs by digging a stock pond.

There is a reason stock ponds are popular in the dry western half of the U.S. — they are a manmade but very necessary reservoir of (mostly) surface runoff for agricultural or fire control needs.

In our case, with a very deep well, no consistently-available surface water, and dry summers, we knew we needed a steady backup source of water for both our livestock and for our extensive garden. A pond fit those needs. It would also serve as a last-resort solution to household drinking and washing needs.

Accordingly, we knew the pond had to be located in a place convenient for all these needs (garden, livestock,

household). It would be difficult to take full advantage of a pond's potential if it were located a quarter-mile away.

My husband, who has a fair bit of engineering experience, considered the location of the pond carefully. In addition to proximity to the house, garden, and livestock, the pond needed to be on a fairly flat piece of land with a slight slope. Most importantly, my husband considered the soil conditions in our target area — a spot that was mostly clay would hold water without the need for a lining.

But no matter how much forethought went into the pond, we didn't know what was actually underground until the digging began.

We decided on a square 50x50-foot pond, about 13 feet deep at one end and shallow at the other. We engaged the services of a skilled contractor with a track hoe. This man had long experience in building stock ponds, and he would know within a few minutes of breaking ground whether the pond would hold water or not. To our relief, the clay went down greater than the pond depth, making for a very watertight hole.

A neighbor, impressed with our aquatic undertaking, decided to have the same equipment operator dig him a pond as well. The neighbor chose a spot in a draw which would provide ample rain runoff. However, the subsurface proved to be too rocky and would not retain water, so the neighbor was forced to relocate the pond closer to his house on high ground, which had a similar clay layer to us. That pond was successful.

Initially, we thought our pond would need to be filled by shunting roof runoff from the barn. However, the clay layer proved useful in that the surface water funneled itself into the pond without any effort on our part. It has remained nearly full throughout the driest summer months and is a valuable addition to our homestead. At its fullest, we estimate the pond holds about 85,000 gallons of water.

Not everyone is blessed/cursed with heavy clay soil, however. If your subsoil stratum consists of limestone, sand, or some other porous medium, you'll need to line the pond. If the pores are small enough, a layer of bentonite may be used. Bentonite is an absorbent clay that swells upon contact with water and forms an impermeable barrier, rendering a pond watertight. Bentonite can also be "sandwiched" between synthetic materials (plastic or vinyl) to line a pond.

If the substratum is too porous for bentonite, then a pond liner (a thick layer of plastic, rubber, or vinyl) may be necessary to hold water. These are available commercially. For smaller ponds, an old billboard tarp (available online) may suffice as a liner.

A couple of final notes on stock ponds. First, our pond cost a *lot* less than we thought it would. We contracted with the track hoe operator during his off-season (January) when he was willing to do the job for less than he might otherwise charge during his busier season. He dug us a 50x50-foot hole in the ground for $1000. It took five hours of actual digging time.

It is also important to realize that, at first, our "pond" was nothing more than a great big hole in the ground. A pond is not a proper pond until (a) it's full (duh) and (b) it has an inflow and an outflow. Inflow proved to be easy due to surface runoff. But for a pond to be healthy, it needs an outflow. Therefore a pipe needs to be buried on the downhill side of the pond that will allow for controlled outflow to limit erosion.

Water purification

There may come a point where you need to filter or purify water for safe drinking, such as when the power is out, your well doesn't work, and you need to use surface water. Whatever the circumstances, it's important to keep a number of filtering or purification methods on hand.

First of all, don't think it's macho to cup your hands over a mountain stream and drink deeply. No matter how pure the water may look, you never know if there's a dead elk upstream just around the bend, rotting in the water and contaminating it for a long distance downstream. Believe me, a bout with Giardia or dysentery is no picnic.

There are a number of effective ways to purify water, including boiling, filtration, and chemical treatments. These methods are effective for typical surface water such as ponds, puddles, roof runoff, streams, and lakes that may have viral or bacterial pathogens. Often it is recommended to combine two or three purification methods for greatest efficacy and safety. *These methods assume the water has no chemical impurities such as toxic waste or pesticides/herbicides.*

Boiling is an acceptable and age-old method of water purification. Bring water to a rolling boil (cover the pot for the greatest efficiency) for at least one minute. A rolling boil doesn't mean tiny bubbles; it means the water is furiously boiling.

Filtration can be as simple as pouring water through a folded bandana (known as membrane filters) or as comprehensive as pumping water through a carbon or ceramic filter (known as depth filters). If the water is muddy or cloudy or has debris in it, it is best to filter out as many impurities as possible by membrane filtration before using an additional purifi-

Many filtration systems are do-it-yourself.
Annie Tuttle installed this water filtration system on her farm.

cation method. Your choice of depth filter may depend on what types of organisms are most common in your area.

For household (as opposed to backpacking or camping) use, a freestanding filter such as a Berkey unit is an excellent means of passively filtering water.

Bio-sand filters are an excellent passive filtering technique. They are the modern modification of the slow-sand filter technique that's been in use for centuries. Bio-sand filters remove pathogens and sediments and are becoming common in developing nations. Plans can be found online and bio-sand filters can often be constructed for less than $100 using a 55-gallon drum. YouTube has a number of clips on how to make bio-sand filters.

Chemical purification is done using chlorine (bleach) or iodine. Effectiveness of chemical purification depends on a number of factors, including temperature, pH, and clarity of the water. Cooler and/or cloudier water requires higher concentration of chemicals to disinfect it.

If you use household bleach, it should not be scented, colorsafe, or have added cleaners. It should be less than a year old (or it loses efficacy) and 5.25% sodium hypochlorite. Add bleach at the rate of 16 drops per gallon of water. Stir and let stand for 30 minutes. If the water does NOT have a slight bleach-y odor at the end of 30 minutes, repeat the dosage and let stand another 15 minutes.

Iodine is another method for purifying water, but overall it is less recommended than bleach. Iodine is light-sensitive and should be stored in a dark bottle. It works best if the temperature of the water is 68° F or higher. While iodine is better than bleach at inactivating Giardia cysts, many people are allergic to iodine (often the same ones who are allergic to shellfish). Iodine should not be used by pregnant women.

If using liquid 2% tincture of iodine, add 5 drops per quart when the water is clear, 10 drops per quart when the water is cloudy. Shake and let sit for one hour. If using another form of iodine, follow the manufacturer's instructions.

Rule of Three

As mentioned earlier, you should employ the "Rule of Three" for water. This means three backups to your main water supply.

In our situation, our main water supply is through our well, powered with an electric pump. Our three backups, both current and nearly completed, are:

• Stored water. We have about 40 gallons of water in either one- or five-gallon jugs with a bit of added bleach. We rotate this water once a year. We also have four or five gallons stored without bleach, which we rotate more frequently. This allows us immediate water during short-term power outages.

• A 1,500-gallon water tank. This will be hooked up to roof runoff from our barn, and used for longer-term household and livestock use.

• A 50x50-foot stock pond. This can be used for watering the livestock and garden and, during a long-term emergency, household use after proper filtering. We also have a Berkey filter and are working on a bio-sand filter.

You should have water sterilization or filtering options on hand at all times. Bleach, water purification tablets, and/or a water filter (such as a Berkey) are all necessary items.

Miscellaneous points

• Remember, water weighs about eight pounds per gallon.

• When storing drinking water for emergency household use, darkness is essential to discourage the growth of algae and bacteria.

• Never believe a realtor who claims a piece of property has a "year round" creek or stream. A great majority of

creeks and streams dry up in the hot dry months. Realtors may not know whether a stream is seasonal or not.

• Ditto this caution about sellers — they may not be entirely forthcoming about a well's reliability. Test the well before you submit to buying a property.

• It might be illegal to irrigate a field from a well designed for household use. Irrigation rights are different than household water rights. Part of the reason behind this is irrigation may deplete water availability for your immediate neighbors. When water is pumped out of the ground too rapidly, it creates a "cone" of temporary deprivation that may affect the water flow into the neighbor's well. Quite simply, if you try to irrigate a corn field out of a well, you may be causing your neighbor's well to run dry.

• There are riparian laws in effect in many parts of rural America that limit the proximity of livestock to water (streams, creeks, rivers, ponds). Herbivorous consumption can damage delicate riparian areas by waterways, and hooves can contribute to bank erosion. You may have to install fences to keep your livestock away from surface water sources.

• The EPA estimates that 37% of household water is used to flush toilets. If you live in an area with limited water, consider a composting toilet.

• Just because you live rural doesn't mean your surface or groundwater is pure. Agricultural chemicals (fertilizers, pesticides, etc.) as well as livestock waste contaminate enormous amounts of water. Modern farming techniques, thankfully, are working to minimize these contamination sources, but pollution still happens. Even the rock salt used to improve conditions on snowy roads is washed into the regional drainage systems and can contaminate water.

• Always assume that surface water is contaminated. Giardia is a common protozoan that can cause multiple complications in people who get infected. Something that died upstream and fell into the water can make even the purest-looking downstream water deadly.

• While shallow wells have multiple advantages for getting water to the surface, they can also be more subject to contamination. Deep wells, more complicated to access, usually (but not always) have the advantage that the water is generally purer.

• Some locations in proximity to the ocean may be subject to saltwater intrusion at certain times (high tide, etc.) or to sinkholes.

• The Internet (including YouTube) is the modern homesteader's best friend when it comes to learning specifics about certain projects such as bio-sand filters or ram pumps. Make lavish use of someone else's expertise!

In conclusion...

Back in the old days when we lived in the city and began thinking through all those "What if?" questions, we were stymied because any solutions or backups (except for some personal water storage) depended on someone *else* to provide. But here in the country, it's up to us to provide our own water under whatever circumstances.

There's a rule of thumb called three-three-three. You can only live three minutes without oxygen, three days without water, or three weeks without food. Assuming your homestead has air, your greatest immediate concern is water.

Make sure you've got it. Δ

A Backwoods Home Anthology
The Fourteenth Year

❋ Use Wallo' Water and gain a
   month of growing season
❋ A packing crate mini-barn
❋ How to butcher a chicken in
   20 minutes or less
❋ Pemmican
❋ Mane and tail tools
❋ The vanishing outhouse
❋ Preparing garden soil in winter
❋ Install a mobile, solar-powered toilet
❋ Portable fence panels: the
   homesteader's friend
❋ Hingeless gate
❋ Mountain and winter driving
❋ A comfortable base camp
❋ Home canning equals fast,
   easy, tasty meals
❋ Brooder in a box
❋ A pleasant surprise:
   the asparagus bean

❋ Preparedness for travelers
❋ Jackie Clay's basic "grab & git"
   emergency kits
❋ The home citrus orchard
❋ Making dandelions palatable
❋ How to select the right
   backup generator
❋ Growing & storing herbs
❋ Successful cold storage
❋ A simple backwoods hay baler
❋ Battery powered weekend retreat
❋ The art of wood splitting
❋ Keeping cats out of the garden
❋ Want more fruit from less space?
   Espalier your trees!
❋ Living with wildlife
❋ Tomato canning tips
❋ Traditional trail foods —
   transportable calories
❋ Piccalilli — a late summer bonus

Ayoob on Firearms

Just because

I generally recommend that people buy guns the way they'd buy power tools, or automobiles, or homes. Assess your needs, analyze your budget, correlate it all with your ability to utilize the thing you're buying, and you'll probably be happy with your purchase and get a lot of productive use out of it.

It's the logical thing. Unfortunately, we humans are not always creatures of logic. Sometimes, we are creatures of emotion, and anyone who has dealt with emotion-driven arguments that are without logic — oh, most of the "gun control" arguments, for example — know the downside of that. But emotion isn't *always* a bad thing.

Consider the emotion of "sentiment." Anything can go bad on you, but sentiment is less likely to do that than most other emotions, so long as it is leavened with logic.

I'm sitting here writing this in Connecticut at the moment, up to my hips in sentiment mixed with logic, applied to the gun. It's the last week of a month-long training tour teaching firearms and deadly force, a tour that has taken me through multiple states which have "assault weapons bans" which limit magazine capacity. Some of those states have a ten-round cap, and one, New York, allows no more than seven rounds to be in a ten-round magazine unless one is on a shooting range. Since I'm legal to carry under the Law Enforcement Officer Safety Act of 2004, but bound by local laws as they would apply to private citizens, those limits apply to me.

I'm carrying a gun of relatively ancient design, a 1911 pistol, specifically a Nighthawk T-3. All my magazines are seven-round Wilsons; no one can ever accuse me of carrying more than seven New York State Compliant cartridges in any of them, since more than that simply won't fit. *Logic*. But, since a World War I vintage Colt 1911 my dad gave me for my twelfth birthday in the year 1960, I have bonded with this style of handgun. *Sentiment*. I've won more than my fair share of trophies and championship titles with this type of gun, thanks to that habituation, and the fact that it fits my hand and my shooting style well. *Logic*. But that fact gives me confidence in it, and in the potency of its .45 caliber cartridge, should I ever need it for self-defense. Is that logic, sentiment, or equal parts of each? I dunno … you tell me.

The "Grail Gun" factor

Collectors speak of their "grails," the things they've always wanted and longed to attain. This stamp for the stamp collector, that particular rare Elgin or Waltham for the watch collector, and so on. When I was a little boy, a copy of the Stoeger *Shooter's Bible* from within a year of my birth sat in the bookshelf in my bedroom. A gun that was highlighted in it was the Smith & Wesson .357 Magnum, with the main image of it the one with the 83/8-inch barrel, and an inset of the version with the 3½-inch barrel. You know, I kind of "imprinted" on those at a most impressionable age.

My dad bought me one with the 83/8-inch barrel — known by then as the Model 27 — when I was in my early teens. I hunted with it, shot matches with it in the Centerfire division of NRA bulls-eye shooting, and had a 6-inch barrel put on it when I

Massad Ayoob

was a rookie policeman shooting the primary law enforcement gun game of the period, PPC (Police Pistol Combat). Six inches was the maximum barrel length at the time, and I wasn't making much money, so re-barreling a gun I already owned made more economic sense than buying a new one. I won my first state championship with that gun, in PPC, when I was 25. Sentiment? You bet.

I never did buy the 3½-inch barrel version back then, much as I wanted one; for police duty, our revolvers had to have at least 4-inch barrels, and there were more modern and efficient .357 Magnum revolvers by that time. I carried the Colt Python and for a while the S&W Combat Magnum, which was much lighter than the Model 27. But I hungered for a 27 in my later years, and when late-onset mid-life crisis hit me in the 21st century, I wound up with two: a classic five-screw "pre-27" made not long after that edition of Stoeger's *Shooter's Bible* had been published, and a stag-handled Model 27-2. I cherish them, and carry one or the other as "barbecue guns" on special occasions. Sentiment? Yes … but from the logical side, you are never less than well-armed when you carry a classic Smith & Wesson .357 Magnum.

Classic rifles

At *Backwoods Home Magazine*, our most popular writer is Jackie Clay. That's largely because of her encyclopedic knowledge of self-sufficient living, which after all is what *Backwoods Home* is all about. But if you just dig a little bit deeper, you find that a lot of the whole self-sufficiency thing goes past the "prepper's" concern about SHTF survivalism, and back to the nostalgic days when people lived off the land in a simpler fashion than modern society allows most of its inhabitants. The log cabin, the home you've built yourself on a plot of land you've carved out of the wilderness, is the very embodiment of independence, and of American heritage.

Jackie and her husband feed their family with food they raised *themselves*. With meat they raised *themselves*. And, yes, with venison they harvested from the forest *themselves*.

Last I knew, Jackie's choice of deer rifle was the venerable Winchester Model 94, caliber .30-30. It's a lever-action carbine that weighs less than seven pounds, fast to the shoulder and fast to the second follow-up shot, if that should be needed. Its name comes from the year of its introduction, 1894. The .30-30 cartridge introduced American hunters to high velocity, flat-shooting rifles which extended their effective range. It was eclipsed more than a hundred years ago by still-faster and flatter-shooting rifle/cartridge combinations, which were also more inherently accurate. Yet millions of Winchester .30-30s, and still more equivalent Marlins and other clones of the concept, remain in the field and in American homes and farmhouses. There is a heritage there: *Sentiment*. But these guns are light and easy to carry all day, perfectly balanced when carried with one hand firmly grasping the receiver in front of the lever: *Logic*.

For many years now, I've limited my hunting to the use of handguns.

I'm in it for the sport when the spirit to hunt moves me, not for the meat. And I simply don't have much time to hunt anymore.

Most of what I do with a rifle, whether competition or teaching, is in the law enforcement and personal protection function. We focus on the AR15, and similar rifles such as the Ruger Mini-14. High speed, low drag semi-automatics, geared to lawful anti-personnel work but also now ruling the world of sport target shooting, except for cowboy action matches, where the nostalgia factor kicks in again.

I gotta say this: if the Zombie Apocalypse came to pass tomorrow, I would have my semiautomatic Springfield Armory SOCOM-16 rifle in the front seat of my van or SUV. I would be expecting the zombies to be coming in vehicles of their own, and a .308 caliber semiautomatic will turn such a vehicle into a colander. A zombie apocalypse without heavy sheet metal and safety glass surrounding the threat? I'll take one of my semiautomatic AR15s, thank you very much. They're the gun of my generation today, and of several other generations — the modern American Rifle. Long distance zombies? My Savage police sniper rifle would come out, along with its Harris bipod, to neutralize the threat from the farthest, safest distance with .308 bullets.

But, if I was to find a weekend to hunt deer with a rifle in the swamps or the thickets, there's no question in my mind that I'd take a Winchester '94. Even if I never saw a deer, it would take me back to when I was a young boy, lugging a long-barreled Model of 1894 in one of its original calibers, .38/55, which felt like a BAR at the time and was about proportional to a little kid's size and weight. Yes, I still have that gun. *Sentiment* and *nostalgia*? I confess to both.

If you have been reading *Backwoods Home* for any length of time, you have noticed that the editors, this writer, and the magazine itself are all fans of the Appleseed Project. Appleseed seeks to remind Americans of their heritage as a Nation of Riflemen, and mixes Revolutionary War history with a

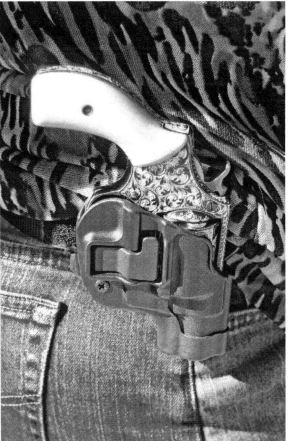

A gift from someone who loves her, engraved and fitted with ivory grips, this S&W Chief Special Airweight .38 is worn on special occasions by a Backwoods Home reader ... just because.

solid curriculum of rifle marksmanship. Their course of fire is relatively fast, extremely accuracy-intensive, and definitely challenging to any shooter.

Most competitors use semiautomatic rifles. Hell, I used one — a Ruger 10/22, built for butt-kickin' by Kay Miculek of Clark Custom, in a stock from Brownell's — to win the coveted Rifleman's Patch.

But, you know what? The legend at Appleseed says that the record score on their demanding course of fire was set by an old man with an old rifle. I'm told it was a Winchester Model 52, an exquisitely accurate bolt action .22 which dates back to before World War II. It requires four movements between shots — bolt up, bolt back, bolt forward, bolt down — and then the firing hand has to acquire its grasp again and find its way to the trigger. With a semiautomatic, of course, there's nothing you need to do but keep your finger on the trigger, let it come forward to the re-set point, and press it again while that unforgiving clock is ticking.

How could an old geezer with a bolt action rifle outshoot all the rest of us with semiautomatics? Maybe because

Nickel plated with ivory stocks, this classic .38 Colt Detective Special is a touchstone that reminds the author of friends and role models, and he sometimes carries it ... just because.

the years had taught him timing. Maybe because he was focused more on perfection than on speed. Or maybe, simply, because an old person with an old rifle had mastered the Old Ways enough to beat all of us whose skills and technology came later.

Sentiment or ***logic***? Once again, I leave it for you to determine.

The "Just Because" factor

As a kid, I first became aware of Chic Gaylord reading my dad's "men's magazines" of the 1950s, *True* and *Argosy*. Gaylord was a fast-draw champion and the greatest holster-maker of his generation, creating designs that set the stage for modern concealed-carry holsters. The original designs are still available from Bell Charter Oak Leather, and are as serviceable then as they were now. Gaylord went on the popular mid-20th century TV show *I've Got A Secret*, and his secret was that he was carrying 13 handguns concealed from the collective eye of the audience. While he used some Smith & Wessons, and set his speed records with a .22 caliber High Standard revolver, Gaylord was a Colt man down to his bones. One of his signature guns was a snub-nosed Colt .38, nickel plated and wearing ivory grips. I saw that as a lad and said to myself, "I'd like to have a gun like that some day."

Gaylord's record of 13 concealed carry handguns was beaten decades later by my friend John Bianchi,

With grips reminiscent of General Patton's, this mid-20th Century Smith & Wesson .357 Magnum is one of the author's "grail guns" ... just because.

widely considered the greatest holster-maker of *his* generation. John got into the upper twenties of concealed handguns, and then beat his own record by getting into thirty-some.

I never got to meet Gaylord, though I cherished my friendship with Bianchi, and in February of 2013 I paid homage to both by going for a new record. I managed to conceal 52 loaded handguns for the Panteao training film *Ayoob on Concealed Carry*, now available on DVD or computer streaming at www.panteao-productions.com. On the way back from the filming with my significant other, I told her how much Gaylord and Bianchi had inspired me, and mentioned that someday, I'd like to have an ivory-handled, nickel-plated Colt Detective Special like Gaylord's. I believe I mentioned also that another friend, the late Charles "Skeeter" Skelton, had owned such a Detective Special and showed pictures of it in his first gun magazine article. I had read it when I was in my formative years. It appeared in *Guns* magazine in the 1950s. I later became handgun editor for that publication, a position I've proudly held for thirty-some years now.

In more recent times, Sheriff Jim Wilson and I got to know each other, as roommates at a seminar held at Clint Smith's famed Thunder Ranch firearms training facility. Later on, I ran into Jim again in the Midwest, and damned if he wasn't carrying an ivory-gripped nickel Colt Detective Special like Gaylord's and Skelton's. There were a lot of touchstones there.

To make a long story short, this past summer I had a landmark birthday, and my sweetie, the Evil Princess, presented me with a mint condition, nickel-plated Colt Detective Special from that period. Yes, it has *huge* sentimental value. But, you know, back in my twenties I figured out that these little D-frame, six-shot Colts were the most accurate and effective of sub-

Since 1894, this style of Winchester has been an American Classic, and nostalgia and tradition are reasons enough for many to hunt with it ... just because.

compact .38 Special revolvers, and this one groups very tightly.

On the increasingly rare day when I'm at home and just wearing a pair of shorts, it fits very comfortably on my belt. It rides in a Bucheimer holster from the 1950s, and when I glance down at it, its nickel finish and ivory grips bring me back to a time in my life that is very important to me. It reminds me of a lot of good people who are also important to me.

There is value in that.

How we decide

A friend of mine in the Pacific Northwest owns many motor vehicles, including the latest and greatest. Yet the one he prefers to drive, the one which pleases him most, is a Chevrolet built in the mid-1950s. It reminds him of a time in his life which he cherishes. And, you know what? It gets him where he needs to go.

The .45 caliber 1911 pistol on my hip at the moment has helped the nation I love win wars since the eponymous year of its introduction. Yes, there are more modern guns which are lighter and sleeker and can fire more shots before they need to be reloaded. I absolutely believe that every law-abiding citizen in our nation has the right to own the most modern and efficient firearms of their time, and for various reasons not germane to this article I expect to be carrying high speed, low drag, high-capacity firearms of that kind next month.

Logic? Certainly, it can't be denied. Indeed, it has to be integral to any decision making process. *Sentiment*, as opposed to generic emotion? Well, one thing we all have to remember is that if our collective experience with the given thing wasn't good or positive, we probably wouldn't have developed a sentimental attachment to it in the first place.

If you think about it, this is one of the many ways in which the world of the gun is an allegory to the rest of the world we live in.

Sentiment and logic can co-exist comfortably. That co-existence, after we've given it some thought, can be natural and efficient ... and pleasing, an element which carries an intangible value which only the individual can weigh and value.

Just ... because. Δ

Lenie in the kitchen
Turkey lentil soup

By Ilene Duffy

One of my favorite holidays is Thanksgiving. I enjoy all the preparations including baking some bread earlier in the week to be used for the stuffing. I do my best to save an acorn or a butternut squash from the garden to add to my favorite side dish, a roasted vegetable casserole. The canned cranberry sauce doesn't hold a candle compared to fresh cranberries cooked on the stove with sugar, orange juice, and a jigger or so of orange liqueur. When I have a good crop of pumpkins, my boys are especially happy to get pumpkin pies for dessert. And even when we don't have a houseful of people for Thanksgiving, I still get a nice big turkey to roast. The leftover meat is so good for next-day sandwiches, casseroles, and especially soup.

I found a beef lentil soup recipe online and modified it so I could use up some of the leftover turkey. This soup took only a little more than an hour to prepare and cook and it got rave reviews from all my taste testers. This one's a keeper.

Turkey lentil soup

3 Tbsp. olive oil
1 large onion, chopped
2 large carrots, chopped
3 stalks of celery, chopped
8 cloves of garlic, coarsely chopped
64 oz. chicken broth
2 tsp. Italian seasoning
½ tsp. pepper
3 cups cooked turkey, chopped
2½ cups dry red lentils
½ cup chopped fresh parsley
salt and pepper, to taste
Parmesan cheese, grated, for serving

This is my kind of soup. It uses lots of the leftover turkey, is fast to prepare, and it's hearty and delicious for a quick winter meal.

Preparation:

Heat olive oil in large stock pot. Add onion, carrot, and celery and cook until onion is translucent, stirring occasionally, about 6 minutes. Add garlic and cook about 2 minutes more. Add broth, Italian seasoning, pepper, and turkey. (I like to add some nice, big bones like a leg or a thigh bone to give the broth more flavor.) Wash and drain lentils and add them to the pot. Stir and cover the pot and cook until lentils are tender, about 40 minutes. Stir occasionally and add more broth or water if the soup gets too thick. Add parsley and cook 5-10 minutes more. Add salt and pepper to taste. (I used Better Than Bouillon to make the broth, so I didn't need to add any salt.) Add grated Parmesan cheese to each serving, if desired. Δ

Husband Dave gets the first taste of hot lentil soup while he works on this issue at our dinner table.

More great recipes are in
Backwoods Home Cooking

Tips for older homesteaders

By Jackie Clay-Atkinson

Over and over again, concerned older folks ask me, "Am I too old to think about homesteading?" My first impulse is to laugh. After all, I'll see 70 all too soon. And our old-time homestead gurus, Helen and Scott Nearing, were hand-building stone buildings in their 80s and 90s. But I realize that older folks' fears and concerns are real and definitely not to be laughed at. After all, how many of us have heard shocked remarks at our own choice of lifestyle? At 50 or 60, years of age a lot of homesteaders are starting to feel vulnerable and fearful for their futures. I'll tell you right here that the one biggest asset for anyone considering a later-in-life homesteading lifestyle is *attitude*!

I can't climb on an unbroken horse and ride him out anymore. But I sure as heck can keep the weeds out of our garden, feed the chickens, clean the barn, and do a million other homestead-related chores. Just because you have a physical handicap, such as arthritis, a hip replacement, chronic illness, or a heart condition, doesn't mean you have to quit. I won't bother you with all the details of my various ills and pains. (I'm sure you remember my bout with a very serious form of cancer seven years back and our injuries after my husband and I fell off our barn a couple years ago.) But like when I used to rodeo at a much younger age, I've learned to suck it up and deal with life.

We all get tired and have days we hurt. Learn to work slowly and steadily. If you need a break, take one and go back to work. I do it every day and still get a lot done. Need a nap some days? Take one and don't feel guilty.

Will and I enjoy sitting on our front porch and watching the homestead around us. What a satisfying feeling that is.

You'll be more productive for it and life will seem brighter.

I will admit to doing all I can to make each and every single chore on the homestead as easy on me as possible. I'll share what I have learned about making homesteading life easier so you can maintain your lifestyle even at an advanced age. One thing that Mom, with all her severe health issues (including crippling rheumatoid arthritis), taught me is that you stay healthier doing constructive things rather than sitting around wishing. After all, homesteading involves gentle exercise every single day: walking to the garden, bending to pull weeds, planting seeds and harvesting vegetables, stretching to pick fruit from trees, squeezing your hands while milking a goat, and steering a tractor, golf cart, or wheelbarrow.

Of course, we haven't even begun to consider other health benefits of a homestead lifestyle such as breathing clean, unpolluted air; eating fresh, chemical-free foods; relaxing in the evening, sitting on the porch remembering the day and listening to your homestead breathe around you. The very lack of stress is huge. Although some people blow off stress as inconsequential, it is a big cause of high blood pressure, stroke, ulcers, and heart conditions. A homesteading lifestyle, lived right, can suck the stress right out of you. Daily doses of laughing at the baby chicks, eating the first sweet cherry of the year, waking to birdsong, and going to sleep listening to the frogs and crickets quickly makes the rat race life of the city seem far away.

Besides better health and well-being, homesteading life is cheaper. At an older age, many of us are on a limited income and sure watch those pennies. But with frugal living on a homestead, we can easily raise most of our own healthy, gourmet quality food, perhaps burn wood off of our own place, and drink well or spring water. There is no sewer fee for having a septic tank, yet you can still have a "modern" flush toilet.

There are hundreds of labor and back-saving tips that are invaluable to older homesteaders. And, as I've learned a lot in my own lifetime, I'll share with you.

Homestead mobility

Our four wheeler (ATV) saves my bad knee from miles of walking every day. Our homestead is pretty spread out and our barn and garden are at opposite sides of our house. So we hop on our ATV and drive where we want to go instead of walking. (Yes, we do get plenty of walking exercise every day, even using it!) While Mom and Dad were living, my oldest son, Bill, brought an electric golf cart up for them to use as they were in their 90s and it was very hard for them to get around. I loved it too and will

someday have one of my own. They are extremely easy to get in and out of, where the four-wheeler does require you to hoist your leg over the back while you are getting on. And the electric golf cart uses no gas, is easily charged up by plugging it in, and is quiet. I took Mom and Dad for "walks" in the woods (way down our wooded driveway and through our pastures). Not only could they keep up with what was going on around the homestead, but they also enjoyed watching the deer and other wildlife up close as the animals weren't scared off by noise.

Of course, a golf cart or ATV can also haul buckets of feed, milking pails and equipment, garden produce, and dozens more handy things around the place.

Can't afford a golf cart or ATV? Don't discount your riding lawn mower. For many years we used ours as sort of an ATV. With a garden trailer (complete with a dump box) hooked on behind, we hauled water, hay, straw, sawdust, firewood, lumber, rocks, gravel, and even Dad and the grandkids as sort of a miniature hayride. If you don't have a riding lawn mower, think about picking up a good used one. Around $300 will usually

buy a larger used riding lawn mower, especially if you buy it in the fall.

Gardens and orchards

I used to pick fruit standing on a stepladder or even propping up an extension ladder onto a tall tree's branches so I could reach the apples or pears way up in the sunshine. Now I don't even like to stand on a chair! Grandma and Mom couldn't climb anymore, either so they used a fruit picker. Now I have a one, too. This is just a wire basket on a long pole with several prongs on the front that rake the fruit off of the branches. The fruit gently rolls down into a padded wire basket which holds several fruits. When the basket is full, you just work your way up the pole, pick the fruit out of the basket, and put it into your larger container. You can stand flat-footed and safely reach even high branches.

And how about weeding in the garden? I used to be able to bend easily or kneel down and creep along on my knees, pulling weeds. I can't even get on my knees now! I can still bend, but after half an hour, even that's not such a great way to spend time.

Luckily, there are alternatives to bending and kneeling. Will bought me one of those little wide-wheeled, tractor-seated garden seats and I love it. I can pull it down the rows, then sit down to weed or pick vegetables. When I want to move on down the row, I just "walk" my feet to propel it onward.

When I face the task of filling my 50 or more Wall O' Waters to protect our tomato plants from late frost, I use a little plastic seat a friend sent me that fits down onto the top of a five-gallon bucket. It's easy to pick up by the handle and carry down the rows and oh, so comfortable to sit on instead of that painful rim on the bottom of the upside down bucket. I use it while weeding and harvesting, too.

Another handy garden help is the reversible padded kneeling bench.

An electric golf cart makes getting around on a homestead easy, quiet, and fun. My oldest son, Bill, used to take Mom to see what was going on in our garden. Without the cart, she couldn't get down the hill.

I find plenty of use for my little rolling garden seat and my handy plastic seat. It fits onto a five-gallon bucket so I can sit to weed or harvest.

The legs are able to be used as handles to help you get up after kneeling down to weed or harvest, or you can flip it over and have a comfortable padded stool to sit on for the same chores. How useful, especially to us aging gardeners!

Raised beds are even easier to weed with less stooping over and deep bending making it easier on tender knees, backs, and hips. In her late 80s, Mom switched to raised beds for all but her potatoes and green beans, which she changed over from rows to wide beds. One of my friends gardens solely in raised beds, raised up two feet high as he uses crutches to get around. With the tall raised beds, he doesn't have to bend or kneel to get down to weed or harvest. And he grows enough that his wife is kept busy canning all summer and fall.

Consider alternative containers for your raised beds. While many raised beds are made of lumber, treated lumber, railroad ties, logs, or plastic planks, you can also use livestock watering tanks, old wheelbarrows, washtubs, bathtubs, or just about any deep container that will hold dirt.

Do you live in town or have little room or ability to have even a raised bed garden? Consider gardening in containers. Virginia, a friend of mine in a neighboring town, has done won-

ders by gardening in five-gallon buckets hanging from her deck. She cuts a hole in the bottom large enough to insert a tomato plant, held in place by a coffee filter until its roots become strong. And she plants the top of the buckets with carrots, onions, or beans. Two crops from one bucket. As the tomato grows, it hangs down and the smaller crops on the top grow upward. She also grows squash, beans, carrots, onions, tomatoes, and more in her many lush buckets, hanging conveniently from her back deck. There's no weeding, and they are easy to water and harvest.

Another helper is my little CobraHead hoe. I have both a short-handled version and a long-handled hoe. Each is lightweight, sharp, and extremely handy for a huge variety of garden work. I can reach across my flowerbeds to remove weeds under my perennials without bending or stretching, make shallow rows for carrots and beets, hoe under plants without damaging leaves, and even lean on it while tired. It's much lighter than a regular hoe and more versa-

A little Mantis tiller is great for tilling small areas, digging fruit tree holes, and cultivating between plants in the garden. This is my second in 20 years and I sure plan on buying another when it's worn out.

347

A simple old-time fruit picker saves me from climbing ladders to pick fruit on the top of the trees. It's much easier and safer.

tile. I even use my short-handled cultivator to plant tomatoes, peppers, and bedding plants and bulbs in the fall.

Are you reluctantly thinking you'll soon have to give up your big garden because your back won't stand the pounding your front-tined tiller gives it every year? Here are a couple of other choices I've found real helpful. The first is a TroyBilt rear tined tiller. I'm on my second big 8hp Horse tiller and have had one for more than 40 years. But it is a bit big and heavy to turn at the end of rows. I can see where I'll probably have to downsize to a smaller Bronco version in the future for this reason. Both till very beautifully, without pounding you to death. Then the soil is fluffy and wonderful after tilling and ready to plant. And, yes, just like the advertisements, you can walk along next to the tiller, letting it do all the work.

For those of you who have smaller gardens or raised beds, consider the Mantis tiller. This little 20-pound wonder does everything from tilling your small and medium-sized garden or raised bed to weeding and even helping you plant trees and shrubs. It's really powerful for its size, reminding me of a mad weasel. There's even an electric version for those of you who need something for a few beds around the house.

I had to save a year to buy my new TroyBilt. But it's one of the best investments we've ever made. You can usually find a good used one locally through your free shopper or on a local Craigslist for a very reasonable price.

Livestock

The type of livestock you have when you become older usually differs from what you raised as a young homesteader. Downsizing not only applies to a change in home size but also in the number and kind of animals and poultry we want to keep in later life. I would never want to be without homestead critters. But I do realize that having lots of mouths to feed (summer and winter), tons of manure to shovel, and heavy chores to do daily can take its toll on us aging folk. No, I don't advocate hauling all our animals to the auction barn. But looking at things realistically, we probably don't need 40 goats, 10 milk cows, 200 chickens, six horses and a dozen sheep when we're 90 years old. As time passes, we usually just cut back on the animals to the ones we love, enjoy, and can take good care of.

Chickens

There's a huge difference in the amount of time, feed, and effort that goes into 200 chickens compared to just a dozen or two.

I used to raise 50 meat birds in a summer and butcher them all in two days' time, but now my tender hands really only want to do about three birds a day. So we just do three birds a day for several days instead. It works fine and saves me from dreading a big job.

Hauling feed and water are two chores that get really old. So I've switched to a hanging feeder that holds a five-gallon pail full of feed; I only have to fill it twice a week and the birds waste so much less feed because they can't scratch it out. And it stays cleaner because they can't poop in it. The water issue is something else we changed. Instead of hauling water every day, we plumbed an automatic chicken watering bowl onto a 55-gallon plastic barrel. Now I only have to take a hose and fill the barrel once every two weeks and the chickens have clean water all summer. I still have to haul water in the winter, but they drink much less because it's colder. Living off-grid, we can't use a heated watering container but those of you who do have electricity can consider it.

Milk cows and goats

As we age, our balance and strength often decrease. I know mine have. In my younger days, I didn't really mind fighting a heavy milking cow or goat

Using an automatic poultry water cup keeps the birds in fresh water at all times. It is plumbed to a larger barrel which only needs filling once or twice a summer.

enced person check out your new purchase and adjust the unit, if necessary, then show you how to use it.

Using a milking machine, you only have to wash the udder, place the bucket in place, and attach each cup to each teat. When finished, you take the milker off and dump the bucket into a strainer over a clean stainless steel bucket and filter the milk. Done.

If you can't find or don't want to buy a used outfit, many companies sell new milkers. One of these is Nasco and you can get a catalog or check them out online.

The milking machine does weigh quite a bit, sometimes a little more (especially full of milk) than you want to handle, but don't despair. A new device called the Udderly EZ is a lightweight, hand-held, pump-up vacuum bottle. You squeeze a handle several times to establish a vacuum, then just hold the quart bottle in place until it fills with milk. Many handicapped homesteaders say they couldn't milk a cow or goat without one. After each quart bottle is full, you simply pour it out into a clean pail and reattach the

that kicked and thrashed about during milking, but now I want a gentle critter that stands placidly while being milked. Is your milker not so nice? Think strongly about buying a very gentle animal that you don't dread milking instead of getting out of the milking business. Even if you have to spend a little more money on an extremely mellow milk cow or goat, do it. Your enjoyment and safety are worth every single penny.

Maybe you've always milked by hand but lately you've had trouble with arthritis or carpal tunnel. If you have upper body strength, your best option would probably be getting a milking machine and vacuum pump. This electric unit consists of a vacuum pump which looks sort of like an air compressor and sits on a shelf or out-of-the-way place and creates the vacuum required to run the milking unit or "bucket." Two common brands are DeLaval and Surge. There are two types of bucket; one hangs from a belt around the cow's or goat's belly and the other sits on the floor next to the animal with a claw consisting of four

lined cups that suck up onto each teat. Buying a used complete milking unit is usually fairly easy if you shop Craigslist or other farm advertising places. Have a farmer or other experi-

By filling our hanging chicken feeder twice a week, I eliminate daily feedings — a great labor saver.

349

milker, pump it up, and fill the bottle again until finished milking. You can also find an electric goat milker at Hoegger Supply Company, but they aren't exactly cheap.

Livestock fencing

One of the greatest challenges with keeping animals is fencing. I've found through the years that if you build a good fence, you won't have to chase animals or have predators in your pasture. As we are entering our "older years" of homesteading, this is becoming more important to us. When younger (and less smart, I think), we often put up with temporary or cheap fencing that would usually hold in the animals or poultry. And guess how many times we had to chase escapees? Now we're working at building good fences all over the homestead so we don't have this problem any more.

For example, you can certainly fence chickens in with chicken wire. But a much sturdier fence can be built using 2x4-inch welded fence six feet high. And this fence can be quickly built using steel T-posts driven into the ground for the wire to be fastened onto. If you will be having chicks or other baby poultry in your poultry yard, add a bottom row of 3 foot high, 1-inch chicken fence to keep them from escaping the yard and becoming targets for nearby predators. In areas with flying predators such as hawks and owls, you can also add a top to your run made of larger-mesh chicken wire or netting to keep your birds safe from attack from above. Built right, your fence will last for decades with minimal maintenance.

Likewise, building strong fences for your goats and other larger livestock is essential as we age. Not many 80-year-old homesteaders cherish chasing escaped livestock … nor do your neighbors enjoy them on their front yards.

You'll find directions for building long lasting, strong fences for all of your livestock and poultry in a previous article I wrote for *Backwoods Home Magazine* (Issue #77 Sept/Oct 2002), available in the *13th Year Anthology*. Two keys to a good fence are strong, braced corners made of heavy posts and correctly stretched, adequate wire.

Livestock housing

As we get older, we appreciate having easy-to-clean animal and poultry pens. Will and I planned on this when building our new barn. All of the pens have partitions and gates that swing out of the way so when we clean the barn, we can put animals outside in their pens, swing the partitions flat against the wall, and clean the whole side out with the tractor, driving through, from end to end.

If you don't have this many animals, consider wide doors to the pens so you could use a skid steer loader or smaller tractor with a loader to clean pens.

Instead of using a wheelbarrow for your daily chores in the pens, you might consider using a two-wheeled garden cart such as Carts Vermont's medium- or large-sized cart. I've had one for more than 30 years and other than replacing some of the plywood, it's been my trusty helper all around the homestead.

These large, spoke-wheeled carts are easy to push or pull over rough terrain, don't accidentally dump, can lever heavy loads by standing up on the flat "nose" and sliding the bulky object onto it, then just tipping the handle down. I've hauled big rocks, lumber, firewood, hay, straw, garden produce, potted trees, dirt, gravel, compost, mulch, fencing, and even our canoe on mine. It sure saves my back.

If you have larger livestock to water and you have electricity, consider installing an electrically-heated livestock watering fountain. This is a small unit and uses less energy than an electric stock tank heater. It con-

nects directly to your water line and provides your horses, cattle, sheep, or goats with fresh water, year-round, with no labor on your part. You can also install one between pens so different animals can share the same waterer. You can find these in many farm catalogs or local farm and ranch stores.

As we live off grid, we use large stock tanks filled with a hose year around. But in the winter, we keep the water from freezing by using a wood-fired stock tank heater that my husband, Will, built from scrap water heaters from the dump. Tossing a few sticks into the heaters sure beats chopping ice out of our northern Minnesota frozen livestock tanks. And I'm sure our horses and cows appreciate warmer water, too. You can learn more about this old-time way of keeping ice out of your stock tanks by reading "Build a wood-fired stock tank heater" (Issue #138 Nov/Dec 2012).

Heating with wood

A lot of homesteaders cut and split their own wood for "free" heat. We always have. But as you get older, that heavy, powerful chainsaw and splitting maul seem to become heavier and harder on your back. My husband, Will, used to be a faller with a commercial logging company. He used a big powerful saw to cut down big trees all day long. So when he came here and looked at my Husqvarna chainsaw with its little 16-inch bar, he kind of raised his eyebrows. But after cutting with it for a year, he came to appreciate its lightness, which is easier on his back.

Will had also always hand-split wood. He split many cords every year not only to heat his house, but also to sell for Christmas money. When I bought my tractor-powered, three-point wood splitter from my oldest son, Bill, youngest son David and I used it happily for two years before Will joined us. But for the first year

Our garden cart gets plenty of use and is much easier to handle than a wheelbarrow. I bought this one 35 years ago and it's still usable.

here, Will continued to hand-split wood until one day he gave in and "let" me hook up the tractor splitter. On finding out how much easier on the back it was, we just about quit hand-splitting wood and began using a hydraulic splitter exclusively. It splits a cord of hardwood in about an hour with the two of us working. And we can still walk the next day!

If you're having trouble cutting and splitting wood the "old" way, try using a smaller saw (keep it sharp) and consider using either a tractor-mounted or trailer-type hydraulic wood splitter.

Canning

As we age, sometimes it's a necessity to make our chores easier in order to keep on homesteading. For example, I have an old, huge pressure canner. When I had eight children at home, I filled it, double decked, with quart jars several times a day during heavy-canning season. And it weighs something like 30 pounds, empty.

As I got older, hauling that old, trusty canner out, washing it, and put-

ting it on the stove really bothered my several-times injured back. So finally I saved up and bought a new All American canner that holds fewer quarts (I'm canning for only three now and use mostly pints) and it weighs only 10 pounds, empty. I have no problem at all getting it up on the stove and into the sink to wash. What a blessing! I still occasionally use my old canner when I'm canning big batches of some crop that's come in all at once. But for my day-to-day canning, I use my smaller canner and I enjoy working with it.

Around the house

There are a lot of improvements we can make inside our homes to make homesteading easier when we are older. For instance, we've found that when we added a ramp to make access into our log home easier for Mom and Dad, it was simply too valuable to take down after they passed away. I know that when I had knee surgery recently I was sure glad that the ramp was still in place. It made it so much easier to get in and out of the house.

During the winter, we use a wheelbarrow to bring our firewood into the house for the wood boxes. It's sure easier than carrying it in our arms.

Here, Will cuts a huge log with our "little" saw with its 16-inch bar. He just cut one side, then the other, neatly cutting the 34-inch tree.

(Even easier is a two-wheeled garden cart.) With the ramp, there is no problem at all bringing in enough wood for a day and night, all at one time.

We can also wheel in furniture or appliances with our handy little moving dolly, right up the ramp with no struggling, mashed toes, or strained backs.

Getting rid of carpeting is a relief to us older homesteaders. It's just about impossible to keep clean on an active homestead. A good-quality, rolled-sheet, vinyl flooring looks great and is easily swept and mopped clean in a flash. A few area rugs work well, also. When they are dirty, you can take them outside and beat them free of grit, or wash them on the front lawn, if necessary. When they get yucky, you can find another use for them.

Adding a few grab bars in the bathroom next to the toilet or in the shower/tub area sure makes things easier on those "aches-and-pains" days. I know that I was glad I did when I took my first bath following knee surgery.

And speaking of the bathroom, how about replacing that low toilet with a taller one? We were taking care of Mom and Dad when we built our log cabin, so we installed tall toilets to make things easier for them. Now we're glad we did. I know every time I use one of those low toilets at a store or someone's home, I say a silent prayer of thanks that ours are so much higher and easier.

Do you have trouble getting up out of bed? We discovered a transfer bed handle which is basically a piece of hardboard that slips between the mattress and box springs with a round metal handle that loops up about 18 inches. We bought it for Dad, but I used it myself after I fell off the barn roof and split my sternum and compressed three vertebrae. You can find one at most handicap accessory stores.

Do you struggle with a hand-operated can opener? I did too until I went can opener shopping at a local Amish store. I bought one for about $10. Yes, it's more expensive than the WalMart variety, but it's worked great for more than 15 years. It opens cans easily with very little pain to the fingers and wrist. You also might consider an electric can opener. These are even easier to use and even folks living off grid will appreciate their low energy consumption. But don't throw away your hand-held can opener for times when the power goes out.

The "living area" in many homes (the living room, dining room, kitchen, and bathroom) is on the lower level, while the bedrooms are upstairs. This is fine until you get older and start dreading those trips to the bathroom at night or even going upstairs with clothes from the laundry to put away. If you have the option or are building a home, consider putting the master bedroom on the ground floor. If you just can't do it, at least try to manage a half bath upstairs.

All stairways in the house should have a sturdy railing on the right side. These can prevent slips and dangerous falls, especially for aging home dwellers. Our railings are peeled balsam poles given several coats of polyurethane to protect the wood and bring out the beautiful grain. They look decorative but sure are handy.

And the laundry room? In our cabin, I used to do our laundry in the basement. But all too soon I discovered that was no longer as easy as it was when I was 50! So when we built our addition to our cabin, I was sure to include a laundry room right off of our entryway. I love it on the main floor. It's only six feet by seven, but it sure cuts down so many steps and possible falls.

Around the homestead

I used to nail most things together on the homestead: gates, pens, plywood, drywall, etc., but then I discovered the 18-volt cordless drill/driver. Now I use this little gem daily. Not only is it much easier on your hands

We use our ATV every day to run around the place, pull our little garden trailer, and haul stuff. Here I'm hauling squash from the garden, saving many steps and my back as well.

and wrists, but if you need to, you can easily take things apart with no damage to the structure. That's great for recycling projects or enlarging them as needed.

Will took this even further, buying an 18-volt cordless impact driver. With this, he can easily and quickly sink large lag bolts for fencing and log work, as well as very long log screws. He used it building our storage barn, our training ring (made of railroad ties and 2x6-inch lumber), our calf barn, our new barn, and the log work on our front porch. Before, he did it by hand and it really took a toll on his hands, wrists, elbows, and shoulders.

Here's a really simple change you can make on your gate fasteners that arthritic fingers will love. We used to use a short length of chain with a thumb-worked snap on it. Not only did my arthritic thumb balk some mornings, but the snaps would freeze shut when we had freezing rains. So we changed the snaps to a spring-loaded, broad-tongued snap that you just push in with your thumb to unfasten. It works easily and doesn't freeze shut all the time. Such a simple thing and so cheap, too. (You do use a length of chain around your gates, don't you? Animals quickly chew through ropes.)

Having a plastic sled or two around the homestead is a real help, especially in the winter. We have a big one that is made for ice fishermen called a "Big Otter." This black, heavy, plastic sled hooks behind our four-wheeler and we often haul hay, bedding, feed, water, and firewood in it during the winter. We also have a child's plastic toboggan I bought on sale for $5. I use that often to haul smaller loads by hand here and there, both summer and winter. You'd be surprised at how easily it pulls along on the lawn, making flower bed clean-up super easy. And in the winter it's just as handy hauling a bale of hay or bedding or a

Here's our little wheelchair ramp. As our entry is fairly low to the ground, it didn't take much. Mom and Dad's old house sat higher and required a longer ramp, running next to their deck, complete with railings.

couple buckets of feed or water here and there on the homestead.

If you live in snow country and are an aging homesteader, please consider getting a snowblower. Until we moved here, we never owned one. We shoveled lots of snow from hundreds of feet of driveway, the paths around the buildings, and to the generator shed and outhouse. While shoveling snow can be good exercise in moderation, it can also kill you. Each year, dozens of people have heart attacks while shoveling snow, especially older folks. I'd always kind of laughed at people having snowblowers. But when we faced plenty of snow here we saved up and bought one. Ours comes with an electric start, but it starts so easy that I haven't used the electric starter in five years. One or two easy pulls and it roars to life.

The snowblower is self-propelled, easy on the back and arms, has several forward and reverse speeds, and really moves tons of snow easily. With it, we can keep the paths to our

buildings cleared without piles of snow from shoveling being built up on the sides. We keep the areas around the buildings clean so it is easy and safe to walk around at chore time without stumbling through drifted snow and icy ruts. You can pick up a good used snowblower in the spring for a couple hundred dollars. It sure makes winter life much easier.

Final thoughts

Just because some of us homesteaders are gathering a few years doesn't mean we're ready to be put out to pasture. After all, during those years we've become smarter about our work and have learned easier ways to accomplish homestead tasks. I enjoy my homestead life so much that I hope to be doing it for the rest of my life. I can't imagine anything else so fulfilling. I hope these hints have given you some ideas, too. And for you not-so-aged homesteaders planning your homestead, consider incorporating these ideas in the new homestead you are about to build to make your own future brighter. Δ

Eye-catching signs with mirrors

By David Lee

Need a sign? Do you want people to find your residence, your mailbox, your veggie stand, your yard sale, your business, or anything else you want to be discovered?

If that's a yes, then you need to give them a sign.

It should be a sign that draws attention. It would be most effective if it stands out from the array of signage already out there. It would be outstanding if it used some special effects. It would be most functional if the information on it could be changed when necessary. It would be convenient if made with easily acquired, inexpensive materials. It should be very practical and economical if you build it yourself.

Let's cut right to the chase and reveal the special effects we're talking about: mirrors.

You can find old mirrors free or for low cost at yard sales, secondhand stores, or perhaps even right in your home. I've often found very high-quality mirrors for little or no money just by keeping an eye open for them. Broken mirror pieces work well, too. New mirrors are not very expensive. A 16x48-inch piece is about $12 at my favorite hardware store and can be used to make several small signs or a big one. Some mirrors are tinted in nice colors.

Mirrors are made of glass and are delicate, so it's important to mount the mirror in a sturdy framework that will not warp, will protect the edges, and can withstand an outside environment.

Construction

First, make a backing panel of plywood or pine board that is about a

The reflected image in the mirrored letters give a "see-through" illusion to the sign and the tree. Stained glass nuggets add flashes of color.

quarter inch larger than your mirror in height and width. Next, build a four-sided frame around the panel that turns it into a shallow box. I usually make the top frame piece wider than the sides and bottom to shed rain from the sign. I also make the top piece longer in order to provide a place to attach hanging hardware or to attach the sign to ground posts. You can make this simple casing or create something more elaborate. I avoid using paint on the wooden parts of my signs, preferring natural weathering as a finish.

How you attach the glass mirror to the wood panel is important. Wood expands and contracts with the weather. Glass, not so much. Lay the mirror in the shallow box on the backing panel and use a bead of silicone glue around the edge of the glass and into the space where the framework meets the backing panel. This provides a flexible connection between the wood and glass.

Do not use any glue to bond the back of a mirror to anything. Eventually it will ruin the reflective coating and makes removing the mirror intact nearly impossible. Silicone glue around the edges is durable, elastic, and holds the mirror in place just right. Silicone is available in a variety of colors, so its exposed application can coordinate nicely with the rest of the decoration on your sign. If the mirror ever needs to be replaced, the silicone can be easily sliced away with a sharp blade.

Okay, you have your special effects sign ready to be mounted on posts, screwed to a tree, hung from a limb, attached to a wall, or perhaps even fastened to the tailgate of your truck or the side of a van.

Decoration

Now you have a place to put your message. If the message needs to be changed often, use materials that can be easily removed from the glass. Magic markers or paints work very well because they can be wiped off or scraped clean from the glass and will tolerate short periods of time outdoors. Longer lasting, more impressive lettering or artwork can be done with silicone glue. Use it right from the tube to write your message, just like decorating a cake with frosting from a tube. It stands up to considerable weather abuse, yet is easily scraped off with a razor.

Stick-on and glue-on letters available from craft and hardware stores work okay, but I think these make the sign look too ordinary (plus, they are expensive). Consider cutting out your own letters from wood with a saber or band saw. Color them with wood stain or leather dye and attach them with good old silicone glue.

You can be really creative and make the letters or artwork on your special sign out of clay. I like sculpting the type of clay that you shape, bake, and paint. This will give your sign a deep, textured effect that is doubled by the mirror. Use silicone to secure them in place. If the clay or wood letters need to be removed, a thin wire drawn between the glass and the pieces will slice them off.

I prefer wood signs with the letters cut out to expose the mirror in the background. There is a good reason for this. At night when car headlights sweep across a sign, the lettering stands out in the reflected light to make the message conspicuous and very easy to read. It's as good as artificially lighting the sign. Better in fact; it uses no electricity.

Other considerations

If your sign needs to be seen from opposite directions, build it with back-to-back mirrors and put the message on both sides. Put some scientific thought into your sign placement. Just above the eye level of car drivers is the best height. A slight angle to your mirror will affect what the observer sees. Your sign can have a straight-back reflection or you can tilt the mirror to reflect the sky.

After 12 years, this sign has weathered to natural shades. The mirror, though cracked, is still attractive and attention-getting.

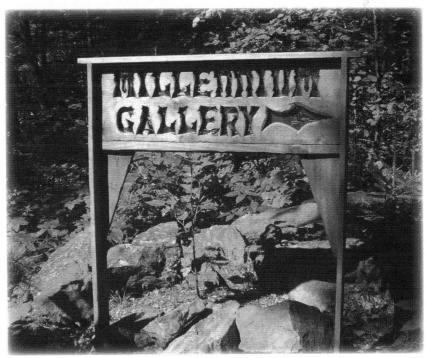

A sign with a mirror behind the hand-carved, cut-out letters gives great texture and depth while pointing the way.

I've seen signs made from various items like horse collars and tire swings. Anything with a big enough opening would work even better by adding mirrors. Over the years, I've built several dozen signs using mirrors. Sign making has been a profitable part-time business. All my sign-making commissions have been from people who first noticed the ones I use for our gallery and our home.

Making signs that are swanky and attention-getting for your home or occupation is entertaining and could get you started on a home business. Δ

SURVIVAL/UTILITY VEST

By David Eddings

When we were younger, my friends and I would go deer hunting, starting as soon as the season opened. We would always go the day before the season opener and scout out the territory where we intended to hunt. The hardest thing about deer hunting is the scouting; we were in pretty good shape because we always covered a lot of territory. When all the leaves have fallen and after a rain, the footing is especially treacherous. A hunter who has never taken a fall while scouting hasn't done a lot of scouting. You haven't lived until you have been slapped in the face by a branch that someone let go before you could get a hand on it. One of my friends even fell out of his tree stand. I asked him how far he fell and he replied, "All the way to the ground."

There are many ways we could have gotten hurt while we were out in the woods and I guess we were just lucky that none of us were ever seriously injured. Minor bumps, bruises, and scrapes were all we ever got, which was good because we never even carried so much as a Band-Aid.

One day, while browsing through one of the many sporting goods flyers that I receive in the mail, I spotted a vest with a lot of pockets. I realized that it would be the solution I was looking for in order to carry just about anything I wanted and still keep my hands free. That was how my utility vest came about. The first thing I purchased was a small first-aid kit. After that I would add an item here and there until I had a pretty useful utility vest. At the time I never thought of it as being a survival vest.

My fully-loaded vest is a perfect companion to a "grab-and-go bag."

There have been many articles written about so-called "bug-out bags," "grab-and-go bags," etc. All I have read about are very good. My problem is, if I needed something, I would have to rummage through the bag to get whatever I needed. I think my survival vest would be a perfect companion to the bags. Everything you might need in a hurry would be right at your fingertips, plus you could wear the vest while hiking or hunting. When not in use, it can be kept in a vehicle for other emergencies. With the vest, you always have your hands free to carry other things.

The vest

Vests come in all different colors and patterns. Picking one out is simply a matter of personal choice. Some vests that I looked at didn't appear to be strong enough to hold up under rough conditions, and a lot of them had nylon mesh built into their construction. I would avoid one of those because the mesh would be likely to snag on things. My vest is a Moose Creek brand and is 65% polyester and 35% cotton. It feels like canvas, is very strong, and has taken a lot of rough treatment. But you can see from the pictures that it still looks great.

The vest I have has nine front pockets: two with zippers, three with double snaps and Velcro, and four with Velcro-only closures. It is highly unlikely that any item in these pockets will ever be lost by accident. There are four inner pockets: two with zippers that hold both of my handguns and two other pockets that have Velcro closures. On the back of the vest there is a large pocket with a zipper that will hold larger items. The front pockets are more like pouches since they will expand to allow a lot of stuff to be loaded into them. The entire vest is made of two layers of material for added strength. The vest is not insulated, which I think is a good feature. This allows me to wear a loose-fitting winter coat over the vest and still have good freedom of movement.

Vest contents:

- 7x7-foot tarp
- small first-aid kit
- signal mirror
- 52x84-inch Mylar space blanket
- Silva orienteering compass
- two triangular bandages
- small bottle of insect repellent
- Russian Dynamo flashlight
- Gerber bypass pruning shears
- folding lockblade knife with saw blade
- Simmons 8X binocular (folding type)
- Gerber Suspension multi-function tool
- magnesium fire starter
- military poncho
- magnifying glass with case
- FM 21-76 U.S. Army Survival manual
- two semi-automatic handguns*
- Storm emergency signal whistle
- parachute cord

*With the exception of the two handguns, I store all the other listed items in the vest at all times.

Handguns

The photo shows the vest zipped down and two semi-auto handguns placed in the zippered pockets located inside the vest in a perfect position for easy reach. Although they are shown partially inserted into the pockets, they will fit entirely inside. If we had to leave in a hurry, both of these weapons would be in the vest. The gun on the left is a Walther P-22 in 22 caliber. The gun on the right is a Glock Model 27 in 40 caliber. The .22 can be used for hunting small game. The 40 caliber is for personal defense and can be used for hunting larger game. For safety reasons, these weapons are carried without a loaded chamber. If your state issues carry permits, I suggest that you obtain a permit. I have a carry permit, but even if I didn't have a permit, I would not hesitate to go armed in an emergency. I selected the two guns because of their small size and their reliability. I believe that a person without an obvious weapon seems like less of a threat to other folks.

Pruning shears

Some might think that including a pair of pruning shears is a little odd. I have found that the shears are one of the most versatile tools that I carry. You can cut dead limbs for a fire, make a pole for fishing, and do other things that you might ordinarily do with a knife. Cutting saplings for an emergency shelter is a snap with this tool — much easier and faster than with a knife.

Russian Dynamo flashlight

I included the Russian Dynamo flashlight because it does not use battery power. The energy needed to power the light is supplied by pumping the grip. I have had this one so long, I didn't know if anyone still sold it. But Nitro-Pak Preparedness Center, Inc. still sells them at www.nitro-pak.com/russian-dynamo-flashlight or call at 800-866-4876. This is a tough little light and it has two settings. A switch on top changes the light from beam to flood. It isn't as bright as a regular flashlight, but it is nice to have when you need it and it will get you to where you want to go at night.

U.S. Army Survival Manual

This is one of the most comprehensive survival manuals that I know of and I believe it is a must-have book for anyone expecting to be outdoors for any length of time. It covers water, food, firemaking, and survival in special areas. There is a chapter covering hazards to survival. I keep my copy stored in a Ziplock bag with all the air pressed out. Paper will absorb moisture, but after several years, mine still looks brand new.

Military poncho

When it comes to staying dry in wet weather, I don't think you can beat a military poncho. The poncho is roomy enough to cover a backpack and your body down to your knees. It has a hood with a drawstring and you can keep your hands inside it for warmth. They even make a blanket liner for additional warmth. Most sporting goods stores carry the plastic variety for limited use, but for a survival situation I recommend that you get one that will stand up to heavy use. Cheaper Than Dirt (www.cheaperthandirt.com, 800-421-8047) has the poncho and the blanket liner if you are interested in adding it to your vest.

Fire starters

I carry a medium-sized prescription bottle full of cotton balls saturated with petroleum jelly. When I want to start a campfire I use one of the cotton balls to start the fire. They will light instantly with a match or lighter and will burn for a long time — long enough to get a fire going pretty good. These fire starters are simple to make and are lightweight to carry in the vest. If you make these, just be sure *not* to hold them with your fingers when you light them or you might get a nasty burn. Place one on the end of a stick before lighting and then place it in the kindling. In a few minutes you will have a nice fire going. Another option is to purchase a magnesium fire starter.

Parachute cord

I always carry several feet of parachute cord in my vest. You can use the cord to make an emergency shelter, to lower yourself down a slope, or for anything else where you would need a rope. It is another item that stores well in a Ziplock bag.

Simmons binocular

The Simmons binocular folds into a small package and has a case. I selected it because of the size. It is a little difficult to use because of the small size, but the trade-off is worth it. Anything larger would not fit into the vest.

Emergency whistle and other small tools

I always carry a Storm emergency signal whistle. It is very loud and can be heard up to half a mile away. The whistle has even been tested under water and can be heard for 50 feet. Go to www.wind-storm-whistles.com or call 314-830-4887 if you would like to purchase one of the whistles. The whistle sells for $5.50 plus shipping. It is something that you would rather *have* and not need than *need* and not have. This whistle is used by the military and other government agencies.

You might want to carry several extra Ziplock bags. They are excellent as water or food containers in an emergency and they add very little weight to your equipment. Cut a length of heavy-duty aluminum foil, fold it and place inside the survival manual. You can mold it into an emergency drinking cup and even boil some water in it to make it safe to drink. At some point I plan to add a small fishing kit.

Conclusion

If you are thinking that this vest is heavy, you are right. However, a few minutes after you put it on, you don't notice the weight because it is pretty well distributed.

My utility/survival vest has served me well over the years. It has given me a sense of well-being knowing that if I ran into a difficult situation, the vest would be there when I needed it. Because I enjoy getting out into the woods, I like having something that will make my stay there a lot more comfortable. With the vest, I

With the exception of the handguns, all other items are stored in the vest.

can make an emergency shelter, build a fire to stay warm and dry, and if necessary, feed myself.

If you want to make one for your own use, you can expect to pay around $50 for a good vest. Surf the net and you will find several different vests to choose from. Some look very good and others I wouldn't waste money on. You might want to buy one that is slightly oversized so you can wear extra layers of clothing underneath it during cold weather. After you get the vest, take time to measure the pockets so you will know what size tools will fit in them. Pick tools that you are comfortable using and don't scrimp on quality when you purchase them. Buy something that you are willing to stake your life on because some day you might have to.

After you have bought your vest and stocked it, why not make one for other members of your family? If the time comes when you have to bug out, you won't be doing it without the family. Young boys and girls would like to have their own, I am sure, so give it some thought. You might someday be glad you did. Δ

Other titles available from Backwoods Home Magazine

The Best of the First Two Years
A Backwoods Home Anthology — The Third Year
A Backwoods Home Anthology — The Fourth Year
A Backwoods Home Anthology — The Fifth Year
A Backwoods Home Anthology — The Sixth Year
A Backwoods Home Anthology — The Seventh Year
A Backwoods Home Anthology — The Eighth Year
A Backwoods Home Anthology — The Ninth Year
A Backwoods Home Anthology — The Tenth Year
A Backwoods Home Anthology — The Eleventh Year
A Backwoods Home Anthology — The Twelfth Year
A Backwoods Home Anthology — The Thirteenth Year
A Backwoods Home Anthology — The Fourteenth Year
A Backwoods Home Anthology — The Fifteenth Year
A Backwoods Home Anthology — The Sixteenth Year
A Backwoods Home Anthology — The Seventeenth Year
A Backwoods Home Anthology — The Eighteenth Year
A Backwoods Home Anthology — The Nineteenth Year
A Backwoods Home Anthology — The Twentieth Year
A Backwoods Home Anthology — The Twenty-first Year
A Backwoods Home Anthology — The Twenty-second Year
A Backwoods Home Anthology — The Twenty-third Year
Emergency Preparedness and Survival Guide
Backwoods Home Cooking
Can America Be Saved From Stupid People
The Coming American Dictatorship — Parts I-XI
Hardyville Tales
Creative Home Improvement
Chickens — a beginner's handbook
Starting Over — Chronicles of a Self-Reliant Woman
Dairy Goats — a beginner's handbook
Self-reliance — Recession-proof your pantry
Making a Living — Creating your own job
Harvesting the Wild: gathering & using food from nature
Growing and Canning Your Own Food
Jackie Clay's Pantry Cookbook
Homesteading Simplified: Living the good life without losing your mind
Ask Jackie: Animals
Ask Jackie: Canning Basics
Ask Jackie: Food Storage
Ask Jackie: Gardening
Ask Jackie: Homestead Cooking
Ask Jackie: Homesteading
Ask Jackie: Pressure Canning
Ask Jackie: Water Bath Canning